Unexplained Mysteries of the 20th Century

Unexplained Mysteries of the 20th Century

JANET and COLIN BORD

CB

CONTEMPORARY
BOOKS

CHICAGO

Library of Congress Cataloging-in-Publication Data

Bord, Janet, 1945–
    Unexplained mysteries of the 20th century / Janet and Colin Bord.
      p.   cm.
    Includes bibliographical references.
    ISBN 0-8092-4113-7
    1. Curiosities and wonders.   2. Supernatural.   3. Occultism.
I. Bord, Colin.   II. Title.
AG243.B63   1989
001.9′4—dc20   89-71295
                                                            CIP

Published by Contemporary Books, Inc.
Two Prudential Plaza, Chicago, Illinois 60601-6790
Manufactured in the United States of America
International Standard Book Number: 0-8092-4113-7

Contents

Introduction and Acknowledgements

Having written *Modern Mysteries of Britain* in 1986, we immediately embarked on this companion volume, *Unexplained Mysteries of the 20TH Century*, which covers the whole of the twentieth century up to mid-1988, and literally the whole of the world. Mysteries do not occur only in Western civilizations but also in remote parts like Siberia (USSR), the Congo (Africa) and Greenland, and 111 separate countries are represented in the Gazetteer. We have also included some British events which update *Modern Mysteries of Britain*.

As soon as we began writing this book we realized that the main problem we experienced when compiling its predecessor, namely an excess of material, was now even more pronounced. Consequently we have had to be selective in our choice of subject-matter, and have concentrated mainly on mysteries that are place-linked rather than those that are person-linked. This criterion is obviously not infallible, because some of the mysteries we have written about, like poltergeists and religious phenomena, perhaps others like UFO close encounters and ghostly voices, may on investigation also prove to be more closely linked to the person than to the place. But the line had to be drawn somewhere, and we have therefore tended to concentrate also on those mysteries which intrigue us most. As a result we have not covered subjects like telepathy and similar psychic phenomena, demonstrations of psychokinesis (e.g. metal-bending), reincarnation, out-of-body and near-death experiences, fire-walking, mediumship/spiritualism, clairvoyance, mysterious deaths and disappearances, Bermuda and other 'triangles', animal mysteries such as homing cats and dogs. That may seem a long list of excluded subjects, but our seventeen chapters cover others of equal or greater strangeness. Each chapter contains details of many cases, but we could not include them all. Extra cases will be found briefly described in the world-wide Gazeteer at the end of the book. Should any readers have similar first-hand experiences to report, they can contact us care of the publishers, Grafton Books, 8 Grafton Street, London WIX 3LA. We are also glad to hear from anyone with photographs relevant to the Fortean Picture Library, our pictorial archive of mysteries and strange phenomena.

A book such as this would be impossible to compile if there were not dedicated researchers around the world pursuing their own special interests and publishing the results of their researches. We admire and acknowledge the work of all the authors named in the Bibliography and Notes, but most especially William R. Corliss, whose *Sourcebook Project* is incomparable and invaluable, and Bob Rickard, who is recognized world-wide for his twenty years of single-minded devotion to the Fortean cause (study of strange phenomena). His magazine *Fortean Times* goes from strength to strength and is *essential* reading (for address see page 401); as are the books he is now publishing under his Fortean Tomes imprint. Other friends, colleagues and fellow researchers whom we wish to thank for their help are Anthony R. Brown (Scotland), Ray W. Boeche (USA), Bill Chalker (Australia), Loren Coleman (USA), COUD-I and members (USA), the late Tim Curry (USA), René Dahinden (Canada), Lucius Farish (USA), Cynthia Hind (Zimbabwe), Norman O. Josephsen (USA), Ulrich Magin (West Germany), Gary Mangiacopra (USA), Shin-ichiro Namiki (Japan), Scott Parker (USA), Stephen C. Pratt (England), Ronald Rosenblatt (USA), Anthony 'Doc' Shiels (England), Bob Skinner (England), Dennis Stacy (USA), Lars Thomas (Denmark), Pete Wayne (Scotland). Especial thanks for prompt assistance whenever needed are due to Dr Karl P. N. Shuker in the field of cryptozoology; and in the field of religious phenomena to Tristan Gray Hulse, who will one day write his own book . . .

1 *Things that go bump in the night . . .*

. . . are known as poltergeists by the parapsychologists. A rough literal translation of 'poltergeist' is 'noisy spirit' and noisy they certainly are, but whether or not spirits are involved is still very much open to question. Like other paranormal phenomena, there are records of poltergeists having been experienced for hundreds of years, and in all kinds of situations, from mud huts in Africa, to modern apartments in New York City; but unlike some other phenomena, which are only transitory and merely a curiosity, such as falls of frogs, a poltergeist is to most victims a terrifying experience, and they do everything they can think of to persuade the unwelcome visitor to leave. But it is rarely keen to go.

A poltergeist might first announce its presence by rapping or banging on the walls. This can be so loud that it is heard some distance away. At Fougères-sur-Bièvre in France, beginning in December 1913, strange noises were disturbing not only the Huguet-Prousteau family but the neighbouring houses too.

> One evening the noise was so great that it was heard distinctly not only in the neighbouring houses, but across the road, over 60 yards away. The house was shaken from top to bottom, the partitions vibrated violently, the doors and windows rattled with singular vehemence. It was found necessary to open them for fear of their glass being broken. According to reliable witnesses, the noises accompanying the vibrations of the house resembled the reverberations of distant thunder. On the other hand, the curtains of the bed were in constant agitation, as if moved by a strong draught, though everything was shut.
>
> Inside the house, several people unconnected with the family made some experiments. They struck a definite number of blows on the wall. Immediately a similar number would answer, but with peculiar sonorousness. The noises were loud and muffled,

and seemed to emanate from the whole house.

One night some determined men went up to the garret. They had hardly got there when the noise commenced and the house began to tremble. Their lights were nearly extinguished, and the men hurried down again.[1]

In a more recent case, at Pinetown, Natal (South Africa), on New Year's Day 1984, fourteen-year-old Wendy Roos heard a loud noise: 'I thought the house was caving in. It sounded as if a large boulder had crashed on to the roof.' Nothing was found, nor was any damage done during other poltergeist disturbances before and after this event.[2]

Mysterious bangings in the house structure are annoying enough, but it can be equally nerve-racking to lie in bed at night listening to noises below, and suspecting you have intruders bent on all-out destruction. A Boer family living in Boshof (South Africa) in 1901 were woken at midnight by the sound of pots and pans being thrown around in the kitchen, and dishes being smashed. After a couple of minutes all was quiet again, and in the morning they were surprised to find nothing broken and everything in place. This happened for three nights, more severe each time, and with the noise of furniture being overturned and broken, but nothing was ever harmed.[3] This is not always the case, however. Poltergeists are usually destructive, and household goods do get smashed, and furniture broken. A destructive poltergeist outbreak was reported from Ireland in 1916, the victims being a farmer and his family. The farmer told a sergeant of the Royal Irish Constabulary:

Sergeant, I am in great trouble. I came to town today to arrange for the funeral of my youngest child. I am suffering terrible annoyance in my house night and day for almost a week. Some unseen spirit is wrecking my house, throwing cooking utensils about and breaking delf. It flung a bottle of ink over my dying child, hurled a heavy glass salt-cellar at a mirror in the sick-room and broke a valuable tea set of old china that my wife was carrying downstairs for safety. She was about half-way down the stairs with the china in her apron when the whole lot was completely smashed in my presence as well as in that of a few friends who had come to the wake. The day previous to the death of the child, myself and servants were churning in the kitchen, when the butter was taken from the churn and some of it thrown against the ceiling ten feet high. I found some of the broken china in my byre some thirty yards distant.

The sergeant went to visit the farm, having a certain degree of natural suspicion about the reported events. He sat in the kitchen with the farmer, his wife and daughter, and waited for some convincing activity on the part of the poltergeist.

Being an old warrior, I was still unsatisfied with what I saw, and I came to the conclusion in my own mind that if some one of the seven or eight flitches of bacon that were suspended near the ceiling, or if one of the two horse-collars which were hanging on pins in the wall over the fireplace should be thrown down, I should then be satisfied as to the reality of the spook; but I took care not to betray what was passing in my mind, either by look or otherwise, to anybody that were present.

. . . I stood up to go. The woman and children said they would not remain when I left, so they started for the back door – the servant first, followed by the two children, then the farmer's wife, next the farmer, and I bringing up the rear. I had got across the kitchen near the end of the obstructing wall, and was turning into the passage, but still in full view of the kitchen, when suddenly one of the horse-collars was flung from its position, high up on the wall, the whole length of the room, landing on the floor with a smack. The farmer turned, and after we had both examined the collar, he said: 'You must now believe'; to which I assented. We passed into the yard, going towards the road, when a graip (dung-fork) was thrown across the yard by unseen hands.

In the end, the farmer had a new dwelling built at some distance from the old.[4]

The events just described, with household goods being thrown around, are very typical of poltergeist activity, and are usually a sure sign that a poltergeist has taken up residence. The mere fact of items being moved around by no human agency is puzzling enough, but there are even stranger aspects to these happenings. Sometimes the objects moved are very heavy, and could not be lifted by one, two or even three hoaxers working together. In Pearisburg, Virginia (USA), in the home of an elderly widow, Mrs Beulah Wilson, and her nine-year-old foster-child, dishes were being smashed and furniture moved in a poltergeist outbreak beginning on 19 December

1976. The police investigated, and Trooper Pritchett reported: 'The furniture was big . . . old-timey chairs . . . and the kitchen cabinets must have weighed 200 pounds or more. She and the boy and Cardwell couldn't have moved them . . . all pulling together.'[5] In a poltergeist outbreak in Ascot, Berkshire (England) in 1975 the family cars were sometimes moved as they stood parked outside. One of the cars was moved nightly for many weeks, as much as nine feet sideways, silently across gravel, with the doors locked and the handbrake on.[6]

Smaller objects, seen moving around inside a house, will sometimes appear to be travelling unnaturally slowly, and they also change direction and turn corners while in flight. Sometimes they have even been seen to pass through closed doors – not literally seen, because the actual transition of solid object through solid object was not observed by the witness, only the result of this happening. Some examples will clarify this. The Poona (India) poltergeist of 1927–30 was a particularly active and unusual one. One of the witnesses was Miss Kohn, who lived in the afflicted Ketkar household and kept a

Guy Lyon Playfair was investigating a poltergeist outbreak in Ipiranga (Brazil) in 1973 when a stool slid downstairs, after having passed through a closed door.

record in her diary of various happenings attributable to the poltergeist. On 19 July 1928 she wrote:

> At 9.30 p.m. while D[amodar] was going to bed, some of his toys
> became active. My sister took care that the lid of his wooden
> toy-case was properly shut. D. and I got into bed, when a wooden
> wheel came pelting on to his bed, and he dodged it, as it went very
> near his head. (He is compelled to dispense with a mosquito net,
> owing to the furious nature of the occurrences last April, when
> stones and toys would appear inside his net just after he had been
> tucked safely in – the memory of these horrors has made him
> nervous of mosquito nets for the present.) The wheel was fol-
> lowed by a spinning-top.
>   I got 'fed-up' and fetched an enormous German dictionary
> weighing about five pounds. I placed this upon the toy-box, and
> got into bed again. Two minutes had not elapsed when another
> top (not the same one as before) came towards us, again out of the
> toy-box. I called my sister's attention to the heavy dictionary. She
> looked into the box to see what toys were there. After a moment,
> when she had just left the room, the same top as at first, came out
> as if to mock our vain imagining that a mere dictionary would
> prove an obstacle.[7]

A similar occurrence took place in Vachendorf (West Germany) in
1948. A refugee family from Bohemia was lodging in one room of an
old mansion, and was there suffering from poltergeist activity. On
this occasion, the two beds in the room were bombarded by stones,
tools and other objects. The mother put the tools away in their box,
closed it and sat on it. To her amazement, as she sat there she saw the
tools reappear one by one in different parts of the room. On another
occasion, her husband was hit on the head by a wooden shoe which
came out of a closed glass cupboard.[8]

In the Nicklheim case (West Germany) of November 1968 to
February 1969, objects which went missing indoors would later be
seen falling outside, and one of the investigators decided to test this.
He placed perfume bottles and pill bottles on the kitchen table, sent
everyone outside, closed all doors and windows, and then joined the
others. Soon a perfume bottle was seen, and then a pill bottle. They
were first seen at roof level, as they moved earthwards in a zigzag
motion.[9]

In many poltergeist cases, objects appear inside a closed room, first noticed at or just below ceiling height as they fall to the ground. In 1952 the mayor of Neudorf (West Germany) experienced a poltergeist outbreak at his home, and one day he, his son and daughter-in-law saw a number of nails appear about eight inches below the bedroom ceiling and fall to the floor. They came from a locked cupboard in the kitchen. In the Poona case, a jar flew into Miss Kohn's bedroom which Damodar had taken to school two days before and had left there.[10] In a New York poltergeist outbreak in 1907–9 the witness reported:

> On one occasion I was making my bed, and entirely alone on that floor of the house, when a penny dropped squarely in the middle of the bed, and a few minutes later another dropped at my feet.
>
> To my certain knowledge there was not a penny in the house, as, shortly before that occurrence, I had searched everywhere for pennies to buy a stamp.[11]

Similarly, though on a larger scale, coins fell before startled witnesses in Finland in 1917 or 1918. Two buttons fell first, then a coin, clicking on the parquet floor. Then more coins fell at five-, ten- or fifteen-minute intervals, and the two frightened students fetched more witnesses. As they watched, the coins kept pouring down. They placed them on the mantelpiece and left to spend the night elsewhere. Next day, the coins were still where they had placed them. The coins were found to be genuine and no one claimed them, so the lucky recipients went out to celebrate with friends at a restaurant.[12]

In these last two cases, the coins did not belong to anyone in the household and were genuine apports, similar to the objects that mediums would cause to materialize in their spiritualist seances earlier this century. From what the witnesses say, it is clear that objects which appear in closed rooms, or leave locked boxes, somehow dematerialize and then rematerialize. We are certainly now way beyond the boundaries of the scientifically acceptable, but we are not there solely on the evidence of one hysterical witness. Many people have *seen* objects suddenly appear and disappear in empty space. Miss Kohn, careful witness in the Poona case, wrote in her diary for 26 July 1928 of how she and Damodar were sitting in her room in the evening with heads close together watching a wick burning in a small bowl.

All of a sudden, quite quietly a round glass button (which belongs to an old set in our possession) was dropped deliberately into the small bowl (*wati*) in which the wick was burning. It did not fall from a height, but appeared only one inch above the edge of the *wati*, i.e. the 'spirit' must have been hovering quite near to our very faces, to produce this act.[13]

During the infestation by the Lieserbrücke poltergeist (Austria) in 1922, the Kogelnik family experienced many unusual happenings, and once Mrs Kogelnik saw an axe disappear, in good light in the late morning.[14]

However unlikely the materialization and dematerialization of inanimate objects might seem to be, at first sight the dematerialization of living people seems impossible. But this too has been reported, certainly not frequently but more than once. It happened several times in the Poona case, when young boys were teleported from one location to another. Damodar was more than once taken into the car which was in a shed, and at least once the shed was closed, so that he had to open it from the inside in order to get out. His elder brother was also teleported, as witnessed by Miss Kohn's sister, who was an intelligent woman and a scholar. Here the event is described by Miss Kohn:

> At 9.45 a.m. on April 23rd, my sister says in a letter, the elder boy 'suddenly materialized in front of me in your doorway like a rubber ball. He looked bright but amazed, and said "I have just come from Karjat". He didn't come through any door.' My sister describes the posture of the boy as having been most remarkable. When she looked up from her letter-writing, she saw him bending forward: both his hands were hanging away from his sides, and the hands hanging limp – his feet were not touching the floor, as she saw a distinct space between his feet and the threshold. It was precisely the posture of a person who has been gripped round the waist and carried, and therefore makes no effort but is gently dropped at his destination.[15]

It is difficult to explain why teleportation should happen, but at least we must be thankful that the poltergeists do return the people they so mysteriously spirit away. (But perhaps they sometimes don't . . . maybe some of the people who disappear without trace have been teleported into a limbo and left there, forgotten by some absent-minded poltergeist . . .)

If we continue to view the poltergeist as alive in some way, it is possible to see other evidence for a sort of human intelligence. Mrs Kogelnik was one person who experienced the poltergeist's particularly unfriendly nature (Lieserbrücke, Austria, 1922). You might think that breaking china and causing household chaos was bad enough, but poltergeists can also be downright spiteful. Mrs Kogelnik tried hard to carry on despite the poltergeist's activity, but it must have been difficult. As her husband, Commander Kogelnik, wrote:

> I must now relate that for a fortnight I had been unable to find an inkstand, which always stood on my desk. All search for it had been in vain . . . Whilst my wife was up under the roof, and Hannie close by her was engaged in cleaning and sweeping, suddenly there was a whistling sound from the further end of the large space where no one had been standing. Then came a crash, and the inkstand fell at my wife's feet, shivered to fragments, the ink it had contained running about over the floor. Shortly afterwards, pieces of coal were thrown, and as my wife and Hannie were not daunted, but continued their sweeping, an old, unused flower-pot came hurtling through the air from a corner in which it had long rested, the earth with which it had been filled being sprinkled over the newly-swept part of the floor. After this the work of cleaning was stopped . . .[16]

However, some poltergeists seem to have a sense of humour, too. A Birmingham (England) family was terrorized by a poltergeist in 1974, but it seems the 'spirit' was enjoying playing games with them. The wife said: 'It's nerve-racking living here. I have to keep my purse and pills on me. If I don't, the poltergeist hides them!' Her husband added: 'He loves to have fun with my underwear. He throws them downstairs, and if I don't pick them up he creates chaos in the kitchen. Once I had a bath and asked my wife to get my pants but she couldn't find them. The next morning I was astonished to see them hanging on a branch at the top of a tree at the back of the house.'[17] During the Vodable (France) poltergeist outbreak in 1914, a bust of the former owner of a big house was found tucked up in bed, its head on the pillow and the bedclothes pulled up round its chin. Later it was found in another bed.[18] In Newark, New Jersey (USA), where William Roll was investigating a poltergeist outbreak in September 1961, he told the family 'It doesn't hit people', and was

promptly hit on the head by a small bottle which had been standing on the table.[19]

The last event indicates that poltergeists can respond intelligently to the spoken words of witnesses. Also they have shown a telepathic ability, for in the Irish case recounted earlier the sergeant only *thought* that if a horse-collar was moved from the wall he would accept the spook's reality, and this soon happened. Another example of responsive intelligence occurred in the Lieserbrücke case, as Commander Kogelnik reported:

> The same afternoon, our teabox lid was missing, and on discovering the loss I said: 'Now wouldn't you be kind enough for once to bring back what you have taken away?' After some minutes the said lid came rolling in from the hall! At this time there were with me in the kitchen both the cook and Hannie, and I had both under observation.[20]

In the Poona case, this time during Miss Kohn's absence, someone put out some fruit and invited the 'spirits' to eat it and then leave them alone. The fruit disappeared and sounds of eating were heard, with lip-smacking noises. Then the rinds reappeared, bearing toothmarks.[21] The Ascot (Berkshire, England) poltergeist would listen in to telephone calls, causing loud interference whenever the

Only seconds after the stool fell downstairs (see page 12), a drawer full of clothes was thrown from an upstairs window, the result photographed by Guy Lyon Playfair, who was convinced that no human agent was responsible.

mysterious activities were discussed. One of the witnesses tested it on several occasions by asking it to buzz twice if it was listening, and always got a double buzz in response.[22]

On the face of it, such behaviour as just described would strongly suggest a human type of intelligence at work. To reinforce this, poltergeists sometimes write or speak to their victims. Writing is less common, but a poltergeist which plagued the family of sub-magistrate A. S. Thangapragasam Pillay in Nidamangalam (southern India) from 3 to 19 March 1920 was fond of communicating in this way. Its first message appeared on 8 March on the lavatory wall and read, in Tamil: 'My name is Rajamadan [chief mischief maker]. I will not leave you.' One of the people who went to look at this message wrote below it, in English: 'Reply sharp. If you don't run away from this house, I would recommend you to my goddess for punishment. Signed ——' Later was found the poltergeist's reply, again in Tamil: 'I will kill the man who wrote these lines. Don't you know that I am the King? I will not leave this house, whatever the inmates do.' To which the now terrified man who had instigated this outburst replied: 'Please excuse me. I beg your pardon.' More writings were found, including a message ostensibly from the sub-magistrate's dead daughter, in her writing. Then on 19 March appeared a message which overjoyed the household, for it told them that the poltergeist intended to leave them and never reappear.[23]

Voices are more often heard during poltergeist outbreaks, but rarely conveying long or coherent messages. Eerie or childlike laughter was heard from the Pittsburgh, Pennsylvania (USA), poltergeist of 1971–2,[24] while the Ivybridge, Devon (England), and Santa Fe (Argentina) poltergeists, both during 1984, were prone to screaming.[25] More coherent vocal communication came from the North Vancouver, British Columbia (Canada), poltergeist of 1977, but he only talked to three-and-a-half-year-old Jason McIntyre, whose mother could not hear what was being said. Not that she really tried: 'I just hide under my bedcovers . . . it's really scary.'[26] In a very strange case from Leesburg, Florida (USA), which took place in January 1978 and throughout that year, the poltergeist at first took the form of unexplained voices over the telephone. There were the usual poltergeist disturbances in the house, where a grandmother, mother and two daughters aged ten and six lived, but the events began with voices on the phone and later developed with voices coming out of the walls and from the ten-year-old girl. The phone voices would demonstrate knowledge of the caller before he identified himself, and would sometimes also describe his clothing or his plans. It would also use foul language and make threats. People using the phone could often see the other members of the household and no one was speaking into an extension phone; no physical explanation was ever found.[27]

In some poltergeist cases, apparitions are seen, though not always as fully-formed figures. In the Pittsburgh, Pennsylvania (USA), case of 1971–2, misty figures were seen – 'a dancing cloud in the middle of the room', and a shadow that was not a shadow but had depth, and moved.[28] 'Vague forms like smoke haze' were seen by the victims of the Ivybridge poltergeist in 1984, and in the Olive Hill, Kentucky (USA), case in 1968 both hazy and clear apparitions were seen. Mrs Callihan saw a ghost in her bedroom, of someone she recognized whom she knew to be dead, and she also saw a white form, again in her bedroom. This, which she likened to a 'large white Catholic nurse', moved towards her, causing her to jump out of bed. She said the shape felt cold when she came into contact with it.[29] Of course some apparitions seen by poltergeist victims, who are not

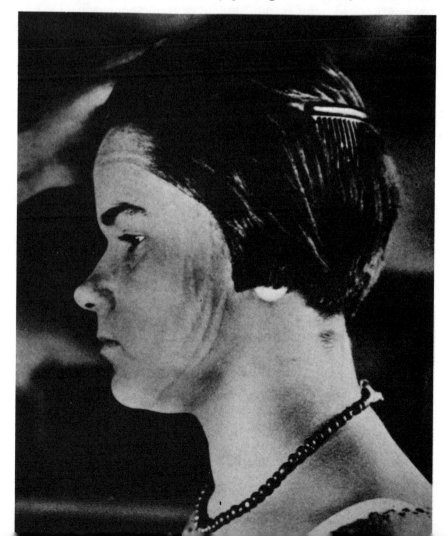

Eleanore Zügun with her face marked by her invisible assailant.

unnaturally in an overwrought state, may be there as a result of expectation rather than as a facet of the phenomenon. Victims may be interpreting light and shadow from external light sources as human shapes, in much the same way that other people see shapes which for them take on the form of religious imagery (see Chapter 15).

There may also be a link with religious phenomena in the cases where a poltergeist has allegedly assaulted a victim. The assault can take a variety of forms. Being hit by a flying object is not common, and when it does happen may be accidental in that the poltergeist did not necessarily intend to hit anyone. In the Poona case, Damodar was bitten and slapped, his sister was cut and pricked and her bib was so tightly knotted she was nearly strangled. Dr and Mrs Ketkar were scratched, smacked and pinched, and also smeared with a thick saliva.[30] The Comeada (Portugal) poltergeist of 1919 in Homem Christo's rented house slapped Mr Christo so violently he screamed out, 'for it seemed to him that fangs hooked his flesh to tear it out', and four red marks of fingers were seen on his cheek immediately afterwards.[31] A similar punishment was meted out in 1974 to Anthony Rossi of East Hartford, Connecticut (USA), who shouted 'You're nothing but a toy!' at a Raggedy-Ann doll said to be possessed by the spirit of a dead girl. Immediately he felt a burning pain on his chest and found seven bleeding clawmarks slashed across his body.[32]

Perhaps the best-known victim of this type of poltergeist assault was Eleanore Zügun, who was the focus of poltergeist activity in Romania in 1925 and the next year in Vienna. She was pricked, scratched and bitten by an invisible assailant on many occasions, these attacks often seen by reliable witnesses.[33] The investigators compared the marks with the stigmata suffered by other people in a religious context, for example bleeding wounds in the palms of the hands at Easter time. Padre Pio was the most famous stigmatic, but there have been many others. Just as those with a strong religious temperament may undergo the stigmata as a result of auto-suggestion, so perhaps may someone suffering a poltergeist visitation self-inflict the injuries by some power of the unconscious mind. But we are running too far ahead with this speculation; and certain it is that the victims themselves usually feel that an outside agency of a paranormal nature is responsible for their afflictions.

We have described a variety of phenomena labelled 'poltergeist', but before we try to throw some light on what may be going on in these cases, we must mention some phenomena of a different kind which do not follow the traditional poltergeist routine but nevertheless may be linked. These are the mysterious flows of blood and water which people have reported from time to time. At a hospital in Nuoro, Sardinia (Italy), in 1972, water was flowing through the floor of every ward to which nine-year-old Eugenio Rossi was moved. Plumbers could find no explanation.[34] Water appeared on the floors, on a piano, even in closed drawers, at a house in Ayersville, Ohio (USA), during 5–10 July 1975, but the ceilings and walls were never wet. A plumber searched for a day for a leak but found none. He was mystified. 'I'd open a wooden kitchen cabinet drawer and there'd be half a gallon of water in it. I picked up a rug with an 18-inch wet spot . . . but the floor underneath was dry. It was really eerie!' Another expert who examined the house said: 'Right before my eyes, little puddles formed all over the bathroom floor! It's a mystery to me!'[35] A similar case was reported from Windsor, Vermont (USA), in September 1955 when the Waterman family found beads of moisture on their furniture which returned however frequently it was removed. A shallow dish being carried from one room to another filled with water on the way. In the Martins' case, their watery affliction followed them from one home to another. When they lived in Methuen, Massachusetts (USA), water spurted from various places as well as seeping from walls and ceiling, and when in 1963 they moved, the same thing happened at their new home.[36]

The three recent reports we have to hand concerning blood appearing in people's houses are even stranger. Why blood, and where does it come from? Does this phenomenon have any links with the bleeding religious images described in Chapter 15? In the case of a house in Aboro, a district of Abidjan (Ivory Coast), blood spurted out of the walls on 12 March 1985. Police and reporters saw bloody clothing, kitchen utensils, a shower and some doors. It was also reported that the blood followed the occupants around – each footstep left a trace of blood. The blood smelled bad, but none of the occupants was wounded.[37] Not many months later, a couple living in St Quentin (France) found tiny red droplets all over the living-room walls and carpet. This was in January 1986. In February they reappeared, and the same night the sound of smashing crockery was heard downstairs, but nothing was damaged. The following day the couple awoke to find their pillows and the kitchen table covered with tiny red stains. The next night the stains reappeared on the bedclothes and also on their pyjamas. The couple moved out of the house for several weeks. The stains, when analysed, were found to be dried blood, but we have no information as to whether it was human or animal blood.[38] In the case of the mysterious blood flows at an Atlanta, Georgia (USA), home in September 1987, tests showed the blood was human and was type O. No source could be discovered for the blood, which was found splattered on the walls and floors in several rooms of an elderly couple's home. William Winston (blood type A) said: 'I'm not bleeding. My wife's not bleeding. Nobody else was here.' His wife told how she had stepped out of the bath and found the floor covered with blood.[39]

The phenomena gathered together under the poltergeist umbrella can be quite varied, as the brief case details given in this chapter show, and no two cases are exactly alike. So-called poltergeists can also overlap with the traditional haunted house phenomenon, as seen by the numerous occasions when people with resident poltergeists have claimed to see apparitions, and this overlap will again become evident in Chapter 5, dealing with ghosts. But the main divide between the two types of phenomenon is that ghosts are place-focused, and poltergeists are people-focused. Some poltergeists even follow the family when they move house hoping to escape, whereas a traditional ghost will stay put and will manifest to whoever happens to be living in the haunted house. There are some people-focused ghosts, usually ghosts of close family members who appear at the time of death or soon afterwards, but this is a separate category of paranormal phenomena, and one usually without poltergeist overtones.

We have said that poltergeist cases vary considerably, but whatever the type of activity which occurs, there is usually one factor which links the cases: there can usually be found one member of the household on whom the poltergeist seems to focus its attention, and that person is usually, though not always, quite young. If he or she leaves the premises, the activity usually stops, though in the case of the Eastern Passage, Nova Scotia (Canada), poltergeist of 1943–4, when Mrs Hilchie took her two daughters to visit their grandmother, they were followed by rapping noises wherever they went – in a restaurant, at the taxi office, and at grandmother's home.[40] Also in Canada, three families in Forest Hill Village, a suburb of Toronto, Ontario, were plagued by poltergeist activity early in 1947, and the link between them was that they all employed the same young domestic servant. In one of the houses, explosions blew large patches of plaster off the walls, resulting in a $3000 repair bill, quite a sum 40 years ago. When the girl was dismissed all the phenomena ceased.[41]

Quite naturally, the young people at the centre of the activity are often suspected of being the intentional cause of it, and sceptical investigators will do their utmost to 'prove' their guilt. They are sometimes helped along by the young person's own behaviour, for it seems that often, when a genuine poltergeist outbreak starts to flag, a youngster may encourage it along by faking some phenomena, also perhaps doing this to keep happy the investigators whose attention they are enjoying as a break in dull family routine. In some cases, however, hoaxing seems to be done in a dissociated state; in others, 'confessions' of hoaxing are extorted in cases where it would have been impossible for a child to have been guilty. For example, when heavy furniture was moved at Bridgeport, Connecticut (USA), in 1972–5, the police reported that ten-year-old Marcy had confessed to a hoax. As Paul Eno, who investigated the case, commented: 'Of course the silliest accusation of all was that a 10-year-old child could fool large numbers of reliable, highly trained people for days by tossing around huge objects in a tiny house without being seen. How such incredible suggestions were in any way more believable than the simple facts of the case is beyond my comprehension.'[42]

In the Newark, New Jersey (USA), case of May to September 1961, thirteen-year-old Ernest Rivers was taken to Duke Parapsychology Laboratory for testing by poltergeist expert William G. Roll, and while he was there, on 18 December, Roll had clear proof that Ernest was a hoaxer. Through a one-way mirror he saw him take two measuring tapes from a table and hide them under his shirt. Later he threw them after his grandmother as she left the room, and then denied knowing how the tapes had moved. Knowing that Ernest had manufactured this event, Roll planned to give him a lie-detector test and ask him about this incident and also about the earliest events at Newark, which Roll thought were genuine poltergeist activity. The result was that there was no evidence of lying when Ernest answered questions on both the early activity and the tape movements. Ernest was also hypnotized, and again denied any knowledge of the tape movement. Therefore the researchers decided that Ernest was in a dissociated state when he threw the tapes and was not doing it consciously.[43]

Here we have a clue that unusual mental states may be operating when poltergeist phenomena occur. A number of the children on whom poltergeists focus are approaching or at puberty, at which time they are subject to internal conflicts and emotional upheavals. Also the majority of poltergeists break out in family settings of some kind, usually adults and children together, and there is sometimes clear evidence that family tensions have built up. In the Icelandic poltergeist case of 1964 the location was a farmstead where parents and grown-up daughter lived. The mother wanted her husband to give up the farm, the daughter intended to get married and live in Reykjavik but was needed to help on the farm: two sources of tension which could have created a build-up of uncontrollable energy.[44]

Sometimes the tension seems to be caused by religious conflict. A Catholic family living in Lee, Massachusetts (USA), were attacked in 1981 by a 'demonic spirit' which decapitated religious statues, threw a crucifix downstairs and stuck a butcher's knife in a kitchen table.[45] The Molignon (Switzerland) poltergeist of 1914 was also anti-Catholic. An eleven-year-old boy suffered convulsions, and poltergeist-type phenomena occurred in his presence. The family tried to overcome it by the power of religion, which spurred the poltergeist to even greater efforts. As a Capuchin friar was pouring holy water into a stoup, the vessel was broken with a stone, and a blessed medal fastened round the boy's neck unfastened itself and was thrown into the air. The arrival of four more priests, reading prayers and invocations, failed to dispel the poltergeist, which continued to pelt the boy with stones.[46] In the case of the Nidaman-galam (India) poltergeist, the afflicted family of the sub-magistrate was Catholic, and attempted to fend off the poltergeist using crucifixes and religious pictures. But the pictures were thrown down and broken, the crucifixes burned or thrown away. Some of the poltergeist's written messages have already been given, but another read in part: '. . . The inmates of this house have done nothing against me. I will not leave them alone unless they become Hindus.' The sub-magistrate replied:

O Devil, You think it easy to convert me to Hinduism by your threatening writings. Beware, I am the child of God; I give you to understand clearly this moment once for all that I am ready to lose my property, wife, children and all that I possess and my life too. But don't think I will ever lose my soul. I am ready to die a martyr for the sake of my Saviour, Lord Jesus Christ.[47]

This exchange suggests that there was some hidden conflict either in

SORRAT members levitate a table.

the household or in certain members of it concerning whether they should have been following the traditional Hindu religious practices rather than the adopted Catholicism.

Most poltergeist researchers would now agree that the majority of poltergeist outbreaks are likely to be caused by repressed emotions within the family, though as yet it is certainly not clear how our emotions can produce sufficient energy to topple heavy pieces of furniture and accomplish the 'impossible' feats briefly mentioned earlier in this chapter, like passing one solid object through another, or teleporting living people from one location to another. Some research is continuing into phenomena of this kind, and the group known as SORRAT (Society for Research on Rapport and Telekinesis), working mainly in Missouri (USA), have produced under controlled conditions phenomena which we believe are relevant to a solution of the poltergeist mystery. They have levitated tables, and they have caused solid objects to move through other solid objects, thus confirming that the improbable is not the impossible.[48]

25

2 *Hairy man-beasts on the North American continent*

Six to eight feet tall, heavily built, covered in short dark hair, walking upright on two legs, and with a human-like footprint – such a creature can be found nowhere in the standard zoology texts. This being, named Bigfoot or Sasquatch, is taken seriously only by cryptozoologists (who search for the 'hidden' animals science ignores) and by those who claim to have seen it. There are a large number of the latter. A few years ago we compiled a list of Bigfoot sightings from 1818 to 1980, which was published in our book *Bigfoot Casebook*, and that contained almost 1000 sightings. Consider how many reports we must have missed, as well as the sightings never reported to anyone, and that 1000 becomes a conservative figure. Also, reports of discoveries of huge footprints without sightings of the creatures that made them are not included.

There is certainly plenty of documentary evidence for the existence of Bigfoot, the majority of sightings coming from the western states and provinces, from British Columbia in the north down through Washington, Oregon and California. However, sightings have been reported from virtually all the states and most of Canada too. Some of the reports include strange features of a paranormal nature, like telepathic communication between Bigfoot and human, or that Bigfoot is invulnerable to gunfire and can dematerialize, or that they are somehow associated with UFOs. As these only feature in a small proportion of reports we do not propose to cover them here, but further discussion of these aspects can be found in our books *Bigfoot Casebook* and *The Evidence for Bigfoot and Other Man-Beasts*. In the space available to us here we intend to bring readers an up-to-date picture of the North American Bigfoot scene in the 1980s. The activity up to 1980 has been well documented in our and others' books, but nowhere else have the post-1980 reports been published yet. The continued reporting of sightings should silence those critics who claimed that Bigfoot was only a 1970s media event.

A still from Roger Patterson's 1967 film of Bigfoot.
Photo Patterson/Gimlin, © 1968 Dahinden.

It is true that there was a big increase in sighting reports in that decade, and that the situation is now quieter again, but Bigfoot has certainly not disappeared, and it should not be forgotten that Bigfoot has been seen for many decades, way back into the last century.

It is frustrating for cryptozoologists that despite this long history of sightings, there is still no solid evidence for Bigfoot's existence – no corpse, no bones, no teeth, only a few hairs which *might* have come from a Bigfoot but which seem to be not much use as evidence because the analysts have no definitive sample of Bigfoot hair with

27

which to compare them. There is not even a photograph which everyone accepts as genuine. The nearest thing we have is Roger Patterson's cine film, shot on 20 October 1967 at Bluff Creek, northern California, and that is still the subject of controversy more than twenty years later. Roger Patterson is now dead, but his colleague on that momentous day, Bob Gimlin, is alive and still maintaining that the film shows a genuine Bigfoot, not a man in a fur suit. In an interview given to the Seattle, Washington, *Post Intel-*

Bob Gimlin holds 14½-inch casts from tracks made by the Bigfoot filmed by his colleague Roger Patterson at Bluff Creek, California.

ligencer in 1985,[1] Gimlin described what actually happened, and how he feels about it all now. He and Patterson were on horseback 40 or 50 miles from the nearest road, searching for Bigfoot after having heard of tracks being found in the area. 'We made the bend and around this big downfall tree, here this thing stood by the creek, just stood. We were on one side of the creek, the creature on the other and our horses went crazy. Roger's little horse just went bananas.' Patterson's horse reared and he slid off its back, pulling his movie camera from his saddlebag.

> As this all was going on, this creature turned and started to walk away from us, just slow like a man would if he were just walking down the street, but as it did this, Roger ran across the creek behind it, but then he stumbled on a sandbar. It was all happening just boom, boom, boom. He was shooting the camera while he was running. He hollered back for me when he stumbled and fell. He said, 'Cover me!' and, naturally, I knew what he meant. So I rode across the creek on my horse and took my 30.06 rifle out of the saddle scabbard and just stood there (pointing but not aiming the rifle at the beast). When I did this, this creature was quite a little ways away from me – about 90 feet – and it turned and looked at me; just turned as it was walking away. It never stopped walking. And then . . . I heard Roger say, 'Oh, my God, I ran out of film.' What he'd been doing was taking scenery-type pictures all the way up, see, and it was one of them old cameras where you had to get underneath something, in the dark, to change the film.

By the time he was able to change the film, the Bigfoot had gone. Gimlin says he has no doubt that the Bigfoot they saw was real. 'I'd have been better off if I said long ago that I believe it was a man in a fur suit because I took so much ridicule about it. But Roger's been dead a long time now, so I kind of feel I owe it to people to tell about what we saw.' Gimlin has no financial interest in the film, and could easily have earned plenty of money selling his confession to the media if the Bluff Creek events were a hoax by him and Patterson. That he has not done so tends to support his assertion that Patterson captured a genuine Bigfoot on film, and there are numerous scientists who think the same.

One scientist who is working in the Bigfoot field is Dr Grover S. Krantz, a physical anthropologist specializing in human evolution, and an associate professor at Washington State University. He

Dr Grover S. Krantz.

became interested after analysing the footprints of an apparently crippled Bigfoot found in the snow at Bossburg, Washington, in 1969. In 1982 he analysed casts of footprints found in the Blue Mountains of southern Washington/northern Oregon by Paul Freeman, who also saw a Bigfoot. These tracks were particularly impressive to Krantz because they showed the fine lines called dermal ridges, which would be extremely difficult for a hoaxer to incorporate in a fake foot. More tracks showing these patterns have been found since 1982, and early in 1987 Krantz saw the tracks themselves, in two locations. Fingerprint experts have examined the casts and the longer they take to look at them, the more likely they are to say that they are authentic. However, veteran Bigfoot hunter René Dahinden studied tracks found near Walla Walla (Washington) in November 1987 and concluded that they were faked, probably made by the hoaxer's hand. In common with other researchers, Krantz is convinced that a physical specimen must be obtained, to prove once and for all that Bigfoot does exist. He plans to fly over Bigfoot territory in a helicopter in the springtime, using an infra-red imager to try to locate the corpse of a Bigfoot that has died from natural causes. The imager would pick up the heat being given off by the decomposing body, a process that would begin in spring when the frozen bodies of animals that died in winter begin to thaw.[2]

With no corpse to examine, it is not possible for anyone to say

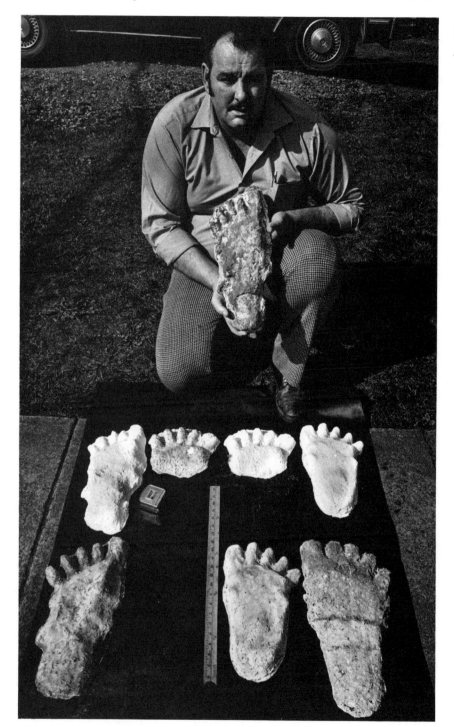

Paul Freeman, who saw a Bigfoot and found many tracks.

whether Bigfoot is animal or human. Some armed witnesses have felt unable to shoot it because it looked human, but appearances can be deceptive and the experts are not in agreement. There are several possible identifications, a popular one being *Gigantopithecus*, a creature which lived in southern China 500,000 years ago – but no one knows whether *Gigantopithecus* was human or animal either. Positive identification of the creature must wait until the scientists have physical remains for analysis, and if they can be obtained without killing a healthy specimen, so much the better.

In the meantime, it is somewhat depressing that most scientists will not concern themselves with the reports that are regularly published in the press, describing new sightings of what may be a unique prehistoric survival. They are right to be cautious, of course, for hoaxes do occur. In 1986, for example, a judge in Pennsylvania fined Craig Alan Brashear $10 plus $50.17 court costs for impersonating Bigfoot. Following reports of strange noises in the woods and bad smells (often reported by Bigfoot witnesses), Brashear dressed in a costume of fake fur and a wolfman mask and stepped into the light from car headlights. Bigfeet are often seen crossing roads, but it is hard to believe that the hundreds of sightings of this kind could all have been of hoaxers in fur suits. Other witnesses may have misidentified native animals like deer or bears, especially in poor light or with only a partial sighting of the creature, but again witnesses are often hunters whom one would expect to be familiar with the appearance of deer and bears, and indeed they are often adamant that what they saw was neither of those. Some of the large footprints may have been hoaxes, but surely not those which are discovered in remote forest areas where few people go.

Hoaxes and misidentifications there undoubtedly are, but is it likely that all of the thousands of creature sightings and footprints recorded over the last hundred years come into these categories? Keep an open mind about the reality of this elusive giant, as you read about some of the most recent, post-1980 sightings.

On 6 February 1981, a 7–8 foot, big, bulky creature was seen behind a restaurant near Rocks State Park (Maryland). It was sorting through rubbish, which included very smelly catfish. Witness Michael Green was on his way to work at 2.30 a.m., and stopped to watch the creature for ten minutes. Finally it walked slowly away.[3] Bigfeet have quite often been seen around homes, usually in rural areas, and it is thought to be the possibility of finding food which attracts them. In this case it may have smelled the catfish, although the report does not say that the Bigfoot was seen eating anything. Bigfeet have been witnessed eating a very wide variety of foodstuffs, including deer, birds, chickens, fish, clams, rabbits, and other small creatures, also apples, berries, corn, grass, twigs and leaves, fruits, roots, vegetables, tomatoes, water plants and convenience foods from rubbish containers at houses or on camp sites.

At the end of February, a couple having a quiet cuddle in their car five miles north of Veedersburg (Indiana) saw an unexpected sight in the car headlights. 'It had just rained that night,' he said. 'It was a nice night, no wind. We both stopped kissing and turned our heads to the front at the same time. That's when we saw it. It was on the outskirts of our lights, about two telephone poles away.'

'Both of us saw it simultaneously,' she said. 'We watched it until it was out of sight. It was only a few seconds. It went from the left side of the road to the right. It crossed the road in about three or four bounds.'

They wondered if it was a cow or a horse, but thought not. 'It was too tall,' he said. 'I saw it from the waist to the back of its shoulders. Its shoulders were what amazed me. It must have been that big across in the shoulders' (holding his arms about 2½ feet apart). 'Its hair looked like the colour of a dirty collie's hair. It looked clumped. The hair wasn't loose. It looked like it weighed 300 pounds easy. And it wasn't 300 pounds of fat – it was a hard body,' he said.

They agreed it was 8–9 feet tall and moved in an upright position. Both also agreed that they had never seen anything like it before, but it was suggested by a naturalist that they had seen a deer crossing the road.[4]

Also in Indiana, two miles south of Spraytown, an 8-foot, dark-haired creature was seen standing outside a house on the snowy night of 16 April 1981. The witness had got up to visit the outdoor toilet, at about 11 p.m., and saw the creature standing about 25 feet away. He also noticed a dirty, mouldy smell. He went inside to fetch more witnesses, but when they returned the creature had gone.[5]

Towards the end of April 1981, a Bigfoot apparently visited a house on the Rocky Boy Reservation in Montana. About 30 large footprints were found outside Jimmy Eagleman's house, in a fenced garden. They had four toes and were around 14 inches long, 8 inches wide, and 2 inches deep in hard soil. Tribal Police Captain Larry Bernard, weighing 200 pounds, was unable to make a dent in the soil when he tried to duplicate the tracks. The trail led off into the

Bearpaw Mountains, and long reddish hairs were found on a barbed-wire fence. Pete Walking Eagle, who was staying in the house, said they had heard noises, but saw nothing when they looked outside. His brother had seen a strange creature a while before; it was 'big and red and running down the road like an ape'.[6]

On 23 May 1981, two fishermen, both described as 'solid citizens', returning home from a fishing trip in the Franklin Section of the Newark Watershed in Sussex County (New Jersey), said they were driving down a dirt road when suddenly a strange creature strode across the road, through their car headlight beams. 'I slammed on my brakes and then quickly turned off the road to follow him down a dirt path. We were about five feet from him when my station wagon got stuck in mud.' They saw the creature was about 6½ feet tall, weighed slightly more than 300 pounds, and was covered all over with reddish-brown hair. It had a flat face and ears like a man and moved with a slight hunch, swinging its arms and clenching its fists. 'He was moving like a cross-country skier would move. I'll go to my grave knowing it wasn't a bear or anyone in a suit. I don't expect to ever see anything like that again.'[7] This is a familiar situation: a great many Bigfoot sightings are made at night, when the creature crosses the road in a lonely rural area, and is spotted momentarily in a vehicle's headlights. In this case, however, the driver followed it and was able to look at it from five feet away, albeit only briefly.

Again in late May 1981, but down south in Louisiana, in the cypress swamp near Ruddock in St John the Baptist parish, Harmon Levron and his sixteen-year-old son Mark were out hunting for poisonous snakes to shoot when they came across an unexpected prey – a Bigfoot. This time the sighting was made in daylight.

> We had each taken about three shots, when I looked at my son and he looked at me. Suddenly, there was a horrible smell in the air. I told Mark that somebody had probably dragged a dead cow into the swamp. So we moved to our right, trying to get out of the path of the smell. As we were walking, we heard a loud noise, like something really big crashing through the branches. Up ahead, about 30 or 40 feet, I saw a tall, shaggy-looking thing with long reddish-orange hair running deeper into the swamp.

They did not investigate further. Levron said, 'I'm telling you, as fast as that thing was running away from us, we were running away from it.'[8] There had apparently been other sightings in the past, and there was to be another about three months later, when eighteen-year-old Danny Simoneaux was on the levee one summer night near the Bayou Steel plant. He was waiting to go hunting in the swamp with his brother when he heard a noise from the direction of the river. 'I shined my light in the direction of the noise, and saw two big red eyes staring back at me. It was about 8 foot tall. I stayed long enough to see that, dropped my gun, and hauled off as fast as I could in the other direction. I still go hunting at night, but never alone.'[9]

Early in August 1981, three youngsters staying in a cabin near Plainfield (Wisconsin) were watched by a mysterious creature at least 7 feet tall and covered with slick, thick white hair. 'The eyes were like deep black hollows in its head and you couldn't see any nose or mouth. I was the only one who saw its eyes,' remembered fifteen-year-old Kim. It (or them, for there may have been two) would walk about outside, look in at the windows, sometimes clawing or pounding on the outside of the cabin, and the youngsters became scared to go outside. The siege lasted over the weekend, but the creature had gone on Monday morning. Returning home and telling their family, they were not at first believed, until their father saw the fear in their eyes. He went to the cabin and discovered human-like tracks 11 inches long in mud near the cabin.[10]

Another white Bigfoot was seen the following month, but in Decker Chapel (Indiana). At 9 a.m. on 25 September, Barbara Crabtree saw a 7–8 foot creature standing in a cornfield behind her home. It had dirty white hair and smelled bad. It also had huge eyes, 'but I couldn't tell you what colour they were because I didn't stand around long enough to look.' She believes it took a chicken which she threw on to the rubbish pile that morning, because it was gone in the afternoon. The same night, when she and her husband were returning from a drive-in movie, Mr Crabtree saw the same creature coming out of woods beside the road. A few days later, Mrs Crabtree heard loud growling outside the house, and the dog was barking. When her husband put on the front porch light, the growling stopped, but began again on the other side of the house.[11] This seems to be another instance of Bigfoot approaching rural houses in search of food. It is interesting that the last two reports were of white-haired creatures: white hair is not as often reported as dark hair, but is not uncommon either.

Also at the end of September 1981, Bigfoot was seen again near Little Eagle (South Dakota), where there were many sightings during 1978, turning this tiny Indian trading post (population 57) into a centre of hectic activity as outsiders flocked in to search for Bigfoot. This new sighting was by three teenagers who were hunting on a ridge ten miles north-west of Little Eagle. Their jeep had stalled and they were walking back to town when they saw three black creatures maybe 10 feet tall. They were moving rapidly, walking upright on two legs. All three boys are seasoned hunters, but were scared by what they saw, and dived to the ground to watch from there.[12]

On a farm in Michigan's Upper Peninsula, thirteen-year-old Tina Barone had quite a surprise when she went into the barn one Friday night in mid-November 1981. There had already been some unusual activity by an unknown creature, with doors ripped off their hinges, grain barrels interfered with, fences damaged, and screaming heard. Then came Tina's experience. She was with her twelve-year-old sister.

> Roxanne was scared to go into the barn because she'd heard noises before. I said I would go first, so I reached for the light. I felt fur. It felt thick and dirty. At first I thought it was a goat or something, so I took my glove off and I touched it again. It didn't look like anything. It was tall with red eyes and big and black and furry and stood on two legs. It had a deep growl.

As she turned to walk slowly from the barn, so as not to provoke the creature, 'it started walking out behind me and I started running'. But it never tried to harm her. Eighteen-year-old David, the girls' cousin, got his shotgun. 'It was some kind of animal,' he said, 'but I can't describe what. It was about 6 feet 6, or 7 feet 6. I didn't shoot to kill. I just shot in the air to scare it away. It was standing on two feet and had real long arms – between a bear and an ape, that's what I think. I've never seen a Bigfoot, so I have no idea if it was one of those.'[13]

Tina's mother, Cindy Barone, saw the creature too, early in December. 'It sort of sits near the barn facing the house so it can look in at us. It's done it before. I think it's after our apples or grain molasses – our bags of grain have been broken into. If it goes into hibernation now and disappears, then we'll know for sure.' She believed it was a pet bear that had escaped from its owner two years before.[14] But the Bigfoot experts were doubtful, because the descriptions given sound much more like a Bigfoot, especially its walking on two legs, which is not usual with bears. Michigan

Department of Natural Resources wildlife biologists were also doubtful about it being a bear, saying that a bear would have been seen more often. 'Bears are very visible. They aren't nocturnal, and they have no natural enemies – so they don't try to hide. It isn't very likely one could be here without someone seeing it.' Another Michigan resident saw a large hairy animal and decided it was a bear. This was early in December, in Lexington Township, about ten miles south-west of the Barone farm. Kathy Hensley's dogs were barking at 6.15 a.m., so she went outside to investigate and in the light from the porch saw an animal over 6 feet tall stand on its hind legs and throw her German shepherd dog, which fortunately survived the attack.[15]

The two law enforcement officials who saw a large hairy creature run across the road ahead of them were quite certain it was no bear, nor a hoaxer. It was about 4.30 on an early February morning in 1982, and the men were on Route 22 in the Adirondacks (New York). The creature they saw was ape-like, 7–8 feet tall, covered in dirty, mangy dark brown fur. It took big strides, and its long arms swung like a human's. It also had highly reflective eyes. 'There's no way in hell that I could believe this was a man in a fur suit!' commented one of the officers.[16]

Bigfoot sightings in the western states of the USA and Canada are not now so frequent as they used to be, and so far none of the 1981–2 reports we have given has come from that area. Our next report does come from Washington state, and has proved to be a very controversial case. The witness was Paul Freeman, a 39-year-old US Forest Service patrolman working in the Umatilla National Forest in the Walla Walla area of the Blue Mountains. At 11.30 a.m. on 10 June 1982 he was alone in the forest.

> Suddenly I saw something step off a bank about 10 feet high and down on to the road. I saw him about the same time as he saw me. He looked like all the pictures I've seen of prehistoric man. He was real hairy – reddish-brown hair. It was so thick you couldn't see through it on his shoulders, arms and legs. But on his face and chest it was thin enough to see his skin, the colour of brown leather.
>
> I was about 65 yards away from him and I just stood there looking at him and he looked at me. I could hear him breathing real heavy as though he'd been running and I could see the muscles in his stomach moving. But that was the only noise he

made. I was scared and I started backing away a few feet. He made the hair stand up on his neck and shoulders just like a dog does when it tries to frighten someone . . . When he saw I wasn't coming any further he turned and walked up the road.

Freeman thought the Bigfoot was at least 8 feet tall, and very heavy. He was convinced that he was not looking at a bear, with which he was very familiar, or a man in a gorilla suit – he could see the muscles moving in its legs, arms and shoulders. 'I've been working in the wilderness for years and . . . never seen anything like it.'

Shortly after telephoning them from a forest service cabin, Freeman was joined by colleagues, and together they photographed and took casts of the footprints left by the creature. They found twenty-one tracks, each 14 inches long by 7 inches wide, and 6–8 feet apart. A week or so later, more tracks were found close by. Some were an inch deep in moist ground, and there were apparently two creatures, each estimated to weigh about 600 pounds. These were the tracks on which Dr Grover Krantz found evidence of dermal ridges, and in the following years Freeman continued to find tracks in the Blue Mountains, which has made some Bigfoot researchers suspicious, though if there really are Bigfeet living in that area, then we would expect there to be tracks also.[17]

Only two days after Freeman's Bigfoot sighting on 10 June, Robert France claims that he too saw a Bigfoot, but in the Chestnut Ridge above the Derry Township village of Hillside, across the other side of the continent in Pennsylvania. France was very familiar with the wildlife of the area, and knew the creature he saw was not a bear or a deer.[18] Don Cunningham, a constable with the Dakota-Ojibway Tribal Council, thought it might be a deer he could see beside the road as he drove his wife and children to Winnipeg (Manitoba) in August 1982. But when it stood erect, he knew it was not. Man-sized and covered with brown fur, it also had a white head and light grey beard. Cunningham chased the creature, which ran like a monkey, and he also found footprints 16 inches across which looked like a human hand.[19]

The same month, a Bigfoot visited a farm at Ellington, Connecticut, and was seen by two farm workers on the night shift. Just after midnight on 23 August 1982, they came face to face with a creature 6–7 feet tall, covered in dark brown hair, and sitting on the edge of a feed bin. Its hand was in the silage inside the bin and it was watching the cows. The two men shouted and ran away, and immediately called the police, but when they arrived there was nothing to be seen.[20]

It was the size of the Bigfoot she saw which most impressed Martha Saulsbury. She and her husband were at Lundy Lake north of Yosemite (California) on 10 September 1982, and it was early in the morning when Mrs Saulsbury picked up her high-powered field glasses and looked at the countryside half to three-quarters of a mile away. She saw 'a big man'. 'Then he walked to the edge of the road and stood there. He looked like a redwood stump, he was so big. I realized it couldn't be a man. He took only two steps and walked behind a switchback. Then he hiked up on a ledge. A pickup truck came along and it looked like a toy cab. The people inside looked like little matchsticks. That's when I realized how big he was.' The people in the pickup never saw him, because they never looked up on to the ledge where he was standing above the road.[21]

Bigfoot sightings were sparse in 1983. One of the few reported took place at Grant's Pass, Oregon, in typical Bigfoot country. A motorcyclist from Nevada, riding through the rain, stopped to report to police that he had seen a 7-foot hairy creature looking like Bigfoot. His headlights showed it standing upright on the road, and as he approached it turned to look at him before running off the road.[22] Another quiet year was 1984, though not for 34-year-old Fred Ranaudo, who was camping in the woods at Lawrenceburg (New York) on 4 June. 'I lit a fire, my truck was parked right beside me, and I was sort of laying there in my sleeping bag. I was on sort of a knob, a high part of the terrain. Down below me toward the road was a creek and a beaver pond. I let the fire go out, and I went to sleep.' He woke at about 3.30 a.m., and heard cries from a wooded area close by.

> I sat bolt upright, and I was looking around. There was no moon, but the stars were out. I didn't have my glasses on, but I could see pretty well. I'd been awake for a while, and my eyes were adjusted to the night . . . I was sitting up, and I turned around to look in the field, and I heard this thing coming through the underbrush. It was making loud thuds. I could hear its feet hitting the ground. I could hear it coming for quite a distance before I saw it, but finally I saw this white shape coming out of the darkness. It was walking at a pretty good pace, but the thing was that it was breathing real hard, like it had asthma, or it had been running real hard. They were big heavy noises, you know, *big* noises, very

loud. My eyes were popping open. It got to be – now I didn't measure the distance; I should have – probably 50 to 75 yards away. I saw it as a large vertical white shape. About the size of a sheet of plywood, so I figure it must have been about nine feet tall. Anyway it was coming up, and it didn't see me yet. It was downwind of me, and the fire had gone out. All of a sudden, it sees me, and it hops up in the air. It was cruising along, and all of a sudden it stops and jumps. It made a big hop, and then it made two little hops after that. It didn't make any other noises other than continued heavy breathing. But when it made its big hop, I hopped too; I jumped out of my sleeping bag and got into my truck. You know this thing was big. It was *very* large, and it was white, and it was furry. I was looking at it pretty closely, and even though I couldn't see it that clearly, I definitely had a feeling about what it was. Anyway, I got in the truck. I rolled the window down and stuck my head out, and I could see it fading back into the darkness. And then it disappeared, and I didn't hear it any more.

Next morning, he found 15-inch footprints where the Bigfoot had been. When he tried to tell people about his experience, he got the usual mixed reactions, but was philosophical about it, saying he wouldn't mind if there was not a rush to find the creature. 'I'd just as soon they leave him alone. I know I believe it. I don't really care if anybody else believes it.'[23]

After these two quiet years, when it looked as though Bigfoot had become *persona non grata* with the media, or, worse still, had reached the point of extinction as a living species, in 1985 a gradual increase in sightings took place. One location of repeated sightings was Colonial Beach, Virginia, where there had been some strange events, notably bad smells and nocturnal screaming, in 1977, 1978 and 1980. The early eighties were quiet, then in 1985 the activity began again, and on 20 June the first creature sighting took place. The family were in the kitchen that night, when they saw a tall ape-like creature in the backyard. Its eyes were glowing white. In August, more sightings were made, of a dark form moving into the woods, and a neighbour saw a dark form sitting on a log in her backyard. It ran away into the woods. Activity continued through 1986 and into 1987, with dark shapes and white eyes being seen at night.[24]

An exceedingly strange Bigfoot encounter was reported in July 1985, from the Greenwater area of Washington state. A couple

camping off the road were attacked before dawn on 6 July by a
bear-like animal 8 feet tall, ugly and smelly, with curly brown hair.
The unusual feature of this case is that the Bigfoot, if that is what it
was, spoke to them. In a high-pitched voice which didn't sound
human, it asked their names and whether they had permission to use
the campsite. They said they had permission, but it told them to get
off the property immediately. As they gathered their belongings
together, it stood on its hind legs and began throwing stones at
them.[25] We have heard of cases where Bigfeet have thrown rocks at
people and done other things to get them to leave, when presumably
the Bigfoot is defending its territory, but cases of talking Bigfeet are
rare indeed. This is one case where a human in a fur suit *must* surely
be the explanation.

In Medinah (Illinois) on 15 August 1985, five golfers saw a
Bigfoot on the golf course at the country club. The creature, 5 feet 6
inches to 6 feet tall, watched them from behind a tree, before walking
along the fence-line, then returning to the tree, climbing it and
vaulting over the fence and away. It was dark in colour, covered in
smooth hair, wore no clothes, and was very agile and wary. It had no
neck, and no snout, its face being pug-like. One witness said,

> At first I thought that this creature was of the ape family, or a man
> dressed in an ape suit. The ape theory was dispelled when I saw its
> walk, which was much more upright than that of an ape and, also,
> its physical proportions were that of a human, not of an ape. The
> human theory was dispelled by the agility with which it climbed
> the tree and jumped the fence. I think it most improbable that any
> human could scale a tree with the speed and agility that this
> creature showed.[26]

Similar physical descriptions were given of a creature seen in East
Pennsboro Township, Pennsylvania, in late September. The animal's head seemed to sit on its shoulders, with no neck being visible,
and it had no snout as a bear's profile has. These two details are
frequently mentioned by Bigfoot witnesses, and are obviously note-
worthy features, in addition to the familiar ones of height, bulk, and
dark body hair. Most people have not read so widely into Bigfoot
reports that they know the creature has no neck and no snout, and so
the fact that they report these features (or lack of them) would
suggest that they are describing something they have really seen, and
not just imagined. The East Pennsboro creature was seen outside a

house, the occupant being drawn to look outside on noticing a bad smell that made him feel sick. The bad smell is another oft-occurring feature of Bigfoot reports, but certainly not one that a hoaxer without Bigfoot knowledge would be likely to think of adding to his story. The creature ran off as the witness shouted. A motorist also saw the Bigfoot, and was as close as 8 feet as he drove by it. He also reported that it had no neck, was 6½ feet tall and hair-covered. It bared its teeth at him, showing long fangs, which other Bigfoot witnesses have also reported.[27]

Early in 1986, truck drivers passing along a lonely stretch of highway north of Tres Piedras (New Mexico) were reporting seeing a huge hairy creature with red eyes. Bears were blamed, but the reports described a more monkey-like creature, and local people said that whatever it was had been in the area for years.[28] An early August report showed that Bigfoot is still around in the Pacific Northwest from where so many reports have come in earlier decades. A five-man construction team building a foot and horse bridge over the South Fork of the Kern River in Inyo National Forest (California) heard loud screams at twilight and saw the shadowy outline of a tall human-like creature. When one of the men fired a warning shot in the air, the creature went over the top of the hill and disappeared. Those of the men familiar with pumas said that the screams were different from a puma's. The scream was so loud it sounded 'like a stadium loudspeaker'.[29]

Later the same month, on 24 August, David A. Brown saw a Bigfoot while searching for ginseng on Taylor's Ridge, Chattooga County, Georgia. He had heard noises and shouted out to what he thought was a friend who had followed him, but there was silence. Then he heard a noise behind him, turned, and saw the Bigfoot 20–25 feet away. It was panting or breathing hard, as if it had been running. 'I was froze to the ground, I couldn't move,' remarked Brown. 'I was afraid it would attack me.' He got a good look at the creature, which he described as 7½ feet tall and weighing 350 to 400 pounds, with a horrible smell. It was covered with hair which fell in thick black locks, and the face looked monkey-like, with large eyes, a flat nose, and thick lips. It seemed to be old and to have no teeth, but that made no difference to Brown because 'I thought it could still eat me.' Its left arm and leg appeared to be hurt, and the left hand had long curved fingernails, but the right hand had short fingernails and appeared normal. Asked if it might have been a bear, Brown responded: 'Naw, it was no bear. I'm sure it was no bear. I sat and

Bigfoot hunter René Dahinden standing beside an 8-foot sculpture of Bigfoot by Jim McClarin, at Willow Creek, California.

stared at him three or four minutes and it was nothing like any bear I've ever seen.' The encounter ended when the creature grunted and walked away down the ridge.[30]

In West Virginia, a father and son claimed they were attacked by

43

two Bigfeet on Dillon's Mountain near Cacapon Bridge, on 25 October. They were hunting wild turkeys when they were surrounded and trapped by a male and a female Bigfoot, which kept circling round them, snarling, growling and lunging at the men. When the father managed to grab his gun and fire into the air, the Bigfeet ran off. This behaviour is not typical: Bigfoot has rarely been reported attacking humans, and some researchers are sceptical of the men's claims.[31] From October 1986 and into the spring of 1987 there were several claimed sightings of Bigfoot in Pennsylvania, including one with glowing red eyes which walked in front of a car in a remote area of Gray Station on 1 February 1987. Another was seen in the same area on 8 April. The 8–10 foot creature came out of woods towards a motorist sitting in his parked car, and was within 30 feet before the man drove quickly away. Two men on a back road near New Alexandria on 16 May saw a Bigfoot standing near an old bridge, blocking their way. Shouts did not bother it, so one of the men fired twice over its head, and it walked slowly away into the woods.[32]

A little earlier in the spring, on 14 March, four men working at night at an oil well in an isolated clearing at Fellers Heights south of Dawson Creek (British Columbia, Canada) noticed a 7-foot Bigfoot skulking in the trees around their work-site. It was peering at them, and circling around. 'It was like we were on his territory and he was checking us out,' one of the men commented. They were sure it was not a bear: its legs were too long and it moved too 'fluidly', and anyway bears were still in hibernation in the bitterly cold weather. Footprints left in the snow were as big as a size 18 men's shoe, and were about 6 feet apart. Bigfoot expert René Dahinden commented, 'Planting footprints in the ground six feet apart in a foot and one-half of snow with no disturbance between the prints is just not that simple [for a hoaxer]'. The creature had also been seen kneeling down, and marks found in the snow confirmed this, with the knees apparently being 3 feet apart.[33]

Multi-witness cases, especially if the report is supported by footprints, are more likely to be convincing than single-witness reports, because if the creature really was a bear, or a deer, or a hoaxer, it is likely that one of the witnesses would be able to identify it. When a group of workmen are all scared by what they see, then the chances are that the creature was as terrifying as they said it was. Another multi-witness sighting occurred on 24 April 1987, when three out-of-work loggers pulled their truck off Highway 89 near

Truckee (California) to eat dinner. They were brewing coffee when they heard a scream, and saw a hairy animal 9 or 10 feet tall, burnt-black in colour, and standing on its hind legs. When it saw them, it moved away, walking with long strides. They drove to Truckee and reported their sighting to the police, who questioned them and established that they were convinced it was not a bear. 'They appeared to be very shaken up,' said Sheriff Moseley.[34]

Witness Walter Bowers Sr has shot four bears and knows what they look like. When he saw a Bigfoot in October 1987 and reported it by phone to the game warden, the man laughed and said it was probably a bear or a moose. When Bowers retorted he knew the difference between what he saw, a bear and a moose, the warden got angry and hung up. Bowers, a retired caretaker, was out pheasant hunting at Salisbury, New Hampshire. As he crossed a field, he felt he was being watched. Then he saw the Bigfoot, out in the field.

> This thing was BIG. I would say at least 9 feet. Maybe less, maybe more, because I didn't stick around too long to do any measuring . . . The whole body was covered with hair . . . I would say it was kind of a greyish colour, from where I was standing. Of course the sun was coming up facing me, but it wasn't that bright . . . The face, I couldn't make that out too good . . . The hands were like yours or mine, only three times bigger, with pads on the front paws, like a dog . . . Long legs, long arms. It was just like, I would say, like a gorilla, but this here wasn't a gorilla . . . I'm tellin' ya, it would make your hair stand up.

The creature ran off towards a large swamp after a few moments. Bowers remembered that only recently a hunter had told him how he had seen two strange creatures walking across this same field.[35]

These recent reports show that the usual explanations of misidentified bears or deer, or hoaxes, will not stand up to examination in most cases. The creatures, often seen clearly, do not look like bears or deer; and hoaxers would be crazy to go wandering through the woods dressed in fur suits, knowing that trigger-happy hunters may take a shot at them. Even if we can discard 50 per cent of the reports as dubious in some way, there are still many good reports by reliable witnesses which cannot be ignored. Their message, incredible though it may seem, is that Bigfoot is alive and well and living in North America.

3 UFOs – mysterious or mundane?

UFOs are real, of that there can be no doubt. It all depends, though, on what you mean by 'real' . . . Thousands of reports world-wide since 'flying saucers' first hit the headlines in 1947 indicate that people are seeing something in the sky and, lacking any immediate explanation, are calling that something a UFO, or unidentified flying object. From that basic starting-point the subject becomes more complex, for there are many possible explanations for what is seen. All the explanations in the world, however, cannot conceal the fact that many sightings remain inexplicable and puzzling. The strangest cases, those involving UFO landings, entities, abductions and contacts, will be dealt with in Chapter 6. Here we will introduce the subject of UFOs by means of the most straightforward sightings of lights or solid craft in the sky.

UFO sightings are reported from all corners of the world – China, the USSR, Australia, Africa, remote locations like Antarctica or Christmas Island in the Indian Ocean – there is nowhere in the world where UFOs have not been seen. So it is not a purely Western phenomenon. Also, sightings pre-date 1947, the year when pilot Kenneth Arnold's sighting in Washington State began the modern media interest in 'flying saucers', as they were called in those more innocent days when 'flying saucer' meant 'visitor from outer space'.

The pre-1947 sightings can be very interesting, because the witnesses describe UFOs which are very similar to those reported in subsequent decades. One problem with UFO reports is that because of the wide media coverage the subject has had over the years, there are now unlikely to be any witnesses who have never heard anything about UFOs. So the reports may be coloured by what the witness already knows of them. Uncontaminated witnesses – those from remote societies where media coverage is small or non-existent, or those who recorded sightings before 1947 – are therefore very valuable. They are also very rare. When the strictest criteria are followed, few cases are eligible, and all those discovered by us when researching this aspect of UFOs involve the presence of entities, so they will fit more appropriately into Chapter 6.

Our research for this chapter has revealed that there are a considerable number of reports of UFOs seen by pilots. Not only are pilots familiar with the sky and what things look like from up there, they are not likely to be easily excitable people and they are also unlikely to be hoaxers, because involvement in a hoax could risk their job. For the same reason, there may be pilot–UFO encounters which have gone unreported, especially if a pilot was alone in the plane and there are no other witnesses to the sighting. However, there are plenty of pilot sightings on record, one of them being the event which began the modern era of UFO sightings in 1947.

The witness in that case was Kenneth Arnold, a civilian pilot aged 32, flying his own single-engine plane over the Cascade Mountains of Washington State (USA) on 24 June 1947. He was an experienced mountain pilot, and so when his attention was alerted by flashes of light and he saw nine bright objects flying in and out of the highest peaks, he knew he was looking at something unusual. They did not look like aircraft, he calculated they were flying faster than was possible for the aircraft of the time, and their motion was unusual: 'they flew like a saucer would if you skipped it across the water.' The press picked up Arnold's story, and 'flying saucers' were born. In the years since, researchers have looked again at Arnold's account, in particular Hans Van Kampen who believes he has found the true explanation. It has been calculated by Dr J. Allen Hynek, a respected scientific UFO researcher, that the size and distance of the objects as claimed by Arnold were unlikely to be accurate, and that they were probably not flying as fast as he estimated. Arnold himself has said that he at first assumed that they were some type of jet aircraft even though he thought their appearance and behaviour contradicted this. Hans Van Kampen has studied Arnold's descriptions, and investigated what terrestrial aircraft were in existence in 1947. He concluded that Arnold may have seen a flight of F-84 Thunderjets, which were at that time still secret. He used his computer to compare the shapes Arnold drew, with the shape of the F-84, and found some striking correlations. So were the first 'UFOs' really jet aircraft?[1]

Another 1940s pilot encounter with a UFO which was given great prominence in early UFO books took place over Godman Air Force Base, Fort Knox, Kentucky (USA), on 7 January 1948. Four jets went up to investigate 'an ice cream cone topped with red', and one pilot, Captain Thomas F. Mantell, radioed back:

> I'm closing in now to take a good look. It's directly ahead of me and still moving at about half my speed . . . the thing looks metallic and of tremendous size. It's going up now and forward as fast as I am . . . that's 360 mph. I'm going up to 20,000 feet, and if I'm no closer, I'll abandon chase.

Nothing more was heard from him, and his crashed plane was found later in the day. Mantell was dead, probably killed by lack of oxygen at 20,000 feet. Everyone was puzzled by Mantell's description of the object he had been chasing: was it a UFO? Only years later did it become known that Skyhook weather balloons, in 1948 a military secret, were being tested in the area at the time, and it was probably one of those he was chasing.[2]

That is two 'UFOs' which were probably man-made artefacts – can the same explanation be ascribed to the unusual craft seen by the pilot and co-pilot of a DC-3 flying at 5000 feet between Mobile and Montgomery, Alabama (USA), on 24 July 1948? At 2.45 a.m. Clarence S. Chiles and John B. Whitted saw a dull red glow ahead of them and thought it was a new army jet. But when the craft passed them about half a mile away, they were not so sure. It had no wings and looked like a cigar 100 feet long and 30 feet in diameter. It seemed to have a cockpit at the front (according to one witness) and glowing windows along the side (according to the other, who did not see the cockpit). It had a blue fluorescent glow below it, as well as the orange exhaust. They heard no sound from it, and they saw it for 10–15 seconds. Several astronomers said it was a bright meteor, but Chiles and Whitted could not accept this explanation, because they had seen the craft perform apparently intelligently controlled manoeuvres.[3]

Only two months later, George T. Gorman found himself chasing a UFO over Fargo, North Dakota (USA). He was in an F-51 fighter that evening when he saw a blinking light which he thought was on an aircraft, but he was unable to catch up with it. It kept turning to avoid him and then coming towards him. Both craft circled and dived at each other for nearly half an hour before the mysterious intruder went straight upwards and disappeared. Other people had also seen the light, but had not seen it manoeuvring. The authorities concluded that Gorman had been chasing a lighted weather balloon or, alternatively, that during the second part of the event Gorman had been chasing a mirage of the planet Jupiter, caused by temperature inversions. Apparently on that evening, Jupiter sank below the horizon at the time Gorman saw the light climb up and disappear.[4]

It is quite likely that these explanations are valid, because under certain atmospheric conditions the unusual appearance of natural phenomena and man-made airborne objects can confuse even the best-trained observer. There is a wide range of natural phenomena that could be misidentified, as we show later in this chapter when we consider some of the explanations which have been suggested for UFO reports. But some pilot reports do remain inexplicable, such as our next case, which concerns a DC-4 airliner flying at 8000 feet in the area of Newport News, Virginia (USA), on the evening of 14 July 1952. Captain William B. Nash was at the controls and Second Officer William Fortenberry was with him. They both saw six red objects moving fast towards them, travelling in formation. The objects were circular and clearly defined, and were about a mile below the plane. The two men saw the objects, plus two more which joined them, for about fifteen seconds as they manoeuvred, still in formation. Nash and Fortenberry later calculated their speed as 12,000 mph. No meteorological or other conditions could be found to account for this sighting, of which there were other, ground-based, witnesses.[5]

Aerial UFO encounters often last only seconds rather than minutes, and this was again the case for Carlos Alejo Rodriguez, whose encounter took place on 5 May 1958 as he was flying his Piper near San Carlos, Uruguay. It was afternoon and visibility was good. Rodriguez's attention was attracted by a bright point of light towards the sea, a light that appeared to be approaching him at speed. As Rodriguez later remembered it:

> More than flying, it seemed to glide through the air at an incredible speed, coming to a stop at a distance of 600 metres (roughly 2000 feet) ahead of me. It remained there, perfectly at rest, giving me the opportunity to see it well. It was like a child's top and its cross section could be compared to a flattened rhomboid. It was spinning really fast, and it appeared to be metallic, reflecting the sunlight as if it were aluminium. I wanted to see it better and I attempted a closer approach. At that time, I could think of nothing but of getting a better view. I was sweating profusely, and heavy drops of perspiration were running down my

forehead. I removed my flying jacket and threw it to the back, to be ready for whatever contingency might occur.

When he was about 1500 feet away, the object disappeared quickly towards the sea and Rodriguez could not keep up with it.[6]

The four witnesses of a UFO over Mansfield, Ohio (USA), on 18 October 1973 were travelling in a helicopter, their commander being Captain Lawrence J. Coyne, a very experienced pilot. It was about 11 p.m. when they saw a red light, which soon appeared to have turned and be heading towards them. To avoid a collision, Captain Coyne began to take the helicopter down; then the light stopped and hovered in front of them for 10–12 seconds, and they could see a cigar-shaped object about 60 feet long, grey and metallic-looking with possible windows. A green beam of light was directed at them, lighting up their cockpit. Then the UFO took off and disappeared in the west. Down on the ground, a woman and four children driving near Mansfield had witnessed the encounter and saw the green light: 'It was like rays coming down. The helicopter, the trees, the road, the car – everything turned green.' Attempts by disbelievers to label the UFO a meteor have been easily countered; nor was the object a conventional aircraft.[7]

In the majority of UFO sightings by pilots, the witness is convinced that the UFO is going to crash into the plane – it comes towards it at speed, as if it has noticed the plane and wants to get a closer look at it. But crashes rarely occur – we cannot say never, for reasons that will soon become clear. Carlos de los Santos Montiel was another pilot who experienced a near-miss. He was flying to Mexico City on 3 May 1975 when he spotted a dark grey metallic disc 10–12 feet in diameter flying just above his wingtip. Looking out at the other wing, he saw another UFO there. Baffled, he looked ahead and saw a third coming towards him at speed. Just before colliding with him, the UFO changed course and flew below him – so close that he felt it scraping the underside of the plane. As the plane lurched, Carlos discovered that the controls no longer worked. But his plane did not crash, and flew along normally. As the two UFOs on either side shot away, his controls were found to be working again and he radioed the airport and learned that the encounter had been tracked on radar.[8]

Floyd Hallstrom, piloting a Cessna 170A over Santa Monica, California (USA), on 1 January 1978, had a very clear sighting of a domed UFO which passed by him just after 1 p.m., in very clear conditions. It was travelling fast below him about half to three-quarters of a mile away, and he at first thought it must be a helicopter. It had no wings, no tail or fins, and he soon realized it had no rotors either. It was also travelling too fast for a helicopter. It was round and of a bright metal, with dark windows. No markings or protrusions of any kind were seen, nor any lights, other than the sun reflecting on the dome. It did not alter course, passing at a speed around 600 mph. Hallstrom knew that by the time he turned his plane, the UFO would be out of sight. Ufologists later traced a ground sighting of a similar UFO from Downey, California, ten minutes after Hallstrom's sighting.[9]

Most pilots live to tell the tale of their UFO encounter, experiencing nothing worse than momentary fear as a collision seems imminent. However, there is a possibility that not all pilots are so fortunate. The mysterious disappearance of twenty-year-old Frederick Valentich on 21 October 1978 has been attributed to a too-close encounter with a UFO. Valentich was flying a Cessna 182 from Moorabbin Airport, Victoria (Australia), across Bass Strait to King Island. He radioed that he had seen a 'large aircraft' with four

A depiction by artist Michael Buhler of the mysterious disappearance of Frederick Valentich.

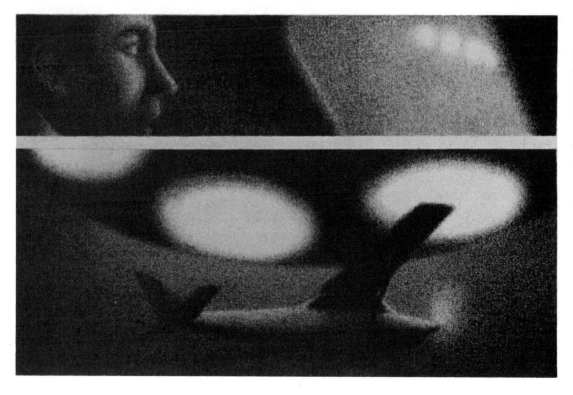

bright lights pass close to his plane. It had then hovered over him, causing engine trouble and a radio blackout. At one point in the conversation, Valentich said: 'It's flying past. It has a long shape. Cannot identify more than that . . . coming for me right now. It seems to be stationary. I'm orbiting and the thing is orbiting on top of me. It has a green light and sort of metallic like on the outside.' His last transmission ended with 17 seconds of a loud metallic sound. Neither Valentich nor his plane was ever seen again, and to this date the mystery has not been solved, but it seems at least possible that a UFO was involved in his disappearance. If he crashed into the sea, it is strange that no wreckage was found.[10]

Only two months later, strange lights were photographed from a plane flying off the north-east coast of New Zealand's South Island. A camera crew was aboard the plane which left Wellington on 30 December 1978, following a UFO sighting nine days earlier by a pilot flying in the same area. Reporter Quentin Fogarty and the camera crew were planning to reconstruct the eventful 21 December flight, never expecting to see UFOs for themselves. But just after midnight, they saw lights above Kaikoura, and the objects were also picked up on radar. The UFOs accompanied them to Christchurch, where the plane arrived 50 minutes later. Lights were also seen on the return journey from Christchurch back to Blenheim. The resulting film was analysed scientifically and many explanations were put forward to explain the lights – such as Venus or other planets, stars, meteors, balloons, aircraft, ground-lights, fishing boats, hoax – but there were convincing reasons for rejecting all these, and the sightings remain unexplained.[11]

The UFO seen over Ontario (Canada) on 18 August 1979 was described as a 'rolling energy ball with a red radiant side and a white radiant side'. The plane, a Cherokee Warrior containing pilot and passenger, was flying 40 miles north-east of Ottawa at 4000 feet when the wings began to glow red. The airspeed indicator fell to zero, and the controls jammed, but the plane kept on flying. The men looked out to see if there was anything outside, and saw the 'energy ball' measuring approximately 300 feet in diameter. It was above them, and the plane seemed to be moving up towards it. For between five and eight minutes the instruments and controls went haywire, until the light moved away and disappeared at speed.[12]

A huge UFO, twice as big as an aircraft carrier, was seen by a Japanese pilot carrying French wine to Tokyo. Late in the afternoon of 17 November 1986, Captain Kenju Terauchi's plane was over north-east Alaska (USA) and travelling south-west at 35,000 feet. He saw in the distance unusual lights which seemed to be travelling along with the plane. He reported: 'It was about seven or so minutes since we began paying attention to the lights when, most unexpectedly, two spaceships stopped in front of our face, shooting off lights. The inside cockpit shined brightly and I felt warm in the face.' The UFOs flew along with the plane, just ahead and to the left, giving off bright lights, some steady and some flashing. The plane's radar picked up the objects. Later in the journey, the captain could see the silhouette of a 'gigantic spaceship'. Another pilot taking off from Anchorage was asked to see if he could see anything behind the Japanese plane. He reported: 'he has traffic following him, sir. It's unknown traffic . . .' As he got closer, the spaceship disappeared. Debunkers contended that Jupiter and possibly Mars were responsible for the sightings, but these were ruled out. Other planets and stars were also ruled out, as were hallucinations.[13]

Unusually, the Alaskan UFO encounter lasted over half an hour. As we have seen, they are usually much briefer. A sighting over Kazakhstan (USSR) was much shorter, more like a UFO fly-past. The date was 22 April 1987, and the witnesses were British, five crew members of a British Airways jumbo jet flying from London to Bangkok. First officer Anthony Colin described what happened.

We were changing over duties on the flight deck. All five of us were together. Suddenly we saw what appeared to be another aircraft away to our right. It was displaying two white lights just like an aircraft would. We watched it carefully and then noticed that there was a green light where there should have been a red port-side navigation light. It was clear that it was coming towards us at about the same level so we turned towards it to ensure that we passed behind it. As we did so it accelerated across our nose, displaying a long line of small lights. They were vaguely phosphorescent and vanished off to our left at high speed. It was impossible to say exactly how far away it was but I would guess it was about a mile. It was definitely not an aircraft, of that I am positive. None of us had ever seen anything like it before. We are all bitter, cynical aviators who like to find a scientific explanation for everything. But this has got us foxed.

The director of the artificial satellite section of the British Astronomical Association had an explanation:

Everything fits with a satellite re-entering the earth's atmosphere. It is a standard description with the greenish glow as the parts of the satellite break up. Although for the moment I cannot say exactly which satellite it was I am sure it was one. They normally burn up about 80 miles up and the aircraft was only ten miles high. It must therefore have been an optical illusion with the actual lights being much further away.

This explanation may be valid, but in the light of other pilot sightings of UFOs, we are not so sure. The precise satellite could not be named, and the burn-up would have taken place much further from the plane than the object seemed to be, both of which count against the proposed explanation.[14]

A 25 June 1987 sighting near Charleston, West Virginia (USA), took place during daylight hours and a solid craft was seen. The Boeing 737 was at 29,500 feet when the pilot saw a 'missile' heading straight for the jet. It passed to the side and slightly below, and the pilot saw a rocket-shaped object about 4 feet long, with fins. A weather balloon was suggested, but the sighting was twenty-five minutes before the day's launch from the nearest launching station, and the wind was not strong enough to make a weather balloon move fast. Also, the pilot would have recognized a weather balloon seen so close.[15]

These cases, just a sample of pilots' reports of UFOs, are all intriguing. They demonstrate that in the majority of cases, no straightforward explanation can be found. Debunkers' explanations often involve unfounded assumptions and do not take into account the experience pilots have of judging natural and man-made phenomena seen from an aerial viewpoint. Ground-based witnesses are not always such reliable observers, and may quite possibly not be able to identify meteors, satellite re-entries, mirages of astronomical bodies, or even relatively common sights like planets, stars and the moon. Other natural explanations for UFOs invoke phenomena that are very rare and not yet accepted scientifically, like plasmas, ball lightning, earthquake lights, and miscellaneous electrical phenomena. Some reports contain details which suggest that a rare natural phenomenon has been witnessed, for example, the UFOs that were reported emerging from the ground in Poland. Henryk Kowalski reported that he and a colleague, Mr Cichoki, saw 'a puff of rosy light' shoot up from the ground at Czerniakov on 12 July 1982 at 7 p.m. Mr Cichoki photographed it, and the picture seemed to show an object.[16] The red light seen at El Abrojal, Rivera (Uruguay), at 10 p.m. on 30 October 1976 may also have been a natural phenomenon of some kind. Seen first over a field, the light was about 300 yards away. After a few minutes it began to move towards the two witnesses at a height of about 100 yards and made a loud noise like the wind. The light became bright like sunlight and dazzled the witnesses. A gust of hot wind knocked them down and they lost consciousness for five minutes or so. Next day they were ill with dizziness, nausea and vomiting, and eye irritation. The light was also seen by other witnesses nearby, who reported a red 'zeppelin' form perhaps 50 yards long, but lacking any definite details. They too heard loud noises and felt a gust of hot air. It emitted coloured lights, predominantly green, and was seen for twenty minutes. There had been a storm earlier in the day, so this UFO could possibly have been some rare electrical phenomenon, perhaps akin to ball lightning.[17]

In the early days of 'flying saucers', all UFO reports were automatically believed to be evidence of extraterrestrial visitors, but fortunately today the best investigators are more detached in their approach. Scientific explanations are looked for, and often found, but sometimes even the scientists are puzzled, and it is then that the debunkers resort to claims of hoaxing. How often hoaxing occurs is difficult to assess, but probably less often than the debunkers like to believe. UFO witnesses are often ridiculed, and certainly rarely achieve fame and fortune: even Whitley Strieber, who topped the US bestseller lists with his abduction story *Communion* and must have made a small fortune from it, has had to face plenty of sceptical and cynical media interviewers. Possibly mental aberration is a more common occurrence than hoaxing, and a witness may believe he or she is seeing something but is really hallucinating or imagining it. This applies more to UFO landings, entity sightings, abduction and contact cases, where there is rarely more than one witness; for examples of these events see Chapter 6.

Hallucinations cannot be invoked to explain photographs of UFOs, but hoaxes are of course immediately suspected, and often confirmed. Photographs of UFOs prove nothing, because virtually any UFO photograph could be faked by a skilled photographer. However, analysts are equally skilled, yet some photographs have not been conclusively proved to be hoaxes. The four we illustrate here have all survived intensive analysis, though there is still not total agreement as to their genuineness.

*The McMinnville
UFO, 11 May 1950.*

Perhaps the best-known UFO photographs are the two taken by Paul Trent at his farm at McMinnville, Oregon (USA), on 11 May 1950. Mr and Mrs Trent did not seek to publicize their photographs, which suggests they did not fake them in order to gain money or fame. Everyone who interviewed them came away with the impression that they were not the kind of people to want or be able to perpetrate a hoax. Numerous technical analyses have shown different conclusions as to the photographs' validity, but the balance of opinion is in favour of their being genuine. It was estimated that the object was some distance away, perhaps more than a kilometre, and was around 100 feet in diameter by around 12 feet thick. An almost identical UFO was photographed by a French military pilot near Rouen in 1954.[18]

The Barra da Tijuca sequence of photographs was taken near Rio de Janeiro (Brazil) on 7 May 1952 by press photographer Ed Keffel. Reporter João Martins was also present, and it was he who first spotted what he thought was an aeroplane, except that it was flying sideways. When he realized it was something strange, he shouted at Keffel to 'Shoot!', and Keffel grabbed his Rolleiflex and took five photographs in about a minute. One analyst discovered a possible internal inconsistency in lighting detail, but the Brazilian Air Force analysis resolved the problem by taking on-the-spot photographs for comparison. It was also suggested that the pictures had been faked by throwing a model up and photographing that, but all five

One of the Barra da Tijuca UFO photographs, 7 May 1952.

photographs were consecutive frames on the film. When the Brazilian Air Force tried to duplicate the photographs using a model, they found it impossible, and these facts do not support the hoax theory. Also, when the negatives were developed, a lieutenant-colonel was waiting outside the darkroom to receive them; a hoaxer would work in secret so that he could discard the negatives if on development they were found to be unsatisfactory.[19]

Another Brazilian sequence of photographs aroused considerable controversy. The location was Trindade Island, 600 miles east of Rio de Janeiro in the South Atlantic Ocean, and the photographer

One of the Trindade Island UFO photographs, 16 January 1958.

was Almiro Barauna, on board the *Almirante Saldanha*, which was fitted up as a hydrographic research unit. On 16 January 1958 the ship was due to leave for Brazil after several days at the island, and the deck was full of sailors and officers. Someone noticed the UFO and called to Barauna, who was on the ship as a civilian photographer. He had a camera with him, and located the UFO by a flash of light.

> It was coming over the sea, moving toward the point called the Galo Crest. I had lost thirty seconds looking for the object but the camera was already in my hands, ready, when I sighted it clearly silhouetted against the clouds. I shot two photos before it disappeared behind the peak Desejado . . . The object remained out of sight for a few seconds – behind the peak – reappearing bigger in size and flying in the opposite direction, but lower and closer than before, and moving at a higher speed. I shot the third photo. The fourth and fifth ones were lost, not only because of the speed the saucer was moving, but also for another reason: in the confusion produced as a result of the sighting, I was being pulled and pushed by other persons also trying to spot the object and, as a

consequence, photographed the sea and the island only – not the object. It was moving out to sea again, in the direction from which it had come, and it appeared to stop in mid-air for a brief time. At that moment I shot my last photo (the last on the film). After about ten seconds, the object continued to increase its distance from the ship, gradually diminishing in size and finally disappearing into the horizon.

He added that the UFO was metallic-looking, dark grey in colour and with a greenish vapour around it. He developed the film straight away, but could not make prints as he had no printing paper with him. Later analysis by the Navy showed that the object was about 120 feet in diameter and travelling at 600 mph. UFO disbelievers were certain the photographs were a hoax, one of their several reasons being that Barauna had previously published fake UFO photographs, though in that instance he had not tried to pass them off as genuine. The sceptics suggest that double exposure was the method used, with a model UFO being photographed against a dark background, then the film reloaded for reshooting at Trindade Island. We do not know whether any tests have been performed to try to prove or disprove this theory. If it was a hoax, it was a skilful one, as the photographs have an air of authenticity about them.[20]

Our fourth photograph is much more recent, and somewhat different from the others, because there is only one photograph, not a sequence, and the photographer did not see the UFO when she took the photograph. Normally, a witness is responding to a visual contact when he or she tries to capture on film what is being seen, but there are a few UFOs which have turned up fortuitously on photographs. The usual explanation is that the 'UFOs' are in fact lens flares or film or processing faults which just happen to look like UFOs, but in this case the answer may not be so simple. The photograph has been exhaustively analysed by Dr Richard F. Haines, who is a research scientist for NASA, and he ruled out both a hoax and a fault with film or camera. The circumstances in which the picture was taken suggest reasons why the photographer did not see the UFO. Mrs Hannah McRoberts was with her husband and baby on Vancouver Island, British Columbia (Canada), in October 1981, and was determined to prove to her husband that she could take a sharp photograph. She was attracted by the cloud and mountain, which looked like a volcano (Mount St Helens had erupted the year before), and was concentrating hard on capturing

The Vancouver Island UFO, October 1981. This is an enlargement of a section of the original photograph.

this effect and keeping the camera steady when she took the photograph. The UFO is so small in the frame that it is not surprising neither she nor her husband saw it, as they were not thinking about or looking for UFOs at the time.[21]

In all these photographs the UFOs look like solid objects, and not just 'lights in the sky', though there are plenty of photographs of those, too. There is other evidence for at least some UFOs being material objects. Witnesses have very occasionally touched the solid craft, and one good example of this comes from France in 1954, the year of a great UFO wave in that country. One afternoon towards the end of April, Roger Mougeolle, aged 37, was logging in the forest at Bois-de-Champ near Bruyères, Vosges. He was accompanied by another man, and together they were lopping off branches when they heard a loud noise, like a train going across a metal bridge. It became quiet again, and then they saw three cigar-shaped objects coming towards them. Two passed silently over, but the third came down towards the clearing where they stood. It had a smooth, grey, metallic surface, with no markings or protuberances, and was over 600 feet long. It stopped and hovered just above the ground. By this time Mougeolle's colleague had fled, but Mougeolle walked up to and underneath the object, putting out his hand to touch it. It felt cold, hard and smooth. Then he raised his axe and hit it to see what would happen. The axe made a dull sound as it struck, and Mougeolle was thrown back 20 feet. He lay on the ground unable to move, being totally paralysed. After a few minutes the UFO lifted and disappeared, and Mougeolle's paralysis also went. He suffered no after-effects.[22]

With this and other similar reports, all the scientists have to work with, if they wish to use the information in their attempts to solve the UFO mystery, is the written and spoken word of the witnesses. They could of course be lying or hallucinating: they cannot produce any solid evidence to support their incredible claims. Very occasionally, UFOs have left traces at landing sites (see Chapter 6) or have deposited some solid matter which can be analysed. One famous instance is the Ubatuba (Brazil) UFO event of 1957. The witness, who was never traced, wrote a letter to the press saying he had seen a 'flying disk' explode over the beach at Ubatuba, and metal had fallen from the sky. Some was collected, and the writer enclosed three small pieces. They were analysed, and one sample was found to consist of pure magnesium. Another sample of the magnesium was not so pure, and contained an unusual amount of strontium, not usually present in conventional magnesium. Further analysis showed that the magnesium had been manufactured in a way only being researched at the time of analysis (1969) and not known at the time of the events (1957). There was other evidence resulting from the analyses to suggest that if this was a hoax, it was a very sophisticated one.[23]

Of course the only way to prove conclusively the existence of the advanced spacecraft which some UFOs seem to be, would be to have a specimen available for study. Some ufologists believe that the American authorities have had one or more crashed 'flying saucers' under wraps for decades, and there is an ongoing research campaign to try and prove the truth of their assertions. Until they succeed, we cannot be sure that *any* UFOs are solid craft. However, one thing we can be sure of is that there are many valid explanations for the phenomena lumped together by the name 'UFO'. There are natural explanations, as we have already mentioned, like misidentification of common or rare natural events; there are psychological explanations, like hoax or hallucination; there are esoteric explanations. The most common of these is that UFOs are extraterrestrial spacecraft from some distant planet, and who are we to say that this is not true? We simply need rather more evidence than exists at present to convince us. If some UFOs are solid craft, there are other places they could come from, like the centre of the earth (unlikely); or under the sea (possible – see Chapter 10 which gives some intriguing evidence in support of this theory); or from the future (a concept beyond man's grasp, but not therefore impossible); or from a parallel universe which coexists with ours though we are unaware of it (if this were true, it would provide a useful solution to many mysteries); or even from terrestrial sources – advanced and secret aircraft from any of the great powers, or even from an unknown civilization living in a little-explored region such as the Himalayas, central Australia, the Arctic or Antarctic regions, or the South American jungle. The possibilities are many; the certainties remain tantalizingly elusive.

4 *Spontaneous human combustion and other mysterious fires*

Death by burning is a grisly subject, not included here for its morbid fascination but because the deaths we are dealing with have some inexplicable features in common. The most notable features of deaths tentatively classed as due to spontaneous human combustion are: there was no source of fire; almost total combustion of the flesh and skeleton, leaving only extremities undamaged; burning being very localized, limited only to the victim and his/her chair, sometimes leaving clothing undamaged. Researchers claim to have found other common factors, but there seem to be exceptions to all of them, for example: it is always the living who combust (but there is one instance of a corpse spontaneously combusting); generally old persons (but all ages are represented); women more often than men (debatable); the victims were usually alone (but not always); all led an idle life (untrue); and so it goes on. It seems that any attempt to categorize spontaneous human combustion in order to find its cause is inevitably unsuccessful, and the most enthusiastic in these attempts are the disbelievers who do not accept that these deaths are at all mysterious.

In order to demonstrate the mysterious aspects of spontaneous human combustion, we will detail some of the most interesting cases this century. It will soon be noticed that all our cases come from the USA. This does not necessarily mean that spontaneous human combustion happens nowhere else: we have detailed a number of British cases in *Modern Mysteries of Britain*. There have probably also been cases elsewhere in the world, but no one interested in the subject has recorded them. However, the concentration of cases in the USA and Britain may indicate that this is a phenomenon of the northern rather than the southern hemisphere, perhaps because in northerly latitudes people live more of an indoor life – though not all victims met their deaths indoors.

In these cases of death by fire, the victim is not invariably reduced

63

to ashes. When Thomas W. Morphey, owner of the Lake Denmark Hotel near Dover (New Jersey) found his housekeeper Lillian Green lying burned on the floor, at the end of December 1916, she was still alive but unable to explain what had happened. The floor where she lay was slightly scorched and her clothes were burned, but nothing else was damaged nor was there any visible source of fire.[1] Conversely, in the case of Mrs Stanley Lake who died at Kingston (New York) in January 1930 it was reported at the coroner's inquiry that 'Although her body was severely burned, her clothing was not even scorched.'[2] This sounds impossible, but is not unique in reports of spontaneous human combustion. Aura Troyer, aged 59, who worked as a janitor in a bank at Bloomington (Illinois), was another victim who was able to speak before he died, but like Lillian Green was unclear as to what had happened to him. He was found in the bank's basement in 1942 with all his clothing burned off, and before he died said only 'It happened all of a sudden.'[3] Also like Lillian Green, Allen M. Small of Deer Isle (Maine) was found lying on the floor, with the floor and carpet scorched but no other burning evident, and no source of fire. His pipe was on the shelf, and the stove lids were all in place. This death happened on 13 January 1943.[4] Only a short while later, on 1 February 1943, invalid Arthur Baugard was found dead at home in Lancaster (New York); only the body was burned, beyond recognition.[5] Police discovered the burned body of Mrs Ellen K. Coutres at her home in Manchester (New Hampshire) in December 1949 and commented: 'There was no other sign of fire, and although . . . the woman must have been a human torch, flames had not ignited the wooden structure.' The fire in her stove had been out for some time.[6]

So far we have an equal number of men and women dying mysterious deaths by burning, all indoors and in quite similar circumstances, those victims who were found before they died being unable to explain how they came to burn. None of these cases appears to have been minutely investigated by either proponents or opponents of the theory of spontaneous human combustion, but that is certainly not true of our next case, which may be the most famous case of possible spontaneous human combustion in the records. The victim was Mrs Mary Hardy Reeser, who lived in the city of St Petersburg on the west coast of Florida. A widow of 67, Mrs Reeser lived in a one-room apartment, but she was not a recluse. She was, according to Vincent H. Gaddis, a 'cheerful, plump, motherly woman', and on the day of her death, 1 July 1951, she had lunched

Mrs Mary Reeser.

with her son and his family. Her son, Dr Richard Reeser, had also seen his mother at 8.30 p.m., when she told him she was planning to take two sleeping pills and go to bed. The last person to see her alive was her landlady, who called in at 9 p.m. and said Mrs Reeser was sitting in an overstuffed easy chair, wearing a rayon nightgown and housecoat, with black satin bedroom slippers, and smoking a cigarette.

Eleven hours later, the landlady called again with a telegram, and was alarmed to find the doorknob was hot. She called two painters, who were working nearby, and they entered the apartment where they found a wooden beam on fire, but no trace of Mrs Reeser. Firemen were called, and it was they who discovered the pile of ashes that was all that remained of Mrs Reeser, all that is except for her foot in a slipper, a charred liver attached to a piece of backbone, and a shrunken skull the size of a baseball. The chair was burned away and

Cleaning up after the mysterious death of Mrs Reeser.

also everything in a circle of 4 feet around it, with smoke damage in the apartment only above a height of 4 feet. Plastic items close by had melted, but the linen on a daybed 5 feet away was untouched, nor was a pile of newspapers only a foot outside the circle burned. Everyone was at a loss to explain how Mrs Reeser's body could have burned away to ashes. There was no smell of burning flesh, no trace of any chemical that could have helped the burning, and it seemed unlikely that one dropped cigarette could have had such incredible consequences. But could it?

Joe Nickell and John F. Fischer, forensic analyst, launched an in-depth investigation into Mrs Reeser's death and other possible cases of spontaneous human combustion and decided that her death was easily explainable. Drowsy after having taken sleeping pills, Mrs Reeser may have dropped her cigarette which ignited her clothing, and she was unable to react in time to save herself. As the fire took hold, her body fat melted and helped fuel the flames – the 'candle effect'. A coating of grease was found on the floor round the body.

The main argument on which hangs the theory of spontaneous

66

human combustion is whether or not such a fire, once burning, would be capable of reducing a body to ashes. Dr Wilton M. Krogman, who had worked on many fire investigations and had experimented with burning corpses in a number of ways, said he had watched a body in a crematorium burn at 2000°F for over eight hours and still leave recognizable bones. 'Only at 3000 degrees, plus, have I seen bone fuse or melt, so that it ran and became volatile. These are very great heats – they would sear, char, scorch, or otherwise mark or affect anything and everything within a considerable radius.' Another source states that a heat of only 1600 to 1800°F for 1½ hours is needed to cremate a body; and that if a longer time were available, the cremation could take place at a lower temperature. As D. J. X. Halliday of the Fire Investigation Unit of London's Metropolitan Police Forensic Science Laboratory put it: 'Cremation is intended to destroy a body in the shortest possible time and is therefore carried out under extreme conditions, but a relatively small fire can consume flesh and calcine bone if it is allowed to burn for a long time.'[7] We have not however heard of any experiments being undertaken specifically to test these two hypotheses. Another inexplicable feature of the case of Mrs Reeser, the shrinking of the skull, may also have had a logical explanation: it was not the skull that was found, that having exploded, but the 'roundish object identified as the head' was in fact a 'globular lump' from the musculature of the neck where it is attached to the base of the skull.[8]

An explanation not involving spontaneous human combustion may be valid in Mrs Reeser's case, for we know that she was smoking a cigarette when last seen, so that a source of fire is known. However the reports of many similar cases specifically state that no source of fire could be found – so how did the victim ignite? Some of them could have been smoking, the evidence having been destroyed in the conflagration, but surely the investigators would have noticed the presence of cigarettes and matches in the room. Also there is a limit to how often we can accept that such a deadly conflagration can result from a dropped cigarette: most people would be able to retrieve it before it caused any damage, and even if it did drop unnoticed it would not necessarily cause clothing to blaze up, as fabrics vary in their flammability. Some reports to come later in this chapter will suggest other, less mundane, causes for outbreaks of fire; but first some more recent reports of possible spontaneous human combustion.

There are at least four cases of mysterious fires in cars. On 3 May

1951, Carl C. Blocker was found in a ditch beside a road near Wabash (Indiana). He was burning, and died in hospital. His car was on the roadside, with minor fire damage, confined to the area of the driver's seat, and examination of the car revealed no origin for the fire.[9] On 1 March 1953, Waymon P. Wood of Greenville (South Carolina) burned to death in his car, and again the fire was confined to the front seat, with no clues as to how it started.[10] In October 1964, Mrs Olga Worth Stephens, a former actress, burst into flames as she sat in a car parked in Dallas (Texas). She died of her injuries but the car was hardly damaged.[11] The strangest car death was that of Billy Thomas Peterson. Peterson, aged 27, apparently committed suicide by carbon monoxide poisoning in his car at home at Pontiac (Michigan) on 13 December 1959, but when his body was found it was badly burned. His clothing, however, even his underclothes, was not damaged or even scorched, and his hair was unsinged – undamaged hairs even protruded from his burnt flesh. The heat had melted a plastic religious statue on the car's dashboard, but the car itself did not burn. One of the doctors at the hospital where the body was taken remembered a few years later that it was 'covered with inexplicable internal and external third-degree burns . . . No explanation was available then, and so far as I know, none is now. I haven't seen a case like it since, and it is still baffling to me.'[12] Peterson probably burned after he was dead, and a similar case was reported from Hoquiam (Washington). Mrs Betty Satlow died of carbon monoxide poisoning on 7 December 1973 and her body was taken to the mortuary. There, on the following day, she began to burn inside her coffin.[13] We wonder if carbon monoxide could be implicated in any other of the mysterious fires. But if it were in some way responsible, why are not more car suicides followed by burning?

In these cases, the victims' bodies were not reduced to ashes, but that aspect of spontaneous human combustion is not the inexplicable part, since as we have seen, some scientists contend that under certain circumstances a body could be reduced to ashes after several hours' steady burning at lower temperatures than is generally realized. The real mystery of spontaneous human combustion lies in the first word, 'spontaneous' – in most cases no origin for the fire is found, despite thorough investigation. Such was the result in the case of Mrs Martin, who died in the basement of her home in West Philadelphia (Pennsylvania) on 18 May 1957. Her son found her lying in front of the coal furnace, but there was no fire in the furnace and it was cold. Her legs and feet had become ashes, and only her

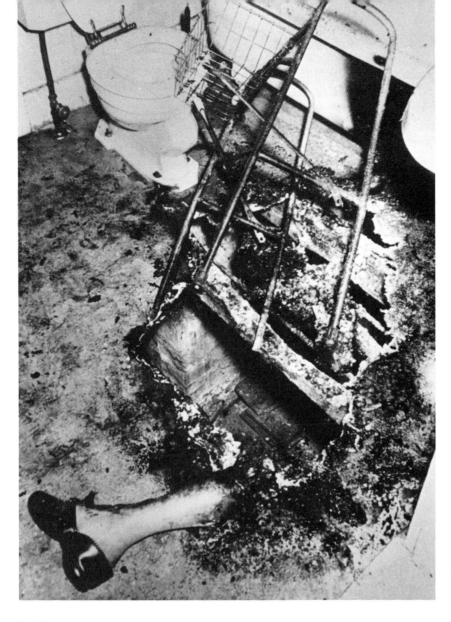

All that remained of Dr John Irving Bentley.

badly burned torso remained. Newspapers stacked two feet away were not scorched, and floor joists overhead were not burned, though they were stained with oily soot.[14]

In the case of Dr John Irving Bentley, who died at Coudersport (Pennsylvania) on 5 December 1966, a source of fire was known, but there is still some mystery surrounding the case. The victim was a 92-year-old retired doctor, who moved with the aid of a walking frame. He was a pipe-smoker, and it was theorized that sparks from either his pipe or his matches ignited his dressing-gown. He then went into the bathroom, where that garment was later found smouldering in the bathtub. But since he managed to remove the burning clothing, why did he then die? As the photograph shows, very little of Dr Bentley was left when he was discovered next morning by the gas meter reader. The burning was confined to a small area of floor which burned through, and a pile of ash was found in the basement below. A sooty film covered the bathroom window, and the man who was first on the scene noticed no smell of burning flesh, only a light-blue smoke that smelled 'somewhat sweet' or like 'an oil film burning'.[15]

In a more recent case, the 195-pound body of Mrs Beatrice Oczki was reduced to about 40 pounds as she sat watching TV on the night of 24 November 1979 at her home in Bolingbrook (Illinois). When she was found next morning, the TV was still on, and a newspaper 3 feet from the body was undamaged, but the ceiling paint had peeled in the heat above her, a beer can had exploded, and a tape in the video recorder on top of the television had melted. Also the fire had consumed all the available oxygen, resulting in the deaths of two dogs in the house, and the pilot lights had gone out.[16] Even if Mrs Oczki was smoking as she watched TV, we are again faced with the mystery of how a cigarette could cause such a conflagration. It is likely that the physical condition of the victim has a part to play, in that some people may be more prone to combustion than others. Mrs Oczki was overweight and a diabetic; it has been suggested that alcohol consumption is also relevant in some cases, as is the taking of liquid paraffin as a laxative, both being highly inflammable substances. If the clothing were inflammable and were set on fire and not quickly removed or the flames put out, perhaps the fire could spread easily to a body impregnated with fatty substances. Then the 'candle effect' would begin, the fat melting and fuelling the fire, which, burning steadily for many hours, would reduce the body to ashes. This could be the explanation, but ideally experiments should be undertaken to establish definitely whether or not it is the right one.

We are still left with the 'spontaneous' aspect. Some victims were found in flames, like Jack Larber who was a patient at a home in San Francisco (California). On 31 January 1959 he had just been given a glass of milk. Five minutes later someone glanced into the room and saw Larber covered in blue flames. He neither smoked nor carried matches.[17] In Lockland (Ohio) on 3 August 1962, Mrs Mary Martin, aged 74, was sitting in a kitchen chair when someone heard her scream, and found her clothing on fire.[18] Both these people succumbed to their burns, but others discovered in similar circumstances have survived. Jeanna Winchester was riding in a car in Jacksonville (Florida) on 9 October 1980 when she suddenly burst into yellow flames, and suffered severe burning. The car crashed as the driver attempted to beat out the flames. When the car was examined, there was little fire damage. Officer T. G. Hendrix commented: 'The white leather seat she was sitting on was a little browned and the door panel had a little black on it. Otherwise there was no fire damage. I've never seen anything like it in twelve years in the force.' He also said that there was no spilled petrol. Jeanna could not remember anything between being in the car, then waking up in hospital. She said: 'At first I thought there had to be a logical explanation, but I couldn't find any. I wasn't smoking anything. The window was up, so somebody couldn't have thrown anything in. The car didn't burn. I finally thought about spontaneous human combustion when I couldn't find anything else.'[19]

California resident Mr Jones found himself smoking one evening late in 1980. His wife said: 'I looked down and smoke was billowing from his arms as though something was on fire. We both started frantically trying to put it out. Suddenly it was gone.' Mr Jones said it had happened before, when he was driving his car. There was no burning, just smoke. Similarly, a Chicago (Illinois) woman found herself enveloped in smoke coming from beneath her blouse sleeve, on two occasions in May 1981. Some time early in the 1940s, Paul V. Weekly of Sioux City (Iowa) was 'awakened by an itching foot' at 3.30 a.m. Throwing back the bedclothes he saw his bed was on fire. He put it out and went back to sleep, only to go through the whole routine again an hour later.[20] These victims were lucky by comparison with Jack Angel, who in November 1974 was inexplicably burned while he was sleeping in his motor home at Savannah (Georgia). He went to sleep on 12 November and awoke four days later, with his right hand burned black. He was also burned on the arm, chest, legs and elsewhere, but only in spots. There was no trace of fire in the van, and no cause was found, even though the van was dismantled in the search for an explanation.[21]

Perhaps the genuinely spontaneous fires which afflicted these victims have some link with the mysterious outbreaks of fire reported down the ages in people's homes. These, sometimes called 'fire-spooks', are thought to have links with poltergeist activity (see Chapter 1), because sometimes the fires occur alongside such phenomena. There is an interesting parallel: the fire-spooks attack buildings and their contents, sometimes resulting in total destruction; the fire of 'spontaneous human combustion' attacks people, again sometimes resulting in total destruction. As already recounted in Chapter 1, the poltergeist outbreak at Nidamangalam (India) of March 1920 involved an assortment of phenomena, one of which was mysterious fires. Clothes were found burning, even when wet, religious pictures were burnt, two broomsticks, and a thatched shed.[22] Half-way round the world, in Nova Scotia, Canada, a fire-spook descended upon a lonely farmhouse at Caledonia Mills, 22 miles from Antigonish, early in January 1922. Alexander Macdonald, aged 70, lived there with his wife and their fifteen-year-old adopted daughter Mary Ellen. Fires started breaking out all over the house; during one night between 5 p.m. and 8 a.m., 38 separate fires began and were extinguished by Macdonald and three of his neighbours. One of the latter, who had been an electrician, described what he saw:

> We were there probably twenty minutes, when the whole house seemed to become illuminated as suddenly and as brightly as if a short circuit had occurred on a high tension wire. This is the only way I can describe it. Though the blaze seemed brighter, I saw in

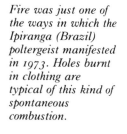

Fire was just one of the ways in which the Ipiranga (Brazil) poltergeist manifested in 1973. Holes burnt in clothing are typical of this kind of spontaneous combustion.

an instant that it came from the parlour, and made a dash for it. A green window-blind was enveloped in flames. I tore it off the wall and saved two little strips of it. The flame was a pale blue. The only thing I ever saw resembling it was a short circuit. The flame was not hot. It did not singe the hair on the back of my hands or on my eyebrows. Five or ten minutes afterwards a blaze broke out on wet wallpaper in the dining-room. The next blaze was in the parlour on a cardboard picture directly opposite the blind.

The next night, 31 fires erupted. Soon the house was wet through with water used to put out the fires, but still they broke out. 'I saw paper burning when it was wet. I picked a piece off the wet floor, and it caught fire. There must have been three inches of water on the floor when a rag was picked up and it was soon ablaze,' reported one of the neighbours turned fire-fighter. The family, by now exhausted, moved out to stay with neighbours. One investigator suspected Mary Ellen of starting the fires, though witnesses gave reasons why this could not be so, one of them having watched her and seen nothing suspicious.[23] If these phenomena are, like poltergeist phenomena, dependent on the presence of a human agent, Mary Ellen certainly fits the bill. Perhaps she was the catalyst but not the instigator, though it is possible that she may have started some of the fires to keep the excitement going. She certainly could not have started all of them, for five adults in the house could not keep up with all the fires that were breaking out.

In another case the same year, at Alva, Oklahoma (USA), the catalyst was probably a 23-year-old woman. The *New York Times* report of 14 March 1922 began:

Blue flames, their origin a mystery, which seem to burst from the air itself, threaten a horrible death to Mrs Ona Smith, 23, an invalid, who lies paralysed on a bed in a little cottage here.

The authorities are completely baffled by the outbreaks. Bedside watchers, who are keeping vigil day and night, can only leap to the rescue as the mysterious fires burst out at intervals in the bedding, clothing worn by Mrs Smith, wall draperies, or any inflammable material in the room.

Two mattresses have been reduced to smouldering ruins, a calendar on the wall has been ignited, a shawl worn by the invalid has burst into flames and several other blazes have started in bedding in the last few days.

A new mattress burst into flames in the presence of several witnesses including a newspaper reporter. They said of the fires that they seemed to start in the air, blue flames jumping and crackling. There seems little opportunity for a human fire-raiser to be working unseen in this tiny cottage. The blue flames described are already familiar from earlier reports, and will be seen again in this chapter. A good example is the Bladenboro (North Carolina) outbreak of January 1932, which began when a cotton dress being worn by Mrs Charles H. Williamson burst into flames. She was not smoking, nor standing near any source of fire. Her husband and daughter tore the charred rag from her body – Mrs Williamson amazingly did not have a single burn, nor did her rescuers. Later that day, a pair of Mr Williamson's trousers burned to ashes in a cupboard, and the following day a bed burst into flames, curtains and other objects were destroyed, without the flames spreading. Outsiders who witnessed the strange fires included the mayor, a doctor and a health officer. They saw bluish flames giving off no smoke and little odour. They appeared out of thin air and vanished just as strangely, burning fabrics but not harming the people who put the fires out. No electrical faults were found in the house, no gas leaks, and after five days the phenomenon ended as suddenly as it had begun.[24]

Bluish flames were also seen in an outbreak of mystery fires at the Dominion Golf and Country Club near Windsor, Ontario (Canada),

Spontaneous combustion was a feature of the Suzano (Brazil) poltergeist case in 1970. When Guy Lyon Playfair went there to interview witnesses in 1975 one told him: 'If I live to be a hundred, I'll swear that the calendar hanging on the wall in front of my nose caught fire by itself. I even put my finger in the flame, to make sure it was real, and I burned my finger.'

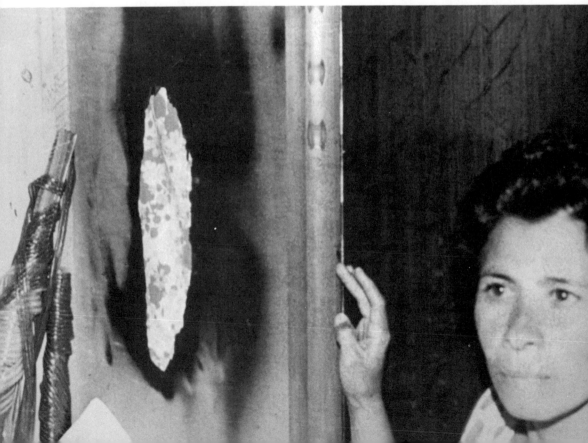

in December 1941. Pieces of paper, tablecloths, towels, curtains were all bursting spontaneously into flame. When the manager grabbed the telephone directory from his desk drawer to call for the fire brigade and opened it, flames leapt out. Next morning an insurance investigator asked the manager, 'Do you mean to tell me that various things just burst into flames? For example, like that broom over there?' He stopped, jumped from his chair and shouted: 'Put out that broom! It's on fire!' Some of the 43 fires were noted to have blue flames: at one point all the tablecloths in the dining room were covered with tiny dancing blue flames. No one seems to have been injured.[25]

The fires at a farm near Odon, Indiana (USA), were equally inexplicable, there being no obvious source for them. The house had never been wired for electricity, and there was no fire burning in the range. The date of these events is uncertain, but was probably 1941. Fires began to break out all over the house. An insurance company report commented,

> Some were so strange as to tax the belief of the most credulous persons who visited the place. A calendar on a wall went up in a quick puff of smoke. Another fire started in a pair of overalls on a door. A bedspread was reduced to ashes while neighbours, standing in the room, stared in amazement. A book taken from a drawer of a desk was found to be burning inside, though the cover of the volume was in perfect condition.

Twenty-eight fires broke out the first day and extra fire-fighters had to be called in. The solution settled on by William Hackler, whose house it was, was to demolish the building and use the wood to build a new one.[26]

However diligent the fire-fighters, some mystery fires get out of hand. At a farm south of Macomb, Illinois (USA), fires began breaking out on 7 August 1948 – small brown scorch-marks on the wallpaper. When these got hot enough they would burst into flames. Tearing off the wallpaper did not help, for the bare wooden boards would ignite, as would the ceiling. Macomb Fire Chief Fred Wilson commented: 'The whole thing is so screwy and fantastic that I'm almost ashamed to talk about it. Yet we have the word of at least a dozen reputable witnesses that they saw mysterious brown spots smoulder suddenly on the walls and ceilings of the home and then burst into flames.' Curtains also burned, and an ironing board on the outside porch – 200 fires broke out in one week. On 14 August there were too many to control and the cottage was destroyed. Next day a barn burned down, then a second barn. The farmer's thirteen-year-old niece who lived with the family 'confessed' under interrogation, but reporters who had been on the scene were not convinced of her guilt. As Vincent H. Gaddis commented: 'Forgotten were the witnesses who had watched brown spots appear, spread, and burst into flames. Forgotten were the fires on the ceilings. I haven't bothered to try it, but I'm certain I could flip matches at ceilings all day with perfect safety.'[27]

More recently, beginning on 31 January 1988, fires kept breaking out in the home of Jerry Siciliano in Clifton, New Jersey (USA), but always in electrical fixtures, outlet boxes or switch-plate boxes. All the electrical appliances, including the refrigerator and the stereo, have had their wires melted. These fires cannot be caused by sudden power surges, because they happened even when the power to the house was cut off. Damage to the house was minor, but Siciliano, having used up several fire extinguishers, moved his family out, just in case. The local fire chief admitted defeat: 'I'm up against the wall with this thing. I'm at the end of the road. I can't figure out what's going on in there. So I just called all the agencies I could think of. Maybe they'll figure it out.'[28]

Fire-spooks usually content themselves with terrorizing one family and their home, but in the summer of 1983 the West Virginia (USA) coal town of Wharncliffe and nearby Beech Creek were plagued by mysterious outbreaks of fire. Houses were burnt to the ground, and in another flames shot out of electrical sockets. But these were not electrical fires, for they continued when the power was disconnected. Clothing in a trunk burned, and wasps were found with burned wings. No arsonist was discovered, nor any other solution to the mystery.[29]

If there is any link between fire-spooks and spontaneous human combustion, we would expect the two to occur together, but so far we have come across only one case of poltergeist fires that resulted in a human death. During the Lucknow (India) poltergeist outbreak, the home of a CID inspector was the focus of inexplicable phenomena, including the burning of clothes and bedding. On 1 July 1975, Shanti, the inspector's wife, was heard screaming 'Help, help, I am burning!' and although her son threw a quilt over her, the fire was not extinguished, and she cried 'The evil spirit is burning me!' The fire was put out with water, but Shanti died that night.[30]

Other residents of fire-spook-infested homes have burst into flames but not been injured, like Mrs Williamson of North Carolina, as described earlier. Another case of this kind happened in Rome (Italy) in an office, when a nineteen-year-old secretary's skirt suddenly burst into flames. She had serious burns to her leg, but survived. In this summer of 1984, other fires broke out in the office, each lasting only a few seconds, but very hot and followed by a gust of wind.[31]

In the cases where the clothes of a particular individual suddenly burst into flames we may be seeing the same phenomenon at work as in cases of spontaneous human combustion, though the latter are usually fatal, perhaps because the victims are older, less able to react quickly, and their bodies may be highly inflammable. There are some reports which suggest that mysterious fires are definitely attracted to certain people. On Antigua (Leeward Islands) in 1929, there was a girl living in the village of Liberta whose clothes would often burst into flames, at home or while she was walking in the streets. Her bedclothes would also burn around her, but causing her no injury.[32] A few years earlier, in 1921, a thirteen-year-old boy living in Budapest (Hungary) also attracted fire. Furniture moved and fires broke out when he was present, and as he slept flames flickered over him and scorched his pillow.[33] Some people have been called 'electric' people because of strange phenomena happening in their presence, like Anna Monara in Trieste (Italy) in 1934, from whose breast a blue light was said to flash as she slept.[34] Also in Italy, ten-year-old Benedetto Supino of Formia could set objects on fire simply by gazing at them. It began in 1982 when a comic he was reading caught fire. One morning he woke to find his bedclothes on fire, and himself burned. All manner of objects would begin to smoulder as he passed by, and pages of books were scorched where he touched them. He also seemed to affect electrical objects, which would malfunction in his presence, and the power supply even failed sometimes. His hands have been seen to glow when machinery failed. Benedetto's down-to-earth comment was: 'I don't want things to catch fire. But what can I do?'[35] In the same year that Benedetto discovered his dubious skill, a Scottish nanny, Carole Compton, was in jail in Italy under suspicion of attempting to murder her young charges. She was said to be responsible for mysterious fires which broke out in the household on the island of Elba. Poltergeist phenomena also happened in her presence. Although found guilty of arson at her trial in December 1983, Carole was freed from jail where she had spent seventeen months awaiting trial. In February 1983, on the Indian Ocean island of Réunion, a twelve-year-old girl was the centre of suspicion when fires kept breaking out in her apartment building. One flat was gutted, and mattresses and linen burnt. The girl's clothes were said to catch fire repeatedly, so it is unlikely she was consciously responsible for the fires.[36] As in other similar cases, she may have been unconsciously responsible for the poltergeist which expressed itself through fire.

People whose presence starts a fire, fires that plague homes, people who burst into flames and are totally consumed . . . Is there any link between them? That is the burning question to which we do not have the answer.

5 Ghosts and hauntings

Those people who have never seen a ghost or heard ghostly footsteps may be forgiven for wondering if it is 'all in the mind' – but there is nothing like a personal brush with the supernatural for swiftly changing doubt to certainty. Some eerie experiences could certainly be imaginary, brought on by suggestion, by being in an allegedly haunted place, or alone in spooky surroundings. But when a child too young to understand about death and ghosts sees his dead mother, we must acknowledge that something other than imagination is at work. Walter Landry, living in Cambridge, Massachusetts (USA), was nearly three years old when his mother died in May 1906. He was told that she had gone away and would come back some day. A nurse was in charge of him at the time of the funeral, and she heard him screaming downstairs. She rushed down and found him terrified and almost in convulsions. He screamed, 'Look at the lady!' When asked 'What lady?', he replied, 'There's mamma!' He pointed as he followed her movements across the room. He later said his mother had motioned to him and tried to take him in her arms.[1] It is intriguing that Walter should be so terrified of his mother, if he did not know about ghosts. Why did he not think it was his mother returned in the flesh, if he thought she was coming back?

Ghosts and hauntings have been reported for centuries, and in all parts of the world, so these experiences are common to people of all nationalities and religious persuasions. The cases we report here and in the Gazetteer are only a tiny sample, but we hope that they give a representative survey of the kind of experience reported this century. There is some overlap with poltergeist phenomena, already described in Chapter 1, because some poltergeist victims also see ghosts in their houses, and some of the domestic ghosts in this chapter may be accompanied by other phenomena which are usually linked with poltergeists, like unnatural movement of furniture or smaller objects, and thumps, bangings and other noises. The two phenomena may actually be quite closely linked, with a human catalyst being needed to trigger domestic hauntings, just as they seem necessary to trigger poltergeist outbreaks.

One popular theory to explain ghosts is that they represent a re-run of past events in the house, usually events which resulted in an outpouring of grief or strong emotion of some kind. This energy somehow imprinted itself on the place, in the fabric of the building perhaps, and a visual – or auditory, or even olfactory – replay takes place when the circumstances are right. This may involve the presence of a psychically sensitive person, who may be the trigger which sets the haunting off. We stress that all this is theoretical, and there will be numerous accounts in this chapter which cannot be explained by this theory. Some ghosts appear conscious of their surroundings, like Mrs Landry whose appearance to her young son we have just described, and cases like this may provide support for those people who believe in the survival of some part of our consciousness after death. The truth is that there are many aspects of ghosts and hauntings which have not been and are not being investigated scientifically, though such investigation is long over-due.

The most common ghostly events take place in ordinary domestic

When the oil tanker S.S. Watertown was at sea in December 1924, travelling from the Pacific coast of America to the Panama Canal, two men died in an accident and were buried at sea. Next day and for many days following, two phantom faces were seen to be following the ship. The faces would appear and disappear, lasting only a short while, and were always the same distance from the ship.

surroundings, and a sample of cases follows to show what some unfortunate people have to put up with. An elderly couple, Albert and Ivy Cardwell, moved to a ground-floor council flat in Rotherham, South Yorkshire (England), in July 1986 and after a few weeks began to notice strange noises, like knocking and scratching on the outside wall of the main bedroom, and sudden drops in temperature although there was nothing wrong with the central heating. Other people heard the noises, but Mrs Cardwell was the only one to see a ghost. She was sitting alone in the living-room one night when she saw the faint silhouette of a woman, which disappeared as she tried to alert her husband. Sometimes council officials suspect victims of hauntings of having made it all up in order to engineer a move to another property, but that certainly did not apply here. Mr Cardwell said, 'We love the flat and really wanted to come here. But this has spoilt it all.'[2]

The ghost Mrs Cardwell saw was insubstantial, but often they are solid, looking like living people. One seen in an old house in Dunstable, Bedfordshire (England), on several occasions in the summer of 1966 by the nineteen-year-old Valerie Haywood was 'an old man dressed in rusty black Victorian clothes and with a gold stud at his collar'. She gave further details of the haunting.

He appears in a bedroom at seven or eight o'clock at night. He has grey hair and he just stands there in the room. He doesn't look evil, but he terrifies me. Even our spaniel, Lassie, won't go into the room. She whimpers when she passes the door . . . We were warned by people who had lived here before not to take over this house, but we laughed at them. We have been told a man went insane in that bedroom many years ago and it is his ghost which haunts it.[3]

If the information the Haywoods were given is correct, this ghost was a former resident. This seems very often to be the case – it is as if a person has developed such a close attachment to the place, from either affection or hatred, that part of him or her remains there after death. There seems rarely to be any reason to fear such ghosts, for they usually do not interact with the living witnesses in an unfriendly way. Two young men who bought a large and imposing mansion in Grand Rapids, Michigan (USA), in 1973 found the house to be haunted by a former owner. After hearing strange sounds for many months, in autumn 1976 they saw the ghost, an elderly man dressed in an Edwardian-style brown tweed suit, standing leaning against the mantelpiece. They also saw him wearing a bowler and carrying a cane or umbrella under his arm. Looking like a businessman about to leave for the office, he tipped his hat and walked through the closed door.[4] Frances Little found a photograph of her house's ghost in the garage. The adobe house, which Mrs Little and her husband bought in 1968, was in the desert in California's Kern County (USA). After only a few weeks there, Mr Little saw a woman wandering round the house, whom he thought at first was his wife. Later Mrs Little was alone in the house one night when she saw a 'tall thin woman in a long dark old-fashioned dress come out of the back room and enter my bedroom. She hesitated at the foot of my bed but never once turned to face me. Then she moved into the family room and I could see her form clearly.' After this encounter she found the photograph and was able to identify the ghost as Alice Margaret Kolitisch, who with her husband had built the house for their retirement in the 1920s. Her furniture was still in the house when the Littles bought it, and it seemed she was still anxious about the house she had loved.[5]

It is probably easier to come to terms with the ghost of a former owner, especially if he or she does nothing but put in an occasional appearance. On the other hand, ghosts which cannot be identified, and whose reason for being there is unknown, might seem more threatening. Such was the case at a house in Stockton, a suburb of Newcastle, New South Wales (Australia), rented by a young couple with a baby daughter. They experienced a fortnight of weird events before moving out in February 1970. They had found rumpled beds, toys moved about, a door knob shook loudly, and the baby sat up as if pulled upright by an invisible person. Friends of the Cookes, the haunted family, had seen and heard strange things, and previous tenants had also experienced the haunting: one was woken by someone shaking his shoulder, another woke to find someone peering at him. What finally decided Michael and Dianne Cooke to leave was a sight of the ghost, here described by Michael Cooke. 'Last night I saw a horrible white face looking out of one of the windows as I walked past. The eyes were white with green in the middle. I was so scared the tears just ran out of my eyes. That was the end. I was thinking of buying the house, but I'll never live there again.'[6]

In a number of cases, witnesses report ghostly smells as well as ghostly noises. In an old house in Lampasas, Texas (USA), Friday was the time when the Bradleys would smell frying liver and onions. They decided it must have been the favourite dish of Adelaide

Higdon, who had lived there for 56 years. The Bradleys also heard a door slam loudly, right by their heads as they lay asleep in bed, and later discovered that there used to be a door in the wall at that point. Mrs Bradley stopped talking to the ghostly Adelaide, to whom she had been giving progress reports on their restoration of the house during the early 1980s, when she learned that Adelaide had been in the habit of throwing plates at her husband, and had been considered very mean. Mrs Bradley commented: 'Now we don't smell liver and onions any more.'[7]

Historic buildings can usually boast a ghost or two. The White House in Washington, DC (USA), has had more than its fair share of famous people passing through its portals, but former president Abraham Lincoln seems to be the most active of the ghosts recorded there.[8] In Britain the many stately homes and castles are usually said to be haunted, for example the atmospheric ruins of Ewloe Castle in Clwyd (Wales), where a recent custodian has heard ghostly singing and seen a ghost which passed through a hedge. The presence of this ghost so frightened a dog that it died two days later with the vet being unable to trace a cause for the death other than severe shock.[9] A very

Ewloe Castle, Clwyd (Wales), haunted by a singing ghost.

clear ghost was also observed in 1934 by two girls playing in the ruins of Hardwick Hall, Derbyshire (England). He looked real, but was floating in mid-air, presumably on the level of a former floor, and disappeared after crossing in front of them. Mrs Winifred Chambers remembered the occasion clearly:

> I can still see him, he looked so real. He had a rosy smiling face and grey hair. He was dressed in buckled shoes, knee-length stockings and riding breeches, open-neck shirt with the sleeves rolled up and an apron. Also he carried a tray full of tankards. He looked like an old-fashioned inn keeper or servant. As my friend and I talked about it we both realized it must have been a ghost and we decided not to tell anyone in case they made fun of us.[10]

Also clearly seen were the figures which peopled the Versailles (France) scene for Miss Annie Moberly and Miss Eleanor Jourdain during their visit on 10 August 1901. So clear were they, that the two ladies were sure at the time that they were real. In fact the ladies may have somehow gone back in time and been seeing the gardens as they were between 1770 and 1774. Other people claimed to have had similar experiences at Versailles.[11]

In Britain, there are many churches, some of them fine buildings hundreds of years old, and they are favourite places for ghosts to appear. One representative encounter, between an unsuspecting church cleaner and a solid-looking phantom, took place on 30 March 1915 at Lytchett Matravers church, Dorset (England). The cleaner was sweeping the chancel when she looked up and saw a little old lady, dressed in black and with a black poke bonnet hiding her face. She bowed to the altar, went slowly into a seat and knelt down. The cleaner was surprised to see this complete stranger, so queerly dressed, but had no suspicion that she might not be real. The cleaner took her eyes away from the woman for a moment, then glanced back at her – but she was gone. She commented later: 'If she had flown she could not have got out of the church in the time.' The cleaner ran out of the building and bumped into a lady coming in to arrange the altar flowers. Together they searched but could find no trace of the old lady, nor had she been seen by the sexton who was outside cutting the grass.[12]

Britain is rich in historical ghosts, presumably because the history of England, Scotland and Wales goes back over many centuries and is full of battles and intrigues. We described some phantom battles in

Modern Mysteries of Britain. Horsemen in period costume are sometimes seen, like that seen by rally drivers in the late 1960s in the lanes on the Lincolnshire/Leicestershire border south of Denton. Two drivers independently saw, on different occasions, a cloaked figure on horseback, but he was not seen by others in the cars.[13] At Easter 1965, across the country in Shropshire, a couple driving near Chatwall saw a cloaked rider on a large black horse, and they slowed to look at him. As they watched, he galloped away. The wife said that horse and rider disappeared, though her husband said they had gone over the brow of the hill. Both agreed that the pair were colourless, only grey, black and white being seen, and that they had heard no sound as the horse and rider 'thundered' past only yards away, although the car window was open.[14]

A ghost seen in 1904 was believed to be of a fugitive from the Battle of Sedgemoor in 1685. The witnesses were a group of schoolchildren going for a walk up Marlpit's Hill near Honiton, Devon, accompanied by their teacher. They were looking apprehensive, and on being asked why, they described seeing a tall, wild-looking man coming down the hill towards them. He wore a broad-brimmed black hat and a long brown coat, and his clothes were muddy and torn. He looked dazed, and stared straight ahead as he passed by. The teacher could not see him, but the children were insistent and their descriptions very clear. It was discovered that a man who had taken part in the battle had once lived in a cottage on the hill, and he had come home a fugitive, only to be killed by army troopers as he greeted his wife and children. A man claimed to have seen the same ghost in 1907, on a bright moonlit night.[15]

As the foregoing examples show, ghosts are not confined to buildings, and often appear out of doors. Ghosts in cemeteries are not uncommon – like the eight or nine figures in 'monk-like garb' seen in a Chicago, Illinois (USA), cemetery by a police officer late in 1977. As he ran into the cemetery to arrest them, he found they had gone.[16] Hooded figures looking like monks are often seen in Britain, usually at night when little detail can be made out, and often by motorists who encounter them on country roads, as for example along St Mary's Lane near Cranham in Essex. One witness, Richard Sage, described his Christmas 1977 sighting:

The Christmas before last I was driving with three other friends when this figure dressed like a monk appeared out of nowhere, crossed in front of us and disappeared. The friend sitting in the front with me saw it, but the two in the back did not. Then the other night [December 1979], about the same spot, the vision appeared again and did the same thing.

Dee Goss supported his account. 'The figure wore a sort of hood or cowl. It seemed to have no legs and just floated across the road in front of us. I saw it very distinctly.' The police thought a local tramp was responsible for the reports, but the witnesses disagreed. The ghost was also seen at Christmas 1976 and 1978.[17] More recently a hooded figure was seen on a new bypass being built near Stocksbridge, South Yorkshire (England). Two security guards patrolling at night in September 1987 saw a hooded figure on Pearoyd bridge. They drove closer, and the beam from their headlights shone straight through it. Two nights earlier, one of the guards claimed to have seen three children dancing round an electricity pylon in the middle of the night.[18]

Another common highway ghost is the so-called 'phantom hitch-hiker', a figure who has become a part of modern folklore worldwide.[19] However, she/he is not completely fictional, for there are reports, claiming to be factual, of people actually having given lifts to ghostly hitch-hikers. We gave some English cases in *Modern Mysteries of Britain*; here is one further English report, plus others from overseas. The location was Lakenheath Air Force Base in Suffolk, the date early 1951. An American security policeman was driving around the base at night when he saw an RAF pilot in uniform who was hitching a lift. He stopped and the pilot got in. After a while, he asked for a cigarette, which the driver gave him. The pilot then asked for a light, and the policeman handed over his lighter. Stopping to get clearance to proceed further, he saw the flick of the lighter out of the corner of his eye. Turning towards his passenger, he found the seat empty, only the lighter lying there.[20]

In Oklahoma (USA) in the winter of 1965, Mae Doria picked up another hitch-hiker who spoke to her, but who turned out to be a phantom. She was driving on Highway 20 east of Claremore when she picked up a young boy eleven or twelve years old. They chatted until reaching Pryor, when the boy asked to get out near a culvert.

At that point [said Ms Doria] I started slowing down but since I didn't see any houses in the area and only a few bare trees, I asked him where he lived. When almost on top of the area, he said 'over there' and as I turned my head to the right to see where he meant, he had disappeared, the seat next to me was bare, he had vanished! Immediately I stopped the car and, jumping out, ran all around the automobile almost hysterical. I looked everywhere, up and down the highway and to the right and left, but to no avail, he was gone.

Two years later she was talking to the gas man about psychic experiences, he having noticed her books on psychic phenomena, and she told him about the ghostly hitch-hiker. He identified the place where she had picked him up, and said he had heard of a phantom boy hitch-hiker being picked up as long ago as 1936.[21]

Another case where at least three separate drivers picked up a phantom hitch-hiker comes from South Africa. While driving his motorcycle near De Rust one night in April 1978, Dawie van Jaarsveld saw a girl standing by the road. He offered her a lift to the next town, but couldn't hear what she mumbled in reply to his question about where she wanted to be dropped. He assumed he

Dawie van Jaarsveld, who gave a lift to a ghost.

would find out when they arrived at Uniondale. He gave her a crash helmet to wear, and a transistor radio earplug so she could listen to the music as he was doing. After ten miles he thought his back wheel was skidding and stopped to check his tyre. He was amazed to find his passenger gone, the helmet strapped on to the seat, and the earplug fixed into his other ear, although his crash helmet was firmly in position. He commented: 'I can tell you, the moment I realized these things I could feel the hair stand on end on my head and I had cold shivers up and down my spine.' Researcher Cynthia Hind checked the man's story, by visiting the café in Uniondale where he called immediately after the unnerving experience and his girl-friend's home where he had been heading that night. Everyone confirmed that he had looked as if he had seen a ghost, and when he told his story, they told him about the famous ghost of Uniondale, because it seemed that other drivers had had a similar experience to van Jaarsveld's. One of them was Anton Le Grange who picked the ghost up in his car on 12 May 1976. Mrs Hind spoke to the policeman who saw Le Grange when he came in to report the incident, and he confirmed that Le Grange was deadly serious and got the policeman to go with him to the car, where he saw the door open and close of its own accord. After Le Grange's experience was reported in the press, a pilot revealed that his fiancée, Maria Roux, had been killed in a car

Myra, a University of Missouri student who died around 1869, communicated with members of SORRAT (see Chapter 1) via a rap code, and later appeared to them on 27 June 1967 when this photograph was taken of her.

crash on 12 April 1968 at the spot where the ghost was seen. Le Grange identified her photograph as very like the girl he had picked up. She had also been wearing the same clothes Maria had on when she died. She seems to appear only around the time she died, and only to single young men.[22] On 4 April 1980, Andre Coetzee, aged twenty, was motorcycling past the accident site when he felt 'someone or something put its arms around my waist from behind. There was something sitting on my bike.' He accelerated to get away from whatever it was, but this only seemed to annoy the ghost, which struck him three times on his helmet. Only when he had reached 100 mph did the passenger disappear. When Coetzee stopped at a café he could hardly speak.[23]

Encounters with ghosts seem to have that effect on people, which is hardly surprising, when their appearance is usually so totally unexpected. The White Lady of Elfin Forest, near Escondido, California (USA), although harmless enough in appearance, usually had a striking effect on people once they realized she was a ghost. She has been seen by numerous people during daylight hours in recent years. One of them was James Harrelson, who was on a family picnic and had wandered off on his own to look at the trees.

> I went about a mile, then sat down to rest. Suddenly I felt a lingering touch on my shoulder. I looked up to see a woman standing in front of me. She was real composed and had a pleasant look on her face. I smiled at her and said hello but she just stared at me with the most penetrating eyes I have ever seen. It was as if she looked right through my eyes and into my soul. It was eerie. Suddenly she started to fade and I knew she was not of this world.

He hastened back to his family and drove them quickly from the forest. Another witness, Roberta Boren, saw a woman walking ahead of her and went to catch her up to talk to her. As she got nearer, the White Lady floated towards a house, and Ms Boren watched her pass right through a wall. Others have seen her on more than one occasion, including a retired minister, Corrine Pleasant, who lives nearby. She too said the White Lady floated about 15 inches off the ground, rather than walking.[24]

The ghost Craig C. Downer saw in the jungle close to the Alto Anchicaya Dam (Colombia) in June 1978 was much vaguer in appearance and could never be mistaken for a living person. He described it as 'luminous, transparent, cloudlike, whitish with a

89

slight greenish cast. The vague but clearly human form stood, or floated, barely above the ground.' It got to within 60 feet of Downer and his colleague, at which point they hurried away and back to their camp. Downer learned later that there had previously been a bad accident at the bridge near where they had been, and that lights they had seen just before the ghost appeared were probably part of the haunting, which was an echo of the tragedy.[25]

So far the only haunted buildings we have mentioned have been people's homes, castles, and churches. But from the evidence we have gathered, it would seem that virtually any building could be haunted. We have heard of a haunted opera house (at Oshkosh, Wisconsin, USA), a haunted fire station (at Virginia Beach, Virginia, USA), a shrine in Tokyo (Japan) haunted by ghostly soldiers, a haunted bar at a US Army officers' club in Katterbach (West Germany), haunted ballrooms where the sounds of ghostly dances are heard (the Fairley-Lampman building at Cripple Creek and the Town Hall Arts Center in Littleton, both in Colorado, USA), haunted hotels and inns (just one example of many being the Gadsden Hotel in Douglas, Arizona, USA, where a ghost in khaki uniform is sometimes seen walking in the basement corridors), haunted university buildings (at Lincoln, Nebraska, USA), haunted theatres (for example Loew's Theater at Syracuse, New York, USA), a haunted prison (at Asheville, North Carolina, USA, where in April 1908 the prisoners at the county jail signed a petition appealing for protection from demons and evil spirits, after seeing ghosts leering at them and hearing strange noises),[26] and haunted factories, one of many being a furniture factory at Thomasville, North Carolina (USA) where night-shift workers claimed to see a 6-foot figure, wearing a check work-shirt and khaki trousers. The workers nicknamed him Lucas, and Victor Couch, one of the owners, claimed to have seen him many times. He said Lucas did no harm and had never spoken to anybody. 'He's the best watchdog I've ever had. He doesn't have to carry a gun to scare somebody off.'[27] There are also haunted libraries, a recent example being the New Hanover County Library at Wilmington, North Carolina (USA). Sometimes the ghost was only heard and not seen. Librarian Beverly Tetterton reported: 'Early in the morning, I will be reading the newspaper and hear noises of books moving on the shelf, books falling over. It sounds like someone is there in the back using the room. But there is no one.' One man saw her in 1982 and 1983, and said he believed her to be a friend and fellow genealogist who used to use the library before her death. 'I was looking through the top of the shelves and I could see her over the books. I called her name. She looked at me, then turned real quickly and flew down to the end of the stacks.' When he followed, there was no trace of her. A woman saw the ghost in 1985. Beverly Tetterton reported: 'She said she put her hand out and said aloud, "What's this?" and the spot where she reached was cold.'[28]

Because of their enclosed and eerie atmosphere, mines are a likely place for people to experience strange happenings. In March 1937 two gold mines in northern Ontario (Canada) were the scene of frightening events. At Bankfield, three miners on the night shift dropped their tools and ran out, after seeing 'something' there. One reported: 'I sure saw something there all right. People are telling me today it must have been some gas formation; but it was the most human-looking formation I have ever heard tell of.' At Little Long Lac, the miners saw flashing lights underground, and the hydraulic air valves were opened when no one was at the controls.[29] In an English coal mine, Silverwood Colliery near Rotherham, South Yorkshire, miner Stephen Dimbleby saw a ghost.

> It just appeared from nowhere – the figure of a body, and I couldn't see through him. He was just like an ordinary bloke, and my first instincts were that it was just somebody mucking about. And then it hit me: he'd come from nowhere, just appeared. And when I shone my light in his face, there were no features on his face. And then I just dropped everything, and set off running out.

He never went back into the mine.[30] A similar encounter was experienced in October 1987 by nineteen-year-old miner Garry Pine while he was underground at Cotgrave Colliery, Nottinghamshire (England). He was inspecting a conveyor belt when he heard groans, and looked up to see a figure standing close by. 'He was wearing a black helmet and dark overalls, but I couldn't see a face at all. At first I thought it was someone messing about, but then he glided away and walked straight through a solid wall at a dead end.' Garry had to be carried from the pit on a stretcher in a hysterical state, and later declared himself 'scared witless' by the encounter.[31]

In 1984, a man was exploring disused mineshafts at Dylife in Powys (Wales) when he heard a strange humming noise, 'like somebody's voice'. He called out, but got no response. He switched off his lamp, and he saw 'a white or a pale blue shape about the size of a small man. It gave off a sort of glow, but not like a torch.' When he switched on his light again, he could see nothing, and quickly left the mine. Talking in the local pub that evening, a man told him that he and friends had more than once seen lights emerging from that mine at night, rising slowly into the air and moving away.[32]

So far, all the ghosts in this chapter have taken human form, although sometimes only a vague human shape. Phantom horses have also been mentioned, and there are plenty of reports of other phantom animals. Rarer but certainly not non-existent are reports of inanimate objects being seen in phantom form, including phantom buildings. Some phantom houses, cottages and landscapes are featured in *Modern Mysteries of Britain*, and since writing that book another British case of recent date has come to our notice. This is a phantom cottage seen beside Loch Mullardoch near Cannich, in the Highland Region of Scotland. The two men who saw it, while climbing in the mountains in May 1987, were both very experienced climbers, being members of the Lochaber Mountain Rescue Team. Donald Watt is team leader and George Bruce is a member of the team. While descending Beinn Fhionnlaidh they noticed a two-storey cottage on the loch shore below. It was made of granite and looked in good condition, but was in the opposite direction from the hut they were heading for. George Bruce said:

Donald Watt and George Bruce, experienced mountain walkers who saw a phantom cottage in Scotland.

The cottage was on the shore. There was ground behind it and the loch behind that. Donald and I had a conflab as we hadn't seen it on the map and didn't know of its existence. We decided to head for it. It caught us completely by surprise. We headed on down towards the cottage, discussing it. We kept it in our sights for some time and then lost view of it. We assumed that we would see it again when we got over the crest of a hillock but when we joined the path along the shore there was no cottage to be seen.

They kept walking but there was no cottage round the next corner, either. George continued: 'We looked back up the hill to get a line from where we had descended in case our bearing might be out. Round a corner we went, and another, and another. But no cottage. Eventually we reached the wooden hut. Then we had a bit to eat. The cottage was so real we just can't explain it.' Afterwards they found that there had been a lodge at the loch, but it was now under water since the area was flooded and dammed in the 1950s. George concluded:

What I would like to see is a picture of the house to discover whether it relates to what we saw. I'm 45, quite fit, have 50-50 vision. I've been known to find pennies on the hill – being an Aberdonian. I will swear blind I saw this cottage. Thank goodness Donald was there to back me up. This has shaken us. I have an open mind but this defies all explanation as far as I'm concerned.[33]

It was also a hiker who saw a phantom hotel at Mount Lowe in California (USA). Bo Linus Orsjo was walking in the area in June 1974 when he saw 'a large green building (probably a hotel) . . . It had an atmosphere of "closed for the season" but there also was a maid sweeping the big staircase.' Afterwards he discovered that a hotel had stood there, and he recognized a picture of it in a book. An Alpine village with hotel and guesthouses had been built as a tourist attraction with a railway leading up to it, but the project had been abandoned after storms and fires, and the hotel had burned down in 1937. On revisiting the area in 1976, Bo Linus Orsjo found only picnic tables, a camp site and ruins with fully grown trees in them, where two years earlier he had seen the phantom hotel.[34]

If phantom buildings seem unbelievable, what are we to make of ghostly transport: horse and carriage, motor car, aeroplane, train, ship – probably most vehicles have been seen in ghostly form. This may be acceptable in the case of a bicycle, where it is being ridden by a ghost, but with planes, trains and ships any humans are almost incidental. The existence of ghostly vehicles tends to support the theory that many ghostly events, whether involving people or not, are re-runs of something that happened in the past. Examples of ghostly vehicles will be found in the Gazetteer; here we have space only to feature two phantom ships reported from the seas off eastern Canada. In November 1910, Captain Ralph and the crew of the *Victor* witnessed the appearance of a phantom schooner in Conception Bay, off St John's, Newfoundland. It was a dark night and two lights ahead were seen by the *Victor*'s lookout. A third appeared, then others, until the craft was ablaze with light. The *Victor* moved closer, and the captain and his men watched as figures in oilskins moved silently about the decks. The main boom seemed to be broken. The watchers could hear no sounds – no voices, no flapping of canvas or creaking of rigging. Suddenly, the lights vanished and the phantom ship had gone.[35] Nova Scotia's Northumberland Strait also claims a phantom ship, and on the night of 10 January 1979 a family claimed to have seen it between Pictou Island and Bayview. Seen through binoculars, it looked like something on fire as it drifted towards Pictou Island. A member of the Royal Canadian Mounted Police also saw it. This was the area where a sailing vessel had burned and sunk, and they believed they were seeing a ghostly re-enactment of that disaster.[36]

If a ghost, be it human in form or an inanimate object, does nothing unusual, like walking through a wall or disappearing, there is a good chance that any witnesses will never realize that they are seeing something extraordinary. How many ghosts might we all have seen without realizing it? And another point worth thinking about: do ghosts appear when there is no one to see them?

6 *UFO landings and close encounters*

Literally thousands of UFOs have been seen around the world since 1947 when pilot Kenneth Arnold's sighting report made newspaper headlines. Although it may seem as if UFOs suddenly came into existence at that time, this was not the case, for subsequently researchers have unearthed many pre-1947 reports. But their high media profile definitely dates from 1947, and in the decades that followed, the idea of 'flying saucers' (as they were originally named) became a familiar one to almost everybody living in the modern world.

People's awareness of UFOs has changed subtly in the last 40 years, and in some ways so has the phenomenon. Through the decades there have always been sightings of 'lights in the sky', and it is likely that many of these are nothing unusual at all, but mis-identifications of natural or man-made objects. But in the 25 years or so following 1947 there were many thousands of reports of UFOs as solid craft being seen at close quarters, either in the sky, as we have already described in Chapter 3, or on the ground. Landings were not uncommon at all in the 1950s and 1960s, and many witnesses of landed UFOs also saw the occupants of these mystery craft. Some people even claimed to have established communication with the entities, and to have been given messages. Today reports of landings and entities are rare, but reports of people being kidnapped and taken aboard UFOs are much more frequent. Have the ufonauts changed their tactics, or is some other mechanism at work here? The answer to this question may become clear as this chapter progresses.

Over the years so many weird accounts of UFOs and entities have been recorded that it is impossible for us to do more than present a handful of representative cases. An early and dramatic UFO landing took place in October 1952 in France, a country seemingly much favoured by UFOs in the 1950s, if the quantity of sighting reports is anything to go by. This particular event took place at Marignane airport, Marseille, and the only witness was M. Gachignard, a customs officer. The time was 2 a.m. on 27 October, and the witness was sitting on a bench out of doors about to eat a snack, and certainly wide awake. He could see the whole airfield, and noticed a light approaching which he thought at first was a shooting star, until it passed in front of him and landed on the runway. It stopped dead from a speed of 150 mph, and M. Gachignard knew it was not a plane. He walked towards it, and as he got closer could see a dark object, shaped like a rugby football with pointed ends, around 3 feet high and 9 feet long. Light came from four square windows in line along the side of the craft. The light was flickering: 'It was neither steady nor bright, but ghostly and soft, almost milky at times.' When he was 150 feet away, a stream of white particles shot from under the rear end to his left and the craft took off suddenly. M. Gachignard froze in terror, wondering if the machine was going to burst into flames or run over him. But he was not injured, and in a matter of two or three seconds it had disappeared from sight. As M. Gachignard commented: 'Its terrific speed on take-off was as noticeable as its low landing speed. It did not seem to accelerate at all. It was stationary one moment and travelling like lightning the next.' He soon discovered that no one else had seen anything, because in both its arrival and departure the UFO had come in at a low height below that of the control tower.[1]

In the absence of any ground traces and any other witnesses, we have only M. Gachignard's report to rely on in this case, but often a witness can point to traces left where the UFO landed – holes, burn marks, unusual substances, damaged plants. In a catalogue of such cases published in 1975, over 500 reports described UFOs seen at close quarters and associated physical traces found.[2] But in only a few of these cases has any scientific analysis been made in an attempt to establish what caused the physical traces. Two cases where analysis has been undertaken are the Delphos, Kansas (USA), landing of 1971 and the Trans en Provence (France) landing of 1981. The main witness at Delphos was sixteen-year-old Ronald Johnson, who was working on the family farm at 7 p.m. on 2 November 1971 when he heard a rumbling noise and saw an object about 10 feet high, hovering 2 feet off the ground among trees 75 feet away, and glowing brightly. The light was so bright it hurt the boy's eyes, and for some days afterwards they were painful and he had headaches. After a few minutes the UFO began to move away and Ronald fetched his parents. They saw the light receding into the distance, and a ring of soil that glowed in the dark where it had been hovering. They touched the soil and it felt cool and crustlike; their fingers also felt numbed, and this effect took time to wear off. Fortunately UFO researchers were quickly alerted and soil samples were obtained for analysis. Ted Phillips reported that 'Unique icicle-shaped crystals 0.01 to 0.05 microns long were found, as was a previously uncatalogued crystalline structure of low atomic weight.'[3] Dr Erol A. Faruk, an English chemist who analysed the soil, came to the conclusion that it had been sprayed with some aqueous solution of a chemiluminescent compound while the UFO was hovering, but results of further analyses are still awaited.[4]

In the Delphos case no firm conclusions have been reached as to the identity of the UFO which paid a brief visit to the Johnson farm; in France, too, the identity of the Trans en Provence UFO has not been established despite scientific analysis of traces left. This landing took place at 5 p.m. on 8 February 1981, on the property of M. Collini, who was working in his garden at the time. He heard a low whistling sound and turned to see something coming down to a terrace at the bottom of the garden. It was an ovoid object, and M. Collini moved forward to see it better as it landed. Only a minute later, it took off again, still making a low whistling noise, and departed. M. Collini found circular marks and a crown-shaped imprint on the ground, and called the police. A team from GEPAN (the official French UFO study group) obtained samples of soil and vegetation, and these showed biochemical disturbances to plant life, as well as evidence of ground-heating to between 300° and 600°C and possible deposition of traces of phosphate and zinc.[5] These cases show that even if proper scientific analysis is undertaken, this by no means ensures that a satisfactory, or even any, solution to the mystery will be found.

In another fairly recent event with unusual features, the Livingston, Lothian Region (Scotland), incident of 9 November 1979 where forester Robert Taylor encountered a UFO in the forest, attempts were made to explain it in terms of natural events, but the explanations were unsatisfactory because they did not follow closely enough the events as described by the witness. The dark grey rounded object about 20 feet across from which emerged two smaller spheres with several legs was 'identified' first as an example of ball lightning, and later as the top half of a daytime mirage of Venus, the light from this triggering an epileptic seizure in which Taylor hallucinated the two spheres rolling towards him and attaching themselves to his legs, pulling him towards the UFO. His torn trousers and the marks left on the ground had no connection with Taylor's experience, according to this explanation. Not surprisingly, Steuart Campbell's valiant attempts to explain Robert Taylor's experience and many other UFO events in natural terms have met with disbelief from most other ufologists, and as T. R. Dutton commented in his personal response to Campbell's latest explanation of the Taylor encounter: 'We should not allow ourselves to be content with trite explanations for mystifying and complex events of this kind, not least because they impugn the integrity of the witness.'[6] Robert Taylor's was indeed a mystifying and complex experience, and one which deserves continued study.[7]

Robert Taylor saw no entities, though the spheres which pulled him towards the UFO may have seemed to him to be under

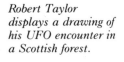

Robert Taylor displays a drawing of his UFO encounter in a Scottish forest.

conscious control, in the moments of fear before he lost consciousness. In numerous other cases, UFOs have landed and entities have emerged, then later physical traces have been found at the landing site, showing that the event was unlikely to have been caused by some natural phenomenon, for these do not usually contain humanoid pilots. But if we are disinclined to accept the reality of such events as described by the witnesses, we can always fall back on another theory: that natural electromagnetic fields may cause lights which a witness sees, this triggering the thought of a 'UFO'. Then the brain is affected by the electromagnetism and the witness hallucinates the rest of the event – seeing a solid craft land and entities get out and perform the various often incomprehensible acts they have been reported as doing. It is doubtful whether this theory has more than a passing relevance to the weird tales we are about to relate, but it is a useful safety net for those to whom these accounts are unbelievable but who consider it improbable that all the witnesses of UFO entities (thousands over the decades and around the world) are liars.

Two very bizarre reports involving entity sightings, from the many on record, were the Flatwoods, West Virginia (USA), case of 1952, and the Kelly/Hopkinsville, Kentucky (USA), case of 1955. The entities seen in these two cases were totally different in appearance. At sunset on 12 September 1952, a 'meteor' was seen to land on a hill at Flatwoods by several boys, who decided to investigate. Mrs Kathleen Hill, her sons, and seventeen-year-old National Guardsman Gene Lemon joined the party. They saw a large globe 'as big as a house', and when one of the party flashed his light into the trees close by, they also saw a huge figure 10–15 feet tall, with a blood-red face and glowing greenish-orange eyes. It floated towards them, and all present wasted no time in hurtling down the hillside. People who searched the area next day found marks on the ground, flattened grass, and a strange smell close to the ground.[8]

By contrast, the entities seen at Kelly on 21 August 1955 were about 3½ feet tall, and they besieged a rural farmhouse, terrifying the occupants. Billy Ray Taylor, one of the residents, was the first to realize that something unusual was afoot, when he saw a silver UFO fly overhead and land in a gully not far away. No one took him seriously, and no one went to investigate. An hour later the first little man was seen approaching the house. He had huge eyes with no pupils or eyelids, no nose, a slit mouth, and large pointed floppy ears. His body was very thin, he had webbed fingers and talons, and

*A dramatic
representation of
what was allegedly
seen at Flatwoods.*

stick-like legs. His skin was silvery and metallic-looking, he was bald, and he glowed. Altogether non-human, both in appearance and in behaviour. The men in the house reached for their guns and shot at him as he stood twenty feet away, but he was unhurt and just 'flipped over' backwards and ran into the shadows. They soon discovered that there were more of the little men, and tried to shoot them out of the trees, off the roof, and away from the windows. One on the roof grabbed Billy Ray Taylor's hair as he started to go outside

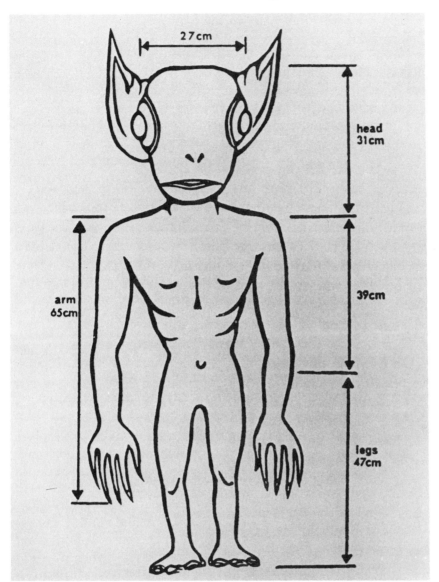

27cm

head
31cm

39cm

arm
65cm

legs
47cm

to see if they had killed any. After several hours under siege, the eight adults and three children at the farm piled into two cars and went to Hopkinsville (they had no phone, so could not call for assistance). There they alerted the police, and policemen and newsmen went back with them, but there was nothing to be seen. Several hours later, all the investigators had gone again – and the little men, who had kept away, reappeared. But the second invasion was less dramatic, and by dawn the little men had gone for good. This amazing story was investigated by numerous people, and no one found any evidence of a hoax. It seems certain that the eleven witnesses did see something strange that August night more than 30 years ago.[9]

As we have seen from the last two cases, UFO entities do not have a uniform appearance. They range in size from 18 inches to 10 feet tall, but the greatest number are between 3 and 5 feet tall. Entities who would easily pass for earth people have been reported by some witnesses, such as Salvador Villanueva Medina, a Mexican cab-driver who spent a night in August 1953 sitting in his broken-down vehicle with two oddly dressed strangers who had appeared on the scene while he was examining his disabled car. One spoke good Spanish and during the night told him, 'We are not of this planet.' In the dawn light Medina accompanied them to their craft. Refusing their invitation to join them, he watched them board the 40-foot wide, shining, lenticular UFO, which then lifted into the air and rapidly flew out of sight.[10]

Of an entirely different appearance was the hairy dwarf with glowing eyes which attacked Gustavo Gonzalaz at Caracas (Vene-zuela) in November 1954. When he struck it with his knife the blade glanced off as if from a steel plate. A few entities have been reported as having one eye, and others with three eyes, and in one report a blackish, shrub-like creature with a single golden eye in its head also had 'other smaller eyes located up and down the body'. Some reports describe entities with long noses, pointed ears, and sometimes protuberant eyes – indeed with so many variations in appearance that it is surprising that descriptions of UFO entities from different cases are ever the same, but they sometimes are. Derogatory press reports sometimes refer to 'little green men', and some UFO re-searchers have stated that green entities are never seen, but this is not true. Jan Wolsky, a 71-year-old farmer who was taken aboard a UFO in Poland in 1978, is just one of many witnesses who saw 'little green men'. As he described them: 'Their faces were a grey-green colour. They had big slanted eyes and their hands were webbed and also green. They wore little one-piece suits.'[11]

The clothing worn by the entities is often described as being a one-piece seamless garment with no apparent openings or fasten-ings. Often they wear a belt which glows or has glowing pieces inset. Sometimes the glowing objects are on their gloves or fingers. Sometimes witnesses describe entities in divers' suits with helmets:

this sounds more like our own ideas of astronauts' equipment. But there are also reports of transparent or cellophane suits being worn. One land-survey worker saw hairless 7-foot entities wearing inflated baglike transparent suits, while their clothing underneath looked like brightly coloured paper. What might the significance be of the great variety of appearance and dress? Perhaps the entities are coming from a number of different places; or are they insubstantial, and able to materialize in whatever form takes their fancy? If the experiences are a form of hallucination, then clearly the details would vary with each percipient.

Much of the observed activity of UFO entities is of a fleeting nature and is of poorly observed figures briefly seen, usually as they scurry into a UFO before a rapid take-off. But there are a number of cases in which the activity seen by the witness is more comprehensive and interesting in human terms. UFO entities have on occasion been seen to examine plants and rocks and sometimes take samples, as occurred in May 1966 at Caracas (Venezuela) when a man watched as two entities, who appeared to be bright and transparent with oversized hands, examined plants with strange instruments. They returned to their oval craft by floating along a beam of light. Brazilian Jose Alves was quietly fishing one night in November 1954 when a UFO landed nearby. He watched three little men in white clothing and close-fitting skull-caps emerge and proceed to collect samples of grass, herbs and tree leaves, while one filled a shiny metal tube with river water. Witnesses have also reported seeing UFOs hovering over creeks and lakes with a flexible hose lowered into the water, apparently suctioning water into their craft. Besides collecting specimens of leaves, water and stones, the UFO entities also take an interest in animal life. They have been seen trying to capture dogs on several occasions, and in January 1978 in Cheshire (England) four poachers watched as silver-suited entities placed a paralysed cow in a cage-like object apparently with the intention of measuring it.

Are all of these activities to be taken at face value? For how long is it necessary for the UFO entities to go on collecting soil, rocks and plants? Perhaps they are not connected with one another, coming from widely different worlds and unaware of each other's presence. Or perhaps they are not really concerned with the continual collection of samples, but are using this activity as a ploy to distract the witness's attention from their real interests.

A frequently observed activity of UFO entities is the inspection of

On 24 November
1978 Angelo
D'Ambros met two
small beings in the
woods near Gastagh
(Vicenza, Italy),
where he had gone to
gather firewood. They
were suspended in
the air, and made
strenuous efforts to
seize the witness's
machete, until he
threatened them with
a piece of wood.
Chasing after them
when they fled, he
saw a domed craft
about 6 feet high
standing on legs,
which then took off at
speed.

a landed UFO, when the occupants are seen to get out and examine the exterior, usually taking off again very soon afterwards. A variation of this occurred on 18 October 1954 when M. Labassiere of Royan (France) was driving with his wife. They saw two UFOs land close together in a field, and from each issued a small entity which walked purposefully across the intervening space without stopping as they passed each other. They continued until they reached the other craft, both UFOs taking off soon afterwards.

A few witnesses tell us that entities have been seen carrying luminous or brilliantly glowing spheres or wands in their hands. Whether these are simply to provide illumination or have some subtler purpose, such as being a portable source of energy, is a matter for conjecture, as they have never been seen to put these objects to any particular use. Consider for example the report from Brazilian witness Adilon Azevedo, who on an evening in July 1965 saw two UFOs land near him on some waste ground. Crouching behind a wall, he saw three entities emerge from one machine and two from the other. For about five minutes they grouped together and conversed in a sibilant language. One held a brilliant luminous wandlike object in his hand, and each group then walked around its machine three times, sometimes bending down to examine the surface of the craft closely. Then they re-entered the machines which rapidly rose into the sky and were lost among the stars.

There are also cases where entities appear to be carrying out repairs on the outside of their craft. Sometimes these take but a few minutes, while others take much longer. A lengthy and difficult repair apparently took place on the night of 24–25 November 1964 at New Berlin, New York (USA). Mrs Mary Merryweather and her mother-in-law observed the crews of two landed UFOs, between ten and twenty entities, working beneath one of the craft for over four hours, cutting lengths of cable to fit a large, heavy object which they had lowered from beneath the UFO. From a little more than half a mile away the two women watched with the aid of binoculars as the tall entities, estimated to be between 6½ and 8 feet in height, laboured to replace the object. Eventually they were successful and soon afterwards the two UFOs rapidly flew away. Later Mrs Merryweather and her husband examined the area and found marks and depressions which confirmed the activity she had witnessed. They also found a 3-inch long piece of cable which appeared to be of unusual construction. Later when investigators asked to see this artefact no one was sure what had happened to it and it could not be found.

There are also numerous cases where the witness, often driving alone at night, suddenly comes upon a landed UFO, sometimes straddling the road. After a few moments of shocked reaction by the witness, figures may be seen hurrying into the craft, which then rapidly takes off. UFO researchers have speculated on the significance of this scenario and have suggested that it may, along with the other activities described, only be designed to attract attention. In the same way, UFOs flying at night are very often brightly illuminated, though there seems no obvious reason why they should carry any lights at all, especially if they are here for clandestine purposes. So the light displays may also be an attention-attracting device. However, there is an alternative explanation for the light displays. In recent years researchers into the electrical rhythms of the brain have discovered that experimental subjects who watch lights flashing at certain regular rates will experience various mental states ranging from drowsiness to deep hypnosis or epilepsy, and this suggests that UFO witnesses who start an encounter by seeing a UFO with flashing lights are being programmed for the subsequent experience, perhaps an abduction, of which we shall say more later in this chapter.

Some witnesses have actually met and communicated with UFO entities. Sometimes food, drink or an artefact is asked for or given. A classic case is that of Joe Simonton of Eagle River, Wisconsin (USA), who in April 1961 saw a UFO land in his farmyard. He walked towards it and a hatch opened. Inside were three dark-skinned 'men', and one handed Joe a silvery jug while making a drinking motion to indicate that he wanted water. When Joe returned with the filled jug he saw that one of the entities was cooking cakes or biscuits on a griddle and he indicated that he would like one. He was given four. Later Joe tried one and told UFO investigators that it tasted like cardboard. An analysis of another revealed that the ingredients were ordinary corn and wheat flours and other unexceptional substances. Another request for water was made to Maria Josa Cintra who was on night duty at Lins Sanatorium (Brazil) in August 1968. She was awakened by a knocking at the front door and there found a woman of normal height but of foreign appearance who spoke in an unknown language and handed her a mug and a beautifully engraved glass bottle. These Maria filled with water, and after handing them back was amazed to see the stranger enter a bright, pearl-shaped object that quickly rose into the air. In May 1978, the Polish farmer Jan Wolsky was invited into a UFO with an all-black interior; he was first given a medical examination and then offered a transparent substance, which his hosts ate but which he declined. Carl Higdon, who was hunting elk in Medicine Bow National Forest, Wyoming (USA) on 24 October 1974, was offered a packet of four pills by a friendly stranger, a preliminary to being taken into a UFO and then having some very strange experiences.

Other witnesses have been given apparently solid objects, but interestingly none of these has ever survived for long. In Massachusetts (USA), Betty Andreasson, who claimed she was abducted into a UFO in January 1967, exchanged a Bible for a blue book which the leader of the UFO entities gave her. The blue book contained formulae, riddles and poems which could be 'understood only through the spirit'. Nine days later she could not find it, but this did not surprise her as the entities had told her that she would only have it for a limited time. Betty Hill, who along with her husband Barney was allegedly abducted into a UFO in 1961, asked for and was given a book by the leader of the UFO entities, but before she could leave some of the crew members objected to her having it and so reluctantly she had to leave it behind. Other UFO witnesses say they have been given metal discs or ingots which sometimes mysteriously disappear at a later date. Other variations on this theme include the case of an entity who snatched a scarf from a terrified Argentinian motorcyclist, and another who poured the contents of an amazed rail worker's oilcan into a bottle. Here again the actions of these entities range from the inexplicable to the incredible.

The presence of UFOs or UFO entities can often produce a state of temporary but total paralysis in a witness. Maurice Masse, who found two small entities with large craniums examining his lavender plants in Valensole (France) in July 1965, was made completely immobile when one of the entities pointed a small tube at him, though he still retained all his other faculties. There are numerous cases where light beams have been used to immobilize witnesses, usually harmlessly, but close proximity to UFOs can cause more injurious effects. Amateur geologist Stephen Michalak was engaged on some prospecting near Falcon Lake, Manitoba (Canada), in May 1967 when a glowing UFO landed nearby. After a cautious approach and watching it for more than thirty minutes, he went up to the craft which was radiating a lot of heat. A blast of hot air from the grille in the side of the UFO set his clothes on fire and as he tore off his burning shirt and vest the UFO lifted off and flew away. He soon felt nauseous and had a bad headache. Vomiting and feeling very weak, he made his way back to the highway and eventually reached home. Over a year later, Michalak was still seeking medical help for his recurring symptoms, and although his illness was diagnosed as not being due to nuclear radiation, its exact cause could not be found.[12]

In December 1980 two women, Betty Cash and Vickie Landrum, with her grandson Colby Landrum, were driving along a country road near Houston, Texas (USA), when a glowing, flame-belching UFO appeared and hovered over the road just over 100 feet in front of them. Unable to proceed, they stopped and got out of the car to watch. The heat radiating from the object was intense, making the car too hot to touch, and it was nearly ten minutes before the hovering UFO finally lifted up and moved away from the road. The witnesses suffered severe symptoms including vomiting, diarrhoea, reddened skin, loss of hair, loss of appetite, stomach-aches and faulty vision.

But the physical effect of UFOs on witnesses is not always for the worst. There are a few accounts where the witnesses claim that after a UFO sighting their health was improved. A deputy sheriff of

Damon, Texas (USA), found that a severe wound on his arm, which had been caused earlier in the day by a bite from a pet alligator, was immediately healed after a close encounter with a UFO. A 73-year-old gaucho in rural Argentina suffered some unpleasant after-effects, such as temporary loss of hair and itching skin, after a UFO hovered overhead in December 1972, but investigators later found that several new teeth were growing in his gums. These effects on the health of the witness are very likely to be unintentional effects due to some type of radiation (experiments in Canada show that electro-magnetic radiation may be beneficial in speeding up the healing process in wounds), but there are many cases where illness or injury seem to be the result of deliberate and aggressive acts on the part of UFO entities.

Sometimes this aggression is in answer to an initial aggressive act on the part of the human witness, but at other times it seems quite unprovoked. Such was the case with James Flynn, who in April 1965 was on a hunting trip in the Florida Everglades (USA). Seeing a strange, glowing, cone-shaped object descend on to the swamp, he drove near to it and then walked to within a few yards. He raised his arm and waved. Immediately a beam of light shot out from the UFO and struck him squarely on the forehead. When he recovered consciousness 24 hours later he was partly blind due to internal haemorrhage. Later, investigators examined the scorched grass circle and burnt tree-tops where the UFO had hovered. In October 1973 truck-driver Eddie Webb poked his head out of his cab window and looked back at the rainbow array of lights which were rapidly gaining on him as he drove to Cape Girardeau, Missouri (USA). Immediately he did so, a yellow/red beam of light struck him in the face and temporarily blinded him. The frame of his spectacles was warped and melted, and he was in hospital for seven days recovering his sight. He successfully claimed insurance compensation for his injury.

Whether this type of attack is a calculated act by an intelligent and malign entity or a programmed reaction from an unmanned probe type of craft is a matter for conjecture, as no entities were seen in either of the previous cases. Sometimes entities are seen, as in January 1970 when two skiers in southern Finland stopped for a breather in a forest glade. A metallic UFO arrived and projected a yellow beam of light on to the ground. Within this appeared an entity holding a black box from which a brilliant yellow light pulsed. The entity pointed this at the witnesses. When the UFO had left, the two men were partially paralysed for a while, and for several weeks suffered from symptoms indicative of radiation sickness. Investigators and journalists who later visited the site were also ill afterwards.

There are a few reports in which the witnesses have initiated attacks on UFOs or entities, usually with rifle fire. In the least hostile reaction, the UFO has moved away while the bullets could be heard ricocheting from its metal surface, but sometimes the reaction has been more aggressive, as in the Brazilian case of August 1967 when Inacio de Souza, a farm manager, saw a UFO in one of his fields. Three entities wearing tight-fitting yellow jersey suits were 'playing about like children'. When they saw de Souza they ran towards him, and he started to shoot at them with a rifle. As he did so, a beam of green light streaked from the UFO and hit him in the chest, knocking him to the ground. The entities retreated to the UFO which quickly took off. In the ensuing days de Souza experienced nausea and tingling of the body as well as general numbness. He lost weight quickly, and blood tests showed that he had severe leukaemia. Within two months he was dead from radiation poisoning.

The principal weapon of the UFOs appears to be a visible coloured beam which can be employed with extreme accuracy, speed, and deadly effect. Fortunately such occurrences are only a small percentage of the mass of UFO reports on record.

Solid objects landing and leaving burn marks and other physical traces, entities that feel solid enough when witnesses come into physical contact with them . . . but there are also reports which suggest that sometimes the phenomena are of a less than solid nature. UFOs have been reported as looking glasslike and translucent, changing shape in mid-flight, and sometimes completely fading away from visibility. In November 1978 four men hunting at night in Seville (Spain) observed a landed UFO with an entity moving about near it. Some of the witnesses saw only the lower half of the entity, while the others could see it only from the waist up. This report is an example of those in which the entities are only partially visible. Very often their lower legs and feet appear to be transparent or missing, or they are standing in long grass or undergrowth which effectively hides the possible absence of lower limbs. Sometimes they are seen to float or glide about and pass in and out of their UFOs without the need for any opening doorway.

There is a strong element of the paranormal in many UFO events and parallels can be found between them and traditional accounts of apparitions and various areas of folklore. After a UFO experience witnesses sometimes find that they have developed psychic abilities, and they may be plagued with poltergeist manifestations. Abductee Betty Hill claims numerous poltergeist occurrences around her home since her experience, and some witnesses report seeing shadowy apparitional figures around their houses or visits from shadowy entities while they lie in bed. Some cases seem to suggest that UFOs 'choose' those who have some psychic ability, but there is also the possibility that a UFO experience will cause latent psychic abilities in a witness to manifest.

Some witnesses have claimed not only to have seen UFOs land, but to have talked to their occupants and gone for a ride in the craft. Named 'contactees' by ufologists, such people were especially common in the 1950s, but today new contactees are rare. Some famous names among contactees are George Adamski, Orfeo Angelucci, Truman Bethurum, Dan Fry, all based in America. Since the Betty and Barney Hill abduction case in 1961, most close contact with UFOs has been in the form of abductions, and this has become the main talking point in the 1980s, especially since the massive success of Whitley Strieber's book *Communion*, which describes his own experiences. However, just as there was doubt about whether contactees had really been aboard UFOs or had only imagined it, so today there is doubt in some ufologists' minds as to the reality of abduction experiences. The abductees are sincere enough, and seem to believe that they have been abducted, but in most cases the details of the abduction have been retrieved from the unconscious mind by means of hypnotic regression, and there is considerable uncertainty as to the reliability of information obtained in this way. So there is a rift between ufologists over abductions, some believing that they prove conclusively that UFOs are from outer space and are here for nefarious purposes involving maintaining their breeding stock; others believing that the abduction experiences reflect the anxieties in the victims' psyches, and that the basic material for these stories is part of humanity's collective unconscious, the form in which it emerges varying according to the time and the place. As UFOs and abductions emerge as a dominant theme in the Western consciousness, so people's inexplicable experiences will tend to adopt this format. The people investigating abduction cases, not being aware of the historical precedent for this type of experience, unwittingly encourage belief in the reality of these bizarre stories which, when publicized, encourage even more people to imagine that they too

Charles Hickson (left) and Calvin Parker photographed in 1986 as they answered questions about their abduction by UFO entities. This allegedly occurred on 11 October 1973 down by the river at Pascagoula, Mississippi (USA), when the men were fishing.

have been abducted. So we are likely to see an increase in abduction reports until some other phenomenon replaces it. It is possible that the 'contactee syndrome' was the equivalent theme of the 1950s.

Whether all the UFO landing and entity sighting reports can also be classed as imaginary events instigated by media reporting of similar cases is very difficult to determine. Whereas most abductees and contactees were alone when their experiences took place, very often witnesses of UFO landings and entities were not alone and there is someone else available to confirm their report. Some witnesses have emerged from peasant backgrounds in remote countries, with little access to radio, television or newspapers, and these would appear to be 'uncontaminated witnesses', meriting a high rating for authenticity. There are also, of course, the inexplicable physical traces sometimes left by landed craft. Despite our personal scepticism about certain aspects of the UFO phenomenon, we are not unaware that there are many puzzling reports still awaiting explanation. Some UFOs may be natural or man-made phenomena misinterpreted, some may be hallucinations, some UFO experiences may be consciously or unconsciously self-engendered, but some UFOs may be 'real', i.e. really inexplicable by our present science. If that is so, we cannot even begin to discuss what the nature of that 'reality' might be, for the possibilities are many, and the implications uncomfortable to contemplate.[13]

7 *Monsters in lakes, rivers and seas*

Although Nessie, the monster in Loch Ness (Scotland), is by far the most famous lake monster, she is only one example of many, for monsters have been reported from lakes and rivers around the world. However, their distribution has a definite pattern to it, the long-necked type of animal being concentrated around isothermic lines 10°C in both northern and southern hemispheres; and, as Dr Bernard Heuvelmans pointed out, 'One could hardly wish for better circumstantial evidence of their existence.'[1] There are other types of animals reported, from all parts of the globe, but there are likely to be many different types of creature responsible for the reports, some known, and possibly some as yet unknown. The same applies to monsters seen in the seas, to which we shall turn later in this chapter.

In the northern hemisphere, a line joining Canada, Ireland, Scotland, Norway, Sweden, Finland and the northern USSR indicates where lake monsters are most likely to be seen, all these countries having an abundance of sizeable lakes. Canada's best-

Looking across Lake Okanagan, British Columbia (Canada), towards Squally Point and Ogopogo Island, where many sightings of lake monster Ogopogo have been made.

OGOPOGO'S HOME

Before the unimaginative, practical whiteman came, the fearsome lake monster, N'ha-a-itk, was well known to the primitive, superstitious Indians. His home was believed to be a cave at Squally Point, and small animals were carried in the canoes to appease the serpent.

Ogopogo still is seen each year – but now by white men!

DEPARTMENT OF
RECREATION & CONSERVATION

known monster is Ogopogo, who lives in Lake Okanagan in British Columbia. Of course, if any of these monsters do exist as unknown species, there must be a breeding colony in each lake, not a single specimen, so it is misleading for them to be given a singular nickname in this way. But if there are breeding colonies in the lakes, why are the monsters not seen more often? A possible answer to this question will be suggested later in this chapter. The Indians who lived in British Columbia before the white settlers arrived included a giant serpent in their legends about the lake, and Arlene Gaal, who has been investigating Ogopogo since 1968, has on record over 200 sightings. A recent one was made by Lionel Edmond, who was fishing on the lake on 20 July 1986 when he heard a loud rushing of water behind him. 'It looked like a submarine surfacing, coming up toward my boat. As it came up perpendicular to the boat we could see six humps out of the water, each hump about 10 inches out of the water and each one creating a wake.' He estimated it at about 50 or 60 feet long.[2]

A few photographs have been taken, and some cine film, but none of these shows the creature clearly, so its identification remains uncertain. Even if clearer photographs were available the mystery

F. W. Holiday (right) and Lionel Leslie, two now-deceased monster-hunters, working at Lough Auna, County Galway (Ireland) in 1969.

would not be solved, because if they showed some creature unknown to science they would be dismissed as hoaxes, exactly as has happened at Loch Ness. Only a carcass will satisfy everybody, and that is the one thing that has never been found. Most monster lakes are far too large to be systematically searched, but in Ireland there are some very small lakes where monsters have been seen, and in the 1960s attempts were made to net them and therefore trap any strange creature lurking there.

One of the lakes chosen was Lough Nahooin in County Galway. It measures only 100 by 80 yards, and a monster had been seen very recently, on 22 February 1968, by farmer Stephen Coyne who lived close to the lough. He had gone down to the water to fetch some dry peat that evening, with his son and their dog. He saw a black object swimming around in the water. It had a pole-like head and neck about a foot in diameter, which it sometimes put underwater, and then two humps were seen, and sometimes a flat tail. This was sometimes seen near the head, showing that the body was very flexible, perhaps eel-like. It came towards the shore as if irritated by the dog which was barking at it. Mrs Coyne and the other children came to see what was happening, and Mrs Coyne noticed two horn-like projections on the head, but no one saw any eyes. The interior of the mouth was pale, but no teeth could be seen. They saw the creature clearly from as close as 25 feet, watching it until dusk when they went back home. However, when the search was mounted in July, only a few months later, there was no sign of the creature, estimated by the Coynes to be 12 feet long. Neither netting nor the use of 'monster-rousers', echo-sounder or fish-stunners produced any evidence of the presence of anything large in the lough. The answer may be that it had moved on, for there is some evidence to suggest that the Irish monsters, and the Scottish, and perhaps others too, sometimes venture on to land, and may be in the habit of moving from one lake to another.[3]

One of the visitors to Lough Nahooin that July was Georgina Carberry, who had herself had a dramatic sighting in 1954 when fishing in Lough Fadda. She and her colleagues saw at close quarters a creature very similar to that described by the Coynes, with two humps, a long neck, and a big open mouth. She remembered that 'the whole body had movement in it' – it was 'wormy', 'creepy', and made a vivid impression on Miss Carberry, so much so that it was six or seven years before she went back to the lake, and she never returned alone.[4]

Large-scale scientific searches for lake monsters are not often undertaken, probably because of the great difficulties to be faced. Organized investigation at Loch Ness began in the early 1960s and has continued intermittently ever since, but very little has been achieved in 25 years as far as positive identification of Nessie is concerned. In America, Joseph W. Zarzynski has worked tirelessly since 1974 to protect and search for Champ, the monster of Lake Champlain. Elsewhere occasional investigations are undertaken, and interested people collect sighting reports and interview witnesses, but without funding large-scale investigation is impossible. Many of the lakes, like those in Scandinavia, are remote and rarely visited except by local people, so all kinds of rare creatures could be living there without anyone knowing. Perhaps it is too late to start looking for them. Many Scandinavian lakes are now dead because of poisoning from acid rain. No fish can survive in acid waters, as has been discovered recently in North Wales where fish put in lakes to stock them have died after a few days because of acidity. If no fish can survive, neither can the predators which feed on them, and we must assume that lake monsters take fish as part of their diet. Therefore not only are Scandinavian lake monsters doomed, but also others like the Loch Ness Monster, and monsters anywhere where acid rain is a problem.

As the entries in the Gazetteer show, there are many other bodies of water south of Canada and Scandinavia where monsters have allegedly been seen. Most American states have at least one, Wisconsin having the greatest number with New York not far behind. South America has so much unexplored territory, though now sadly being rapidly invaded by industrial concerns greedy for profit, that all kinds of unknown creatures could be living there, and indeed rumours have emerged from time to time of water monsters, but no expeditions have yet attempted to track these rumours to their source. The continent of Africa is also a likely place to find unknown creatures, and recent expeditions to the Congo in search of Mokele-mbembe have brought back convincing evidence that this creature still survives, and indeed may be a prehistoric survival unlike anything else living on this planet. (For further details see Chapter 17.) Australia has her bunyip, a legendary creature that sounds like a water monster. Whether the bunyip still survives is uncertain, for few water monster reports come out of Australia today. Other countries around the world from where lake monster reports have come this century include China, France, Greenland, Italy, Japan,

Malaysia, New Zealand, Papua New Guinea, Poland, Switzerland, and Tibet.

It is clear that a lot of people have seen something that they suspect is a water monster – but what have they really seen? Not many witnesses get a close look at the creature, seeing only some splashing or a dark shape at a distance. If the lake is one renowned for its monster, like Loch Ness or Okanagan, then they will jump to obvious conclusions. But there are many possible explanations for what is seen, all of which are feasible in certain circumstances, and must be considered before labelling the sighting a monster. There are several species of fish which, if left undisturbed in a lake with a plentiful food supply, will grow very large in size. Perhaps the best example is the sturgeon, averaging 10 feet in length but often growing much bigger. Reports of giant fish being seen in Lake Seton in British Columbia (Canada) have occasionally been made, and in 1965 two Indians fishing from a canoe saw a sturgeon 22 feet long. In June 1966 a couple on the lake in a 25-foot boat sailed alongside a giant fish. Paul Polischuk said: 'It was a giant sturgeon, a good ten feet longer than my boat. It swam close to the surface for quite a long time before turning and heading for deep water. There is no question of a mistake.'[5] In 1984 the monster reportedly lurking in Stafford Lake near Novato, California (USA), was exposed when the lake was drained for dam repairs – it was a 6½-foot white sturgeon, possibly 50 or 60 years old.[6] In November 1987 an 11-foot sturgeon weighing nearly half a ton was found dead in Lake Washington, Washington State (USA), where there had been rumours of a huge, duck-eating monster.[7] In the USSR a sturgeon caught in the Volga River was 24 feet long and weighed 3241 pounds.

The largest wholly freshwater fish today is reckoned to be a rare giant catfish found in Eastern rivers. It can measure up to 9 feet 10 inches long. The European catfish or wels used to be the biggest, at 8–15 feet, but these have now been overfished and large specimens are not thought to survive. However, they might, and could be responsible for some European and Scandinavian lake monster reports. In China, giant red fish were reported from Lake Hanas in the Xinjiang Autonomous Region in 1985. Reports of giant fish in this lake go back at least to the 1930s. Professor Xiang, a biologist, watched them through binoculars and could see the head, spiny rays and tail fin. He said the fish were over 30 feet long. Their heads were the size of car tyres, and about 60 were seen together. It was suggested that they were a species of giant salmon.[8] It is clear from these reports that where a lake monster is imperfectly seen, a large fish of known species is likely to be a strong contender rather than some unknown species. Also other animals like seals or otters may be misidentified, or swimming deer. Sometimes the 'monster' may not be a living creature at all. Several ingenious theories have been put forward to account for sightings, for example whirlpools, temperature inversions, dead trees, mats of rotting vegetation, and these may indeed sometimes be responsible, especially if the viewing conditions are bad and the witness is hoping to see a monster. Even more exotic 'monsters' sometimes come to the surface. This report describes an event which took place in England on 7 January 1934.

A furore was caused near Birkenhead and Liverpool today when a crowd gathered around a large pond at Spital, in which, it was reported, a strange animal with a queerly shaped head was disporting itself.

The 'monster' was dragged from the pond after being lassoed. While the crowd fearfully retreated to a safe distance, more intrepid spirits approached and discovered it to be a child's over-sized rocking horse, with a head painted red and a long black mane. Covered with slime and weeds, it presented a terrifying appearance.[9]

There have been plenty of occasions when a witness got a good view of the monster, and later described a creature bearing no resemblance to any known species. The long-necked type are most often seen, and there have been many suggestions as to what they might be. Prehistoric survivals are among the possibilities put forward, for example the plesiosaur, which is what the Loch Ness Monster might be, and the zeuglodon, a type of whale long extinct which has been suggested for Champ and other monsters. But without more evidence as to the nature of the creatures, it is fruitless to speculate on what they might be.

We mentioned earlier the possibility that some lake monsters may be able to move about on land. It has also been suggested that they might, where feasible, come into the lakes from the sea, and also go out again, as the mood takes them. Loch Ness is connected to the sea by the River Ness, and monsters have been seen in the river. Also, some sea monster reports sound very similar to lake monsters. So could some of the lake monsters actually be sea monsters? Ulrich Magin, who suggested this possibility,[10] went on to say that his

In October 1987 Operation Deepscan was held at Loch Ness, in an attempt to perform a complete sonar scan by means of a fleet of sonar boats moving in line abreast down the loch.

theory explains various features of the Loch Ness Monster reports: many sightings may occur when there are creatures visiting the loch, quiet years may indicate there are none visiting. Also, the variety of shapes and colours reported may be because different types of creatures enter the loch, not just one type. And the question of breeding colonies is answered by Ulrich Magin's theory. To ensure regular sightings over the years, a breeding colony would be required, not just one or two individuals, but if there were a breeding colony in the loch, why are sightings not more frequent? Magin replies, 'There is no breeding herd of monsters in the loch, but there are, regularly, marine visitors.' This theory sounds feasible, and could be applied equally well to other lochs connected to the sea by a short river. It becomes less feasible the longer the river connection, we feel.

Another fact which seems to link sea and lake monsters is that so often long-necked animals are reported. One of these was photographed a few years ago, off Falmouth, Cornwall (England), where in the mid-1970s there were many sightings of sea monsters which were nicknamed Morgawr. A woman took two close-up photographs

A sonar chart in the wheelhouse of one of the sonar boats involved in Operation Deepscan at Loch Ness.

of Morgawr in February 1976, one of which is shown on page 120. This creature has a long neck and a humped body, as so often described by people who see lake monsters and sea monsters. The photographer also wrote a description of the creature:

> It looked like an elephant waving its trunk, but the trunk was a long neck with a small head on the end, like a snake's head. It had humps on the back which moved in a funny way. The colour was black or very dark brown, and the skin seemed to be like a sealion's . . . the animal frightened me. I would not like to see it any closer. I do not like the way it moved when swimming.

This brings to mind Georgina Carberry's description of the creature she saw in Lough Fadda, as 'wormy', 'creepy', and 'the whole body had movement in it'. Her monster, too, was long-necked and had two humps. Was it perhaps the same species as Morgawr?

The Morgawr photographed was only 15–18 feet long, the witness estimated, but sea monsters are usually much bigger than that. A few sample descriptions from the many hundreds of reports made this century will help to give a clearer picture. Sea monsters have been seen all over the world, hundreds of miles from land as well as close inshore. The latter are seen by fishermen in small boats, yachtsmen,

One of the February
1976 photographs of
Morgawr, the Cornish
sea monster.

and by people on land; the former, of course, from larger vessels. Nowadays sightings from ships are fewer than in the last century and earlier, possibly because sailing ships travelled much less noisily. Today sea monsters have more warning of the presence of vessels and can keep out of sight. Sometimes, however, the monster seems positively curious about interlopers into its territory, and approaches them, and has even been known to dive beneath a small boat and come up underneath it, lifting it from the water and almost capsizing it. This happened to Captain Alexander S. Banta, a pilot who was off City Island, New York City (USA), where he was to lead a vessel through Hell's Gate. The date was 10 August 1902. Twice the creature, black and much bigger than a whale, attacked the boat, then was distracted and made off in the direction of a steamer passing by. Captain Banta hurriedly took his leaking boat back to shore.[11] Also apparently curious was the monster which approached a group of fishermen working four or five miles off Hermanus (South Africa) in 1903. One of them described what they saw.

> I looked across the sea, and, to my horror, I saw the most awful-looking monster with its head about four feet above the water, rapidly approaching our small boat. We were petrified and there was nothing we could do.

*The sea monster
photographed by
Robert Le Serrec in
1964.*

Suddenly, about ten yards away, the snake-like creature raised its head still further to a height of more than 20 feet and looked down on us with eyes like saucers – not once but three times – for periods of about 15 seconds, and it was at least 120 feet long. It had a head the size of a paraffin tin and was covered with long hair that looked like seaweed. It appeared to be the thickness of an 8–10 inch water pipe. The body a black-brown, and the throat a whitish brown colour; it swam very fast and then very slowly. It suddenly made one terrific dive and that was the last we saw of it.[12]

During World War I, the sinking of the British steamer *Iberian* by the German *U28* in the North Atlantic resulted in a sea monster sighting by the commander of the *U28* and some of his officers. Some seconds after *Iberian* had been torpedoed and sunk, there was an explosion underwater.

A little later pieces of wreckage, and among them a gigantic sea-animal, writhing and struggling wildly, were shot out of the water to a height of 60 to 100 feet . . . We did not have the time to take a photograph, for the animal sank out of sight after 10 or 15 seconds . . . It was about 60 feet long, was like a crocodile in shape and had four limbs with powerful webbed feet and a long tail tapering to a point.[13]

In more peaceful circumstances, at least three sea monster sightings were made in 1923 in the Pacific islands of New Caledonia. The 22 September sighting was in the main harbour of Nouméa by two women from Freycinet Isle who were in a boat on a fishing expedition. They heard a prolonged whistle and saw a strange animal which shot a jet of vapour then a spout of water vertically into the air. It was dark, almost black, and looked like a sea horse with a crest down its back. Its head was 30 feet out of the water, and it kept lifting its head and tail and hitting the water with a loud noise. The women were, not unexpectedly, terrified, and sped home, seeing the creature three more times on the way. A retired policeman also saw the incident from his home on Freycinet Isle. He concluded his description: 'I did not see the head; but at each appearance, I heard this tremendous noise like the trumpeting of an elephant, followed by the sound of the wash like many sheets of metal falling. It was flat calm.'[14]

Native island-dwellers are usually familiar with the sea and know when they are seeing a rare and unusual creature. Similarly professional seamen, who have spent many hours watching the seas. One such, the commander of a Coast Guard patrol ship, saw a strange creature off Long Island, New York (USA), where there have been other sightings. It was some time in 1929.

We were running from Bermuda and on reaching a point about 20 miles south of Montauk Point, on the east coast, we stopped the engines and lay to. I was on the bridge when I sighted something in the water' about a half-mile off starboard bow. As it came nearer, I saw that it was a strange creature with a long neck and a serpent-like head. It was moving through the water at about 10 to 12 knots. I called the helmsman and he summoned four or five men, all of whom started for a boat with the intention of launching it and capturing the creature. I immediately countermanded that intention because from what I could see of the creature's head and neck, it was quite apparent that it was big enough to swamp the boat. It eventually passed within about 200 yards of us and I could establish that the head was about 2 feet in diameter and was 8 to 10 feet out of the water. The front of its neck was very black and shiny like satin, glistening as if it had recently been under water. I could plainly see the wrinkles on the skin where the eye that was turned toward the ship must have been two or three inches across.[15]

In the same general area, but 120 miles out to sea, to the east of Pollock, the crew of the scalloper *Noreen* had a close sighting of a monster on 3 September 1959. The cook, Joseph H. Bourassa, was one of six men on deck, and he said he had never seen anything like it during his twenty years at sea. His description reads:

He had a large body and a small alligator-like head. The neck seemed to be medium size, matching the size of the head. The body was very large, shaped somewhat like a seal. There was a mane of bristly hair or fur which ran down the middle of his head.

He would surface the upper part of his body and glide out of the water with the lower part of his body remaining submerged. The portion of his body which was visible measured about 40 feet in length. We estimate his weight to be between 35 and 40 tons over all.

At no time did the whole body show. He stayed on the surface no longer than 40 seconds at a time. You could hear the heavy weight of his upper body when he dove below, creating a large splash and a subsequent wake. He surfaced four times in 20 minutes during which we were trying to stay clear of him. The Captain changed course to steer away from him and the queer fellow surfaced on our starboard beam . . .

Another peculiar thing about him was that when he'd surface he would turn his head looking towards us and it seemed to us he was playful and curious. Another point was that on the upper part of his body there were two flippers, similar to those of a seal.[16]

Further north, there have been numerous sea monster sightings around Nova Scotia and Newfoundland, two large islands off the eastern coast of Canada. In July 1976 there were three sightings off the southern side of Cape Sable Island, Nova Scotia. Keith Ross and his 24-year-old son Rodney, anchored in foggy waters off Pollock's Ledge several miles offshore, saw a 50-foot creature emerge and make for their boat. Rodney compared it to a huge sea horse.

I never seen crocodiles other than on television, but its head was sort of like that coming out of the water. Peaked at the top, with a big wide mouth, its neck was full of things that looked like gigantic barnacles. Its eyes were in sockets, but popped out of the side of its head, and it had two tusks maybe two or three feet long and four inches or so round . . . I didn't think it was a whale. Not with a head like that and those tusks.[17]

The other main location where sea monsters are seen off the eastern coast of North America is the Chesapeake Bay area of Maryland and Virginia. 1978 was a particularly good year for Chessie, as the monster is called. One sighting was made from Bay Quarter Shore, Heathsville, Virginia, by a retired CIA employee, Donald P. Kyker. He was sitting on his porch when he saw something undulating in the Potomac River, 75 yards off shore. He saw 'a 25–30 foot long sleek body, dark grey, 8 inches in diameter and about to move at 7 to 8 miles per hour'. He called his friends Howard and Myrtle Smoot, who lived downstream, and they also saw the monster. Three more appeared, one larger than the Smoots' 36-foot porch. Mr Smoot shot one of the smaller ones in the neck, and they all submerged. The Smoots' next-door neighbour, C.

Phillip Stemmer, also saw them. He said they moved 'like self-propelled logs. They weren't just three somethings floating there. They were moving faster than the water, they were making waves.'[18]

Off the west coast of North America, monsters are sometimes seen off California, at places like Stinson Beach, Redondo Beach, San Francisco Bay. Further north, the monster seen in the seas off Vancouver Island (British Columbia, Canada) is known as Cadborosaurus or Caddy, since one of its haunts is Cadboro Bay. There were many sightings in the 1930s, including at least three close sightings in the last three months of 1933. Early in October, Major W. H. Langley, clerk of the British Columbia Legislature, and his wife, saw a creature 80 feet long in Cadboro Bay, which reared its head out of the water and scratched its neck on barnacles on the rocks.[19] Later the same month, on 21 October, First Officer A. E. Richards on the bridge of the liner *Santa Lucia*, off Sheringham Point near Victoria, in the dawn light saw what he thought was a wreck, until he saw seven humps.

> Then I saw this great eel-like monster rear its head like a Scotch terrier struck by curiosity. Its eyes were red and green, like the port and starboard lights of a ship. It was about ninety feet long. As we approached within 200 feet, it rose out of the water, with its seven humps like a camel and its face like a cow, and didn't make any noise, but I thought it should have mooed. Then it uttered an eerie bellow, like a bull whale in its last agony and reared up, perhaps thirty feet, perhaps fifty, and flopped over on its back. Along its flanks was a phosphorescent glow. By this time we had five searchlights on it, and it turned to the side and dived. Maybe it went under the ship.

The captain also saw it dive and said it was 'Certainly the most unusual sea monster I ever saw.'[20]

Cyril B. Andrews of Pender Island in the Gulf of Georgia (British Columbia) claimed a very close sighting of Caddy, also at the end of 1933. He signed an affidavit that said that in the company of thirteen others he saw the monster rear its head out of the water and gulp down a duck, within ten feet of them. It was at least 40 feet long, and had a head like a horse's, and they watched it for some time until, 'with a queer undulating movement, it submerged and disappeared.'[21]

However close a sighting is, if the creature is in the water the witness does not see its whole body. Very occasionally, a sea monster is seen on land. This happened on the west coast of Tasmania (Australia) in 1913, as related here by Hartwell Conder, Tasmanian State Mining Engineer.

The animal was seen by Oscar Davies, foreman prospector, and his mate (W. Harris), who are working under myself . . . I have known both of them for a considerable number of years, and can guarantee absolutely their sobriety, intelligence and accuracy. They were walking along the coast on April 20, just before sundown on a calm day, with small waves rolling in and breaking on the shore, when at a distance of about a half-mile they noticed a dark object under the dunes which surprised them by showing signs of movement.

They advanced toward it and finally came within gunshot. When about 40 yards off it rose suddenly and rushed down into the sea. After getting out about 30 yards it stopped and turned round, showing only the head above five seconds, and then withdrew under the water and disappeared.

The characteristics are summarized as follows:

It was 15 feet long.

It had a very small head, only about the size of the head of a kangaroo dog.

It had a thick, arched neck, passing gradually into the barrel of the body.

It had no definite tail and no fins.

It was furred, the coat in appearance resembling that of a horse of chestnut colour, well groomed and shining.

It had four distinct legs.

It travelled by bounding – i.e. by arching its back and gathering up its body, so that the footprints of the fore feet were level and also those of the hind feet.

It made definite footprints. These showed circular impressions, with a diameter (measured) of nine inches.

There was no evidence for or against webbing . . . The creature travelled very fast . . . When first discovered it reared up and turned on its hind legs. Its height, standing on the four legs, would be from three feet six inches to four feet.

Both men are quite familiar with seals and so-called sea leopards that occur on this coast. They had also seen before and subsequently pictures of sea lions and other marine animals, and can find no resemblance to the animal that they saw.[22]

Bernard Heuvelmans commented on this sighting in his classic book *In the Wake of the Sea-Serpents*, and says that the animal reminds him of a sea-lion except that there are none in Tasmania (though stray specimens from Australia or New Zealand could end up there), and no sea-lions are more than 8 feet long. Their footprints would not be so big nor their heads small, and the witnesses were positive it was not a sea-lion.[23]

Even such a close sighting as this takes us no nearer to an identification. Photographs might help, but photographs of sea monsters are rare. The photographs of Morgawr, showing most of the body of that particular monster, have not helped either, because it seems that the clearer and closer a photograph of any subject in the field of the strange and mysterious, the more likely it is to be dismissed as a hoax. That may seem somewhat illogical, but it happens all the time. Photographs (see page 121) taken by Robert Le Serrec on 12 December 1964 off Hook Island, off the Queensland (Australia) coast, are also controversial. Le Serrec claimed that they show a sea monster like an enormous tadpole with a big head and a body about 75–80 feet long. He also shot some cine film underwater, but this was too blurred to show any details.[24]

If photographs cannot be used to identify sea monsters, what about corpses? There have been plenty of those over the years, huge mounds of flesh washed up on remote beaches. The problem with these is that they are often badly decomposed when found, and are in remote places where there are no scientists close at hand. When analysis has been undertaken, or even the remains simply examined by a competent person, they have often been identified as known sea creatures such as whales or sharks or squids. But sometimes an identification is uncertain and the possibility remains that the creature is an unknown species. In two recent cases identification is uncertain because the carcass is no longer available for examination. A Japanese fishing boat located about 30 miles east of Christchurch (New Zealand) brought up a large carcass in its nets in April 1977 and after measuring and photographing it, it was dropped back in the sea again, for it smelled very bad and would contaminate the catch. Its overall length was about 33 feet and it could have been any number of things – giant sea-lion, giant shell-less turtle, basking shark, plesiosaur . . . The corpse found on Bungalow Beach in the Gambia in June 1983 was also not available for analysis by the people who tried to identify it. It was found and examined by Owen Burnham, but he had no camera with him, so was able to bring back only a description and measurements. Working from these, Dr Karl P. N. Shuker short-listed six possible identities: pliosaur (short-necked plesiosaur), mosasaur (giant marine lizard), thalattosuchian (sea crocodile), Shepherd's beaked whale, archaeocete (primitive whale), ichthyosaur (fish-like reptile). He decided that the pliosaur and thalattosuchian were the closest contenders, but sadly it will remain for ever uncertain whether or not the Gambian sea monster really was a species believed extinct for millions of years.[25]

The seas are so vast that there is more than a possibility they could be harbouring such 'extinct' species. The coelacanth found in 1938 may not have been a 'monster' in size, but it had been 'extinct' for 70 million years. Previously unknown marine species keep being found, like Shepherd's beaked whale (1937); Japanese beaked whale (1958) – an all-black whale up to 12 feet long; Cochito (1958) – a new porpoise found in the Gulf of California; Megamouth (1976) – a new kind of shark, and the world's third largest; Prudes Bay killer whale (1983) – a separate Antarctic species. These are not small creatures by any means, but their existence was unknown until this century. Of course some 'monsters' may be known species but not readily identified by the witness who probably is not familiar with the rarer species. Some species likely to be called sea monsters include oarfish (ribbon-like body up to 23 feet long); Steller's sea cow (a sirenian like the dugong or manatee, known in the eighteenth century along the Kamchatka coast of the USSR and elsewhere in northernmost latitudes, but possibly also occasionally even further afield like the west Canadian coast); leopard seal (10–13 feet in length, snakelike and reptilian in appearance, moves overland by wriggling, but confined to Antarctica and seas around Australia, New Zealand and South America); frilled shark (rare but with a long body known to grow to at least 12 feet). There are plenty of others, especially the giant versions of well-known species. There is now good evidence that turtles, octopus and squid can all grow to huge sizes. A dying giant squid with tentacles 24 feet long was found in August 1983 in a bay near Bergen (Norway)[26] and it is claimed that they can reach 200

A giant squid, 20–24 feet long, was seen off Tenerife on 30 November 1861, but the crew of the French gunboat Alecton *failed in their attempt to capture it.*

feet overall. So there are plenty of known contenders before we even begin to think about unknown creatures which might exist in the seas. Some are extinct rather than unknown, and the best contenders were listed earlier as possible identifications of the Gambian corpse: the plesiosaur, mosasaur, thalattosuchian, ichthyosaur and archaeocete (the zeuglodon, a snakelike whale up to 70 feet long that existed 25 million years ago). In addition to all these, Dr Heuvelmans has analysed almost 600 sightings of sea monsters from the years 1639 to 1965 and has described five new species: Egede's super-otter (an extremely primitive pre-zeuglodon archaeocete which was confined to colder northern latitudes and probably is now extinct, no recent sightings having been reported); the 'many-humped of New England', the sea-serpent seen off the eastern USA, which may also be a form of zeuglodon; Aelian's cetacean centipede, another archaeocete, found in tropical and sub-tropical waters; *Megalotaria longicollis*, or 'the big sea-lion with a long neck', the most common sea monster reported and the one which in northern latitudes is also seen in lakes; and a giant sea-horse with enormous eyes adapted to deep water.[27]

It is unlikely that our zoologists will be able to study these creatures, alive or dead, at close quarters, for even the monsters in relatively small bodies of water, the inland lakes, have proved impossible to observe, capture or kill. Barring world-wide oceanic pollution, sea monsters will thankfully be safe from mankind for a long time to come.

8 Ball lightning and spook lights

Although there are hundreds of good reports of ball lightning on record, many made by scientists, it has taken a long time for this phenomenon to gain scientific respectability. It still cannot be explained, however, and remains a mysterious, often frightening, enigma. Ball lightning can take numerous forms: 1 inch to 5 feet (or possibly even more) in diameter, though small luminous spheres 5–15 inches in diameter are most common. The colour is most often yellow, red, bluish-white, but purple and green fireballs have also been reported. They sometimes make a hissing or buzzing noise, and sometimes leave behind a smell of sulphur. They can move freely, sometimes against the wind, and enter houses. They can 'live' for anything from a few seconds to ten minutes or longer, and either simply disappear or explode; they can also be destructive to property and occasionally cause injury to people. Although their occurrence is not always associated with thunderstorms, they sometimes do appear when there is one in the area, and this helps to identify a 'fireball' as ball lightning. If there is no storm, the 'fireball' may still be ball lightning, or it may be another kind of mystery light, which we will describe more fully later in this chapter.

Some witness descriptions of ball lightning sightings will show what these compact balls of energy are capable of. The first account is by a scientist.

One afternoon in the spring of 1923, following a rather severe thunderstorm, I was surprised to see, from my home in Chevy Chase, Maryland [USA], a ball of light about the size of a toy balloon approximately 125 feet away in the adjacent woods. It was 8 feet, roughly, from the ground, and in a few seconds had moved in my direction 100 feet, or so, when, at the height of 7 feet, it came in contact with a tulip tree. At this place a cloud of dust was formed by a dynamite-like explosion so loud that neighbours came

out of their houses to see what had happened. I immediately
examined the tree and found that the explosion had occurred
where two nails had been driven into the trunk. There were no
wires or connections of any kind attached to the tree. The bark
was shattered at the place struck and so loosened from the trunk all
around that the tree died.[1]

Ball lightning does not always damage or destroy whatever it
touches, but it would seem that sometimes the energy of which it is
composed is so powerful as to be able to cause considerable damage.
In South Australia in 1920, a hissing noise heralded the arrival of a
spherical ball, about 12 inches in diameter, from the sky over
Parkside. It bounced along the cement floor of a veranda, and the
witnesses saw that it was like a ball of smoke 'with glowing "comma
shaped" electrical "worms" wriggling about'. At the end of the
veranda it lifted up into the air and flew over the next-door house.
They heard a crash as it hit another house, and it then apparently
bounced over to Fullerton where it demolished a house.[2] In the
previous year, a similar event had taken place in Salina, Kansas
(USA), on 8 October. Witnesses described seeing 'a ball of fire as
large as a washtub floating low in the air' in one of the main streets of
the town. It struck the corner of a building at a height of 35 feet,
about halfway up, and demolished a window and tore out some
bricks, then it exploded with a bang, showering baseball-sized balls
of fire into the air.[3] More recently, on 11 June 1987, a 'thunderbolt'
hit a cottage in North Wales – at Cwmyglo in Gwynedd – demolishing the chimney stack. Villagers saw a red ball flashing
through the sky just beforehand. The occupants, Alec and Audrey
McLellan, first knew of it when they heard 'an almighty bang' at
1.15 p.m. as they were sitting down for lunch. Mr McLellan said: 'I
thought an aeroplane had hit the top of the roof. There was a colossal
noise inside the house as if a bomb had fallen, but it was all over in
seconds.' As well as demolishing the chimney stack, the fireball also
caused a tremendous surge of electricity which blew a fusebox off the
kitchen wall. Mr and Mrs McLellan were shaken but otherwise
unhurt, as were their cats and dogs.[4]

Smaller lightning balls seem to have a less destructive, more
exploratory nature. If this makes them sound alive, that is the
intention, because sometimes these balls do seem almost intelligent
as they 'explore' the interior of a building. In 1961, Mrs Doris Will of
Cheltenham, Gloucestershire (England), was watching a thunder-

storm from her kitchen, when she felt as if something was watching her. She turned, and saw a fireball inside the room. In alarm she ran through the dining room and up the stairs. The fireball followed her and passed her on the stairs. In her confusion, she followed it, and saw it enter a bedroom and shoot out of the open window, making a 'crash like thunder'.[5] During a storm on 2 August 1921 at Hohen-schaftlern in Bavaria (West Germany), the nine-year-old witness was indoors with an uncle when they saw a lightning ball 8 inches in diameter enter through the open window and fall to the floor. It jumped up and down once or twice, then rolled slowly across the floor towards the observers. It was translucent and changed colour rapidly through green, red, light blue and pale yellow. They also saw protrusions from its surface. When it was near the table, the youngster got up to take a closer look, but was pulled back. The ball rolled across to the tiled stove, up the iron parts leaving a deep groove, and then exploded in the airvent leaving a smell of ozone.[6]

Ball lightning often enters a house through an open window, but will get in wherever it can if the windows are closed. What compels it to enter a house is unclear, but perhaps it is attracted to electricity, in a house or even in a person. In the last-mentioned case the ball lightning rolled towards the witnesses, in the previous one it followed a woman when she ran upstairs. We are reminded also of the 'UFO' event at Livingston (Scotland), already mentioned in Chapter 6, where Robert Taylor saw a large sphere in the forest, from which two smaller spheres rolled towards him and grabbed his trousers. Was this in fact another example of ball lightning with a similar attraction mechanism at work? To return to the ways in which ball lightning enters a house: on 8 September 1981 during a thunderstorm at Te Ngaere (New Zealand), the witness inside a house felt the building shake during a loud thunderclap and saw a 'flow of light' come in under the door. It had no true shape but was 3 or 4 inches long and 2 inches wide, moving along the floor like quicksilver. It was bluish-silver in colour, brighter at the edges than in the middle. Arms flowed out 'like runs of oil' among the tools laid out on the floor. Eventually the 'blob' went out again under the door. This was not exactly ball lightning, but obviously a similar type of phenomenon.[7]

The fireball which visited the Blumenthal family at their home in Washington, DC (USA), during a storm in the spring of 1953 gained entry through the keyhole. They heard a loud sizzling noise at the patio doors, then saw a vivid light at the keyhole which became a pencil-sized rod of light as it entered the room, turning into a ball of fire about 10 inches in diameter. It hovered momentarily, then shot above them and exploded as it made contact with the brick fireplace, leaving a small black mark.[8] Even stranger is the ball lightning which entered a room through a closed glass window pane, without damaging it. This occurred on 27 July 1952 at Hamburg (West Germany), seconds after a flash of lightning. The witnesses saw a gleaming purplish sphere outside the window, then it was in the room. It made a 90-degree turn parallel to the wall and floated into the room where it exploded.[9]

Ball lightning has also been known to enter aeroplanes in flight, and here too it must enter through a solid surface as planes do not usually have open windows or keyholes. In the spring of 1958 an Aer Lingus Constellation was flying between Shannon and Gander (Newfoundland). St Elmo's Fire was seen dancing on the exterior of the plane, which was not unusual, but then it concentrated itself in one spot and there was a crashing noise from the cockpit. As the First Officer later reported, '. . . a large (about 2 feet in diameter) orange ball of something slowly emerged from the area between the pilots' seats. It emitted a crackling sound, as flame would, and it had what could be described as licks of flame emitting from its surface, but there was no heat from it. There was the distinct odour of ozone in the cockpit.' The orange ball moved through the plane, startling a hostess who ran screaming through the cabin. The First Officer followed in the hope of calming everyone down. 'The hostess mentioned had leaped on to a seat as the ball floated straight down the aisle, at floor level, past her. I watched fascinated as it went to the rear bulkhead of the cabin and passed through it. At that time a snapping sound was heard. When it was close to me in the cockpit, it emitted a hissing sound, and everyone could feel some sort of a powerful static charge in our scalps.' He concluded: 'Apparently, this sort of thing is encountered by airliners around the world several times a year.'[10] We have several similar events on file, including one in 1984 when a fireball flew over the heads of the passengers and out of the tail section of a Soviet airliner flying over Sochi on the Black Sea (USSR).[11]

Sometimes, rather than flying through the plane as if it were not there, the ball lightning collides with it. This happened on 12 August 1956 over Tambosk (USSR) while the airliner was flying through a cold front containing dense thunderclouds. The crew saw a dark red fireball approaching rapidly, and it collided with the blade

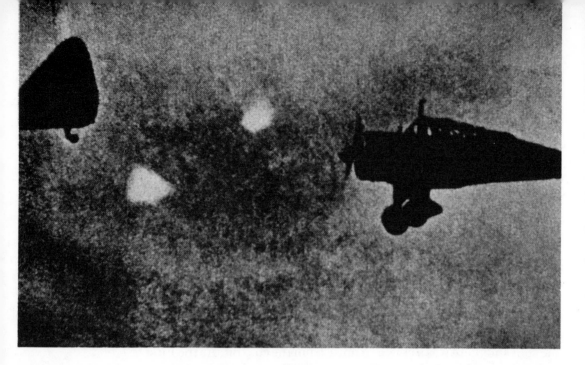

of the left propeller, exploding in a blinding flash. Little damage was caused.[12] Land-based vehicles also sometimes collide with ball lightning. On the road between Tiistenjoki and Laitomaki (Finland) a truck-driver travelling during a storm on 30 August 1969 saw a fireball moving 3 feet off the ground which shot in front of his truck and struck it, exploding as it did so.[13] The report does not mention any damage, so presumably none was caused. Rather more destructive was the fireball which collided with a car on the road between Osakis and Eagle Bend, Minnesota (USA). Richard Vogt was driving home on the night of 10 May 1961 when, shortly before midnight, he saw 'a ball of fog about 3 feet in diameter' descending out of the sky in his direction. It was travelling so fast he could not escape it, and it struck the car on the bonnet and windscreen. It sounded like a shovelful of fine gravel hitting the car. There was also a blast, and the car interior instantly became unbearably hot. Vogt stopped and got out, and found that some damage had been caused: the windscreen was cracked, and was too hot to touch, and there were burn marks on the bonnet. This sounds like a ball lightning strike, though the sky was clear that night.[14]

Instead of hitting buildings, trees, planes or cars, fireballs sometimes hit people, or strike close enough to cause injury, although fortunately such cases are fairly rare. One such was at Gatineau Point, Ontario (Canada), in September 1925. Two men took refuge in a log barn when a storm came up, one sitting on a log just inside the open door. Suddenly a fireball came in at the door and hit the end of the log, which was splintered. The fireball circled round inside the barn before knocking out some boards at the far end and exiting. The man sitting on the log was knocked unconscious and stayed that way for eight hours. He was partially paralysed for a while afterwards. The other man was not in such close contact with the fireball, but was still thrown 15 feet out into the field.[15]

The power of fireballs can obviously vary greatly, for some people have been struck by them, but not injured so severely as the man at Gatineau Point who was knocked unconscious. In Bremerton, Washington (USA), Robert Burch was standing in his room at the YMCA on the evening of 6 November 1951 when he saw in the mirror the reflection of an orange-red fireball coming towards him through the open window. It exploded in a blinding flash and with a loud noise and he felt a pain in his arm as he fell to the floor. He was taken to hospital suffering from shock and second-degree burns on his arm. In his room, the contents of a wastepaper basket were set on fire, luggage beneath the window was charred and smoking, two radio cabinets were burned and the windowsill was black and hot. A policeman outside saw the fireball flash through the sky and into the room.[16] Mrs Patricia Townsend was also struck by ball lightning. She was at home at Haymarket, Virginia (USA), on a summer's day in 1977 when a storm was threatening, and she was talking on the telephone in her kitchen when a brilliant flash lit up the outside of the house, accompanied by a loud report. She heard a hissing noise, the phone became alive in her hand, and the kitchen was bright with lightning. She continued:

> Anyhow, almost at the same time as the lightning zoomed across my kitchen and the phone started vibrating in my hand, a large red ball (with yellow and white somewhere) appeared in front of me and hit me on the chest with the force of a large man hitting me with his fist. I fell to the floor and I believe the phone was still in my hand. I'm still not sure if I was knocked unconscious or not. I couldn't swear I was and couldn't swear I wasn't. The ball hit me with the accompanying sounds of smacking and crackling, kind of like a string of fire-crackers being set off.

The ball seemed to be made of a soft burlap-type surface with a fuzzy texture. Mrs Townsend had chest pains for several days, but fortunately recovered.

Amazingly, a year later, the incident was repeated. On 21 June 1978 she was in the kitchen and a storm was raging outside. A fireball about a foot across with jagged yellow and white edges hit her in the face. It felt like being slapped with an open hand. She collapsed and later suffered neck pains and slurred speech, but again soon recovered her full health.[17]

We noted earlier that ball lightning sometimes seems to show intelligence. Vincent H. Gaddis also thought so, for he said in his book *Mysterious Fires and Lights*:

Moreover, they display an independent will and curiosity, circling objects and human beings, entering and exploring houses, and, perhaps, returning to bathrooms to melt chains. They exhibit either innate intelligence or control by intelligence at possibly an animal level. In the electrified fields of a thunderstorm, they can enter the range of our limited sight and sound. After brief visits they must return to their invisible, natural habitat, and their temporary vehicles explode or fade away.[18]

The bathroom incident he referred to dates from the summer of 1921, and the witness was the Revd J. H. Lehn, of York, Pennsylvania (USA). He was in the bathroom during a thunderstorm when

. . . a ball or globe of lightning came through the screen in the otherwise open window without in any way damaging or affecting the screen so far as my eyes could judge by later inspection, and descended to the floor. It was about the size of a grapefruit and yellow in colour, similar in hue to sodium flame, though it did not dazzle my eyes. It swiftly and deliberately rolled about my feet and then hopped up into the bowl of the wash basin and melted into two portions the steel chain holding the rubber stopper and then disappeared, I presume down the drain. It made no sound at any time. The whole event took but a few seconds.

Several weeks later I was standing in the same bathroom . . . during another electrical storm. Exactly the same kind of event occurred. The ball of fire of approximately the same size and colour circled my feet after it had come through the screen with no visible effects on the wire. After the globe of fire circled my feet, it went beyond for some short distance and then hopped up into the bathtub and, as it descended, it melted into two pieces the steel chain that held the rubber stopper.

The Revd Mr Lehn 'sensed both of these presences as friendly' and added, 'maybe the second sphere wanted a chain of its own to melt in two – at any rate, that's what it did.'[19]

If these incidents demonstrate intelligence or curiosity, then the next case certainly demonstrates aggression. If true, it is an exceedingly strange event. Five mountaineers were camping 12,000 feet up in the Caucasian mountains (USSR) on 17 August 1978. Victor Kavunenko reports what happened:

I woke up with the strange feeling that a stranger had made his way into our tent. Thrusting my head out of the sleeping bag, I froze. A bright-yellow blob was floating about one metre from the floor. It disappeared into Korovin's sleeping bag. The man screamed in pain. The ball jumped out and proceeded to circle over the other bags now hiding in one, now in another. When it burned a hole in mine I felt an unbearable pain, as if I were being burned by a welding machine, and blacked out. Regaining consciousness after a while, I saw the same yellow ball which, methodically observing a pattern that was known to it alone, kept diving into the bags, evoking desperate, heart-rending howls from the victims. This indescribable horror repeated itself several times. When I came back to my senses for the fifth or sixth time, the ball was gone. I could not move my arms or legs and my body was burning as if it had turned into a ball of fire itself. In the hospital, where we were flown by helicopter, seven wounds were discovered on my body. They were worse than burns. Pieces of muscle were found to be torn out to the bone. The same happened to Shigin, Kaprov and Bashkirov. Oleg Korovin had been killed by the ball – possibly because his bag had been on a rubber mattress, insulating it from the ground. The ball lightning did not touch a single metal object, injuring only people.[20]

Ball lightning is not the only light phenomenon to show intelligence and awareness of people. Various other 'balls of light' have been reported as showing similar attributes; these balls have been named BOLs by Hilary Evans, who has taken a special interest in them.[21] We too shall refer to them as BOLs here, as this abbreviation serves as a handy description of a puzzling collection of data. One group of lights, referred to prosaically by William Corliss in his 'Catalog of Geophysical Anomalies' as 'low-level nocturnal lights', has been documented for centuries, and was in past ages in Britain known more colourfully as will-o'-the-wisp, jack-o-lantern, corpse light or corpse candle. The standard explanation for these was 'swamp gas' – that methane gas given off by swampy ground spontaneously ignited – but it is clear that this easy explanation is unsatisfactory. The lights are quite often seen over marshy ground, though not always; but no one has yet been able to duplicate them experimentally. In Britain they became part of folklore, the name corpse light or corpse candle arising from the belief that they would visit a house where someone was dying or soon to die, and take the route the coffin would later follow. Jack-o-lantern indicates that the light is similar to a lantern, carried by an invisible figure; will-o'-the-wisp its insubstantiality. Nowadays these lights are less often seen in Britain than they used to be, perhaps because a lot of the marshy ground has been drained. One 1933 report came from a marshy area in the Vale parish of Guernsey (Channel Islands), the witness being a young girl who was cycling home late on a misty night along a lane. 'Looking back before turning into my gateway, I saw to my fright, what could only be described as a ball of fire, bouncing along at a fast pace along the top of the hedge.'[22] This is not exactly typical, because she called the light 'a ball of fire', and will-o'-the-wisps are usually pale or soft lights, yellow, white or blue in colour. But this emphasizes the danger of arbitrarily dividing these lights into categories.

Another, equally uncategorizable, incident, which may or may not have been a will-o'-the-wisp, took place in the summer of 1952, while the witness was taking a quiet evening stroll along a country lane near Coventry, West Midlands (England).

A short way off and coming in my direction I saw, floating in the air, something that I first took to be a soap bubble, about the size of a golf ball. I looked around to see if any children had come along as I had been lying down [on the grass verge, smoking a cigarette], but seeing no one about I turned to where I had seen the object, and to my curiosity, though seemingly in motion, it hovered just beyond me, then it carried on. And carried on is the right word! For there was a gentle breeze blowing, but the bubble was not travelling with it, it was going in the opposite direction!

I thought that some speck or something had settled in my eye and the movements of my eyes had made me see this bubble, but that it was not so became apparent when I stood up, for this explanation would not fit what I now saw. A number of bubbles were now round me, circling, going up and down and hovering over me. Then came the amazing part, for, supposing that they were satisfied that I was of no further interest, the bubbles drew together and somehow seemed to be drawn into each other, until the resulting bubble had become something I can only describe as a goldfish bowl, dirty inside the glass. Then it was away, but so quickly that it was there, and then it wasn't.[23]

Again we get the hint that the bubbles were intelligent. In folklore will-o'-the-wisps were said to lure people into marshy ground by waiting for them, then moving ahead as they went to investigate. Such events also happen in more modern settings. Somewhere in Maryland (USA), on 16 July 1952, two policemen in a car saw a yellow light coming straight for them on the road ahead. They stopped and the light stopped, hovering about 20 feet in front of them. As they moved slowly forwards, the light retreated. When they speeded up, it did so too. After matching their speed for a while, it seemed to tire of the game, and took off at speed.[24] Although these lights are usually elusive, and sometimes even go out if approached too closely, we came across one report of a man who touched one. It was in 1929 or 1930, when he was walking home from Coldwater to Greenleaf in Mississippi (USA). Suddenly a ball of light came over the fence and down to the road. It was about the size of a plate, and was moving slowly, at ground level. The witness got down on his hands and knees and put his hand through it as it moved past, but he felt nothing.[25]

So these lights evidently are not filled with energy like the lightning balls described earlier. It is not always easy to tell the difference. Some time earlier this century, possibly in the late 1920s, two men were walking along a dirt road on Brown's Mountain in West Virginia (USA). They saw a flash of light in the sky, and then three or four lights hovering above the ground. They were different colours – yellow, blue, and one like a gas flame. One man ran back in fear of the Devil, but the other carried on past the lights – and heard voices jabbering, though he could not tell what they were saying. He heard the voices all the way to the top of the mountain, an hour's walk, and he saw floating lights all the way. When he got to the top, one light exploded and the rest vanished.[26] Ball lightning? Will-o'-the-wisp? Or what? We have not come across any other reports of BOLs where voices were heard – but voices have been heard in conjunction with UFO sightings, so could these lights have been

The ball of light photographed at Uzès in 1974.

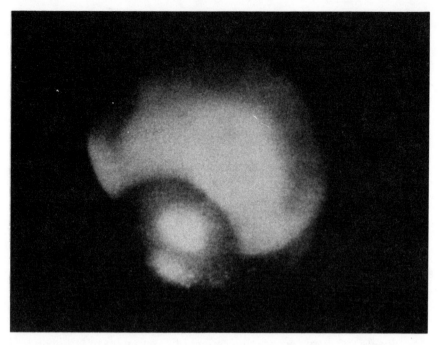

some kind of UFO? Some so-called UFOs are unidentified formless lights rather than unidentified flying objects, and Corliss designates them 'high-level nocturnal lights', which is a sensible description as it avoids the 'spacecraft' connotation too often inseparable from UFO reports. Many UFOs are in fact BOLs, and are probably closely linked to the light-ball phenomena we are discussing here.

One example of a UFO which may have been ball lightning or some unknown kind of electrical phenomenon was the sighting of a large translucent ball by sixteen-year-old Christophe Fernandez at Uzès, Gard (France). He was alone at his home outside the town on the evening of 19 November 1974, and saw from the bathroom window a brightly shining ball standing motionless beside the road about 100 feet away, despite a strong wind blowing. Its diameter was about 6 feet. Christophe bravely went outside to photograph it (one of the resulting pictures is shown here) and heard a sound like that of a bottle being emptied. The globe seemed transparent, for he could see the stone wall behind it. After he had gone back indoors, he saw the globe rise about 15 feet in the air and a bright 'cylinder' emerge from beneath it. Then the UFO shot upwards and disappeared at an incredible speed, leaving a feeling of heat at the landing site. This incident was presented as a UFO, but it bears a strong resemblance to the light-ball phenomena described in this chapter. The 'cylinder' which emerged can be likened to the small light balls sometimes given off by ball lightning.[27]

If BOLs can be identified as UFOs by some witnesses, they can also take human form when seen by others. There is at least one report on record of a BOL taking human shape, and this case again occurred on a mountain. The witness was climbing in the Bavarian Alps (West Germany) around 1950 and she got lost. 'All of a sudden I noticed a sort of a big ball of light, and this condensed into the shape of a tall, rather Chinese-looking gentleman . . . He bowed, spoke a few words, led me by a small path to the tourists' way, and disappeared as a ball of light.'[28] On another occasion a BOL guided lost people off a mountain. This took place in November 1977 on Mount Snezka, Czechoslovakia's highest mountain. A couple were climbing on a sunny day when it began to snow and they lost their way.

> Then suddenly I looked to the left and saw a big blue ball, which was very near me and shone with a clear and warm light. I was very surprised, and I must admit I was also very frightened. I shut my eyes, but when I opened them the ball was still there. I asked my husband if he could see it, but he could not. Then, when I stepped forward, the ball moved with me, then it turned to the right and moved slowly away from me. I followed it, as if hypnotized by it. My husband asked why I had changed direction and said it was the wrong way, but he followed me although he still couldn't see the ball. All the way, the ball showed us the right direction and after two hours we arrived at the town. As soon as I could see the first houses, the ball disappeared.[29]

There are certain locations around the world where BOLs are seen regularly, and have been for many years. The lights are called ghost lights or spook lights, but are clearly not a separate category, being very similar to the BOLs we have just been describing, especially to the British will-o'-the-wisp. The most famous ones are probably the Saratoga Light and the Marfa Lights, both in Texas, the Brown Mountain Lights and Maco Light, both in North Carolina, the Hornet Spook Light of Missouri (all USA) and the Min Min Light of Queensland (Australia), but there are many (hundreds?) others of lesser fame.

Saratoga's Light is seen on Bragg Road, an 8-mile stretch of dead-straight sand road in the heart of the Big Thicket. Debbie Collier was a teenager with a carload of friends when she saw it around 1970. It was a glowing ball of light, and 'It looked like it was about head high, about 300 yards in front of us.' As the driver sped forward, the light moved ahead. Then it went out. 'Then we happened to look behind us, and it was behind us, heading towards us, and I really got scared then.'[30] Other witnesses tell of it looking like a lantern light, swaying as if being carried. Bragg Road follows the line of a former railway, and ghost light sites do often seem to be on or near old railway tracks. From this, and the light's similarity to a lantern, has grown the legend that it is a lantern carried by the ghost of a headless brakeman, murdered for some forgotten reason. Texas's other well-known ghost lights, at Marfa, do not have this explanation, for they do not restrict themselves to any one stretch of road or railway. They are most often seen in a sparsely populated area called Mitchell Flat, and they look like lanterns twinkling in the foothills of the Chinati Mountains 30 miles away. Among the many witnesses are two geologists who were prospecting for uranium. On 19 March 1973 they were sitting in their car about 10 miles east of Marfa at 10 p.m. Suddenly some horses in a field whinnied and bolted. Moments later, the two saw a ball of light rapidly moving in

The Marfa light photographed by James Crocker in September 1986.

from the south-west, with another one behind it. The lights, which 'appeared to be about one-half the size of a basket ball', moved 'behind some bushes and in front of other bushes' and hovered briefly a few hundred feet away before vanishing.[31] The local people are proud of their lights, and do not take kindly to disbelievers. As Julia Plumbley, whose father's sighting in 1883 was the first written report of them, said, 'We all got kind of mad when a reporter from Houston said they were just mercury-vapour lights on ranches. The light I've seen over the years isn't a range light. It's a soft, small kind of ethereal-looking light. You can't get close to it. And there's really nothing to say about it except that it's real and it's there.'[32]

Neosho (Missouri) is the nearest town to the site of the Hornet Spook Light (also known as the Ozark Spook Light), about 17 miles to the north-west. The stretch of road, known as Spooklight Road, is a straight country road lined with trees, rather like Bragg Road in Texas. At least two investigators have proved that lights on US66 over 10 miles away, seen through shimmering air close to the ground, are responsible for the ghost lights; but the locals quickly remind us that the lights were seen before there was any US66 or motor vehicles. Experiments have also been conducted into the Brown Mountain Lights in the Blue Ridge Mountains of North Carolina, and they have shown that lights seen above the crest of the mountain are refractions of artificial lights. However, the smaller lights, seen briefly flitting through the trees, have not been explained. In an effort to discover if they are seismic in origin, small charges were detonated on the mountain in July 1981, but no lights were seen.[33] North Carolina's other famous ghost light, at Maco, follows the course of the Seaboard Coast Line railway tracks, and the familiar ghost story is also present. This time the ghost is a conductor who was decapitated by a train in 1868, and the ghost is looking for his head. Sceptics ascribed the lights to car headlights on a nearby highway, so in an experiment all the traffic was stopped while investigators watched for the light – which duly appeared.[34]

In Arkansas, the Gurdon Light also has a ghost story, this time of a railway foreman bludgeoned to death with a spike maul by an employee on the railway tracks where the light now appears.[35] At Screven, Georgia, the light, 'a glowing clear-white ball that floats and swings side to side along the tracks, its light often flashing bright, then dimming', is the lantern of a railway flagman killed in a train accident. The ghost is looking for his head, severed in the accident.[36]

143

Leaving aside these colourful explanations for the lights, there are several possible natural explanations. It is probable that in some cases car headlights in the distance are being seen, the eerie effects produced by the particular circumstances of the location and the atmospheric conditions. Experimenters at the site of the Paulding (Michigan) lights concluded that headlights along Highway 45 nearly 4 miles away were responsible. One man drove along the road, another stayed at the ghost light viewing site.

> With their CB radios the men communicated with each other as to when the headlights of the car were turned on and off. They coincided with the mystery light. When the headlights were turned off the light disappeared, and when they were turned on it showed to the naked eye as one bright light, but through the telescope as two. They checked out the lights of other motorists as well, continuing to communicate by CB radio. When a car was travelling north, away from Paulding, the viewer could see a red light. When the car approached the city he saw a white light. Even the yellow lights of the cab of a truck were identified.[37]

In other places, lights from towns, villages, and even individual farms and ranches, could be mistaken for mystery lights in the right atmospheric conditions. Yet some lights appear in places where there are no highways or towns, for example, the 'money lights' in the Peruvian Andes (said to indicate the location of buried gold), the Min Min Light of Alexandria Station (an 11,000-square-mile ranch) in Queensland, Australia, the Waimea Lights in Hawaii.[38] For them, an explanation such as earthquake lights, biological luminescence, lights from radioactive mineral deposits, marsh or swamp gas, may be offered. Or perhaps electrical phenomena like St Elmo's Fire, or others even less well understood, are responsible, or even ball lightning. Trying to force all the varied phenomena of BOLs into neat pigeonholes is a task doomed to failure. For there lingers that suggestion of intelligence, noted by some of the BOLs witnesses. Is there perhaps a life form unknown to us which can make itself visible as a ball of light? William Bathlot might well have answered 'Yes' to that question. At the beginning of this century, he often saw balls of light around his farm in Beaver County, Oklahoma (USA). One night, when he was returning from Liberal, Kansas, with a wagonload of lumber, a globe of light frightened the horses. Bathlot walked over to the place where it had disappeared, and saw nothing, but said 'I felt some sinister thing was watching my every move and cold chills ran up my back.' On another occasion, while out looking for a lost cow, he and his companion saw a globe of light which moved away when they tried to approach it. And when they backed up, it moved forward.

Then we just stood there with that thing about a dozen feet in front of us as silent as death itself. It was transparent. We could see a bunch of sage brush right through its body. It hovered in the air approximately eighteen inches above the ground. We could see no body resembling bird or animal, nor could we see anything resembling legs to hold it up. It was just a ball of light.

Yet apparently this strange object could see us, and it checked our every move. The deadly unnerving stillness of the thing seemed to paralyse us. Finally I raised the shotgun to my shoulder and let it have both barrels. The light went out.[39]

9 *Winged people and other non-humans*

Apart from ghosts and UFO entities, covered elsewhere in this book, there are many reports from people who see living human-like creatures which are apparently not human. Without trying to categorize them here, as the reports are so varied, we will simply present a selection of reports in chronological order, with comments where appropriate.

It is fitting that we begin with a flying being, for there have been numerous sightings of men and women flying around, some of them with 'built-in' wings. If one person claims to have seen such a thing, it is easy to dismiss the report as misidentification of some big bird, but can 240 people all be wrong? They all saw a woman in white, without wings, flying around over Voltana (Spain) on at least five occasions in June 1905, always in the daytime. Sometimes she was flying against the wind, and one woman said she heard singing as the 'angel' passed overhead. Two Englishmen were among the witnesses, so the sightings could not be ascribed to a vivid peasant imagination. No one could find any evidence of a hoax.[1]

An unusual encounter which took place in May 1913 was not revealed to the world until 1978, by which time the witness was a grandfather. He stuck to his story through intensive questioning, remembering the time he was twelve years old, chopping cotton with his two brothers on the family farm near Farmersville, Texas (USA). They heard the dogs howling and, when they went to investigate, found a little green man only 18 inches tall.

> He didn't seem to have on any shoes but I don't really remember his feet. His arms were hanging down just beside him, like they was growed down the side of him. He had on a kind of hat that reminded me of a Mexican hat. It was a little round hat that looked like it was built onto him. He didn't have on any clothes. Everything looked like a rubber suit including the hat.

146

The dogs jumped on him and tore him to pieces, and he seemed to have human internal organs. Next day when the boys visited the spot where the bloody remains had lain, there was no trace of them.[2]

Twenty little men were seen near Barron, Wisconsin (USA), on a summer's night in 1919. Harry Anderson was a thirteen-year-old boy travelling in a car with others when the car ran out of oil. Harry walked to a farm to fetch some, and as he was walking back he saw twenty little men walking along towards him in single file. They had bald heads and white skins, and wore leather 'knee-pants' held up by braces over their shoulders. They were mumbling but not talking to each other, and they paid no attention to the terrified boy.[3]

A little ET-like entity surprised an Australian family when it unexpectedly appeared in their house one night in 1930. This was at Mandurah in Western Australia, and Beryl Hickey, who was a teenager at the time, remembered the event clearly.

> It was the most frightening thing I had ever seen. My father, who was religious, was terrified. He thought it was the work of the Devil and threw a prawning net over it to drag it outside. It had big ears, a wide slit mouth and glistened as though it was wet or covered in oil. It stood about half a metre tall, with bulging eyes covered with a film.
>
> It was obviously not human, yet it had perfectly formed little hands and feet and was pink like a baby. It made a frightened squeaky noise when it was caught under the net. Our father told us never to speak about it or tell anyone. But I told a friend and she reminded me about it after reading about the film.[4]

However incredible these accounts may sound, the witnesses all stand by the truth of what they have reported. Many, like Beryl Hickey, do not speak of their experiences for many years, for fear of ridicule. It was only the release of the film *ET* which prompted her to speak about what she had seen: 'I hadn't thought about it for ages until I saw the film and I just wanted to let people know there really might be funny things around.'

Mrs E. E. Loznaya's experience also made a lasting impression on her. She was a fifteen-year-old in the winter of 1936, and one morning as she went to school by a lonely road in the Pavlodar region of Kazakhstan (USSR) she saw, moving rapidly through the air, a man-like figure dressed in black.

This 'man' was, to my mind, of medium height and his black clothes covered him completely, like overalls. His head (more exactly – something like a helmet) and massive ('square') arms tightly fixed to his body were perfectly visible. I saw no hands and feet. I could see behind his back an oval thing like a rucksack.

As he flew towards her, she could see that in place of a face there was 'an entirely black surface'. A rumbling noise was heard, and he was only about 40 yards away. Frightened, she looked around for somewhere to hide, and when she looked back to the man, he had gone.[5]

Ireland's most famous non-human inhabitants must be the fairies, or Little People, who are not merely characters in fairy-tales, but are still being seen today, in Great Britain as well as in Ireland. Some recent British encounters are described in our earlier book *Modern Mysteries of Britain*. Here we have an Irish case from 1938, the location being a crossroads between Ballingarry and Kilfinney, six miles from Rathkeale, County Limerick. Schoolboy John Keely claimed to have seen a fairy walking along the road, but his story was received with disbelief and amusement, so on being told by his friends to go back and talk to the fairy, John did so. He asked where the fairy came from and was told: 'I'm from the mountains and it's all equal to you what my business is.' Next day, John met two fairies at the crossroads, with a group of men watching secretly from the bushes. The fairies were seen skipping with a rope. They were about 2 feet tall, had 'hard, hairy faces like men, and no ears'. They wore red clothes, including knee-breeches, and one had a white cape. John approached them and held the hand of one. The three of them began to walk down the road, but the fairies suddenly noticed the hidden onlookers, and ran away. The men chased them, and said that although the fairies went through hedges, ditches and marshes, they stayed quite clean.[6]

Another flying man was seen on 6 January 1948, this time over Chehalis, Washington (USA). Mrs Bernice Zaikowski was one of several people to see him, including young children on their way home from school at 3 p.m., who wanted to go into her garden to watch him. She saw him hovering about 20 feet over her barn. He had long silver wings fastened over his shoulders with a strap, which he manipulated by means of controls on his chest. He flew in an upright position, making a sizzling or whizzing noise.[7] Only three months later, on 9 April, Viola Johnson and James Pittman saw *three* flying men, circling above the city of Longview, Washington. They had no propellers or motors attached to them, but the witnesses could hear motors. Their feet dangled down, and their heads moved as if they were looking round, and they appeared to have helmets on. Mrs Johnson had thought they were gulls until they got closer and she saw they were men.[8]

A similar initial misidentification occurred early in the 1950s, when two winged men were seen at Pelotas in the state of Rio Grande do Sul, southern Brazil. Luiz do Rosário Real and his wife Lucy Gerlach Real took a walk one night in a wood beside the sea. Suddenly two fast-moving shadows crossed their path, which was lit by the full moon. Looking up, they saw two gigantic 'birds' (as they thought) flying at treetop level. When the 'birds' descended vertically and landed near the witnesses, they saw that the figures looked human and were about 6 feet tall. The 'birdmen' then crouched down on the ground. The witnesses felt they were being observed, and Luiz, being curious, wished to get nearer, but his wife prevailed upon him to leave, and they did so.[9] These 'birdmen' were presumably winged, in contrast to the earlier reports where the flying entities either had no wings or strapped-on wings. That these creatures are not 'real' birds is shown by the fact that the witnesses in this and the previous case originally thought they were looking at huge birds, until they got closer. In the next case, too, a giant bird could not have been responsible, for the creature disappeared. A private on guard duty one night at Camp Okubo near Kyoto (Japan) in 1952 saw a giant bird coming down towards him. On the point of firing at it as it hovered, he felt its eyes on him and looking more closely he could see it was not a bird. It had a man's body and was well over 7 feet from head to toe, with a similar wingspan. The young man began firing but when he looked to see if he had killed it, there was nothing there. The sergeant told him that another guard had seen something similar a year before.[10]

A strange sighting, again of a winged man but this time with a bat's wings, was made in Houston, Texas (USA), on 18 June 1953. It was 2.30 a.m. on a hot night, and three people sat talking on a front porch. Suddenly, about 25 feet away, Hilda Walker saw 'a huge shadow across the lawn. I thought at first it was the magnified reflection of a big moth caught in a nearby street light. Then the shadow seemed to bounce upward into a pecan tree.' She told her companions and they all saw 'the figure of a man with wings like a bat. He was dressed in grey or black tight-fitting clothes. He stood there for about thirty seconds, swaying on the branch of the old pecan tree. Suddenly the light began to fade out slowly.' They had time to see the man in detail and described him as about 6½ feet tall, wearing a black cape, skin-tight pants, and quarter-length boots. 'He was dressed in a uniform like a paratrooper wears. He was encased in a halo of light,' said one witness. Mrs Walker added, 'I could see him plain and could see he had big wings folded at his shoulders. There was a dim light all around him.'[11]

Following that rash of winged beings, we now have an entirely different kind of entity. The witness was Eberto Villafañe, who was sleeping in an improvised bed of sheepskins at his cousin's mica mine at Cerro del Valle (Argentina) one night in 1953. He woke up suddenly and saw a beautiful woman approaching him. He thought at first he must be dreaming, but what followed convinced him he was fully awake. He got up and saw that the woman was signalling at him to stay. She was wearing a tight-fitting green elastic-mesh garment, and her feet were strange, looking like serpents' heads with shining slanting eyes on the insteps. Villafañe fled, but looking back, he saw that the woman was settling down on the sheepskins. When he showed the skins to someone later, they were not white but yellow, as if scorched.[12]

Quite a lot of the non-human entities reported sound similar to the entities seen close to landed UFOs, but on these occasions the witness sees no UFO, so there is no certainty that the entities came from a UFO. In truth, it is difficult to be certain of anything with cases like these: all we have to go on are the witness reports. The entities seen by Mrs Margaret Symmonds at 3.30 a.m. on 3 July 1955, as she drove the family car en route to Florida (USA), were engaged in that kind of puzzling, inconsequential activity which UFO entities often seem to demonstrate. But Mrs Symmonds saw no UFO, only the entities. She was driving at 60 mph when, near Stockton, Georgia, she saw in the headlights four objects she thought were pigs. She slowed down, not wanting to hit them. As she got closer, she saw they were little figures 3½ or 4 feet tall, grey in colour, wearing capes and standing huddled in the road as if about to dig into it with the stick one of them was holding. One of the entities stepped aside to get out of her way, and looked right at her. He had a roundish head, with a sort of slouch hat on. The eyes were big, like saucers, and reflecting red. The nose was long and pointed, the mouth seemed small, and she saw no lips. His legs were short, and the body was hidden by the cape. Mrs Symmonds swerved past them, then screamed out in her fear, waking her husband who was sleeping in the back of the car. When she told him what she had seen, he wanted to go back, but she refused.[13]

1955 was a good year for strange entities. In addition to Mrs Symmonds's sighting in July and the Kelly (Kentucky) UFO entities siege (described in Chapter 6) in August, there was also a strange sighting near Branch Hill, Ohio (USA), where in March a man driving a truck over a bridge at 4 a.m. saw three small figures kneeling by the road. They were 3 feet tall and had frog-like faces, and were greyish in colour. The driver stopped the car because he thought someone was hurt. One of the entities was holding a dark chain or stick giving off sparks, and when the witness got out of his vehicle one of them moved as if signalling him to stay where he was. So he watched for about three minutes, and the next thing he knew he was driving back towards Loveland.[14] Other strange frog-like creatures were seen in the same area in 1972, as described in Chapter 14.

In the autumn of 1956, an incident took place in Falls City, Nebraska (USA), which has several similarities to the Chehalis incident of 1948, described earlier. It was a fine afternoon and the witness was outside at his pickup truck when he noticed what he thought was a kite in the sky. As it came closer, he realized it was a winged creature, 8 or 9 feet tall, flying only 15 feet above the ground. Its wings, which were like polished aluminium, and had coloured lights along the underside, were attached by a shoulder harness, which had a breast plate with dials which the entity manipulated with its hands (as did the Chehalis flying man). The creature's face was 'very frightening, almost demonic'. It had large watery blue eyes, and leathery wrinkled skin. As it approached, the witness found himself temporarily paralysed until it had passed overhead. As it did so, he heard a hissing sound (as at Chehalis).[15]

Back now to the Little People, with a tale from New Hampshire (USA). This 'dwarf' however, only 2 feet tall, is very different from the traditional Little People of Britain and Ireland, who are much more human in appearance, and presumably have no relationship to the dwarf of this and other accounts. Tiny entities have been reported from all over the world, with and without UFOs, but how can we tell if there is any link between them? The New Hampshire dwarf, seen at Derry on 15 December 1956, was not very human in appearance. He was green in colour, with a wrinkled skin like elephant hide, and his head was high and domed. The ears were like a bloodhound's, the eyes had a film over them like a snake's, there were simply two holes for a nose. His arms and legs were short, the hands like stumps and the feet lacking toes. Nor did he have any clothes. The man who saw this strange little entity was gathering Christmas trees in a wood. He watched it for twenty minutes before trying to catch it, at which it made a screeching sound, and the witness fled. In a different account he said it vanished when he bent to pick up a bundle.[16]

To what can we ascribe the infinite variety of entity descriptions? A multiplicity of creatures passing briefly into visibility from their own normally invisible worlds; or entities from who knows where assuming any arbitrary garb for their brief appearance here; or a richness of imagination on the part of human witnesses? We make no attempt to judge the accounts, but simply describe what the witnesses say they saw. This chapter contains only a small sample of the reports available, chosen by us for their intrinsic interest and aura of strangeness: like the two 'Michelin Men' seen on a road near Jerez de la Frontera (Spain) in May 1960. The witness was motorcycling from Prado del Rey to Jerez during daylight hours when he saw a being on the road 500 feet in front. 'He was completely red, from head to foot, and suddenly appeared at the edge of the highway, rather tall, something like two metres [6½ feet] or more, having trouble walking, and his walking was like a mechanical doll, that is to say, like a robot, with stiff arms.' Don Miguel Timermans Ceballos stopped his motorcycle, and then saw another entity appear suddenly and follow the first. He was about 4 feet tall, dressed similarly except he had on one black boot. They crossed the road at an angle, and Timermans decided to go closer. But when, only moments later, he reached a curve in the road approaching the slope where he had seen them, they had disappeared. Being alone, he did not venture off the road in search of them.[17]

In an incident similar to that reported by Mrs Symmonds in 1955, a woman driving the family Cadillac to California with her husband and children sleeping in the car, saw a non-human entity on the highway about 15 miles east of Globe, Arizona, about midnight one day in early June 1960. It stood on the right side of the road, as if about to cross, and she slowed the car. The figure turned to face her, and then ran off into the brush. She reported,

> The second I saw that thing my heart came up in my mouth and my stomach turned a flip-flop . . . The little figure . . . was small

[about 3 feet tall], broad-shouldered, with long arms, dark in colour, and it had a head shaped somewhat like a flattened ball – almost like a pumpkin. In this head were two yellowish-orange glowing 'eyes'. I recall that when it was in side view there was a light beaming out beyond the face. I saw no nose, or mouth or ears. The body was not as well defined as the head, and I got the impression of hair or fur.

Like Mrs Symmonds's husband, this witness's husband also wanted to go back, but the driver wisely refused.[18]

Our catalogue of winged entities continues with a sighting in 1960 or 1961 in West Virginia (USA), when a woman driving her father along Route 2 by the Ohio River saw a tall man-like figure on the road in the Chief Cornstalk Hunting Grounds.

I slowed down and as we got closer we could see that it was much larger than a man. A big grey figure. It stood in the middle of the

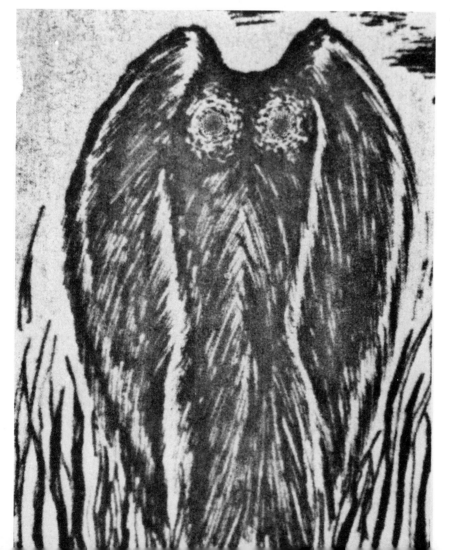

An artist's impression of Mothman.

road. Then a pair of wings unfolded from its back and they practically filled the whole road. It almost looked like a small airplane. Then it took off straight up . . . disappearing out of sight in seconds. We were both terrified. I stepped on the gas and raced out of there. We talked it over and decided not to tell anybody about it. Who would believe us anyway?[19]

It was in this same area that the incredible 'Mothman' appeared a few years later. 'Mothman' was the name given to a winged being 5–7 feet tall, armless but with wings which folded back when not in use. He had no head as such, but luminous bright red eyes 2–3 inches in diameter were set in his 'shoulders'. He was grey in colour, though it is not known whether this was the colour of his clothes or his skin/fur, as no one saw him closely enough. In flight his wings did not flap, but he could move fast, over 100 mph. He also made a mouse-like squeaking noise. A very strange-sounding entity indeed! UFOs were also reported in the area of West Virginia where Mothman was being seen, mainly around Point Pleasant and especially near the disused TNT area, a World War II ammunition dump, during the last two months of 1966.[20]

An extraordinary 'bird woman' was seen near Da Nang, Vietnam, in July or August 1969. The main witness was Earl Morrison, at that time serving with the US 1st Division Marine Corps. At 1–1.30 a.m. on a still night he was on guard duty with two other men and they were sitting on top of a bunker, talking and looking around. Suddenly they saw a figure in the sky, coming slowly towards them. It was a naked woman, black in colour, but glowing with a greenish cast. She had huge bat's wings, and flew silently over them at a height of only 6–7 feet, so they could see her form clearly. When she was about 10 feet away, they heard the sound of her wings flapping.[21]

From Sweden comes a report of a 'little man' seen by several people. Three of the witnesses were in a car on a dark and rainy night (19 August 1970), driving through the forest a mile south of Narken, when they saw a little man no more than 3 feet tall standing on a path. When the car headlights shone on him, he raised his arms to cover his face. They heard a sound like a shot, and saw a white flash. They kept on driving, and discussed the little man they had all seen, wondering if he had aimed a weapon at them. They noted he was wearing what appeared to be a greyish raincoat and a helmet or sou'wester. Later they heard that other people in the area had seen a little man. Early the following year, on 16 February 1971, Åke

Westerberg, living at Stråken near Överkalix, 40 miles south of Narken, also saw what sounds like the same entity, near his house.

It was about six o'clock in the evening. I had to go by bus to a neighbour to buy some milk. When I left my home it was already dark. At the bus stop my eyes fell on a dark form in the middle of the road, approximately 15 metres away. It looked like a little man to me. I couldn't see his face; there was just a grey spot there.

The little man didn't move at all and seemed to be rooted to the ground. I became curious and stepped closer. Then I heard a sudden growl come from him. Afraid, I retreated, but he did not move. Without warning, an intense white light appeared, so bright I had to tightly close my eyes. The light lasted for 5 or 6 seconds. When I carefully opened my eyes again, the little man was gone.

Mr Westerberg had a very blurred impression of the entity's clothes. 'He was black and looked clumsy in a way. The thing on his head was difficult to discern, but he wore something on his stomach, a lamp or box of some kind.'[22]

In Mexico, two bricklayers were working on a house at Ixtapalapa when 'We heard a faint humming noise, and we looked over towards the road and saw two beings approaching, who were nearly two metres high, wearing silvery, scaly clothing. They had no noses or mouths, and seemed to be floating in the air. They came right up to about fifteen metres from where we were, and we were able to see that their backs were green.' They moved away when a woman came by on the road.[23]

'Little People' usually refers to entities 4 feet or less in height, but occasionally very tiny entities are seen, like those 8 inches in height seen by four boys outside the town of Ibague in Colombia. The boys were searching for botanical specimens in a muddy riverbed, when they saw four small beings standing under a little stone footbridge and apparently looking for something in the mud. They were dressed in white, and had tiny grey caps on their heads. As the boys walked towards them, they disappeared 'as though by magic'. The boys searched the place and found tiny footprints.[24]

It was also a young boy, eight-year-old Tonnlie Barefoot, who first saw the tiny entity of Dunn, North Carolina (USA), when he was playing in a field of dried cornstalks near his home on 12 October 1976. He saw the little man 'not much bigger than a Coke bottle',

Tonnlie Barefoot who saw a tiny entity in 1976.

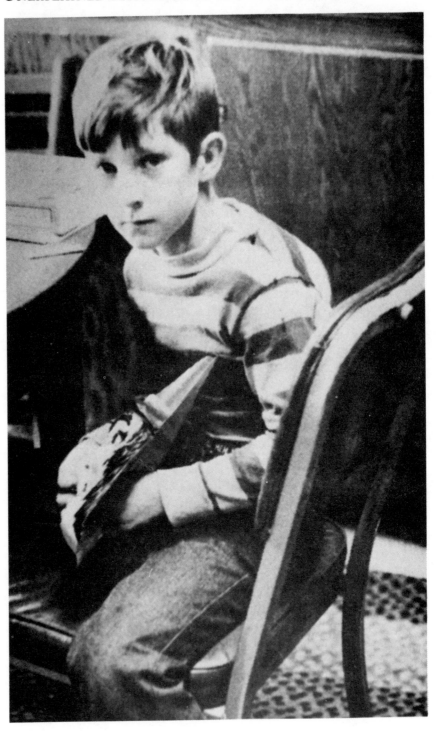

dressed in black boots, blue trousers, and a blue shiny top, with a black 'German-type hat' with a pretty white tie. He seemed to be reaching for something in his back pocket, then froze, squeaked like a mouse, and ran off fast through the cornstalks. He left some footprints 2¼ inches long and 1 inch wide with bootmarks in them. On 25 October, twenty-year-old Shirley Ann McCrimmon also saw a little man, as she came home from a party just before daybreak. He wore boots and a thin garment, and his skin was light brown. He shone a tiny bright yellow light across her eyes, and ran away when she screamed. The dogs also barked at him. Footprints were again found, in hard ground, but none in the soft ground where he had stood, and as in the cornfield the footprints ended abruptly.[25]

Why should youngsters so often be the ones to see the Little People? Is it simply coincidence, or are they more open to psychic phenomena, more able to see things not visible to adult eyes? The only witnesses to catch sight of the 'Dover Demon' were all teen-agers. Bill Bartlett, with friends Mike and Andy, all seventeen, was the first to see the strange creature which suddenly appeared around Dover, Massachusetts (USA). It was a clear, dry evening on 21 April 1977 and at about 10.30 p.m. the three friends were driving along a road bordered by trees, fields and widely spaced houses. Suddenly the headlights illuminated a strange creature which Bill at first thought was a cat or dog picking its way along a low stone wall beside the road. When he saw it more clearly, he realized it was definitely no cat or dog.

It had a large head shaped like a watermelon, from which shone large eyes 'like two orange marbles', but Bill could not make out any ears, nose or mouth. A thin neck joined the large head to a thin body. The arms and legs were long and thin, with long fingers and toes. Seemingly hairless, the creature had a peach-coloured skin with a rough texture. Overall it was 3 to 4 feet tall. As an amateur artist, Bill was observant, and the creature's strange appearance impressed itself on his memory as he drove past at a distance of about 20 feet. The sighting was later estimated to have lasted for five or six seconds, and after they had driven past Bill immediately said to his friends 'Did you see that?' Neither of them had, Mike looking out at the other side of the road, and Andy in the back talking to Mike. When Bill described what he had seen, they wanted to go back and look for it, but Bill had been frightened by the creature's weird appearance. 'No way, no way,' he responded. 'When you see something like that, you don't want to stand around and see what it's going

Bill Bartlett's first pencil sketch of the 'Dover Demon'.

to do.' However, after a mile he was persuaded to turn around and drive back, but they saw nothing. When they got home, Bill was still upset, as his father later told investigators. He straight away made a drawing of the creature, while the details were still clear in his memory.

Meanwhile, later that same evening, another young Dover resident had a close encounter with the 'Demon'. It was just after midnight when fifteen-year-old John Baxter set out to walk, or hitch-hike, home from his girlfriend's house. He was just over a mile away from the site of the Bartlett encounter, about which he of

John Baxter with his drawing of the 'Dover Demon'.

course knew nothing, when he saw someone walking towards him on the same side of the road. As it was very dark he could make out no details and from the person's height thought it might be a kid he knew. So he called out, but there was no answer. The figure stopped when it was 25 feet away, and John stopped too, calling out 'Who is that?' The figure suddenly scuttled off down a wooded gully and John went after it for a short distance. When he stopped he could see it standing about 30 feet away with the long fingers of both hands gripping a tree trunk and its toes curled around a rock. Like Bill he could see two light eyes but no other facial features. As they stood

159

watching each other, John felt nervous and went back up to the road, walking as fast as he could away from the spot. He too drew a sketch, and later, when the stories got out, he showed it to Bill Bartlett who was amazed at its remarkably close resemblance to the creature he had seen.

Nearly 24 hours after John Baxter's sighting, two more Dover youngsters saw what was almost certainly the same creature. Eighteen-year-old Will Taintor was driving fifteen-year-old Abby Brabham home at about midnight on 22 April. Will knew about Bill Bartlett's sighting as the two were close friends, but Abby had heard nothing about it. She was the first to see the 'Demon', and she got a better look at it than Will, who only saw it fleetingly. It was crouched on all fours beside the road, and they passed about 8 feet from it. It had a large oblong head, a hairless tan or beige body, and no nose, mouth or ears were noticeable. Abby remarked on its round bright green glowing eyes – as contrasted with the orange eyes described by Bill. As with the earlier witnesses, neither Will nor Abby wanted to stop and get a closer look, indeed Abby asked Will to drive faster. This plainly demonstrates that the creature was something unfamiliar – it is unlikely that all four witnesses would have failed to recognize a dog or cat or goat, or other often-seen creature.

But what was it? Various suggestions were put forward, somewhat half-heartedly – a monkey, a sick animal that had lost its hair, an escaped laboratory animal – but none of them really fits the description given by the witnesses. The other possibility is a hoax concocted by the witnesses, who all attended the same high school, but the investigators, being well aware of this possibility, took pains to check up on all of them and found that they were generally considered reliable, and not likely to stage a hoax. Also, none of the witnesses was putting forward wild theories to explain what they had seen, like a creature from outer space or a supernatural manifestation. They were all trying to think of a rare terrestrial creature which would fit the description, perhaps something that lived in the water, because on all three occasions it was seen not far from water. However, no one seems to have come up with anything at all likely, and as one of the investigators commented, it would be surprising if a native creature of such a large size was seen only during that one day and never before, or since.[26]

It was once again youngsters who saw the little green entity of Arnold, Pennsylvania (USA), at the end of February 1981. Five boys aged eleven to sixteen were spending their Saturday afternoon in the railway yard when eleven-year-old Chris saw the little creature squatting down with its back to him. He crept up on it, determined to catch it: he grabbed it and lifted it up, shouting for the others to help. It wriggled and twisted and squealed so much he was forced to drop it, and it ran into a drainpipe. The boys agreed that the strange creature was green in colour, naked and without hair or fur, but with wrinkled 'elephant' skin which felt dry and rubbery, like elastic. It was just under 3 feet tall, humanoid in shape, with nipples, large ears, and a tail one inch long, and it walked upright on two legs.[27]

Looked at rationally, all the reports in this chapter seem unbelievable, the result surely of misidentification of unfamiliar wild creatures, or of hallucination or hoax. It is more comfortable to be able to rationalize them in this way . . . but are we really justified in doing so? For most people, the only really convincing proof would be to see a non-human entity for themselves, but then, like all such witnesses, they would find themselves in the position of trying to convince the doubters and disbelievers that they were speaking the truth. Eleven-year-old Chris took the right action when he tried to capture the Arnold creature. Had he managed to do so, there might now exist incontrovertible proof that non-humans (at least of the little green-skinned kind) are real – but he failed, and the question remains: what did all these people see?

10 USOs – unidentified submarine objects

The seas and oceans of our world are far greater in extent than the land masses, covering 70 per cent of the earth's surface, and in some areas the water is very deep – as much as 7 miles deep in the 'trenches', although these do not cover a very great area. However, depths of 3–4 miles are reached over large areas of ocean. Man rarely penetrates into these depths and, as we have already seen, there may be many kinds of creatures living there which are as yet unknown to science. Because of the difficulties man has in entering and living in the oceans, the submarine regions are little explored, and hardly used – by humans. But the following reports which describe unknown craft entering, leaving, or travelling within the oceans may suggest that there are other intelligences on this planet to whom the underseas are familiar territory.

Since there must be an observer present before a report can be made, it is impossible to judge how widespread is the behaviour described here. Out on the oceans away from land, there could be very much more activity that is not witnessed. The fact that more reports come from land-based witnesses seeing activity just offshore is probably due to there being far more potential witnesses on land than on the sea. Also the geographical distribution of reports is probably dependent on the degree of development of the witness's country, those in underdeveloped countries not having any official to report to. So the distribution of reports does not really tell us much, other than that these phenomena are seen all over the world.

We can, as usual, only give a selection of reports here, but others will be found described in brief in the Gazetteer. As hinted earlier, the reports fall into three categories, some of which, potentially, are more easily explained than others. If a witness reports seeing a UFO flying down to the sea and then submerging, there are numerous possible explanations: that he/she did see an unidentified craft submerging, though it could be crashing rather than intentionally going under water; that he/she saw a meteorite, a plane, or space debris crashing into the sea, but was unable to identify it correctly because of distance; or that he/she saw an astronomical body (star, planet, moon, sun) on the horizon which appeared to be a solid object entering the water as it went below the horizon. If a witness reports seeing a UFO emerging from the sea and flying away, there is not really any straightforward explanation for there is no natural phenomenon that behaves like this. When witnesses report uniden- tified submarine craft, they may of course be seeing terrestrial submarines, secretly exploring foreign waters, or they may be seeing sea monsters. However, some reports do not easily fit into either of these categories, as we shall see, and then the witnesses might be seeing UFOs which have temporarily submerged (conceivably some of these craft might be capable of travelling just as easily under water as in the air), or they might be seeing submarine craft which are not man-made but originate from an underwater civilization. Making such a suggestion is to take a great leap into speculation: but considering how little we know about the ocean's depths, it is not inconceivable that some intelligent life form finds the sea a congenial environment, and successfully lives there, unknown to mankind.

But that's enough speculation for a while. We will present some of the most interesting reports from this century, and you can judge for yourself whether anything strange is happening beneath the surface of the ocean, or whether all these reports can be explained in natural terms. We will begin our tour in northern Europe, where there have in recent years been many reports of mystery submarines – around Greenland, Iceland, Norway, and especially Sweden. In April 1988, Bengt Gustafsson, Supreme Commander of the Swedish Army, announced that there had been 30 cases of unidentified foreign submarines in Swedish waters during the previous six months.[1] Since the Scandinavian reports are almost certainly of terrestrial submarines, even sometimes imaginary submarines resulting from rumours and panics, or misinterpretation of underwater cliffs and other topographical features of the seabed, we will not linger over them. In the Baltic Sea in 1959, soldiers near Kolobrzeg on the Polish coast saw the sea become agitated and then a triangular object with sides about 12 feet long came up out of the water, circled over the barracks, and flew away.[2] By no stretch of the imagination could this have been a terrestrial submarine. Nor could the sighting which occurred over Norway's Namsenfjorden in 1959. At 10 p.m. one December night, Lorentz Johnson was going home to Skomsvoll when he saw a cigar-shaped object 150 feet up in the sky. It had windows and gave off a reddish glow. Suddenly it dropped two long objects into the fjord. Another witness was across the fjord, and he saw nothing strange, but heard splashing noises. Five years afterwards, a man fishing in the same area snagged something on the bottom. A colleague who had sonar on his boat located a sizeable object. This was confirmed four years later, in 1968, when a Norwegian UFO group used sonar to detect an object 20 feet long at a depth of 300 feet, but it did not prove possible to reach it with divers.[3]

In late February 1963, 30–50 miles off the north coast of Norway in the direction of Spitsbergen, a very strange radar/sonar event occurred. Ships from the British Royal Navy North Atlantic Fleet were engaged in exercises, and on this particular morning, the witness was in charge of the radar–sonar room on a frigate. A blip denoting a solid object appeared on the radarscope, and the indications were of an object 100–120 feet across at a height of 35,000 feet. It appeared suddenly, an impossibility for a conventional aircraft, but the witness said conditions were not favourable for the anomalous propagation of false targets. It was learned that the same target was also on the scope of the nearest ship, but outside the witness could not locate the object through binoculars, nor could he make contact with it by radio. Jets were sent up to intercept the object, and when they were 10–15 miles from it, the men in the radar–sonar room saw its radar blip make a steep angular descent at great speed, crossing all three radar screens and going below the radar horizon of 750–1000 feet, all in 2–3 seconds. Following loss of radar contact, an underwater target was picked up on sonar, indicating an object moving fast at about 10 miles distance, and in the same direction as the radar target had been moving. The object dropped into deeper water, moving fast in a zigzag path away from the ship, and after a few minutes contact was suddenly lost. The ship steamed to the point where the object had entered the sea, but nothing was seen and no further contact was made with it.[4]

Reports of possible USO activity have also come from all the coasts of Britain – off England, Wales and Scotland. Lifeboats have frequently been called out when flares have been sighted offshore, but nothing has been found and the flares remained unaccounted for. This seems to occur regularly off the English coast of East Anglia (Norfolk and Suffolk). In May 1975 something more solid was found, by accident. A dredger 30 miles off Gorleston (Norfolk) struck a submerged object in water nearly 150 feet deep. The propeller was slightly damaged. The ship went back, using echo sounders, but nothing could be found.[5]

A strange sighting from the west coast of Britain was reported by Gavin Gibbons in his book *The Coming of the Space Ships*.[6] The location was the coast of Dyfed (Wales), and the date was 24 March 1955.

> It was at 7.15 p.m. that Mrs Harding, a farmer's wife of Aberarth, was called outside by her young daughter, who was pointing excitedly at the evening sky. She gazed out over the sea in the direction that Rosalyn, her daughter, indicated. There, to the north-west of where they stood, and well out to sea, was a large orange ball giving out a black trail and zig-zagging downwards. They remarked that it looked very like the sun except for the movement and the long, black, smoky trail that streamed out behind. As they watched, it exploded and, still in the shape of an orange ball, plunged into the sea. The strange thing was that they could still see it glowing beneath the surface of the water, and this continued for upwards of an hour after the object finally struck. The trail that it had left behind changed from black to grey before it dispersed: neither of the two watchers had heard any sound from the ball, either in the air or in the sea.

A similar object was seen that evening from a coastal position some miles north, near Tywyn (Gwynedd). The two witnesses reported that after dropping into the sea, the bright orange object shot up into the sky again, leaving a grey trail behind it. But it is not clear whether or not they were watching the same object as was seen by the witnesses at Aberarth.

Across the English Channel to France, where off the Normandy coast the crew of a French fishing boat saw 'a large, black, bird-like object' fall from the sky one July day in 1910. It fell into the sea, bounded back, fell again and disappeared leaving no traces.[7] South to Portugal, where on 6 July 1965 the commander and crew of a Norwegian tanker saw a cigar-shaped object fly out of the sea off Puerto La Cruz. It was glowing blue, and had a row of portholes with yellow lights.[8] Sixteen years later, a short distance to the south, and just over the Spanish border at Isla Cristina in the province of Huelva, two boys saw a light emerge from the sea about 1000 feet offshore. It was the night of 8 February 1981, and their attention was first caught by a light rising up from the depths. 'This light was getting brighter and brighter, which made us think of a submarine, but suddenly it came out of the water and stayed still at a height of about 500 metres (1600 feet), disappearing without a trace soon after.'[9]

Further east, in the Mediterranean, there has been a considerable amount of USO activity over the years. On 26 July 1970 a diver fishing off Alcocebre in eastern Spain was in water 25–30 feet deep and 200 feet offshore when he found a strange metallic cylinder about 20 feet long lying on the sea bed. He examined it closely, tried unsuccessfully to move it, and was also unable to scratch it with his knife. Early the following morning he was rowing in the same area when his companion saw something leaving the water. A few hours later when the diver went down again, the cylinder had gone. He was sure he was in the same spot, and was a very experienced diver.[10]

Eight years earlier a very strange encounter with a USO had taken place in the Mediterranean, one of the very few such cases involving entities. The location was the fishing port of Le Brusc, between Marseilles and Nice in southern France, and the witnesses were fishermen. Three of them were out in two boats late at night on 1 August 1962 when they saw what seemed to be a submarine moving slowly along the surface of the water. Some 'frogmen' were climbing out of the sea on to the craft. One of the fishermen called to them with a loud-hailer (they were about 1000 feet away), but they did not respond – except for the last man, who turned and waved his arm. Then after he had gone inside, the craft rose above the water and hovered there, with red and green lights shining. A white searchlight beam shone towards their boats. Then all the lights went out, the craft glowed orange and began to rotate, faster and faster, until it shot off at speed and vanished among the stars. The fishermen were flabbergasted and very puzzled. 'Apart from the noise of the waves, we had heard no sound from it, and you can well imagine that we asked ourselves what it could possibly have been. It was not a submarine, nor a helicopter nor a seaplane, we would have certainly seen if it was any one of those.'[11] Not many witnesses get as close as this to a USO, or see its occupants, and if true this is an extraordinary tale. We say 'if true' because of course it is impossible for us to verify every account we use, and we must therefore rely on the integrity of the journalists and investigators whose work we are quoting. Of course we do not use material from sources known to us to be dubious.

USO activity has also been reported off Italy's long coastline, especially during the Italian UFO wave of 1978. In October of that year, fishermen were seeing 100-foot columns of water forming in clear, calm weather, and a dark body longer than their boats emerging briefly from the sea before quickly resubmerging.[12]

Leaving the confines of the Mediterranean Sea and moving south again, it seems that little USO activity has been reported around the African continent. The only report we have for the western side dates right back to 1902, when on 28 October in the early hours of the morning the lookout on the SS *Fort Salisbury*, located in the Gulf of Guinea some distance off West Africa in the South Atlantic, saw a huge dark object to starboard. He called the second officer, and together with the helmsman they watched the strange submarine craft. Second Officer Raymer later recalled: 'It was a little frightening. We couldn't see too much detail in the darkness, but it was between five and six hundred feet in length. It had two lights, one at each end. A mechanism of some kind – or fins, maybe – was making a commotion in the water.' The surface of the craft 'appeared to be scaled' rather than smooth, and the object was slowly sinking. This sounds almost like a giant sea creature, except that at 500–600 feet it would be impossibly huge, and also it is unlikely to have had a light at each end.[13] Is it likely to have been a terrestrial submarine? They were being developed around this time – the first British submarine was launched in 1901 – but it is unlikely that these early craft could travel so far away from land.

To the east of Africa, the only recorded location of USO sightings we know of is the island of Réunion, where on 10 February 1975 a man at Petite Ile saw a very bright object come up out of the sea and fly off very fast.[14] Further east, somewhere in the Indian Ocean, the fourth officer on board *Queensland Star* saw a white UFO in the sky which dropped and entered the sea, making the water very bright. Particles of a white substance fell into the sea after the UFO had sunk. This happened on 18 September 1961.[15]

Mysterious submarines have also been seen around Australia and New Zealand. On 11 April 1965 two men on the cliffs at Wonthaggi, Victoria (Australia), watched two 'strange craft' for fifteen minutes. They identified them as submarines by their conning-towers, but a Navy spokesman commented: 'A preliminary investigation of the report suggests, in view of the locality and configuration of the coastline, that the objects are unlikely to have been submarines.' Only four days later, two youths saw two cylindrical objects off

Coolum (Queensland) and three days after that two fishermen were chased by a big vessel off Mooloolaba near Brisbane (Queensland). There was a further sighting of two objects in the sea off Fraser Island (Queensland) on 6 June 1965: they were dark, narrow, and up to 100 feet long. The witnesses, in a plane, saw two or three smaller objects near the bigger ones.[16]

Mystery submarines were also seen off New Zealand in 1965, and the first sighting predated the Australian ones, taking place on 12 January in Kaipara Harbour, north of Helensville. A DC3 was flying at 500 feet over the harbour when the captain saw a 'stranded whale' which on closer examination he saw to be a metallic structure about 100 feet long and resting in 30 feet of water. The Navy confirmed that it could not have been a conventional submarine because of the inaccessibility of the location.[17] Later that year, on 13 November, two fishermen on their way to tend cray pots off Rugged Islands at the north-west of Stewart Island, saw a strange 'tower' emerge from the sea 300 yards away. There was a 'box' close to it. After a few seconds the water surged and the objects disappeared. The men were sure they had not seen a submarine conning-tower, or whales or logs, and the Navy confirmed that it was an unlikely place for submarines to operate because of the rocks in the area.[18]

An unidentified submarine surfaced off Coomlieyna Beach near Ceduna (South Australia) on 28 December 1976, and was seen by about twenty Aboriginals who were fishing at the beach. The craft was about 90 feet long and had a white conning-tower, a black centre line and a red stripe at the water-line. But a Royal Australian Navy spokesman said that submarines are usually dark in colour, and the details did not match any of the submarines in the world's navies. Also, no craft were operating in those waters at the time.[19]

Further north, USOs have been reported from various places off East Asia, the most southerly being Vietnam where on 16 June 1909 an elongated 'bolide' (meteor/fireball) was seen by fishermen over Dong Hoi city, Annam, in the early hours of the morning: they saw it fall into the sea after it had been visible for eight or ten minutes, which rules out its being a meteor.[20] The crew of an American craft off Inchon (South Korea) saw two objects with smoke trails which struck the water at great speed, sending up huge columns of water.[21] This happened in December 1950, and a few years later, on 15 January 1956, a large object glowing blue-grey was seen to fall into the water off Pusan (South Korea). The glow was visible for an hour and a half as the object floated on the surface before sinking.[22]

Strange objects were seen descending into the sea off Japan in both 1956 and 1957, and a more recent sighting of a USO took place in 1980. On that occasion, actually on 18 August 1980, the captain of a Russian research vessel in the Sea of Japan saw a metallic-looking cylindrical object rise slowly from the sea and hover nearby before shooting away.[23]

We now cross the Pacific Ocean to the Americas, where some very strange goings-on have been reported. Our first stop is the Aleutian Islands (USA) in the far north, where in the summer of 1945 the crew of a US Army transport ship taking supplies to Alaska saw a large round object emerge from the sea, a mile or so distant. They saw it climb straight up, then circle the ship before flying off to the south.[24] There were two independent witnesses to an incident in the Strait of Juan de Fuca, Washington State, on 9 March 1960. Two lorry-drivers, both east of Port Angeles, reported seeing a large flaming object descending into the water. Nothing was found, nor were any planes reported missing.[25] There have been numerous other reports of objects seen crashing into the sea off Washington, Oregon and California. Although in most cases nothing is ever found in the sea, an object was traced on the sea bed following a splash-down off Lummi Island, Washington, on 27 July 1984. It was egg-shaped, metallic, and orange or gold in colour. One diver who stood on it said it was humming, and when he surfaced his boots were covered in a reddish dust. When the divers returned a few days later, the object had gone.[26]

An unusual submarine was seen off Avalon, Catalina, California (USA) on 28 July 1962, by the captain and a crewman of a fishing boat. The captain saw lights low on the water just before dawn, and went closer to investigate. Through binoculars he saw a squat, lighted structure which appeared to be the stern of a submarine, with men working on it.

> We could see five men, two in all-white garb, two in dark trousers and white shirts, and one in a sky-blue jump-suit. We passed abeam at about a quarter-mile and I was certain it was a submarine low in the water, steel grey, no markings, decks almost awash, with only its tail and an odd aftstructure showing.

It came towards them and swept past at speed, heading for the open sea, still on the surface. It was assumed to be a new type of Russian submarine, but there are doubts about that identification.[27]

Surprisingly, we have only one report from the western coast of the South American continent. This was a sighting from a fishing vessel twenty miles off the coast of Chile near Tocopilla in the north. There were many sightings of a UFO on 23–24 September 1971, including police witnesses. After about eight hours, the UFO, 'a red ball', was seen by the ship's crew as it flew round the ship for several minutes. Then they watched it sink into the sea about 3 miles away.[28] The absence of cases from the western side of the continent is more than compensated for on the east. The Argentine coast in particular seems to attract USOs. Our earliest report here dates from June 1950, when a man on a long-distance walk from Tierra del Fuego to Buenos Aires was walking along the Atlantic coast between San Sebastian and Rio Grande late at night. He heard a noise like water being disturbed, and saw a luminous oval object emerge from the sea about 1500 feet offshore. It flew off towards the land. A fortnight later the same witness saw a similar occurrence when he was between Rio Gallegos and Santa Cruz. This time four UFOs came out of the sea.[29]

An unidentified submarine was perplexing the Argentine Navy in June 1959. They had it confined in Buenos Aires harbour but were still unable to identify it. It was shaped like a huge fish (perhaps it *was* a huge fish), silver in colour, with a large tail like the vertical stabilizer on a B-17. It moved and manoeuvred very quickly. Divers got close but could not identify it as any known submarine. We do not know what happened to it.[30] In the following year they had problems with two submarines in the Golfo Nuevo, a partly enclosed area of water 20 by 40 miles in size many miles south-west of Buenos Aires. In February 1960 the Navy tried every way they could think of to track down the submarines. There was only one at first, then after a few days a second appeared. They could stay under water for several days, and could move quicker than the ships on the surface. The Argentine Navy were assisted by US Navy experts, and they used many tons of explosives, but the submarines disappeared as mysteriously as they had arrived.[31] A lorry-driver who claimed to have frequently seen luminous craft entering and leaving the sea around this time commented: 'It is absolutely certain that in the depths of the Gulf of San Matías there is a flying saucer base. These happenings are common knowledge throughout a large region of Patagonia, where it is a regular and quite a normal thing for people to be heard speaking of the Martians.' The Golfo San Matías is just to the north of the Golfo Nuevo.[32] To the south is the Golfo de San

Jorge, and on 30 September 1964 a man driving near Comodoro Rivadavia saw three or four UFOs which went into the sea one after another. A few miles further on his journey, he saw more luminous objects, perhaps the same ones, emerging out of the sea and circling around at great speed before climbing into the sky and disappearing.[33]

A few miles south of the Golfo de San Jorge a farmer saw a large cigar-shaped UFO on 18 March 1966. It was very close to him, less than 100 feet away, and he thought it was 65–70 feet long. It was metallic, grey-black, and smooth with no markings or windows. Grey smoke was coming from its rear end, and it seemed in difficulties as it was 'chugging along' and making noises. He ran for cover as it began to vibrate as if about to explode. While over the sea it crashed into the water. 'It did not float at all. It just hit the water with a huge splash and went down quickly.'[34]

The quantity of UFO and USO sightings off the Argentine coast suggests that the idea of a submarine UFO base in the South Atlantic may not be too crazy after all. There has also been some activity off the Brazilian coast further north. On 10 January 1958 an army captain was sitting in the porch of a house near Curitiba, and examining an unfamiliar 'island' through binoculars. The 'island' turned out to be a strange object in two sections joined by vertical shafts or tubes. The whole thing sank as he and others watched; then fifteen minutes later, after a ship had passed by, it rose again, finally disappearing after a few more minutes.[35] Rather more dramatic was the event witnessed by an eight-year-old girl living near Iguapé. On 31 October 1963 she heard a roaring noise and saw a silvery object in the sky, which flew overhead, hit a palm tree, and fell into the Peropava River. Other witnesses came on the scene in time to see the water and mud boiling where the UFO had crashed. A group of fishermen on the far shore of the river also saw the UFO crash. They said it was like polished aluminium, and about 25 feet in diameter. There were numerous attempts to locate the UFO by divers, but they were hampered by the 12 feet of mud into which it seemed to have sunk. It is possible that the craft could have been repaired underwater and escaped in darkness, or it could be resting deep in the mud where it fell, or it could have travelled upstream or downstream under water. At any rate, no trace of it was ever found.[36]

On 20 July 1967 the captain of the Argentinian ship *Naviero* witnessed a classic USO while his ship was 120 miles off Cape Santa

Marta Grande (Brazil). The captain was called to the deck and saw a cigar-shaped UFO around 110 feet long, glowing blue and white. It paced the ship for fifteen minutes before diving into the water, passing under the ship and disappearing into the depths. He could see it glowing brightly as it moved under water.[37] In Amapa in the north of Brazil, a UFO was seen to emerge from the Araguari River in late 1980, witnessed by at least 70 people waiting for a ferry across the river. The craft appeared solid, about 15 feet in diameter. It hovered 15–20 feet over the river before rising slowly, then speeding off towards the ocean.[38]

Some USO activity has also been reported from Venezuela on the north coast of the South American continent. A cone-shaped UFO, 'giving off strange flares', was seen descending from the sky and entering the water, leaving it turbulent and brightly coloured, north of Orchila Island on 13 December 1959, the witnesses being on board a Swedish ship.[39] In 1967 there was considerable activity, several witnesses on the mainland seeing UFOs come out of the sea. One man on the beach at Catia la Mar on 27 August saw the ocean 'boiling', and then three grey discs emerged and flew off.[40] In a sighting on 29 March 1973 near Carayaca, a man saw a tiny figure like a five-year-old child at a small window in a UFO which came down on to the sea a few yards from the shore. His wife saw two UFOs land in the sea, and one submerged for a while before they both took off again.[41]

Some time in 1963, a sonar operator on a destroyer taking part in a US Navy anti-submarine exercise off Puerto Rico, some miles north of Venezuela across the Caribbean Sea, reported that one of the submarines chased an unknown submarine object travelling at more than 170 mph. This mystery craft was tracked on sonar by thirteen ships, and it was traced for four days as it went down to depths of 27,000 feet. No terrestrial submarine can move so fast or descend so deep underwater.[42]

Moving north again, across the Gulf of Mexico to the southern coast of Mississippi (USA), we find reports of a small USO, 3 feet long, 3 or 4 inches wide and shiny like stainless steel which was playing hide and seek with coastguard officers at the mouth of the Pascagoula River on 6 November 1973. Two fishermen reported seeing the object, which had an amber light on it. The coastguard officers and the fishermen tried beating at the craft with oars and boathooks, but it evaded them by putting out its light, moving away, then lighting up again. They lost it after 40 minutes. This event took place in the same area and less than a month after a widely publicized UFO abduction case had occurred.[43]

As on the west coast of North America, there have also on the east coast been numerous reports of large objects seen splashing into the sea, but these might well be crashing planes (though unlikely if none reported missing?) or space debris or meteorites. In the summer of 1954 a Dutch government ship arrived in New York and reported that the crew had seen a flat object emerge from the sea about 80 miles offshore. The captain had looked at it through binoculars and said it was greyish at first, but turned brighter on the lower part. There were also bright spots like lights around the edges.[44] On 22 June 1957, a large object seen to fall into the water of Long Island Sound (New York) had two white lights and one red light, so it was unlikely to have been a meteor. Nor, at that early date, would it have been space debris.[45]

An interesting early report from the *St Andrew* somewhere in the North Atlantic shows the difficulty of distinguishing between meteors and UFOs. On 30 October 1906 the ship passed through a meteoric shower about 600 miles north-east of Cape Race (Newfoundland, Canada). In the words of the chief officer:

On Tuesday afternoon the weather was clear and bright, although there was little sunshine. Just after one bell, 4:30 o'clock, I saw three meteors fall into the water dead ahead of the ship one after another at a distance of about five miles. Although it was daylight, they left a red streak in the air from zenith to the horizon. Simultaneously the third engineer shouted to me. I then saw a huge meteor on the port beam falling in a zig-zag manner less than a mile away to the southward. We could distinctly hear the hissing of water as it touched. It fell with a rocking motion leaving a broad red streak in its wake. The meteor must have weighed several tons, and appeared to be 10 to 15 feet in diameter. It was saucer shaped which probably accounted for the peculiar rocking motion. When the mass of metal struck the water the spray and steam rose to a height of at least 40 feet, and for a few moments looked like the mouth of a crater. If it had been night, the meteor would have illuminated the sea for 50 or 60 miles. The hissing sound, like escaping steam, when it struck the water was so loud that the chief engineer turned out of his berth and came on deck, thinking the sound came from the engine room. I have seen meteors all over the world, but never such a large one as this.[46]

The witness's description of the meteor as saucer-shaped, falling in a zigzag manner and with a rocking motion, does cause some doubt as to whether this really was a meteor, or a UFO, which of course in 1906 was a concept the witness would not have been familiar with. But if meteors really can behave in this way, then perhaps a good number of the 'UFOs' seen to fall into the sea were in fact meteors?

It was definitely not a meteor that fell into Shag Harbour, Nova Scotia (Canada), on 4 October 1967. The object, seen at night by witnesses on land, had several reddish-orange lights which went on and off in order, and it slowly disappeared into the water. Then the witnesses saw the lights change to a single white light and the object was bobbing on the water about half a mile off shore. Police witnesses also saw the light flashing on the water. Boats went out to it, but found only a large patch of bubbling water and yellowish foam. A two-day search found nothing, and no planes were reported missing.[47]

As if all these reports of USO activity were not strange enough, we

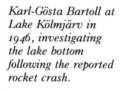

Karl-Gösta Bartoll at Lake Kölmjärv in 1946, investigating the lake bottom following the reported rocket crash.

have a number of reports of similar activity *inland*, in rivers and lakes. Being particularly rich in lakes, Scandinavia also has proportionately more of these cases. During the summer of 1946, thousands of people reported seeing unknown rocket-like objects crossing the sky or crashing into lakes. They were widely believed to be from Russia, but this was never proved. One of the 'ghost rocket' crashes was investigated recently, with the main witness, farmer Knut Lindbäck, being interviewed in 1984. He and his maid were haymaking by Lake Kölmjärv in the extreme north of Sweden on 19 July 1946 when they heard a humming noise in the sky. Lindbäck looked up and saw a long, grey, rocket-like object diving towards the lake. As it fell into the water it sent up a tall column of water, and then another. Describing the object, Lindbäck said it was about 6 feet long 'and had a snub nose, while the stern was pointed. I thought there were a few small winglike protrusions on the side, but I am not sure. Everything happened so quickly!' He went to the lake and rowed out to the spot where the object had sunk. Weeds and water lilies had been torn up by their roots and the water was muddy. The water at that point was only about 6 feet deep, but an intensive search by military personnel failed to locate the rocket in the deep mud.

Other similar cases that summer were reported from Lake Kattistjärn (14 miles north-east of Kölmjärv) where a boy fishing saw something hit the water close to him, raising a tall column of water. This happened about fifteen minutes before the Kölmjärv incident. There was another sighting of an aerial object at the same time, over Bölebyn in the north. It was likened to a shining milkcan, and according to the report was in view for fifteen minutes, so it could not have been moving very fast. Three weeks later, on 13 August, an object with small wings crashed into a lake in mid-Norrland; and on 18 July, the day before the Kölmjärv crash, *two* cigar-shaped rockets with wings fell together into Lake Mjösa in mid-Norway.[48] Predating the world-wide publicity for UFOs which began in 1947, these Scandinavian 'ghost rocket' reports remain among the most puzzling UFO phenomena. If they really were experimental machines launched by the Russians, then there must have been a production line and continual launches, to account for the number of reported sightings, and yet no wreckage was ever recovered.

In more recent years in Scandinavia, there have been reports of huge holes torn in thick ice on lakes, for example a hole 60 by 90 feet in ice 3 feet thick on Lake Uppramen (Sweden) in 1968.[49] A dark or grey object was actually seen tearing a long channel in the ice on Lake

Siljan (Sweden) on 30 April 1976.[50] In Finland, a hole 8 by 10 feet appeared in the ice on Säkkiä Lake on 8 December 1983, after villagers had seen whirling lights in the sky. The same thing happened again in the winter of 1984.[51] In the USA and Canada, there have also been similar reports – from Upper Scott Lake in Michigan (1 January 1970), from Wakefield, New Hampshire (10 January 1977),[52] and from Wyandotte County Lake in Kansas (mid-March 1978),[53] for example – and there have also been several instances of UFOs diving into rivers and lakes, or even occasionally emerging from them. A shiny sphere studded with spikes, as big as a bowling ball, descended as if controlled into a 5-acre lake near Concord, North Carolina (USA), in September 1962 and, watched by policemen, began to disintegrate into a mass of shiny wire or shredded aluminium.[54]

The strangest report must surely be that from a man who was fishing in the Thompson River at Kamloops, British Columbia (Canada), on 16 May 1981. It was a bright, sunny afternoon, and a small boat had just passed by when he heard a noise 'like water being poured into a frying pan', and the water 100 yards away began to bubble. A 'typical flying saucer' then rose slowly out of the river, up into the air, and flew away. A rain of pellets fell on him, presumably from the UFO, and he collected some of this material for analysis. Unfortunately we have no information as to the results.[55]

A rare photograph of a USO was obtained in 1964 by Frank S. Kinsey, former Air Force pilot during the war, who was in November of that year paying a brief visit to the newly completed Casitas reservoir near Ventura, California (USA), with his brother-in-law. It was a dismal, overcast morning as they stood on the water's edge. Suddenly,

> I heard sort of a loud noise and water splashing, and I looked out into the lake and here's this object coming out of the water. I was so flabbergasted . . .
>
> I had a camera [with infra-red film in it] around my neck, but I completely forgot the camera due to the fact that I was so astounded to see something like this coming up out of the water. It came out of the water, I'd say about twenty or thirty feet, and hovered . . . I happened to remember that I had my camera . . . and just as I was getting the camera up to my eyes, this object started moving away, and I just barely got it near the edge of the film; then, within a few seconds it disappeared out over the

mountains . . . As it was speeding up, it started changing colours, from a real dark lavender colour up to a real bright orange-yellow, and that's the last I saw of it.

Frank S. Kinsey's photograph of the UFO which emerged from Casitas Reservoir.

Before taking the photograph, Mr Kinsey had looked at the object through his binoculars, and could see what appeared to be an entity staring back at him.[56]

Can all these strange reports be dismissed as hoaxes, hallucinations or natural phenomena? Some undoubtedly would be identifiable if more information were available, but what about those cases where solid objects were seen or found? Curiously, none of these objects was ever retrieved for analysis. Either they had disappeared when a second visit to the spot was made, or were irretrievably lost in deep mud. As with UFO phenomena, the USOs remain ephemeral, tantalizing, for ever beyond our reach. They serve to remind us that although man likes to think himself master of the planet, there are many mysteries still to be solved. We tend not to think too deeply about such things, for they are disturbing to our equilibrium. USOs must surely come into the category of subjects which bring about this feeling. How often have you heard or seen this subject discussed in the media? Very likely never, yet, as this chapter has shown, there has been continuing activity in the world's oceans by solid craft of whose origins we remain completely ignorant. We can speculate, as Ivan T. Sanderson did in his book *Invisible Residents*, that there is intelligent life in or under the oceans, but we are totally unable to test this speculation. If underwater civilizations do exist, all they need fear from mankind is that we will pollute them out of existence.

11 *Ghostly voices*

Ghosts are not usually communicative beings. They move in silence and often seem unaware of the witness. It is true that many people have reported hearing phantom footsteps in their home, but we know of no instances where a ghost has been seen and footsteps heard simultaneously. Yet there are numerous accounts on record of ghosts speaking, although as a proportion of the total ghost sightings the figure would be very low. But as the psychic researcher G. N. M. Tyrrell commented when describing the 'perfect apparition' in his classic work on this subject, *Apparitions*: 'The apparition might speak to us, and possibly it might go as far as to answer a question; but we should not be able to engage it in any long conversation.'[1] Andrew MacKenzie, in commenting on this aspect in his own book *Hauntings and Apparitions*, suggests that many of the communications from ghosts may be telepathic in nature: 'that what is interpreted as speech from an apparition is often a communication received telepathically and converted by the recipient into language.'[2] There have been instances of foreign ghosts conversing easily with witnesses who spoke only English, suggesting that the communication took place telepathically, even though the witness may not have realized this. However, the majority of ghosts do not speak, indeed seem loth to speak, and will not reply if spoken to.

There are, however, reports of ghostly voices which are not associated with a visible apparition but are simply heard. These voices may be hallucinatory in nature – but on occasion the witness has been able to record them, and therefore they certainly had some objective reality. Other types of ghostly voices include phone calls received from dead people; the voices produced by direct-voice mediums; as well as voices which are not directly audible but only recorded on tape. We will provide examples of all these in this chapter, beginning with cases where a ghost was seen and heard to speak. Around 1955, a woman attending a performance at the Metropolitan Opera in New York found she had an irritating neighbour – a woman who wore a rustly silk outfit and who nudged the witness in the ribs and hissed 'Flat, flat, *flat!*' every time the soprano sang. She went to complain to the management, but the usher who returned with her found no one in the seat. It was believed that the woman had been the ghost of the soprano Frances Alda, who had behaved in the same way when alive.[3]

In Finland in 1957, two women claimed to have seen and spoken to the ghost of their president, Dr Juho Kusti Paasikivi, who had died four months before. On 19 April they were approaching the elevator in an apartment building in Helsinki, on their way to visit someone, when they both saw President Paasikivi standing by the elevator door. One of the women, Mrs E. Sinisalo, opened the door and the President said, in Finnish of course, 'After you, ladies, please!' Mrs Sinisalo commented: 'He looked a little younger and thinner than when I had last seen him. But he still spoke in the big, almost raucous voice for which he was famous.' They all got into the elevator and ascended to the fourth floor where, as the door was opened and he began to leave, he said: 'Ladies, you must certainly be wondering why I am here when I should be in the grave. But it is really so!' He left the elevator and as the two ladies continued up to the next floor they saw him standing smiling at them through the glass door. It is interesting that the President never operated the elevator himself. Mrs Sinisalo opened the door at ground level, it stopped at the fourth floor without anyone pressing the button, and Mrs Sinisalo again had to open the door for the President to leave. But why did the two ladies not realize immediately on first seeing the President that they were seeing a ghost? They recognized him, and must have known he had been dead for four months. Yet Mrs Sinisalo said later: 'I did not quite realize that he was a dead man until he announced it himself . . . But I still think it is curious that neither Aunt Maja nor I remembered when we were in the elevator with him that we knew Paasikivi was dead.' It would seem that, for some reason, on entering the apartment building they simultaneously entered a kind of trance state and shared a hallucination of the dead President. If this explanation seems far-fetched, so too does the possibility that the President's ghost really did ride in the elevator with them.[4]

Apart from one further Finnish case, the rest of our speaking ghosts come from England, a country rich in ghosts both legendary

President Paasikivi photographed in the early 1950s.

and factual, so it is not surprising that a certain proportion of them prove to be communicative. It was a ghostly priest that Ivor Potter saw at Poundstock church, Cornwall, on 2 March 1971 when he was attending a funeral service there. He described how,

> for about four minutes I saw a priest I assumed was going to take part in the service, standing beside the vicar in the porch. We even wished each other 'Good afternoon'. It was only later I discovered

he did not exist . . . I always thought they were supposed to be misty, gossamer creatures. But the ghost was absolutely solid. He answered me back and I walked all round him.[5]

A phantom monk was seen by several people in the 1970s near the old St John's church in Chester, and he spoke to at least two of the witnesses. One of these encounters took place in December 1973, when the witness was walking home late at night along a cobbled footpath by the church. Suddenly he saw a monk in a black robe and cowl. The figure spoke in what seemed like German, but although the witness knew German he could not understand what was said, and thinks it may have been a dialect. The man told the monk, whom he had no reason to believe was not a living person, that he could not understand him, and the monk seemed upset. The witness walked round him to continue along the path, but immediately thought he ought to try and help him, so turned round – but there was no one there, and there was nowhere he could have gone to so quickly. Even so, the witness refused to believe he had seen a ghost. He wrote to a local newspaper about his experience, and another man replied that he too had had a similar experience when using the path late at night. 'When I was about half-way down, I met a man dressed like a monk, i.e. in a black robe and wearing sandals. He spoke to me in some outlandish language which I could not understand, and I said so. He seemed to repeat his request, but it was no use, I didn't understand him.' This failure to make himself understood saddened the monk and he turned away. Again the witness moved on, then turned to find the monk no longer there. The church dates back many centuries, and seems a likely place for such a haunting. We can only wonder what the ghostly monk was asking for. It is unlikely that his communication was telepathic, for had it been, the witnesses would have understood him.[6]

Very rarely does a witness have the opportunity to speak to the same ghost on more than one occasion, but this happened to Matthew Manning, psychic and healer, when he was a teenager living at home in Linton, Cambridgeshire. It all began in 1971, when Matthew saw a ghost on the stairs. He apologized to Matthew for frightening him, and added that he needed to walk to ease the pain in his legs. He allowed Matthew to draw a quick sketch of him, before he climbed upstairs and disappeared out of sight on the landing. The following year Matthew saw him again in one of the bedrooms. He shook hands with him, though he felt nothing – 'my hand passed straight through his'. Again the ghost complained about his legs. This time Matthew saw him actually disappear.

> It was as though I was watching a colour television screen from which the colour was gradually fading. I noticed that the figure of Robert Webbe was losing its colour around the edges, so that his outer areas were greyish, while the main central areas of his body were still showing colour. While I watched, I could see the colour vanishing . . . Within less than thirty seconds, I estimated, all the colour had gone and I was left facing a shadowy grey figure. Then the grey became fainter, and I realised that he was vanishing – into the air.

Although Matthew did not see the ghost very often, and so was rarely able to communicate face to face, the ghost did write at considerable length through Matthew's hand, and answered his questions. The ghost was also responsible for the writing of hundreds of old signatures on a bedroom wall. Matthew obtained tape recordings of muffled voices, and dinner-time noises, complete with belches. The richness and complexity of this case make it one of the most fascinating we have ever come across, and the full details are given in Matthew Manning's book *The Strangers*.[7]

Another case which has certain parallels with Matthew Manning's experiences took place in Dodleston, Cheshire (England), beginning in November 1984. Following poltergeist activity in a cottage that was being renovated, the occupant Ken Webster received a message in the form of a poem on his computer screen. A few weeks later, another message in a Late Middle English dialect was found: 'Wot strange wordes thou speke, although I muste confess that I hath also bene ill-schooled . . . thou art a goodly man who hath fanciful woman who dwel in myne home . . . 'twas a greate cryme to hath bribed [stolen] myne house.' After this, Ken began to reply to the messages, and a lengthy dialogue was opened up with Tomas Harden, who claimed to be living in the mid-sixteenth century, in the Dodleston cottage. As well as using the computer, he also wrote messages on blank paper and chalked on the floor. This is the first such case of communication by computer that we have come across, but we suppose it was inevitable that those denizens of the spirit world (or in this case living in a parallel timeflow?) anxious to communicate would eventually make use of hi-tech. A hoax seems unlikely in this case – it would have involved a vast amount of effort –

and as in the Manning case the implications, if both cases are genuine, are quite incredible. Perhaps for this reason, scientists have so far preferred to ignore such cases.[8] Full details of the Tomas Harden case can be found in Ken Webster's book *The Vertical Plane*.

In another Finnish case which took place on 12 February 1977, a woman holding a reception at her flat in Helsinki had among her guests a woman she later discovered to have been a ghost. The guests were celebrating the award of a doctorate to one of their friends, and about 60 people were present. One woman the hostess did not recognize. She wore old-fashioned clothes and shoes, and had no coat, which was surprising in view of the very cold weather. She seemed to be accompanying one of the professors, and the hostess assumed she was his wife. Later, the woman came to the kitchen and asked if she could help. The hostess declined her offer, and never saw the strange woman again. She later talked about her to some of the guests, but no one else had seen her. It was three years before the mystery was solved. The hostess happened to see a magazine article about the painter Meri Genetz, who had died in 1943, thirty-four years before. She recognized her from her self-portrait and photographs. Meri Genetz had once lived in the flat where the reception was held. She had been interested in spiritualism and had held seances in the flat. The present occupant had already noticed presences there before she saw Meri Genetz, and she had on another occasion elsewhere seen the ghost of her dead dog, so she herself was obviously psychic.[9]

Perhaps the flat was haunted in a mild way by the ghost of Meri Genetz. It is often the case that ghostly voices are heard in houses that are thought of by their occupants as haunted, because of strange things happening there. A woman living in a farmhouse at Thatcham, Berkshire (England), heard a woman's voice say very loudly, in a local accent, 'Mind my pie!' She was in the pantry at the time, and was alone in the house. Several months later, her mother who was visiting saw the ghost of a woman pushing a pram and accompanied by two small children, but her daughter who had heard the ghostly voice could see no one. Her mother had not been told about the voice.[10] In a pub at Bourne, Lincolnshire (England), it was a baby's crying that was heard. The publican's wife had a new baby, but she was sure it was not her baby that she heard crying. However, for obvious reasons she told no one about the ghostly crying until her mother who also lived there remarked that she had heard another baby crying. They discovered that they did not necessarily hear it at the same time, and this, together with the fact that there were no houses adjoining the pub, helped to rule out a living baby as the source of the crying.[11]

Factory workers also seem prone to hearing ghostly voices. During 1973 night-shift workers at a factory in Soham, Cambridgeshire (England), heard mysterious voices and saw shadowy shapes, while in 1974 an early morning cleaner at a factory in Dunston, Tyne & Wear (England), heard 'an awful scream', toilets flushing by themselves, and locked doors banging. Workers claimed to have heard 'Maria' being shouted, and other strange sounds.[12] Some people have heard ghostly singing. In Monkstown, Dublin (Ireland), in 1977 numerous people heard a man's voice singing 'Danny Boy' and 'Old Man River' in the middle of the night, and at the time it was happening, they heard it every other night, sometimes fainter,

Talley Abbey, haunted by ghostly chanting monks.

sometimes louder. At the time of the full moon, it was louder and was heard nightly. One of the witnesses recorded it, and the singing was preceded by a faint voice crying for help. The local people believed the voice to be that of Sir Valentine Grace, who once owned the estate where the houses now stood. He had died 30 years before. They also felt the haunting had been triggered by the cutting down of a tree. At the time the estate was sold, an agreement was signed to the effect that none of the trees should be cut down.[13] Ewloe Castle in Clwyd (Wales) was also haunted by a singing ghost, according to a former custodian who heard the beautiful singing coming from a tower on three occasions, always during a severe thunderstorm. Someone suggested it was the whistling of telephone wires or electricity cables, but there are none at the castle.[14] Also in Wales, the sound of ghostly monks chanting has been heard in the atmospheric ruins of Talley Abbey in Dyfed.[15]

Ghostly voices have also been heard at haunted sites in America, and one such site which seems to be a favourite with vocal ghosts is Point Lookout State Park in St Mary's County, Maryland, and especially the lighthouse and old hotel. Gerald J. Sword, who lived in the lighthouse from January 1973, was to hear many strange

Point Lookout lighthouse.

noises in its twenty rooms – footsteps, crashes, furniture moving, doors opening and closing, and also voices. He would be woken at night by the chattering noise of numbers of people talking, and would get up to trace the sound outdoors to the yard gate, from where it would move to another location, and on to another as he followed the sound. Each time this happened, the route the voices took was the same. There was nothing to be seen. During the Civil War, a prison camp was located in the area, and Mr Sword wondered if the voices were those of sick and dying prisoners. He experienced many strange happenings in the lighthouse, including seeing a ghost, and when the ghostly activity was at its most lively he would leave a tape recorder switched on. One unusual recording obtained in this way was of a female voice saying, 'Let us not take any objections to what they are doing.' A male voice was also heard singing. Psychic researchers who came to investigate the hauntings also captured unusual voices on tape, some of them having an apparent connection with the location, e.g. 'Vaccine', spoken by a female voice in the former hospital area, 'Fire if they get too close to you', said by a male voice on an old road where prisoners used to march. 'Help me' and 'Bad shape' were also heard in the hospital area.[16]

Ghostly voices are not only heard in houses, indeed several of those we have already described were heard out of doors. In July 1924 a strange voice was being heard in a cemetery at Butler, New Jersey (USA). On 13 July an investigating committee of local citizens went into the cemetery late at night, to look into reports that 'for the past ten nights any one who ventured past the cemetery or into the adjoining wood immediately was greeted by a voice that seemed to come from tree tops, the ground or the air overhead.' The first witness was Police Patrolman Thomas Spring. 'He said when on the way home at midnight a scream rang out from the top of a tree, followed by a lingering moan that ended abruptly in a cackle of wild laughter. When he looked up the tree the voice seemed to drift high in the air and descend on another tree several yards beyond. Mr Spring was astonished, but made no investigation.' The voice was heard by many other people subsequently, and some heard threats or 'pleading cries for help'. Mr and Mrs Roland Marcus of Butler were pursued along several miles of road by the voice: 'It was said the voice on this occasion prefaced his moaning by a loud cry of "Help!" followed by a warning of "look out" and a burst of demonic laughter. The voice seemed at times to belong to an invisible man on the road behind them and at others to be suspended on a travelling wire overhead.'

The press report gives no information as to the outcome of the citizens' cemetery excursion, but it does give the local people's ideas as to the voice's possible origin. They clearly scorned a paranormal explanation, except for those who remembered the exploits of the legendary 'Jersey Devil' earlier in the century, and wondered if he had reappeared at Butler. The popular theory was that 'some scientist with advanced discoveries in radio had set up a laboratory near by and was broadcasting the moans, screams and yells with a device that could throw the sounds where he willed. To support this, those who claim to have heard the apparition's cries say the voice sounded hollow, inhuman, as if it came from a mechanical amplifier.'[17] We shall never know what the true explanation was – but if anyone living in or near Butler reads this, and can throw any light on the mystery, we would be delighted to hear from them.

Other inexplicable outdoor voices include the cries for help said to have come from a rock sticking out of Dongting Lake in the Hunan province of China. They may be the cries of drowning sailors which have somehow been recorded in the rock and are played back when the conditions are right.[18] Other cases which parallel this will be discussed later in this chapter. In South Africa a tree in Daveyton, Witwatersrand, was weeping between September and February annually, presumably a natural phenomenon, but there were also claims that it spoke. Unfortunately what it said was not quoted in the report.[19]

The voice which was heard in the cemetery at Arapaho, Oklahoma (USA), from 1972 onwards was immediately identified as that of the just-buried George Smith. He was calling 'Oh no! Oh, my God! Robina has not been saved!' He had never got over losing his nineteen-year-old daughter in a car accident in 1936, and the belief that she had died before achieving salvation haunted him for the rest of his life. He was buried next to his wife and daughter. Local people continued hearing his cries for years afterwards, including Cecil and Sharon Rutherford who were decorating a grave in 1980 and heard 'a deep groan; then a deep masculine voice – very sorrowful – bawled that Robina hadn't been saved.' They heard it again when about 50 feet from the Smith grave, but could see no sign of a prankster. The minister also heard the voice while holding another funeral service in the cemetery on 13 March 1979. Arthur Turcotte, a geologist who undertakes psychical research in his spare time, visited Arapaho in search of a natural explanation and heard for himself the voice as it clearly spoke its message.[20]

Some of the ghostly voices we have described have been heard in places where other strange happenings have occurred, though it is not inevitable that ghostly voices will be accompanied by apparitions or other paranormal phenomena. People suffering poltergeist outbreaks in their homes are likely to hear ghostly voices as just one more way in which the phenomenon manifests. The most outstanding case is strictly speaking ineligible for this book, as it took place in 1889, but it was so extraordinary that we cannot resist the temptation to give it a brief mention. The location was the farm of the Dagg family at Clarendon near Shawville, Quebec (Canada), where poltergeist phenomena broke out in the autumn of 1889. A ghost was seen, taking varied forms, and it also spoke. As well as the local people, Percy Woodcock of Ontario, a successful artist who was also interested in the paranormal and came to investigate the happenings, also heard it. In fact it spoke to him for several hours. The phenomenon seemed to centre on eleven-year-old Dinah, a girl who helped with the chores, but Woodcock was convinced that she, with her high-pitched voice, could not have faked the ghost's gruff voice. Many people gathered at the farm the next day, having heard that the ghost had promised to take its leave, and they all heard it, including a Baptist minister who attempted to exorcize it, whereupon it laughed and told him to stick to photography, his hobby. The voice showed intimate knowledge of everybody, and no one could see who might be faking it, or how. Finally it led the crowd in hours of hymn-singing before departing for good.[21]

We do not know of any more recent case in which a voice has spoken at such length. In most poltergeist outbreaks where voices are heard, they are only brief occurrences. In Santa Fe (Argentina) in March 1984 falls of rocks and stones on to a house were accompanied by locked doors opening, screams, and cries of 'Mother, mother'.[22] A family in Hackettstown, New Jersey (USA), experienced a great variety of poltergeist phenomena during 1973-6, including voices heard in the corner of a bedroom sounding like a group of men talking, though their words could not be discerned, and the sound of a female voice singing.[23] In a poltergeist outbreak at Leesburg, Florida (USA), which began early in 1978, unexplained voices were heard on the phone. A strange voice would interrupt a normal phone call, identify the person on the phone in the house and give other relevant information, sometimes using bad language as seems to be the habit of vocal poltergeists. Several months later, voices also started to come out of the house walls, and then directly from a ten-year-old girl. These events were accompanied by the usual sort of poltergeist behaviour as described in Chapter 1.[24] In a much older case, dating back to 1919, the person on whom a poltergeist in Suri, West Bengal (India), was focused, sixteen-year-old Sisir Kumar, also heard voices. His dead father spoke to him, giving him instructions to help combat the 'spirit' who 'is trying to harm you'. He also heard the female 'spirit', who claimed to have been Sisir's wife in an earlier life.[25] In Spain, a house in the village of Bélmez de la Moraleda, which has become famous for the mysterious faces which appeared on the floor, was also the location for other paranormal phenomena including mystery voices, some of which were recorded. In Spanish were the words 'spirits', 'poor Cico', 'drunkard', 'little grandchild' and 'what will become of your life?' as well as cries and groans.[26]

Sometimes the voices heard seem like recordings from the past, while others are speaking here and now. Examples of the latter given in this chapter include President Paasikivi, the Chester monk, the ghost in Matthew Manning's house, and the 'spirit' who spoke to the Dagg family. Another case which comes into this category concerns Blessed Clelia Barbieri, who founded a religious order, the Suore Minime dell'Addolorata, in the Bologna area of Italy, before she died aged 23 in 1870. On her deathbed she promised her six companions that she would never abandon them. Since her death, she has continued to join in the hymns and prayers of the Sisters in their services in Italy, Africa and India. In each of these countries the local language is used (Italian, Kiswahile, and Malayalam), and Blessed Clelia's voice speaks each with a perfect pronunciation. The voice has even been heard by young novices who had no knowledge of the existence of the phenomenon and who, in fact, were frightened by it until the older sisters explained the background and promise of Blessed Clelia. Her voice is still heard today, as one of the Sisters testifies:

This 'Voice' never speaks alone but joins in with the voices of the other nuns almost as if she were present as a member of the community. I can testify to this feeling of a presence because I am personally among those who hear her and can state that when unexpectedly this voice is united to ours, it is sometimes happy and sometimes sad, it moves from one section of the church to another and really gives the impression that Blessed Clelia is present among us. There is a feeling of a presence which sometimes is so strong in me that I can hardly find the strength to continue because I am so moved. Not all the sisters hear the 'Voice' and those who do are not the 'most saintly'. The 'Voice' has also been heard by non-religious persons who at times did not know of the existence of this phenomenon.[27]

It would be difficult to explain such multi-witness cases in terms of auditory hallucinations, and we would not presume to try to do so. Nor do we think that the voices sounding like recordings are hallucinatory. Indeed it seems far more likely that they *are* recordings, though not of the conventional type we are familiar with. Here are a few more of this kind of case, in addition to the ones already given (like 'Mind my pie!', the crying baby, the Monkstown singing, the Point Lookout voices, and the Arapaho cemetery voice).

A woman staying with friends in their Somerset (England) farmhouse in November 1986 heard voices at night which were preceded by a 'click exactly as of a radio turning on'. The voices sounded like a group of adults talking, but she could not make out the words. After two minutes, the click was repeated and the voices stopped. The same thing happened again the same night, exactly as on the first occasion, and then again later in the morning, when she was trying to catch up on her lost sleep. This time she could hear someone say: 'Don't tell Aunt Emmie [or similar name] on the way to the church.' She later learned that the lady of the house had also been hearing the same thing, about once a week. There seemed to be no obvious explanation for the voices. The house was not haunted, but a jug of milk had been seen to levitate, empty itself and smash, suggesting some source of psychokinetic energy in the house.[28]

The two women's experience sounds very like a replay of a real conversation that took place in the house at some unknown time in the past. It was also two women (though together this time) who heard another recording from the past, in France on 4 August 1951 while they were holidaying at Puys near Dieppe. They shared a bedroom in a house where German troops had lived during the war. They both awoke around 4 a.m. to hear a noise like a storm at sea. 'It sounded like a roar that ebbed and flowed, and we could distinctly hear the sounds of cries and shouts and gunfire.' They went out on to the balcony and heard the sounds coming from the beach: '. . . the separate sounds of cries, guns and dive bombing were very distinct.

Many times we heard the sound of a shell at the same moment. The roaring became very loud.' It suddenly stopped at 4.50, recommencing at 5.05. It continued as it began to get light, stopping and starting again a few times before dying away towards 7 a.m. as the witnesses fell asleep. Similar sounds had also been heard by one of the women a few days earlier, on 30 July, though 'fainter and not so intense', ending with 'a lot of men singing'. The witnesses' statements were written on 4 August while the events were fresh in their minds. What they heard corresponded closely to the sounds of a real battle which took place on 19 August 1942 during a World War II raid on Dieppe. However, since no one else heard the noises, researchers have wondered if perhaps the two ladies had only thought they were hearing the sounds of battle, when in fact they were hearing a combination of natural sea sounds, real aircraft flying along the London–Paris route, and a dredger working in the harbour at Dieppe 1½ miles away.[29] It is impossible now to determine whether this was what happened, or whether they somehow 'tuned in' to a playback of the 1942 Dieppe Raid.

Although it is not yet a scientifically respectable concept, the theory that sounds from the past have somehow been recorded and can be played back if one knows how to switch the recording on, seems to be validated by numerous cases, the most important of them being the events at the Prince of Wales inn at Kenfig in Mid-Glamorgan (Wales). Following the landlord's claim to have heard ghostly voices and organ music in the pub, electrical engineer John Marke and industrial chemist Allan Jenkins undertook a successful experiment in 1982 in which they were able to record the sounds by connecting electrodes to a stone wall in the pub at night after it had closed. They fed 20,000 volts of electricity through the electrodes and switched on tape recorders, and left them in a locked room for four hours overnight. When the tapes were played back they found they had recorded a variety of sounds including voices, organ music, and a clock ticking (there was no clock in the room where the recording was made). The words spoken by the voices could not be understood, and may be in an old form of Welsh. The theory is that the stones in the walls contain similar substances, like silica and ferric salts, to those in recording tapes, and that the stones somehow recorded sounds which can be played back when the electrons in the silica are triggered.[30] Very little research has been done into this amazing yet feasible possibility, so far as we know, but if the Kenfig recordings do prove to be genuine recordings of past

John Marke and Allan Jenkins preparing to record the ghostly sounds at Kenfig in 1982.

activity in the pub, then there is no reason why the same thing should not have happened elsewhere, nor why the experiment should not be repeated in other 'haunted' stone buildings, like churches. A number of cases of ghostly voices could be accounted for in this way, for example the voices coming from the Chinese rock, described earlier.

Tape recordings of voices have been made at other places where ghostly sounds have been heard, as for example at Point Lookout, Maryland (USA), as described earlier. One of the psychic researchers who recorded voices at Point Lookout was Mike Humphries, who is an anthropologist and director of St Clement's Island Museum. He has also recorded ghostly sounds and voices at numerous other locations around Maryland. He never hears the voices at the time of recording, only after the tapes are played back. He asks

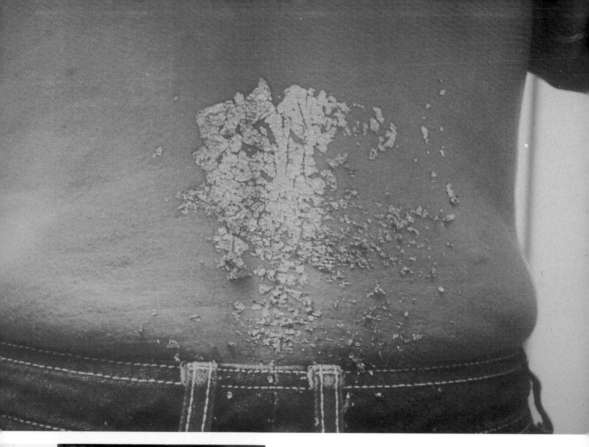

98 per cent copper, 2 per cent zinc foil materialized on psychic Katie's body, during 1986–7 in the Vero Beach, Florida, USA, research room of Dr B. E. Schwarz. Here the foil can be seen on Katie's back. This rare, as yet unexplained, phenomenon may be similar to stigmatization. Dr B. E. Schwarz/Fortean Picture Library

SORRAT psychokinesis experiments, Missouri, USA: three frames of a cine film showing the exit of an aluminium bar through the front glass of a sealed mini-lab, captured on film by the Cox–Calvin RSPK Automatic Filming Device. Dr J. T. Richards/Fortean Picture Library

A frame from a cine film of Bigfoot, taken on 20 October 1967 by Roger Patterson at Bluff Creek, northern California, USA. Photo Patterson/Gimlin, © 1968 Dahinden René Dahinden/Fortean Picture Library

Paul Freeman, who allegedly saw a Bigfoot and its footprints on 10 June 1982 in Umatilla National Forest, near Walla Walla, Washington State, USA. René Dahinden/Fortean Picture Library

Japanese news photographer Tsutomu Nakayama took this photograph of a possible UFO (at top, to right of tree) in Hawaii, 25 April 1974. He never saw the UFO, which did not appear in other photographs of the scene. Tsutomu Nakayama/Fortean Picture Library

Travis Walton, who was allegedly abducted by a UFO on 5 November 1975 while working in Apache–Sitgreaves National Forest, Arizona, USA, here photographed in 1985. Dennis Stacy/Fortean Picture Library

Damage caused by spontaneous combustion in the Suzano poltergeist case, Brazil, 1970. Guy Lyon Playfair/Fortean Picture Library

This photograph shows a possible ghost inside Lincoln Cathedral, England (in central doorway). Photographer T. C. Raybould says no one was around as he took the photograph, some time in 1971. T. C. Raybould/ Fortean Picture Library

Anthony Shiels took this photograph on 21 May 1977 from the ruins of Urquhart Castle beside Loch Ness, Scotland. The creature, which was only above water for a few seconds, cannot be identified and is therefore probably Nessie, the famous Loch Ness Monster. Anthony Shiels/Fortean Picture Library

A fanciful model of Ogopogo, the lake monster believed to live in Lake Okanagan, at Kelowna, British Columbia, Canada. René Dahinden/Fortean Picture Library

Bill Bartlett's painting of the 'Dover Demon', the strange creature he and others saw in April 1977 at Dover, Massachusetts, USA. Loren Coleman/Fortean Picture Library

Will Taintor and Abby Brabham at the place where they saw the 'Dover Demon' in April 1977 at Dover, Massachusetts, USA. Loren Coleman/Fortean Picture Library

The Blue Mountains of New South Wales, Australia, where yowies and thylacines have been seen. Lars Thomas/Fortean Picture Library

Fortean researcher Loren Coleman with a video crew interviewing witnesses who saw a red 'ape' in the Bridgewater area of Massachusetts, USA. Loren Coleman/Fortean Picture Library

A weeping statue of the Virgin Mary, in Brooklyn, New York, USA, in 1984. Fortean Picture Library

A bleeding statue of the Virgin Mary, in Porto San Stefano, Italy, 16 October 1972. Fortean Picture Library

questions of long-dead occupants of houses, and hopes to record their replies. Once a voice said: 'this side after death'. On another occasion, 'he could not determine the source of a mysterious clicking sound that kept appearing. Upon checking back with the owner of the allegedly haunted house, he was told that the previous owner, whose ghost was suspected of haunting the place, had suffered a stroke and before he died communicated through a series of clicks.'[31] Lori Mellott and Lynda Andrus are two Maryland women who tape-record ghostly voices, working through their organization Southern Maryland Psychic Investigations. Their prime concern is to 'aid spirits stuck between here and the hereafter. A lot of time they don't realize they're dead. Our goal every time is to make contact and explain to the spirits that this is the 20th century. Many times when you explain that to them, they're happy to move on.'[32] In late 1986 the group investigated an old house in Calvert County, Maryland, said to be haunted. They recorded several voices, male and female, saying things like 'I'm up here', 'I can help you', 'I like you', 'They're going to kill me', 'I killed for you', and 'It's near his vault.'[33]

When similar recordings are obtained unexpectedly, they are far more frightening than when obtained in experimental conditions. In August 1986 thirteen-year-old Dawn Dearden found a message on an old tape at her home in Kilnhurst, South Yorkshire (England). The tape should have had recordings of Dawn when she was seven, but at one point another child's voice was heard saying, 'Born again never to die. Born again into your family. I'm born again, born again.' No one recognized the voice. The tape had been locked away in a case for six years. Dawn's mother said: 'Dawn and Clare came running downstairs as though they had seen a ghost. They were extremely upset. We had been listening to the tape three weeks before and the message was certainly not there then. There is no way anyone could have got it on to the tape without first wiping off the recording of Dawn. The tape has never left this house and we don't have the sort of equipment needed to superimpose the voice over Dawn's.'[34]

Where are these recorded voices coming from? Are they consciously or unconsciously placed on the tapes by the people who 'discover' them? Are they somehow recorded by means of the psychic energy of the people involved? Are they recordings from the past? Or are they the voices of the dead? Throughout this century there have been experiments and claims that the dead sometimes speak to us. In the early years this communication allegedly happened through direct-voice mediums. A darkened seance room and the presence of an entranced medium were necessary before the dead could communicate, often through trumpets floating unsupported through the air, their location signalled by luminous marks; sometimes through ectoplasmic trumpets which were produced by the medium. Viewed objectively, this seems to be a most unlikely means of communication by the dead, and certainly plenty of fraudulent mediums have been exposed over the decades; but there remains a possibility that some mediums were indeed able to open a channel through which the dead could speak. A modern case which happened in Chicago, Illinois (USA), demonstrates that it would be unwise to deny this possibility. Teresita Basa was found stabbed to death in her apartment on 21 February 1977. During the following July, Remibios Chua, who had worked with the dead woman, three times became entranced and spoke in the voice of Teresita Basa. She told Dr Jose Chua that she had been murdered by Allan Showery, who also worked at the same hospital. Showery was arrested and charged after the police had checked the evidence supplied by Mrs Chua, and he confessed to the murder and to stealing Ms Basa's jewellery.[35] It is possible that Mrs Chua, consciously or unconsciously, picked up clues while working alongside Showery that led her to suspect him, and that she acted out the trances in order to avoid direct personal involvement in convicting him. It is also possible that the dead Teresita Basa spoke through her.

Another way of communicating directly with the dead may be through EVP – electronic voice phenomenon. This was discovered by Friedrich Jürgenson in Sweden in 1959, and independently in the States by Attila von Szalay, a psychic who researched into it with the parapsychologist Raymond Bayless over a number of years. Jürgenson's work in Europe was continued by Dr Konstantin Raudive, a Latvian living in Germany, until his death in 1974. He recorded many thousands of 'spirit voices', and others have continued to investigate this strange phenomenon. The voices are picked up on tape using various procedures too complex to describe here. They can even sometimes answer questions posed by the researchers. But whether they really are the voices of the dead is still uncertain. Other alternatives are that the researchers themselves unconsciously imprint the voices on to the tape by means of psychokinetic energy, or the voices are formed by the psychic rearrangement of the 'white noise' sound from the radio which the tape records. (It has been found that the voices come through better if 'white noise' is used as a background.) Whatever the explanation, this phenomenon is a very real and puzzling one, with the voices often sounding very clear, and delivering meaningful messages.[36]

Somewhat similar to EVP is a project called Spiricom. This was developed in the United States by William O'Neil, a psychic and electronics experimenter, supported by George W. Meek's Meta-Science Foundation of Franklin, North Carolina. In 1980, O'Neil established contact with Dr George Jefferies Mueller, who had died in 1966. He communicated for eighteen months, leaving his voice on tapes which have been analysed. One investigator believes the voices were faked using an artificial larynx, but this has not been proved conclusively.[37] The latest development in communication is via television, researchers in Luxemburg and West Germany claiming to have video-taped recognizable moving images of the dead from television screens.[38]

Mediums' trumpets, tape recorders, Spiricom device, television – the dead seem keen to communicate at all costs. Have they even tried to use the telephone? Incredible though it may seem, there are numerous accounts on record of people who have received phone calls from the dead. Sometimes the recipients knew the callers were dead, but not always. A recent case will give a flavour of the experience; many more cases, with discussion of the mechanics and implications of the phenomenon, can be found in D. Scott Rogo and Raymond Bayless's book *Phone Calls From the Dead*, which also discussed other electronic methods of contacting the dead. In October 1987, there was a disaster at Indianapolis, Indiana (USA), when a pilotless jet plane crashed into the Ramada Inn hotel and exploded. Christopher Evans, aged 21, was working at the hotel's front desk on that fateful day. A relative rang his parents to say that there had been an accident at the hotel, and they were preparing to go there to see if he was safe when the phone rang again. 'I said "Hello",' Mrs Evans recalled. 'He said, "Hello, Mom." I said, "Is that you, Chris?" He said, "Yes." I said, "Are you hurt?" He said, "No, Mom, I'm OK."' The Evanses were relieved, but went to the hotel to fetch Christopher. They learned that he was missing, and later he was confirmed dead. Officials speculated that Mrs Evans was talking to her son at the time the jet hit the hotel, and they were cut off because of the crash, but Mr and Mrs Evans were sure they received the phone call half an hour after the disaster.[39] A truly puzzling occurrence, but similar to those which many other people have also experienced.

12 *Hairy man-beasts around the world*

Most people in the Western world will have heard of the Yeti, or Abominable Snowman, and many people now also know that there is said to be a similar man-beast in North America, the Bigfoot or Sasquatch (dealt with in Chapter 2), but very few realize that there are similar reports from many other parts of the world. However, as we shall see, they are not all describing the same kind of creature. Some are more man-like, some more animal-like, and they also vary in height. In Central America, especially Belize and Guatemala, they are 'little people' known as Dwendis or Duende, 3½ to 4½ feet tall, with thick brown hair like a dog's all over their bodies and flat yellowish faces, who live in the forests.[1] In Ecuador and Colombia, they are known as Shiru, while in Guyana, Surinam and French Guiana they are the Didi. As recently as 1986 or 1987, an American looking for fungi in the forests of Guyana heard footsteps on the dry leaves, and looking up, saw a person who 'had fur from his head down to his toes'. This 5-foot apeman 'moved and sounded like a human, yet it wasn't'. It moved slowly past, making an occasional 'hoo' noise, and had obviously not noticed the mycologist lurking close by.[2]

Further south, in Brazil, the Mapinguary is a much larger and more fearsome creature. It lives mostly in the provinces of Amazonas, Mato Grosso and Goyaz, as well as Guaporé and Acre on the Bolivian frontier, and cattle found dead with their tongues pulled out are believed to be its victims. A Brazilian who was a member of a ten-man expedition in 1930 saw what he believed to be a Mapinguary. They were in the jungle near the Urubú watershed when he became separated from the others. Night was approaching, so he climbed into a large tree. Suddenly he heard a loud cry, somehow like a man's, which was coming closer. He loaded his gun as he heard loud footsteps, then saw in the clearing 40 yards away a dark, man-sized silhouette. When it roared again, the watcher fired at it, whereupon it leapt for cover and growled threateningly. The gunman fired again, and the creature fled into the forest, still growling. At dawn he found blood among the broken bushes, and smelled a 'sour penetrating smell' which reminds us that some Bigfoot witnesses also report a bad smell.[3]

The explorer Lieutenant-Colonel P. H. Fawcett came across 'savages', which were fur-covered yet man-like for they were using bows and arrows. This was in the Cordilheira dos Parecis in Brazil, near the border with Bolivia, some time in 1914. The 'savages' lived in a village of primitive shelters in the forest, and when Fawcett and his companions came across it, they saw 'great ape-like brutes who looked as if they had scarcely evolved beyond the level of beasts', making arrows or just idling. Fawcett describes what happened next.

I whistled, and an enormous creature, hairy as a dog, leapt to his feet in the nearest shelter, fitted an arrow to his bow in a flash, and came up dancing from one leg to the other till he was only four yards away. Emitting grunts that sounded like 'Eugh! Eugh! Eugh!' he remained there dancing, and suddenly the whole forest around us was alive with these hideous ape-men, all grunting 'Eugh! Eugh! Eugh!' and dancing from leg to leg in the same way as they strung arrows to their bows. It looked like a very delicate situation for us, and I wondered if it was the end. I made friendly overtures in Maxubi, but they paid no attention. It was as though human speech were beyond their powers of comprehension.

Fawcett avoided disaster by firing into the ground, then into the trees, while the 'savages' shot their arrows at the intruders, who finally retreated. The local people knew of these 'savages' and called them Maricoxis.[4]

Moving south again to Argentina, we find stories of the Ucumar and Ucu, hair-covered creatures seen most often around the foot of Umahuaca and throughout the state of Salta.[5] In southern Argentina, members of the South Patagonian Ice-cap Expedition found strange footprints in the snow in the Andes in 1976. They were made by a creature walking on two legs, and measured about 6 inches long by 4 or 5 inches wide.[6]

Across the South Atlantic to the African continent, where we note Ivan Sanderson's comment that 'Relics of goodness knows how many races could still be lingering on in the montane forests of

Africa.'[7] This is confirmed by research carried out in Kenya by Jacqueline Roumeguère-Eberhardt, of the Centre National de la Recherche Scientifique in Paris, who in 1978 announced at a press conference in Nairobi that she had over ten years collected reports of unidentified forest-dwelling hominoids, which she referred to as 'X'. She had categorized five types of 'X', some using clubs to kill prey, others eating tubers, berries and mushrooms, and another carrying bow and arrows. A bow and arrows seized from an 'X-5' was shown to the press. The local forest tribes had not seen similar weapons before; and they also said that the 'X-5' did not respond to Masai, Swahili and other languages shouted at him. As well as the bow and arrows, this hominoid was also carrying leather bags for storing nettles and honey. One witness had been held captive by an 'X' for more than an hour. He said, 'His eyes, his nose, his mouth were those of a man, and his face was not covered with hair, but his forehead was very low, rather like that of a baboon.' Another witness saw a hominoid with long hair almost to his heels: 'He had so many stones and twigs in his hair that, if he had not moved, I would have taken him for a rock.' Mme Roumeguère-Eberhardt had collected reports of 33 encounters in eleven forests, and planned an expedition to try to learn more about the forest hominoids, whom she thought might be a link between modern man and fossil men.[8]

The problem with many of Africa's mystery hominoids is that they might in fact be undiscovered or misidentified apes. Anyone interested in the full story should read Bernard Heuvelmans's *Les Bêtes Humaines d'Afrique*, unfortunately not yet translated into English.[9] Apart from reports of ape-like creatures, there are also some fairly reliable reports of hair-covered pygmies. In the west these are known in the Ivory Coast, where the Séhité are dwarfs with reddish fur, living in the forests. In 1947, a young African saw one close to the Institute of Education and Research at Adiopodoumé, only twelve miles from Abidjan. There was thick forest around the Institute, but this was regularly traversed by natives, who knew of no pygmies living there, so the report was unexpected. But the witness was certain of what he saw, and it fitted in with other reports from elsewhere in the region. The sighting was brief – a little man with long reddish fur and long hair on his head appeared among the roots of a silk-cotton tree, and on noticing he was not alone, he fled. Further east, hairy pygmies are also believed to live in Tanzania, where the little men 4 feet tall are known as Agogwe.[10] All these pygmies may be ancestors of the modern pygmies, or they may be the descendants of Australopithecines, who lived in southern Africa around 500,000 years ago and whose fossil remains have been found.

There are many different kinds of hairy hominoids believed to be still living in Asia, the best known of which is of course the Yeti, whose territory is the Himalayan mountain range of India, Nepal and Tibet. Most mountaineering expeditions these days seem to come back with reports of having found strange footprints in the snow, though the creatures that made them are rarely seen. (Brief details of some of these reports are given in the Gazetteer.) Don Whillans saw what may have been a Yeti when he was on Annapurna in June 1970. He found footprints in the snow, and then the same night he looked out of his tent, because he felt the creature might still be around nearby. In the moonlight, which was bright enough to read by, he saw a movement. A creature was bounding along towards a snow-covered clump of trees, where it pulled at some of the branches. He watched for twenty minutes, and could make out a black ape-like shape through binoculars. 'Then, quite suddenly, it was almost as if it realized it was being watched, it shot across the whole slope of the mountain.'[11]

Visitors to the Himalayas rarely get closer than this to a Yeti. It is the local people whose encounters are more likely to be eyeball to eyeball, as happened in July 1974 to a Sherpa girl tending yaks near Pheriche in Nepal. While sitting near a stream, she heard a noise and turned to see a Yeti with black and red-brown hair, large eyes and prominent cheekbones. It grabbed her and carried her for a short distance, dropping her as she screamed and struggled. It then killed two yaks, one by hitting it, the other by breaking its neck.[12] This Yeti's abortive attempt to kidnap a young girl is interesting, because in Canada there have been a few similar reports of people being kidnapped, and also from China, where peasants have claimed they were raped by hairy wild women. Another close encounter between 'Yeti' and native took place in late January 1987, when a seventeen-year-old youth living in a village in northern Kashmir (India) stepped outside at 9.30 p.m. carrying his fire-pot (a clay pot containing embers) and was attacked by a 4-foot hairy creature standing on two legs. He hit it with the fire-pot, it squealed and ran away. Two villagers who heard the squeal and looked out, saw the creature running away on two legs, and jumping a ditch in a man-like way. Eighteen fine red hairs found attaching to the fire-pot were sent for analysis. Ten days earlier, a similar creature had woken villagers with high-pitched squeals in the mountains 100 miles to the west.[13]

The hair which was analysed was found to come from a Himalayan brown bear.[14]

Sceptics have come up with natural explanations for the many 'Yeti' footprints found in the snow: animal tracks which have become distorted due to melting of the snow, making them appear larger; or the tracks of holy men who sometimes go barefoot. It is certain that the Yeti's existence will not be proved on the basis of footprints alone, and it is the sightings of the creatures themselves which will provide information as to the nature of the creature, together with the few physical samples that are sometimes obtained, like hairs and faeces. The so-called Yeti scalps held in monasteries are probably made of goatskin, though they are not deliberate hoaxes in that to the monks they are ancient relics which were made as wigs to be worn by dancers representing the Yeti in ritual dances.[15]

A complicating factor in any analysis of the Yeti reports is that the native peoples believe there are several different types of Yeti, including the small *yeh-teh*, the larger *meh-teh*, and the giant *dzu-teh*. The small and medium specimens may be monkeys or apes. There are several species of langur monkeys living in the Himalayas which could be mistaken for the Yeti.[16] Bigger Yetis might be a kind of orang-utan, living on the ground rather than in trees. They can stand erect, and in the snowy mountainous habitat may have adapted to walking upright too. There have been reports of Yetis dropping down on to all fours when in a hurry. The very big Yetis may be a form of Gigantopithecus, the giant primate identified from fossils found in China, and very similar to the North American Bigfoot and Sasquatch. Alternatively they might simply be misidentified bears, as in the Kashmir incident of 1987. The red bear is a local Tibetan version of the European brown bear, standing 6½ or more feet tall and leaving large man-like footprints. They are also known to live at high altitudes in the cold months when they are not feeding and are sluggish.[17] However, people who have seen Yetis close to are sure they are not bears, or indeed any other known local animal. Until close-up photographs, or even better, corpses, are obtained, the Yeti will remain the mysterious giant of the snows.[18]

To the north and west of the Himalayas is the vast Union of Soviet Socialist Republics, where there are many sparsely populated regions, an ideal habitat for undiscovered creatures. For obvious reasons, the man-beasts we are hunting in this chapter have survived only in such uninhabited areas of the world: the man-beasts of Europe, for example, now survive only in legend. As man 'tames' more and more of the wilderness areas of the world, so the survival of such creatures becomes ever more precarious. It is likely that some of these magnificent prehistoric survivals will be extinct by the end of the century. In the USSR they may be safe for a little longer, since their territories are often inhospitable to man, but even so, re-searchers believe that the populations are under threat. The areas most actively researched in recent years are the Caucasus (including Daghestan), the Pamirs (including Tadzhikistan), the Urals and Tien Shan mountains. The other main area is in the cold northern Siberian region, from where some reports have come, and parts of Mongolia (Inner Mongolia is an Autonomous Region of China, Mongolia is a People's Republic). We will begin our survey of this vast area in the north, for less is known about the Siberian creature, known as the Chuchunaa, which has been seen mainly in the Yakutia area based on Verkhoyansk and in the Chukot Peninsula to the east. They have also been seen in the region of the Ob River, 3000 miles to the west. In Yakutia, 55-year-old Tatyana Ilinicha Zakharova told how she saw a Chuchunaa in the 1920s while berry-picking.

He was also picking berries and stuffing them into his mouth with both hands. When he saw us, he stood up to his full height. He was very tall and lean, more than two metres [7 feet] high, they say. He was dressed in deerskin and barefoot. He had very long arms and on the head, he had shaggy hair. He had a very large face like that of a man but much darker. His forehead was small and protruded over his eyes like the peak of a cap. His chin was large and wide, much larger than that of a man and he was very similar to a human being except he was much taller. After a second, he ran away. He ran very quickly, leaping high after every third step.[19]

This is a more human-like type of Chuchunaa, wearing rudimentary clothes, but the 'wilder' type are also reported in Siberia. Two hair-covered, 6-foot man-beasts with glowing dark-red eyes were seen near the Ob River in 1960 or 1961 by a man whose dog bolted for the village after the creatures had gone. These wore no clothes, and had projecting faces, long arms, and an unusual way of walking, turning their legs out.[20]

Further west there have been reports from the Urals, and from areas even further west also. In August 1986, Nikolai Avdeyev led an expedition to the Timansky Ridge in the Komi republic, and collected eyewitness reports from the local people who were familiar

Nikolai Avdeyev.

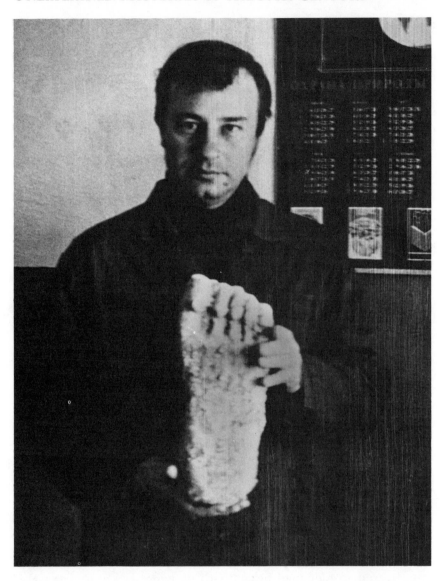

with the Yag-mort, as they call the creature. Sightings were happening regularly, including one in the month of his visit, when a man haymaking was frightened by a Yag-mort which opened the door of a hut where the man was spending the night with his colleagues. It stood in the doorway for a minute, then turned and went away. It was covered with light grey hair and had glowing eyes. The dogs had been barking when it arrived, but had then disappeared, and did not reappear until the next day. In September 1986, another witness saw a Yag-mort family of father, mother and child. The male was over 6 feet tall, the female was smaller, with long hanging breasts. Avdeyev flew back to the area on receiving this report, to visit for himself the cave near Kedva where they were seen. He found some tracks in the sandy soil close by, but was sent packing by some local person who was firing his gun and shouting at him to leave. He was later told that the locals believed the Yag-morts should be left alone, for to interfere with them would bring misfortune to the Komi people.[21]

Also in Western Siberia, in a settlement in the Tyumen Region by a tributary of the River Ob, Maya Bykova, a member of the recently formed Association of Cryptozoologists in Moscow, saw a hairy man-beast in August 1987. She had travelled to the remote hunting cabin in a cedar forest after being told that a humanoid creature was being seen there. The witnesses called him Mecheny and he had red-brown hair all over his body except for his left forearm where the hair was white. She first saw him at dawn, as he stood 15 feet away from the cabin leaning against a dead tree. She could see his white forearm and glowing red eyes. He was about 6 feet tall, and she described him as very similar to the creature caught on film by Roger Patterson in the USA (see photograph in Chapter 2). After only a minute or so, a dog with the party came running round the cabin barking, and Mecheny disappeared into the forest.[22]

Further south, one of the most active areas for man-beast sightings has been the Caucasus Mountains, between the Black and Caspian Seas. Over a period of more than 30 years, Dr Zh. I. Kofman has been actively researching in the Caucasus, and she has obtained many valuable eyewitness reports.[23] In this area the creature is called the Kaptar, or Almasty, is well known to hunters and others who spend time in the mountains, and is not considered dangerous. It is around 5 feet tall, covered with brown hair, walks upright and has a protruding face. They live in the dense forests on the mountains and valley slopes, but occasionally come into the villages to steal food from crop fields, just as has been reported of the Bigfoot in North America. They are even said to barter with traders sometimes, exchanging vegetables for trinkets. Two sightings in 1979 took place at the Chegem River, the witnesses being two men cutting wood. On the second occasion, one creature was seen lying in the grass from a distance of 30 feet, and his back except for his buttocks was covered with hair. He sat up and ran away when approached. In the earlier sighting that year, the witnesses said that the creature had an overhanging forehead, slant eyes, and an aquiline nose, and Dr Myra Shackley remarks that this sounds very Neanderthaloid.[24] Some researchers believe that a population of Neanderthalers has survived in Asia, and that these sightings of 'man-beasts' are the evidence supporting their beliefs. Dr Shackley discusses this possibility in her book *Wildmen*. Unfortunately no corpse is available for study, so the theory cannot be either proved or disproved. A possible Kaptar was shot and killed in 1941, but the whereabouts of the corpse is not now known. It happened near Buinaksk (Daghestan), where an infantry battalion was stationed. A man was brought in as a suspected spy, and Lieutenant-Colonel V. S. Karapetyan examined him in the shed where he was kept, because he sweated profusely in a warm room. Karapetyan remembered that the creature was covered with dark brown shaggy hair 1 inch long, with the palms and soles free of hair.

Lieutenant-Colonel V. S. Karapetyan (second from left) photographed in 1972 with Russian hominoid researchers Dmitri Bayanov (left) and Dr Zh. I. Kofman (right). René Dahinden, Canadian Bigfoot investigator, is the fourth member.

He was bearlike in some respects but definitely not apelike. I noticed that his hands were very big and his fingers unusually strong. At first his face confused me because of the absence of beard or moustache. His nose was not broad, squashed-looking, or protruding; in fact, it also looked human. The face was oval-shaped, the hair on the head wavy but not long. His face was covered with a light fluff – like that of a calf. His genitals appeared human. His eyes focused on something that wasn't there; his look was dull and vacant. He blinked occasionally.[25]

Russian man-beast hunter Igor Bourtsev holds a cast of a footprint 13½ inches long found in the Gissar Range of the Pamirs on 21 August 1979.

Karapetyan used tweezers to pull hairs from the creature's body. He flinched but was silent. Karapetyan realized it was his own skin and not an animal pelt worn for disguise. He told the partisans who had captured the creature that he was probably a wildman, and that theirs was the decision as to what to do with him. He later believed the wildman had escaped, but learned that in fact he had been executed by firing squad.[26]

Further east, still inside the USSR but close to the borders with China and Afghanistan, lies the Pamir mountain range, a remote, inhospitable area of glaciers, ice-fields, mountain peaks, and some alpine meadowland. In recent years amateur expeditions have gone regularly into the lower-level Gissar range of the Pamirs, and have found considerable evidence for the survival there of large man-beasts, with many footprints found, reports of eyewitness sightings, and even sightings by expedition members. One was in August 1980, by Nina Grinyeva, who was with Igor Tatsl's expedition on the Siama River, and another was in September 1980, by Lake Pairon. Two female members of the Tatsl party saw a female hominoid from 30 feet away. They were spending the night out of doors under a tree on the lake shore, and the creature sat on a boulder watching them and making munching sounds for a long time.[27]

Earlier this century, Major-General Topilski got a very close look at one of these creatures, which had been shot. In 1925 he and his men were pursuing retreating soldiers in the Pamirs. The fugitives were trapped in a cave in the glaciers, and some of them came out as snow and ice fell from a cliff, burying the cave entrance. They had a strange story to tell. Inside the cave they had encountered some 'hairy man-like creatures' which had attacked them with sticks. One creature had been shot, and now lay buried under the snow. General Topilski's men cleared away the snow and found the body. At first he thought it was an ape, but it looked very man-like. The creature was 5½ feet tall, covered with brownish hair on the chest and greyish hair on the belly. The hair was thick, though there was little of it on the buttocks, and the knees, soles and palms were hairless. The creature had no beard or moustache, but there was thick matted hair on the back of its head. Its eyes were dark, and its teeth were large, even and shaped like a human's. The lower jaw was massive and the jawbones protruded. The brows were also powerful, but the nose was flat. The men buried the creature under a cairn of stones, being unable to take the body with them for further examination.[28] Only a few years later, in 1934, a geologist called B. M. Zdorick came across a sleeping Dev (as the locals called the creatures when he told them what he had seen) lying on a mound of newly turned earth. The description is very similar to that of the creature shot by the fugitives.[29]

Further north, approaching Mongolia, are the Tien Shan mountains, which are half in the USSR and half in China. The Kirghiz range is also in this area, in Kazakhstan, and in both these mountainous regions man-beasts have been seen. In July 1972, a teacher and two pupils who were walking in the Kirghiz mountains were followed for over a week by what appeared to be 'an old male hominoid who made sounds as if he was asthmatic'. He would try to steal food from their tents at night by reaching in a hairy arm. One night he stepped out of the shadows towards their fire, and was as close as 12 feet away, but the teacher panicked and they never saw the hominoid again.[30]

Wildman research in the USSR has been well served by a few dedicated researchers who have devoted decades of work to the subject, like Professor Boris Porshnev and Dr Kofman, though there are also others. Over the 1970s and 1980s, people like Igor Tatsl, Dmitri Bayanov and Igor Bourtsev have led amateur expeditions into the mountains in search of evidence, and early in 1988 it was announced that an Association of Cryptozoologists had been formed in Moscow and that scientists from this society would follow up wildman reports. Perhaps it will be in the USSR rather than in the USA that the existence of hairy hominoids will first be officially recognized.

Moving north and east, we pass over the border into China, through Dzungaria where man-beasts have been seen, and into Mongolia, from where many reports have come, thanks to dedicated researchers like Dr Rinchen who studied the Almas for 50 years until his death in 1977. Earlier this century they were widely reported in the Gobi desert and Altai mountains, but recent reports suggest that sightings are now restricted to the provinces of Hovd and Bayanolgy in the west, with obvious conclusions about their dwindling numbers being unavoidable.[31]

Only in the last ten years have we in the West learned that there have for many years been persistent rumours of 'wildmen' in China. The tales go right back to ancient literary works with references to big, hairy, man-like creatures living in the forests of central China, especially the Shennongjia mountains in Hubei province, from where many of the modern reports come. Other provinces from which reports have come in recent years are Zhejiang, Hunan,

Zhou Guoxing in Shennongjia, 1977.

Gong Yulan, the woman by the tree, saw a wildman at this spot in Shennongjia forestry region on 19 June 1976.

Shaanxi, Sichuan, Fujian, Anhui and Yunan. Large research projects were undertaken in 1961, 1977 and 1980, the 1977 expedition lasting nearly a year and involving 110 people. So far, no conclusive proof of the existence of wildmen has been obtained. The 1980 expedition to Jiulong mountain in Zhejiang province located the hands and feet of a 'wildman' – but these turned out to have come from a stump-tailed macaque, a kind of monkey. A 'wildman' was captured in Hunan province in 1984, but again this was identified as a stump-tailed macaque. Does this mean that all Chinese wildmen are misidentified macaques? Zhou Guoxing thinks not. He is the vice-director of Beijing Natural History Museum and an expert on Chinese wildmen. His research indicates that there are two kinds, a small one about 3 feet tall, and another between 6 and 7½ feet tall. The smaller specimens are almost certainly stump-tailed macaques, he believes, and there are also numerous misidentifications of bears to confuse the issue. But he also believes that the larger ones are descendants of Gigantopithecus, such as we have already encountered elsewhere.[32]

208

A biologist saw a dead wildman in the Ganzhou area in 1940. It was a big-breasted female, about 6 feet tall and covered in greyish-brown hair. In 1950, a geologist saw a mother and son in a mountain forest in Shaanxi.[33] In June 1977 commune team leader Pang Gensheng had an hour-long very close encounter with a 7-foot 'hairy man' which he met in the forest when he was cutting wood in Dadi Gully, in Zhouzhi county of Shaanxi province. As it approached, the frightened witness backed up until he came to a cliff and could retreat no further. The wildman was as close as 5 feet away, and they both stood motionless for over an hour. Finally, Pang Gensheng groped for a stone and threw it at the wildman, striking him in the chest. He howled and rubbed at the spot, then wandered away mumbling, but made no effort to retaliate against his attacker. The latter had plenty of time to memorize the wildman's physical appearance, and gave this description:

> He was about seven feet tall with shoulders wider than a man's, a sloping forehead, deep-set eyes, and bulbous nose with slightly upturned nostrils. He had sunken cheeks, ears like a man's but bigger, and round eyes also bigger than a man's. His jaw jutted out and he had protruding lips. His front teeth were as broad as a horse's. His eyes were black. His hair was dark brown and more than a foot long, and hung loosely over his shoulders. His whole face, except for the nose and ears, was covered with short hairs. His arms hung down to below his knees . . . the hair on his body was short. He had thick thighs . . . he walked upright with his legs apart.[34]

Only a few weeks later, Yang Wanchun also saw a tall 'hairy-man' at the same place, and said, 'While we were facing each other, the hairy-man uttered 11 or 12 different sounds, which seemed to imitate a sparrow chirping, dog barking, pony neighing, leopard growling, and an infant crying. He changed his call incessantly for over one hour.' Again he saw the creature clearly, and said it was 'definitely not a black bear, golden monkey, *zongyang* nor giant panda!'[35]

There are many more sighting reports, and it seems feasible that if Gigantopithecus survived anywhere, it was in the mountains of China, the place where he is known to have lived in the middle and later Pleistocene periods, roughly 500,000 years ago. The environment has remained stable, and there are still primeval forests, where both flora and fauna from the time of the Gigantopithecus have survived, for example the Malaysian tapir and orang-utan, as well as the giant panda. The Gigantopithecus may have spread outwards from this area to the Himalayas where it became the larger species of Yeti, and northwards and east across the Bering Isthmus into the North American continent, where it became the Bigfoot or Sasquatch.[36]

Further east and south, there are also reports of man-beasts from Japan, and in countries south of China as far down as Malaysia and Indonesia. It is difficult to know what to make of the Japanese reports. There is still plenty of remote habitat, for example in the Mount Hiba area where the 'Hiba-gon monster' was being reported in the early 1970s. Farmers working in the foothills would claim to see a 5-foot hairy creature, but whether it really was a Bigfoot-type creature or simply some kind of large monkey is unclear. To the south of China, hairy wildmen have been reported from Burma, Thailand, Laos, Cambodia, Vietnam and down into peninsular Malaysia. The deep-frozen hominoid exhibited in the USA in the 1960s was said to have been shot in Vietnam. Just exactly what these wildmen are, whether Gigantopithecus or 'merely' unknown giant apes, remains to be discovered. Across the sea in the Indonesian islands of Sumatra and Borneo, and possibly on smaller islands too, there would appear to be small hairy hominoids still surviving, known as Sedapa or Orang pendek in Sumatra, and Batūtūt in Borneo. The Malayan bear may often have been misidentified as an Orang pendek,[37] but sometimes a witness got a close look at the creature and was unable to identify it, except for noting its human-like characteristics. In 1923 a Dutch settler on Sumatra named Van Herwaarden saw a Sedapa or Orang pendek in the jungle. It was a 5-foot female, and it retreated into a tree, where he got a good look at it. In his description are several references to its human-like features – 'The eyes were frankly moving . . . like human eyes . . .' 'I was able to see its right ear which was exactly like a little human ear . . .' 'There was nothing repulsive or ugly about its face, nor was it at all ape-like . . .' When it escaped from the tree and ran for cover, Van Herwaarden took up his gun. 'Many people may think me childish if I say that when I saw its flying hair in the sights I did not pull the trigger. I suddenly felt that I was going to commit murder. I lifted my gun to my shoulder again, but once more my courage failed me.' Dr Heuvelmans notes that the only non-human features were the 'relatively long canine teeth and extremely long arms'.[38] Modern reports from this part of the world are rare, and a cryptozoological expedition is needed to ascertain whether the creatures are still being seen and, if so, what exactly they are.

East of the Indonesian islands are yet more islands, a whole belt of them across to the north of the Australian mainland, and even in such relatively small land areas there are rumours of hairy men: on Malaita and Guadalcanal in the Solomon Islands, for instance, on some of the New Hebrides islands, and in Fiji.[39] New Zealand too has its Moehau Monster or Coromandel Man, said to live in the Coromandel peninsula east of Auckland on North Island. But in Australasia the most frequent reports of man-beasts in recent years have come from Australia. Most zoologists would pooh-pooh any suggestion that hairy man-beasts 7 feet tall are living on that continent, and would explain away any sightings as being the result of over-active imaginations, reading too much about the Yeti and Bigfoot, or simply misidentifying native species like the wombat (a burrowing marsupial up to 4 feet in length, which lives in the eastern mountains and looks vaguely badger-like; it could only be called a hairy man-beast by someone who caught a brief glimpse of one among the trees on a dark day – unless of course there are also 7-foot wombats walking about on their hind legs). There are not supposed to be any apes in Australia, so these cannot be used to explain away sightings. However, there is a definite tradition of large hairy bipedal hominoids going back at least to the mid-nineteenth century, and the creature, whatever it is, was known to the Aboriginals. Today it is called the 'Yowie', though the origins of this name are obscure. The majority of sightings this century have been in New South Wales and Queensland, and the majority of reports were made in the 1970s. One very interesting early report came from the Bombala/Bemboka area of New South Wales, where on 12 October 1912 a man riding along a track saw a strange creature on all fours drinking from a creek. It was covered with grey hair, and witness George Summerell's first thought was: 'What an immense kangaroo'.

> But, on hearing the horse's feet on the track, it rose to its full height, of about 7 feet, and looked quietly at the horseman. Then stooping down again, it finished its drink, and then, picking up a stick that lay by it, walked steadily away up the slope to the right or eastern side of the road, and disappeared among the rocks and timber 150 yards away.

Summerell described the face as being like that of an ape or man, minus forehead and chin, with a great trunk all one size from shoulder to hips, and with arms that nearly reached to its ankles.

. . . about a score of footprints attested the truth of Summerell's account, the handprints where the animal had stooped at the edge of the water being especially plain. These handprints differed from a large human hand chiefly in having the little fingers set much like the thumbs . . .

. . . A striking peculiarity was revealed, however, in the footprints; these, resembling an enormously long and ugly human foot in the heel, instep, and ball, had only four toes – long (nearly 5 inches), cylindrical, and showing evidence of extreme flexibility. Even in the prints which had sunk deepest into the mud there was no trace of the 'thumb' of the characteristic ape's 'foot'.

Beside perhaps a score of new prints, there were old ones discernible, showing that the animal had crossed the creek at least a fortnight previously.[40]

Sixty-five years later, and only 22 miles away, greengrocer Kos Guines shot at a Yowie near Pambula (New South Wales) while out with his son hunting rabbits. Hearing a crashing sound in the bracken beyond him, 'I swung around, anticipating a kangaroo, and saw a large hairy creature 30 metres away.' He had never heard of the Yowie. 'All I could think of was: my God – a gorilla.' He shot at the creature's back. 'There's no way I could have missed at that range; the gun was loaded with rabbit shot, and if the gorilla felt any discomfort he didn't show it. He didn't even flinch or make a noise, but just charged away through the bracken.' The animal moved on two legs and was ape-like, like a small man only broader. 'My clearest mental picture was of the back of its hair-covered dome-shaped head, which sat right down on its shoulders.'[41]

These incidents took place in the extreme south-east of the state, near the Victoria border. Many sightings have been made in the Blue Mountains further north, around Sydney, and also in the far north-east of New South Wales and into southern Queensland, in the Gold Coast area. Around Springbrook in the Gold Coast a National Parks worker had a close sighting of a 7-foot Yowie early in 1978. The man was cutting timber when he heard a grunting noise. Thinking a pig was loose, he went into the forest to look for it.

Then something made me look up and there, about 12 feet in front of me, was this big black hairy man-thing. It looked more like a gorilla than anything. It had huge hands and one of them was wrapped around a sapling. It had a flat, black shiny face, with two big yellow eyes and a hole for a mouth. It just stared at me and I stared back. I was so numb I couldn't even raise the axe I had in my hand. We seemed to stand there staring at each other for about 10 minutes before it suddenly gave off a foul smell that made me vomit – then it just made off sideways and disappeared.[42]

Three years later, on 20 May 1981, three boys aged eleven, thirteen and fourteen who were bush-walking in isolated hill country west of Dunoon saw a hairy man-like creature cross the path 20–25 feet ahead of them. Soon afterwards a second creature appeared, and the boys saw them for long enough to describe them as about 5 feet tall, with long brownish hair all over their bodies. They appeared to have no necks, but rounded heads which 'seemed to just sit on their shoulders'. They were not wild pigs, nor wallabies, nor gorillas. The eldest boy commented: 'Gorillas are black and bow-legged. These had straight legs and were brown, more human-like.'[43]

There have been many (thousands?) other sightings of the Yowie, too many for them all to be dismissed as misidentification or imagination or hoax. It seems likely that some kind of unknown creature is sharing at least the eastern part of the country with the Aboriginal natives and the white settlers. But is it some kind of animal – a species of ape, perhaps, which has somehow evaded scientific discovery – or a human? There is ample evidence that early man lived in Australia, and it is now known that men with *Homo erectus* features survived until 10,000 years ago. Has he in fact survived much longer, to the present day? The *Homo erectus* finds were at Kow Swamp in Victoria, not a very great distance really from the location of the first of our Yowie reports.[44] Recently (in 1987) stone tools 43,000–47,000 years old have been found along the Nepean River near Sydney (New South Wales), another Yowie stronghold. These tools pre-date by 5000 years the previous earliest occupation site known in Australia.[45] There may at one time have been a land bridge linking northern Australia with New Guinea, and early man may have migrated southwards, just as he may also have moved into the North American continent across the Bering land bridge.

If we can accept the possibility that the Bigfoot reports of North America are based on sightings of some genuine unknown hairy hominoid, there is no reason why we should not also accept the Australian reports as well as those from China, the USSR, and all the other countries covered in this chapter. The most depressing part of this saga is the scant attention paid to the reports by most scientists. We cannot see how they can fail to be excited, or at least intrigued, by the reports, but it is left to cryptozoologists with usually minimal resources to endeavour to find out the truth before it is too late. And soon it may be too late, for all the evidence indicates that the hominoids are barely surviving in many areas and will soon be irrevocably extinct.

13 Unexpected objects falling from the sky

The old lady who rang the weather bureau to ask if the end of the world had come when beans started to fall from the sky in St Louis, Missouri (USA), in September 1945[1] can perhaps be forgiven her over-reaction. It must indeed seem as if the world has turned topsy-turvy when someone who has never come across the phenomenon before suddenly realizes that frogs, fishes, or one of the many other reported substances are descending from the clouds. Events of this kind are admittedly rare; but they have happened frequently enough for them to be accepted as something other than an aberration on the part of the witness. Disbelievers have claimed that 'frog falls' are nothing more than showers of rain which have tempted tiny frogs hidden in the undergrowth out into the open – conveniently disregarding those cases where people have *seen* them fall, or felt them pattering down on to themselves or their vehicles.

In April 1986 a huge block of ice fell in a field at Wiston near Haverfordwest, Dyfed (Wales). Beryl Voyle heard a whistling noise as it fell, and here displays just a small portion of the possible ice-meteorite.

The most commonly reported fall is of chunks of ice, sometimes very large, like the 100-pound block which fell through Edith Turner's roof in Stuart, Florida (USA), in July 1982 as she sat drinking coffee in the kitchen. She said it sounded like 'the sky was falling in'.[2] There are so many reports of 'ice-bombs' that we have not listed them in the Gazetteer: they are now almost a common occurrence. Also, many of them may have a straightforward explanation. Often they smell of chemicals, and are coloured blue or green; sometimes they even appear to consist of frozen human waste products. In such cases it seems clear that the ice comes from aeroplane toilets: leaky seals allow the disinfectant and waste to seep out on to the fuselage where it freezes, falling to earth when the plane enters warmer air. Not all ice-bombs are composed of sewage, however, and fresh-water ice also falls. This too may have broken off a plane's fuselage, but planes usually have de-icing equipment to prevent the problem, and there are ice-falls which pre-date planes, so there is clearly some other phenomenon at work too. Ice-bombs are not simply large hailstones: they are different in composition. Sometimes the ice-bomb is very large – 20–50-pound chunks are not rare, and even bigger ones are on record, as we have already seen. They sometimes break up on impact with the ground. One theory is that the chunks of ice are actually meteorites made of ice instead of stone. Some scientists say this is not possible, because ice entering the earth's atmosphere would melt. Perhaps the chunks that fall have partially melted and were originally much larger. Scientists are usually unable to make tests on the evidence: there is rarely anything left to analyse because melting occurs quickly once the ice-bomb has crashed to earth. However, a man who was nearly hit by a falling lump of ice in Kazan (USSR) in August 1984 put the ice in a refrigerator so that it could be preserved for analysis, and scientists decided it was part of a 'frozen gas meteorite'.[3] In the West, where planes are a handy scapegoat, reports of falling ice continue to be largely ignored. Nevertheless, ice-meteorites remain a likely explanation in many cases.[4] It has even been suggested that the earth's oceans may be largely composed of water from ice-comets which bombarded earth several billion years ago, and that the water level is still being 'topped up' by small ice-comets.[5]

There are occasionally strange aspects to reports of ice falls which cause one to wonder if sometimes paranormal forces are at work. For example, early in September 1978 in Lake Worth, Florida (USA), Mrs Helen Goddard kept hearing noises as if something was falling on her roof. After three or four days, she heard a 'loud report' and found chunks of ice scattered in her garden. 'They're small cubes, about an inch or an inch-and-a-half long and three-quarters of an inch deep. It looks exactly like an ice cube from an extremely small tray, not your ordinary household tray.' Later more ice was found after she heard noises. Mrs Goddard doubted that anyone was throwing the ice. 'The porch is on the back of the house, away from the street. You wouldn't think a kid could throw ice so far. There is an alley behind the house but I have a German shepherd so we don't have much traffic in the alley.' She concluded: 'You wouldn't believe the sound that ice makes when it hits that aluminum roof. I'm not living in fear of ice cubes falling on me but it does get to bother you.'[6] Somewhat similar, but nastier, was the report from South Burnaby, British Columbia (Canada), in February 1986, that for three days in a row, slime fell from the sky on to the elementary school. It spattered on the building and on cars parked there. 'It smelled like dung,' said a teacher's aide. A local health official attributed the mess to a jet flushing its holding tanks, but is this really likely to have occurred at exactly the same place three days in a row?[7] The repetitions in these cases bring to mind the repeated showers of stones at many locations, with possible poltergeist connections, which are reported in Chapter 16.

Second in frequency to ice falls are falls of fish, frogs and toads. Unlike ice-meteorites, these are very unlikely to have come from outer space, and there is a straightforward natural explanation to account for this phenomenon. The fish, frogs and toads are often still alive when they land, so clearly they have not been in the sky for very long. The explanation seems to be that a whirlwind or waterspout sweeps them up into the sky, carries them a short distance, then drops them as the wind dissipates.[8] The frogs and toads are always small specimens, and the fish usually. Baby frogs and toads are found together in large numbers in nature, since they start that way as spawn, and 'grow up together'. Sometimes the weather seems to support the whirlwind theory. On 25 October 1947, early in the morning, fish fell into streets and gardens in Marksville, Louisiana (USA). Although the weather was foggy and calm, the previous day had seen numerous small twisters or 'devil dusters' in the area. The fish were identified as fresh-water varieties found in local waters; although dead, they were fresh and many of them were turned into meals.[9]

Very often witnesses report a violent rainstorm at the time of a fall, as happened on 2 July 1901 in Minneapolis, Minnesota (USA). In one part of the city, frogs and toads fell in the rain, as was reported in the press.

> When the storm was at its highest and the wind forced sheets of rain against the shattering window panes the air suddenly turned dark and threatening. There appeared as if descending directly from the sky in the direction of the wind a huge green mass.
>
> Then followed a peculiar patter, unlike that of rain or hail. When the storm abated the people found, three inches deep and covering an area of more than four blocks, a collection of a most striking variety of frogs. Small frogs and toads of all kinds and descriptions. So thick was the consignment of 'quackers' that in some places on the sidewalks and in the street travel was impossible.[10]

Witnesses sometimes see a 'special' cloud from which the fall emerged, as for example Louis Castoreno who was at work in his back yard in Fort Worth, Texas (USA), early in May 1985 when fish began to fall from the sky. There was thunderstorm activity in the area that morning, and Castoreno said the fish fell 'right after a dark cloud passed over'. He thought someone was throwing the fish at him and looked around, but saw nothing, not even a plane they could have fallen from. He commented: 'It scared me. When you see fish coming down out of the sky, and there's nobody around, that's scary.' The fish, 34 of them, were about 2 inches long, and the recipient lives less than a mile from Trinity River, where he and his sons have gone fishing unsuccessfully.[11]

The weather was clear and hot in April or May 1956 on the day when live fish fell from the sky on a farm at Chilatchee near Uniontown, Alabama (USA). The witness and her husband were surprised to see a small, very dark cloud forming in the sky. It was almost overhead when it started to rain, the rain falling in a very small area about 200 feet square, and as the rain fell, so the cloud turned from dark to almost white. During the fifteen-minute rain shower, three types of fish were seen to fall, catfish, bass and bream, all local fish. They were alive and flopped about on the ground. When the rain stopped, the cloud dispersed. The witnesses could not account for the event. Since the fish were alive, they had clearly not been in the sky for long. But there was no unusual weather in the area, and no whirlwinds or tornadoes were reported. If they were picked up from the nearest creek a mile or two away, how did it happen? Perhaps they had been carried from further afield, but the whole process must have happened quickly for them to have stayed alive.[12] Although the whirlwind theory seems feasible enough, there are obviously some events that are difficult to account for by means of that theory. Another one concerns three fishermen from a tiny Pacific island in the Kiribati group. In 1986 they survived 119 days adrift in an open boat after their engine broke down. They lived by catching and killing sharks, drinking their blood and eating them

Louis Castoreno with some of the fish that fell in his yard at Fort Worth in 1985.

raw. When they were finally rescued, they told how, one night while they were praying for a different kind of fish as they were tired of eating raw shark, something fell into the boat. It was a rare, blackish fish which never comes to the surface, living over 600 feet deep in the ocean. How did *this* come to fall from the sky? Was it in answer to their prayer?[13]

Fish, frogs and toads are not the only creatures to have fallen from the sky, but no other species falls so frequently. Dead birds have been reported falling, but we shall not concern ourselves with these reports, since although their deaths may be mysterious and sudden, there is no mystery about their being in the sky, as there is with alligators, crabs, eels and clams. The alligator fell at Evansville, Indiana (USA), on 21 May 1911: 'During the hard rain here today an alligator two feet long fell from the clouds and, landing on the step of the home of Mrs Hiram Winchell, tried to crawl in at the front door. The visitor was killed by Mrs Winchell and several other women with bed slats.' (So much for Indiana hospitality!)[14] Late in 1960, a 5-foot crocodile was found in a back yard at Long Beach, California (USA), after the occupants heard a heavy thump and a loud grunt, and they assumed it had fallen from the sky since there seemed to be no other explanation.[15] Equally mystifying was the discovery of a small dead monkey in a back garden at Broadmoor, California, early in the morning of 26 October 1956 by Mrs Faye Swanson. The 4 by 4-inch post holding her clothes-line had been splintered, presumably when struck by the falling creature. It was theorized that the monkey had fallen from a plane, but an airport spokesman said no planes had been carrying monkeys that night.[16]

Starfish, crabs and clams, all salt-water species, have been recorded falling at inland locations: starfish fell on St Cloud, Minnesota (USA), on 21 April 1985, and they were identified as originating off Florida, a long way away;[17] crabs fell on Laidley in Queensland (Australia) on 12 May 1930, a location 50 miles from the sea;[18] and one clam fell in Yuma, Arizona (USA), on 20 August 1941,[19] about 60 miles from salt water. That these sea creatures, and maybe even crocodiles and alligators, could be picked up in whirlwinds and carried some miles is just about feasible, but what about the admittedly rare reports of falls of flesh and blood? It was reported that on 27 August 1968, meat and blood fell over an area of one square kilometre for five to seven minutes between Coçpava and São José dos Campos in Brazil. The meat, in chunks 2–8 inches long, was violet and spongy and drops of blood also fell. No aircraft or birds were seen in the sky at the time, indeed the sky was clear.[20] The origin of this meat was not immediately obvious – but in March 1986 a recognizable piece of flesh fell from the sky: a human finger. It landed with a thump on a car roof in West Berlin (Germany) as the owner was getting into the car. He thought it was a joke (some joke!) and left the finger by the roadside, but later that day he notified the police who collected it, and started looking for its owner.[21]

If we turn to falls of inanimate objects, the range of things that have fallen is incredibly wide, and only in desperation do we turn to the whirlwind theory for an explanation. First of all, the foodstuffs which have fallen include peaches, which fell on a house-building site in Shreveport, Louisiana (USA), on 12 July 1961. The workmen could see that the peaches, hard and green, the size of a golf ball, were falling from above and not being thrown. They also saw a thick cloud overhead, which is where the fruit presumably fell from, but the weathermen said that there had not been the right conditions that day for the fruit to have been lifted in strong winds.[22] The other foodstuffs which have fallen this century have consisted of smaller items, like the rice which fell on parts of Mandalay (Burma) in January 1952,[23] the seeds which fell on Savannah, Georgia (USA), in February 1958,[24] the navy beans which fell in a hail shower on Van Nuys, California (USA), on 6 March 1958,[25] the beans and peas which fell on Blackstone, Virginia (USA), in August 1962,[26] and the beans which fell on a ranch at João Pessoa, Brazil, in July 1971. The rancher boiled some of the beans, but said they were too tough to eat.[27] We also included some strange British falls of vegetable matter in *Modern Mysteries of Britain*: hazelnuts falling in Bristol (Avon) in March 1977, eggs falling on Wokingham (Berkshire) in December 1974, mustard and cress seeds, maize, peas and beans falling on Southampton (Hampshire) in February 1979. None of these falls can easily be accounted for. Where are beans and peas, etc., stored in the open so that they can easily be lifted by a whirlwind?

Even more puzzling is the case of the falling corn kernels, though a somewhat weird explanation for this has recently come to light. The corn was falling almost daily on Evans, Colorado (USA), beginning around 1982. It fell only in a 50-foot area, around twenty kernels a day on average, but some days as many as 100.[28] This continued for several years, amounting to considerable quantities of corn. In July 1987 a local man claimed that he had been shooting kernels of corn into the air with a slingshot. Although this just might be the answer, it seems strange that anyone would waste time and money in this way. Where did he get all the corn from, and why did he do it? Local residents were sceptical of the claim, and maybe corn is still falling on Evans.[29] Our final edible fall is the bags of cookies which landed on the garage roof and back garden of a house in Louisville, Kentucky (USA), in November 1965. They probably fell from a plane, but none reported the loss.[30]

Every now and then, there is a most welcome fall – of money. On 17 June 1940 silver coins worth several thousand copecks fell in the Gorki area of the USSR during a storm.[31] Thousands of 1000-franc notes fluttered down on Bourges (France) in 1957,[32] while a solitary French coin, a shining 2-franc piece, fell into a garden at Gastonia, North Carolina (USA), in October 1958. Mr and Mrs McGee were working in the garden when it fell – they looked up but could see no plane from which it might have dropped.[33] In December 1975, dollar bills began falling from the sky over LaSalle Street in Chicago, Illinois (USA), $588 being collected by eager searchers – and turned over to the police.[34] The paper money that fell over Limburg (West Germany) in January 1976 was appropriately German marks, and two clergymen gathered 2000 marks which they saw descending from a clear sky.[35]

Apart from all these recognizable items, there are many reports of falls of strange objects or substances which might or might not be man-made or result from man's industrial activities. We will give a selection here, and others can be found in the Gazetteer. Today, with so many bits of man-made junk hurtling around above us, anything metallic which falls from the sky could simply be some of this space debris. So reports pre-dating the first terrestrial satellite – Sputnik 1, which was launched on 4 October 1957 – are the most interesting. Especially intriguing is the hot, molten rain which fell on the beach area of Santa Cruz, California (USA), on 6 January 1909, one witness being Mrs W. H. Burns.

Mrs Burns's attention was engaged and her curiosity aroused yesterday afternoon by the peculiar antics of a number of barefoot children who were playing in front of her house. When she asked them what was the matter they told her that the air was full of electricity and that hot shot was falling from the clouds. She then noticed a clatter on the house-top that sounded like hail, and looking in the direction of the grandstand of the casino ball grounds, she saw little white threads of smoke rising from the roof wherever these little red hot metal globules struck the damp boards. Every roof in the vicinity showed the same peculiar condition.

This molten rain continued from about 2 to 4 o'clock in the afternoon and varied in intensity. At times, however, children who were bareheaded and unshod were compelled to take cover. One boy carried a burn on his finger as the result of being struck by one of these hot pellets. One theory to account for the phenomenon is that the molten rain was due to a passing meteor that had been disintegrated. Mrs Burns has saved a few of the little pellets. They are about the size of a No. 8 shot, and resemble lead.[36]

In the summer of 1910, what was described as a white marble cylinder, 12 inches long and weighing 3 pounds, fell on farmland at Westerville, Ohio (USA). Whether this symmetrical object was manufactured or just an unusual meteorite is unknown.[37] Fragments of something resembling china fell during a thunderstorm over Portland, Oregon (USA), on 21 July 1920,[38] while on 25 January 1923 something fell into a large haystack at Quetta (Pakistan) during a violent thunderstorm. A native watchman saw a huge white ball of fire come down from the sky and start a fire in the hay. This could have been a 'straightforward' case of ball lightning, but the strange thing about it was that the fire burned for two days and left over 5 tons of glassy slag. Some of the wires which had held the hay bales were found embedded in the slag. If the slag somehow burned because of high temperatures, why did the wire not melt?[39] In 1930, a partly fused iron bar fell from the sky during a thunderstorm at Hunstanton, Norfolk (England), striking a chimney;[40] while in New Haven, Connecticut (USA), in 1953 a billboard was damaged by a 'fiery object' which came down and crashed through it, before apparently rising into the sky again. Some fragments left by the mysterious object were analysed and found to consist of almost pure copper.[41] Red-hot pieces of cast iron fell on Woodside, California (USA), in the summer of 1954;[42] and nails fell on Raritan, New Jersey (USA), in July 1955.[43]

All these reports pre-date the first satellite launch. We must be more cautious with succeeding reports, but even so, some of them are decidedly strange, and unlikely to represent falls of satellite debris. When an 18-inch length of heavy chain fell on to a bulldozer in Rock Hill, a suburb of St Louis, Missouri (USA), on 15 May 1959, driver Wallace Baker looked up and saw a vague something

Joseph Barbieri saw a fiery object pass through this billboard at New Haven, Connecticut (USA) in 1953.

streaking away high in the sky – plane, or UFO? Wouldn't he have been able to identify a normal plane passing overhead? Would a plane have been carrying a length of chain of this kind (see photograph on page 226)? Also the chain was very hot, and made Mr Baker's gloves sizzle when he tried to pick it up.[44]

And what about the golf balls which fell from the skies over Punta Gorda, Florida (USA), on 3 September 1969? There were literally hundreds of them rolling around the streets – a field day for golfers but a mystery for the police, who could find no one who had lost the balls or could throw any light on their strange arrival in Punta

Gorda.[45] Equally strange was the fall of papers on to North Green-bush in the Albany area of New York (USA) which was witnessed by Bob Hill, manager of radio station WHRL, on 24 July 1973. He watched them flutter slowly down. 'I'm certain the things must have been above 10,000 feet. The sky was crystal clear. There was nothing to interfere with my observation. It took something like half an hour to 45 minutes for the objects to land.' He managed to retrieve a couple of sheets and found them to contain complex mathematical formulae, but his later research did not manage to track down their owner.[46] In Indianapolis, Indiana (USA), the paper which fell from the sky on 16 May 1984 was not at quite such a high intellectual level: it was rubbish. One witness saw 500 or 600 pieces of scrap paper and other rubbish – newspapers, computer printout, cardboard, plastic cups – falling from the sky. It was traced back to a landfill site a mile away, but the weathermen were at a loss to know how it had been lifted into the sky, since the nearest storm was hundreds of miles away, and it was not warm enough for 'mini dust devils' to arise.[47]

One of the strangest falls of recent years took place in 1984, actually on 1 January, when a World War II shell weighing 22 pounds crashed out of the sky into Fred Simons's patio in Lake-wood, California (USA), leaving a 4-foot crater. Fortunately it contained no explosives. No one had seen or heard a plane, though neighbours did hear a whistling noise as the shell came down.[48] Could this be a case of teleportation, with the shell somehow having been held in limbo since the last war? It's a very way-out explanation, but the facts are pretty way-out, too!

Although we are not aware of it, around 1000 tons of matter falls on to the earth every day. We have all seen shooting stars or meteors: when these fall to earth they are known as meteorites. Apart from the meteorites which are big enough to see and handle, tiny particles or micro-meteorites are constantly floating down, and it is these which make up the estimated 1000 tons. Only around 500 meteorites of any size land on the earth each year, many of them falling into the sea, so only about ten are actually recovered annually.[49] There was a time, and not so many years ago, when scientists denied that stones could fall from the sky, as there were none there to begin with. Now meteorites are familiar to everyone. But there are still anomalous falls of rock and stones. When these happen repeatedly at a certain location, they are clearly paranormal, and as such will be dealt with separately in Chapter 16. Here we describe only single falls: but we must be aware of the possibility that a stone discovered after an apparently linked event, like a thunderbolt, may not have fallen from the sky at all, but may have been lying there all the time, only being noticed after the dramatic event which gave rise to the belief that something had fallen. The following reports do not always give sufficient information, but are worth repeating nevertheless.

At Holbrook, Arizona (USA), on 19 July 1912, there was a loud explosion and stones fell from the sky – at least 14,000 of them. Some were very small.[50] Two dissimilar stones cemented together fell on to Cumberland Falls, Kentucky (USA), on 9 April 1919.[51] A limestone ball fell and exploded at Bleckenstad (Sweden) on 11 April 1925, the events being witnessed by several people. Fragments were analysed and said to contain fragments of marine shells and a fossil like a trilobite. The limestone was not like any in Sweden.[52] A boulder measuring 30 by 30 inches fell on Dundalk, Maryland (USA), on 27 January 1956;[53] a much smaller rock, 4 by 3 inches, fell in front of a man gardening at Aston, Birmingham, West Midlands (England), on 12 May 1969, but this rock was described as 'warm and sticky'. It also seemed to expand as it cooled.[54] On 12 July 1975 black and sticky stones rained down on to a street in Etterbeek (Belgium).[55] A lump of porous rock, sparkling with what looked like

The chain which fell from the sky at Rock Hill, Missouri (USA), in 1959.

melted glass and white flecks all over the black material 'resembling slag', crashed on to a patio in Toronto, Ontario (Canada), on 20 August 1978. It was warm, and may have caused a small explosion; it broke on impact. Geologists at the Royal Ontario Museum said it was not a meteorite.[56] A similar description was given to a rock which burned the grass and left a crater when it fell at Marshfield, Massachusetts (USA), on 4 November 1983. No one saw it fall: it was the hole with smoke rising from it which drew people's attention. Police said a live power line had come down and caused the fire and the hole and melted a rock, but Robert Lang, who pulled a piece of smouldering rock out of the hole, disagreed, saying there were no wires down. There were several pieces of the rock, which Lang described as porous: 'On one side it looks like slag from a welder's wire. And it looks almost like silver or aluminum spread through it.'[57]

So far in this chapter, the only objects falling from the sky which may have originated 'up there' are ice-meteorites and lumps of rock. Our next category of falls – slimes, goos and jellies – might also be extraterrestrial in origin – or at least some of them might. There are plenty of possible terrestrial answers, the most likely being slime-fungi, substances regurgitated by animals or birds, or waste material from industrial processes, which has somehow been dumped where it should not have been. Let us see how many of the reports seem to be truly mysterious: you will see that it is not always easy to tell whether a case has a mundane explanation or not. A substance smelling like glue fell on Sart (Belgium) on 8 June 1901,[58] and a salty white goo came down on to Salt Lake City (appropriately!), Utah (USA), on 25 March 1955,[59] but we do not have enough information on either event to be able to identify what fell. A reddish oily liquid spattered down on to a garden in Cincinnati, Ohio (USA), on 22 July 1955. Warm and sticky and somewhat like blood, it began to sting Ed Mootz's hand. It also caused his peach trees to shrivel and die. During the noxious shower, Mr Mootz looked up and saw a small cloud, a turbulent mixture of red, green and pink.[60] This may have been a fall of effluent which had somehow been discharged in liquid form from a chemical plant. A green slime which fell on a six-block section of Foggy Bottom in Washington, DC (USA), on 5 and 6 September 1978 also caused problems, killing plants, making cats and dogs ill, and damaging car windscreens. It undoubtedly fell from the sky, because the roof of a twelve-storey building was coated with it. The scientist who analysed the slime said: 'It's a green material – it's soluble in water and it's soluble in alcohol. When this stuff hit, it was very fluid.' Later it thickened and turned black. Its principal components were nickel sulphate, iron sulphate and manganese, and it was a 'product of combustion', but was not jet fuel nor pesticide.[61]

There are plenty of similar reports of mystery liquids which hardened, or dissolved, and were unidentifiable, some of them apparently stranger than others. Three particularly puzzling cases date from the 1950s. On 26 September 1950, two police patrolmen driving in their patrol car near Philadelphia, Pennsylvania (USA), saw something fall into a field. When they investigated they found a six-foot-long object giving off a misty purplish glow. One of the men touched it and found it to be a jelly-like mass. Within half an hour it had evaporated.[62] It was also a policeman who witnessed the fall of another strange object, this time in his Miami, Florida (USA), garden on 28 February 1958. It fell from a clear sky, and was a transparent globe with a glittering surface. 'It seemed to be made up of thousands of minute cells resembling those of a honeycomb, and it was pulsating over its entire body.' The witness stuck his fingers into it. 'To my amazement I could feel nothing. I withdrew my finger at once and saw that I had left a hole in the material the size and length of my finger. This was the first time in my life that I had been able to see and touch an object, yet be unable to feel it.' He managed to gather some of the material into a jar, as it began to spread across the lawn and shrink, but his sample also dissolved, leaving a dry, empty jar.[63] Five 'strange, floating foam-like objects' were seen at Charlotte, North Carolina (USA), on 20 March 1957, drifting in the sky, and one of them came to earth 60 feet away from the witnesses. It was like a thick liquid or 'ice breaking up', was shiny and cool when touched, and numbed the fingertips. There was a faint odour like burned matches.[64]

In earlier centuries, such mysterious blobs were known as 'star jelly', 'pwdre ser' (the Welsh name), or 'rot of the stars', and were believed to be gelatinous meteors, or shooting stars which had landed.[65] As noted earlier, there are numerous natural explanations, but whether they can account for the strangest cases remains debatable. Three purple blobs found on a lawn in Frisco, Texas (USA), on 11 August 1979 initially defied scientific analysis. But later it was claimed they were the chemical residue from a battery reprocessing plant. True? Or merely a way of sweeping troublesome data under the carpet?[66]

There may be some link between 'star jelly' and 'angel hair', the latter being sticky fibres allegedly dropped by UFOs, but claimed by disbelievers to be nothing more than spiders' webs. In many instances this explanation is undoubtedly the correct one, for there are certain types of spiders which become airborne on a floating mass of webs. But there are also other cases which cannot be explained so easily. A witness in Monterey, California (USA), saw 'spaceships' like jellyfish quivering in the sky over the bay on 4 October 1971, and they left behind floating fibres when they shot away.[67] On 22 October 1973, a woman in Sudbury, Massachusetts (USA), saw a shining globular UFO in the sky at the same time as she saw sparkling fibres on the wires and leaves. She collected some of the sticky material, and sealed it in a jar in her refrigerator. Analysis showed that the fibres were not spiders' webs, and they could not be identified.[68]

Also unlikely to have been spiders' webs were the strange lines which stretched up into the sky in three American locations in the 1970s: Caldwell, New Jersey, in August 1970, Elberton, Georgia, in mid-June 1972, and Greensburg, Ohio, in September 1978. Several lines or wires were hanging from the sky over Caldwell, in actual fact stretched taut at angles between 30 and 50 degrees to ground level. The reports published in *Pursuit* give the relevant facts, and we quote:

> Neither the upper nor the lower ends were ever seen, or located, even when they finally fell. They just came out of the sky from, apparently, down low at one end, and went up overhead and then on up into the sky to a point of invisibility, even when traced with powerful binoculars. In one case the line remained taut for a month, through several severe electrical storms and several other days of high winds. Then, for no apparent reason, one 'end' of the line gave way and a pile of the stuff was found in a front yard. The owners pulled in a large amount, but the line snapped farther up and the upper end remained invisible. In another case, four boys spent *one hour* hauling in a line which had dropped during the night; again, this snagged and broke before the entire line could be pulled in. And in all cases, when the line fell it immediately curled up, just as did the nylon fishing lines on 2″ spools, bought by us for comparison.[69]

No pattern could be discerned in the distribution of the lines, and despite numerous efforts, no ends could be found. Some of the material retrieved was analysed by the DuPont Company 'who stated that it was chemically a type 6 Nylon (caprolactam) or possibly a copolymer such as type 6 and type 66, but that it was not of their manufacture.' A sample was also analysed by a Dr Vargas at Rhode Island University, where another mystery developed. 'These lines had a fine hollow tube running through their length. When Dr Vargas first examined the specimens this was empty, but after a time in a vacuum jar he found to his amazement that this tube was filled with some other solid substance, and this defied analysis so far as we can make out.'[70]

Two years later, a similar line, single this time, was seen in Elberton, Georgia. Newspaperman Herbert Wilcox was alerted by the initial witness, and he went over to see the thing for himself.

By the time I got there, the sun had come up and the moon had gone down, but the line was still mounting the sky and shimmering in the light of the early morning sun as far as the eye could see. An earthy guess was that it might be a kite string. If so, it was the longest and fanciest kite string ever seen around here. Besides, there was no kite in sight to hold it way up in the air. Another guess was that it was some sort of hot line laid out by a plane, or maybe a parachute had disintegrated way up yonder and that this was what was left of it. This still didn't explain how it managed to stay up there. During the day, Eddie Boswell . . . got on the roof, where the line was at its lowest point. He pulled in yards and yards of it but never saw a thing to indicate what it had been fastened to. There were two kinds of material in the line. That pulled from the west was a fluffy, shiny, white substance. That from the east was a tiny, hard-finished green material something like a fishing line. Both were hard to break.[71]

The third line we know of (there may be more) was seen at Greensburg, Ohio, in September 1978. A man who found it snagged on a bush behind his house began pulling it off, and had to call his neighbours in to assist. Using fishing reels, they collected 1000 feet, filling eight reels, before the line broke and floated away. It could still be seen stretching up into the sky, and the theory again was that children had been flying a kite using fishing line. But although this explanation was invariably trotted out, no one has ever reported seeing the elusive kite, or finding anyone who had been flying it.[72]

14 Out-of-place big cats and other mystery animals

Although man has successfully managed to exterminate many wild animals from areas where their requirements conflict with his, nevertheless there is ample evidence to suggest that some animals have been able to secretly recolonize territories where they are officially believed to be extinct. Perhaps the best example is *Felis concolor*, the puma, cougar or mountain lion, which until 100 years ago was widespread in the eastern USA. Today the only state where there is an officially recognized small population is Florida, but persistent reports have come from other eastern states, i.e. Georgia, Alabama, Mississippi, Louisiana, Oklahoma, Arkansas, Tennessee, South Carolina, North Carolina, Virginia, Kentucky, Missouri, Wisconsin, Iowa, Illinois, Indiana, Michigan, Ohio, West Virginia, Maryland, New Jersey, Pennsylvania, New York, Connecticut, Massachusetts, Vermont, Maine. (More details of the areas where sightings have been made, and when, can be found in the Gazetteer.) The animals are so elusive that conclusive evidence of their existence in these states is difficult to obtain. Disbelievers claim that witnesses are misidentifying other creatures, such as large dogs, bobcats, and feral cats, and it is true that in poor viewing conditions such mistakes can easily occur. However, it is certainly feasible that *Felis concolor* has taken up residence in the wilder areas of the eastern states, and that there is really no mystery about this species' ability to survive, whether they are escaped pets or circus animals (as some of them may well be), or survivors of original wild populations. The mysterious aspect is in the big cat reports describing lions, or black panthers.

There should certainly not be lions living wild in the USA, unless they have escaped from captivity, or are something else masquerading as a lion. In Waukegan, Illinois, in November 1985 a lion hunt was called off when it was discovered that the 'lion' was a German shepherd dog which had been shaved to emphasize its lion-like appearance, so that it seemed to have a lion's mane and a tufted tail.[1] In other lion hunts – as in central Illinois in July 1917; Elkhorn Falls, Indiana, in August 1948; near Kapuskasing, Ontario (Canada), in June 1960; near Roscoe, Illinois, in May 1970; in Tacoma, Washington, in July 1976; and in Fremont, California, in November 1979 – the descriptions were clearly of a lion-like animal: e.g., 'a male African lion about eight feet long with hair growth at the end of its tail and a mane' (Roscoe, Illinois).[2] These and other similar sightings have led researcher Loren Coleman to theorize that there might be a relict population of the giant American lion of 10,000 years ago still surviving in North America, *Panthera leo atrox*.[3]

The other enigmatic big cat reports are those describing *black* cats. These are a complete mystery, because black (melanistic) pumas are very rare. There are known to be black jaguars (*Panthera onca*), but very few and restricted to southern US states like Arizona.[4] The leopard (*Panthera pardus*), whose habitat is Asia and Africa, is sometimes black, and is then called a panther. There are very many reported sightings of 'black panthers' in the eastern USA – can there be whole families of escaped panthers living wild? It is unlikely, but what else might the witnesses be seeing? Sometimes they could be misidentifying a black labrador dog, or a creature called a fisher (*Martes pennanti*). This is a member of the weasel family, and it can be found across Canada and into the north-eastern USA; it is known to live in the Adirondacks and as far south as Oneida Lake (New York) and in the northern part of Maine. Perhaps it has also spread further south. One was reportedly seen as far south as Florida, in January 1984.[5] The animal is slightly smaller than a fox, with a bushy coat and long tail, and is dark in colour.[6] On balance, though, the most sensible explanation for the reports of big black cats is that melanism is for some reason becoming more common in the puma species, even though this is officially denied in the absence of any black corpses.[7]

In Britain, totally unexpected big black cats have been caught and killed, but they are not pumas: to further complicate the issue, they are an as yet unidentified species, possibly a cross between Scottish wild cats and feral cats. We have written at length on the mystery cats of Britain in *Modern Mysteries of Britain*, so will only summarize the facts here briefly. There have been persistent reports of big cats, often described as pumas, being seen in Britain since the 1960s, and hardly any area of the British mainland seems to be without at least some sightings. As mentioned, black cats have been killed

and trapped in Scotland. For the most up-to-date account of the zoological findings, and indeed for a highly readable and interesting survey of mystery big cats around the world, Dr Karl Shuker's book *Mystery Cats of the World* should be consulted. Elsewhere in Europe, big cats are sometimes reported, but as in the States none is yet available for study. The most recent European sightings have been in France, Denmark, West Germany, Switzerland and Italy. The lynx (*Felis lynx*) is native to Europe, but is becoming rare in many areas, and is now found mainly in the Pyrenees, the Alps and the Jura mountains. An unsuccessful attempt was made to reintroduce them into the Vosges mountains of France in 1984, where they became extinct a century ago, but other attempts, kept secret to protect the animals from human predators, may have been more successful. There are wild cats (*Felis sylvestris*) still living in some areas of southern Europe, and there are grey wolves in Spain, Italy, France and East Germany. So some of the 'pumas' reported may be rare native animals, or feral cats, or big dogs, while others may be pumas which have escaped from zoos, circuses, or private houses. And, as in Britain, there may well be unknown species of cats roaming the wilder parts of Europe.[8]

A rare photograph of a mystery black cat on Exmoor (England), taken in 1987 by Trevor Beer who has been in search of the 'Exmoor Beast' for several years.

The third area of the world where mystery cats have been widely reported is Australia. Since there are no native cats in Australia, the animals being seen today cannot be survivors of earlier wild populations, but they might, of course, not be cats at all. As in the USA, officialdom is dubious about the validity of the reports, but the local people are convinced there are big cats living wild. There are several areas in New South Wales where pumas or black panthers are seen. Most of the reports date from the last twenty years, but similar animals were apparently seen around Tallong in the late 1920s and early 1930s. The Southern Highlands area in the south-east of the state is the focus for sightings today, especially around Nowra and in Kangaroo Valley. One example from many was the sighting at the beginning of June 1978 by Mrs Robin Neale and Mrs Janice Bruem, near Kangaroo Valley township. The animal they saw 'had a long, cat-like tail and its head was cat-like and was about two feet tall and five feet long from the head to the end of its tail . . . We are both convinced it was a giant, cat-like animal. We're intrigued and we want to know what it is.' (They are certainly not alone in that.) It ran away with a graceful lope. Both women had seen big cats before in

A thylacine in captivity.

234

recent years.[9] At Emmaville in the north of the state it is a black panther that is seen, the first reported sighting being on 19 February 1958 near Coolatai.

Sightings of big cats in Australia are 'explained' as a puma lost from a travelling circus – or as wartime servicemen's mascots let loose – or as misidentified dogs, dingoes and feral cats – yet the sightings of 'pumas' and 'panthers' continue.[10] The situation is further complicated by the fact that there might also be other, native, species of unknown or 'extinct' animals living in the bush in several parts of Australia. One of them is like a big dog, has distinctive stripes across its body, and also has a pouch, therefore being a marsupial like the kangaroo. It is known as the thylacine or Tasmanian wolf or Tasmanian tiger, and is supposedly extinct in Tasmania although occasional sightings are still reported. The mainland version is also supposed to be extinct. Also found in the fossil record is a marsupial 'lion', which may have survived to the present day too. Sightings of striped animals may therefore indicate that some form of thylacine is still around. In January 1979, for example, a Mr and Mrs Barlow were driving at night near Forster

Miss Rilla Martin took this photograph of a mystery animal in Victoria (Australia) in 1964.

(New South Wales) when a striped dog-like animal ran across the road in front of them, causing them to stop suddenly. In the lights they could see it clearly: about 5 feet long, almost 2 feet tall, with a body like a greyhound, and a row of blackish stripes on its mousy-brown fur.[11]

Further north, in Queensland, striped 'cats' are also seen, the reports going back to the 1870s.[12] These animals may be an as yet unrecognized species, the marsupial tiger-cat.[13] 'Black panthers' are also seen, as for example at Miles, 150 miles north-west of Brisbane. Mervyn Platz saw one at dusk late in January 1983.

> I pulled my utility up about 15 metres from it. At first I thought it was a black dingo. It was about two feet high, five to six feet from its nose to tail and had a cat's head about three times as big as a normal cat, with yellow eyes. We watched each other for about five minutes, before it slunk away in the grass. It showed no fear at all.

Farmers in the area had recently had animals (dogs, cats, sheep and goats) killed.[14]

In Victoria the same situation as in Queensland and New South Wales can be found, with sightings both of big black cats and of striped ones which are possibly thylacines. The black cats are seen frequently in the Grampian mountains south of Horsham, while in Gippsland, a large black dog hit by a car near Trafalgar in February 1979 was thought to have been responsible for numerous sightings in that area. It was 3 feet 10 inches tall at the shoulder and very thin, apparently not finding too good a living in the wild.[15] Although the 'modern' wave of sightings of 'pumas' began in the 1950s, there were earlier reports, and there may have been more sightings than we are now aware of – possibly such reports did not reach the papers as often as they do today. In November 1933 three men working in the hill country at Gunyah near Trafalgar 'heard a strange call and saw a large fawn-coloured beast moving slowly in bracken fern. It had a large cat-like head, and appeared to be about 6 feet long. All had a good view of the animal, which bore the appearance of a lioness. Tracks of the animal were discovered later, with a distinct claw impression.' Other farmers in the region had seen a similar beast.[16] Thylacine-like creatures have been seen at widely separated locations in Victoria: around Portland in the south-west, in West Wimmera, around Lang Lang in Gippsland, and on the Victoria/

New South Wales border, where in 1977 farmers were observing a pack of the animals including one carrying a baby in its pouch.[17] The animals are most often seen as they cross roads. Two men driving north of Benambra on a fishing expedition late in December 1980 saw one from a distance of only 35 feet. The driver stopped to watch as it sauntered across the road. 'It was about half a metre high, a metre from nose to tail and definitely had stripes. It was mainly grey with a bit of brown fur and had a tail that was thick and long; it wasn't bushy like a fox or tapered like a dog's tail.' The witness was sure he knew what the animal was. 'I've been travelling the eastern alps for 25 years and as sure as apples it was a Tasmanian tiger. I've seen plenty of wild dogs, dingoes and foxes, but never one of these before.'[18]

Thylacines are also being seen on Tasmania, where they were a familiar native species until the beginning of this century. Because they were believed to be responsible for excessive sheep killing, a bounty was offered for scalps and the thylacine rapidly declined until it became officially extinct in the 1930s, when the last specimen died at Hobart Zoo. However, sighting reports have continued regularly since then, although despite numerous expeditions no positive evidence of the thylacine's survival has been obtained. One reliable sighting was made in March 1982 by a park ranger, Hans Naarding, somewhere in the north-west of the island. He was sleeping in his van, and when he awoke he scanned the woods with his spotlight, as was his habit. He saw, standing in the rain, a dog-sized striped animal with a thick, rigid tail.

> My camera bag was out of immediate reach so I decided to examine the animal carefully before risking movement. It was an adult male in excellent condition with 12 black stripes on a sandy coat. Eye reflection was pale yellow. It moved only once, opening its jaw and showing its teeth. After several minutes of observation I attempted to reach my camera bag but in doing so I disturbed the animal and it moved away into the undergrowth. Leaving the vehicle and moving to where the animal disappeared, I noted a strong scent. Despite an intensive search no further trace of the animal could be found.[19]

It is almost certain that populations of thylacines do still live in Tasmania. Whether they also live in Western Australia is less certain. Five photographs taken somewhere in the state in November 1985 by Kevin Cameron, a tracker of Aboriginal descent, purport to show a thylacine, but there has been considerable controversy as to the photographs' validity.[20] Over the years, various big cat-like animals have been seen in Western Australia, notably on sheep farms where they have been killing the animals. 'Black panthers' were reported at Kulja north of Koorda early in 1972, where the farmers were trying unsuccessfully to trap it or them.[21] In August 1982, Dr Per Seglen, a Norwegian research scientist visiting Australia for a conference, saw a big cat crossing the road ahead of him between Badgingarra and Nambung National Park, north of Perth. He reported: 'I saw this big cat about 100 metres ahead. It was loping along and then it disappeared into bushes. Had I been in Africa I'd have said it was a leopard from its gait and size. I could not see whether it had any spots but it had a long, spotted or heavily striped tail.' Later, he failed to find the animal in Perth Zoo or in any book on Australian marsupials. 'The whole thing was very puzzling. I wasn't expecting anything except, perhaps, a kangaroo. But then I sighted an animal which does not belong on this continent at all.'[22]

The Wisconsin kangaroo or wallaby, photographed in 1978.

Doubtless the arguments about whether big cats and thylacines are living in Australia will continue until the creatures are filmed or photographed by an unimpeachable witness, or, best of all, carcasses

are obtained. The very elusiveness of the animals naturally causes disbelievers to doubt their existence: but perhaps it is this very quality of elusiveness that has helped them to survive for so long.

If pumas and panthers are being seen in Australia and Europe, then they are 'out-of-place' animals – animals seen in habitats where they do not normally live. There are other animals than big cats which are quite often seen in unexpected places, like kangaroos. When they are seen in England, they are usually wallabies, which are also Australian marsupials and look very much like kangaroos, but smaller. In England there are colonies of wallabies living wild, some escaped from captivity in recent years and some (in Derbyshire) the remnants of a colony living on an estate which became neglected about 1940. They seem to live quite successfully in the wild, so long as the winter weather is not too extreme. This may also be the case in the USA, where 'kangaroos' have been seen often since the mid-1960s. Sightings are not usually close up, but two policemen got very close to the beast they were chasing in Chicago (Illinois) on 18 October 1974. Patrolmen Byrne and Ciagi cornered a 5-foot kangaroo in a dark alley at 3.30 a.m., but it was not intending to come quietly, and started to scream as Patrolman Byrne tried to handcuff it. A scuffle ensued, in which Patrolman Ciagi was kicked in the legs, and the kangaroo escaped down the street.[23]

These out-of-place kangaroos are rarely, if ever, captured. Often they seem to disappear as mysteriously as they appeared, after having been seen by a few bewildered citizens. But during the Wisconsin outbreak of 1978, a photograph was taken of the creature. Not a very good photograph, admittedly, but clear enough to show something unusual. The kangaroo was first seen on 5 April 1978 at Waukesha. Sightings at Pewaukee Township, Brookfield Township, and around Waukesha followed, then on 24 April two men in the bush near Menomonee Falls took two Polaroid photographs of the kangaroo. Loren Coleman, who saw a colour print, said the creature could be a Bennett's wallaby or swamp wallaby,[24] and as in England, these creatures could be escapees from private animal collections or zoos, living wild. Elsewhere in the world, 'kangaroos' have been reported in New Brunswick, Nova Scotia and Ontario (all in Canada – for locations see Gazetteer), around Morange-Silvange in France, and on the northern border of Hungary. That these animals are probably escaped wallabies is shown by the occasional records of escapes. In May 1979, for example, a 'kangaroo' seen in Nashua, New Hampshire (USA), was caught and found to be a wallaby that had escaped from a carnival that had recently left town.[25] Another possible identification for smaller 'kangaroos' is a native North American animal, the coati (*Nasua narica*), which is a carnivore in the raccoon family. Sightings of 'kangaroos' not more than 2 feet tall (plus a 20-inch tail, which stands erect with a curl at the top) are likely to be of coatis.[26]

Although kangaroos and wallabies can be dangerous to humans if cornered or threatened, crocodilians are even more potentially harmful. There is a native species of crocodilian in North America, the American alligator which lives in the marshes, rivers and swamps of the south and south-eastern states, no further north than Louisiana. Yet crocodilians have been seen, caught and killed at many other locations much further north and west: in Arizona, California, Colorado, Connecticut, Delaware, Washington, DC, Illinois, Indiana, Kansas, Maryland, Massachusetts, Michigan, Minnesota, New Jersey, New York, Ohio, Oklahoma, Texas, Virginia, Washington and Wisconsin (for fuller details, see Gazetteer). It is likely that many of the creatures seen are discarded pets, which could survive until the cold weather. Caimans (from Central and South America) are the smallest crocodilians, and these are sold in exotic-pet shops. But some of the creatures seen have been quite sizeable, which suggests they may have been surviving and growing in the wild over many years. They seem to like living in sewers, perhaps because this is a warmer environment with rats available for food. 'Alligators in the sewers' may be thought of as an urban folk-tale, but they really have been found there. (Whether they were discarded pets flushed down the toilets is another matter.) In 1935 the *New York Times* reported the finding of an alligator in a New York city street. Boys shovelling snow into a manhole on East 123rd Street saw movement in the hole, and using a rope pulled out an 8-foot alligator, which was clearly in poor health. They killed it with their shovels, and it was found to weigh 125 pounds.[27] More recently, in May 1983 a crocodile emerged from a storm drain in Cairns, Queensland (Australia), and grabbed the leg of a passing man. He was fortunately wearing cowboy boots, and so was not injured. In Paris (France), municipal workers in the sewers found a young crocodile wandering through the tunnels in March 1984. The 2½-foot creature was captured and taken to the much more pleasant environment of a vivarium in the Jardin des Plantes.[28]

Other out-of-place creatures preferring a watery environment include eels. In a case somewhat similar to the 'alligators in the sewers', several 4-foot eels were found in the water pipes of an apartment house in Medford, Boston, Massachusetts (USA), after residents complained of low water pressure. Officials said that they would have had to swim 100 miles through water mains from Quabbin Reservoir.[29] Nile monitor lizards, which are around 6 feet long, tend to stay near water – but not usually in the USA, as they are native to Africa. In the summer of 1981, three Nile monitors were caught in Florida in just over three weeks, and another had been found near South Bay two years earlier. One was found on the golf course at Royal Palm Beach, another was in a garden at Hypoluxo, and the third was found lying across the engine of a car when a North Miami man lifted up the bonnet.[30] Then, in February 1984, a teenager shot and killed a 6-foot Nile monitor he found in a pond at Findly, Ohio.[31]

It is possible, of course, that the Nile monitors were escaped pets. But that is a difficult explanation to pin on salt-water creatures found alive in fresh-water environments, like the octopus that was pulled out of the Kanawha River near Charleston, West Virginia (USA), on 24 December 1933 by two men fishing from a boat. They became aware of it when its tentacles flopped into their boat. From its head to the tip of its largest tentacle measured 3 feet.[32] We also have four reports of sharks being found in fresh water: in Rivieres des Prairies, a stream in Montreal North, Quebec (Canada), on 14 July 1968 (4 feet long, weighing 20 pounds);[33] in a creek in Arlington, Texas (USA), in July 1976 (a 3½-foot sand shark);[34] in East Lynn Lake, West Virginia (USA), on 18 August 1977 (2 feet long and weighing 10 pounds);[35] in the filter of the water-intake entrance to a power plant at Detroit, Michigan (USA), in late June 1978 (the shark was dead, and we have no size details).[36] Is it significant that they were all found in the same six weeks of summer?

Some strange land animals have also been found in unexpected places, like the 8-pound armadillo (origin, southern USA, Central and South America) found wandering across a lawn in Holliston, Massachusetts (USA), on 23 December 1978,[37] though this and the lemur (origin Madagascar) found dying in a Lincoln, Nebraska (USA), garden on 12 November 1931 could have escaped from zoos or private collections.[38] Zoos usually own up when they lose animals, especially big ones, but no origin could be found for the bear seen wandering around in Hamburg (West Germany) in September 1974. It was seen by more than 30 people, and police found footprints and hair samples, but since no bear had been lost, and the animal seemed to have disappeared, they concluded that it must be a hoax.[39] The small elephant reported wandering in the Bay Ridge section of Brooklyn, New York (USA), on 2 May 1979 was equally elusive.[40]

It is unlikely that elephants are living wild in the USA, but monkeys/apes/chimpanzees might be. There are known to be naturalized monkey populations in Florida and Texas, and Loren Coleman believes that there are primates living wild in other areas too.[41] There have been numerous sightings of them – and it is possible that some so-called 'Bigfoot' sightings may be of out-of-place apes. Places where apes have been spotted include an island in a lake in southern Massachusetts (June 1980); Gum Creek bottom near Mt Vernon (summer 1941) and Enfield (April and May 1973), both in Illinois; Hamburg, Arkansas (1968); Trimble County, Kentucky (1962); Calumet, Oklahoma (1967–70, when a man was feeding a 'chimpanzee' he wanted to capture); and in North Huntingdon Township, Pennsylvania (autumn 1987).[42] After several sightings in the farmland of Honeybrook Township in Pennsylvania beginning in early October 1987, a monkey was shot early in November, and the corpse persuaded the disbelievers that the local people really had been seeing a primate. It was about 2½ feet long, weighed about 50 pounds, and had reddish-brown fur and inch-long canine teeth, but specialists at the University of Pennsylvania School of Veterinary Medicine could not identify the species. Nor did the authorities know where it had come from.[43]

The out-of-place animals we have been describing so far are reasonably identifiable, even if the exact species is uncertain. However there are also many media reports of weird and wonderful creatures which it would tax even the most competent of zoologists to identify. Some of the reports are so vague and garbled that we must ignore them. Others are more detailed, and intriguing enough for us to ponder over what the witnesses might have been seeing. Some of these creatures seem to have dog-like features. At this point it is worth commenting that some sightings of what are thought for various reasons to be big cats are described in dog-like terms, in Great Britain as well as in the USA. The witnesses' uncertainty about what animal they have seen, and the finding of dog-like tracks with claw marks, often causes the authorities to blame the sightings on large dogs, but as some of these cases show, the answer is often not so straightforward.

In 1951, Mrs Lawrence Laub, living on a farm at Calumet,

Oklahoma (USA), saw an animal that 'looked like a cross between a wolf and a deer'. It had four thin deer-like legs, and its head and body were also deer-like. Its feet were 'huge pads', and it had long hair, a bushy tail, and small pointed ears. It was bigger than a dog or wolf. Her husband had also seen a similar creature two years before.[44] In 1975, an unidentifiable wolf-like animal was biting the ears off pigs in Jasper County, Mississippi (USA).[45] In the spring of 1978, a 'doglike animal, larger than a fox, tan with a long dark tail' leapt on to the back of a pony in Prestonburg, Kentucky, severely injuring it.[46] In 1982 near Cheyenne, Oklahoma (USA), two cattlemen saw an animal they could not identify. 'It was bigger and broader than a dog would be. Its head pretty much sat down on its shoulders, and it walked on four legs,' said Alex Inman. George Springer added, 'It wasn't fuzzy or furry, but slick haired, like a pig. It was kind of smooth moving. It didn't bounce any. It was pretty heavy, and had a pretty big body.' When they honked their horn, it ambled off unconcernedly into the brush.[47]

It is possible that some of these strange animals are crosses or hybrids. Coyotes and wolves, both members of the dog family, live in certain areas of the USA, and both these are known to have successfully mated with dogs to produce hybrids: coyotes and wolves together have also produced hybrids.[48] The offspring of a dog and a coyote are known as coy-dogs. One was killed at Williamsville, Virginia (USA), on 2 October 1977, after it had been terrorizing livestock in the area for several years.[49] It is likely that many of these dog-like creatures are in fact hybrids. Another possible identification is the grey fox (*Urocyon*) which is quite different from the red fox (*Vulpes*) in proportions, gait and habits as well as in colour.[50] There are other members of the dog family which could be responsible for these puzzling sightings, except that these creatures are not native to the USA: the maned wolf, for example, with its long thin legs (the Calumet creature?), lives in South America. Wild or feral dogs could certainly survive in areas where coyotes and other predators live; and they would be big animals, as competition in the wild favours the bigger breeds, but feral dogs usually hunt in packs and these mystery animals are always seen alone.

However, some of the animals described are unlikely to be any species of dog. Dogs, coyotes and wolves do not usually jump, but some of the 'monsters' do. On 2 July 1924, an animal seen near West Orange, New Jersey (USA), was causing some excitement at the police station, after one of their patrolmen rang in to report it. 'I have just seen an animal that has a head like a deer, that runs like a rabbit and has fiery eyes. What do you think it is?' Mrs Clyde Vincent also saw it: 'We were picnicking on the road a while ago, when an animal that had a head like a deer, that ran like a rabbit and had fiery eyes came along and jumped over us.' A farmer at Livingston had seen 'the devil' jumping about his fields. The police thought the creature might be a kangaroo escaped from a circus or zoo, but they found nothing when they searched.[51]

The strange animal that was stealing chickens from a farm at Greenwich, New Jersey (USA), in December 1925 was cornered and shot by the irate farmer, but even when he had the corpse immobile in front of him, neither he nor the hundreds of others who came to view it could identify it. According to the press report, it was

> the size of a grown Airedale with black fur resembling Astrakhan. It had not run when he pursued it, but had hopped kangaroo-fashion. Its fore-quarters were higher than its rear and the latter were always in a crouched attitude. Its hind feet had four webbed toes. Its eyes were still open and very yellow and its jaw is neither dog, wolf, nor coyote. Its teeth are most curious, as the crushers in the lower jaws each have four prongs into which the upper teeth fit perfectly.

This too could be a dog-family hybrid, except for its hopping gait.[52] Another jumping animal was puzzling police near Concord, Delaware (USA), in September 1979. Witnesses described seeing a black four-footed animal less than 3 feet tall, with a 2-foot long tail that was not bushy but tapered, and curled at the end. Instead of running it leapt 'like a kangaroo'. Strange tracks 4 by 4½ inches were also found.[53] The mystery animal seen around Old Lyme, Connecticut (USA), in July–September 1986 was described as a cross between a dog and a rabbit. It had a dog's body and a rabbit's head, with long floppy ears, and it hopped like a rabbit. Standing more than 18 inches tall, it was thin like a greyhound (perhaps starving through indecision as to whether it should be carnivorous or vegetarian), had short grey hair and a long thin tail. It seems highly improbable that a dog and a rabbit could mate successfully. One suggestion was that the animal was a European hare, but no member of the rabbit family has a long thin tail.[54]

The coati, mentioned earlier as possibly responsible for some sightings of 'kangaroos', is not a familiar animal in most parts of

The coati killed near Falls City, Nebraska (USA) in 1968.

North America, although the range of the white-nosed coati (*Nasua narica*) is wider than is generally realized. Hence the puzzlement when a specimen was killed near Falls City, Nebraska (USA), late in October 1968.[55] It was seen to walk briefly on its hind legs, and apparently coatis can do this; they can also climb trees. The animal was likened to both a raccoon and a dog, and the witnesses were on the right track, for the coati is a member of the raccoon family and raccoons are thought to be closely linked to dogs and bears in the evolutionary line.

Earlier in this chapter we reported on the discovery of some large reptiles in the USA – 6-foot Nile monitor lizards and crocodilians up to 10 feet or more long. There have been a few other reports of giant reptiles and amphibians which may or may not turn out to be known species: like the giant 8-foot salamander reputedly caught in the Trinity Alps in northern California in 1960 by animal trainer Vern Harden and a companion. They used a shark hook, and held the creature for long enough to measure it, before letting it go as a storm approached. Other explorers claim to have seen giant salamanders lazing around caves and ponds in the rough wilderness country 25 miles north-west of Weaverville.[56] The largest known North American salamander is the up to 29-inch Hellbender (which, however, is not a Californian species), although some Asian salamanders can reach 5 feet. We know of no more recent reports of 8-foot salamanders; there has, however, been more than one report of bipedal man-sized lizards. In the 1970s the 'Lizardman' was seen near Wayne, New Jersey (USA). A motorist who drove past it saw in his headlights a towering greenish body covered with scales, a reptilian face with bulging frog-like eyes and a broad lipless mouth.[57] In October 1975, a 'giant lizard' 15 feet long with a foot-long forked tongue and big bulging eyes was seen near Milton, Kentucky (USA), by numerous witnesses in Trimble County. It was dull white in colour, with black and white stripes across its body and speckles over it.[58]

The so-called 'Loveland Frog' was probably not a frog at all. It was first seen on Riverside Road near Loveland, Ohio (USA), on 3 March 1972 by a police officer who saw in his headlights a 3–5-foot, leathery-skinned creature with a frog's or lizard's face, which leapt over the guardrail after looking at him for a few seconds and went over the embankment into the Little Miami River. A fortnight later, another police officer saw it on the same road. There were reports of a large frog living in the river going back to the 1950s, and in 1985 two boys claimed to have seen a big-dog-sized frog by the river.[59] One possible identification for the 'Loveland Frog' is an iguana, and the common iguana (*Iguana iguana*) can reach 6½ feet in length. Living mainly in Central and northern South America, it can also be found in Florida, but whether it could survive in the colder, more northerly Ohio in March is another matter. All other North American iguanas are only a few inches long. The Lizardman of New Jersey could also have been a common iguana, but New Jersey is also a long way north of Florida. Alternatively, they might all, including the 'giant lizard' of Kentucky, have been Nile monitor lizards. These have definitely been seen and captured in the States, although they are not native species. They stay near water (the Loveland Frog was near water), they can climb trees (the Loveland Frog climbed over a guardrail), they have forked tongues (the Kentucky lizard had a forked tongue), they are striped and speckled (as was the Kentucky lizard). There are also dissimilarities in the descriptions as well as similarities, not to mention the rarity of Nile monitor lizards in North America – but this is the closest identification we can find. Over to all you readers with more zoological knowledge than we have . . .

The 'Loveland Frog',
seen in Ohio in 1972.

Mysterious giant reptiles are not only found in North America. There are persistent reports that monitor lizards 30 feet long are living successfully in Australia – in the forests of northern Queensland, and further south in New South Wales and Victoria, as well as in New Guinea. These creatures are not yet officially accepted, but there have been numerous reliable sightings, and they are thought to be a native species, not out-of-place animals like the Nile monitors found in North America. On 27 December 1975, a farmer saw a monitor lizard at least 30 feet long in scrubland on his Cessnock (New South Wales) farm. It stood about 3 feet off the ground, had four powerful legs, a 2-foot neck and 3-foot head. It was mottled and greyish, with dark stripes. Early in 1979, herpetologist Frank Gordon was driving in the Wattagan mountains of New South Wales in his Land Rover, and while searching for skinks in a swamp in an inaccessible region he saw a large 'log' which suddenly got up on four legs and ran into the forest. It was about 27–30 feet long. In 1975 two farmers stopped their vehicle to remove a 'log' blocking their road, but it obligingly removed itself. This again was in the Wattagans. These are only a few of the reports collected by Rex Gilroy, in his search for the Australian giant lizard.[60]

Giant reptiles have also been seen in recent years in parts of Europe. Over the 50 years from the 1930s to the 1980s there have been intermittent reports from Italy of giant lizards, like the 8-foot 'dragon' with a green and yellow body seen at Monterose north of Rome in 1935. It was seen in a forest, and an old man said he had been seeing it every ten to fifteen years since he was a boy.[61] More recently in Italy, there have been many sightings of a 'huge scaly thing at least 15 feet long. It walked on thick legs and its breath was searing hot. I ran for my life and it followed me for a couple of hundred yards.' This creature was seen in July 1969 near Forli; a few years later the Goro Monster appeared. In June 1975 a farmer hoeing tomatoes saw a large snake with legs, over 10 feet long and as thick as a dog. The police found tracks, but no monster. Apparently the creature was also seen in earlier years.[62] A 12-foot fur-covered reptile-like creature with four legs was reportedly seen at Cosenza in July 1981, again by several witnesses, but the police could find no trace of it.[63]

Further north, there have for centuries been reports of a large unknown reptile 3–6 feet long, living in the Swiss, Bavarian and Austrian Alps, and known as the Tatzelwurm. It looks like an oversized lizard, and is whitish or light brown in colour, with powerful three-toed feet and a cat- or fish- or salamander-like head, a wide mouth with sharp teeth, and a forked tongue. Sightings are now infrequent. One was seen near Rauris (Austria) in the summer of 1921, the creature being 2–2½ feet long, grey in colour, and it leapt 25 feet at a height of 9 feet in the direction of the witness, who escaped.[64] Numerous identifications have been put forward: an otter, a pearl lizard, a glass snake, a myth . . . or a giant salamander, which seems feasible in view of the fact that salamanders can reach 2½ feet in America (the Hellbender) and 5 feet in Asia. Why not a European mountain salamander reaching 3–6 feet? There may also be Tatzelwurms in the Pyrenees between France and Spain. There were reports of a giant lizard near Ossum (France) in the late 1890s, and again in May 1939, when it was seen by women picking berries. The folklore of the area contains legends of giant lizards with crests.[65]

Giant snakes have also been seen in Spain. A green snake 6 feet long crossed a road from a sugar field and was killed by a car, at Chinchilla, Albacete, on 22 July 1969. In the following summer a 6-foot snake was seen regularly on a farm near Alcoy in Alicante, and another at Orihuela.[66] There have been numerous sightings of giant snakes in America, too, and although it is likely that a good proportion of them are escaped pets, it is also possible that these creatures, or even unknown native species, could live successfully and unobtrusively in the sparsely populated regions. In the Appalachian mountains of Pennsylvania, for example, a 40-foot snake first reported by hikers in 1919 has been intermittently seen ever since. It is believed to spend the cold winters in warm coal-mine shafts.[67] Another area with sightings spread over decades is the Hockomock Swamp in Massachusetts.[68] In the summer of 1944 an 18-footer that became known as the Peninsula Python was seen by numerous people along the Cuyahoga River, Ohio.[69] More recently, a huge snake nearly caused Eileen Blackburn to crash her car near Cascade, Montana. In late October 1978 she was driving on Interstate Highway 15 about 2½ miles south of Cascade when she saw the snake.

> It was between 20 and 30 feet long and its coils were at least three feet across. It covered my side of the freeway. It was standing, with its head up, and it was taller than the hood of my car.
> I tried to slow down and I'm sure I hit it or it struck at the car

because it hit high on the lefthand side of my car. It appeared to be a sort of a grey-white in colour with a tan strip.

It had a flat head that came down to a point and the head was wider than the body. The body was about six inches in diameter at its widest point and, from the way it stood and the shape of the head, it looked like a cobra. I've seen rattlesnakes, bullsnakes and cobras and this looked like a cobra.

Her daughter also saw the snake, as did others on the road, but the police chief who went to look for it found nothing.[70]

We have travelled a long way in this chapter from out-of-place big cats to huge snakes, via kangaroos, crocodiles and giant lizards, but there are even more monsters to report on in Chapter 17: the 'extinct' species which may not be extinct at all. Watch out for pterodactyls, dinosaurs, and mammoths!

15 *Religious phenomena, including visions of the Virgin Mary*

Early in 1988, Cardinal Sin was blaming visions of the Virgin Mary on hunger, saying: 'When you are hungry you see visions, so my advice is to eat. When you are not hungry you will not see visions.' This assertion followed claims that the Blessed Virgin Mary had appeared to crowds in Manila (Philippines).[1] If he had been referring to spiritual rather than physical hunger, the Cardinal's comment might have made more sense. We must charitably conclude that he is not aware that thousands of people have claimed to have seen visions of the Blessed Virgin Mary in this century alone, of whom only a small proportion are likely to have been hungry at the time. Far more relevant to the search for an explanation of the visions is the fact that the majority of witnesses were Catholics. However, it should not be thought that the Catholic authorities somehow engineer these apparitions, or at least encourage them, in order to increase the devotion of their flock; on the contrary, the Catholic Church is very loth to endorse apparitions, and the miracles and cures which often follow, and, like Cardinal Sin, attempts to dissuade believers from taking an interest in such events. So these happenings are outside the control of the official Church, and the believers who flock to the places where visions are seen are not doing so with Church approval. They may seem, indeed, to be disregarding Church instructions, even transferring their allegiance from the official Church to the religious figures whose apparitions they see. Perhaps it is this loss of control over their flock which most concerns the Church officials.

Whatever the Church thinks about the apparitions, they have continued to appear regularly over the decades. The visionary figure is usually the Blessed Virgin Mary in one of her many guises, sometimes alone, sometimes with the infant Jesus, and/or angels and saints. She appears in a wide variety of costumes, the details of which are usually minutely remembered by the witnesses. The initial witnesses are often children or teenagers, though adults may also witness later visions. She often has messages, sometimes secret, which she tells to the chosen recipients. She sometimes provides signs to prove her presence to the faithful, especially in those cases where only a few chosen witnesses can actually see her. There are many cases of single-witness visions where no signs are given, and we have not concerned ourselves with those visions here, because it is possible for hoaxes to occur, and for ardent Catholics to let their imaginations run away with them. So we are only including those visions with more than one witness, or where the signs at least are seen by many, even if the Virgin herself is not. Even these events could be lacking in external reality, of course, in that the witnesses could be sharing an imaginary experience, based on expectations.

There is a school of thought which believes all such events to be either hallucinatory or illusionary, and that it is 'the loss of loved ones or repressed sexual feelings' which bring about visions of the Blessed Virgin Mary.[2] But this is a simplistic interpretation of what are complex psychic events. Whether Catholics are indeed hungrier, more grief-stricken or more starved of sex than other mortals is doubtful. We suspect that the tendencies that cause people to see visions are inherent in most of us, but they express themselves in different ways: Catholics see visions; others see UFOs or are abducted by UFO entities. If we search hard enough, we can find in all civilizations ways in which this desire to make contact with higher beings manifests itself.

The most important question, as yet unanswered, is whether any external, objective intelligence has a hand in this kind of experience, or whether the visions, encounters, or whatever are solely personal, self-induced events. There are certainly some puzzling factors to be considered. Our Lady's liking for trees and springs is noticeable. Would an uneducated peasant child consciously locate his or her vision in such a spot? The most famous series of visions of the Blessed Virgin Mary took place at Fatima (Portugal), beginning in the spring of 1916 when an angel appeared to three children tending sheep. There were two further appearances, and then on 13 May 1917 they saw the Blessed Virgin Mary herself, again while they were watching the sheep. Her arrival was heralded by a flash of lightning, and as they hastily drove the sheep down the hill, fearing a storm, they saw a beautiful and dazzling woman standing in the foliage of a small oak tree. Later apparitions again took place at the oak tree.[3] The visions seen at Beauraing (Belgium) beginning on 29 November

1932 were always located close to a may tree,[4] at San Damiano (Italy) the Virgin appeared over a pear tree,[5] and there are others where the vision was located at or in a tree.

Springs are even more important. The famous events at Lourdes (France), which began on 11 February 1858 at Massabielle when Bernadette Soubirous saw a vision of a lady in white, resulted in the water of Lourdes being used for healing up to the present day. Our Lady directed Bernadette to a damp patch of earth in the grotto where she appeared, and at that point a spring arose which soon yielded more than eighteen gallons of water daily, becoming the focal point of the Lourdes shrine.[6] An earlier vision at La Salette (France) in September 1846 was followed by cures from spring water,[7] and at Banneux (Belgium), Our Lady directed twelve-year-old Mariette Beco to put her hands in a small spring or stream, saying, 'This stream is reserved for me.' On the next occasion, she again went to the stream, and the apparition said 'This spring is reserved for all nations. To relieve the sick.' There were eight apparitions in all, during January to March 1933, and Banneux is now a centre of pilgrimage and healing.[8] On 2 July 1947, the Blessed Virgin Mary appeared to Clara Laslona in her home at St Emmerich-Berg (Hungary) and showed her a spring which was to be used for healing the sick, while in 1964, Our Lady caused a well to be dug next to the pear tree where she appeared at San Damiano and the water was used for healing purposes.[9]

Trees and springs have been objects of ritual worship for thousands of years, and in Britain, for example, there are many holy wells surviving which were believed to have healing properties. Some are still visited for healing purposes, such as St Winefride's Well at Holywell (Clwyd, Wales), which is also a Catholic shrine.[10] Trees and springs are important symbols occurring universally in mystical, visionary and religious experience, but the precise nature of their significance to the visionary is too complex to explore in this short chapter.

There are many supernatural elements at work in religious visions. The signs seen by witnesses could be considered supernatural, like the showers of rose petals which fell at Lipa (Philippines), following a series of visions of the Virgin experienced by a Carmelite novice, Teresita, beginning on 12 September 1948. The petals were believed to have healing powers.[11] At San Damiano the pear tree where Our Lady appeared burst into blossom in late autumn, as a 'sign', on at least two occasions in the 1960s, and many photographs

This photograph is said to show an appearance of Our Lady at San Damiano (Italy) on 16 October 1967.

were taken of strange light effects when the sun appeared to spin and throw out coloured shafts of light.[12] A similar miracle, 'the dance of the sun', took place at Fatima on 13 October 1917, witnessed by about 70,000 people who had gathered for the expected apparition of the Blessed Virgin Mary. One eyewitness was Father Ignatius Lawrence Pereira who was a nine-year-old boy at the time, and was attending school when the teachers and pupils heard shouts outside.

Our teacher rushed out, and the children all ran after her. In the public square people wept and shouted, pointing to the sun, without paying the slightest heed to the questions of our teacher . . . it was the great solar prodigy with all its wonderful phenomena which was seen distinctly even from the hill on which my village was situated. This miracle I feel incapable of describing such as I saw it at that moment. I looked fixedly at the sun, which appeared pale and did not dazzle. It looked like a ball of snow turning on itself . . . Then suddenly it seemed to become detached from the sky, and rolled right and left, as if it were falling

Part of the huge crowd which witnessed 'the dance of the sun' at Fatima on 13 October 1917.

upon the earth. Terrified, absolutely terrified, I ran towards the crowd of people. All were weeping, expecting at any moment the end of the world . . . During the long minutes of the solar phenomena, the objects around us reflected all the colours of the rainbow. Looking at each other, one appeared blue, another yellow, a third red, etc., and all these strange phenomena only increased the terror of the people. After about ten minutes the sun climbed back into its place, as it had descended, still quite pale and without brilliance. When the people were convinced that the danger had passed, there was an outburst of joy.[13]

On the same occasion, before 'the dance of the sun', a shower of white flower petals fell at the place where Our Lady appeared, but they disintegrated before landing.[14] With regard to the validity of the phenomenon known as 'the dance of the sun', one person can hallucinate, two together *might* share a hallucination (though psychologists do not agree about whether that is possible) – but it is beyond all possibility that 70,000 people could share a hallucination. Nor were the witnesses all simple peasants – there were many sceptics, disbelievers and scientists among the crowd, and they too saw the phenomenon.

One of the people present at Fatima on 13 October 1917 was Monsignor John Quareman, and he saw the orb of light which appeared when Lucia claimed the apparition was coming to the oak tree. Remember that at Fatima only the three children could actually see Our Lady. Monsignor Quareman said, 'To my surprise, I saw clearly and distinctly a globe of light advancing from east to west, gliding slowly and majestically through the air . . . My friend looked also, and he had the good fortune to see the same unexpected vision. Suddenly the globe with the wonderful light dropped from sight.'[15] If we did not know that he was describing the arrival of the Blessed Virgin Mary, we might easily think he was describing a UFO sighting.

We have already suggested that where some people see visions of Our Lady, others would see UFOs. This is illustrated by events in Quebec (Canada) in the summer of 1968, when UFOs and entities were being seen. In one case, at St-Stanislas-de-Kotska on the evening of Sunday 28 July 1968, five children saw 'a sort of circle surrounded by a bright red halo', and then a second one; the first landed in a cornfield close to the house. They went out to investigate, taking a flashlight, and in its beam they saw a creature less than 45 feet away. It was about 3½ feet tall, with an ugly black face with rough, furrowed skin, and on seeing it they dashed back to the house in panic. One boy saw the creature's face looking in at him through a window, and it was knocking on the glass and making a mooing sound. Shortly afterwards they saw the UFO with its red halo ascending slowly into the sky. Next day, the landing site was seen to be an area of flattened oats.[16] On the same night, at Upton, Quebec, three hours later, a family saw a sparkling, rotating 'cloud' in their garden, and several 3-foot entities chasing the cows in a nearby field.[17] Whether these were the same entities as the one the children saw is impossible to judge, because at Upton they were not close enough for the witnesses to see them clearly. In late July, at St Bruno in Quebec, five to thirteen children on a farm saw a cloud come out of the sky, and from it stepped the Blessed Virgin Mary who spoke to them about peace and brotherhood. One of the families set up an altar in the backyard, and many people gathered on 7 October when she had said she would return, but they waited in vain.[18]

Something strange was obviously happening in Quebec at the end of July 1968, but what? Although all the witnesses saw the craft as clouds or lights, as UFOs are often described, when it came to the associated events those from a religious background saw the Blessed Virgin Mary, and the other children saw a UFO entity. Does this indicate that when an encounter is triggered by some stimulus, what is seen depends very much upon the witnesses' own beliefs and mental images? Some researchers believe that seismic activity is the trigger, or more specifically, that when there is seismic (earthquake) activity in the area, electro-magnetic phenomena result, and these may react with the human bio-electrical system, causing distortions in the brain's electricity. With the brain thus stimulated, the witness will see monsters, humanoids, UFO entities, visions . . .[19] The seismic activity may also produce luminosity, and these free-floating lights could be interpreted as UFOs, or as heralding the arrival of the Blessed Virgin Mary (as at Fatima and elsewhere). At Zeitoun, a suburb of Cairo (Egypt), between April 1968 and May 1971, hundreds of thousands of people witnessed luminous phenomena over St Mary's church. It began on 2 April 1968 when two Muslim car mechanics saw a white figure which they thought was a nun standing on top of the church. It disappeared after several minutes, but crowds began to gather hoping for a reappearance, which happened a week later. Then it appeared two or three times a week. Its arrival was heralded by flashes of light, then the figure would form, human in shape, and white in colour (sometimes bluish-white), wearing flowing robes of light. It was sometimes accompanied by 'doves of light' which flew around without flapping their wings. The figure was interpreted as the Blessed Virgin Mary, and that is what people then saw: they claimed to see her bowing to them, pacing back and forth, hands raised in blessing, garments swaying in the wind.[20] How much of this detail was grafted on to an amorphous luminous shape by the awestruck crowd? Was the Blessed Virgin Mary really present at all?

Researchers into the association between such phenomena and seismic activity have found that, during 1969, seismic activity within a radius of less than 500 kilometres was ten times greater than normal, and they conclude that this supports their hypothetical link between luminous phenomena and seismic activity.[21] However, the Zeitoun appearances were most strong from April to summer 1968, and were waning by 1969, so the temporal link is not quite as close as the scientists would like to think. Also, a radius of 500 kilometres gives a very large area. But if their theory is valid, it does not necessarily rob the Zeitoun (and other similar) phenomena of all paranormal content. It could be that the psychic energy of the crowds was responsible for forming the luminosity into human shape; or if there is an exterior force or intelligence behind such appearances, it too could use the luminous seismic phenomena as a means to facilitate its appearances, clothing itself in the garb most easily accessible from the preconceptions of the eager witnesses. And there is a third possibility: the strength of the apparition could have created the seismic disturbances, rather than the other way round.

Luminous phenomena above a Zeitoun (Egypt) church in 1968.

More recently, Our Lady has been appearing at another Cairo church, that of St Damiana the Martyr in Shoubra. The first vision occurred on 25 March 1986, on the roof as at Zeitoun. On succeeding nights thousands came to see the apparitions. In addition to the Virgin, a fiery cross appeared, and St Damiana herself. Miracle cures have been reported. If both the Shoubra and the Zeitoun apparitions are merely natural luminous phenomena, why do they appear on church roofs rather than anywhere else?

Whatever may be the reality behind religious apparitions, it is clear that many devout Catholics would greatly welcome, albeit fearfully, their own personal encounter with Our Lady, or some other saintly figure. Therefore they might tend to interpret in a religious way images which non-religious people would see differently. Many such occurrences are recorded in the press, the image usually taking the form of Christ's face or the outline of the Blessed Virgin Mary, for example at Sault Ste Marie, Ontario (Canada), where an image of the Virgin Mary was found in 1985 when a large branch was lopped off a tree, and a constant flow of pilgrims came to visit this natural icon.[22] In Beauport, Quebec (Canada), Canon Cyrille Labreque died on 8 March 1977, and when he was lying in his coffin one of the sisters of the Adoring Missionary Dominican Sisters saw an image of Christ on the sole of his shoe.[23] In April 1974 the parishioners at Castelnau de Guers (France) saw the face of Christ on a napkin covering the ciborium on the altar. It lasted for about fifteen minutes, and was also seen by the priest. 'I had just knelt before the altar. As I rose I saw, on the fine white napkin covering the ciborium, the face of Our Lord. His right eye was closed, the left open. The nose was bruised and swollen and the face bore an expression of pain.' The church afterwards became overrun by seekers after relics.[24] In Italy, an image of Jesus on a window pane at Supino in September 1987 was pronounced an optical illusion caused by dirty glass, but the believers still came to look.[25] A butterfly fish, bought at Dar es Salaam (Tanzania) market in 1965, had Arabic writing on its fin, which was deciphered as 'Divine Universal Truth. There none but God to be worshipped.'[26] In Mount Shasta, California (USA), a fluttery white angel's image was being seen on the screen of a faulty television set in August 1987, said by a prosaic television repairman to be the result of a faulty capacitor.[27] At Lake Arthur, New Mexico (USA), a woman frying tortillas in October 1977 found that one was marked with Christ's face, and now it is visited by pilgrims at its shrine in a local church.[28]

We could continue indefinitely with accounts of religious imagery. The quantity of reports confirms mankind's ability to see meaningful images in fortuitous marks – a variant on the children's game of seeing castles in the clouds, or pictures in the fire. The problem lies in separating these 'Rorschach blot' pictures from the truly supernatural images, of which there are undoubtedly some. Perhaps the most intriguing was the case of the hailstones of Remiremont (France). At the time of the miraculous hail shower, there was upset in the town because an outdoor procession in honour of Our Lady of the Treasure had been banned. Then, on 26 May 1907, a fierce hailstorm was followed by a second storm, in which hailstones as large as tomatoes and hen's eggs fell. The large hailstones fell from 5.30 to 6.15, and some were collected afterwards. They were found to contain a portrait of the Virgin Mary. A villager took some to show to a local priest, Abbé Gueniot.

> In order to satisfy her, I glanced carelessly at the hailstones, which she held in her hand. But since I did not want to see anything, and moreover could not do so without my spectacles, I turned to go back to my book. She urged: 'I beg of you to put on your glasses.' I did so, and saw very distinctly on the front of the hailstones, which were slightly convex in the centre, although the edges were somewhat worn, the bust of a woman, with a robe that was turned up at the bottom, like a priest's cope. I should, perhaps, describe it more exactly by saying that it was like the Virgin of the Hermits. The outline of the images was slightly hollow, as if they had been formed with a punch, but were very boldly drawn. Mlle André asked me to notice certain details of the costume, but I refused to look at it any longer. I was ashamed of my credulity, feeling sure that the Blessed Virgin would hardly concern herself with instantaneous photographs on hailstones. I said, 'But do not you see that these hailstones have fallen on vegetables, and received these impressions? Take them away: they are no good to me.' I returned to my book, without giving further thought to what had happened. But my mind was disturbed by the singular formation of these hailstones. I picked up three in order to weigh them, without looking closely. They weighed between six and seven ounces. One of them was perfectly round, like balls with which children play, and had a seam all around it, as though it had been cast in a mould.[29]

Quite as strange as the image of Our Lady is the fact that the hailstones were seen to fall slowly. This is a characteristic of poltergeist phenomena, as we have seen in Chapter 1 and will again encounter in the next chapter, dealing with showers of stones. If the facts of Remiremont have been accurately reported, there seems no straightforward explanation for the miraculous hailstones.[30]

The reports of weeping and bleeding religious images are equally puzzling. There are hundreds of these on record around the world: anywhere there is a devout Catholic community the phenomenon seems likely to happen at any time, though Italy and the United States of America are the places where a high proportion of the cases have occurred. Statues or paintings of the Virgin Mary and of Christ are the usual focus for this phenomenon, but any saint could be the focus and even non-saints: in January 1974 a plate with pictures of Pope John XXIII and President John F. Kennedy began to ooze drops of blood in Pescara (Italy).[31]

Weeping images can result in outbreaks of religious fervour, as occurred in Syracuse in Sicily (Italy) in 1953. In August of that year Antonietta Januso was pregnant and bedridden after suffering seizures, blindness and fainting spells. On 29 August she had a series of fits and following that noticed that a plaster statue of the Madonna was weeping. News of the miracle spread rapidly, and crowds gathered. Samples of the tears were analysed and found to be indistinguishable from human tears. The Church officially recognized the miracle, and a shrine was erected where the statue is still venerated by pilgrims.[32] Disbelievers have of course found ways of denying the strangeness of the phenomenon. It has been suggested that plaster statues are coated with plastic and if this is punctured at the eyes the water naturally held in the plaster will seep out producing 'tears'.[33] An enterprising scientist in America, Shawn Carlson, has devised six ways to make an image weep. In one experiment he used salt crystals to make a copy of the Mona Lisa cry.[34] There is no mention of his having made any images cry tears indistinguishable in composition from human tears. The Syracuse Madonna wept real tears, and in other cases where analysis of the liquid has been performed, they were pronounced to be real human tears. As if weeping real tears were not strange enough, in one instance the tears vanished when they reached the bottom of the frame in which the weeping portrait of the Virgin was mounted. A priest confirmed that this was happening (in Island Park, New York, USA, in March 1960).[35] Of course hoaxes do occur. In Lomello near

A weeping statue of Our Lady at Maasmechelen, Belgium.

Pavia (Italy) in August 1980 a plaster Virgin was seen to be weeping coloured tears, and it was rumoured that the owner had been seen squirting pink water on to the statue from his son's water pistol.[36]

Bleeding images are perhaps harder to fake, particularly when the blood is analysed and found to be human. A representative case took

262

place in January 1971 in Maropati (Italy), when a lawyer woke up
and found that a painting of the Madonna hanging over his bed was
dripping blood. First of all he found blood spots on the pillowcases,
but neither he nor his wife had cut themselves.

> After the blood spots appeared a few more times, I was dumb-
> founded to discover that they were dripping from under the glass
> of the painting. The bloodlike liquid was coming from the
> Madonna's eyes like tears, and from her heart, hands, and feet. It
> was also dripping from the hands and feet of the two saints
> kneeling beside her. Some of the red liquid began to form crosses
> on the white wall below the painting.

After the bleeding had occurred daily for a while, it later became
more intermittent. Police searched for signs of hoaxing, but found
none. They took the painting and placed it in a locked box at their
headquarters, but next morning when they looked at it they found
blood on the painting again. Analysis proved it was human blood.[37]
When the blood from a statue of Christ was analysed in Pennsylvania
(USA) in 1975, it was found to be human blood but in an advanced
state of decomposition, the red cell count being very low.[38] Miracle
cures have followed some bleedings, as at Baguio City (Philippines)
where in 1983 the exposed heart on the breast of a 10-foot statue of
the Virgin was bleeding, the blood soaking a white sheet placed
below the statue. The sculptor of the statue, one of many who were
cured, recovered from cancer.[39] Even bleeding phenomena can be
hoaxes, however. In Canada in December 1985 and January 1986 a
statue of the Virgin was allegedly weeping and sweating blood at
Ste-Marthe-sur-le-lac, in Quebec, but a TV crew member who
scraped some of the blood from her face had it analysed and found it
was composed of pork dripping, beef fat and vegetable oil. Someone
later admitted that he had regularly applied fat and his own blood to
the statue.[40]

Sometimes the substance which is secreted by the image is neither
tears nor blood, but oil of some kind. A statue of St Charbal (a
Lebanese saint canonized in 1977) oozed oil in Concord, Sydney,
New South Wales (Australia), beginning on 15 March 1985 and
continuing for a week. A plastic statue of the Virgin Mary in
Ramallah (Jordan) was oozing olive oil in October 1987, whenever it
was touched by ten-year-old Samaher Hnout. Countless times she
climbed on the table at her home to reach the statue which stood on a

A bleeding picture of Christ in a church at Mirebeau-en-Poitou, France, in 1911–12.

wall unit, touched the statue, then rubbed her oily fingers on the hands of the pilgrims who had gathered to see the miracle.[41] The liquid seeping from a statue of the Virgin Mary at Rmaïch (Lebanon) in November and December 1983 was said to be a mixture of blood and olive oil.[42] In Montreal (Canada) an icon of the 'Mother of God' which came from Mount Athos in Greece began to stream with fragrant myrrh in November 1982.[43]

A clue to the mechanism by which religious images produce tears,

264

blood or whatever can perhaps be found in a case which occurred at Templemore, County Tipperary (Ireland), in August 1920. The phenomena centred on sixteen-year-old James Walsh, a devout Catholic. All his religious images began to bleed, and statues in another house bled after he visited. At the same time as the images were bleeding, poltergeist phenomena were occurring, with furniture and other objects moving of their own accord.[44] D. Scott Rogo, in his excellent book *Miracles*, has commented on the links between poltergeist phenomena and the occurrence of bleeding and weeping images. It would seem that whereas for some people repressed emotions give vent to traditional poltergeist phenomena (as described in Chapter 1), when these people are devoutly religious the phenomena can take the form of bleeding or weeping religious images. Those people who suffer from the stigmata (bleeding in the places where Christ suffered at the Crucifixion, most often in the palms of the hands) sometimes find that religious images in their homes are also bleeding. One such was Sister Elena Aiello of Cosenza, Calabria (Italy), who suffered bleeding stigmata on her hands. One day some of the blood splashed on to the wall near her bed, and it formed a picture of Jesus's face. This could not be washed away, even by use of detergents, and it flowed with fresh blood, which tests showed to be human. The blood began flowing on 29 September 1955 and continued until 13 October, thereafter flowing intermittently until Sister Elena's death in 1961.[45] Enzo Alocci was another Italian stigmatic at whose home in Porto Santo Stefano religious images would bleed.[46]

Sister Elena Aiello of Cosenza (Italy) photographed some time during 1955–61. The stigmata on her hands are covered, but she displays the face of Jesus formed of blood which appeared in her bedroom.

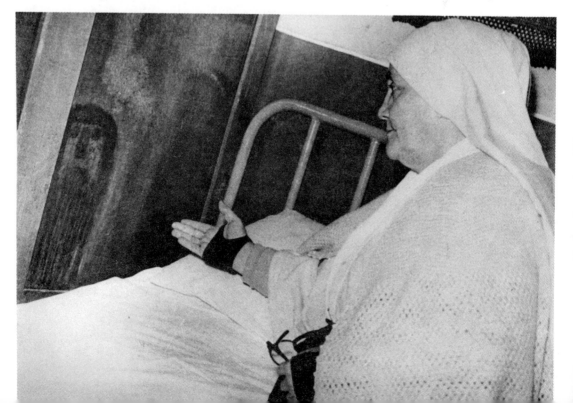

Natuzza Evolo's 'haemographs' or blood pictures are perhaps the most extraordinary. She is a stigmatic living in Paravati (Italy), and she is illiterate, so she cannot be consciously responsible for the words in foreign languages which form in her blood. An example of the production of a haemograph is given by Giovanna de Chiara, a schoolteacher.

It was Holy Monday three years ago. Natuzza was at Catanzaro at my house, and besides her and me, there were my sisters Nella and Rosetta. All of a sudden we noticed that the wound on Natuzza's wrist was bleeding; so we asked her to produce a haemograph for a young man who I knew wanted an example. Natuzza held a white handkerchief that I had given her on her wrist for about 10–15 minutes. It had the name of the owner written on it. After that she gave me back the handkerchief. I opened it and saw some bloodstains. I put it on the table and we all waited for the formation of the design.

Slowly the blood started to move to one side of the handkerchief and vertically spell out the name S. Valeriano Martire. The bloodstain that was left started then to move as well and formed the figure of a saint whom we assumed to be S. Valeriano. When we read his name Natuzza exclaimed, 'Who is this saint? Does he exist?' When I gave the handkerchief to the owner, I found out that he was devoted to that saint.[47]

The evidence is strong enough to show that although hoaxes can and do occur, the majority of weeping and bleeding phenomena are likely to be genuine, and are somehow linked to poltergeist phenomena.

There are other religious phenomena involving blood which also lack obvious explanations. The 1700-year-old bones of St Maximina are kept at St Adrian's church in Chicago, Illinois (USA), and in May 1970 they were found to be oozing a watery blood.[48] This sounds very similar to the 'perspiration and blood' oozing from the incorrupt body of St Charbal Maklhouf whose remains are kept at the Monastery of St Maro, Annaya (Lebanon). The miraculous phenomena accompanying St Charbal began at his death, for a bright light surrounded his tomb for 45 days following his burial. On exhumation, his body was found to be perfectly preserved, despite frequent heavy rains resulting in the body being found floating in mud. The bloody exudation was first discovered at the exhumation. Since that day in 1899 the flow has continued. The body was buried for 23 years from 1927 to 1950, when pilgrims to his shrine noticed liquid seeping from the tomb. When the saint's body was again exhumed, it was found to be still incorrupt, flexible and lifelike, the garments stained with blood. Now the body is examined annually, when the fluid is found to be 3 inches deep in the coffin. Many thousands of pilgrims visit St Charbal's shrine, and miraculous healings occur frequently.[49]

Somewhat different but equally inexplicable is the miracle of the liquefaction of the blood of St Januarius. St Januarius was a bishop of Benevento, beheaded by the Romans in AD 305. His relics included two phials said to contain his blood, and these are today held, along with his skull, at the cathedral in Naples (Italy). The phials are fastened into a silver and glass case, which cannot be opened without destroying the relics. Several times a year, the reliquary is displayed in ceremonies held in the saint's honour, and the blood, normally dried, liquefies, sometimes bubbling and foaming. On the few occasions when the blood fails to liquefy, the citizens of Naples expect a disaster of some kind, like the severe earthquake which struck Italy in 1976 just after the non-liquefaction. In 1970, Dr Giorgio Giorgi, a Naples doctor, watched the demonstration from only a yard away. He later described how the archbishop had held up the reliquary and rotated it slowly, asking the saint to produce the miracle.

> After about four minutes, certainly no longer, I was disconcerted to see just in front of my nose, at a distance of little over three feet, that the clot of blood had suddenly changed from the solid state into that of a liquid. The transformation from solid into liquid happened suddenly and unexpectedly. The liquid itself had become much brighter, more shining; so many gaseous bubbles appeared inside the liquid (shall we call it blood?) that it seemed to be in a state of ebullition [boiling].

On kissing the case, Dr Giorgi found that it was cool, proving that heating had not caused the liquefaction, which, it seems, happens regardless of the temperature in the cathedral. Sometimes the blood is already liquid when taken from its vault, at others the process of liquefaction takes more than 24 hours. All scientific attempts to explain the miracle have proved negative.[50] Although St Januarius' miracle is by far the best known, there are also other examples of saints' blood liquefying in a similar way. A phial of the blood of St

Aloysius Gonzaga at Gesù Vecchio church in Naples becomes fluid on the feast of St Aloysius, 21–29 June, and the blood of St Pantaleone at Ravello also liquefies.[51]

There are so many religious phenomena which appear to defy all known scientific laws. In the Eucharistic miracle, the bread and wine of the Eucharist have literally turned into real flesh and blood. This is said to have happened at several European locations between AD 595 and 1730, one of them being Lanciano (Italy) where in the eighth century the priest celebrating Mass 'doubted the Real Presence of Our Lord on the altar', and 'before his astonished gaze almost the entire host was changed into Flesh, while a small portion of it remained bread. At the same time the wine became Blood, which clotted and split up into five little pieces of different shape and size.' Twelve centuries later, these relics remain intact, and are on view in an ornate altar in San Francesco. This ancient miracle might be regarded simply as a piece of Catholic folklore, were it not for the fact that in 1970 the relics were scientifically examined under a microscope and in the laboratory. Dr Odoardo Linoli, Professor of Anatomy, Histology and Microscopy at Arezzo, reported that

> the Flesh is real flesh and the Blood real blood. The Flesh, without any possibility of doubt, is heart muscle (myocardium). Heart muscle and blood both belong to the human species and to the same blood group AB. The Blood contains the substances normally found in fresh blood. The preservation of Flesh and Blood, left in their natural state for 12 centuries and exposed to atmospheric and biological physical agents, is a phenomenon that defies explanation.[52]

However, we must add a cautionary note to that unequivocal statement: there is no *proof* that the flesh and blood were once bread and wine; so in that respect the 'miracle' fails to convince the disbeliever.

When we turn to the phenomenon of incorruption, there is incontrovertible proof, in the form of perfectly preserved bodies. There are many records of saints' bodies being dug up years after burial, and being found incorrupt. This phenomenon is not confined to Catholic holy men or women, but there are more on record because of the custom of exhuming saints. A good example of the phenomenon is St Catherine Labouré, who died in 1876 in Paris (France). Her body was buried in a triple coffin in a chapel crypt in the city and lay undisturbed for 56 years until it was exhumed on 21 March 1933 in preparation for her beatification. A surgeon who witnessed the exhumation reported:

> The body was carefully taken out of the coffin and placed on a long table.
>
> The face on account of its first contact with the air had slightly darkened since the day before [when the saint's body was first revealed]; the clothing perfectly preserved was carefully removed . . .
>
> In examining the body we noticed the perfect suppleness of the arms and legs. These members have merely undergone a slight mummification. The skin throughout was intact and like parchment. The muscles were preserved; we could easily dissect them in a study of anatomy.
>
> We cut the sternum on the median line. The bone showed a cartilaginous, elastic consistency and was easily cut by the surgeon's knife. The thoracic cavity being opened it was easy for us to remove the heart. It was much shrunken but it had kept its shape. We could easily see within it the little fibrous cords, remains of the valves and muscles. We also took out a number of the ribs and the clavicle. We disjointed the arms – these two will be conserved apart. The two knee caps were taken out. The fingers and toe nails were in perfect condition. The hair remained attached to the scalp.
>
> The eyes were in the orbits; the eyelids half closed; we were able to state that the ball though fallen and shrunken existed in its entirety, and even the colour, bluish grey, of the iris still remained. The ears were intact.
>
> To ensure the preservation of the body we injected a solution of formaldehyde, glycerine and carbolic acid.[53]

Other Christian religious figures whose incorrupt bodies have been exhumed this century include Blessed Maria Assunta Pallotta, the Curé of Ars (St Jean Vianney), St Bernadette Soubirous (the visionary of Lourdes), Blessed Paula Frassinetti, and St Charbal Maklhouf (mentioned earlier); more details of these and many other pre-twentieth-century incorrupt Catholic saints can be found in *The Incorruptibles* by Joan Carroll Cruz. A very recent example, post-dating Ms Cruz's book, is that of the discovery of Cardinal Schuster's incorrupt body at Milan (Italy). He died in 1954, and was an

The incorrupt body of St Bernadette Soubirous.

admirer of Fascism and a friend of Mussolini, so his incorruption is somewhat embarrassing to the Church; there were allegations that it was not a genuine incorruption, but that the corpse had been injected with preservative immediately after death.[54] Incorruption also occurs in other religious traditions, for example it was said that when the Chinese Communists opened the shrine which housed the mummy of Tsong Kha-pa (a Tibetan Buddhist leader who died in 1419) the body was undecayed and still warm.[55]

Miracle cures have followed the discovery of blood oozing from saints' remains, and the same has happened after miraculous flows of pure water. A fourth-century stone sarcophagus at Arles-sur-Tech, Pyrénées Orientales (France), produces a flow of pure water which is taken out by means of a small pump. The tomb stands on supports above the ground, and there is no obvious explanation for the annual flow of 80–150 gallons. This water is placed in small phials and used to heal the sick.[56] A similar source of healing water (called 'oil' in this instance) is the stone sarcophagus of St Walburga, housed in a shrine to the saint at the Abbey of St Walburg, in Eichstätt (West Germany). Every year, water drips from the tomb into a dish, beginning in October and continuing until the end of February, and flows regardless of atmospheric conditions. The water is collected and poured into glass phials, for it is said to have healing properties.[57] The water (called 'manna') which oozes from the bones of St Nicholas, kept in a basilica at Bari (Italy), is said to be sweet-smelling and able to cure illness if drunk. It is bottled, after dilution with ordinary water (because there is not enough to satisfy demand), and sold to pilgrims.[58]

There are many other well-attested inexplicable phenomena associated with religion and mysticism, such as stigmata, levitation, bodily elongation, the odour of sanctity, prolonged fasting, bilocation (being seen in two places at the same time) and other miraculous happenings. Until someone writes a definitive study of all these phenomena, and the ones we have briefly covered in this chapter, we must guide those with whetted appetites to two reliable books already published which cover some of them – D. Scott Rogo's *Miracles* and Herbert Thurston's *The Physical Phenomena of Mysticism*. Both are well worth delving into. D. Scott Rogo gives one good reason why the definitive book has not yet been written: 'Such an endeavour would take a lifetime of research, and the results would fill more than a dozen books.'

16 *Stones thrown by invisible assailants*

> The Invisible Wights which haunt houses seem rather to be some of our Subterranean Inhabitants (which appear often to men of second sight), than Evill Spirits or Devils, because tho they throw great stons, pieces of Earth, and wood at the Inhabitants, they hurt them not at all, as if they acted not maliciously like Devils, but in Sport like Buffoons and drols.

Robert Kirk wrote these words in 1690, as part of his *Secret Common-Wealth*, a treatise on supernatural happenings,[1] and the quotation shows very clearly that the phenomenon of showers of stones was well known in the seventeenth century and earlier. A pamphlet published in London in 1698 was entitled *Lithobolia, or the Stone-throwing Devil*, and described a poltergeist outbreak including the throwing of missiles 'by an Invisible hand' in New Hampshire (USA).[2] But little or no progress has been made in finding a solution to the mystery, probably because there has been no scientific investigation of it. Whenever it happens the police are baffled; they assume that someone is throwing the missiles, but cannot explain how they escape detection. The police usually do not realize that the pattern is a familiar one: they believe it to be a singular event. This chapter will show that it is far from being a unique occurrence, but is both world-wide and happening regularly.

The phenomenon clearly has poltergeist links – usually (but not always) other poltergeist phenomena are reported as happening at the same time. There is often one person on whom the stones seem to focus, as in poltergeist phenomena. There is also an interesting overlap with the 'falls' phenomenon we described in Chapter 13: sometimes the stones fall vertically as if from the sky. Whether they are indeed falling out of the sky, or 'merely' materializing a few feet up, is not easy to determine. If apparent falls of stones are indeed a poltergeist-type phenomenon, then maybe other 'falls' are not really falls at all but poltergeist showers. It might be fruitful to re-examine the cases in Chapter 13 in that light. A rundown of the best of the twentieth-century stone-throwing cases that we have on record will perhaps give some clues as to why and how this puzzling phenomenon occurs.

In October 1901 stones were falling on Harrisonville, Ohio (USA), as reported here in the *Buffalo Express* of 27 October 1901:

Pomeroy, O., Oct. 26 – The little village of Harrisonville, eight miles from this city, is terribly wrought up over the mysterious stoning of houses and people there in broad daylight. It began on Sunday afternoon, October 13th, when a small boulder came crashing through the window of Zach Dye's house, a half-mile out of town. The family were all at home, and at once ran out to see who had thrown the stone, but no one could be found, notwithstanding the house stands in the open and several hundred yards from any object large enough for a man to hide behind. While the members stood about in the yard in open-mouthed wonder, other stones pelted the house, coming from where no one knows.

On Monday afternoon, at about the same hour, a shower of stones fell right in the heart of the little village. The first intimation the citizens had of it was when a piece of rock came through the plate-glass door of a store, and when the proprietor and the customers ran outside to see who had thrown it, there was no one in sight. An alarm was given and the citizens came out with their guns, and, notwithstanding the stones continued to fall about them, they were unable to tell whence they came. One man, William Alkire, was hit a glancing blow on the arm, but was not seriously injured, while James Clay, a one-legged man, who was standing in front of his house shouting to the excited populace that it was probably nothing more than a lot of mischievous boys, had his crutch knocked from under him and broken by a large boulder, which struck it about midway.

On the third day, when the stones began to fly through the air, the entire population thronged the streets. They were lined up and counted, to see who it could be that was throwing the stones. Every man and boy in the village was found to be in the line, and still the dangerous missiles flew through the air.[3]

By having all the male population in view, these resourceful villagers proved that the stone-throwing was not a local prank. (Presumably they thought a female could not be capable of such a thing.) That it had poltergeist origins is suggested by the incident of James Clay's broken crutch, which is an example of the mischievous humour typical of poltergeists.

Two years later, in September 1903, an equally puzzling yet different type of stone-throwing poltergeist briefly afflicted W. G. Grottendieck, who was living at Dortrecht in the Sumatran jungle (Indonesia). He wrote:

> At about one o'clock at night I half awoke, hearing something fall near my head outside the mosquito curtain on the floor. After a couple of minutes I completely awoke and turned my head half round to see what was falling on the floor. They were black stones from ⅛ to ¾ of an inch long. I got out of the curtain and turned up the kerosene lamp, that was standing on the floor at the foot of the bed. I saw then that the stones were falling through the roof in a parabolic line. They fell on the floor close to my head-pillow. I went out and awoke the boy (a Malay-Pelambang coolie) who was sleeping on the floor in the next room. I told him to go outside and examine the jungle up to a certain distance. He did so whilst I lighted up the jungle a little by means of a small 'ever ready' electric lantern. At the same time that my boy was outside the stones did not stop falling. My boy came in again, and I told him to search the kitchen to see if anybody could be there. He went to the kitchen and I went inside the room again to watch the stones falling down. I knelt down near the head of my bed and tried to catch the stones while they were falling through the air towards me, but I could never catch them; it seemed to me that they changed direction in the air as soon as I tried to get hold of them. I could not catch any of them before they fell on the floor. Then I climbed up the partition wall between my room and the boy's and examined the roof just above it from which the stones were flying. They came right through the 'kadjang' but there were no holes in the kadjang. When I tried to catch them there at the very spot of coming out, I also failed . . .

He added that he could see the boy standing in front of him while stones fell behind. Also,

> the stones were hotter than could be explained by their having been kept in the hand or pocket for some time . . . they fell rather

slowly . . . it seemed to me that they were hovering through the air; they described a parabolic curve and then came down with a bang on the floor. The sound they made in falling down on the floor was also abnormal because, considering their slow motion, the bang was much too loud.[4]

This account contains many paranormal features familiar to poltergeist reports: apparent materialization of stones, or their passage through a solid object (the roof), his inability to catch them, their slow fall, their heat, the unexpectedly loud bang they made . . . There is no indication that the phenomenon was repeated after that night. Was it perhaps focused on his 'boy' rather than on Mr Grottendieck himself?

In Port of Spain, Trinidad, stone showers inside a boarding house, as well as an outdoor bombardment, were just part of a whole range of poltergeist phenomena which began on 12 November 1905. Furniture moved, potatoes flew from a basket, and other objects were thrown about. A girl lay ill in the house at the time, possibly the focus of all this unnatural activity.[5] In Magilligan, County Derry (Northern Ireland), the phenomena seem to have been triggered by Mr McLaughlin cleaning his chimney. Beginning on 9 January 1907, flows of soot in the rooms were accompanied by showers of stones hitting the house and breaking windows. There were three women in the house, any one of whom could have been the trigger for the events.[6] There is no indication of how long the phenomena lasted.

At a house in Marcinelle near Charleroi (Belgium) they lasted for precisely four days. When the stone-throwing was first reported, on 30 January 1913, the police began to watch the house. One of the watchers said,

I have seen a stone arriving in the middle of a large window-pane, and then came others in spiral round the first point of impact, so that the whole of the glass was broken up methodically. I even saw, in another window, a projectile caught in the fragments of glass of the first hole it made, and subsequently ejected by another passing through the same point.

In other words, the aim of the unseen assailant was extraordinarily accurate. Mr Van Zanten, who lived in the house, commented:

But what surprised us most was that not one of the 300 stones thrown hit anybody. The first day my little boy was in the garden and my little girl was sleeping in her cradle near an open window on the first floor. They were not disturbed in any way. The nurse, it is true, was struck on the head by a piece of brick, but she was not much hurt. My father-in-law was hit on the arm and cried: 'Well! I did not feel anything.'

Although the police searched four houses from where they judged the missiles could be coming, they found nothing suspicious. On 2 February, the bombardment stopped.[7]

A case which supports the theory that poltergeist manifestations focus on or are triggered by a young person took place at Molignon (Switzerland) in April 1914. For a week or so, an eleven-year-old boy was 'seized by nervous crises': he suffered what sound like convulsions, accompanied by the movement of objects in the room. Sand and stones were thrown into the room, and the boy was hit by stones as he lay in bed.[8] During the 1919 poltergeist outbreak at Suri, West Bengal (India), bricks were thrown into the house through the windows. A female ghost was seen, and one of the witnesses said she saw this ghost stooping to lift bricks, and was able to warn other members of the family before a brick came flying in.[9]

The stone-throwing poltergeist in the Ardèche region of France, whose activities began early in September 1921, seemed to focus on a farmer, as the stones followed him into the fields, 220 yards away from the farmhouse. The stones fell at all hours, and the three children, aged twelve, seventeen and twenty-two, were suspected and watched, but never caught out. A clergyman who was brought into the case by the farmer reported:

I was anxious, first of all, to satisfy myself as to the facts. The next day, at five o'clock in the evening, I was in the farmyard, having two of the children with me, and facing me, when a stone the size of a hen's egg came down vertically, grazing one of the children. A little later another stone grazed me in the same way, about 52 yards from the house. The children were in sight close by me, and they could not have been the cause. The stones fell slowly, and gave one the impression of falling from a height of about 6 feet only. This was often remarked. It is incomprehensible.

He also saw apples strike the window shutters, and some came inside through a hole they knocked in the shutter.

> . . . They arrived in a horizontal direction with considerable speed. It would have been humanly impossible for anybody to hide in broad daylight in front of the window, which opens on to an empty field 440 yards long.
> The most able man, unless he were quite near the window, would never have succeeded in throwing an apple through a hole of an inch or so, however well he aimed.

Again we see the uncanny accuracy, impossible for 99 per cent of humans to achieve so regularly. The phenomena continued for four months, until January 1922.[10]

Several stone-throwing cases clustered together in the early 1920s. Simultaneously with the Ardèche events, stones were falling on to Chico, California (USA). The falls were said to have begun in July 1921, and continued until the end of March 1922. Large, smooth rocks 'seemed to come straight from the clouds', usually falling on two adjoining warehouses; the rocks were warm (remember that the stones which fell in Sumatra in 1903 were also warm), and there were other clues to the poltergeist nature of the phenomena. In the Charge warehouse, fifty bags of wool were mysteriously moved overnight to the place where Mr Charge had been planning to move them. Mr Charge also said that almonds, pieces of fruit and other small objects fell on to and into the warehouse, as well as the rocks. Miriam Allen de Ford, who came to Chico in company with many other interested witnesses in March 1922, reported: 'While I was discussing it with some bystanders, I looked up at the cloudless sky, and suddenly saw a rock falling straight down, as if becoming visible when it came near enough. This rock struck the roof with a thud, and bounced off on the track beside the warehouse, and I could not find it.' So although on the surface this sounds like a 'straightforward' case of stones falling from the sky, in fact there are numerous features which cause it to be classified as a poltergeist manifestation.[11]

The Roodeport (South Africa) stone-throwing episode of 1922 was also clearly the work of a poltergeist, although the police tried to pin it on a housemaid, and claimed to have been successful in so doing. For several months stones showered on to a chemist's house, and when the maid was sent into the garden stones fell around her.

Police searched but found no one, so as the stones seemed to be associated with the girl, they decided that obviously she must be responsible. She allegedly confessed, implicating others, but from the details we have it sounds very much like the usual poltergeist manifestation focusing on the unfortunate maid.[12] Missiles were flying again in Africa the following year, at Weti on the island of Zanzibar (Tanzania), as witnessed early in 1923 by Bishop Weston of Zanzibar, who wrote that he saw

> large pieces of earth violently plucked from the walls [of the hut built of kneaded clay] and thrown into the air. As will be easily understood, I went to the place absolutely sceptical on the matter, and I demanded that everyone should leave the hut, which I then had surrounded by a cordon of guards. In spite of this, several large pieces of earth continued to be violently detached from the walls and projected against the ceiling. Several of these pieces were even thrown outside the door; one of them hit me on the head. I then went back to the house and began the exorcism, pronouncing the ritual prayers. The manifestations ceased at once. The house has now been repaired, and no disturbing phenomena have reoccurred.[13]

Although it was not stones that were thrown here, the mechanism is presumably the same; and in this case, as in a few others later in the chapter, the projectiles were actually seen at the start of their movement. The bishop did not say if any particular person seemed to attract the phenomenon, but he was presumably not interested in investigating what occurred, simply in bringing it to an end. This he claims to have successfully achieved by means of exorcism, therefore he must have believed that evil spirits were responsible.

A very varied stone-throwing/poltergeist outbreak took place on one day in August 1927 in rural Czechoslovakia. The details were reported by the parish priest, and the description as given by Father Herbert Thurston in his *Ghosts and Poltergeists* includes all the important details.

> On 11 August 1927, a young man and a boy of thirteen had been fishing in one of the streams running from the Tatra range. They were on the point of returning home when suddenly a stone fell near them. It was followed by a second, and by others in succession. They grew frightened and hastily decamped. Then

they seemed to encounter a continuous shower of stones which only came into view when they were 30 centimetres (i.e., about a foot) away and which did not strike with any great violence . . . They took shelter in a tavern, but the stones pursued them there, and the pair were promptly ejected on the ground that they must be possessed by the devil. When they reached home, there were further manifestations. Stones seemed to fall from the ceiling. In one of the rooms the boy's father had made a collection of curious pebbles and geological specimens. These now started flying from one room to another and dropped on the ground. The next day a piece of coal in the kitchen sailed out and broke a glass panel in the door. In the afternoon a pack of playing cards flew up from the table and scattered among the visitors who were present. Finally, on the third day some pieces of money dropped from nowhere – between ten and twenty coins in all – and there was also a twenty-kronen note in paper. It was afterwards discovered that this money belonged to one of the people in the house. The stones which fell were of a type common in the district. It is stated that the thirteen-year-old boy had taken part as a medium in various seances in other parts of the country; but these particular manifestations were new and had only occurred in this, his native village.[14]

Clearly the phenomena were following the boy and were therefore probably triggered by him, albeit unconsciously, but there is no suggestion that they recurred and it is puzzling why they should confine themselves to this one day, especially as such powerful and frequent phenomena were reported: we would have expected the events to have continued for much longer.

The very active and long-lived Poona (India) poltergeist of 1927–30, described in Chapter 1, also sometimes indulged in stone-throwing, as for example on 23 May 1928 when stones apparently fell from the roof. The day was Damodar's ninth birthday, and Miss Kohn, who was in charge of him, watched him closely to see that he was not picking up and throwing the stones. Having ascertained his pockets were empty and he had not picked any stones up, she would find another stone being thrown: she would check his pockets again and find them full of stones. She took these away, and the procedure would be repeated. It looked as if Damodar were guilty, but Miss Kohn knew he was not, and that somehow the stones had been magically transported into his pockets by the poltergeist, who often showed other signs of intelligence, meddling, and a strange sense of humour.[15] It was also in 1928 that the late Ivan T. Sanderson, an active Fortean researcher in his later years, experienced paranormal stone-throwing. He was on the island of Sumatra (Indonesia), sitting on the veranda of an estate house with his host and hostess, when a small, shiny, black pebble sailed in out of the darkness. More followed, and Sanderson enquired who was throwing stones. His host replied that the same thing occurred nightly, but no one was ever hit by the stones.

> Our host invited us to pick up some of the stones and mark them with chalk (which he provided), lipstick, paint, or anything, and then toss them as far as we could into the surrounding garden. This garden was extensive, with sweeping lawns, shrubbery and beyond, acres of secondary tropical growth – a tangle so thick you could not force your way through it. We threw the small stones, duly marked, far out into this peripheral tangle. We must have thrown over a dozen such marked stones.
> Within a minute they were all back!
> Nobody, with a powerful flashlight or super-eyesight, could have found those little stones in that tangled mess, in that length of time, and thrown them back on to the veranda. Yet, they came back, all duly marked by us![16]

Such an experiment surely proves that human agency was not responsible for the stone-throwing.

We have three cases on record for the 1930s, all from the middle of the decade. On the island of Grenada (West Indies), among other strange happenings at a cottage were falls of stones, as here described in *The West Indian*:

> Police have climbed to the roof from the windows and seen the stones dropping on the roof. Another puzzling feature of the stone-throwing is that the missiles fall as if dropped from the skies and yet remain stationary where they fall. The stones up to the present have injured no one, though crowds press thickly round the cottage each night. They vary in weight between two ounces and a pound.

The outbreak began on 17 September 1934 at the cottage 'at the Botanic Station end of Lowther's Lane', and the stone-throwing continued for a couple of months until the occupants moved out. On 15 January 1935 the cottage burned down.[17]

As the Grenada events were coming to an end, so the Burgess, Ontario (Canada), poltergeist was gathering steam. In January 1935 there were reports of strange happenings at a farmhouse in Burgess Township, and people who went to see for themselves found the ten windows of the log house all broken. In addition to mysterious stone-throwings, James Quinn and family had experienced other poltergeist manifestations, especially with objects flying around indoors. Neighbours had also seen the strange happenings. After a fortnight of disturbances, the final one occurred on 15 January, and shortly thereafter the family moved away. It was quite possibly family tensions that caused the phenomenon, with Mrs Quinn and the children wishing to return to a more civilized environment: but probably the victims did not fake the phenomena, as has also been suggested, for they follow too closely well-established patterns with which the family are unlikely to have been familiar.[18]

A man prospecting at the deserted mining camp of Howells (near Prescott, Arizona, USA) in the summer and autumn of 1936 witnessed some strange poltergeist phenomena including stone-throwing. As is usually the case, the stones did not hurt if they hit anyone. However, very unusually, they were accompanied by weird lights like small 'gobs of pink jelly' when seen close to, and like red car tail lights from a distance.[19] In 1942, at Lovington, New Mexico (USA), another unusual case involving a strange light is said to have occurred. The location was an adobe range house, where one night the informant Mrs D. T. Spears saw 'a very red orange light', as if someone was 'carrying it about shoulder high and walking or running all around the barn'. Others came out to see it, and for two hours they watched and tried to get close to it. After they gave up and went back indoors, at 1 a.m., they heard a noise and went to the windows from where they saw

hundreds of rocks about baseball size all around the house. They were falling from the top of the house. We all rushed up to the roof and saw the red fireball as we called it taking off across the range, real low this time and twice as big.

Anyway it stopped and we all went outside again, and it came closer and closer. We stood still for a while and when it looked like it was just across the earth tank we all took out after it. However, it was still a good ways off and when we started running it shot straight up and stayed over us as long as we were outside. And as long as the moon was bright, every night the rocks fell from above. We always cleaned them away every day and it was never the same rocks.

The police were called out, but they thought someone was playing a trick. The rock-falls lasted for five or six nights. There was more to the story, but Mrs Spears never revealed what else they saw in the yard: 'it would just sound too ridiculous'.[20]

This was obviously something rather different from the usual poltergeist outbreak, for weird lights, similar to the balls of light described in Chapter 8, have never been recorded in poltergeist outbreaks, so far as we know. The Howells lights, too, are equally puzzling. We cannot even begin to try and explain these two events, so we move on quickly to the 1950s and back to Indonesia, where in November and December 1950 a Dutch couple and their family experienced a poltergeist outbreak consisting mainly of stone-showers. The stones sometimes fell in closed rooms: some turned at sharp angles in the air to avoid obstacles, and they were seen to 'float'. It was also found that if a stick was thrown away, it immediately returned.[21] In Australia in 1957, a young Aborigine farm-worker at Pumphrey, Western Australia, was attracting showers of stones. For five days stones rained around him, and two witnesses in a closed tent with the man saw stones fall at their feet. 'Freak winds' was the explanation from scientists whose knowledge of stone-showers was obviously zero.[22]

From the 1960s, 1970s and 1980s we have too many reports to include them all here. Possibly the phenomenon is not occurring any more frequently, but is now better reported. In March 1963 a guest house at Brooklyn, Wellington (New Zealand), was showered with stones and coins. The bombardment began on 24 March and lasted overnight for over seven hours. The residents and police had a sleepless night, trying to find the owner of the guilty catapult. Nearly every window was smashed, and people were hit but not seriously injured. No other house was touched. Among the stones were four New Zealand pennies, a large copper coin. The attack was repeated the following night; and on the third night 600 people were waiting for the show. After three hours the phenomenon ceased and never restarted.[23]

During a poltergeist outbreak in the small town of Jabuticabal (Brazil) which began in December 1965 there was considerable activity from flying bricks and stones. Pieces of brick fell inside the house, and continued falling even more frequently after an attempted exorcism by a Catholic priest. Eleven-year-old Maria was taken away to a neighbour's house, and there stones began to fly around indoors, 312 being counted during a period of intense bombardment. During a meal in another nearby house,

> a stone descended from the ceiling and split into two about four feet from the ground, the two parts proceeding in different directions as they fell to the floor. One of the women present immediately picked up the two pieces of stone and noticed that they fitted together like pieces of a three-dimensional jigsaw puzzle. Moreover, they seemed to snap together as if magnetically attracted to each other. The stone was passed around the table, and everybody noticed the strange magnetic effect, which soon weakened and disappeared.

Maria continued to be the focus of poltergeist attacks for over a year, sometimes suffering considerably from the unwanted attention, as for example during the period when needles would suddenly appear deep in the flesh of her left heel. Once 55 needles were extracted at the same time.[24]

An Indian poltergeist began throwing coal and stones in 1963 but later progressed to a much more varied output. The location was Karol Bagh near New Delhi, and the poltergeist was most active in December 1968, when 'fistfuls of *dhal* (pigeon peas) and *gram* (chick peas), lumps of coal, *pedas* made of moist flour, onions, tomatoes, safety matches began falling in the courtyard.' After seventeen days a reporter from *The Indian Express* came to see for himself what was happening, and wrote:

> . . . the invisible imp keeps pelting the courtyard with his un-solicited gifts, undaunted by prayers and curses alike. Today, after raining *gram* and *dahl* on the courtyard floor in the morning, he switched over exclusively to coins later in the day. Two-*paise*, 10-*paise* and 25-*paise* coins clinked and tinkled on to the floor from nowhere as this reporter watched in the broad daylight of five o'clock in the afternoon.[25]

There had been other poltergeist outbreaks involving stone-throwing earlier in 1968. In Kuala Lumpur (Malaysia) in January

1968 stones fell inside and outside a house, and objects mysteriously caught fire.[26] In an Osceola, Indiana (USA), poltergeist outbreak in October 1968, among all the other destruction and confusion, stones were seen to rise from the ground and crack windows;[27] while in the Nicklheim (West Germany) outbreak, which began in November 1968, stones fell in closed rooms. One felt warm when picked up by a priest who was blessing the house at the time the stone fell.[28]

In late October 1973 stones began showering down on to two fishermen at Skaneateles Lake, New York (USA), in a similar outbreak to that in Czechoslovakia in 1927. The rain of pebbles followed them back to their car, and when they stopped on the way home to change their clothes, stones fell on them again. Stopping further on for a drink, they were bombarded when they came out of the bar. Even at their home town of Liverpool (New York), stones fell as they parted company. Later analysis of some of the stones showed they were of local origin.[29]

The psychic investigator Guy Lyon Playfair personally witnessed an outbreak of stone-throwing in Brazil in September 1974. It was happening in a slum area near Carapicuiba and when he arrived on 24 September the bombardment had been in progress for more than three weeks. Six small houses were the focus of attention, and as Playfair talked to two of the affected residents,

> a hail of stones or pieces of brick fell out of a cloudless blue sky, rebounding off the roof of one house on to another at a lower level. I cannot say how many stones there were; I clearly saw a small puff of tile dust as a projectile struck the roof directly in my line of vision about ten feet from where I was standing, and a small piece of broken tile landed at the feet of the woman I was talking to. I picked it up at once; it showed signs of having been recently broken.

OPPOSITE *Guy Lyon Playfair at the scene of the stone-throwing outbreak at Carapicuiba (Brazil) in 1974. The large loose tiles had been placed on the roof to hold broken tiles in place, this roof having been bombarded several times.*

No one had received a direct hit from any of the missiles. Even a couple standing only feet apart inside their house by an open door were not hit when a stone flew between them. In addition to stones, heavy blocks of concrete were also falling, one having done so only minutes before Playfair arrived on the scene. He soon ascertained that it was difficult to lift, let alone throw.[30]

Police were called in to investigate the outbreak of stone-throwing in Spokane, Washington (USA), beginning on 30 August 1977 and afflicting only the Billy Tipton home. It continued at least until 6

September and possibly longer. By that date 100–150 stones had fallen on to the house. The police were 'baffled': they suspected a prankster but could find no trace of one. Two rocks fell while Police Captain Charles Crabtree was on the roof to get a better view of the surroundings. 'It's impossible to say where the rocks are coming from or who is doing it,' was his verdict. There were 50-foot-tall trees in front of the house, so the police theorized that a rocket-launcher was being used. We can be certain that no one was apprehended, since this is a classic case of 'stone-throwing by invisible assailant'.[31] The following year he had moved to Hazlet, New Jersey (USA), where in June 1978, on twenty consecutive days, a house on Elm Avenue was bombarded with large rocks and concrete debris. Windows were broken and cars were damaged. In apparent desperation, police arrested a youth seen throwing a pebble at his garage door, believing he was working in collusion with others, but we doubt it. How could they be projecting rocks up to 5 pounds in weight, so that they appeared to fall straight down, and landed only on one house? And without anyone else being aware of their activity?[32]

Only a month later, a garage in Galax, Virginia (USA), was bombarded with nails for four days. Mechanics collected 300–400 nails, and police who saw them falling from their roof-top vantage point commented, 'There are hundreds of them every day. There are roofing nails and concrete nails and ten-penny nails, every kind.' The bombardments were periodic, beginning on 10 July and ceasing on 13 July 1978. Damage was done to windscreens and the buildings; but no one was hurt. Police again believed that a person must be responsible, even though they could see no one when they watched the events from the roofs.[33]

During the 1980s there were several stone-throwing outbreaks on the African continent, beginning in July 1980 at Pietermaritzburg (South Africa) where two teenage friends travelling there to take part in the tennis championships met a witch-doctor on the railway station. They annoyed him by their attitude; and then blamed their later experiences on the encounter. While they were practising their game, stones began to fall around them, and later they fell inside the boys' bedroom while they were in bed. The stones stopped only when the boys left for home.[34] The following year, stones began to rain on to a garage in Aversa (Italy) during February, and police were so scared that they fired into the air with their machine guns. The report does not say if this put a stop to the showers, but it is probably the first time a poltergeist has been warned off by a burst of fire from the police.[35] Also during 1981, a Belize (Central America) couple and their thirteen-year-old granddaughter were singled out as the target for stone-showers, experiencing them while out walking, indoors eating dinner in a closed room, and in church.[36]

British readers of this book may be wondering if this phenomenon has ever happened in Britain, since we have not included any British cases in this chapter. In fact there are several recent cases, which are recorded in our earlier book *Modern Mysteries of Britain*, including the spectacular Ward End, Birmingham (West Midlands), case which went on for several years beginning in 1979, and left the police 'completely baffled' after 3500 man-hours of investigation.

Another long-lasting outbreak took place in Kenya, beginning on 23 December 1982 and lasting at least six months. The Kavoi family, living at Machakos, were being terrorized by the stone-showers, which began with a shower of stones on the roof of their house while they were all inside eating supper. It happened again next morning, but on neither occasion could anyone be seen throwing the stones, which seemed sometimes to be falling straight down, at others to be moving horizontally. Just as in similar cases in the United States and elsewhere, the authorities were called in but could find no culprit. Sub-chief William Ndunda was even struck by a stone himself. He also saw 'a big stone fly up from the ground and hit the roof with such force that it shattered'. Peter Kavoi noted other strange aspects of the phenomenon: 'Sometimes I actually saw the stones seemingly materialize out of thin air. They would suddenly appear out of a tree or over a roof and plunge into our yard. Sometimes they would fall very gently, just pitter on to the ground. At others they would fall with such force that they shattered.' The bombardment continued while prayers were said and hymns sung, nor was a witch-doctor able to stop them. Mr Kavoi was, not surprisingly, fed up:

I can tell you honestly that we are being driven mad by what is happening. Hundreds of people have come to the house promising help but nobody has been able to do anything. We have prayers said and we have had witch-doctors performing strange ceremonies. Nothing has helped. Even the government say they don't know what else they can do. All I am doing is placing my trust in God. If I keep praying, sooner or later I believe the stones will stop.[37]

An outbreak of stone-throwing equally disturbing for the family involved took place in the desert 15 miles from Tucson, Arizona (USA), beginning in September 1983. The pattern of events so familiar to readers by now was again repeated: the Berkbigler family of parents and three children aged twenty, nineteen and fifteen were moving into their partially completed 'dream house' when the bombardment started. The property was surrounded by cactus and brush, with no nearby neighbours, and despite intensive searches including helicopter surveillance, no prowler was apprehended even though the rocks were falling daily. They were of local granite, some pieces fist-sized, and cars parked outside were often dented. When the heavy bombardments were taking place, the family were trapped indoors, only able to venture out protected by makeshift shields and wearing helmets. During three months, there were 79 episodes of rock-throwing, and damage estimated at $7200 had been caused. A psychic investigator with much experience of poltergeist cases, D. Scott Rogo, visited the Berkbigler home early in December, and saw the events for himself just a few days before they stopped for good on 7 December. He was convinced that a 'rock-throwing poltergeist' had been at work and not a prankster.[38]

Back in Kenya, in early 1986 the rural settlement of Ngoliba was being haunted by poltergeist phenomena, including showers of stones. The inhabitants were also being hit by tree branches which appeared out of nowhere. They were hoping that a medicine man would be able to exorcize the demons.[39] Outbreaks of stone-throwing in out-of-the-way places like Ngoliba, a community of peasant farmers living in mud huts in the Kenya countryside, that are identical to outbreaks of stone-throwing in the jungle of Indonesia, in an English city, and in the Arizona desert . . . coupled with the obvious fact that police forces around the world are not familiar with the phenomenon but reject suggestions of poltergeists and look instead for a human agent, even though they are *always* unsuccessful in finding one . . . coupled with the frequently reported paranormal features of extra fast or slow travel, appearances inside closed rooms, stones being lifted from the ground, the return of marked stones thrown out into the jungle, and so on . . . all these factors, together with the sometimes parallel occurrence of poltergeist phenomena, indicate that the stone-throwing is also an aspect of such activity, utilizing the same energy which is involved in poltergeist events when furniture is overturned and household objects sent flying around. No human agent could be capable of many of the things poltergeists do; and also the events reported world-wide are very similar, which cannot be explained by publicity given to such cases if even the police are not aware of the existence of similar cases. In the spring of 1987 the police in Itapeva, São Paulo (Brazil), saw rocks pulled out of the soil and thrown against houses and dropped on roofs. Furniture and rubbish bins were taking flight, and during a special service in the cathedral, where they hoped to get rid of the phenomena by means of prayer, the attempt worked in the opposite way to that intended, when a rock weighing one kilo fell from the sky and through the cathedral roof, landing in front of the congregation.[40] A phenomenon like this, which has been happening all over the world for at least 300 years, would seem to demand some determined investigation on the part of the scientific community, not for each outbreak to be treated with amazement as if it were unique, as invariably happens.

17 *Is extinction the end?*

Extinction sounds final, but the evidence shows that man is often premature in proclaiming species of animals extinct, simply because no sightings of them have been made for several years. They have a nasty habit of popping up again and surprising those who have written their epitaph. Many examples could be cited, but space allows us only a few, such as the hispid hare and the pygmy hog, which in the early 1970s were both believed to be extinct; both were rediscovered living in Assam, and small populations of the hispid hare were also found in Nepal and India.[1] Early in 1986, the Cuban ivory-billed woodpecker was seen in Cuba, having been thought to be extinct for 30 years after logging had reduced its favoured habitat.[2] The disappearance of habitat and food supplies caused by man's encroachment on wilderness areas is, sadly, the principal reason for so many species becoming extinct in our time, and many more are threatened. Another to reappear was a bamboo-eating lemur, rediscovered in mountainous rain-forests in Madagascar during the autumn of 1986, although it remains one of the most endangered primates in the world.[3]

Sometimes the reappearance of once-native creatures is less straightforward, like that of the British boar. There have been recent sightings, and killings, of boars in Britain, and boars were once native to the island, but it is not necessarily feasible to conclude that the species is no longer extinct in Britain. The boar is believed to have become extinct around the seventeenth century, but in the summer of 1972 there were several sightings, including a capture and a killing, in Hampshire. Four years later, in March 1976, a year-old wild boar was run over and killed on a forestry road near Nairn (Scotland), but the Highland Wildlife Park, which had a breeding pair, claimed that no boars of theirs had gone missing. Boars seem to be attracted to domestic gardens. The Hampshire capture was in a garden where the animal was eating young trees, and in December 1979 one was causing annoyance to householders by rooting about in gardens in Basildon (Essex, England) during the night. It was never caught, though it was seen several times, once grazing in a field with some horses.[4]

Other once-native creatures have been seen in Britain in recent years, such as bear, lynx, hyena, wolf and wolverine, all of them long extinct there and, like the non-native species that have also been seen (monkey, jackal, kangaroo and wallaby, crocodile, and others), there are several possible explanations that do not involve the reappearance of extinct species: zoo or circus escapes, escaped or abandoned pets, misidentification. We can also add jokes or hoaxes, following the great auk hunt of 1986. The great auk has been extinct since 1844, but recently reports of sightings began to filter south from the Orkney Islands (Scotland). In May an expedition set out to hunt the bird, followed by a band of eager journalists. But their excitement turned to disillusionment when they realized that it was simply a publicity stunt, and the great auk remained as extinct as the pterodactyl (and how extinct *that* is will be considered later).[5]

The Tasmanian wolf or thylacine is another supposedly extinct creature still being seen, and with over 1000 sightings since 1936 this reappearance is not likely to be a hoax. We have already written about the thylacine in Chapter 14. It became extinct on the Australian mainland around 2000 years ago, and on Tasmania fifty years ago, but it is still being seen in both places, and ends our list (which could be much longer) of recently 'extinct' creatures still being seen.[6]

The most famous example of long-extinct creatures rediscovered alive and well is the coelacanth. Until its discovery in 1938 it was known only from the fossil record. As with the dinosaurs, it was thought to have been extinct for 65 million years – until fishermen off the Comoro Islands near Madagascar trawled it from the depths of the sea. Since that first specimen in 1938, more than 80 have been caught. Unfortunately they cannot be kept alive, because they live in the cold, dark ocean depths and die after only a day in captivity. Recently, marine biologists working from a two-man submarine at a depth of 100 fathoms off the Comoro Islands have been able to obtain film of coelacanths living in their natural habitat.[7]

If the coelacanth has continued to live so successfully for millions of years, how many other creatures from the age of the dinosaurs may also have survived? An attempt will be made later to answer that tricky question, but there are certainly some creatures, like the

Bulmer's fruit bat which was discovered in a New Guinea cave in 1977 by the zoologist J. I. Menzies, which have survived over many thousands of years. Not quite the millions of the coelacanth, but still a long time for sizeable creatures to remain undetected by man. The fruit bat was known from 10,000-year-old fossils, also found by Menzies in New Guinea. To his surprise, he discovered the live specimens soon after he found the fossils, but sadly the whole colony was killed or driven from its cave by a hunter before Menzies' return later in 1977. In 1972 a species of peccary (a pig-like mammal), thought extinct since the Ice Age, was found in Paraguay, and in Australia in 1966 a mountain pygmy possum, known only from fossils 20,000 years old, was found alive and well in the kitchen of a ski-lodge high in the Victorian Alps 130 miles from Melbourne.[8]

New species discovered in recent years are probably also survivals from thousands of years ago. The mere fact that large creatures are still found proves that man is less familiar with what lives on our earth than he would like to believe, and it also leaves the way clear for further spectacular discoveries. The many new finds include the banana bat of Mexico (1960), a new honey-creeper on the Hawaiian island of Maui (1973), the African peacock (1936), and many other bats and birds. The kouprey, a wild forest ox, found in Cambodia in the 1930s, the 10-foot-long Komodo dragon of Indonesia, first recorded in 1912, and the onza, a puma-like cat found in Mexico in 1986, are three examples of much larger land creatures which remained undetected until the twentieth century; in the seas there must lurk countless unknown species. In 1986 a previously unknown kind of shrimp was located living near geysers of hot water on the floor of the Atlantic Ocean, and a six-sided creature about the size of a silver US dollar, covered with rows of black dots, was also found, until 1986 known only from rock fossils more than 70 million years old.[9]

Not only new small creatures are discovered in the sea. In 1976 a previously unknown shark 14¾ feet long, was hauled out of the Pacific off Hawaii. It was nicknamed Megamouth, and later christened *Megachasma pelagios*, because of its huge cavernous mouth, though in fact it feeds on plankton. A second specimen was netted off California in 1984. The discovery of Megamouth proves beyond doubt that unknown creatures of very large size are awaiting discovery in our oceans, and it is possible that some of them will prove to be prehistoric survivals. Over the centuries sailors have reported seeing monsters in the seas, and they are still seen today, as reported in more detail in Chapter 7. Just as sea monsters may be unknown or 'extinct' species, so too might the lake monsters, also described in Chapter 7. Possible identifications for the Loch Ness Monster include the plesiosaur, a long-necked marine reptile sup-posedly extinct for 70 million years. There are points for and against this identification, and the mystery will remain unsolved until such time as there is a corpse available for scientific examination. The same applies to Champ, the monster of Lake Champlain in the USA. Among other explanations, it has been suggested that Champ too is a plesiosaur, though others prefer to identify it as a zeuglodon, a snake-like primitive whale extinct for 20 million years.

Both Nessie and Champ are well documented, so far as sighting reports are concerned: both lakes are easily accessible and witnesses are able to report their sightings without difficulty. Our third lake creature is rather more inaccessible, requiring considerable organ-ization and determination on the part of would-be witnesses even before the habitat can be reached. This monster is Mokele-mbembe, reportedly living in the Likouala swamps and Lake Tele in the People's Republic of the Congo in Africa. Reports of large unknown animals in Central Africa go back 200 years, but early explorers had enough problems without trying to follow up such reports, though some of them did come across large unidentified footprints. In 1913, Captain Freiherr von Stein zu Lausnitz led an expedition to the Likouala district and afterwards described what he had heard about an animal called Mokele-mbembe:

> The animal is said to be of a brownish-grey colour with a smooth skin, its size approximating that of an elephant; at least that of a hippopotamus. It is said to have a long and very flexible neck and only one tooth but a very long one; some say it is a horn. A few spoke about a long muscular tail like that of an alligator. Canoes coming near it are said to be doomed; the animal is said to attack the vessels at once and to kill the crews but without eating the bodies. The creature is said to live in the caves that have been washed out by the river in the clay of its shores at sharp bends. It is said to climb the shore even at daytime in search of food; its diet is said to be entirely vegetable. This feature disagrees with a possible explanation as a myth. The preferred plant was shown to me; it is a kind of liana with large white blossoms, with a milky sap and apple-like fruits.

It was not until the 1970s that determined efforts began to find out the truth behind all the reports and rumours. James H. Powell, Jr, a recognized authority on crocodiles, was one of the researchers who went to the region where the reports were emanating from, in order to talk to people living near Lake Tele, and he was able to hear some first-hand sighting accounts. Schoolteacher Mambombo Daniel claimed to have seen a Mokele-mbembe as recently as 1977, when it stuck its neck out of the river. He said it looked very like a picture of a Brontosaurus he was shown. He saw it from only 30 feet away: it was grey in colour, with a neck as thick as a man's leg. It was not a snake, because he saw part of the body. The witnesses generally were frightened by the Mokele-mbembe, and felt it was bad luck to talk about seeing it. One fisherman recalled how a Mokele-mbembe was killed in about 1959, and those who ate the meat died. James Powell, who interviewed this man, commented: 'He said some of the large stakes used to trap the animal were still there. When Roy and I expressed our interest in going to the site to look for bones or other remains, our informant was incredulous. He seemed to consider us mad for contemplating so foolhardy an act.'[10]

The 'Roy' referred to is Dr Roy Mackal, who was with James Powell during this 1980 expedition. In 1981, Dr Mackal conducted

What Mokele-mbembe might look like if it were a small sauropod dinosaur.

another expedition to the Congo, but was unable to reach Lake Tele. In 1983 the Congolese zoologist Marcellin Agnagna led an expedition to the Likouala region, and claimed to have been successful in seeing the creature called Mokele-mbembe for himself. He was with two local villagers close to Lake Tele, when one of the men began shouting that he could see a strange animal in the water. All three men waded into the shallow water until they were about 700 feet away from the animal, which was looking towards them. They saw 'a wide back, a long neck and a small head', the whole being about 15 feet in length visible above the water. They watched the head and neck for about twenty minutes before it submerged completely. Unfortunately they had run out of film. They took a canoe out to where it had been seen, this time armed with video equipment, but there were no further sightings.[11]

In his book *A Living Dinosaur?*, Dr Mackal describes vividly his travels in the Congo in search of Mokele-mbembe, and in the chapter headed 'Mokele-mbembe: What could it be?' he outlines the possible identifications of this elusive yet apparently real jungle monster. It is 15–30 feet long including the long neck and tail, has four short legs, with claw marks visible in its 1-foot diameter footprints, and is a herbivore. No known mammal corresponds to what is known of Mokele-mbembe, but the descriptions sound like a small sauropod dinosaur. However, it might also be a large lizard, though there are

Dr Roy Mackal and colleagues used a giant dugout in their search for Mokele-mbembe.

no known lizards corresponding exactly to the features of Mokele-mbembe. Dr Mackal seems to favour the sauropod dinosaur, but until there is a specimen available for study this identification remains controversial, and even the existence of such a creature as Mokele-mbembe is doubted in some quarters. In his book Dr Mackal also describes other unidentified animals reported in the Likouala region. The Emela-ntouka has a large curving horn on its head, and although in some ways similar to Mokele-mbembe, it lacks the long neck. It eats foliage, but is known to kill elephants, buffalo and hippopotamus. It might be an unknown species of rhinoceros, or it might be a Ceratopsian dinosaur like Monoclonius or Centro-saurus which both had a horn.[12] Yet another unknown animal is called by the natives Mbielu-mbielu-mbielu, and this one has 'planks growing out of its back' – possibly large plates like those which ridged the back of the Stegosaur, a dinosaur which might be responsible for the modern sightings of Mbielu-mbielu-mbielu.[13]

Dr Mackal points out the difficulties in making positive identifi-cations of all these mystery animals, another of which is Nguma-monene, the 'most mysterious' of them all. It is a giant snake 130–195 feet long, with a serrated ridge running along its back. It was seen in 1961 in the Mataba River by a woman bathing. A snake-like head and neck emerged from the water 50 feet away from her, and her cries brought villagers who watched the giant animal for 30 minutes as it moved around in the water. It never emerged, but they saw the ridge or frill along its back, and its forked tongue. A similar creature was seen by a missionary, Pastor Ellis, in November 1971, and Dr Mackal visited him to learn the full details. He saw it crossing the Mataba River and out into the jungle, and judged it to be 30 feet long, though it must have been much longer as he did not see the head or tail. He also saw its ridged back. Could it be a giant lizard, possibly a primitive type and a surviving link between lizards and snakes, wonders Dr Mackal?[14] The existence of giant lizards is scientifically acceptable: the Komodo dragon is 14 feet long, and in Chapter 14 we described sightings of 30-foot monitor lizards in Australia.

Giant turtles (Ndendeki) 12–15 feet in diameter have also been reported in the Likouala region, and giant crocodiles (Mahamba) over 50 feet long.[15] The Likouala region is very inaccessible, being mainly swamp and forests, and man rarely penetrates it. The flora and fauna are largely unresearched, and it seems that if prehistoric monsters are able to survive anywhere, this remote part of Africa is a

better place than most. There are enough reports of strange creatures to tantalize even the most conservative zoologist; and there are
likely to be many more expeditions by the most determined of them,
in an effort to get to the bottom of the Mokele-mbembe mystery,
which Dr Bernard Heuvelmans, father of cryptozoology, calls 'the
zoological craze of the 1980s'.[16]

Sea monsters and lake monsters can at least hide themselves under
water when they wish to escape the too-curious gaze of man, but land
animals are more exposed to view, and for this reason the experts are
even less inclined to accept that unknown species of large size are
living on dry land. It certainly seems incredible to suggest that
prehistoric winged creatures – pterosaur/pterodactyl/*Pteranodon* –
may not have become extinct 65 million years ago but survived to the
present day. However, three schoolteachers driving to work near
San Antonio, Texas (USA), on 24 February 1976 saw a huge 'bird'
with a 15–20 foot or more wingspan swooping over their cars.
Patricia Bryant said: 'I could see the skeleton of this bird through the
skin or feathers or whatever, and it stood out black against the
background of the grey feathers.' David Rendon added the information that the creature glided rather than flew, and that the huge
wings had a bony structure. Later they found their 'bird' illustrated
in an encyclopedia, where it was captioned '*Pteranodon*'. This was
during a spate of similar sightings in south-east Texas: the previous
month a man at Raymondville investigating a noise like the flapping
of batlike wings and a strange whistling late at night felt something
grab at him with big claws. Seeing what it was, he ran for cover,
nearly scared to death. What Armando Grimaldo saw was a 5–6-foot
'bird' with a 10–12-foot wingspan. It had a bat- or monkey-like face,
large red eyes, no beak, and dark leathery skin without feathers.
Although the creature managed to tear his clothes, his skin was not
scratched. The Texan mystery bird was never identified positively,
but some witnesses were sure they had seen a *Pteranodon*, which was
a kind of pterosaur.[17]

On 14 September 1983 another Texan had a close-up view of 'a
large bird-like object' when it flew over Highway 100 near Los
Fresnos close to the Texas/Mexico border. 'Its tail is what caught my
attention', said ambulance-driver James Thompson. 'I expected
him to land like a model airplane. That's what I thought he was, but
he flapped his wings enough to get above the grass . . . It had a black
or greyish rough texture. It wasn't feathers. I'm quite sure it was a
hide-type covering . . . I just watched him fly away.' The creature's

body was 8–10 feet long, and it had a wingspan of 5–6 feet. It had a hump on the back of its head, almost no neck, and a pouch near its throat. Thompson afterwards referred to the creature as 'a pterodactyl-like bird'.[18]

Early in 1972, a student unearthed the skeletal remains of a pterodactyl with a 51-foot wingspan. This was in the Big Bend National Park east of Terlingua, Texas (USA),[19] and shows that pterodactyls did once fly in this area, even if it was a long time ago. So what did James Thompson and the earlier witnesses really see? Some of the giant birds or pterodactyls might in reality have been giant bats. Ivan T. Sanderson saw what he believed to be a giant bat in the Assumbo Mountains of Cameroun in West Africa when doing zoological work there in 1932. The creature, with at least a 12-foot wingspan, dived at him after he fell into a river, an event graphically described in his book *Investigating the Unexplained*.[20] However, this may in fact have been a pterodactyl: elsewhere in Africa there are traditions of 'flying dragons' which are perhaps pterodactyls.[21] The Texan sightings of giant birds cannot easily be explained in terms of known birds like pelicans, blue herons, condors or storks, but if there really were pterodactyls still surviving we would expect there to be far more sightings. As the Texan sightings were in an area very close to the Mexican border, perhaps the creature or creatures responsible had strayed temporarily from their usual home in the mountains of Mexico, a remote area where they would be rarely seen.

We have written about some other winged monsters in our earlier book *Alien Animals*, but one we did not cover there is the giant penguin of Florida (USA), which caused an uproar in 1948 but has not been seen since. The mystery was investigated by Ivan T. Sanderson, zoologist and Fortean researcher, who collected details from 24 people who actually saw the creature. The first sign of its existence was a set of tracks found on the beach at Clearwater, Florida, in February 1948. Similar three-toed, bipedal tracks with claws, measuring over 13 inches long, were found subsequently on other beaches in the area, and also 40 miles up the Suwannee River. The beast thought to have made all the tracks was seen both on the shore and swimming in the sea and river. One witness was a lady out on a boat trip with her husband. While walking on the beach on a small uninhabited island she saw something in the bushes, and when it started waddling down the beach to the sea she saw that it was 15 feet tall and had 'a head like a rhinoceros but with no neck. It sort of flowed into its narrow shoulders. It was grey and covered with short thick fur. It had short, very thick legs and huge feet, and from its shoulders hung two flippers. It didn't run into the water, or dive in; it sort of slid in half sidewise.' Ivan Sanderson himself had a brief and tantalizing glimpse of the creature from a plane above the Suwannee River: 'some enormous dirty-yellow coloured creature roiling about on the surface of the water, making a huge lozenge-shaped patch of foam on the dark waters all around it'. He was able to make a detailed study of the tracks and the descriptions, and concluded that the creature must be a giant penguin 15 feet tall. The fossil remains of a 7-foot penguin have been found in New Zealand, and even today there are 3-foot penguins, the Emperor and King Penguins. As Sanderson concluded:

> Finally, be it noted that most of the reports of Three-Toes [as he called the creature] hail from the southern hemisphere and penguins are southern-hemisphere animals, though one species lives on the Galapagos Islands just north of the Equator. Further, all penguins spend most of their lives on the high seas, congregating once a year at special places and often on distant islands to breed. They are shy creatures when at sea and they float just below the surface with their heads sticking out, and usually duck under and swim long distances when they feel the throb of an approaching propeller. There could be thousands of giant penguins afloat in the Antarctic and sub-Antarctic oceans and a modern powered ship would never get near enough to them to spot them. And it is interesting to note that not a few descriptions of the heads of alleged 'great sea-serpents' were, in the olden days of sail, described as looking like those of horses, camels, or rhinoceroses. A thick-billed penguin, fifteen feet long, on the coast of Florida is admittedly pretty horrid, but I don't think we can legitimately any longer laugh it out of court.[22]

If there is indeed a 15-foot penguin lurking in southern waters, it joins the list of newly discovered, sizeable creatures like the kouprey, the Komodo dragon, the onza and the Megamouth shark. Might there be even bigger birds as yet undiscovered? A 1985 press report headed 'Living in fear of a giant chicken' amusingly suggests that there might:

MILAN [Italy]: Terrified farmer Gianpiero Balzi, 39, rushed from his field and called the police. For as he had been walking through the field in Brescia, near Milan, checking the growth of maize, he had found four huge footprints. 'They were the exact shape of a chicken footprint,' he said. 'But enormous, as if some gigantic bird had swooped down, landed and then taken off again.' A police spokesman said: 'The footprints are eight feet long, five feet wide and 16 feet apart. And the whole area is covered in a grey powder. We are protecting the prints until experts arrive, but so far we can see no reason for them. There was no sign of any other activity.'[23]

It is hard to see how a bird with 8-foot footprints could go undetected for long. By comparison, 15-foot penguins on the beaches of Florida sound positively normal. However, in 1988 Tony Signorini of Clearwater admitted to hoaxing the footprints. So what was the creature people saw?

Another sizeable creature whose survival may have gone largely unnoticed because of its watery environment well away from civilization is Steller's sea-cow. This is an aquatic mammal of the Sirenian order, like the dugong and manatee, first discovered in 1741 off the coast of the Siberian Kamchatka peninsula (USSR). It was believed to have been exterminated by 1768, but may also have inhabited other northern waters: indeed it has even been suggested that a type of Sirenian with a long neck may be responsible for lake-monster

A young Steller's sea-cow.

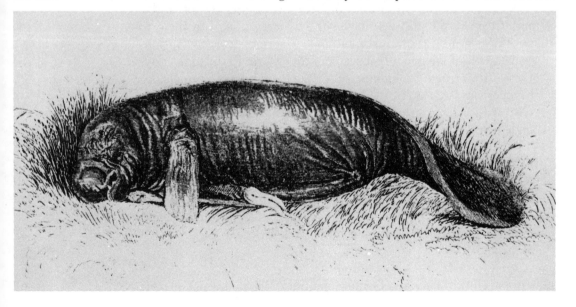

reports in northern latitudes. There were numerous reports of surviving sea-cows in the 1800s,[24] and some sighting reports have also been published this century. A whale harpooner told Dr S. K. Klumov in the early 1950s about an animal he had seen on several occasions near the Commander Islands (Komandorskiye Ostrova), again off the Kamchatka peninsula.

> This animal appears almost always in the same place, and we observe it at the same time: generally in the first part of July. The place is not far from Bering Island, about 50 km in the Southeast . . . Of course, it is not a whale. We know the whales by their appearance, by their fins and by their blowing. This animal does not make any water jet, and it does not show its head out of the water, only the upper part of its back. The back is wide, large, smooth, without any fin, and black . . . Nobody could find any sensible explanation. Maybe a big fish? It was about 10 metres long.[25]

In July 1962 the crew of a whaler near Cape Navarin on the north-east part of Kamchatka saw what may have been sea-cows:

> The witnesses, most of them seasoned hunters and whalers, all agreed that the animals were unlike any known cetacean or pinniped. They were from 20 to 26 feet long, varying no doubt according to age. Their skin was very dark, with a small head clearly separated from the body. The upper lip was divided in a hare-lip and overlapped the lower one. The tail was remarkable in being edged with a fringe. The beasts swam slowly, occasionally dived for short periods and then rose above water in a very marked way. They formed a compact group, all swimming together in the same direction.[26]

A corpse was found in the summer of 1976 at Anapkinskaya Bay,[27] and in the early 1980s Soviet researchers were said to be actively searching for live specimens off Kamchatka, so it is likely to be only a matter of time before Steller's sea-cow is pronounced 'alive and well', and not extinct after all.[28]

Siberia, traditionally thought of as a barren area, may not be so lifeless and uninteresting as it is usually pictured. In its waters may dwell the 'extinct' Steller's sea-cow, in its forests may live giant hairy man-beasts (see Chapter 12), and yet more 'extinct' and 'unknown' species may also lurk there. Among the allegedly extinct prehistoric species, a good candidate for resurrection is the mammoth, that 10-foot-tall giant of the Arctic Circle. Everyone has heard of the huge corpses of mammoths deep-frozen in the Siberian earth with their last meal still intact in their stomachs. People have been finding these remains for hundreds of years – nearly 5000 specimens have been discovered over the last 300 years, and 500,000 tons of tusks are believed to lie buried along the Arctic coast[29] – and in this century scientists have been able to study them in order to learn all about this monster which has been extinct since the last Ice Age – or so it is believed. In 1984 the US publication *Technology Review* published an article describing how egg cells from a frozen mammoth found in Siberia had been fertilized by sperm from an Asian elephant and implanted into female Asian elephants. Two elephant/mammoth hybrids had been successfully born and were being reared in Irkutsk in the USSR. However, this startling breakthrough was soon revealed to be nothing more than an April Fool's prank played by a biochemistry student at the Massachusetts Institute of Technology.

The mammoth.

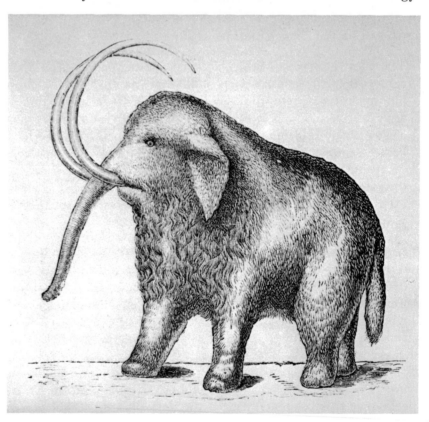

Mammoths were once widespread, their remains having been found in Europe, and they were also contemporary with man. It is clear that as the climate grew warmer after the Ice Age, they retreated northwards, but the reason for their eventual disappearance even from Siberia, and why so many should have been so suddenly overtaken by death that their bodies were preserved intact, is unknown. One suggestion is that those which perished had ventured on to the marshy plains and sank into the icy mud, or were caught unawares and overwhelmed by the first snows and frost of the winter when they were away from the shelter of the forests. Others may not have been so unfortunate but carried on living and breeding in what seems to be ideal conditions for them, the forests of northern Siberia, which cover nearly 3 million square miles. There are so few people living there that whole herds of mammoths could thrive unseen; and in fact the forest-dwellers have reported seeing them. In 1922 the Evenks, the indigenous people of Siberia, described to Russian scientists how they had hunted the 'shaggy elephant', and they were able to give accurate details of its diet, appearance and behaviour. They also produced well-preserved mammoth skins.[30]

A Russian hunter also claimed to have seen mammoths in 1918. He was exploring the forest in the Siberian taiga when he came across huge tracks, the footprints in the mud being about 2 feet across and oval in shape. He followed them and found a 'huge heap of dung' made up of vegetable matter. He also noticed broken branches 10 feet up, as if a tall animal had passed by. He followed the tracks for several days through the bitterly cold forest, somewhat nervous at what he might find.

One afternoon, it was clear enough from the tracks that the animals weren't far off. The wind was in my face, which was good for approaching them without them knowing I was there. All of a sudden I saw one of the animals quite clearly, and now I must admit I really was afraid. It had stopped among some young saplings. It was a huge elephant with big white tusks, very curved; it was a dark chestnut colour as far as I could see. It had fairly long hair on the hindquarters, but it seemed shorter on the front. I must say I had no idea that there were such big elephants. It had huge legs and moved very slowly. I've only seen elephants in pictures, but I must say that even from this distance (we were some 300 yards apart) I could never have believed any beast could be so big.

The hunter did not know about mammoths, which is why he referred to the beasts as elephants. When he returned to the spot the next day they had gone, and it was too cold for him to follow them again.[31]

Considered logically, there seems no reason at all why mammoths should not have survived to the present day and be quietly getting on with their lives in the wild Siberian tundra. There are many other hints and rumours around the world of survivals of 'extinct' species and discoveries of new ones, some feasible, others not so likely. Among the latter are recent reports out of the Kamchatka peninsula region of Siberia, concerning a new mystery animal, the Irkuiem. This is said to be a 1-ton polar bear which crawls along the ground, having a small head and long narrow body like a caterpillar. It may be related to a species of bear extinct for 10,000 years, *Arctodus simus* or the 'short-faced bear'. Reindeer breeders have claimed several recent sightings, and in 1987 an expedition of hunters set out to find the creature. A giant bear that is unable to run but moves by pulling itself along the ground sounds unlikely, to say the least, but we wait with bated breath and open minds for further news of the expedition, which has not come to hand at the time of writing.[32]

Any of the remotest, barely habitable regions of the world might be a last refuge for some truly remarkable creatures. Reports of 'giant rabbits' were brought back by gold prospectors from the interior of Australia. Were these the same as the 12-foot-tall kangaroos reportedly seen, or something else, perhaps the hippo-sized Diprotodon, a prehistoric wombat-like creature which is believed to have survived until at least 2000 or 3000 years ago?[33] It coexisted with man, because an aboriginal painted carving found in a cave in northern Queensland, and dated to about 10,000 years ago, clearly depicts the Diprotodon.[34] From Africa there are enough reports of surviving prehistoric creatures and other mystery animals to fill a book – indeed Bernard Heuvelmans has written one, though unfortunately it is as yet only available in French: *Les Derniers Dragons d'Afrique*.[35] South America, too, is the source of many tantalizing stories, like that from the guide who had lived among the Indians in remote rain-forests for many years, and was told that prehistoric animals still lived in the jungle. Once he had travelled up the Amazon (Brazil) and seen a 'prehistoric animal' rising from the water and smashing his canoe.[36] Then there was the Liverpool man, J. Harrison, who was travelling on the Manuos, an Amazon river estuary, some time around February 1947 when he and others saw five strange birds flying overhead. 'The wingspan must have been at least twelve feet from tip to tip. They were brown in colour like brown leather, with no visible signs of feathers. The head was flat on top, with a long beak and a long neck. The wings were ribbed.'[37] In 1977 a team of explorers were planning to climb Mount Antana in a remote jungle region of Venezuela, in search of a 'dinosaur' – a large lizard said to live in a cave near the top of the mountain, but we have no report that they found anything.[38] In neighbouring Guyana, there may also exist large reptiles in the highlands,[39] and again in the Mato Grosso region of Brazil.[40] In southern Brazil, the *minhocao* might be a surviving Pleistocene glyptodont, a type of huge armadillo; while in Patagonia (Argentina) the Smilodon, or sabre-toothed tiger, might still survive. Also in Patagonia, the Mylodon or giant ground sloth might just possibly still be around: it was still in existence when the earliest Indians arrived.[41] We must of course add to this growing list of possible prehistoric survivals world-wide the many humanoids great and small which we have already described in Chapter 12, especially Neanderthal Man and Gigantopithecus.

Any complacency felt by scientists that they have identified and catalogued all the large living creatures of the earth will surely be dealt a severe blow if any of the monsters seen and described by so many eye-witnesses are ever brought into the laboratory as corpses for examination. We have mixed feelings about such a development and the resulting enormous publicity: would it mean that the creatures would then be hounded into genuine extinction? Perhaps it would be best for them to remain undiscovered, protected by the mockery of the 'experts' who do not trouble to search for creatures that cannot exist.

Gazetteer of Strange Events

ALEUTIAN ISLANDS

US sailors saw UFO rise from the sea; March 1945

ALGERIA

AIN-EL-TURCK Small man with glowing eyes seen on beach; 24 October 1954

NEAR BÉNOUD Giant snake 120 feet long reportedly killed by nomads and French soldiers

JEAN-MERMOZ Domed UFO giving off yellow and blue lights like searchlight seen; 20 October 1954

LAVARANDE, ORAN Two lorry drivers ran away across fields after a large disc-shaped UFO flew over the road; 11 October 1954

ANTARCTICA

ADMIRALTY BAY Brazilian meteorologist and five others saw reddish egg-shaped UFO which travelled slowly and split into two separate objects identical to the original. They changed to bluish-white, brightened, then vanished; 16 March 1961

ARGENTINA

ATACAMA DESERT Giant beings left footprints in snow on mountains; 1956

NEAR BAJADA GRANDA, NEAR PARANÁ Student on motorcycle attacked by round-headed being with white hair and three eyes; having grabbed boy's collar, the entity did a 'half turn, like a robot' and departed; 28 July 1962

BUENOS AIRES HARBOUR Navy chased unidentified submarine object; June 1959 (see Ch. 10)

CERRO DEL VALLE, SAN JUAN Man sleeping rough at his mica mine saw beautiful woman in green; 1953 (see Ch. 9)

CHUBUT TERRITORY Rumours of monsters in PATAGONIA: gold prospector named Sheffield found trail of flattened vegetation and, 'I saw in the middle of the lake an animal with a huge neck like that of a swan, and the movement in the water made me suppose the beast to have a body like that of a crocodile'; 1922

COMODORO RIVADAVIA   Man saw UFOs descend into sea, and later saw luminous objects emerge and fly off; 30 September 1964 (see Ch. 10)

CORREA, NEAR ROSARIO   Rancher discovered dead cow near seven burned circular patches of grass; a few days later, fungi the size of basket-balls were growing there. Neighbours saw strange lights in the sky around the date of cow's death; 14 October 1968

NEAR DESEADE   Farmer saw cigar-shaped UFO, *c.*70 feet long, chugging along giving off grey smoke; it crashed into the sea and sank; 18 March 1966 (see Ch. 10)

LAKE NAHUEL HUAPI   Lake monster reports

GOLFO NUEVO, CHUBUT   Navy pursuing USOs over 15 days; February 1960 (see Ch. 10)

NEAR PAJAS BLANCAS AIRPORT, CÓRDOBA   Motorcyclist saw UFO 60 feet wide hovering ahead of him, and hid in ditch. Entity in diver's suit came and fetched witness into UFO, then took him back, placing hand on man's shoulder in farewell; April 1957

PINAMAR COAST, BUENOS AIRES   Man saw rotating UFO emerge from ocean and follow him for a short distance before climbing out of sight; 31 May 1971

PUERTO GARIBALDI   Foil/tinsel fell from sky; *c.*17 January 1965

QUILINO, PROVINCE OF CÓRDOBA   Air Force man saw UFO and was unable to draw his revolver; voice from UFO told him in Spanish not to be afraid and that they had bases in SALTA REGION – they were here to warn people of dangers of atomic energy; 20 August 1957

SALTA   Schoolchildren saw small green entities which tried to catch them; *c.*4 October 1965

SALTA, CHACO, EL CHORRO, UMAHUACA   Legends and rumours of Ucumar or Ucu, big hairy man-beast (see Ch. 12)

GULF OF SAN MATÍAS   Strange luminous craft often seen entering and leaving the sea; early 1960s (see Ch. 10)

SANTA FÉ   Poltergeist activity with showers of stones and voices including screaming; March 1984 (see Chs 1 and 11)

TIERRA DEL FUEGO   Between SAN SEBASTIÁN and RIO GRANDE: man walking along coast saw oval UFO emerge from sea and disappear overland; June 1950. A fortnight later, near SANTA CRUZ, he saw a similar event (see Ch. 10)

AUSTRALIA

New South Wales

BETWEEN BOMBALA AND BEMBOKA   Man riding along track saw strange man-like animal drinking from creek; probably a 'Yahoo' or 'Yowie'; 12 October 1912 (see Ch. 12)

BOYD TOWN BEACH, NEAR EDEN   Carcass of sea animal found, 8 feet long with horse-like head; similar to another found not long before at nearby Narooma; May 1935

CESSNOCK   Farmer saw monitor lizard at least 30 feet long in dense scrub; 27 December 1975 (see Ch. 14)

COFFS HARBOUR   Fall of frogs on to roof, and on naval vessel at sea; 1944

CONCORD, SYDNEY   Oil oozed from statue of Lebanese saint, St Charbal. Crucifix touched with the oil later began dripping oil and blood. A picture of St Charbal also dripped oil; statue began dripping oil on 15 March 1985, continued for a week. Other events in 1986 (see Ch. 15)

NEAR DUNOON   Three boys saw two Yowies (hairy man-beast) in thick scrub in hills; May 1981 (see Ch. 12)

EMERALD BEACH Truck-driver saw bright circular object rise up near highway at night; it had flames along the bottom. UFO slowly descended again, and witness drove away in fear. Site was investigated three years later, and burnt tree limbs and circles of poor grass growth found; June 1970

EMMAVILLE AREA Sightings of big black cat; beginning 19 February 1958 (see Ch. 14)

EWINGSDALE Thousands of frogs fell in rain; 6 April 1939

NEAR FERNVALE Brothers saw disc-shaped domed UFO pass overhead, lighting up the valley, before landing nearby. Circle of scorched grass found next day; 1927

NEAR FORSTER Striped animal, possibly thylacine, seen crossing road; January 1979 (see Ch. 14)

GROSE VALLEY, NEAR KATOOMBA (1976), OXLEY ISLAND NEAR TAREE (1977), WOODENBONG (1977) Yowies seen at these and other locations during the 1970s, an active time for reports of these creatures

HAWKESBURY RIVER Gigantic dark animal seen in river: through binoculars witness saw two large humps, two sets of flippers below the surface, and a tail. The head then surfaced, revealing snake-like features, and neck extended 9 feet above water; May 1979, and numerous other sightings in 1970s

HUSKISSON Multi-coloured fireball 10 feet in diameter burst through wall of hotel bar; 19 March 1978

KEMPSEY Much UFO activity over the town beginning 1971

LISMORE Cross in cemetery glowed brightly at night; began c.1918? until 1978, when smashed by vandals. Sightings of water monster in lagoon north of Lismore since the beginning of the century – furry, barrel-shaped body, 3–6 feet long, dog-like head and small ears, with a whining voice

NEAR ORANGE Woman and son saw UFO on their farm at night. Next day ground traces were found; 26 May 1977

NEAR PAMBULA Man hunting rabbits in hilly forested area saw Yowie and shot it in the back, but appeared not to have hurt it; 1977 (see Ch. 12)

PORT STEPHENS Long-necked sea monster (neck 8 feet long) seen from steamer; body had five 'loops' and was dirty yellow; seen for 15 minutes; 2 February 1925

QUIRINDI Fall of fishes from tornado-type cloud; 12 November 1913. Other locations of fish falls in the state include SINGLETON (shrimps, 1918), MULLUMBIMBY (1921), GULARGAMBONE (c.1920), RANDWICK (long marine worms, 1927), ADELONG (29 October 1932), VAUCLUSE (13 January 1941), GOSFORD (16 April 1946), BELFIELD (winkles, August 1952), WOODBURN (April 1959), LISMORE (17 July 1959), WOOLOOWARE GOLF COURSE (November 1959)

SCARBOROUGH 80-foot sea monster with long neck seen; mid-1930

SOUTHERN HIGHLANDS Many reports of panthers or pumas since 1966, especially around NOWRA and in KANGAROO VALLEY (see Ch. 14)

STOCKTON, NEWCASTLE Couple left their haunted house: white face seen looking out of window, beds disturbed, toys moved, figure seen; February 1970 (see Ch. 5)

WATTAGAN MOUNTAINS Sightings of giant (30-foot) monitor lizards going back to 1830; recent witnesses include two farmers in 1975, and herpetologist in 1979 (see Ch. 14)

Northern Territory

CORROBOREE ROCK, NEAR ALICE SPRINGS Revd R. S. Blance, visiting this aboriginal ritual site, took a photograph on which a strange figure appeared; 1959

DARWIN Long-necked sea monster

more than 75 feet long seen by policeman fishing in Bynoe harbour; February 1980

KILLARNEY STATION   Three rains of fish in a fortnight on cattle farms 200 miles from sea; February 1974

MELVILLE ISLAND   Sea monster seen about 5 miles south-east of island: at least 40 feet long with huge head which witness, in boat, tried to hit with an oar; June 1916

WAVE HILL STATION   Hundreds of fishes fell from the sky; 1951 or 1952

WEARYAN RIVER   Nursing sister travelled into remote area to help man who had been shot in the leg. While she was attending to the wound, two men appeared wearing white operating theatre gowns and helped her. When she looked up to thank them, they had gone. Several aborigines witnessed this event; February 1941

Queensland

BOUGAINVILLE REEF   Pilot photographed UFO which paced his plane; 28 May 1965

BOULIA AND WINTON   Occasional appearances of the Min Min Light – oval and luminous, moving irregularly close to ground or higher (see Ch. 8)

CAIRNS   In city street, crocodile locked jaws round man's leg; he kicked it away and it dived into storm drain; May 1983 (see Ch. 14)

CUNNAMULLA   Delta-winged 'aircraft' with no tail, windows or sound, zigzagged over golfers and trail-bike riders – RAAF claimed no known delta-wing aircraft in that area; late September 1984

EMERALD   Black panther seen, and chased at 45 mph; 23 September 1979; other reports from WARBURTON, HEALESVILLE, MONTROSE, MT EVELYN, NEERIM, BEENLEIGH, MILES (January 1983). Some sightings may be of an

unrecognized species, a marsupial tiger-cat (see Ch. 14). Also at Emerald, a man-beast (Yowie) which left footprints 12 inches long, pursued witness and bounced his car up and down; August 1979

ETON RANGE, NEAR MACKAY   Three men saw circular UFO, 30 feet in diameter, which made a buzzing noise; it carried another disc, and had tripod landing gear and headlights. Damaged trees and landing traces found by police; 23 May 1965

FRASER ISLAND   Long black objects up to 100 feet long seen floating in the sea; 6 June 1965. Other sightings of USOs that year off Coolum and Mooloolaba (see Ch. 10)

HOOK ISLAND   Sea monster photographs taken by Robert le Serrec; 12 December 1964 (see Ch. 7)

HORSESHOE LAGOON, NEAR TULLY   Man driving tractor saw grey-blue UFO, 24 feet in diameter, rise from lagoon, spinning like a top, and fly off fast; flattened reeds found; 19 January 1966

NEAR KILCOY   Two teenagers camping in gully caught glimpse of Yowie and found large footprints in soft sand; February 1980

LAIDLEY, TOOWOOMBA DISTRICT   Falls of crabs in rain, 50 miles from sea; 12 May 1930 (see Ch. 13)

MARYBOROUGH–MORETON BAY   Sea monster sightings along coastline since late last century

NEAR NAMBOUR   Boy saw tiny disc, c.12 inches diameter, hovering close by; it made a humming noise and had whitish mist around it. Afterwards he felt ill and developed large blisters on his hands; 1932 or 1933

NEAR NEBO   Group of young people saw strange lights and objects in trees, heard loud explosion; in following days unusual marks found on the ground; 22 March 1975

PRINCE OF WALES ISLAND   Hunters saw red UFO land; others saw similar object; 14 July 1959

SPRINGBROOK, GOLD COAST Man cutting timber saw 7-foot Yowie; 1978 (see Ch. 12)

MOUNT TAMBORINE, GOLD COAST HINTERLAND Three horsemen were stalked by a Yowie on mountain slopes – it was large and grey and scared the cattle dogs; May 1981

TOWNSVILLE Sea monster with three humps covered with scales and barnacles seen by fishermen beyond Fairway Beacon; other sightings off Mourilyan Harbour and Mackay; August and September 1934

WARWICK Fall of gudgeon from the sky; 1901. Other fish-fall locations in the state include: COOPER'S PLAINS (1906), VICTORIA PARK, BRISBANE (1907), CALOUNDRA (February 1909), IPSWICH DISTRICT (12 May 1930), NEAR PRAIRIE (February 1944), CLONCURRY (6 February 1949), TOWNSVILLE AIRPORT (1 April 1959), BRISBANE SUBURBS (1959), HUGHENDEN (16 April 1971)

South Australia

OFF COOMLIEYNA BEACH, NEAR CEDUNA Aboriginals saw unidentified submarine about 90 feet long; 28 December 1976 (see Ch. 10)

PARKSIDE Ball lightning bounced among houses, demolishing one at FULLARTON; 1920 (see Ch. 8)

STUART RANGE Giant reptile seen by opal-hunter; 1931

Tasmania

BOOBYALLA Huge banana-shaped UFO seen just above ground; 25 May 1974, during period of many UFO reports in Tasmania

CRESSY AREA UFO flap, including sighting of 'mother ship' and accompanying smaller objects; October and November 1960

KETTERING Man saw 'plane' coming down at night and went to investigate; found dome-shaped object with bright light coming from windows. Humming noise was followed by UFO taking off. Next day he went back and found circular area of scorched grass; February 1976

LUNE RIVER Thylacine/Tasmanian tiger/Tasmanian wolf seen by bushwalkers; February 1986. Recent sightings of this 'extinct' animal have been reported at various locations on the island, including BLACK RIVER (February 1977), BETWEEN GLADSTONE AND DERBY (19 August 1977), and MOLE CREEK. Over 1000 sightings since 1936, with 104 during 1970–80, but no positive proof of its existence yet obtained (see Ch. 14)

MURCHISON HIGHWAY, BETWEEN QUEENSTOWN AND BURNIE Former policewoman in car saw bright green light in sky – her watch and clock in car stopped, car lost all power and brake would not work, which effect lasted for several minutes until green light vanished. Watch started again at Burnie, and she found she had used extra petrol; 20 August 1979

LAKE SORELL Two men saw three UFOs as they camped by the lake. An intense light shone down on to the lake, before the objects departed 'in a flash'; 26 February 1975

WEST COAST Mining officials saw four-legged sea monster on shore; 20 April 1913 (see Ch. 7)

Victoria

BASS STRAIT Two planes searching for missing schooner saw lights; one plane flew into large cloud and was never seen again, nor was the schooner; 1920. RAAF Beaufort bomber crew flying at 4500 feet saw 'dark shadow' flying alongside only 100–150 feet away, with flame belching from its end. During 18–20 minutes the plane's radio and direction-finding instruments would not work, until UFO accelerated away; February 1944. Frederick Valentich disappeared on a flight to KING ISLAND; 21 October 1978 (see Ch. 3)

NEAR BENAMBRA Thylacine seen crossing road; late December 1979. Other sighting locations include the LANG LANG area of Gippsland, in WEST WIMMERA, and the PORTLAND area (see Ch. 14)

GRAMPIAN MOUNTAINS, SOUTH OF HORSHAM Many sightings of big cats since 1950s (see Ch. 14)

GUNYAH, NEAR TRAFALGAR Large fawn-coloured cat 6 feet long seen by men working in hill country; November 1933 (see Ch. 14)

HEYFIELD, GIPPSLAND Fish fall; 25 July 1933

LAURISIOR RESERVOIR, KYNETON Animal with long shaggy ears which it used to propel itself 'at tremendous speed' seen in water several times by people living nearby; August–September 1949

RAM HEAD Sea monster seen by steamer crew: 30–35 feet long, with four fins 5 feet high, head bigger than seal's; 13 July 1902

NEAR ROSEDALE Farmhand woken at night by cattle bellowing, went out and saw domed UFO moving just above paddock. It had no wings or tail, and he saw orange and blue lights on the 15-foot-tall craft. It hovered over water tank before landing in paddock. Farmhand went over to it on motorcycle, and as he approached he heard a whistling noise and felt like jelly. As he watched from 40 feet, UFO made a screaming noise and took off, sending out a blast of hot air. Next day he found the landing site clearly marked, and 10,000 gallons of water had gone from the tank; 30 September 1980

WONTHAGGI Two unidentified submarines seen offshore, Navy could not identify them; 11 April 1965 (see Ch. 10)

WYCHEPROOF Car headlight beams seemed to bend to right, and driver saw conical light beam in field. Object producing it flew away; 5 April 1966

Western Australia

CLAREMONT Four fish fell from sky; 20 June 1945

CORDERING AREA, EAST OF BUNBURY Many reports of mysterious cat-like animals; sightings reached a peak in 1978. Other cat sighting locations include KULJA (1972), NAMBUNG (August 1982), ENEABBA (24 August 1982), TRAYNING (October 1985) (see Ch. 14)

MANDURAH Tiny, glistening, hairless human-shaped creature entered house; 1930 (see Ch. 9)

NEAR MOORA Two young men saw object like two saucers face to face sitting on legs in paddock; it had oval windows and shimmered; when they returned several days later it was not there; 1925

NULLARBOR PLAIN Woman driving on lonely road with three sons said the car was chased by an eggcup-shaped UFO, lifted from the ground, and covered in ash; astronomer said it could have been a large meteorite shower; 20 January 1988

PUMPHREY Pebbles and rocks fell from sky over several days, and at a location 150 miles away; March 1957 (see Ch. 16)

UPPER SWAN VALLEY Fall of fishes; 1 July 1927

AUSTRIA

EGGENBERG, GRAZ Poltergeist outbreak; 25 October–early December 1929

EISENBERG   Aloisia Lex saw visions of the Blessed Virgin Mary, who gave her messages; beginning 1946 when she was in a coma. In 1947 her father saw a beautiful woman dressed in white in the garden. In 1956, a grass-cross, visible sign of proof, was imprinted on to her land. Messages continued into the 1980s

GÜSSING   Poltergeist outbreak; September–December 1925 and intermittently for three years

LADING   Poltergeist outbreak; 1916–18 (about)

LIESEBRÜCKE, KÄRNTEN   Poltergeist activity at inn and house where young maidservant employed; 24 November 1921–31 January 1922 (see Ch. 1)

NEAR RAURIS   Tatzelwurm (giant lizard) seen; summer 1921 (see Ch. 14)

VIENNA   Poltergeist outbreak in smithy, with movements of tools, coal and iron; July–August 1906

VÖST, NEAR PEUERBACH   Poltergeist outbreak; 26 January–5 February 1932

THE BAHAMAS

NASSAU (60 miles east of)   Officers and passengers on board the *Mauretania* saw 60-foot sea monster with undulating humps and large head lying flat on water; 6 March 1934

BEAURAING   Five children saw 33 apparitions of the Blessed Virgin Mary, with messages; began 29 November 1932 (see Ch. 15)

BRUSSELS   Luminous area 25 feet long, 5 feet high, seen in street; it became phosphorescent green, vibrated, changed shape and moved away; it was formed of tiny luminous particles; 24 January 1970

ETTERBEEK   Small stones, black and sticky, fell from the sky for several seconds; 12 July 1975 (see Ch. 13)

HUY   Cigar-shaped UFO landed and two entities were seen on board; 9 October 1954

RIVER MAAS, NEAR OMBRET   3-foot 'crocodile' seen in river – discarded pet alligator?; 6 August 1979

MARCINELLE, NEAR CHARLEROI   300 stones thrown at house over four days but no human agent found although the police investigated; 30 January–2 February 1913 (see Ch. 16)

SART   Substance that smelled like glue fell from sky; 8 June 1901 (see Ch. 13)

NEAR WARNETON   Man driving at night saw landed UFO in field, then two entities approaching car, both wearing helmets; they seemed to try to communicate before returning to craft; 7 January 1974

BETWEEN WASMES AND AUDEMETS   Man's clothing burnt when he approached UFO landed on road at night, giving off bright light; 14 November 1954

WILSELE   Rains of stones on four houses; May–July 1973

BELGIUM

BANNEUX   Eight apparitions of the Blessed Virgin Mary; January–March 1933 (see Ch. 15)

BELIZE

MAYA MOUNTAINS   In forest at foot of mountains, local forestry officer saw 'little people' below 4 feet 6 inches

tall, hair-covered; known as
Dwendis, who live in the forests of
the south
SAN ANTONIO   Couple and
granddaughter pelted by small
stones, outdoors and indoors; 1981

BOLIVIA

LAKE ORIGUERE   Reports of gigantic
'fish' which capsized canoes
ORURO   Radio technician claimed
abduction by UFO entities who
examined him and gave him a
message; 15 August 1980

BORNEO

LAWAS RIVER   Reports of monster with
cow-like head, eyes like lightbulbs
and big neck – dugong?; May 1985

BRAZIL

ARAGUARI RIVER, AMAPA   Many people
saw UFO rise from river, hover,
then fly out to sea; November 1980
(see Ch. 10)
BARRA DA TIJUCA   Press photographer
Ed Keffel took five pictures of
UFO; 7 May 1952 (see Ch. 3)
BAURÚ   Survey worker saw 150-foot
disc-shaped UFO land, standing on
three legs. Three 7-foot entities tried
to get him inside; he hid and

watched as they tossed huge stones
and leapt about; 23 July 1947
BRASÍLIA   Poltergeist outbreak; 18–19
September 1960
CARAPICUIBA   Stones, bricks and
concrete falling on six slum houses;
September 1974 (see Ch. 16)
NEAR COÇPAVA   Meat and blood fell
from the sky for five or so minutes;
27 August 1968 (see Ch. 13)
CORDILHEIRA DOS PARECIS   Explorer
Col. Fawcett and companions saw
naked hairy 'savages' who threatened
them with bows and arrows: called
locally Maricoxis, and possibly
primitive men; 1914 (see Ch. 12)
NEAR CURITIBA   Strange object seen on
sea, which sank, then rose, then
sank again; 10 January 1958 (see
Ch. 10)
FERNANDO DE NORONHA   Sea monster
seen off this island; its head was as
big as a cow's and witness also saw
one coil of its body, 30 feet away
from head; 1905
NEAR FRANCISCO DE SALES, MINAS
GERAIS   23-year-old farmer Antônio
Villas Boas was taken from his
tractor into a UFO by several
entities, forcibly undressed, and
blood was taken by cupping. A
naked female entity later entered and
made advances to which Villas Boas
responded and they had intercourse.
Before leaving the craft, he
attempted to take an object as proof
of his experience, but the entities
stopped him; 14 October 1957
IPIRANGA, SÃO PAULO   Poltergeist
outbreak with a wide range of
phenomena, including stool passing
through closed door and sliding
downstairs, rapping noises,
outbreaks of fire including inside a
plastic bag of clothes, clothing and a
floor being soaked with water and
equally mysteriously drying out,
objects moving about and
disappearing. The poltergeist
followed the family through four
homes, and stopped when the
daughter got married; 1968–73 (see
Chs 1 and 4)

ITAPEVA   Rocks mysteriously flying at houses; one fell through cathedral roof; May 1987

JABUTICABAL   Poltergeist outbreak centred on young girl named Maria, involving stones and eggs flying indoors, materialization of objects, crockery thrown and broken, Maria being slapped and having furniture thrown at her and being suffocated at night and having needles stuck in her heel and her clothing burned; began December 1965 and continued for at least a year (see Ch. 16)

JOÃO PESSOA   Beans fell from the sky; June 1971

LINS SANATORIUM   Woman on night duty gave water to female UFO entity; August 1968 (see Ch. 6)

MANUOS, AMAZON RIVER   Traveller saw five 'birds' with leathery bodies and wings; c.February 1947 (see Ch. 17)

MATO GROSSO   Reports of humanoid creature known as Mapinguary, which killed cattle and pulled out their tongues (see Ch. 12)

NEAR MINDURI   Two giants c.18 feet tall, clothed in red, seen from behind as they walked up the side of a hill; August 1958

RIO NEGRO   Explorer Major Percy Fawcett killed 62-foot anaconda; normally these snakes are at most 25–30 feet long; 1907. In the late 1940s, two photographs were taken of the *sucuriju gigante*, a 60–150 foot monster snake with glowing green eyes said to live on the RIO ARAGUAYA

PELOTAS, RIO GRANDE DO SUL   Couple saw birdmen; early 1950s (see Ch. 9)

PERNAMBUCO/RECIFE (40 sea miles offshore)   Officer on merchant vessel saw sea monster about 180 feet long, overtaking ship 'with the speed of an arrow off a bow'. It had large dorsal fins; 1906

PEROPAVA RIVER, NEAR IGUAPÉ   Disc-shaped UFO plunged into river; 31 October 1963 (see Ch. 10)

PIATA BEACH   Motorcyclist saw UFO over the sea and took four photographs showing markings on underside; he then entered a trance state and wrote a message as if from the UFO, calling for an end to atomic tests; 24 April 1959

NEAR PONTAL   Fisherman saw UFO land and three small entities come out and collect leaves, grass, and water in a tube; 4 November 1954 (see Ch. 6)

PONTA PORÃ   Poltergeist outbreak; 1969–73

PORTO DAS CAIXAS   In church, 300-year-old life-size painted wooden statue of Christ on the Cross dripped human blood; miracle cures followed; beginning January 1968 and for at least ten years

RIO DE JANEIRO (100 miles north of)   Fishermen reported two sightings of sea monster with long neck and dark green scales, 100 feet long; August 1982

OFF SANTA MARTA GRANDE   Unidentified submarine object seen by crew of cargo ship; 30 July 1967 (see Ch. 10)

SÃO PAULO   Poltergeist outbreak; July 1972. Paranormal movement of rocks and other objects; spring 1987 (see Ch. 16)

SÃO PAULO, SÃO JOSE DOS CAMPOS, RIO DE JANEIRO   Multi-coloured UFOs, likened to ping-pong balls, seen in the skies and on radar, and fighter jets were sent up to chase them; one was surrounded by thirteen coloured lights; 19 May 1986

SOROCABA   Poltergeist outbreak; several weeks from mid-July 1972

SUZANO   Poltergeist outbreak, with several incidents of spontaneous combustion; 1970 (see Ch. 4)

TRINDADE ISLAND   Marine photographer took four pictures of UFO seen from Brazilian Navy ship; 16 January 1958 (see Ch. 3)

UBATUBA   UFO exploded over sea and some debris was retrieved for analysis – it was very pure magnesium; 10 September 1957 (see Ch. 3)

URUBÚ RIVER WATERSHED AREA
Expedition member saw and shot at
'thick-set black figure' standing
upright; he thought it was a
Mapinguary; 1930 (see Ch. 12)

BULGARIA

SOFIA   Bright, spherical UFO flew
slowly at a great height over the
city; 1908. Conical UFO seen;
9 April 1967. Bluish neon UFO of
trapezoidal shape seen moving
against the wind; 21 November 1967

BURMA

COMILLA   Thousands of small fish fell
in heavy storm; World War II
MANDALAY   Rice fell from the sky;
January 1952 (see Ch. 13)
MEKONG RIVER   Tall, dark, hairy
'monkey-men' seen near
Burma/Thailand/Laos border; July
1969

CAMEROUN

ASSUMBO MOUNTAINS   Zoologist saw
giant bat or pterodactyl; 1932 (see
Ch. 17)
LAKE BAROMBI MBO, KUMBA   Children
saw two monsters in lake with necks
12–15 feet above water; 1948 or
1949

CANADA

Alberta

BANFF NATIONAL PARK   Midges encased
in ice fell from the sky; 16 February
1952. Bigfoot was seen in the Park
in August 1968; other locations in
Alberta of pre-1981 Bigfoot sightings
include NORTH SASKATCHEWAN
VALLEY (March and July 1969), BIG
HORN DAM, NORTH SASKATCHEWAN
RIVER (August 1969), NEAR ROCKY
MOUNTAIN HOUSE (summer 1972),
NEAR SEVEN PERSONS (autumn 1972,
October and December 1983), NEAR
BIG HORN DAM (May 1974), NEAR
SEXSMITH (October 1975), NEAR
COLD LAKE (summer 1976), NEAR
CAROLINE (September 1976), NEAR
ROCHESTER (October 1976)
BATTLE RIVER, CLEARWATER RIVER,
NORTH AND SOUTH SASKATCHEWAN
RIVERS   Water monster reports
BOWNESS LAGOON, COLD LAKE, HEART
LAKE, LAKE MCGREGOR, LAKE
MINNEWANKA   Lake monster reports
CHRISTINA LAKE   Reports of lake
monster 30–40 feet long with 3-foot
hairy neck, horse-like head and big
eyes; June 1984
SADDLE LAKE   100 sightings of lake
monster during 1974–84; 75–150
feet long with horse-like head

British Columbia

BENNET LAKE, CHADBURN LAKE, LAKE
COWICHAN, LAKE HARRISON, LAKE
KAMLOOPS, LAKE KATHLYN, LAKE
KOOTENAY, MARTIN'S LAKE, LAKE
OSOYOOS, SETON LAKE (see Ch. 7),
LAKE SKAHA, LAKE SOMENOS, LAKE
TAGAI, WILLIAMS LAKE   Lake
monster reports
CAMPBELL RIVER AREA   Site of possible
first Bigfoot sighting in British
Columbia this century, in 1901.

Timber cruiser Mike King watched Bigfoot washing roots in water and placing them in neat piles. Many other sightings in British Columbia up to 1980, for example at COUGAR LAKE (1915), where prospectors watched Bigfoot eating berries; the case of Albert Ostman kidnapped by Bigfoot in summer 1924; MORRIS CREEK (July 1936), where Bigfoot threw rocks at an Indian in a canoe; MICA MOUNTAIN, where William Roe had a close view of a Bigfoot eating leaves (October 1955); BELLA COOLA, where female Bigfoot and two youngsters seen (April 1962); ROSCOE INLET (July 1973), where fisheries patrolman watched Bigfoot on beach

CHILLIWACK   Poltergeist outbreak characterized by loud rappings in the walls; several months from October 1951

DUNCAN   Burning mass fell from sky, landing on asphalt road. Samples of rock-like substance taken for analysis; 11 March 1984

NEAR FELLER'S HEIGHTS   Four members of oil crew saw Bigfoot in remote forest clearing; 14 March 1987 (see Ch. 2)

NORTH VANCOUVER   Poltergeist centred on three-year-old boy who had a ghostly friend; 1977 (see Ch. 1)

LAKE OKANAGAN   Home of lake monster 'Ogopogo' (see Ch. 7)

BETWEEN PRINCE RUPERT AND KAMLOOPS   Two Bigfeet seen at night crouching under tree, third standing upright nearby. It appeared 11–12 feet tall and weighing 800–1000 pounds; 24 December 1983

SAANICH, VANCOUVER ISLAND   Teenage boys reported seeing 8-foot hairy creature in the bush; February 1982

LAKE SHUSWAP   Lake monster reports, e.g. Griffiths family saw seven dark greyish humps while out sailing, c.20–25 feet long and moving quite fast; June 1984

SOUTH BURNABY   Slime smelling like dung fell from sky on to elementary school three days running; February 1986 (see Ch. 13)

TERRACE   Schoolboy saw 'little green man' who spoke in an incomprehensible tongue and gave boy a lump of strange substance before disappearing – it gradually shrank and disappeared, or was lost; late February 1970

THETIS LAKE   Monster seen with human-like body, silver and scaly, big ears, razor-sharp points on head; 19 and 23 August 1972

THOMPSON RIVER, KAMLOOPS   Fisherman saw UFO emerge from river and fly away, raining down pellets; 16 May 1981 (see Ch. 10)

VANCOUVER ISLAND   Hannah McRoberts photographed UFO; October 1981 (see Ch. 3). Many sightings of Cadborosaurus or Caddy, British Columbia's sea monster, have been made around Vancouver Island; favoured locations include MACAULAY POINT, CHEMAINUS BAY, STUART CHANNEL, PENDER ISLAND, VALDEZ ISLAND, QUEEN CHARLOTTE ISLANDS, CADBORO BAY (see Ch. 7)

Manitoba

CEDAR LAKE, DAUPHIN LAKE, DIRTY WATER LAKE, LAKE MANITOBA, RED RIVER, LAKE ST MARTIN, LAKE WINNIPEG, LAKE WINNIPEGOSIS   Lake monster reports

EASTERVILLE AREA   Numerous sightings of Bigfoot-type creatures; 1968, 1969, 1970, 1973. Other places in Manitoba where Bigfeet were seen pre-1981 include NEAR REYNOLDS (summer 1970), NEAR POINTE DU BOIS (July 1974), NEAR BEAUSEJOUR (June 1975), NEAR LONG PLAINS RESERVE (July 1975), AGASSIZ PROVINCIAL FOREST (October 1975), POPLAR RIVER (1976), NEAR STEINBACH (10 July 1979), LITTLE SASKATCHEWAN INDIAN RESERVE (October 1979)

NEAR FALCON LAKE Steve Michalak, prospecting for minerals in the woods, saw two UFOs, one of which landed. After 30 minutes of changing colour, a door opened and a purple light shone out. Witness could hear voices and shouted in six languages, with no response. He went nearer, put his head in the opening, and saw a maze of flashing lights. He examined the craft exterior and saw no seams or rivets. He touched the machine and his rubber glove melted and his shirt caught fire. The UFO took off and Michalak went to seek medical help; 20 May 1967 (see Ch. 6)

LONE ISLAND, WHITESHELL PROVINCIAL PARK Two policemen fishing in Whiteshell River saw 8-foot Bigfoot on shore; next morning they were woken by dogs barking at 5.30 a.m., and from their campers saw Bigfoot being attacked by two large wolves, which it grabbed and threw aside; October 1983

NEAR ROSA Man driving on 59 Highway saw 7-foot Bigfoot standing in road; 9 April 1986

BETWEEN SANDY BAY AND WINNIPEG Man chased Bigfoot-type creature which left footprints like a human hand 16 inches across; August 1982 (see Ch. 2)

NEAR WOODRIDGE Ghost light seen in forest; 1950–70

New Brunswick

GRAND LAKE, LOCH LOMOND, LAKE MAQUAPIT, ST CROIX RIVER, SKIFF LAKE, LAKE UTOPIA ('Old Ned') Lake monster reports

NELSON-MIRAMICHI Security guard at mill saw 'baby kangaroo' which bounded into bush; others also saw it; June 1979

ST CROIX RIVER Fishermen on river at Bayside saw sets of fins 20 feet and 50 feet apart; later saw head with huge green eyes; 10 August 1903

NEAR ST JOHN Two men by lake at night saw UFO with red, orange, green and blue lights which came down on to water, making a sizzling noise before submerging completely; next day, water was muddy, and hot near place where UFO sank; summer 1967

Newfoundland

CONCEPTION BAY, ST JOHN'S Phantom ship seen; November 1910 (see Ch. 5). In Conception Bay, as well as HEART'S DELIGHT HARBOUR, WHITE BAY and TRINITY BAY, sightings of giant squids; 1901–35

CRESCENT LAKE, DILDO POND, GANDER LAKE, LONG POND, SWANGER'S COVE Lake monster reports

FLAT ROCK, ST JOHN'S House plagued for two weeks by fire-spook; doll, dictionary, box of religious tracts and sack of sugar burst into flames spontaneously; November 1954

GOOSE BAY, LABRADOR Fiery spherical UFO seen to make right-angle turn by plane crew; also seen from ground; early 1952

OFF NORTH COAST OF LABRADOR Cylindrical UFO with lighted portholes hit the sea and sank; 23 September 1960

PORT-AU-PORT Sea monster 200 feet long, 18 feet diameter and neck 60 feet out of water was said to be destroying fishing gear; August 1936

TRAVERSPINE, NEAR GOOSE BAY, LABRADOR Isolated house often visited by hairy Bigfoot-type creature around 7 feet tall when erect, though it sometimes dropped to all fours. It wielded a stick against the dogs, and stayed around the area for two winters; c.1913

Northwest Territories

DUBAWNT LAKE Lake monster reports

FORT NORMAN Bigfoot seen; November 1973. Also an earlier

report from somewhere in the Northwest Territories in summer 1952 described how a man saw a 9-foot Bigfoot standing watching him from blackberry bushes 75 feet away; it then walked away

Nova Scotia

LAKE AINSLIE, CRANBERRY LAKE   Lake monster reports

ANTIGONISH   Kangaroo seen; October 1986. Other sightings near EASTERN PASSAGE and COLE HARBOUR; January 1987

CALEDONIA MILLS, NEAR ANTIGONISH   Many fires of probable poltergeist origin at an isolated farmhouse – 38 in one night; January 1922 (see Ch. 4)

CAPE SABLE ISLAND   Sightings of sea monster: 40–50-foot creature with 'alligator's head' and big red eyes approached fishing vessel to within 10 feet; July 1976 (see Ch. 7)

EASTERN PASSAGE, NEAR HALIFAX   Poltergeist outbreak with rappings and household objects being thrown around; 24 December 1943–8 January 1944 (see Ch. 1)

GLACE BAY   Mysterious outbreaks of fire in house; beginning 16 April 1963

NORTHUMBERLAND STRAIT   Fiery phantom ship seen; 10 January 1979 (see Ch. 5)

SHAG HARBOUR   Unidentified submarine object over 60 feet long seen; October 1967 (see Ch. 10)

WINDSOR   Poltergeist outbreak; October 1906–February 1907

Ontario

BANKFIELD AND LITTLE LONG LAC GOLD MINES   Mine-workers frightened by lights and ghosts; March 1937 (see Ch. 5)

LAKE OF THE BAYS, BERENS LAKE, CONWAY'S MARSH, LAKE DESCHENES, LAKE ERIE, LAKE HURON, LAKE MAZINAW, LAKE MEMINISHA, MUSKRAT LAKE ('Mussy'), NIAGARA RIVER, NIGHTHAWK LAKE, NITH RIVER ('Slimy Caspar'), LAKE ONTARIO ('Metro Maggie'), RIVER OTTAWA, BAY OF QUINTE, RIDEAU CANAL, ST LAWRENCE RIVER, LAC SEUL, LAKE SIMCOE ('Igopogo'; 'Kempenfelt Kelly'), LAKE SUPERIOR, LAKE TEMISKAMING   Lake monster reports

BURGESS TOWNSHIP, NEAR PERTH   Stone-throwing and other poltergeist activity at a farmhouse; January 1935 (see Ch. 16)

CACHE LAKE, ALGONQUIN PARK   Long, low, moving cloud emitted continuous rumbling noise – no hail or rainfall, no sign of lightning; July 1931

CAMPDEN   Several people saw black, 7-foot Bigfoot and 16-inch tracks found; August 1965

NEAR COBALT   Sightings of Bigfoot nicknamed 'Yellow Top'; September 1906. In July 1923 prospectors saw a Bigfoot in a blueberry patch. Near GILLIES LAKE, woman and son saw Bigfoot with light head in April 1946. Bigfoot walked in front of busload of miners on 5 August 1970

FOREST HILL VILLAGE, TORONTO   Poltergeist activity at three houses which shared the same servant; January 1947 (see Ch. 1)

GALT   3-foot crocodilian caught; 17 June 1929. Others seen and caught at TORONTO (18 June 1929), WINDSOR (20 September 1970), and at GUELPH a woman found 3½-foot alligator under her car; May 1977

GATINEAU POINT   Men sheltering from storm saw ball of fire enter barn; both were injured; September 1925 (see Ch. 8)

GEORGIAN BAY   Eight witnesses saw UFO on water; entities were manipulating hose in water. On seeing witnesses they returned inside, all except one who was still outside when craft took off; August 1914

NEAR GERALDTON   Hiker badly shaken

after seeing tall Bigfoot in woods; *c.*10 October 1978

HAMILTON   Boy saw two UFOs, 8 feet long and with flashing lights, land; touched antenna and received electric shock; 31 March 1966

JORDAN   Following electrical storm, nine-year-old boy's presence caused fruit to fly, clods of earth and buttons to fly around, very like poltergeist phenomena; October 1913

NEAR KAPUSKASING   Man saw maned lion on his farm, 3 feet tall, 5 feet long, with 4-foot tail with bushy end; June 1960

MISSISSAUGA   Molten green flaming mass fell from sky on to table in back garden; 16 June 1979

NIAGARA FALLS   Sightings of planes at a time when none were flying in the area; 1914–16

NIAGARA RIVER   Possible water monster sighting; late 1970s

NIPISSING JUNCTION   Haunted house; early 1937

OTTAWA (40 miles north-east of) Instruments of plane affected by close proximity of UFO; 18 August 1979 (see Ch. 3)

QUEENSTON   Fish fell from sky in heavy rain; some found in tree branches; 11 June 1938

RUTHVEN   Bigfoot seen by boy; 4 June 1977

ST CATHARINES   Fish fell from sky in thunderstorm; 13 July 1927. Poltergeist activity with furniture movement – one chair containing an eleven-year-old boy floated 7 inches off the ground; February 1970. Fall of hot ash, white stuff and smell of sulphur from big black cloud; *c.*14 July 1976

SAULT STE MARIE   12-foot pike pole with spike on one end and hook on the other crashed through a window, presumably from the sky; 7 February 1979

SCARBORO   Kangaroo seen; 31 May 1979

SCARBOROUGH, TORONTO   Poltergeist outbreak; 1968–*c.*1971

LAKE SIMCOE   Ghost light seen on shore near Brechin; 1952

NEAR SMITHVILLE   Truck-driver saw tall, long-armed Bigfoot; 9 August 1965

STOUFFVILLE   Football-sized ball lightning with purplish streak from top came down fast and struck barn with loud noise and flash; 1 May 1933

TILLSONBURG   Bigfoot seen in tobacco fields and 18-inch tracks found; September 1965

TORONTO   Warm porous rock, not a meteorite, crashed on to patio; 20 August 1978 (see Ch. 13). During four hours' sleep at night, 31-year-old woman developed second and third degree burns on thighs and abdomen, needing skin grafting; night-clothes and bed linen were not affected; 19 June 1980

NEAR WIARTON   Police constable saw big cat, possibly cougar; mid-October 1978, following many reports on the BRUCE PENINSULA during the previous year

NEAR WINDSOR   Mysterious outbreaks of fire at golf and country club; tablecloths covered with tiny dancing blue flames; December 1941 (see Ch. 4)

Prince Edward Island

EGMONT BAY   Two men saw 40–60-foot sea monster – dark, serpentine, head 3 feet long; 1956

O'KEEF'S LAKE   Lake monster reports

Quebec

LAKE AYLMER, LAKE BASKATONG, LAKE BLUE SEA, LAKE BOWKER, LAKE BREECHES, LAKE BROMPTON, LAC AUX CEDRES, LAKE CHAMPLAIN ('Champ'), LAKE CREUX, LAKE DECAIRE ('Lizzie'), LAKE DESERT, LAKE MASKINONGE, LAKE MASSAWIPPI, LAKE

MEGANTIC, LAKE MEMPHREMAGOG, MOCKING LAKE, LAKE MOFFAT, LAC DES PILES, LAKE POCKNOCK, LAKE REMI, LAKE ST FRANCOIS, LAKE ST JEAN, LAKE SIMON, LAKE SINCLAIR, LAC TRENTE-ET-UN-MILLE, LES TROIS LAC, LAKE WILLIAMS   Lake monster reports

MONTREAL   Fine white filaments floated down on to ship; it was tough and resilient, difficult to break when stretched, and disappeared after a few minutes, none of these features applying to spiders' webs; 10 October 1962. Small crocodilian found on vacant lot; 28 July 1973. Icon from Mount Athos (Greece) began to stream with myrrh; began November 1982, continued at least four years

LAKE POHENEGAMOOK   Home of lake monster 'Ponik' – up to 80 feet long, three humps seen, or an 'upturned boat' shape

RIVIERES DES PRAIRIES, MONTREAL NORTH   Fisherman caught 4-foot shark in freshwater stream; 14 July 1968 (see Ch. 14)

ST BRUNO   Children on farm saw a cloud from the sky, from which came the Blessed Virgin Mary who spoke to them about peace and brotherhood; late July 1968 (see Ch. 15)

ST LAWRENCE RIVER (65 miles north of Quebec City)   Airline pilot and co-pilot watched submarine for four or five minutes in an area where the Navy said a submarine could not operate; March 1965. UFO with flashing red lights seen by witnesses on Nun's Island to plunge into river; 23 May 1969

ST-STANISLAS-DE-KOTSKA   Children saw UFOs and an entity; 28 July 1968 (see Ch. 15). On same day, UFO and several entities seen at UPTON (see Ch. 15)

TERREBONNE   Flats in big house troubled by fire-spook; fourteen-year-old girl confessed after police interrogation, but confession suspect; January 1948

Saskatchewan

NEAR BEECHY   Ghost light seen in Buffalo Basin district; 1912–25

NIPAWIN   Three witnesses saw landed UFO and watched several little entities in silver suits going up and down a ladder. Square imprints and burnt areas seen and photographed next day; summer 1935

PETER POND, TURTLE LAKE   Lake monster reports

SASKATOON   Four children saw oval UFO hover, then drop something. They went nearer and saw entity 9 feet tall, in 'white monk-like suit' who made noises and held out his hands. They fled; 19 September 1963

TABOR   Tabor Lights seen around cemetery, dating back to 1892 with most activity in November–December 1938

Yukon Territory

LAKE TESLIN   Lake monster reports

CENTRAL AFRICAN REPUBLIC

NEAR BOCARANGA   Eight men watched UFOs for half an hour; 22 November 1952

CHILE

NEAR ARICA   Miner saw UFO land and two entities came out. They asked for water in a mixture of Spanish and English. Witness gave them some, and they then departed; 15 June 1964. Pilot and crew members saw UFO; it was mechanical and came towards plane; 6 September 1985

ISLA DE CHILOE Phantom ship *Caleuche* seen; 1968 and other times

NEAR OSORNO Man trekking in forest saw beam of light and UFO, and became paralysed; then human-like entity *c*.4½-feet tall appeared as if from thin air, wearing wrinkle-free translucent suit; late January 1967

PAMPA LLUSCUMA, NEAR PUTRE Corporal Armando Valdes walked towards light (UFO?) and returned after fifteen minutes with five-day growth of beard and watch calendar advanced five days; 25 April 1977

PELLUCO UFO with violet light landed, then five minutes later took off at speed; trees found uprooted and clear landing circle with mass of soil missing, never found; 31 July 1965

NEAR TOCOPILLA UFO seen by several witnesses, and police who investigated saw luminous object approximately 60 feet in diameter and helicopter-like cabin over sea. Sergeant shot at UFO, which moved fast to within 150 feet and illuminated the area like daytime. After several hours, it sank into the sea, observed by ship's crew; 23–24 September 1971 (see Ch. 10)

CHINA

CHANGBAI, MANCHURIA Monster seen swimming in lake: about 6 feet long, black, reptilian, with oval head and long neck; several sightings, and one witness shot at it and missed; 1980

NEAR CHONGQING (CHUNGKING), SICHUAN PROVINCE Peasant out in fields saw entity with huge head, wearing one-piece 'space-suit' which looked metallic and shone brightly. Head was in helmet, and entity walked stiffly but fast. Witness ran away, but looking back the entity had vanished; end August 1971

DADI GULLY, ZHOUZHI COUNTY, SHAANXI PROVINCE Man cutting wood saw hairy wildman which stood within 6 feet of him for an hour, until witness threw a rock at it and retreated; early June 1977. Shortly afterwards there was another encounter here with a similar creature; 21 July 1977 (see Ch. 12)

DONGTING HU LAKE, HUNAN PROVINCE Cries for help heard from rock; 1981 (see Ch. 11)

GAOLIGON MOUNTAIN REGION, SOUTH YUNAN Anyone who stands by pools called 'The Mysterious Lakes' and shouts, is rewarded by a rain shower: the louder the yell, the heavier the rain; the longer the yell, the longer the rain lasts; 1981

LAKE HANAS Lake monsters identified as giant red salmon (*hucho taimen*) *c*.33 feet long; 1985 (see Ch. 7)

LANZHOU, GANSU PROVINCE Student saw luminous black being in vegetable garden; two others saw him two days later; 29 July 1974. Chinese Boeing 747, *en route* from Beijing to Paris, saw fast UFO pacing plane for two minutes; 11 June 1985

MEISHAN, SICHUAN PROVINCE Noisy, reddish-orange UFO like large straw hat seen hovering at midnight for thirty minutes; 7 March 1987

NORTHERN CHINA At 36,000 feet, mystery falling object broke off part of tailplane of Chinese military plane, which landed safely; 2 November 1983

QIAOSHIANG COMMUNE, HUBEI PROVINCE Woman cutting grass for pigs saw red, hairy creature rubbing its back against a tree; primate hairs were collected; 19 June 1976

QING XIAN, HEBEI PROVINCE UFO with dome, giving out white light, flew 15–20 feet above ground; September 1943

SHANGHAI Statue of the Immaculate Heart of Mary in church on hill near Shanghai wept for three days; 1953. UFO seen over city for forty minutes – 'like an oval plate' or 'comet with a tail like an umbrella' or 'flying orange' – and military aircraft took off to observe it; later identified as excess fuel ejected from booster rocket of Japanese satellite, burning up in the atmosphere; 27 August 1987

SHENNONGJIA MOUNTAINS, HUBEI PROVINCE More than 300 sightings of 'wild men' recorded since 1920s, and expeditions have gone in search of them (see Ch. 12)

TASHKURGHAN (where borders of China, India, Afghanistan, Pakistan, USSR meet, adjoining Tajikistan in USSR where wildmen still seen) Hairy man-beast shot and killed; 1944

TIANCHI/HEAVEN LAKE, BAITOU MOUNTAIN Lake monster reports over last century

TONG-EUL-KIOU Remains of Blessed Maria Assunta Pallotta were found to be perfectly preserved, eight years after her death; April 1913

WUXI 100-pound block of ice fell from sky on to city pavement; scientists proved its meteoric origin by use of satellite picture; 11 April 1983

YUNAN PROVINCE Soldiers killed and ate Yeti-like creature; 1962

ZHANGPU COUNTY, FUJIAN PROVINCE Two large luminous orange objects descended on outdoor cinema audience of 3000 and swept diagonally across, almost scraping the ground, and causing panic; two children died and 200 were injured; 7 July 1977

ZHEJIANG PROVINCE Two lorry-drivers in convoy saw UFO and two strange figures on the road, in two locations; entities were $c.4\frac{1}{2}$ feet tall, wearing helmets and spacesuits with backpacks and cylinders. All disappeared when one driver got out of his cab; 13 December 1979

CHRISTMAS ISLAND (INDIAN OCEAN)

Officers on vessel off west coast saw UFO through binoculars; it was squat and cylindrical, with pale blue light underneath and another light on dome above. It appeared stationary, only disappearing after nearly $1\frac{1}{2}$ hours. Did not look like weather balloon, and too early and too slow for satellite Cosmos 1402; 20 January 1983

COLOMBIA

ANCHICAYA American Peace Corps worker saw luminous ghost in the jungle; June 1978 (see Ch. 5)

ANDES MOUNTAINS Reports of 4–5-foot hair-covered hominoids called Shiru

ANOLAIMA UFO seen from rural farm by eleven witnesses, one of whom got to within 20 feet of it and saw an entity inside; two days later he was taken ill and died from gastroenteritis, possibly caused by exposure to radiation; 4 July 1969

NEAR IBAGUE Four boys saw tiny entities in muddy riverbed; 10 August 1973 (see Ch. 9)

CONGO

LAKE TELE AND LIKOUALA-AUX-HERBES
RIVER Sightings of water monster
known as Mokele-mbembe, a
possible prehistoric survival, and
other mystery animals (see Ch. 17)

CUBA

HAVANA Several reported sightings of
an apparition of the Blessed Virgin
Mary standing on the waters of
Havana bay: a smiling, olive-skinned
woman dressed in white, she has
long dark hair and stretches out her
arms; late 1970s

CZECHOSLOVAKIA

BRATISLAVA Poltergeist outbreak;
11–13 August 1927
BRNO Military men watched light in
sky which would disappear then
reappear elsewhere. Tracked on
radar and jets scrambled, but UFO
always disappeared each time jet
approached, and after an hour
disappeared for good; 1960
HOTIANSKY-NEMCE Retired pilot saw
UFO travelling fast over mountains;
April 1955
KOŠICE Glowing red and black spheres
seen hovering over towns and
villages; 1 September 1965
KOSTEN-STEINHÜGEL Poltergeist
outbreak; August–November 1927
KOTTERBACH Poltergeist outbreak;
several days in July 1927

LNAR Witness saw four shining discs
in straight line, which were replaced
by twelve spheres arranged six by
six. They divided into two, and all
flew away at speed; 14 August 1965
NIKOLSBURG (MIKULOV), NEAR BRNO
Poltergeist outbreak; October 1927 –
summer 1928
SCHICHOWITZ Three girls saw
apparitions of Blessed Virgin Mary;
June and July 1948
MOUNT SNEZKA Couple climbing on
mountain got lost in snowstorm, and
were led to safety by shining blue
ball which appeared near them;
November 1977 (see Ch. 8)
SNOPOUSOV Woman and grandchildren
saw two domed UFOs which came
down, sat motionless in sky for
several minutes, gave off smoke,
then took off, emitting bright light;
1 July 1966
TATRA MOUNTAINS Man and boy
followed by showers of stones,
indoors as well as out; 11 August
1927 (see Ch. 16)

DENMARK

LAKE FURESÖ (north of Copenhagen)
Violent splashing at private boat pier
seen, and boat briefly lifted clear of
the water; several 1-inch planks were
splintered. Was it a giant pike, or
some other monster?; February 1944
RIVER GUDENAA, JUTLAND Snake 6 feet
long seen in water, yellowish-brown
in colour; one person was attacked
by it and had to run away after
trying to defend himself with a
stick; September 1943
HERNING & HOLSTED, JUTLAND
Sightings of big cat; 1971. Other big
cat sightings have been in VEJEN,
ÅLUM (1980 or 1981),
ASSERBØLGÅRD, ÅBENRÅ (January
1965), THY (winter 1968–9)

LAKE KILDEVÆLD, ØSTERBRO, COPENHAGEN Couple strolling by lake saw dark object projecting more than 3 feet which moved across lake and then came back; July 1986

SONDERBORG Mechanic saw UFO land and became paralysed; also birds stopped singing and cows were immobile. Four entities in black with helmets emerged, and others on deck appeared to be making repairs. Eight other objects came out and hovered before flying away; 19 June 1951

NEAR SVENDBORG Man on bicycle saw disc-shaped UFO, luminous and seemingly made of glass, spinning at ground level; it chased him at a height of 20 feet; 15 April 1959

TVED DUNEPLANTATION 'Lynx' seen – greyish yellow with long legs, large head and stumpy tail – no animal missing from zoos. There were several sightings, but it was never caught or shot; winter 1968–9

ULUSHALE FOREST, MÖN ISLAND Strange snake seen, c.4½ feet long, with dark back and light underside, and 'nasty head'; some thought it might be a giant eel taking a walk on land; June 1973

in 1959 on a boating expedition; 22 September 1972

EAST GERMANY

HOPFGARTEN, NEAR WEIMAR Poltergeist outbreak with rappings centred on dying woman; 14–28 February 1921

LEIPZIG Poltergeist outbreak; 4 September–20 November 1931

NEUBRANDENBURG Two apes or monkeys seen several times; none missing from zoos; November 1938

ECUADOR

ANDES MOUNTAINS Reports of 4–5-foot hair-covered hominoids called Shiru

DOMINICAN REPUBLIC

PALENQUE, SAN CRISTOBAL Driver flagged down by three entities in green clothing, with yellow-grey skin. Witness saw oval UFO in bushes. One entity told him he was Freddy Miller, a Dominican who had been rescued from drowning in the sea by a UFO and taken to Venus to live. After a few minutes' talk, the entities left. Miller, a believer in UFOs, had disappeared

EGYPT

SHOUBRA, CAIRO Thousands of people saw apparition of Blessed Virgin Mary on roof of church of St Damiana in Papadoplo; beginning March 1986 (see Ch. 15)

ZEITOUN, CAIRO Hundreds of thousands of people saw luminous apparitions above a church, which were interpreted as the Blessed Virgin Mary; April 1968–May 1971 (see Ch. 15)

ENGLAND (see also *Modern Mysteries of Britain*)

Bedfordshire

CHICKSANDS WOOD   Man walking his dogs saw large black cat-like animal, and found half-eaten rabbits; November 1985

DUNSTABLE   House haunted by man in Victorian dress; summer 1966 (see Ch. 5)

Berkshire

ASCOT   Poltergeist activity with several unusual features – lights flashing inside and outside house, flying objects, parked cars moved soundlessly, ashtray thrown without disturbing ash, telephone phenomena; Christmas 1974–early 1976 (see Ch. 1)

THATCHAM   Ghostly voice heard in farmhouse; ghost of little old woman see later (see Ch. 11)

WINDSOR   Ghost of Cardinal Wolsey seen in house; Easter, early 1920s

Cambridgeshire

LINTON   Ghostly man spoke to witness on two occasions, and recordings were made of conversation and other domestic sounds from an earlier century, in haunted house occupied by psychic Matthew Manning; 1971 onwards (see Ch. 11)

SOHAM   Workers on night shift saw shadowy shapes and heard ghostly voices; autumn 1973 (see Ch. 11)

Channel Islands

VALE, GUERNSEY   In marshy area, ball of fire seen bouncing along top of hedge at night; 1933 (see Ch. 8)

Cheshire

CHESTER   Ghostly monk spoke to man hurrying home at night; December 1973 (see Ch. 11). Man heard and saw sobbing ghost and ghost of man hanging in tree; November 1984. Woman vacating shop heard ghostly voice saying goodbye; 1985. Girl saw man who spoke to her; she later realized he was dead; January 1986

DODLESTON   Poltergeist activity in cottage accompanied by communications on home computer from man living in sixteenth century; began November 1984 (see Ch. 11)

WEAVERHAM   Poltergeist activity in bungalow when young boy present, with furniture moved, messages written in flour, objects falling; October 1975

Cleveland

HARTLEPOOL   Two fireballs (ball lightning?) flew past house-painters and 'disintegrated in a shower of sparks'; 25 October 1979

Cornwall

LOSTWITHIEL   Poltergeist activity at Trout Hotel; early 1987

POUNDSTOCK   Man spoke to priest, who responded; later learned he was a ghost; 2 March 1971 (see Ch. 11)

Derbyshire

HARDWICK HALL   Children saw ghost of smiling man carrying tray of tankards; 1934 (see Ch. 5)

Devon

CHARFORD MANOR   Hotel cellars haunted by ghost of elderly man – footsteps heard, bottles moved by invisible hands, figure seen floating by in dining-room; early 1980s

NEAR DARTMOUTH   Large black cat-like animal ran across road, causing witness's car to collide with hedge; 5 November 1986

DEVONPORT, PLYMOUTH   'Phantom food slinger' was throwing packs of sausages into back gardens, and once a fresh lobster worth £4–5; 1979–83

HONITON   Children on Marlpit's Hill saw ghost of man who may have been killed following seventeenth-century Battle of Sedgemoor; 1904 (see Ch. 5)

IVYBRIDGE   Poltergeist activity, with tappings, smells, screaming, and smoky forms seen; November 1984 (see Ch. 1)

NEAR WIDECOMBE   Asian leopard cat shot by Dartmoor farmer; April 1988

Dorset

LYTCHETT MATRAVERS   Ghost of little old lady seen in church; 30 March 1915 (see Ch. 5)

Durham

DURHAM AREA   Sightings of mystery cat, especially at BOWBURN, THINFORD, FERRYHILL, DEAF HILL, WINGATE; August–October 1986

East Sussex

BRIGHTON   Witness heard ghostly voice early in the morning; January 1973

Essex

NEAR CRANHAM   Ghost of figure in cowl or hood seen on road at night at Christmas time by several drivers; 1970s (see Ch. 5)

HADLEIGH   Phantom Georgian house seen; c.1946

SOUTHEND-ON-SEA   Man saw apparition of living woman; 1983

Gloucestershire

CHELTENHAM   During thunderstorm, ball lightning entered house, followed woman upstairs and shot out of open bedroom window; 1961 (see Ch. 8)

STOW-ON-THE-WOLD   Poltergeist activity which began destructively, then mellowed into singing and joking from the spirit 'George'; 1963–4

Greater London

CLARENCE HOUSE   When occupied by British Red Cross Society, woman working there alone one dark autumn afternoon saw 'greyish, swirling, triangular, smoky mass . . . receding and advancing alternately'; 1940s

ELM PARK GARDENS, CHELSEA   Poltergeist activity centred on young servant girl, mainly thumps and knockings in the dividing wall; 1937

HAMPSTEAD HEATH   Young wild seal caught in pond; 25 August and early November 1926

HOUSE OF COMMONS   Ghost of living
man seen in Parliament; May 1905

Greater Manchester

COLLYHURST, MANCHESTER   Children in
haunted flat saw ghostly woman in
their room, who spoke to them;
12 November 1972

Hampshire

BARTON-ON-SEA   Man and wife on golf
course were surrounded by falling
fish – hundreds of live fish, larger
than whitebait, fell from a cloudless
sky; 1948

HAYLING ISLAND   Fox-size cat run over
by car, identified as Asian swamp
cat (*Felis chaus*); July 1988

Hereford & Worcester

WORCESTER   Poltergeist activity began
when Christmas tree shook
violently; family also heard
footsteps, and ashtray flew across
room; Christmas 1985–February
1986

Hertfordshire

BERKHAMSTED   Ball lightning appeared
in house – it was white with moving
internal structure and a crackling
noise; 13 September 1981

Humberside

BRIDLINGTON   Fishing trawler believed
to be haunted, with the radar
regularly going wrong, the steering

sending the ship round in circles,
lights going on and off, and cabins
cold despite heating; ghostly figure
also seen on deck. The atmosphere
'changed overnight' after a ceremony
of exorcism was performed by a
priest, and the skipper and crew
began landing good catches again;
December 1987

Kent

UPSTREET   Witness sleeping out in tent
woke in gale and saw 'round
globules of fire' bouncing in tops of
apple trees; *c.*1927

Lancashire

MORECAMBE   Specialist in long-distance
TV reception picked up call letters
of station in Houston, Texas, USA
– but these letters, KLEE-TV, had
not been in use for over three years:
had they been transmitted back from
outer space?; September 1953, and a
second incident 23 November 1955

Leicestershire

BREEDON-ON-THE-HILL AREA   Lump of
metal fell from sky and crashed
through car windscreen, injuring
driver; nearby airport denied there
were planes in the area at the time;
August 1987

Lincolnshire

BOURNE   Ghostly baby crying heard in
public house (see Ch. 11)

NEAR DENTON   Rally driver saw ghostly
horseman; 28/29 January 1967 (see
Ch. 5)

Norfolk

ECCLES   Man saw cheetah: 2 feet tall, dark-brown and spotted coat; 16 June 1987

OFF GORLESTON   Dredger struck submerged solid object 30 miles offshore, but when it went back using echo sounders, no object could be found; May 1975 (see Ch. 10)

HUNSTANTON   During violent thunderstorm, partly fused bar of iron fell from sky, striking chimney; 1930 (see Ch. 13)

NORFOLK BROADS   Possible case of spontaneous human combustion; 29 July 1938

Nottinghamshire

COTGRAVE COLLIERY   Miner saw ghost underground (see Ch. 15)

RUFFORD ABBEY   Ghost in monk's habit and carrying crucifix seen by soldier on guard duty; spring 1942

Oxfordshire

MAGDALEN COLLEGE, OXFORD   Students heard and saw ghosts in their rooms; spring 1987

Shropshire

NEAR BRIDGNORTH   Couple out walking saw phantom ruined building; 21 September 1978

CHATWALL   Ghostly horse and rider seen; Easter 1965 (see Ch. 5)

Somerset

BRIDGWATER   Charred peat or compost found in garden after witness saw

bright object descending and heard loud noise; summer 1978

EXMOOR   Big cats seen on the moor over several years; hair from a sheep kill identified as from a lynx, but there is probably more than one cat; sightings and killings began 1983

WYCHANGER BARTON   12-inch long, red-hot cylinder crashed through house roof; no planes flying over at the time; September 1987

South Yorkshire

KILNHURST   Mysterious message found on cassette tape; August 1986 (see Ch. 11)

ROTHERHAM   Noises heard and apparition seen in haunted flat; August 1986 (see Ch. 5)

SILVERWOOD COLLIERY, NEAR ROTHERHAM   Miner at coalface saw ghost; date unknown, probably 1970s or 1980s (see Ch. 5)

STOCKSBRIDGE   Ghosts seen on new bypass; September 1987 (see Ch. 5)

Staffordshire

ALTON TOWERS   In deer park of stately home, man saw millions of frogs ½ inch long falling from sky for at least 1¼ hours; World War II

Suffolk

LAKENHEATH AIR FORCE BASE   Ghosts seen, including phantom RAF pilot who hitched a lift; February 1951 (see Ch. 5)

Tyne & Wear

DUNSTON   Cleaner heard scream in factory's haunted toilet, and workers heard voice; autumn 1974 (see Ch. 11)

West Midlands

ASTON, BIRMINGHAM Warm and sticky rock fell from the sky; 12 May 1969 (see Ch. 13)

NEAR COVENTRY Man walking in country lane saw 'soap bubbles' moving against the wind; summer 1952 (see Ch. 8)

OLDBURY Pupils at grammar school saw ball lightning during thundery weather: 'spherical, glowing object drifted in through window', it was 'yellowish, off-white' and 'resembled a giant glowing thistledown' more than 6 inches in diameter. After ten seconds it touched a metal desk leg and vanished silently, leaving no smell; early 1940s

FIJI

LAUTOKA METHODIST MISSIONARY SCHOOL Students saw little dwarfs 2 feet tall and covered with black hair, who ran away as the boys approached; July 1975

FINLAND

HELSINKI Large numbers of coins materialized inside house, falling on to parquet floor; autumn 1917 or 1918 (see Ch. 1). Ghost of former President spoke to two women; 19 April 1957 (see Ch. 11). Party in apartment visited by ghost of former resident, who spoke to witness; 12 February 1977 (see Ch. 11).

IMJÄRVI Two men out skiing saw UFO slowly descending and sending out beam of light, in which stood an entity 3 feet tall and very thin. It directed a pulsating light at one man, then a thick red-grey mist and coloured sparks came from the UFO, hitting the men. The mist was so thick they could see nothing, and when it cleared the UFO was gone. The men were ill for some time afterwards; 7 January 1970 (see Ch. 6)

KURSU, SALLA Man saw UFO outside backwoods cabin; then inside room, whose door was closed, stood entity in helmet and shimmering clothes, with big eyes. They talked about Apollo 13 before entity disappeared through wall; 15 April 1970

LAKE LOUKUSA, TAIVALKOSKI White lake monster, first seen autumn 1958

PARAINEN ISLAND, NEAR TURKU Sightings of sea monster around the island; June 1978

NEAR PUDASJÄRVI Woman driving on country road entered strange fog and saw domed UFO with portholes; she was taken inside for examination and received message supporting peace and opposing war; 2 April 1980

SÄKKIÄ LAKE, NEAR LÄNKIPOHJA 10 by 8-foot hole appeared in ice and lights in sky seen; 8 December 1983 (see Ch. 10)

BETWEEN TIISTENJOKI AND LAITOMAKI Truck-driver collided with lightning ball on road; it exploded on impact; 30 August 1969 (see Ch. 8)

TYNKA, KALAJOKI REGION During heavy thunderstorm, ball lightning seen travelling along the ground; another cut into a pine tree and damaged a shed; 14 July 1979

YRJO KANTO, NEAR SIKASALO Farmer split open aspen log felled several months before, and found dried fish like a perch, over 16 inches long, in rotten hollow with no clue to how it got there; October 1969

FRANCE

ARDÈCHE DEPARTMENT   Stones and apples were thrown at farm, some falling vertically, some falling slowly; September 1921–January 1922 (see Ch. 16)

ARLES-SUR-TECH, PYRÉNÉES ORIENTALES   80–150 gallons of water annually, used for healing purposes, flow from sarcophagus in abbey (see Ch. 15)

ARS   When body of Curé of Ars was exhumed, 45 years after his death, it was found to be well preserved; 17 June 1904

ATHIS-MONS, SEINE ET OISE   Mme Debord and others saw vision of Virgin and child; 1943

BOIS-DE-CHAMP, NEAR BRUYÈRES, VOSGES   Forestry worker touched hovering UFO; April 1954 (see Ch. 3)

BOURGES   1000-franc notes rained down from sky; 1957 (see Ch. 13)

BRIGNOLES   Thousands of small toads fell from the sky in freak storm; 23 September 1973

CANET-PLAGE, NEAR PERPIGNAN   Thousands of pea-sized frogs fell from the sky just before heavy rain shower; 28 August 1977

CHABLIS, YONNE   Panther seen; early 1980

CHERBOURG   Poltergeist outbreak, with blows and scratchings; 26–28 April 1918

CROLLON, MANCHE   Children saw three apparitions of Blessed Virgin Mary; 16 July 1933

DEUX SÈVRES   Child touched ball lightning with foot; it exploded and killed eleven cattle, but child unhurt; 1904

DOUAI   Poltergeist activity centred on mechanical doorbell, which finally fell off the wall and broke; June 1907

DRAGUIGNAN, PROVENCE   Two pilots saw 'elongated egg' glowing white as it travelled along straight course westwards at speed; also five ground-based witnesses; 6 October 1952

DUGNY   Three workers in a chalk works saw apparition of Blessed Virgin Mary and infant Jesus; August 1951

ENTREVEUX   Man broke plaster statue of St Anne and human blood flowed from the detached hand; 1954

EPINAL, VOSGES   Sheep and cows killed by mystery animals; big black cats seen in the area; 1977

ESPIS, TARN ET GARONNE   Children and adults saw visions of Blessed Virgin Mary, angels and saints; they appeared reliably on the 13th of the month; began 22 August 1946 and continued until 1950

FERDRUPT, VOSGES   Two children had vision of Blessed Virgin Mary with rays shooting from her hands; 2 March 1928

FOUGÈRES-SUR-BIÈVRE, NEAR BLOIS   Poltergeist outbreak with loud banging in house walls; 27 December 1913–February 1914 (see Ch. 1)

GAILLAC   Cigar-shaped UFO seen, accompanied by about ten pairs of discs; they hovered over the town and quantities of 'angel hair' fell from them; 27 October 1952. This followed a similar event at OLORON on 17 October 1952

GRANDE-SYNTHE   Poltergeist outbreak, with knockings, movement of objects, and mysterious fires; late 1985

GRAULHET, TARN   In chapel of Saint-Roch cemetery, mysterious burning of napkins at foot of statue of Virgin Mary, sixteen times in three years; 1980–3

HYDREQUENT, PAS-DE-CALAIS   Ten-year-old boy, and later fifty adults, saw apparition of Blessed Virgin Mary in a cave; August 1953

ILE NAPOLÉON, HAUT-RHIN   Three young boys saw apparition of Blessed Virgin Mary; 1947

L'ISLE BOUCHARD, INDRE ET LOIRE   Four young girls saw apparition of

Blessed Virgin Mary; 8 December 1947

LACHAUD, CORRÈZE Farmer in field heard a bang, then felt sticky dust falling on him which gave him second-degree burns on his arms, hands and face, and giddiness, sight problems and anaemia; 15 July 1966

LE BRUSC, VAR Fisherman saw UFO on the sea, with frogmen climbing aboard before it took off and was lost to view; 1 August 1962 (see Ch. 10)

LIART, ARDENNES Twelve men saw silent vision of Blessed Virgin Mary; 7 December 1948

MARIGNANE AIRPORT, NEAR MARSEILLE Customs officer saw UFO come in to land; 27 October 1952 (see Ch. 6)

MIREBEAU Picture of Christ in church began to bleed from hands, heart and head; tests showed blood was human; 1911 (see Ch. 15)

MONTPINCHON, MANCHE People were seeing a shining 'white lady', identified as the Virgin Mary, along lanes; mid-September 1984

NEAR MORANGE-SILVANGE, MOSELLE 3-foot kangaroos seen; June 1986

MULHOUSE Wide range of poltergeist activity over four years, with physical attacks, noises, an apparition, movement of objects, etc.; 1978–81

MUZILLAC, MORBIHAN Three children had 65 visions of the Blessed Virgin Mary; 1918

NEUVILLE Poltergeist outbreak; June–July 1906

NEVERS When the body of St Bernadette Soubirous, the visionary of Lourdes, was exhumed 30 years after her death, it was found to be incorrupt; 22 September 1909

OFF THE NORMANDY COAST Large, black, bird-like object fell into sea and disappeared; early July 1910 (see Ch. 10)

OSSUM Sightings of giant lizard several yards long; late nineteenth century and May 1939 (see Ch. 14)

PARIS When the body of St Catherine Labouré was exhumed 56 years after her death, it was found to be perfectly preserved; 21 March 1933 (see Ch. 15). Young crocodile found wandering in the sewers; 8 March 1984 (see Ch. 14)

PETIT TRIANON, VERSAILLES Miss Moberly and Miss Jourdain saw people and scenery from the eighteenth century; 10 August 1901. Also later sightings of ghosts in period costume by other witnesses (see Ch. 5)

PLESCOP, MORBIHAN Three children had eleven apparitions of Blessed Virgin Mary; 26 December 1947–1948

GULF OF PORTO, CORSICA Fishermen saw sea monster 200 feet long; October 1907

PUYS, NEAR DIEPPE Two women on holiday heard ghostly sounds of World War II air-raid; 4 August 1951 (see Ch. 11)

QUAROUBLE, NORD Metal-worker Marius Dewilde saw dark object (UFO) on railway track, and two small entities. He tried to stop them and was paralysed by a strong light shone on him; 10 September 1954. A wave of UFO sightings took place in autumn 1954, especially in France, and there were 200 landings of which the Quarouble case is representative

REMIREMONT Showers of hailstones with portrait of Virgin Mary inside; 26 May 1907 (see Ch. 15)

RIVER RHONE Water monsters seen 1954–5; long-necked sea serpent seen at mouth of river in summer 1964

ST JEAN-DE-MAURIENNE Poltergeist outbreak; June 1955

SAINT-QUAY-PORTRIEUX, CÔTES-DU-NORD Three witnesses saw sea monster with black hump, travelling fast, then joined by another; summer 1911

ST QUENTIN, AISNE Tiny red droplets of blood appeared on walls, carpets and bed; noise of crashing crockery heard in kitchen; January 1986 (see Ch. 1)

SERON, HAUTES-PYRÉNÉES Mysterious fires in farmhouse – about 90 in one month; began 6 August 1979

SEYSSUEL, NEAR LYON Poltergeist outbreak; *c.* two weeks in early 1930s

TRANS EN PROVENCE M. Collini watched UFO land at the bottom of his garden, *c.*5 p.m. A minute later it took off, and landing traces were found. Scientific study undertaken; 8 February 1981 (see Ch. 6)

UZÈS, GARD Teenager at home at night saw and photographed bright shining ball in the road; 19 November 1974 (see Ch. 8)

VALENSOLE, BASSES-ALPES Maurice Masse saw UFO land in his lavender field and was immobilized by two 4-foot entities who pointed an instrument at him; 1 July 1965 (see Ch. 6)

VALESCURE, VAR Puma seen and hunted but not caught; February 1983

VILLESANG, PUY-DE-DÔME Noises heard from lake after nightfall gave rise to rumours of monster in lake; 1929

VODABLE Poltergeist outbreak, including bells ringing, pictures moving, and objects placed in the beds; 7–24 September, 17–18 December 1914 (see Ch. 1)

GABON

LIBREVILLE Fisherman saw UFO land, from which strange entity emerged, which made incomprehensible noises before returning to UFO and taking off; it left footprints in sand; 25 December 1963

THE GAMBIA

BUNGALOW BEACH Carcass of strange sea creature washed ashore; possibly a long-extinct species; June 1983 (see Ch. 7)

GIBRALTAR

NORTH FRONT Thousands of small frogs fell during a thunderstorm; May 1921

GREECE

ASTEROUSSIA MOUNTAINS, CRETE Three youngsters out hunting saw giant dark-grey bird flying low. It had bat-like wings with finger-like projections, sharp claws, pelican's beak, and reminded them of a pterodactyl; summer 1986

ATHENS Weeping icon of the Panagia in Russian Orthodox Church of the Holy Trinity; March 1969

CAPE MATAPAN Ship's crew saw sea monster with long neck and humps; spring 1912

MISSOLONGHI Poltergeist outbreak; December 1926–January 1927

NAVPLION Thousands of little green frogs fell in the rain; 1981

THASOS Man in boat saw 'periscope' 5–6 feet out of water and moving fast, too fast for a submarine – may have been a sea monster; May or June 1916

GREENLAND

Soviet pilot saw large pear-shaped UFO flying parallel to him; thought it was American craft so hid in clouds. Forty minutes later, saw it again. It had no wings, antennae or windows, and no smoke. Tried to get closer, but UFO always kept the same distance. After fifteen minutes it shot up into the sky at speed; 1956

DISCO BAY Reports of black water monster; 1954

LAKE NATSILIK Lake monster reports, and in canal linking lake to sea, where women saw huge fin 'as large as a sail'; 1954

LAKE UMANAK Reports of white lake monster; 1954

GRENADA

LOWTHER'S LANE Cottage the focus for showers of stones and other things before being mysteriously burned down; 17 September 1934–14 January 1935 (see Ch. 16)

GUAM

Serviceman saw fish fall in rain, including a tench; September 1936

GUATEMALA

CUBULCO AREA Reports of El Sisemite (hairy wildman) living in the mountains; they would kidnap women, and one man claimed his daughter had been seized from COBÁN in early 1940s

GUYANA

KONAWARUK River gold prospector saw two creatures with human features but covered with reddish-brown fur. They stood upright and retreated into the forest. They may have been Didis, the legendary 5-foot 'wildmen' of Guyana and Surinam; 1910. An American botanist in forest saw 5-foot hair-covered 'apeman'; 1986 or 1987 (see Ch. 12)

HAITI

PORT-AU-PRINCE Statue of the Virgin Mary wept; 26 May 1976

HONG KONG

Students at barbecue on beach saw sea monster offshore; black with green eyes, it was 20–30 feet long and made a loud crying noise; March 1969

HANG HAU AREA OF SAI KUNG Big dark cat-like animal seen by several people, and large dogs were killed by mystery animal; October and December 1976

HUNGARY

ON BORDER WITH CZECHOSLOVAKIA
Villagers saw out-of-place kangaroos;
mid-September 1985

BATA 'Fiery cartwheels' seen rumbling
noisily along the hilltops; ball
lightning? UFOs?; August 1940

BUDAPEST Fires broke out in boy's
presence, and furniture moved; 1921
(see Ch. 4). UFOs seen; 10 June
1947. Poet Laszlo Benjamin saw
UFO emitting an almost blinding
white light, over mountain near city;
20 November 1967

HASNOS Crowd had vision of Blessed
Virgin Mary; 1949

KECSKEMÉT, NEAR BUDAPEST
Poltergeist outbreak; 29–31 July,
13 November 1921

ST EMMERICH-BERG Vision of Blessed
Virgin Mary; 2 July 1947 (see
Ch. 15)

UND Teacher photographed UFO;
27 October 1954

ICELAND

70 MILES SOUTH-EAST OF ICELAND
Officers and men of HMS *Hilary*
saw sea monster with neck 15–30
feet long, head was black and glossy;
it also had triangular dorsal fin; May
1917

LAKE KLEIFARVATN Bird hunters saw
two creatures bigger than horses
emerge from lake; they moved like
dogs but swam like seals and left
footprints larger than horses' and
split into three; November 1984

SAURAR Poltergeist activity with
movement of furniture and smashing
crockery; 18 March–mid April 1964
(see Ch. 1)

VOPNAFJÖRTHUR Two fishermen saw
black, humped sea monster which
surfaced five times; 13 February
1963

INDIA

CALCUTTA Poltergeist outbreak; c. July
1906. Boeing 747 coming in to land
was paced by round, bright, 'pink
neon' UFO; 16 July 1977. Huge
bright UFO surrounded by coloured
lights slowly crossed city on three
nights in November 1986

CHENGANNUR, KERALA Iron statue of
Indian goddess menstruates

CUDDAPAH, MADRAS Poltergeist
outbreak; c. April 1935

DEGAON, MAHARASHTRA Poltergeist
outbreak; c.1967

DHUBRI, ASSAM Woman saw 'luminous
plate' land in field and take off
again; 1 October 1954

NEAR ISLAMPUR TOWN, BIHAR UFO
hovered over school roof and drew
up large sections of roof; 12 July
1979

NORTHERN KASHMIR Workers on
mountain sheep farm heard and saw
4-foot hairy 'yeti'; one boy hit it
with a fire-pot when it attacked him;
late January 1987 (see Ch. 12)

KAROL BAGH, NEAR NEW DELHI Falls of
miscellaneous small items in
courtyard; 1963–8 (see Ch. 16)

LUCKNOW Poltergeist activity, with
smashing of crockery and other
household goods, and clothes and
bedding catching fire – the
house-owner's wife was burnt and
died; 1975–6 (see Ch. 4)

MADRAS Luminous ball (ball
lightning?) appeared, moving fast
and hit coconut tree, exploding 'like
a stick of dynamite'; autumn 1958.
Woman saw 8-foot humanoid
creature with 'shiny skin' in the

moonlight, and then a yellow-red object rising into the sky; 1 July 1976

MANNAR, NEAR DIMAPUR Possible case of spontaneous human combustion: burned corpse of woman found, her clothes unscorched and nothing burned in the room; May 1907

NIDAMANGALAM, TANJORE The Catholic Indian family of a sub-magistrate were plagued by 'the Devil' in the form of a poltergeist whose antics caused them to move house; 3–19 March 1920 (see Chs. 1 and 4)

OLD MAHABALESHWAR, NEAR BOMBAY Many witnesses saw UFOs dancing in the sky at dusk; small red and green globes came from and returned to larger yellowish saucer hovering motionless for forty minutes; 16 May 1974

PILIBHIT Poltergeist outbreak; 1930

POONA Extraordinary poltergeist case centred on two young brothers, with object movements, physical assaults, falls of stones, teleportation, and so on; 1927–30 (see Chs. 1 and 16)

SUNDARBANS (tidal forest at mouths of Ganges, also in Bangladesh) Huge monitor lizards up to 20 feet long said to live here; also were found in Assam (known as the *buru*) but thought to be recently extinct; may also survive in Bhutan and Burma

SURI, WEST BENGAL Poltergeist outbreak with spoken messages from the dead; two months in 1919 (see Chs. 11 and 16)

tall, covered in short hair, which sprang into a tree; may have been a Sedapa (man-beast); 1917

PADANG, SUMATRA Poltergeist outbreak; c.1926–7

NEAR PALEMBANG, SUMATRA In swamp forests, man hunting wild pigs saw 'dark and hairy creature' in tree; he climbed up very close to it and decided it was a Sedapa; October 1923 (see Ch. 12)

LAKE PATENGGANG, JAVA Reptilian lake monster reports

SUMATRA Ivan T. Sanderson experienced stone-throwing poltergeist; 1928 (see Ch. 16)

SURABAYA, JAVA Poltergeist outbreak; six weeks in 1950

WEST KALIMANTAN 9-foot creature, half man, half beast, seen in rain forest; August 1983

IRAN

TABRIZ LAKE Iranian history researcher and wife abducted into UFO which landed by their car. Entities looked like two Egyptian mummies; 20 September 1976

TEHRAN UFO came close to ground and crowd gathered before it took off. Small entity in black was seen at the controls; 12 October 1954

IRELAND

Co. Cork

LOUGH ATTARIFF Fisherman saw long, dark brown monster with large glittering eyes 100 yards away; June 1966

INDONESIA

DORTRECHT, SUMATRA Small stones fell slowly inside room; September 1903 (see Ch. 16)

NEAR MOUNT KABA, SUMATRA Man lost in forest saw creature 5 feet 9 inches

335

BALLINSPITTLE Statue of the Virgin Mary was seen to move super-naturally; beginning late July 1985. During the autumn of 1985 similar events were reported at other Catholic shrines throughout Ireland

BALLYVOURNEY Mystery animal seen crossing road: 'pale grey with shaggy but not long hair', long and slender (2½ feet from nose to tail), tail held straight up, short legs, pointed and tufted upright ears, cat-like face – maybe a lynx; 1980

Co. Donegal

KERRYTOWN Villagers often saw the shining apparition of the Blessed Virgin Mary above the cliffs; 11 January 1939–1946

WASKEL LOUGH Fisherman hooked something large, but saw only a yard of back, brownish-grey with dirty cream blotches; late 1940s

WEST DONEGAL Ten villages hit by freak lightning bolts over two years, with roofs stripped off, windows smashed, and televisions and telephones wrecked; 1983–4

Co. Dublin

NEAR DUBLIN Flying disc 10 inches in diameter landed and child was burned; November 1952

KILLAKEE House haunted by ghostly figures and large black cat; late 1960s–early 1970s

MONKSTOWN, DUBLIN Ghostly singing heard; 1977 (see Ch. 11)

Co. Galway

LOUGH ABISDEALY Long-necked black monster, with looped body like gigantic snake seen, 1914; also man

saw huge eel-like creature crawling out of lake

LOUGH AUNA Lake monster reports, one of a humped creature 30–40 feet long

LOUGH DUBH Schoolteacher and son saw monster that tried to get out of lake to attack boy; it had short thick legs and hippo face; March 1962

LOUGH FADDA People fishing saw monster with large open mouth; 1954 (see Ch. 7)

KILKERRIN BAY Sea monster with 6-foot neck and brown hairy body seen; 1910

LOUGH MASK Lake monster reports

MUTTON ISLAND Lighthouse-keeper shot and killed sea monster 48 feet long and 28 feet round the middle which had been tearing fishermen's nets; 5 May 1935

LOUGH NAHOOIN Lake monster reports; searches unsuccessful (see Ch. 7)

LOUGH SHANAKEEVER Man saw long-necked animal like black foal by lake, which went into the water; c.1955; also later sightings

Co. Kerry

ASDEE Four children saw life-sized statues of Jesus and Mary in church moving: Jesus beckoned and Mary's eyes moved; 14 February 1985

LOUGH BRAN/BRIN Black monster seen, 10 feet long, reptilian and like a cross between giant seal and mythical dragon; summer 1979; seen on shore by fourteen-year-old boy who said it had four short legs; 1940

LACKAGH LAKE Lake monster reports

Co. Limerick

BETWEEN BALLINGARRY AND KILFINNEY NEAR RATHKEALE Boy met and talked with fairies; 1938 (see Ch. 9)

Co. Mayo

SRAHEENS LOUGH, ACHILL ISLAND
Sightings of lake monster; on 1 May
1968 at night, two men saw it run
across the road, and said it was 8–10
feet long. A week later, boy cycling
by lake saw large black creature
crawling out of water

Co. Roscommon

LOUGH REE   Three priests saw
long-necked monster swimming 100
yards away; 18 May 1960

Co. Tipperary

TEMPLEMORE   All the statues and holy
pictures in a home where there was
a sixteen-year-old boy began to
bleed; also poltergeist phenomena
centred on the boy; beginning
21 August 1920 (see Ch. 15)

Co. Waterford

MELLERAY, CAPPOQUIN   People visiting
the grotto saw statue of Virgin Mary
come to life; she gave messages;
began 16 August 1985

Co. Wexford

CAHORE POINT   Long-necked sea
monster seen, which moved like a
big worm; 23 January 1976
ENNISCORTHY   Poltergeist outbreak,
with rappings and movement of
bedclothes; 7–29 July 1910
HOOK HEAD   Sightings by fishermen of
huge lizard-like monster with long
neck and humped back, at least
20 feet long; 1975

Co. Wicklow

LOUGH BRAY   Lake monster seen; 1963

ITALY

ADRIATIC SEA   Fishermen were seeing
strange columns of water *c.*100 feet
high, and long dark objects
emerging and submerging; October
1978 (see Ch. 10)
ANCONA   Poltergeist outbreak;
December 1907–January 1908
ASSISI   Crowd saw statue of Blessed
Virgin Mary move; 11 February
1948
ATRIPALDA, AVELLINO   Photograph of
face of Turin Shroud streamed with
blood; began December 1958
AVERSA   Shower of stones rained on to
garage; early 1981 (see Ch. 16)
BARI   Two pumas seen; 1983. Bones of
St Nicholas exude pure water called
'manna', used for healing (see
Ch. 15)
BOARIA, ROVIGO   Egg-shaped UFO flew
over farm emitting blast of light:
cows panicked, farmer fainted, pond
was dried up and haystacks caught
fire; cattle were burnt; 15 October
1954
BOLOGNA   The voice of Blessed Clelia
Barbieri has joined in the prayers
and hymns of her fellow-nuns since
her death in 1870 (see Ch. 11)
BRESCIA   Farmer found four huge
chicken's footprints; June 1985 (see
Ch. 17)
CAPE MASSULO, ISLAND OF CAPRI   Artist
saw UFO land and four small
entities in coveralls emerge; they
stayed outside for half an hour
before leaving; 17 October 1954
CASERTA/AVELLINO/POTENZA AREAS
Long-hair-covered, 6-foot monster
with bright eyes and large ears seen

in the mountains, sometimes in conjunction with low-level lights; May and June 1986

CEFALA DIANA, NEAR PALERMO, SICILY At least 30 people saw apparition of Blessed Virgin Mary at window of ruined castle, every day for a week; May 1967

LAKE COMO Lake monster reports

COSENZA, CALABRIA Bloody profile of Jesus's face appeared on wall at home of stigmatic Sister Elena Aiello; began flowing blood 29 September 1955, intermittently continued until her death in 1961 (see Ch. 15). 12-foot 'reptile' with long fur and walking on four legs seen by several people; July 1981 (see Ch. 14)

FORLI 15-foot reptile chased witness; July 1969 (see Ch. 14)

FORMIA Objects would catch fire when boy gazed at them, and electrical items were affected; began 1982 (see Ch. 4)

GIARRE, SICILY Photograph of Blessed Virgin Mary wept; 21 August 1954

GORGONA ISLAND, ADRIATIC SEA USO seen; 22 June 1979

GORO 10-foot 'snake with legs' seen; summer 1975

ISOLA, NEAR LA SPEZIA Cigar-shaped UFO landed and three small entities emerged and took away farmer's rabbits from their cages; he aimed his rifle at them, but it failed and was too heavy to hold. He was also paralysed; 14 November 1954

LANCIANO Eucharistic miracle: bread and wine turned to real flesh and blood in eighth century, and these sacred relics are intact twelve centuries later; scientifically examined 1970 (see Ch. 15)

MARINA DI PISA Children and adults saw apparition of Blessed Virgin Mary; 27 April 1948

MAROPATI Painting of Madonna wept human blood from eyes, heart, hands and feet, and blood formed into crosses on the wall below; beginning 3 January 1971 (see Ch. 15)

MARTA, VITERBO Four young girls and adults saw visions of Blessed Virgin Mary in cave; 19 May 1948

MILAN Body of Cardinal Schuster was found to be incorrupt when exhumed 31 years after his death; February 1985 (see Ch. 15)

MONTEROSE 8-foot reptile with green and yellow body seen; August 1935 (see Ch. 14)

MONTICHIARI Visions of Blessed Virgin Mary appeared to Pierina Gilli, and other witnesses saw signs in the sky; began 1947

MOUNT ETNA, SICILY Apparition of 'St Agatha' appeared on the summit; January 1909

NAPLES Bleeding picture of Christ; August 1973. Blood of St Januarius kept in two small phials liquefies several times annually during public ceremonies in saint's honour held in cathedral (see Ch. 15)

NISCIMA, SICILY Statue of Madonna wept tears of blood, and continued when placed in sealed glass case; began 30 August 1980

NUORO, SARDINIA Water seeped through floor of whichever hospital ward nine-year-old boy was in; November 1972 (see Ch. 1)

OLIVETO CITRA Blessed Virgin Mary appeared to twin brothers, and a recording of her voice was obtained

PARAVATI Natuzzo Evolo made 'haemographs' or blood pictures (see Ch. 15)

NEAR PERUGIA Water monster seen in marshes which are linked to the sea by the River Tiber; 1933 or 1934

PESCARA Plate with images of Pope John XXIII and President Kennedy was weeping blood; January 1974 (see Ch. 15)

PIACENZA Eels fell from the sky; 9 June 1957

RIVER PO, PORTETOLLE 20-inch crocodilian caught; June 1973

PO-DI-GNOCCA Farmer watched disc-shaped UFO land; deep crater found at site and trees were burnt; 15 October 1954

ROME The body of Blessed Paula

Frassinetti was found to be perfectly preserved when exhumed 24 years after her death; 1906. Thousands saw UFO manoeuvring over the city, also tracked on radar; 17 September 1954. Poltergeist outbreak; 19 April–2 May 1975. Mystery fires erupted in offices; summer 1984 (see Ch. 4)

SAN DAMIANO   Dying, Rosa Quattrini was miraculously cured by Our Lady; many apparitions followed, and witnesses photographed Her 'signs'; cure and first apparition took place 29 September 1961 (see Ch. 15)

OFF SAVONA   UFO emerged from sea; 3 June 1961

SCHEGGIA, PERUGIA   Four children going to school saw vision of Blessed Virgin Mary; May 1959

SYRACUSE, SICILY   Bleeding limestone crucifix; blood coagulated instantly; 1972

NEAR SYRACUSE, SICILY   11-foot reptile seen; hunted for two days, then found and killed by peasants; carcass burned; December 1933. Statue of Blessed Virgin Mary shed tears; 29 August–1 September 1953 (see Ch. 15). Italian jeweller and his wife, travelling in car at night, saw in headlight beams a little entity 3½ feet tall, in luminous or iridescent garment, diving helmet, and two little wings instead of arms; 19 May 1960

RIVER TICINO   Water monster seen at river mouth; 1934

TORRIGLIA, NEAR GENOA   Nightwatchman Fortunato Zanfretta saw 9-foot entity and UFO and had a time-lapse. He had another encounter later in the month, when he went missing, and under hypnosis recalled being taken aboard the UFO; 6 and 27 December 1978, with further experiences on 30 July and 2 December 1979

TRE FONTANE, ROME   Blessed Virgin Mary appeared several times in grotto to children and their Communist father; 1947

TRENZANO, BRESCIA   Madonna wept tears of blood; 1957. Other cases of bleeding and weeping images in Italy include: NEAR ASSISI (statue weeping, 1972), CINQUEFRONDI, REGGIO CALABRIA (weeping Madonna, 1972), LENDINARA, ADRIA-ROVIGO (weeping picture, 1972), RAVENNA (Fatima statue wept, 9 December 1972), VERTORA, BERGAMO (Madonna wept blood, 1972), CASTEL S. LORENZO, SALERNO (Virgin Mary bled from heart on many occasions), FLORENCE (Virgin Mary wept blood), SAN VITTORINO (Fatima statue in shrine crypt wept, 1972)

TURIN   Poltergeist outbreak in inn cellar, where bottles fell and broke; 16 November–7 December 1900. Luminous, pulsating, colourful ball of light seen in sky above Caselle Airport; this UFO moved fast and performed manoeuvres impossible for a plane; 30 November 1973

NEAR UDINE   Several people saw giant serpent 12 feet long, which made whistling noise; summer 1963

VENUS LAKE, ISLAND OF PANTELLERIA   Noises heard in lake at night, leading to rumours of lake monster; July 1982

NEAR VILLA SANTINA, IN CARNIA, FRIULI   Prof. R. J. Johannis, searching for fossils in the mountains, saw landed UFO and two small entities with green skin, large round eyes, and slit mouth. When he shouted to them, one sent a ray of smoke from his belt and witness fell to ground. They took his pick and left in UFO; 14 August 1947

IVORY COAST

ABORO, ABIDJAN   Blood spurted from house walls; 12 March 1985 (see Ch. 1)

ADIOPODOUMÉ, NEAR ABIDJAN
Educated African boy saw 'pygmy' covered with long reddish fur and long reddish head hair who ran into forest; 1947. There are other similar reports, including one of a creature being killed between Sassandra and Cavally rivers by elephant-hunter; 1947 (see Ch. 12)

JAMAICA

ROEHAMPTON   Poltergeist outbreak; May–c. July 1931

JAPAN

AKITA CITY   Virgin Mary statue shed tears from right hand; 1973. She shed tears and sweated; 1975

CAMP OKUBO, NEAR KYOTO   Soldier on guard duty saw winged man; 1952 (see Ch. 9)

FUJISHIRO   Bank manager driving on bypass with two colleagues saw black car ahead of them disappear in puff of white smoke; 19 November 1963

FUKUOKA PREFECTURE   Stone image of guardian deity shed tears after owner made offerings of flowers and tea; 22 July 1983

MOUNT HIBA AREA   'Hibagon monster' (man-beast) reported; early 1970s. Also similar creatures called 'Yamagon' and 'Kuigon' (see Ch. 12)

HOKKAIDO   'Okiku-chan' doll, in Mannen temple since 1938 when its young owner died, has hair which grows and must be cut in a special ceremony every March. The hair has been analysed and is human hair.

Other similar dolls include one at Kyoto City, and another at Obihiro City.

LAKE IKEDA   Lake monster reports: twenty people saw two humps 15 feet long with 15 feet between them; 1978

SEA OF JAPAN   Captain of Russian freighter saw UFO come out of the sea; 18 August 1980 (see Ch. 10)

KOBE   Explosion heard, 'fireworks' seen on the bay, and two whirling balls of fire were seen to submerge in the sea; 21 November 1956

KOFU   Two seven-year-old boys saw light in the sky and later in a vineyard; they walked around landed UFO and saw unknown oriental characters on it. A ladder came out and an entity in silver emerged, with large head and other strange features. A second entity was seated inside, hand on a lever. As the boys started to run away, the entity spoke to them in a voice like a tape playing fast. They ran home and fetched the parents of one of them, who also saw the light; 23 February 1975

LAKE KUTCHARO   Lake monster reports

NISHIKAWA-CHO, YAMAGATA PREFECTURE   Circular flattened area found in reed bed, and suspected of being UFO-linked; 9 August 1986

NORTH PACIFIC OCEAN   Fishing-boat crew saw two metallic silvery UFOs dive into the sea; 19 April 1957

PACIFIC OCEAN, 180 miles off north-east coast   Four airline pilots saw mushroom cloud billowing to height of 60,000 feet and expanding to 200 miles diameter, in two minutes, then it inexplicably disappeared – looked like nuclear explosion, but no radioactivity found; scientists later suggested that a meteor had shattered on reaching the cloud deck, thus forming a large plume; 9 April 1984

SAYAMA CITY, SAITAMA PREFECTURE   Radio ham Hideichi Amano had driven up a mountain to make radio transmissions; there saw strange lights in and outside the car, and a humanoid creature at the window. A babbling noise came from a 'pipe' in its mouth. After several minutes it faded away and Mr Amano was able to restart his car; 3 October 1978

MOUNT SENOHARA   Glowing lights, orange and blue, seen at various points on the mountain at night over two hours; 31 July 1982

TOKYO   Phantom soldiers seen in compounds of Nari Shrine; summer 1979

TOMAKOMAI, HOKKAIDO   Night security guard saw light over the sea which came down until it hovered at c.70 feet; tube emerged and touched the surface, appearing to suck up water. It then came closer, and witness saw figures in windows. Other objects appeared, and all disappeared into larger object, which flew away; July 1973

JORDAN

BEIT SAHOUR   Apparitions of the Blessed Virgin Mary seen at a grotto at the Lady's Well; began 15 August 1983

RAMALLAH   Plastic statue of Blessed Virgin Mary oozed olive oil; October 1987 (see Ch. 15)

KENYA

KISANANA   Red and black fish fell from the sky during a thunderstorm; early April 1978, following a similar event the same time the previous year

MACHAKOS   Over at least six months, stones showered on to a house, some

seeming to materialize from thin air; beginning 23 December 1982 (see Ch. 16)

NGOLIBA   Hominoids, possibly prehistoric survivals, reportedly seen by 33 natives in 11 forests (see Ch. 12). Poltergeist activity, including flying pots and pans and stones mysteriously thrown; mid April–May 1986 (see Ch. 16)

KOREA, SOUTH

OFF INCHON   Men on ship saw two UFOs hit the water; December 1950 (see Ch. 10)

OFF PUSAN   'Washtub'-sized object seen to fall into the sea and after a while it sank, glowing all the while; 15 January 1956 (see Ch. 10)

LEBANON

ANNAYA-DJEBEIL   St Charbal Maklhouf died 1898 and a bright light surrounded his tomb for 45 nights; when exhumed, the body was incorrupt, and a blood-like liquid was oozing from it, which has continued to the present; miraculous cures occur at his shrine (see Ch. 15)

RMAÏCH   Blood and olive oil flowed from statue of Blessed Virgin Mary; began 18 November 1983 (see Ch. 15)

341

LEEWARD ISLANDS

LIBERTA, ANTIGUA   Girl's clothes and bedclothes would burst into flame; 1929 (see Ch. 4)

LUXEMBOURG

KAYL   Several people saw vision of Blessed Virgin Mary; 1 November 1947

MADAGASCAR

AMBATOLAMPY   Poltergeist outbreak; July–August 1909

AMBOHIBAO   'Blood' spurted from tree being cut down; 19 June 1984

STRAITS OF MADAGASCAR   Passengers on *Llandovery Castle* saw UFO which came down to within 45 feet of the sea, on to which it shone a searchlight; it was a huge metallic cylinder nearly 1000 feet long; 1 July 1947

MALAYSIA

BUKIT MERTAJAM   Schoolchildren saw tiny landed UFO and four 3-inch-tall entities; 19 May 1979. Another tiny UFO seen at Kampung Nagalilit by students who were temporarily blinded when it shone light at them; 26 May 1979

LAKES CHINI AND BERA   Lake monster reports

IPOH   Factory workers saw 10-foot headless ghost; June 1976

KELANTAN   After terrific thunderstorm, small fish seen swimming in ankle-deep water which fell in ten minutes on to hard-baked fields; 1915

KUALA LUMPUR, PENINSULAR MALAYSIA   Poltergeist activity with objects falling out of the air; 27 February–17 March 1955. Stones fell inside and outside house; January 1968 (see Ch. 16)

LAWAS RIVER, SARAWAK   Water monster reports – possibly a dugong?; early 1985

LUMUT   At night, students saw three hairy creatures 10 feet tall, with red eyes; they were said to disappear into thin air; 11 August and succeeding days, 1979

PAHANG STATE   Mysterious hairy creatures 4 feet tall seen in jungles east of Kuala Lumpur; possibly members of Orang Batik, a shy primitive tribe; August 1969

SEGAMAT   'Giant', which left footprints 18 inches long, seen; soldiers on guard duty who saw it at night said it was 18 feet tall; August 1966

SUNGAI SIPUT   Over three weeks, schoolboy pulled over 80 pieces of coloured thread from his right eye. Threads always same colour as shirt he was wearing, but medical profession baffled. After treatment with holy water from Hindu temple, the phenomenon stopped; May 1985

MALI

TESSALIT   Air Force officer saw UFO, dark yellow and almost circular, which descended then accelerated away fast; 4 October 1951

archaeological site saw a pygmy from the group of little people known as the Alux; 1977

MAURITIUS

Poltergeist outbreak, 21–22 September 1937

MEXICO

LAKE CATEMACO   Reports of huge black serpent with two horns on its forehead; 1969

CIUDAD VALLEYS   Taxi-driver met two UFO entities; mid-August 1953 (see Ch. 6)

COATEPEC   Four men separately saw strange figure dressed in black, on Avenida Campillo. He had shining hands, cat's eyes, and was carrying a metal or crystal rod giving off a bright light; September 1965

IXTAPALAPA   Two men saw two flying entities; 18 August 1972 (see Ch. 9)

MEXICO CITY   Pilot in Piper aeroplane was accompanied by 10–12-foot diameter disc at each wingtip, and another flew underneath; 3 May 1975 (see Ch. 3)

GULF OF MEXICO, 50 miles north of Frontera   People on board the *Livingston* saw sea monster at least 200 feet long, dark brown and with head 6 feet long; it made a loud rattling noise as it swam away; 21 June 1908

MONTERREY   Statue of Infant Jesus breathed, perspired and wept; daily crowds of 15,000 came to see; January 1972

YUCATAN   Caretaker at Mayapan

MONGOLIA

ALTAI MOUNTAINS   Russian doctor saw family of wildmen, and learned from his patients that the Almas had been seen by many of them; 1963 (see Ch. 12)

NEAR BULGAN   Man found hair-covered corpse which was not bear or ape or man, but not knowing its significance he left it where it was; 26 June 1953

GOBI DESERT   Military personnel working on irrigation project saw 'great disc of light trailing flames' which landed on the sand, and took off when team of motorcycle troops arrived, leaving 'seared cross' on the ground; mid-April 1968

USSR Reconnaissance unit during Japanese invasion saw and shot two hairy creatures like anthropoid apes, man-sized with reddish hair all over; 1937

MOROCCO

MAMORA FOREST   French engineer in car saw small entity entering UFO which took off; 12 October 1954

OVED BETH   Truck-driver saw circular, flat UFO flying over Beth River; it flipped over, then landed on edge in field. Soon rose and flew off at great speed; 3 November 1954

SAHARA DESERT   Rain of frogs; December 1977

MOZAMBIQUE

BEIRA   Orange disc-shaped UFO landed, and four small entities ran away when craft exploded; 5 April 1960

NEPAL

MOUNT EVEREST   Polish climbing expedition led by Andrzej Zawada found Yeti footprints at about 17,600 feet; February 1980. In the area of Everest, trekker Janusz Tomaszczuk saw Yeti over 6 feet tall; 1975

HIMALAYAS   Edward W. Cronin, Jr., and companions, camped at 12,200 feet, found tracks of large creature (Yeti?) which had walked through their camp overnight; 18 December 1972

HINKU VALLEY   British climbing expedition led by John Edwards heard strange scream and found footprints, possibly made by Yeti, at 17,250 feet; November 1979

NEAR KHUMBU GLACIER   Lord Hunt's expedition found and photographed Yeti tracks 14 inches long; November 1978. Lord Hunt has seen Yeti tracks several times over 30 years and heard high-pitched cries

MACHHAPUCHRE   Mountaineer Don Whillans saw possible Yeti while at 13,000-foot base camp when climbing Annapurna: he saw a black ape-like shape bounding along in snow and pulling at tree branches; June 1970 (see Ch. 12)

MARCHE, NEAR PHERICHE   Girl tending yak herd was knocked unconscious by Yeti – 4–5 feet tall and hair-covered – which also killed the yaks; July 1974 (see Ch. 12)

ZEMU GLACIER   N. A. Tombazi saw Yeti walking upright, stooping to pull at dwarf rhododendrons, and later found footprints 6–7 inches long, at 15,000 feet; 1925. Lord Hunt saw tracks at 19,000 feet; 1937. Sherpa Tenzing Norgay saw tracks on glacier; 1946

THE NETHERLANDS

AMSTERDAM   Poltergeist outbreak; ten days in April–May 1919

THE HAGUE   Poltergeist outbreak; October 1926–April 1927

VORSTENBOSCH   Three eleven- and twelve-year-old children saw an apparition of the Blessed Virgin Mary; 27 June 1947

ZANDVOORT   Sea monster sightings; 1906

NEW CALEDONIA

NOUMÉA   Sea monster sightings; 22 September 1923, and elsewhere in the islands on 28 June and 30 September; also later, e.g. September 1929 (see Ch. 7)

NEW ZEALAND

BLENHEIM   Woman milking cows saw UFO 30 feet in diameter with two strong green lights and jets sending out orange flames. She could see two entities inside glass dome. UFO flew off at speed making high-pitched noise; 13 July 1959

BROOKLYN, WELLINGTON Guesthouse bombarded with stones and some coins overnight, and again the following two nights; March 1963 (see Ch. 16)

CHRISTCHURCH, 30 miles east of: Japanese fishing boat netted carcass of possible sea monster; April 1977 (see Ch. 7)

COROMANDEL PENINSULA Reports of hairy man-beast (see Ch. 12)

KAIAPOI AREA Big cat, possibly tiger, seen, and paw prints and droppings found; July 1977

KAIPARA HARBOUR Unidentified submarine object seen, 100 feet long; 12 January 1965 (see Ch. 10)

LYTTELTON, 24 miles off Crew members of Japanese fishing boat saw sea monster looking like hippopotamus; 28 April 1971. Fishermen at Lyttelton said they too had seen 'funny things' while fishing

RUGGED ISLAND, OFF STEWART ISLAND Fishermen saw strange craft which came up out of the water; 13 November 1965 (see Ch. 10)

SOUTH ISLAND, off north-east coast Wellington Airport saw unidentified targets on radar, and pilot saw lights in the sky, on several nights. They were filmed 30 December 1978, and scientific analysis was able to eliminate all natural explanations like planets, meteors, balloons, aircraft, military manoeuvres, fishing boats (see Ch. 3)

LAKE TAUPO Lake monster reports; 1980

TE KUITI In railway excavations, workman found cavity in newly fragmented rock (sedimentary mudstone) 12 feet down, and imprisoned frog found therein; it was pulled out alive. Later another was found; November 1982

TE NGAERE Patch of light, fluid like quicksilver, entered house during thunderstorm; 8 September 1981 (see Ch. 8)

WAIMATA VALLEY, NEAR GISBORNE Farmer saw landed UFO at night; it glowed bright blue and had bright red interior. Two entities were kidnapping his dogs and he fired at them. They dropped the dogs and ran away; 2 December 1977

WAIPAWA Man saw grey torpedo-shaped airship (UFO?) with three occupants, one of whom shouted to him in an unknown tongue; 3 August 1909 – one case in an 'airship' scare over New Zealand in 1909

WELLINGTON Poltergeist outbreak; March 1963

WHITSTONE, NEAR OAMARU ¾-inch cube of red-hot metal fell from the sky, hitting tractor; 24 March 1961

NIGERIA

KATSINA Fireball (ball lightning?) appeared inside house with thick mud walls and one tiny window; 1956

NORTHERN IRELAND

Co. Antrim

BESSBROOK Blessed Virgin Mary appeared regularly to two people at a grotto in the church, and gave messages to one of them; 1987

PORTGLENONE Farmer saw UFO 6 feet wide cut 40-foot tree in two 9 feet above ground; 28 December 1958

RATHLIN ISLAND Sea-captain saw sea monster; June 1910

Co. Derry

MAGILLIGAN   Stones bombarded house;
January 1907 (see Ch. 16)

MONEYMORE   Couple approached 3-foot
UFO landed in bog: egg-shaped,
bright red with three dark red
stripes. As Thomas Hutchinson
grabbed at it, it rose and flew off.
He had intended to take it to the
police station; 7 September 1959

Co. Fermanagh

COONIAN, NEAR BROOKBOROUGH
Poltergeist outbreak; began 1913

LOUGH ERNE   Large round lights, 'like
motor car lamps', seen near lough
over seven or eight years; 1904–12

NORWAY

GJERSJOEN BRIDGE   Three witnesses
saw UFO which followed their car
and hovered just ahead of them.
They stopped until it took off
vertically. The car paint colour
changed from dark beige to bright
green; November 1953

HESSDALEN, NEAR TRONDHEIM   Strange
lights seen in the mountain valleys;
UFO researchers made extensive
studies using radar, spectral
analysers, seismograph, lasers, and
photography, but no positive
identification resulted; 1981–5

Many Norwegian lakes are reputed to
contain lake monsters, including
JÖLSTERVATN, KRÖDEREN, MJÖSA,
MÖSVATN, SANDSEVATN, SKODJE,
SNÅSA, SÖGNE, STOREVATN, SULDAL,
TORFINNSVATN, TYRIFJORDEN

LAKE MJÖSA   Farmer and family saw
two cigar-shaped craft pass overhead

and fall into the lake together;
18 July 1946

NAMSENFJORDEN   Man saw UFO drop
two long objects into the water;
December 1959. Five years later,
fishermen found object on the
bottom, 20 feet long (see Ch. 10)

NORWEGIAN SEA   Man on frigate 30–50
miles off north coast saw UFO on
radar, which dived into sea and was
picked up on sonar; no visual
sighting; late February 1963 (see
Ch. 10)

OSLOFJORD   Humped sea monster seen
by people in yacht; about 60 feet
long; 4 October 1902

STAVANGER   Woodcutter saw tall entity
emerge from landed UFO, then
return and take off; 4 January 1958

TELEMARK   Man was dazed when ball
lightning exploded close to him;
21 August 1900

TOTEN   Poltergeist outbreak; c.1935

PAKISTAN

QUETTA   During violent thunderstorm,
ball of fire came down and set fire to
haystack; in the ashes, several tons
of glassy slag were found;
25 January 1923 (see Ch. 13)

PAPUA NEW GUINEA

BOIANAI   Revd W. B. Gill, in charge of
mission station, saw UFO and
occupants on three nights, in
company with Papuans; 26–28 June
1959

LAKE DAKATAUA, NEW BRITAIN   Lake
monster reports

PERU

ANDES MOUNTAINS Lake monster reports, with 30-foot monster said to devour sheep; 1974

CUZCO Several witnesses saw tiny silvery UFO land on ancient Inca stone fortress; two tiny beings emerged. On seeing an audience, they retreated and took off at speed; 20 August 1965

HUANACO PROVINCE Student who fell into bog was helped out by four scaly creatures about 3 feet tall with three fingers on each hand, who held out branches to him; January 1977

PUNO Boy saw seven one-eyed beings 32 inches tall, and ran to fetch his family. They saw a bright light rising into the sky. Not far away, sports writer Jorge Chaves saw UFO land on road ahead, then take off; 8 September 1965. On 20 September, shepherdess at Pichaca, District of Puno, saw six entities *c*.32–36 inches tall come out of UFO – they spoke like geese cackling, wore white clothes and gave off flashes of light. Another entity sighting, 32 inches tall and one-eyed, at Arequipa on 29 September – two men nearly ran over it. They also saw a UFO

LAKE TITICACA 12-foot-long water creature reported, resembling seal or manatee

PHILIPPINES

BAGUIO CITY Blood flowed from exposed heart on 10-foot statue of Blessed Virgin Mary in chapel near airport; miracle cures followed; began February 1983 (see Ch. 15)

BAUANG Film crew saw sea monster which surfaced after underwater charges were fired. It had a flat head and long serpent-like body, and bit the steel shaft of an underwater spear while men were trying to get into a boat; December 1966

LIPA Following visions of the Blessed Virgin Mary seen by a nun, there were many miraculous showers of rose petals, witnessed by many people; September–December 1948 (see Ch. 15)

MANILA Visions of the Blessed Virgin Mary reportedly seen by crowds; early 1988 (see Ch. 15)

TABING ILOG, LUZON Poltergeist outbreak; October–November 1964

POLAND

CHALUPY, HEL PENINSULA Man saw two UFO entities in green suits, partially hidden in 'fog'; he also saw 'misty quicksilver' disc-shaped UFO hovering nearby; 8 August 1981

CZERNIAKOV 'Puff of rosy light' shot out of the earth and was filmed, the film showing a solid object, or UFO; 12 July 1982 (see Ch. 3)

EMILCIN Farmer Jan Wolsky taken aboard UFO by little green men; 10 May 1978 (see Ch. 6)

ERNESTOWO Couple duck-hunting saw huge steel-coloured 'cigar' in the sky; it had five windows along the side, the front ones glowing with orange light, and hovered before vanishing rapidly over the horizon; 29 August 1979

KOLOBRZEG Soldiers saw triangular UFO *c*.12 feet wide rise out of Baltic Sea, circle above barracks, then vanish at speed; March 1959 (see Ch. 10)

LUBLIN Statue of Blessed Virgin Mary in cathedral wept tears of blood for two days; July 1949

OSTRALECE Electrical engineer and others saw three silent cigar-shaped UFOs, reddish-pink, moving horizontally along the horizon; 20 March 1959

STETTIN (SZCZECIN) Poltergeist outbreak; January 1931–1933

WOLIN Spherical metal UFO c.90 feet across seen by seven people to land in a field; 31 July 1953

LAKE ZEEGRZYNSKI Lake monster reports, with bathers seeing 20-foot monster with black head and rabbit-like ears; July 1982

PORTUGAL

ALMASEDA, NEAR CASTELIBRANCO Four people saw UFO land from which emerged two entities in shining clothing; they gathered flowers, shrubs and twigs in shiny box before re-entering craft, and tried to invite witnesses on board; 24 September 1954

COMEADA, SUBURB OF COÏMBRA Poltergeist outbreak with loud blows and other noises, physical assault, and a baby moved from its cradle to a table; early October 1909 (see Ch. 1)

CRIACAO DO CABRITO, AZORES Watchmen at air station saw oval UFO with glass tower and balustrade where two entities stood; two others were in the tower. Witness shone a light at UFO, and he was covered in cloud of dust. UFO vanished and witness fainted; 1 February 1968

FATIMA Three children saw an angel, and then later the Blessed Virgin Mary appeared – on 13 May; many people gathered for her promised monthly appearances, and on 13 October they saw a silver disc moving in the sky. She gave the children secret messages; 1917 (see Ch. 15)

PUERTO LA CRUZ Tanker crew saw cigar-shaped UFO fly up out of the sea; 6 July 1965 (see Ch. 10)

SANTA MARIA AIRPORT, AZORES Guard saw UFO land; entity came out and talked to him but was not understood; 20 September 1954

PUERTO RICO

EL YUNQUE MOUNTAIN Nine people were on the mountain at night in search of UFOs, and two saw four entities 5–6 feet tall, with long arms, big eyes, pointed noses and ears. One carried a 'little machine' with lights on it, and they all moved by leaping; 20–21 October 1973

MOCA AREA Mysterious deaths of animals, especially domestic ducks, geese and rabbits, also goats; UFO sightings in same area; February–July 1975

QUEBRADILLAS Small entity dressed in green with helmet seen; it also had a tail; red and blue lights on a box on its back lit up and entity flew away; witnesses watched the lights among the trees, and they were joined by another set of lights as if another entity was there; 12 July 1977

RÉUNION

NEAR ARECIBO Arab merchant gave lift to phantom hitch-hiker; 20 November 1982

PETITE ILE Man saw UFO come up out of the sea and fly away; 10 February 1975 (see Ch. 10)

PLAINE-DES-CAFRES Farmer saw oval UFO just above ground, and 15 feet in diameter. Two small entities stood in object. It vanished in a flash and a blast of hot air; 31 July 1968

ST PIERRE Girl's clothes caught fire, and flats were burnt; February 1983 (see Ch. 4)

VALEA PLOPULUI, POSEŞTI Nightwatchman saw object fall from sky after midnight; marks found at presumed landing site same day: corn stems broken, cylindrical hole in ground, increased radioactivity in soil; 28 September 1972

ROMANIA

BUHAI, TALPA, GOROVEI, and also VIENNA (Austria) Poltergeist activity centred on Eleanore Zügun, including violent physical assault; February 1925–May 1927 (see Ch. 1)

CLUJ Crowd saw vision of Blessed Virgin Mary; 1948

NEAR CLUJ Two couples picnicking in wood saw round, metallic UFO, and Emil Barnea took four photographs; 18 August 1968

NEAMT At monastery, paving stones split to reveal grave of monk whose bones exuded pleasant fragrance; 23 May 1986

PETRILA PETROŞANI Chickens were frightened by circular silver UFO in the sky; it had small protuberances beneath, and dome with antennae on top. It rotated as it flew off, and others saw it; 22 November 1967

SCAIENI (PRAHOVA) Ten children watched strange coloured lights for an hour; burn marks found on grass later and increased radioactivity found by investigator; 29 March 1976

SÎNGEORZ-BĂI Professor of civil engineering saw UFO he thought was meteorite coming to earth, but it slowed down then changed direction, climbing steeply and changing colour, then changing direction again; 4 August 1967

RWANDA

LOCATION UNKNOWN Seven teenagers, especially Marie Clare, saw visions of the Blessed Virgin Mary, who gave them messages; 1980–5

SCOTLAND (see also *Modern Mysteries of Britain*)

Borders Region

PEEBLES Ghostly phenomena in Cross Keys Hotel, centred on Room 3; radio interviewer trying to record ghostly voice obtained only the voice of Donald Duck recorded at high speed; September 1975

Fife Region

ST ANDREWS University student walking across playing fields at night saw three ghostly monks walking above present ground level, who disappeared when 10 feet away; autumn 1979

Grampian Region

OFF GIRDLE NESS, ABERDEEN   Crew of
collier saw red flashing light which
fell into the sea; no wreckage found;
22 November 1963

Highland Region

LOCH MULLARDOCH, NEAR CANNICH
Mountaineers saw phantom cottage;
May 1987 (see Ch. 5)
LOCH NESS   Dwelling place of lake
monster 'Nessie' (see Ch. 7), one of
several lakes in Scotland with
persistent monster reports; others
include LOCH MORAR ('Morag'), LOCH
EIL, LOCH LOCHY, LOCH SHIEL, and
also sea-lochs like ALSH, DUICH,
LINNHE
REDCASTLE, BLACK ISLE   Mystery black
cat which had been taking pet ducks
was trapped by their owner; possibly
a melanistic Scottish wildcat, or
cross between feral cat and wildcat;
February 1988

Lothian Region

LIVINGSTON   Forest worker
encountered UFO hovering above
ground; 9 November 1979 (see Chs.
6 and 8)

Strathclyde Region

GLASGOW   Man saw football-sized
object hovering above the ground,
hissing, glowing red, giving off smell
of rotten eggs – it moved towards
him, then up street, before
vanishing: ball lightning?;
November 1979
LOCHDON, ISLE OF MULL   Ghostly voice
heard in house; summer 1974

MILNGAVIE   'Ball of fire' landed on
house during thunderstorm: this ball
lightning damaged buildings, and
another in Blantyre, 6 feet in
diameter, struck empty petrol tanks;
11 May 1977

Western Isles

LOCH SEAFORTH, HARRIS/LEWIS
Steamer crew saw object falling into
the sea; no aircraft missing;
27 February 1961

SOLOMON ISLANDS

SANTA CRUZ ISLANDS   On three nights,
mysterious flying object seen, like
ball of fire which flew fast below
cloud level lighting up the ground;
one landed, but nothing later found
at the spot; September 1977

SOUTH AFRICA

Cape Province

BLAAUWVLEI   Poltergeist outbreak;
September–October 1921
FORT BEAUFORT   Fiery ball, changing
colour to green, then white, seen
hovering over trees on farm. Bernie
Smit fired several shots at it, with
no effect. An hour later, police
arrived and saw a shiny black sphere
which dodged behind trees when
approached. It turned greyish-white
and darted away over the treetops

when shot at, making a loud whirring noise; 26 June 1972

GROENDAL WILDERNESS RESERVE, NEAR UITENHAGE   Four young boys saw three men in bright silver suits, gliding rather than walking; 1 October 1978

HERMANUS   Fishermen working 4–5 miles offshore saw sea monster; 1903 (see Ch. 7)

KIMBERLEY   Two brown football-sized objects made of a soft material fell from the sky; three days later they had shrunk and turned white; 15 June 1962

KOKSTAD   Spontaneous fires were breaking out in house occupied by 39 people; summer 1983

LANSDOWNE, NEAR CAPE TOWN   Poltergeist outbreak; several days in July 1937

LOXTON   Farmer saw landed UFO and small entities with slanting eyes; hit in the eyes by a beam of light; 31 July 1975

ROSMEAD   Red lights seen over school tennis court at night; holes found in tar surface of court; 12 November 1972

UITENHAGE   On the Flats, man saw frogs and fishes falling in the rain; March 1925

NEAR UNIONDALE   Corporal Dawie van Jaarsveld gave a lift to female phantom hitch-hiker on his motorcycle; April 1978. Similar experience befell another motorcyclist two years later (see Ch. 5)

Natal

PIETERMARITZBURG   An early UFO sighting – 'massive sheet of shining metal, revolving . . . with each turn a great flash was thrown off each side', seen for forty minutes, then it shot upwards at speed; summer 1930. Showers of stones bombarded two youths, indoors and outdoors; early July 1980 (see Ch. 16)

PINETOWN   Loud crashing noises in poltergeist outbreak, but no damage caused; 24 December 1983–January 1984 (see Ch. 1)

ST LUCIA LAKE   People fishing saw 90-foot monster in water; lake communicates with sea, and a similar creature seen offshore the same night; 7 July 1933

TIGER ROCKS   Sea monster more than 60 feet long seen; April 1947. More sightings in the summer, then in September a man walking on the beach at Isipingo saw monster with eyes 'like red searchlights' and making a loud braying noise

ZULULAND   English couple heard footsteps and knocking in their cottage, and ghost identified as former resident; began May 1952

Orange Free State

BOSHOF   Poltergeist outbreak; violent noises heard at night, but nothing broken or disturbed; three nights in 1901 (see Ch. 1)

Transvaal

DAVEYTON, WITWATERSRAND   Tree shed 'tears' annually between September and February, and was also said to speak; July 1982 (see Ch. 11)

GROOTVLEI PUMPING STATION   Water monster reports; also in ORANGE RIVER and tributaries of VAAL RIVER

JOHANNESBURG   Ball lightning seen rolling up incline; it had comet-like tail and saw-tooth streaks of light. It exploded on meeting wall, leaving no damage but acrid smell; *c.*1920

MINDALORE, KRUGERSDORP   Meagan Quezet and son André saw landed UFO; five or six entities came out, speaking in unidentifiable language; 3 January 1979

ORLANDO EAST, SOWETO   Stone-throwing was followed by outbreaks of fires in this poltergeist case: the furniture was burned and wrecked, and windows broken; began 10 May 1978

PRETORIA   UFO landed on road and took off leaving macadam blazing; 16 September 1965. Wooden cross 'wept' resin annually on anniversary of battle

ROODEPORT   House bombarded with stones over several months, sometimes falling vertically; 1922 (see Ch. 16)

VANDERBIJLPARK   Legless ghost of old man seen several times by family; November 1975

SPAIN

OFF ALCOCEBRE (CASTELLÓN)   Diver saw 20-foot metallic object lying on sea bed; next day a friend saw something leave the sea in that area, and the diver later found the cylinder had gone; 26–27 July 1970 (see Ch. 10)

ARROYO DE LA MIEL, MÁLAGA   Object dived into lake, then emerged and flew off; September 1971

BÉLMEZ DE LA MORALEDA, ANDALUSIA   Faces appeared on cement floor; voices also heard; 1971 onwards (see Ch. 11)

NEAR CANTILLANA   Stones shot upward from ground, accompanied by detonation; two hours on morning of 4 May 1910

CHINCHILLA, ALBACETE   Green snake 6 feet long crossed road and was killed by car; 22 July 1969. Other big snakes seen at ORIHUELA and ALLOY in ALICANTE (summer 1970), and near ACEUCHE in CÁCERES (July 1973) (see Ch. 14)

EL PRADO DE EL ESCORIAL, NEAR

MADRID   Blessed Virgin Mary appeared in tree to Amparo Cuevas, and gave messages which other witnesses could hear; began 1981 for at least five years

EZQUIOGA   Children and 150 others (including unbelievers) saw vision of Blessed Virgin Mary with angels and saints; 30 June 1931

HUESCA   'Apeman' seen in the Pyrenees, 6 feet tall and naked, emitting animal-like sounds; threw tree trunk at workers; may have been a feral child rather than relic hominoid; May 1979

ISLA CRISTINA, HUELVA   Boys saw luminous UFO emerge from sea and disappear; 8 February 1981 (see Ch. 10)

NEAR JEREZ DE LA FRONTERA, CADIZ   Man on motorcycle saw two humanoids looking like 'Michelin man'; May 1960 (see Ch. 9)

LA CODOSERA, BADAJOZ   Children and adults, 100 in all, saw several apparitions of Blessed Virgin Mary; May 1945

NEAR LA CORUÑA   Large shining disc-shaped UFO rose with explosive noise and shot away at great speed; 5 November 1954

LÉON   Young woman saw two men with silvery objects on their backs, who flew away; next day seen by several other people; c.1914

MADRID   Statue of Blessed Virgin Mary wept blood from eyes and heart eleven times; 1972

PALMAR DE TROYA   Teenage girls saw apparition of Blessed Virgin Mary in tree; continued for many years with messages given; began 30 March 1968, still continuing 1986

PUENTE DE HERRERA, VALLADOLID   8-foot high UFO with coloured lights seen on ground with entity beside it, seemingly interested in alfalfa field; afterwards road glowed where UFO had stood; 15 August 1970

SAN SEBASTIAN DE GARABANDAL, SANTANDER   Four children regularly saw an apparition of the Blessed

Virgin Mary, and miracles occurred; began 18 June 1961, continued into 1965

VALENCIA   Caravelle airliner made emergency landing after being followed by UFO; 11 November 1979

VILLARES DEL SAZ, CUENCA   Illiterate boy cowherd saw big 'balloon' (UFO) on the ground, out of which came tiny (*c*.26 inches) entities with yellow faces; they spoke but he did not understand and one smacked his face; early July 1953

VOLTANA   Winged woman seen flying over town by many witnesses; June 1905 (see Ch. 9)

ZARAGOZA   Poltergeist outbreak; November–December 1934

SRI LANKA

HEWAHETA   Many witnesses on tea plantations of circular UFOs with side-wings; 17 July 1971

GULF OF MANNAR   Second officer of *Bali* saw long-necked sea monster, neck 15 feet long, grey-green in colour; 31 October 1922

MUTWAL   Schoolboy saw statue of Virgin Mary in grotto move, and others saw movements later; July 1987

SWEDEN

Throughout Sweden, 1000 reports of rocket-like objects seen in sky, or crashing into lakes; summer 1946

BLECKENSTAD   Limestone ball containing marine shells and fossil fell from sky; 11 April 1925 (see Ch. 13)

ERVALLA   Farmer returning home at night was surrounded by cone-shaped dazzling white light which made his hat and hair rise up and gave him a 'suntan'; 10 November 1948

GOTLAND ISLAND   Couple saw disc-shaped UFOs made of a shining metal, the upper part rotating over the lower, and with red lights; they also heard a clicking sound; 5 August 1957

HOGANAS   Two men saw disc-shaped UFO in the woods and were attacked by four grey, 'fluid', entities; but they fled when one man sounded car horn; 20 December 1958

LAKE JALKA   Dark object about 60 feet long seen on the water; March 1974

LAKE KÖLMJÄRV   Mystery flying object seen to crash into lake; 19 July 1946. Similar crashes at Lakes KATTISJÄRN, MJÖSA, and others (see Ch. 10)

LULEA   Army officers saw seven disc-shaped UFOs hovering over field exercise, intermittently over several hours, and one witness felt they were trying to communicate by telepathy; 3 March 1976

MARKIM   Man saw blinding light at night, and later under hypnosis remembered being abducted on to a UFO; 23 March 1974

NEAR NARKEN   Three people in car saw 'little man' and white flash; 19 August 1970. Similar experience reported near ÖVERKALIX; 16 February 1971 (see Ch. 9)

NEAR ÖJEBYN   Car driver surrounded by vertical beams of light; headlights and brakes failed. When beams vanished, driver saw black object rise from field half a mile away; 20 September 1971

BETWEEN ORRESTA AND TORTUNA   Ghost train seen; 1933

PARAJAEVARRA, LAPPLAND   Fireballs fell from an overcast sky, fatally burning one person and badly burning others, destroying five houses and damaging others; July 1938

SERNA, DALARNA   Hole found in lake ice; April 1968

LAKE SILJAN   Object seen tearing hole in lake ice leaving channel *c*.12 feet wide; 30 April 1976

BETWEEN STOCKHOLM AND KALMAR   Jet liner buzzed by luminous, pulsating UFO; 1 September 1977

LAKE STORSJÖN, JÄMTLAND   Lake monster reports

LAKE TORNEA   Black lake monster seen, *c*.45–60 feet long; July 1981

LAKE UPPRAMEN   Mystery hole in ice, triangular, 60 by 90 feet, discovered, but frogman found nothing in the water; April 1968 (see Ch. 10)

VALLENTUNA   Wave of UFO sightings, with hundreds of sightings over a few months; including on 23 March 1974 possible abduction of man from LINDHOLMEN

SWITZERLAND

THE ALPS   During a heavy snowstorm, exotic insects looking like spiders, caterpillars and huge ants fell and soon died; March 1922. Reports of large reptile known as Tatzelwurm (see Ch. 14)

NEAR CHUR, GRAUBUNDEN   Two hunters watched a tiger kill a deer; September 1974

RIVER DOUBS   Sightings of long-necked water monster with blue back and yellow stomach; 1934

GRINDELWALD   Bright balls of light (ball lightning?) appeared from air inlet of large wood-store and disappeared with loud explosion and smell; July 1921

LAKE LÉMAN   A dozen people in boat watched saucer-shaped UFO hovering above them; it made several leaps before taking off at great speed; 16 August 1958

MOLIGNON, NEAR SION   Poltergeist outbreak centred on young boy, phenomena including stone-throwing; 18–27 April 1914 (see Chs. 1 and 16)

SYRIA

DAMASCUS   Statue of Blessed Virgin Mary wept; 1977

TAIWAN

MT SION   The god 'Yehobah' appeared and appointed Elia Hong as his prophet; the event was video-taped; early 1980s

TANZANIA

WEMBARE PLAINS   Lion-hunter saw two little men, 4 feet high, covered in brown fur, walking upright – they were the legendary Agogwe; pre-1937

WETI, ZANZIBAR   Clods of earth fell inside and outside house; spring 1923 (see Ch. 16)

THAILAND

BANGSUE   Poltergeist activity with stone-throwing, floating bar of soap,

crashing objects; servant girl
unmasked and admitted her guilt,
but that may be only a partial
solution; late 1967–1 March 1968

PORT OF SPAIN, TRINIDAD   House
pelted with stones, and poltergeist
activity indoors; began 12 November
1905 (see Ch. 16)

TIBET

CHANGHAI (THE LONG LAKE)   Chinese
scientist saw 10-foot 'miracle animal'
with horse's head and dinosaur or
rhino body; 12 October 1984
FOREST REGION at *c.*13,000 feet
Mountaineer Reinhold Messner saw
a 6½-foot-tall Yeti with shaggy black
fur from a distance of 30 feet; June
1986
LAKE DUOBUZHE   Chinese soldiers were
reported to have killed strange
animal from lake – ox-like, legs like
a turtle's, short curly horns, skin like
hippo's; 1972
WEST OF MOUNT EVEREST   Eric Shipton
and colleague saw and photographed
Yeti tracks; 1951
LHAKPA-LA   Col. C. K. Howard-Bury
saw Yeti footprints at over 20,000
feet; 1921
MENBU LAKE   Farmers and party
officials saw lake monster with long
neck, big head and body; one farmer
rowing on lake was said to have been
dragged down, and a cow pulled in
from the shore; June 1980
MENLUNGTSE   Chris Bonington's
expedition found strange footprints,
possibly of Yeti, at more than
15,000 feet; April 1987

TRINIDAD AND TOBAGO

EAST COAST RIVER   Reports of 'scaly
serpent' 25–30 feet long seen moving
in a way impossible for a snake

TUNISIA

NEAR SOUK EL KHEMIS   People working
in fields saw UFO which stopped
like a disc on edge and swung like a
pendulum just above ground before
flying away; 3 September 1954

TURKEY

ISTANBUL   Rain of frogs; 17 June 1969

UGANDA

ENTEBBE PENINSULA   During
thunderstorm, balls of brilliant blue
light 4–6 cm in diameter entered
room through window, floated across
and left by another window –
windows open with metal screens;
same event occurred again later;
1982

URUGUAY

EL ABROJAL, RIVERA   Rural worker and
wife saw blinding light and heard

loud noise as it moved towards them. Gust of hot wind knocked them down and they became unconscious; afterwards they suffered nausea, vomiting, dizziness and eye irritation. Other witnesses at the local school saw the same object for twenty minutes; 30 October 1976 (see Ch. 3)

SALTO UFO landed on road ahead of car with five people in it. UFO kept changing colours; it was as wide as the road. Inside was a green light and three entities moving about. After a while flames shot from the sides and it took off upwards; 15 August 1965

UNITED STATES OF AMERICA (USA)

Alabama

CHILATCHEE, NEAR UNIONTOWN During localized rain shower, live fish fell; April or May 1956 (see Ch. 13)

FRANKVILLE Hissing noise followed by explosion, and plants flew into the air – but no hole found, and no debris; March 1986

HUNTSVILLE Girls walking home at night saw light travelling along creek bed at car speed; 1934 or 1935

NEAR MOBILE (1948), WALNUT CREEK, NEAR CLANTON (autumn 1960), OLD TAYLOR ROAD, DOTHAN (May 1976), EAST BREWTON, JAY PIPELINE BETWEEN FLOMATON AND JAY, CONECUH RIVER (March 1978), 'BLUE HOLE' CREEK, NEAR ATHENS (August 1978) – locations of pre-1981 Bigfoot sightings

MONTGOMERY Airline pilots Chiles and Whitted saw cigar-shaped UFO; 24 July 1948 (see Ch. 3)

NAUVOO Big black cat, possibly cougar, seen on porches and in gardens; May 1987

QUEENSTOWN Mystery animal (big cat?) killed 250-pound Shetland pony and 130-pound pig; January 1975

NEAR VERNON Ghost light seen on road 10 miles to west of Vernon

Alaska

ANCHORAGE Japanese captain of airliner saw bright lights of two UFOs and silhouette of giant 'mother ship', which followed him for 400 miles as he flew across north-east Alaska to Anchorage; 17 November 1986 (see Ch. 3)

DRY HARBOR 100-foot-long carcass washed ashore, covered with reddish-brown hair two inches long; it also had 6-inch teeth; 1956

ILIAMNA LAKE Lake monster reports; other Alaskan lakes with monsters are LAKE CLARK, BIG LAKE, CROSSWIND LAKE, KALOOLUK LAKE, LAKE MINCHUMINA, NONVIANUK LAKE. Also, ghost lights seen in mountains around Iliamna Lake

KODIAK Navy personnel in patrol aircraft saw UFO, also seen on radar; at 1800 mph it flew faster than contemporary aircraft; 22 January 1950

NULATO (c.1920), NEAR KALUKA (c.1940), DEWILDE'S CAMP, NEAR RUBY (1943), INSIDE PASSAGE (August 1956), WEST OF RUBY (August 1960), NORTH OF HYDER (August 1968), YUKON RIVER, NEAR GALENA (summer 1968), NEAR BRADFIELD CANAL (July 1969), NEAR ILIAMNA AND NEWHALEN (January 1978) – locations of pre-1981 Bigfoot sightings

SECURITY BAY Sea monster seen 'looping along through the water'; April 1947; monster with cow-like head and fins on back seen from

small boat off Pennock Island;
8 May 1947

UMIAT Trappers saw red, disc-shaped
UFO moving up and down, nearly
touching the ground, then circling
before flying away; February 1959

Arizona

APACHE-SITGREAVES NATIONAL FOREST,
NEAR HEBER Six men working in
forest saw large UFO hovering
above clearing. Travis Walton
jumped out of truck and ran towards
UFO, where he was struck by beam
of light. His colleagues left, but soon
returned after seeing UFO in sky.
They could not find Walton, and he
was absent for five days, reappearing
in a phone box 15 miles away. He
claimed to have been taken into the
UFO. This case is controversial, but
many facts are in Walton's favour;
5–10 November 1975

COLORADO RIVER, LOST LAKE 10-foot
crocodilian killed; June 1943. 5-foot
specimen caught at TUCSON; spring
1950. Large crocodilian seen at LA
PAZ SLOUGH, PARKER; early 1950s

DOUGLAS Ghost in khaki seen in
Gadsden Hotel; 1970s

NEAR FLAGSTAFF (1924 and January
1971), LITTLE JEDITO WASH (autumn
1965), YARNELL (1975), POLACCA
(January 1979) – locations of
pre-1981 Bigfoot sightings

NEAR GLOBE About 15 miles east of
Globe, small non-human entity seen
on road; June 1960 (see Ch. 9)

HOLBROOK Loud detonation followed
by fall of stones – c.14,000 collected,
some very small; 19 July 1912 (see
Ch. 13)

HOWELLS, NEAR PRESCOTT Prospector
witnessed paranormal showers of
stones and weird lights; summer and
autumn 1936 (see Ch. 16)

NEAR TUCSON Desert house
bombarded daily by rocks; no one
caught; September–December 1983
(see Ch. 16)

YUMA One clam fell from sky;
20 August 1941 (see Ch. 13)

NEAR YUMA AIR FORCE BASE Scientist
saw UFO, a silvery disc encircled by
dark bands, the latter only seen
through Polaroid glasses; 5 May
1953

Arkansas

BEDIAS CREEK, LAKE CONWAY, ILLINOIS
RIVER, MUD LAKE, WHITE RIVER
Lake monster reports

DIERKS Black panther seen; 1977. Also
in WALTON HEIGHTS, LITTLE ROCK;
November 1976

FOUKE Many claimed sightings of
Bigfoot, and giant footprints found;
from 1953 onwards. Other locations
of pre-1981 Bigfoot sightings are
SPRINGDALE (early 1970s), PINE
BLUFF (June 1973), NEAR HOLLY
SPRINGS (October 1974), NEAR
FORDYCE (October 1974), CAMDEN
(March 1975), SOUTH CROSSETT
(June 1978), BENTON (August 1978)

GURDON Ghost light seen on
Missouri-Pacific railway tracks (see
Ch. 8)

HOPE, DE QUEEN, FULTON, MELA, OLA,
BARESVILLE, LITTLE ROCK and
elsewhere Mysterious loud booms
heard, coinciding with onset of cold
weather; December 1983

MIDLAND Fire spook in house caused
damage to curtains, clothing,
wallpaper and furniture; barn
burned down; 9 September 1945

WYNNE As woman prayed for her
newly dead husband, a 'beautiful
cross' appeared in a glass door, and
was taken as a sign from God;
thousands queued to see it;
17 October 1987

California

BAKERSFIELD Apparitions of Our Lady
of Guadalupe seen in La Loma
barrio; began 24 December 1984

BIG BEAR CITY, SAN BERNADINO
Poltergeist outbreak; June–
c. November 1962

NEAR BLOCK MOUNTAIN, HUMBOLDT
COUNTY   Deer-hunter saw Bigfoot
running towards him; at 80 feet
away it veered off into thicket;
September 1985

BONITA   Fish seen to fall from sky on
to gardens; August 1984

BROADMOOR   Woman found dead
monkey in garden: it seemed to have
fallen from the sky; 26 October 1956
(see Ch. 13)

BRUSH CREEK   Two gold miners saw
UFO land on 20 May and 20 June,
and little entity got out with shiny
pail to collect water; 1953

CARMEL RIVER   Three men walking on
beach near river mouth saw huge
snake-like head 8 feet above sea;
monster was about 40 feet long and
had greyish-green body hair, pinkish
neck and head, and green glassy
spines along back; April 1948

CASITAS DAM, NEAR VENTURA   Men saw
UFO emerge from reservoir;
photograph taken; November 1964
(see Ch. 10)

CHICO   Showers of stones fell
intermittently from sky on to two
warehouses; January–March 1922
(see Ch. 16)

NEAR CISCO GROVE   Three men were
hunting in the mountains and while
one was alone he saw a strange light
at dusk and climbed 12 feet up into
a tree. Three figures approached,
two clad in silvery-grey material; the
third moved like a robot. The first
two tried but failed to climb the
tree; the robot tried to gas the
hunter with 'smoke' from its
'mouth'. He climbed higher and
began to throw down pieces of
clothing which he had set on fire.
The robot let out more gas and the
hunter became unconscious for a few
seconds each time. He also shot
arrows at the robot, which made a
noise as if striking metal. At dawn,
another robot came, and more gas
was released, causing the hunter to
lose consciousness and when he
came round they had all gone. He
found his colleagues again, and they
had seen the light, which may have
been a UFO; 4 September 1964

COMMERCE   Mystery underground
explosions, most noticeable around 3
or 4 a.m.; late 1987 and into 1988

ELFIN FOREST, NEAR ESCONDIDO   White
lady ghost seen by numerous
witnesses (see Ch. 5)

ELIZABETH LAKE, LAKE ELSINORE, LAKE
FOLSOM, HOMER LAKE, LAFAYETTE
LAKE, LAKE TAHOE ('Tessie')   Lake
monster reports

HAGGINWOOD, SACRAMENTO   Stones
and metal pieces falling nightly,
breaking windows; July 1946

INYO NATIONAL FOREST, NEAR MONACHE
MOUNTAIN   Workmen heard screams
and saw Bigfoot-like figure; August
1986 (see Ch. 2)

KERN COUNTY   Desert house haunted
by woman who had built it; 1968
onwards (see Ch. 5)

LAKEWOOD   World War II shell fell
from sky, leaving 4-foot crater in
man's patio; 1 January 1984 (see
Ch. 13)

LONG BEACH   5-foot crocodile found in
back yard after residents heard
heavy thump and loud grunt; late
1960 (see Ch. 13). Ghostly
phenomena on ship Queen Mary, in
retirement since 1967

LOS ANGELES   Possible case of
spontaneous human combustion:
Mrs Esther Dulin (30) died sitting
in a chair and remains fell through
burned floor; May 1953. Poltergeist
outbreak; November 1972–February
1973. Spontaneous outbreaks of fire
in house; 9 March 1976. Six-inch
polished steel cylinder crashed
through house roof; August 1987

LUNDY LAKE, YOSEMITE   Bigfoot seen
through binoculars in forest;
10 September 1982 (see Ch. 2)

LYNWOOD   Poltergeist outbreak;
September 1960

MONTEREY   UFOs and 'angel hair'
seen; 4 October 1971 (see
Ch. 13)

MOUNT LOWE Hiker saw phantom hotel; June 1974 (see Ch. 5)

MUROC AIR FORCE BASE Witnesses saw three silvery spheres or discs; first lieutenant was sure they were not aircraft, weather balloons or birds. UFO seen at ROGERS DRY LAKE 40 minutes afterwards; 8 July 1947

OAKLAND Possible case of spontaneous human combustion; February 1974

ORIFLAMME MOUNTAIN, BORREGO DESERT 'Ghost lights' seen at night on mountain slopes – said to be 'money lights' marking buried treasure and veins of gold

PALM SPRINGS Wheel with tyre dropped on to car while being driven; 16 April 1969

RED BLUFF UFO sightings over six days, with police patrolmen seeing football-shaped craft 150 feet long which dropped from the sky, hovered, then rose again and performed aerial manoeuvres at speed; 13 August 1960

REDONDO BEACH Fishing boat crew saw sea monster looking like a merman 3 miles offshore – it had shiny eyes under broad, smooth forehead, dark hair on its head and under its chin, and it was 10–12 feet tall. It flipped its tail and disappeared as they got a boat out to catch it; May 1935

NEAR RIVERSIDE While crossing Santa Ana riverbed, Charles Wetzel saw monster which clawed at him through windscreen; it had a round head, no ears, protruding mouth, shiny eyes and very long claws, its skin scaly 'like leaves' – Bigfoot or what?; 8 November 1958

SAN FERNANDO VALLEY Poltergeist activity, with radio being interfered with, footsteps heard, etc.; apparitions also seen; November 1972–1973

SAN FRANCISCO Possible case of spontaneous human combustion; 31 January 1959 (see Ch. 4)

SAN FRANCISCO BAY Men sitting in car saw snake-like sea monster chasing seals – it was 60 feet long, dark

green fading to cream beneath; 5 February 1985

SAN LUIS OBISPO Tiny fish came up with water from artesian well 580 feet deep; February 1952

SANTA ANA Ghost in pizza plant; 1970s

SANTA CATALINA ISLAND Unidentified submarine object seen by captain of fishing boat off Avalon; 28 July 1962 (see Ch. 10)

SANTA CRUZ Red-hot metal pellets fell from sky on to beach; 5 January 1909 (see Ch. 13). 50-foot corpse washed ashore; summer 1925

SANTA MONICA Pilot saw round, silver UFO with windows, which flew 1000 feet below him; 1 January 1978 (see Ch. 3)

SANTA SUSANNA MOUNTAINS Man and son on all-terrain cycle on dirt road saw large hairy creature, possibly Bigfoot, watching them. It began to follow them and they crashed the bike, but the creature was not seen after the accident; January 1984. Three men investigating this sighting saw a similar creature, 8 feet tall, in their flashlight; February 1984

SOUTH OF SHASTA, ON OLD HIGHWAY 99 Couple saw two Bigfeet crossing road, one looked in car window; spring 1947. One of many Bigfoot reports from California in the last 40 years. Other locations include BLUFF CREEK, site of famous 1967 Patterson/Gimlin cine film (see Ch. 2), among other sightings, OROVILLE area, HOOPA VALLEY, BLUE LAKE, TRINITY ALPS, CONFIDENCE RIDGE, KLAMATH RIVER, LITTLE ROCK, EUREKA

STINSON BEACH Several people saw humped sea monster about 100 feet long; 31 October 1983. Another, a 'long black eel', seen off COSTA MESA, was 10 feet from man on surfboard and he said it was not a whale; 2 November 1983

THORNTON 60-pound statue of the Madonna wept oily liquid and moved 30 feet; 1981

TRINITY ALPS 8-foot salamander said

to have been caught; January 1960
(see Ch. 14)

TRUCKEE   Three men eating supper off
Highway 89 at dusk saw 9–10-foot
hairy animal on hind legs, possibly
Bigfoot; 24 April 1987 (see Ch. 2)

TULARE LAKE BASIN, CORCORAN   6-foot
alligator seen; summer 1930. Several
sightings of alligators in FOLSOM
LAKE (September 1957–June 1958),
8-foot specimen seen in LAFAYETTE
LAKE (23 October 1975), 4-footer in
KINGS RIVER, FRESNO (23 June
1981), 7-footer in FEATHER RIVER,
YUBA CITY (5 August 1981)

VAN NUYS   Navy beans fell in
hailstorm; 6 March 1958 (see
Ch. 13)

VENTURA AREA   Big black cats seen;
1960s. Other locations of big cat
sightings include MARIN COUNTY (30
sightings during 1957–75), EAST BAY
AREA (1972), SAN JOSE HIGHLANDS
(late 1973), and FREMONT – where
there was a fruitless search for a
large male lion in November 1979

WILSON LAKE, NEAR CHESTER   Off-duty
deputy sheriff hunting deer in
wilderness area came face to face
with 4-foot little man, human in
appearance, with red and gold cap,
close-fitting green pants, gold
long-sleeved jacket, tight boots. No
fasteners were seen on the clothes.
After a minute, he ran up a gravel
slope and disappeared; c. September
1956

WOODSIDE   Red-hot pieces of cast iron
fell from the sky; summer 1954 (see
Ch. 13)

YORBA LINDA   Fourteen-year-old boy
photographed UFO through
window; it was hat-shaped with four
appendages on the rim, and analysis
showed it to be a solid, free-flying
object; 24 January 1967

Colorado

ALAMOSA   Horse called Snippy found
dead on ranchland, mysteriously
mutilated, this event being one of
the earliest and most famous cases of
unexplained animal mutilations;
September 1967

AURORA   3-foot baby alligator found
crawling across city street; August
1984

LAKE COMO, LAKE KATHERINE, TWIN
LAKES   Lake monster reports

CRIPPLE CREEK   Horse, penned in
corral with four others, found dead
cause unknown; corpse mutilated by
clean incision around anus; one eye
clouded over with grey film; spring
1980. Other reports of mysterious
animal mutilations in Colorado, 203
in 1975, the peak year. Also in
Cripple Creek, the Fairley-
Lampman Building was haunted –
voices heard, footsteps, dancing in
the ballroom, an apparition of a
young woman seen, typewriter
heard, perfume smelled; early 1980s

EVANS   Regular falls of corn kernels
from sky; 1982–6 (see Ch. 13)

GOLDEN   Kangaroo seen on outskirts of
town, and chased by police;
12 August 1976

LITTLETON   Town Hall Arts Center
haunted – laughter and music heard,
elevator moved, etc.; late 1986

MT ELBERT (1960s), COLORADO SPRINGS
(summer 1975), NEAR OURAY (4 and
5 July 1976) – locations of pre-1981
Bigfoot sightings

SILVER CLIFF   Ghost lights seen in
cemetery since 1880s

Connecticut

BASILE LAKE, CONNECTICUT RIVER, LAKE
POCOTOPANG   Lake monster reports

BRIDGEPORT   Poltergeist activity began
with pounding noises in the walls
and escalated into the usual domestic
chaos with furniture overturned and
china smashed; early 1972–early
1975 (see Ch. 1)

COLLENDER'S POINT, DARIEN
Crocodilians found; 2 October 1929

EAST HADDAM TOWNSHIP 'Moodus Noises' heard periodically since eighteenth century, sounding like guns, thunder, logs falling. Thought to be from earthquakes close to surface

EAST HARTFORD Raggedy-Ann doll said to be possessed by spirit of dead girl; some poltergeist activity in apartment; early 1973–March 1974 (see Ch. 1)

ELLINGTON Bigfoot seen in farm barn; 23 August 1982 (see Ch. 2)

HADDAM NECK 'Panther' seen, and tracked in the woods; possibly responsible for killing and eating two calves; May 1907. More recent big cat reports come from GLASTONBURY (1939), WEST ROCK (seen ambling through town) and BRANFORD (both autumn 1967), and forests in the HAMPTON, ASHFORD and EASTFORD areas (1980s), although officially cougars have not been in Connecticut's woods for 100 years

NEW HAVEN Fiery object crashed through billboard; analysed fragments were almost pure copper; 1953 (see Ch. 13)

OLD LYME Mystery animal seen, like a rabbit/dog cross; November 1986–January 1987 (see Ch. 14)

OLD SAYBROOK Woman saw 20-foot UFO with brightly lit portholes outside her bedroom window, with three entities inside; it tilted and shot off upwards at speed; 16 December 1957

POMFRET Ghostly sounds heard in ruins of abandoned settlement; investigators heard laughter and sounds of daily life, and took photographs which showed streaks, blobs and faces; investigation 1971

SOUTHINGTON As storm approached, reddish ball dropped from clouds to tops of trees on mountainside and bounced down to next level of treetops, eventually vanishing; summer 1958

TRUMBULL White Bigfoot-type creature seen which could run at 35 mph; 1970

Delaware

NEAR CONCORD Mystery animal, dark in colour with 2-foot tail and jumping like kangaroo, seen; September 1979 (see Ch. 14)

DOVER 5-foot crocodilian caught; 1 April 1982

HARRINGTON Mystery black animal, possibly a big cat, seen by numerous people in the area; summer 1984

District of Columbia

WASHINGTON Presidents have had eerie experiences in the White House, and the ghost of Lincoln has been seen (see Ch. 5). Wave of UFO radar/visual sightings; 19–20 and 26–27 July 1952. During storm, ball lightning entered room through keyhole and exploded on hitting fireplace; spring 1953 (see Ch. 8). Foot-long crocodilian seen walking down Pennsylvania Avenue; December 1962. Acidic green slime fell on city, affecting animals and killing plants; 5 and 6 September 1978 (see Ch. 13). Secret Service officer saw big cat on Massachusetts Avenue N.W.; 10 August 1982

Florida

BARDIN Sightings of 'Bardin Booger', i.e. Bigfoot; 1987

BUCKINGHAM Man found 4-foot cobra in garden wood pile; October 1986

NEAR CLEARWATER AND ON SUWANNEE RIVER 15-foot penguin seen; February 1948 (see Ch. 17)

LAKE CLINCH, LAKE MONROE, ST JOHN'S RIVER, ST LUCIE RIVER, SUWANNEE RIVER Water monster reports

DADE COUNTY Mysterious death of Esther Cooks, a possible case of spontaneous human combustion; January 1975

EVERGLADES, NEAR BIG CYPRESS INDIAN RESERVATION   James Flynn saw cone-shaped UFO and was struck by beam of light; 12 March 1965 (see Ch. 6)

JACKSONVILLE   People on beach heard noises coming from two clouds, like 'someone rattling cellophane' or like 'someone walking on pebbles'; 2 February 1969. Happened again a week later over MIAMI. Girl burst into flames while riding in car; 9 October 1980 (see Ch. 4)

NEAR JACKSONVILLE   DC-6 airliner en route from New York to Puerto Rico nearly collided with 'big fireball' moving fast with roaring sound; 9 March 1957

LAKELAND (1947), BIG CYPRESS SWAMP (spring 1957, February 1970, February 1971), HOLOPAW (1963), BROOKSVILLE (spring 1966, 30 November 1966, summer 1976), NEAR ANCLOTE RIVER (summer and December 1966, summer 1967), ELFERS (January 1967), NEAR DAVIE (1969 and 1971), NEAR FORT LAUDERDALE (9 January 1974), PALM BEACH COUNTY (September 1974), MIRAMAR (23 January 1975), CAPE CORAL (2 February 1975), NEAR GAINSVILLE (February 1975), NEAR LAKE OKEECHOBEE (6 March 1975), DADE COUNTY (24 March 1975), NEAR VENICE (7 June 1975), NORTH FORT MYERS (summer 1975, June 1976), CITRUS COUNTY (November 1975), NEAR GROVE CITY (mid-June 1976), DELRAY BEACH (February 1977), MOON LAKE (February and April 1977), NEAR LABELLE (23 May 1977), NOBLETON (May 1977), KEY LARGO (July 1977), APOKA (October 1977), BELLEVIEW (October 1977), OCALA NATIONAL FOREST (November 1977) – some locations of pre-1981 Bigfoot sightings

LAKE WORTH   Falls of ice cubes on to house; early September 1978 (see Ch. 13)

LEESBURG   Unexplained voices on the telephone were followed by poltergeist phenomena with the movement of furniture and smaller objects, and voices coming from the walls; January 1978–late 1978 (see Chs. 1 and 11)

MIAMI   Globular, pulsating, glittering ball fell into backyard, and dissolved away as people watched; 28 February 1958 (see Ch. 13). Bedclothes and curtains burst spontaneously into flame; late February 1959. Poltergeist outbreak in warehouse, with 224 incidents of goods falling off shelves; mid-December 1966–c. February 1967

OFF MIAMI   Rocket-like object found in 40 feet of water, but Navy said it was not a missile; 27 September 1966

ORLANDO   One ice-cold egg fell from the sky; 19 May 1959

NEAR OVIEDO   Ghost lights seen on State Road 13

PENSACOLA   Ghostly man in check shirt seen frequently in house; beginning c.1963

PORT RICHEY   Hundreds of small fish fell from the sky; 7 September 1971

PUNTA GORDA   Golf-balls rained from the sky; 3 September 1969

ROYAL PALM BEACH   6½-foot Nile monitor found on golf course; 20 June 1981. Another found at a house in HYPOLUXO on 12 July 1981; and a third found lying across car engine parked in driveway, NORTH MIAMI, on 14 July 1981 (see Ch. 14)

ST PETERSBURG   Mysterious death of Mary Reeser, a possible case of spontaneous human combustion; 2 July 1951 (see Ch. 4)

TARPON SPRINGS   Icon of St Nicholas in St Nicholas cathedral wept; December 1969 and 1973

WEEKI-WACHI SPRINGS   John Reeves saw landed UFO and entity, in tight-fitting silver-grey suit, and helmet like glass bowl. Entity drew out black box, which flashed like a camera, and left footprints; 3 March 1965

Georgia

ATLANTA   Human blood seeped from the floors of several rooms in an elderly couple's house; September 1987 (see Ch. 1)

BERRIEN COUNTY   Farmer saw panther with lion's mane chasing his cattle in forested land between Alapaha and Enigma; 1976

NEAR BOSTON (*c*.1951), NEAR KINCHAFOONEE CREEK (1 August 1955), NEAR COLUMBUS (*c*.1956), TARRYTOWN (1965), BLACKBURN STATE PARK (2 September 1974) – locations of pre-1981 Bigfoot sightings

CHATTAHOOCHIE RIVER, NO MAN'S FRIEND POND, SAVANNAH RIVER, SMITH LAKE   Lake monster reports

CHEAHA STATE PARK   Deer-hunter saw possible Bigfoot running away from him on two legs; 24 January 1987

DALE   Poltergeist outbreak in railway telegraph tower; December 1909

ELBERTON   'Shining line' seen stretching up into sky; many yards were pulled in without the end appearing; mid-June 1972 (see Ch. 13)

GRIFFIN   'Golden egg' fell slowly on to lawn, vanishing in smoke and explosion as it landed; 10 September 1973

MOODY AIR FORCE BASE   Aircraft collided with big orange fireball (ball lightning?) causing sharp jolt; 1952

NEAR ROME   'Black panther' leapt against car, leaving muddy pawprints on bodywork; 1958

SAVANNAH   Rain of seeds; February 1958. Jack Angel suffered mystery burns, possibly spontaneous human combustion, and survived; 12–16 November 1974 (see Ch. 4)

SCREVEN   Ghost light seen on railway (see Ch. 8)

STOCKTON   Just south of town, woman driving in early hours saw four small entities in the road; 3 July 1955 (see Ch. 9)

TAYLOR'S RIDGE, CHATTOOGA COUNTY 7½-foot Bigfoot seen; 24 August 1986 (see Ch. 2)

UNION COMMUNITY, PAULDING COUNTY 24-inch footprints, possibly made by Bigfoot, found embedded in road; September 1984

VALDOSTA   Bengal tiger shot by law enforcement officer on highway; February 1987

Hawaii

HONOLULU   Ghost in red dress seen in Hilton Hawaiian Village Hotel; August 1959. Woman saw 'lightning, crumpled with lots of black in the folds' and 25 feet long, dazzling electric-blue, pass through her garden making a sizzling noise; it disappeared, and explosion heard overhead; 22 September 1965

Idaho

BEAR LAKE, LAKE COEUR D'ALENE, PAYETTE LAKE ('Slimy Slim', 'McCall Monster', 'Sharlie'), PEND OREILLE LAKE, SNAKE RIVER, TAUTPHAUS PARK LAKE   Lake monster reports

CHESTERFIELD   Probably earliest twentieth-century sighting of Bigfoot in Idaho, when on 14 January 1902 skaters were chased by an 8-foot hairy creature with a club; many other sightings in the state, for example near PRIEST LAKE (1930s and 1970), FRENCH CREEK (16 June 1968), NEAR MCCALL (autumn 1968, summer 1970, autumn 1972, December 1974), NEAR OROFINO (June 1969, November 1972, June 1973, October 1975), NEAR DIXIE (September 1972), NEAR KELLY LAKE (September 1975), SEIGEL CREEK (July 1976), PAYETTE NATIONAL FOREST (7 April 1980), MINE CREEK, NEAR MALAD (30 August 1980)

NEAR PORTAGE   Cross-shaped hole in ground, 14 feet in diameter, found

in Little Malad River valley on
Idaho/Utah border; clods of soil
thrown out around hole; 1978

SMITH'S FERRY Something fell from
the sky and started small forest fire;
6 August 1961

SNAKE RIVER CANYON Two boys and a
man saw UFO like inverted
pie-plate, 20 feet long by 10 feet
thick, flying through canyon below
its rim; 'flames' were shooting from
the side and it made a swishing
sound; 13 August 1947

TWIN FALLS Rancher claimed UFO
swooped down near where steer was
standing; when it left, steer had
gone too; 7 September 1956

Illinois

BELLEVILLE 5-inch long 'E'-shaped
metal objects fell on to houses;
September 1982

BLOOMINGTON Possible case of
spontaneous human combustion;
1942 (see Ch. 4)

BOLINGBROOK Possible case of
spontaneous human combustion;
24 November 1979 (see Ch. 4)

CENTERVILLE 'Centaur', half man/half
horse, seen; 18 May 1963

CHICAGO 'Watery blood' oozed from
neck, hands and feet of St
Maximina, the 1700-year-old
remains being in a glass coffin in St
Adrian's church; May 1970 (see
Ch. 15). 4½-foot kangaroo cornered
in city alley by police, but it
escaped; 13 October 1974. More
sightings in Chicago, and also in
PLANO (October and November),
FOX RIVER, NEAR MILLBROOK
(5 November), and LANSING
(6 November). In July 1975, 5-foot
kangaroo seen in cornfields at DU
QUOIN, and another at ROCK ISLAND
on 6 April 1976 (see Ch. 14). Paper
money fell from the sky; December
1975 (see Ch. 13). Murder victim
spoke through entranced woman
three times and named her

murderer, who confessed and was
jailed; July 1977 (see Ch. 11). Police
officer saw several phantoms 'in
monk-like garb' 'milling about' in
cemetery; they disappeared as he got
near; late 1977 (see Ch. 5). Woman
survived possible outbreak of
spontaneous human combustion;
May 1981 (see Ch. 4). Statue of
Virgin Mary in St John of God
church wept; May 1984. Painting of
the Virgin Mary in St Nicholas
Albanian Orthodox church wept;
began 6 December 1986. Blue light
seen in overgrown Bachelor Grove
Cemetery

DECATUR Out-of-place crocodiles seen
several times; 30 August 1937,
24 October 1966, 26 June 1967.
Crocodilê caught at OAKLEY early in
August 1971. Small specimen caught
on lake shore at LOMBARD (30 July
1970); one caught on US66 at
CHENOA (22 September 1972);
1½-foot caiman caught in HUMBOLT
PARK, CHICAGO (August 1984)

NEAR EFFINGHAM Possibly earliest
Bigfoot sighting in the state, by two
boys who saw hairy creatures near
their home from time to time
(c.1912). Other Bigfoot locations
pre-1981 include ELIZABETH (25 July
1929), GUM CREEK NEAR MOUNT
VERNON (summer 1941), CREEK EAST
OF DECATUR (November 1962),
STATE HIGHWAY 89 NEAR
ILLINOIS/WISCONSIN BORDER (July
1964), NEAR CHITTYVILLE (11 August
1968), KICKAPOO CREEK (August
1970), PEORIA (June–July 1972),
CAIRO (25 July 1972), NEAR CREVE
COEUR (July 1972), MURPHYSBORO
(1973–5), EDWARDSVILLE (1973),
AURORA (January 1974), CAROL
STREAM (autumn 1974)

NEAR ENFIELD Pink-eyed, three-
legged, grey and hairy monster seen;
first sighting 25 April 1972

FOUR LAKES VILLAGE LAKE, LAKE
MICHIGAN, STUMP POND, THOMPSON'S
LAKE Lake monster reports

HARVARD Ghostly voices and laughter
heard in haunted house; late 1950s

NEAR MACOMB   Mysterious outbreaks of fire on farm – around 200 in a week. Cottage and barns burned down; August 1948 (see Ch. 4)

NEAR MEDINAH   Golfers saw tall, dark, hairy 6-foot creature, possibly Bigfoot, climb tree and then leave the area. It crossed 7–8-foot fence 'like it wasn't even there'; September 1985 (see Ch. 2)

MONTICELLO, DECATUR AND THROUGHOUT CENTRAL ILLINOIS 'Nellie the lion' seen by numerous witnesses – 'a large, yellow, long-haired beast'; summer 1917. Game warden shot at 'black panther' near Decatur on 25 October 1955. Other locations of big cat sightings include CHAMPAIGN, SALINE and LAWRENCE COUNTIES (1963), MACON COUNTY, JASPER COUNTY, SHAWNEE NATIONAL FOREST, WINNEBAGO COUNTY (all 1970), BELLEVILLE (1976), EAST CARONDELET (big black cat thought to have killed several chained-up dogs – December 1986), between DUPO and CAHOKIA (eating carcass on road – 22 February 1987), MILLSTADT (21 September 1987)

ROCKFORD   Possible case of spontaneous human combustion, victim being child; spring 1959

Indiana

BASS LAKE, BIG CHAPMAN'S LAKE, EAGLE CREEK, HOLLOW BLOCK LAKE, HUNTINGTON'S LAKE, LAKE MANITOU (DEVIL'S LAKE), LAKE MAXINKUCKEE, WABASH RIVER   Water monster reports

CARMEL, INDIANAPOLIS   Kangaroo seen; sightings also around RENSSELAER and SHERIDAN; November 1974

DECKER CHAPEL, KNOX COUNTY Sightings of white Bigfoot; September 1981 (see Ch. 2)

ELKHORN FALLS   Family out fishing saw 'lion with long tail'; other sightings in ABINGTON area; August 1948. Other locations of big cat sightings include LA PORTE (August 1985)

EVANSVILLE   Live alligator 2 feet long fell from sky; 21 May 1911 (see Ch. 13)

HARTFORD CITY   Sightings of bright silver humanoid entities 4 feet tall, with egg-shaped heads, gas masks with hoses to their chests, and square feet; they flew off in an upright position; 22 and 23 October 1973

HOUSTON HILL AREA, EAST OF HOUSTON   Bigfoot sightings; July–September 1982

INDIANAPOLIS   Poltergeist outbreak with movement of objects, knockings, and one witness being repeatedly bitten; 10 March 1962–February 1963. Rubbish (cardboard, plastic cups, computer printouts, etc.) fell from sky; 16 May 1984 (see Ch. 13). Phone call from the dead – desk clerk in airport hotel made call to his parents at the time of plane crash in which he was killed; October 1987 (see Ch. 11)

NEAR ODON   Mystery fires broke out at farm, 28 in one day; 1941 (see Ch. 4)

OSCEOLA, SOUTH BEND   Two related families suffered poltergeist activity, with household objects being thrown around and rocks striking the outside of the houses; September–October 1968 (see Ch. 16)

ROACHDALE–ROCKVILLE AREA   Source of numerous Bigfoot sighting reports in 1972; other locations of pre-1981 sightings in the state include THORNTOWN (1949), BLUE CLAY SPRINGS (1962), NEAR RISING SUN (May 1969), SOUTH OF WINSLOW (15 August 1970), SHARPESVILLE (June 1971), AURORA (April 1977), HOOSIER NATIONAL FOREST (August 1979), MONROE RESERVOIR (27 March 1980), JACKSON COUNTY (October–November 1980)

SOUTH BEND   Fish fell from the sky; 16 July 1937

NEAR SPRAYTOWN   8-foot Bigfoot seen standing near house; footprints found; 16 April 1981 (see Ch. 2)

NEAR VEEDERSBURG   Couple in car at night saw Bigfoot in headlights; February 1981 (see Ch. 2)

VINCENNES   Crocodile killed at Mariah Creek; December 1946. One found at FALL CREEK, INDIANAPOLIS, September 1959

NEAR WABASH   Possible case of spontaneous human combustion; victim was in car; 3 May 1951 (see Ch. 4)

Iowa

CEDAR RAPIDS   Poltergeist outbreak; 16 August 1962

CLAYTON COUNTY   Yellow-tan-coloured big cat 4 feet long seen near McGregor; 1974

NEAR MANCHESTER (September and 15 January), NEAR WEBSTER CITY (12 October), MINBURN (15 November), ADEL (early January), NEAR EDGEWOOD (13 January)   Bigfoot sighting locations in 1979–80

MICH COAL MINE, NEAR OSKALOOSA   8–10 foot Bigfoot jumped out of shadows when witness went to sweep snow; December 1977

NEAR MOUNT PLEASANT   Fisherman saw shiny blue translucent egg-shaped UFO land nearby; after fifteen minutes it flew slowly away; 3 June 1920

OCHEYADAN RIVER   Boy saw black, hairy, 6-foot creature, possibly Bigfoot, drinking from its hands at the river. Footprints found later; 22 August 1976

PELLA BRIDGE, NEAR HARVEY (c.25 February), OTTOSEN (27 and 30 July, 11 and 12 September), DEAN BOTTOMS, NEAR MOULTON (28 August), SOUTH OF RENWICK

(27 September)   Bigfoot sighting locations in 1978

SIOUX CITY   Man in bed burst into flames; 1940s (see Ch. 4). Bigfoot sightings; August 1974

SPIRIT LAKE   Lake monster reports

STONE PARK AREA   Bigfoot sightings; summer 1971, January 1972, 1974

TURKEY CREEK AREA, NEAR LOCKRIDGE   Tractor driver saw Bigfoot at night; partially eaten turkeys found; 3 October 1975

Kansas

NEAR ABILENE   Kangaroo seen; 1 November 1971

COLDWATER   Twelve-year-old farmer's son returning from fields on tractor saw tiny man 20 feet away; he had long nose and long ears, and 'floated' to UFO and went inside; craft then took off; September 1954

DELIA   Truck-driver saw Bigfoot; 20 July 1964

DELPHOS   Boy on farm saw UFO hovering close to ground, where it left ring of glowing soil; 2 November 1971 (see Ch. 6)

IOLA   Miners on night shift saw creature having 'horns and long hair, great big eyes and an inhuman look, although standing erect like a man'. Apart from the horns, this could describe a Bigfoot; November 1903

KINGMAN COUNTY LAKE   Lake monster reports

NEAR LEAVENWORTH   Monster seekers saw 7–8-foot light-coloured Bigfoot; summer 1968

NEWTON   10-inch alligator found in basement; July 1970. Others seen in LITTLE ARKANSAS RIVER and 13TH STREET CREEK, WICHITA (July 1978), on INTERSTATE 70, OLATHE (summer 1978), and two boys found a dead alligator or caiman in a creek in south-east JOHNSON COUNTY, early March 1979

POTTAWATOMIE INDIAN RESERVE   Bigfoot sightings; c.1959

SALINA Large fireball struck building, exploded, and showered balls of fire around which floated away; 8 October 1919 (see Ch. 8). Gorilla-like creature left three-toed prints in witness's back yard; 18 July 1977

NEAR TOPEKA Frequent sightings of Bigfoot creature; mid- to late 1960s

WYANDOTTE COUNTY LAKE Hole 6 feet in diameter found in lake ice, and in ice on nearby farm pond; mid-February 1978

Kentucky

CUMBERLAND FALLS Two dissimilar stones cemented together fell from sky; 9 April 1919 (see Ch. 13)

DANVILLE Sightings of big cat – lion or cougar; summer 1966

GODMAN AIR FORCE BASE, NEAR FORT KNOX UFO chased by three F-51 planes led by Capt Thomas Mantell, who crashed; 7 January 1948 (see Ch. 3)

HERRINGTON LAKE, OHIO RIVER, REYNOLDS LAKE Lake monster reports

KELLY, NEAR HOPKINSVILLE Farmhouse besieged overnight by little men or 'goblins', possibly from UFO; 21 August 1955 (see Ch. 6)

LOUISVILLE Unnatural daytime darkness lasted for half an hour and terrified the city; 7 March 1911. Poltergeist outbreak, with objects floating in the air; January 1952. Bags of cookies fell from sky; November 1965 (see Ch. 13)

NEAR MILTON 15-foot 'lizard' running on two legs seen; October 1975 (see Ch. 14)

OLIVE HILL Poltergeist activity followed boy from house to house, including the movement of furniture and smashing of crockery; mid-November–?late December 1968 (see Ch. 1)

PARIS Fire spook burnt bedclothes and children's clothing with thirteen fires in three days; December 1958

PRESTONBURG Dog-like animal, possibly coyote/dog hybrid, attacked pony; spring 1978 (see Ch. 14)

STANFORD Three women driving late at night saw UFO and 'lost' 1 hour 25 minutes; under hypnosis they revealed they had been abducted into the UFO and subjected to examinations; 6 January 1976

TRIMBLE COUNTY Site of Bigfoot activity; June 1962. Other locations where Bigfoot seen pre-1981 include LICKING RIVER (1959), NEAR MOUNT VERNON (July 1962), MURRAY (1968), ALBANY (autumn 1973), HENDERSON COUNTY (1975), NEAR PEMBROKE (spring 1976), SIMPSON COUNTY (January 1977), NEAR OWENSBORO (August 1978), PENNYRILE PARKWAY, CHRISTIAN COUNTY (March 1979), BOONE COUNTY (1 April 1980), MAYSVILLE (October 1980), FLEMINGSBURG (October 1980)

Louisiana

BETWEEN ABBEVILLE AND LAFAYETTE On Highway 167, two men in car saw 1940 black auto, with woman driver and child wearing 1940-style clothes. Driver looked lost, so men indicated she should pull over. They halted ahead of her and looked back, but the car had vanished. Another driver behind the two cars saw the old car disappear suddenly; 20 October 1969

ALEXANDRIA Rain fell from a clear sky on house roof; 11 November 1958

ALGIERS Possible case of spontaneous human combustion: Glen B. Denney (46) had been drinking and was found with some arteries severed but no cause of fire could be found; 18 September 1952

CALCASIEU RIVER Water monster reports

GONZALES Ghost light moved along road and over treetops, dodging anyone who approached it; April 1951

HONEY ISLAND SWAMP Several sightings of Bigfoot-type creature, once coming out of the water and leaving large footprints; 1973. Tracks found 1981. Other places where Bigfoot seen pre-1981 include NEAR EAST BATON ROUGE (summer 1977), NEAR BELVILLE (October or November 1977), NEAR RICEVILLE (January 1978), NEAR CROWLEY (January 1978), NEAR KROTZ SPRINGS (4 June and November 1978)

MARINGOUIN Ghost of headless man often seen on railroad tracks near Bayou Ramah at night; July 1948–mid-1949

MARKSVILLE Fish fell from the sky; 23 October 1947 (see Ch. 13)

METAIRIE 4-foot alligator found on lawns, took an hour for police to capture it; September 1970

NEW ORLEANS Spontaneous combustion of police cars; early June 1980

ST JOHN THE BAPTIST PARISH Man and son shooting snakes in swamp saw tall, shaggy Bigfoot-type creature; 21 May 1981. Other sightings in the area reported (see Ch. 2)

SHREVEPORT Hard green peaches fell from the sky; 12 July 1961 (see Ch. 13)

Maine

BELFAST Round blue object fell from sky, causing fire; 10 May 1963

BOYDEN LAKE, CHAIN LAKES, MACHIAS LAKE, MOOSEHEAD LAKE, RANGELEY LAKE Lake monster reports

CASCO BAY Fishermen cruising 5 miles off Cape Elizabeth saw long-necked monster more than 100 feet long; it turned its head towards the sound of the lightship foghorn; they watched it for 45 minutes; 5 June 1958

DEER ISLE Possible case of spontaneous human combustion; 13 January 1943 (see Ch. 4)

NEAR DURHAM Woman and four children saw 5-foot black Bigfoot-type creature; she saw it again next day, and children had seen it before; July 1973. Other Bigfoot sightings pre-1981 occurred near FREEPORT (July 1974) and near MANCHESTER (22 September and November 1975)

KITTERY POINT Flames seen rising from the beach and surface of the sea; one foot high, they made a crackling noise and gave off sulphurous smell; lasted for more than 45 minutes; 1 September 1905

WESTPORT ISLAND Couple out walking saw black cat 2½ feet long and 18 inches tall; 30 August 1987. Other big cat sightings around WYTOPITLOCK

Maryland

BALTIMORE During thunderstorm, small oblong fireball rose from floor and attached itself to finger of woman standing indoors; it disappeared when lightning shone outside; 19 June 1924. Poltergeist outbreak; 14 January–9 February 1960

CALVERT COUNTY Ghostly voices found on tape after researcher visited haunted house; autumn 1986

CHESAPEAKE BAY Many sightings of sea monster 'Chesapeake Chessie', also known as 'Potomac Patty' (see Ch. 7)

CHEVERLY Technical writer saw UFO, glowing white circular object, which descended from the sky, stopped and was joined by second object; both then ascended again fast; 27 July 1975

CHEVY CHASE Following thunderstorm, ball of fire seen in woods; it exploded like dynamite when it hit tree; spring 1923 (see Ch. 8)

DUNDALK Boulder measuring 30 by 30 inches fell from sky; 27 January 1956 (see Ch. 13)

HAREWOOD PARK   Site of many sightings of Bigfoot-type creatures. Other popular Maryland locations include PATAPSCO VALLEY STATE PARK, WHITE MARSH, CHASE, and PARKVILLE. Researcher Mark Opsasnick of Maryland has recorded over 200 sightings of Bigfoot in the state this century

NEAR HEBRON   Ghost light seen 1 mile west of Hebron; 1902–52

INDIAN HEAD   Scientist at US Naval Ordnance Station and others saw spherical object moving fast between them and jet plane; August 1966

PARKTON   After explosion in sky, non-meteoritic metal fragments fell to earth; 11 August 1965

POINT LOOKOUT   Ghostly voices heard in lighthouse, and heard on tape; 1973–9 (see Ch. 11)

PRINCE GEORGES COUNTY   Hunters trailed wounded big cat which had killed and injured pigs; February 1930

RIVERDALE   4-foot crocodilian caught on sand bar; 4 December 1933. Two seen, one 7 feet long, in Herring Creek, on lower Potomac River; 18 November 1942

NEAR ROCKS STATE PARK   Bigfoot seen sorting through garbage behind restaurant; 6 February 1981 (see Ch. 2)

SCAGGSVILLE   9-foot hair-covered man-beast seen running across field and into wood; 18-inch, five-toed tracks found in nearby garden; 15 January 1988

SILVER SPRING   Intermittent poltergeist activity, including footprints found in sawdust – bare right foot, the left only a scuff mark; c.1966–76

Massachusetts

BOSTON   88 miles south/south-east of Boston lightship, captain of fishing trawler saw sea monster like gigantic eel, longer than his 136-foot boat; 24 May 1925

NEAR BRIDGEWATER   Numerous sightings of a 7-foot 'bear' or Bigfoot type of creature; it picked up the rear end of a police patrol car in the dark, and the officer saw it running away; December 1969–April 1970

NEAR BROCKTON   Small ape-like creature seen on island in lake called 'The Nip'; June 1980

CAMBRIDGE   Three-year-old child saw ghost of mother at the time of her burial; May 1906 (see Ch. 5)

DISMAL SWAMP, NEAR WARE   Sightings of crocodiles 6–8 feet long; 1922. Three crocodiles 1–3 feet long have been caught since then. Small crocodiles also caught on FRANCONIA GOLF COURSE, NEAR PALMER; 18 July 1937

DOVER   'Dover Demon' seen, a small being with a large head; April 1977 (see Ch. 9)

FRIZZLEBURY   Big cat seen; November 1944. Other reports come from REHOBOTH (1972) and TRURO (1981–2)

GLOUCESTER   Sea monster seen off Cape Ann: 70 feet long, slithering on top of water, like huge snake with fins and yellow dots; 7 July 1960. Numerous other sightings off Massachusetts coast, including LYNN BEACH, NANTUCKET, VINEYARD SOUND

HOCKOMOCK SWAMP   Giant snakes seen; e.g. 1939. In 1970 motorist ran over 8-foot boa constrictor (see Ch. 14)

HOLLISTON   8-pound armadillo found on lawn; 23 December 1978 (see Ch. 14)

LAWRENCE   Poltergeist outbreak; c. October–November 1963

LEE   Poltergeist with anti-religious tendencies caused chaos in household; apparitions seen; 1981 (see Ch. 1)

LEICESTER   Live frogs and toads fell from the sky; 7 September 1954

LOWELL   Old house haunted by ghosts of small boy in sailor suit and woman; 1979

MARSHFIELD   Hot porous rock fell from

sky, making a hole in the ground;
4 November 1983 (see Ch. 13)

MEDFORD, BOSTON   4-foot eel found in
water pipe in apartment house, and
two more found later; 14 June 1972
(see Ch. 14)

METHUEN   Water spurted throughout
house, and also wept from walls and
ceiling; 1963 (see Ch. 1)

NEWBURYPORT   Three short-lived
outbreaks of poltergeist phenomena
– strong wind indoors, loud crashing
noises; 1 October 1901, late
September 1903, 29 November 1904

NORTH CHELMSFORD   Shower of small
toads; 21 July 1933

NORTH READING   Blobs of jelly-like goo
found scattered around; 12–18
December 1983

NEAR OAK BLUFF   Man saw 30-foot
luminous cylinder floating on sea;
then it ascended, illuminating beach
and water; 27 March 1979

QUINCY, BOSTON   Mystery animal seen
near stream in cemetery; e.g.
16 November 1964

SOUTH ASHBURNHAM   Betty Andreasson
claimed encounter with UFO
entities who took her into UFO; the
details came back under hypnotic
regression; 25 January 1967 (see
Ch. 6)

SUDBURY   Sparkling, sticky 'angel hair'
drifted from the sky, and witness
saw shiny UFO moving off;
22 October 1973 (see Ch. 13)

NEAR SUDBURY   'Flaming basketball'
fell from sky near barn, which was
then destroyed by fire, and people
linked the two events; 28 April 1965

TWIN LAKES, SILVER LAKE   Lake
monster reports

Michigan

ALPENA   Ball lightning entered house
and moved around room in circles,
smashing holes in walls; 1 August
1907

AU TRAIN LAKE, BASSWOOD LAKE, LAKE
HURON, LAKE MICHIGAN, NARROW

LAKE, NICHOLS LAKE, PAINT RIVER,
LAKE SUPERIOR, SWAN LAKE,
WILLIAMS LAKE   Lake monster
reports

BENTON HARBOR   DC-4 destroyed when
flying on stormy night; people on
the ground saw ball of fire in the sky
beforehand; 23 June 1950

CASS RIVER, NEAR ENOS PARK   Bigfoot
walked in front of car; 1 May 1983

DETROIT   Dead shark found in filter at
Edison's Trenton Channel power
plant; June 1978 (see Ch. 14).
Woman motorist on I-94 at the
Michigan Metropolitan Airport saw
kangaroo hop across road; seen next
day by police; September 1984. One
also seen on campus of MICHIGAN
STATE UNIVERSITY, LANSING;
3 August 1968

FORT CUSTER RECREATION AREA   9-foot
hairy creature (Bigfoot?) seen on
several occasions near KALAMAZOO
RIVER, witnesses including recreation
supervisor and state trooper, who
saw it on a frozen pond; 1981

GENESEE COUNTY   Couple travelling
north from Cavison saw shaggy
black creature, possibly Bigfoot,
walking off road. It walked into
deep ditch as their vehicle
approached and they did not stop;
October 1984

GLADSTONE   Police officers followed
UFO, a glowing orange light
zigzagging across the sky; 12 March
1980

GRAND RAPIDS   Old mansion haunted
by footsteps and other noises, the
scent of roses, and by the ghost of
an elderly man in brown tweed;
ghost first seen autumn 1976 (see
Ch. 5)

LEXINGTON TOWNSHIP   6-foot creature,
possibly Bigfoot, threw German
shepherd dog; 15 December 1981
(see Ch. 2)

MILLINGTON   Boy cycling home at
night saw three Bigfeet walking
beside road; one 14-inch footprint
found; 4 September 1983

OAKLAND COUNTY   Many sightings of
alligators in lakes: 24-inch one

caught in ELIZABETH LAKE, 1953; at least two sightings in LOWER LONG LAKE, June/July 1955, and 57-inch one caught, 10 July 1957; 60–70 inch creature seen in ISLAND LAKE, 9 July 1955; 17-inch alligator caught in HARRIS LAKE, June 1956; 42-inch one caught in SUSIN LAKE, 4 August 1957; 36-inch one in SQUARE LAKE, August 1987. Other sightings and captures at MOUNT CLEMENS (October 1958), HINES PARK, DETROIT (18 November 1960), EAST LANSING (31 May 1967), CAPITOL BUILDING, LANSING (6 June 1968), and at CRYSTAL, ORION and WALLED LAKES

PAULDING Ghost light seen regularly – ghost of railway engineer, UFO, car lights, or what? (see Ch. 8)

PONTIAC Possible case of spontaneous human combustion; 13 December 1959 (see Ch. 4)

SAGINAW RIVER Fisherman suffered a nervous breakdown after seeing man-like creature climb up the bank, lean on a tree, then return to the river; 1937. One of the earliest sightings of a Bigfoot in the state. Other pre-1981 sighting locations include 'GORILLA SWAMP', CHARLOTTE (1951), NEAR MARSHALL (May 1956), SISTER LAKES, CASS COUNTY (May and June 1964), NEAR MONROE (13 August 1965), PORT HURON (24 April 1969), BAY CITY (summer 1973), NEW BUFFALO (autumn 1973), BARRYTON (1977), CARO (September 1977), MASON (1978), FOWLERVILLE (July and August 1978), CONCORD TOWNSHIP (August 1978), EVART (October and November 1978), MILLINGTON (October and December 1978), LANSING (December 1978), MAYVILLE (1979), BATTLE CREEK (7 November 1980)

ST CLAIR COUNTY Thirteen-year-old girl may have touched a Bigfoot in a barn on their farm; mid-November 1981 (see Ch. 2)

ST CLAIR RIVER 50-pound monkfish (salt water species) found alive in freshwater river; 16 June 1963

STURGIS Reports of panther-like animal; November 1947. Other locations where big cats have been seen include LEONARD, CANTON TOWNSHIP (August 1971), NEAR MICHIANA (February 1977), MANCHESTER (black panther on residential streets – May 1984), WIXOM (July 1984), FLINT (black panther – August and December 1984), MILFORD (black panther – July 1986), WATERFORD TOWNSHIP (black panther – August 1986), CLARE COUNTY (black panther – November and December 1986), LOON LAKE, OAKLAND COUNTY (April 1987)

NEAR STURGIS Two women driving at 3 a.m. saw strange phenomenon: rain of brown slime, smell of rotting eggs, car engine stopped, millions of small rays of 'lightning' flashed, reddish fluorescent glow in sky, grass standing straight up and glowing, lines of red light dancing on road, car hot to touch – low-level aurora display?; 10 June 1982

UPPER SCOTT LAKE, ALLEGAN COUNTY Following mystery explosion, hole in ice found, 40 feet across; 1 January 1970

WOODHAVEN Home bombarded by noise like sonic boom, every half-hour or so, which vibrated floor – not gas leak, or sewer gas, or plumbing, but possibly poltergeist?; April 1979

Minnesota

COON RAPIDS Kangaroos often seen in woods; 1957–67

NORTH OF FLOODWOOD Hunter saw a 4½-foot Bigfoot which jumped from a tree and walked into woods; 12 November 1968

GREAT SANDY LAKE Lake monster reports

ISLAND LAKE, NEAR DULUTH Tall white Bigfoot seen walking across yard; 26 January 1973

LA CRESCENT Hunter heard footsteps and saw huge black hairy Bigfoot –

he came up to the middle of its chest. He dropped his shotgun, which went off, and the Bigfoot ran away screaming; 1968

LAKEFIELD   Crocodilian shot at in stream; June 1941

LITTLE FALLS   Foil/tinsel fell from sky; 1 August 1957

NEAR LONG PRAIRIE   Man driving saw rocket-shaped UFO resting on fins in road, and three beer-can-shaped objects 6 inches high which came from under the craft towards him. They seemed to be watching him. Eventually they returned to the UFO, which took off; 23 October 1965

NEAR MARGIE   Man saw reddish Bigfoot in swamp; November 1978

MINNEAPOLIS   Frogs and toads fell 3 inches deep; 2 July 1901 (see Ch. 13). Two men tracking a balloon by plane saw bright glowing UFO, and a second one two hours later; 11 October 1953

BETWEEN OSAKIS AND EAGLE BEND   'Ball of fog' hit man's car like a shovel of fine gravel, with a blast and intense heat; 10 May 1961 (see Ch. 8)

NEAR ROCHESTER   Woman saw 7-foot Bigfoot illuminated in car headlights; 14 December 1979. South of Rochester, driver saw Bigfoot crouching over dead rabbit beside road; early 1969

ST CLOUD   Starfish fell in rainstorm; 21 April 1985 (see Ch. 13)

ST GEORGE   Deputy sheriff Arthur Strauch photographed UFO in presence of other witnesses; it was disc-shaped and silvery with a spinning outer rim; 21 October 1965

NEAR STEPHEN   Deputy sheriff Val Johnson, alone in car, saw bright light which shot towards him. He lost consciousness and skidded across the road. Afterwards, his eyes were irritated, a headlight was smashed, windscreen cracked and aerials bent. Other reports of balls of light 'attacking' cars in northern midwest; 27 August 1979

NEAR TOWER   Several youngsters saw white Bigfoot in woods; July 1972

Mississippi

NEAR BAY SPRINGS   Mystery animal attacked pigs, eating only their ears, but some animals survived the attacks; some farmers saw animal they could not identify: at least 6 feet long and waist high, large head with short ears, shaggy tail, black and grey in colour, and slightly dog-like; January–March 1977

NEAR COLDWATER   Man walking home on clear night saw ball of light come over fence and across road; he put his hand through it but felt nothing; 1929 or 1930 (see Ch. 8)

NEAR MERIDIAN   Truck-driver saw landed UFO with three propellers and three little men who came out of it. They seemed friendly but he could not understand their 'chattering'. They left and UFO took off straight up; 7 November 1957

MISSISSIPPI RIVER, PASCAGOULA RIVER   Water monster reports

PASCAGOULA   Charles Hickson and Calvin Parker saw UFO and entities while fishing in river at night; the silvery robot-like entities grabbed them and took them into craft, where Hickson was examined; 11 October 1973. In PASCAGOULA RIVER, USO 3 feet long with amber light seen moving; 6 November 1973 (see Ch. 10)

NEAR WINONA   Two men driving at night saw 7-foot Bigfoot running along roadside; it had red eyes; November 1966. Other locations of pre-1981 Bigfoot sightings in the state include GREENVILLE (June 1971), NATCHEZ (17 January 1977), JACKSON (August and December 1977), FLOWER LAKE, NEAR TUNICA (9–11 March 1979)

Missouri

NEAR ALTON   Early sighting of 'an animal that walks upright like a man, rather brown hair all over and with a face something like a monkey' – possible Bigfoot; June 1925. Other locations of pre-1981 Bigfoot sightings in Missouri include PINEY RIDGE (1947), KINLOCK (July 1968), HIGHWAY 79 NORTH OF LOUISIANA (July 1971), LOUISIANA (July 1972), NEAR NEW HAVEN (20 July 1972), NEAR O'FALLON (24 July 1972), PACIFIC (October 1975, 18 May 1977), OZARKS, WEST OF ST LOUIS (November 1980)

CEDAR HILL   Ghostly voice and laughter heard in haunted house; early 1980s

NEAR COLLINS   Mystery light called El Dorado Light occasionally seen on farm

LAKE CREVE COEUR, KANSAS RIVER, MISSISSIPPI RIVER, MISSOURI RIVER, LAKE OF THE OZARKS   Water monster reports

FESTUS, ST LOUIS   Small red-hot cylindrical object fell from sky; 26 May 1970

HARTVILLE   Poltergeist activity; June–August 1957

NEAR JOPLIN   Ozark Spooklight has appeared regularly near village of Hornet since 1886; like other ghost lights, it disappears when approached (see Ch. 8)

KANSAS CITY   Object 2 feet long and 1 inch in diameter flew into room with sound of 'crushing glass'; it hovered as it changed into a ball, then dissolved, again with sound of crushing glass but no glass was broken – ball lightning?; 1959

ROCK HILL, ST LOUIS   18-inch heavy chain fell from sky; 15 May 1959 (see Ch. 13)

ST LOUIS   Great quantities of material like spider-webs floated out of the sky, mostly dissolving on touching the ground, which spider-webs would not do; material analysed found not to be of biological origin; October 1969

SPRINGFIELD   Twelve cobras and one boa found in small area; 1953

UNION   Woman driving on Highway 50 felt impact on back of car, then felt it rise by one foot or more. It swayed and vibrated, and she saw a bright light which rose above car and disappeared. Then car returned to ground. Car was unharmed but driver was shocked; 27 July 1978

WASHINGTON COUNTY   7-foot cougar seen crossing road; May 1955. Other sightings in early 1950s, e.g. in OZARK AND LINCOLN COUNTIES. Sightings of big black cat in LONE JACK area; early 1980

WELLESVILLE   During thunderstorm, 'lightning picture', looking like a portrait of church sexton, appeared on ceiling of Episcopal church. He was at home opposite when lightning struck in church; August, turn of century

Montana

BUTTE   Live toad found in rock 200 feet down in silver mine when shaft was being sunk; there was no fissure in the rock; May 1907

NEAR CASCADE   Woman saw huge snake 20–30 feet long which struck at her car; October 1978 (see Ch. 14)

FLATHEAD LAKE, MISSOURI RIVER, WATERTON LAKE   Water monster reports

GLENDIVE   Spontaneous outbreaks of fire in house; January 1958

GREAT FALLS   Nicholas Mariana filmed two silvery discs flying over the ball park, but it has never been determined if they were 'true' UFOs or not; 15 August 1950

KALISPELL   Three hikers saw large ape-like creature, possibly Bigfoot, fording waist-deep river; 9 June 1985

ROCKY BOY   Large four-toed footprints found, and possible Bigfoot seen; April 1981 (see Ch. 2)

SEELEY LAKE   Bear hunter saw 8-foot Bigfoot in the woods, but did not shoot at it; 1959. Other locations of pre-1981 Bigfoot sightings in Montana include LOST TRAIL PASS (November 1962 and September 1969), BROWN'S GULCH (17 May 1964), GRID CREEK (August 1964), NEAR BILLINGS (11 September 1968), NEAR COLUMBIA FALLS (1960s), BITTERROOT MOUNTAINS (September 1974), BOOTLEGGER TRAIL (December 1974), VAUGHN (26 December 1975 and 7 March 1976), ULM (21 February 1976), NEAR GREAT FALLS AIRPORT (22 February 1976), NEAR SUN RIVER (22 February 1976), GREAT FALLS (March and 28 July 1976), EAST HELENA (4 April 1976), NEAR RAINBOW DAM (21 July 1976), PFEILING GULCH (July 1976), NEAR GERBER (spring 1977), SILVER CITY (14 June 1977), BELT CREEK CANYON (20 August 1977)

Nebraska

ALKALI LAKE, MISSOURI RIVER   Water monster reports

NEAR ASHLAND   Police patrolman Herbert Schirmer saw UFO and experienced time loss; under hypnosis he remembered being taken aboard and had talks with entities who said they were getting electricity from power lines; 3 December 1967

COUNCIL BLUFFS   Three falls of blobs of molten metal; 17 December 1977, 5 July 1978, 10 July 1978

FALLS CITY   Man saw human-like form with wings like polished aluminium fly overhead; autumn 1956 (see Ch. 9)

HARLON COUNTY LAKE, REPUBLICAN CITY   12-inch piranha fish found in lake; September 1987

KEARNEY   Reinhold Schmidt claimed to have seen landed UFO 30 feet wide, on four legs, and with staircase down which came two men who took him inside. There were four people, ordinary-looking men and women, inside who told him they were doing no harm, and he would know all about it in a short time. Then they asked him to leave, and the UFO took off; 5 November 1957

LINCOLN   Lemur found 'in convulsions' in yard, and later died; 12 November 1931 (see Ch. 14). Psychical researcher heard ghostly footsteps and felt 'wave of extremely intense energy' followed by 'a pure fear' and he ran from the building, at Nebraska Wesleyan University; early 1972

MACY   Three-toed tracks 15 inches long, possibly made by Bigfoot, found; June 1986

PLATTE RIVER, NEAR GRAND ISLAND   6-foot kangaroo seen around cabin; 28 July 1958. Other sightings at ENDICOTT, STANTON and FAIRBURY

RAVENNA   Boy out hunting saw white Bigfoot with black hands and face; seen same day by independent witness; 13 December 1959. Other locations of pre-1981 Bigfoot sightings include MINERSVILLE (November 1968, August 1969), GERING (September 1972), CRETE (April 1973), FORT CALHOUN (October 1973), OAKLAND (August 1974), YORK (September 1974), NORTH OF NEBRASKA CITY (June 1975), LINCOLN (December 1975, August 1976, July 1980)

SURPRISE   Farmer saw maned lion, and woman saw lion and mate in town; also seen in RISING CITY; summer 1954. On 12 November 1951 there was a lion hunt near CERESCO, not far away

NEAR UTICA   6-foot creature with long hair, glowing yellow eyes, and goat-like from waist down, seen – Bigfoot?; December 1982

Nevada

DIAMOND MOUNTAINS   Bigfoot seen and 15-inch footprints found; early 1960s

NEAR MCDERMITT   Ghost lights seen on Oregon Canyon Ranch

LAKE MEAD, PEGRAND LAKE, PYRAMID LAKE, WALKER LAKE   Lake monster reports

NEVADA TEST SITE   Workman saw dark-haired 6–7 foot Bigfoot walking across road; 23 January 1980

SOUTH-EAST OF LAKE TAHOE   Two couples saw 7–8 foot Bigfoot with long shiny black hair and flat leathery face at roadside; 29 July 1973

WALKER LAKE   Frogs fell from sky in rainstorm; summer 1983

New Hampshire

CENTRAL SANDWICH   Boy saw 6–7 foot 'gorilla-looking' creature, possibly Bigfoot; *c*.1942

DERRY   Man gathering Christmas trees in wood saw green dwarf; 15 December 1956 (see Ch. 9)

EXETER   Huge, silent UFO with flashing red lights followed car for 12 miles before taking off at speed; young man saw similar object, and when he and police patrolmen returned to the site, they saw it together when it rose from behind trees and approached within 100 feet; 3 September 1965, and other similar sightings during the autumn

FITZWILLIAM   During thunderstorm, ball lightning seen by house, 'round, bronze, glistening ball with gleaming rays shooting from the top and sides' like Christmas-tree ornament; 10 August 1937

NEAR FREEPORT   Bigfoot seen in car lights at close range; July 1974

HANOVER/COLEBROOK/WHITE MOUNTAIN   Sightings of big cat – mountain lion, Canadian lynx, or bobcat?; August 1983

HOLLIS   Bigfoot shook camper where family was sleeping; seen in lights, it was 8–9 feet tall and stepped over 4½-foot fence with ease; 7 May 1977

MANCHESTER   Possible case of spontaneous human combustion; December 1949 (see Ch. 4)

PITTSFIELD   Poltergeist outbreak, with small objects moving around; early 1971

SALISBURY   Pheasant-hunter saw Bigfoot; October 1987 (see Ch. 2)

WAKEFIELD   Mystery hole found in ice on pond, and farmer claimed to have seen flat black object 2 feet square in the water below; 10 January 1977

WHITE MOUNTAINS   Betty and Barney Hill saw UFO while driving at night; later under hypnosis they discovered they had been taken aboard for medical examination; 19 September 1961

New Jersey

BARNEGAT BAY   Teenager saw big silvery object splash into the water, making a low rumbling noise; 18 April 1979

BUTLER   Disembodied voice heard in cemetery; July 1924 (see Ch. 11)

CALDWELL   Nylon line seen hanging in the sky; August 1970 (see Ch. 13)

CLIFTON   Fires kept breaking out in house's electrical fixtures, even when power cut off; beginning 31 January 1988 (see Ch. 4)

NEAR DOVER   Possible case of spontaneous human combustion; December 1916 (see Ch. 4)

EVERITTSTOWN   Man saw egg-shaped UFO hovering in front of barn, and 3-foot entity with frog-like eyes who said in broken English that he was peaceful and only wanted the dog. Witness replied: 'Get the hell out of here.' Wife of witness saw UFO but not entity, though she heard the voices; 6 November 1957

GREENWICH   Farmer killed animal which was stealing his chickens, but no one could identify it; December 1925 (see Ch. 14)

HACKENSACK MEADOWS   31-inch alligator killed; September 1929.

Crocodilians seen and killed at PASSAIC RIVER; 11 September 1933. 2-foot alligator captured in streets of GLASSBORO; August 1978. 3-foot specimen caught at LINDEN; November 1978. 5-foot one seen at EDISON; 24 August 1980

HACKETTSTOWN   Poltergeist activity including ghostly entities being seen and voices heard; February 1973–1978 (see Ch. 11)

HAZLET   House bombarded often with large rocks and concrete debris; June 1978 (see Ch. 16)

MAYS LANDING   Small kangaroo seen on farm, and heard screaming; strange tracks often found leading to swamp; 1900

MONTCLAIR   Poltergeist outbreak; April 1918–at least 1925

NEWARK   Poltergeist activity with household objects being thrown; 6 May–September 1961 (see Ch. 1)

NEWTON   Buckshot fell indoors over several days; March 1929

NORTH SHREWSBURY RIVER, PASSAIC FALLS   Water monster reports

LAKE OBERST, GLASSBORO   Spherical glowing UFO landed briefly; crater 18 inches deep found there afterwards; 4 September 1964

RARITAN   Nails fell from the sky; July 1955 (see Ch. 13)

RIO GRANDE   Poltergeist outbreak in gift-shop, often affecting equipment, like sewing machine which started up and began to sew, unattended; 1979

NEAR SALEM   Bigfoot shook car while driver changed tyre; c.1927. Other locations of pre-1981 Bigfoot sightings include PINE BARRENS (1950s), MORRISTOWN (1965, 21 May 1966), LOWER BANK (autumn 1966), VINELAND (July 1972), MIDDLETOWN (22 October 1973), BEAR SWAMP (February 1975), NEAR RUTHERFORD (summer 1975), WHITE MEADOW LAKE (summer 1976), WANTAGE TOWNSHIP (12 and 13 May 1977)

SOMERVILLE   Big cat, variously described as lion, tiger or panther, seen by numerous witnesses; July

1921. Other locations where big cats have been seen include PASSAIC (1931), STANHOPE (black panther – 1977, 1978, 1979), LACY TOWNSHIP (black panther, seen by police officers – November 1983), MAURICE RIVER area, especially VINELAND and PITTSGROVE TOWNSHIP (June 1987), NEW EGYPT (late February–mid April 1988)

SUSSEX COUNTY   Two fishermen saw Bigfoot in car headlights; 23 May 1981 (see Ch. 2)

TRENTON, CAMDEN, WOODBURY, BURLINGTON, GLOUCESTER, and other places on the border with Pennsylvania, and including BRISTOL (PA)   Winged monster 'Jersey Devil' seen; January 1909. Also in Trenton, there was a fall of tiny toads in a rain shower; c.1930

UNIONPORT   Lightning struck woman and left figures on her arm resembling pheasant, snake, and Chinese letters; June 1906

LAKE WANAQUE   Ghost lights seen on hills to west

WAYNE   Poltergeist activity followed family from previous home in Brooklyn – with footsteps, knockings, and objects flying round; 1971. Near Wayne, 'Lizardman' seen in 1970s (see Ch. 14)

NEAR WEST ORANGE   Mystery animal seen, possibly a kangaroo; 2 July 1924 (see Ch. 14)

New Mexico

ANTHONY AREA   Sightings of 'ape with long black wavy fur', possibly Bigfoot; summer 1968

ARREY   Naval scientist and others saw white UFO through theodolite; they were tracking a balloon and were sure the object was no balloon; 24 April 1949

ARTESIA   Black 7-foot Bigfoot with white eyes seen standing in alley; October 1980

CHUSKA MOUNTAINS   Shepherds shot at 8-foot Bigfoot which ran wounded into canyon and was helped by two others; late 1960s, more activity 1971

CIMARRON   Poltergeist phenomena in St James Hotel; 1980s

DULCE   Mutilated cow corpse discovered, and owner also found triangular groups of prints as if a machine (UFO?) had landed; June 1976

NEAR GALLUP   Toads fell in a sudden shower of rain and hail; June 1949

NEAR HOBBS   Two alligators were living in swamp; October 1976

LOS ALAMOS   Many sightings of mysterious green fireballs here and at other top secret facilities in the American south-west; 1948–9

LOVINGTON   Red 'fireball' seen, and hundreds of rocks fell around house; 1942 (see Ch. 16)

ROSWELL   Small portrait of Christ began to bleed; 25 and 26 May 1979

SITTING BULL FALLS   Bigfoot seen by campers; October 1980

SOCORRO   Patrolman Lonnie Zamora saw UFO land in desert, and entity beside it; it took off with a loud roar; 24 April 1964

TUCUMCARI   Fireball came to earth beside 30-foot-high water tank which collapsed, demolishing twenty buildings and killing four people; no meteoritic fragments found; 13 December 1951

VALLECITOS   Explosion heard in field, and mud and grass thrown out a quarter of a mile away leaving crater 8 feet deep and 75 feet across; July 1983

WHITEWATER   Bigfoot ran beside car at 45 mph until occupants shot at it; January 1970

OVER THE DESERT   Jetliner in sky was hit by a foreign body, presumably from above, causing an engine to fall off; 17 April 1985

New York

ALBANY   UFOs seen by civilians, police, military personnel, pilot, and on radar; 20 August 1975. Ghostly phenomena experienced in NEW YORK STATE CAPITOL BUILDING

BLACK RIVER, LAKE CHAMPLAIN ('Champ'), EAST CAROGA LAKE, LAKE GEORGE, HUDSON RIVER, MAZINAW LAKE, LAKE ONONDAGO, LAKE ONTARIO, SILVER LAKE, SPIRIT LAKE, WADING RIVER, LAKE OF THE WOODS Water monster reports

BRONX, NEW YORK   Clothes, jewellery and cash stolen from the Koch apartment. Two days later a light was seen in the apartment when the occupants were out; detectives converged on the building and entered the apartment, to find no one there. But Mrs Koch found that the stolen clothing was back in the closet; May 1903. Poltergeist outbreak; 9 February–c. April 1974

BROOKLYN, NEW YORK   Little elephant seen in Bay Ridge Section, but search found nothing; 2 May 1979 (see Ch. 14)

BUFFALO   Boys found small fishes in puddles in the streets after hard shower; summer 1900. Another fish fall seen on 29 September 1939

CHERRY CREEK   Sixteen-year-old boy milking cows saw beeping UFO landing nearby. 50 feet long and football-shaped, it shot up again after seconds, leaving a strange smell, burned grass and marks in the soil; 19 August 1965

CITY ISLAND, NEW YORK CITY   Sea captain saw big black sea monster which dived and came up under his boat; 10 August 1902 (see Ch. 7)

NEAR CLARENDON   Tiny frogs fell in rain shower; 5 October 1937

COLONIE   Booms like artillery shells heard frequently in house, usually at night, causing vibrations in ground – gas, sewer, water, electric lines checked without success; August–September 1984

CONKLIN   Five young boys saw UFO and entity in field; creature made noise like a kazoo; 16 July 1964

DEXTER   7-foot Bigfoot seen near hardware store; 3 August 1983

DUTCHESS COUNTY   Bigfoot seen on several occasions; 8–9 feet tall, it approached a pick-up carrying a 4-foot stick; January 1971. Other locations of pre-1981 Bigfoot sightings in the state include RICHMONDTOWN, STATEN ISLAND (7 December 1974 and 21 January 1975), WATERTOWN (January 1975 and 10 August 1976), NEAR SARANAC LAKE (June 1975), WHITEHALL (24 and 25 August 1976), NEAR OXBOW (autumn 1976), NEAR THERESA (27 and 28 June 1977)

ELMIRA   Fall of cardboard-like substance from sky; 27 August 1956

HEMPSTEAD   Three icons of Virgin Mary in private house wept for a week or more; March–May 1960

IRVINGTON   Unique octagonal house haunted by two ghosts, one heralded by a delicate scent; 1966

ISLAND PARK   Woman praying before portrait of the Virgin Mary saw the eyes open and tears flow; they vanished on reaching the bottom of the frame; March 1960 (see Ch. 15)

KINGSTON   Possible case of spontaneous human combustion; January 1930 (see Ch. 4)

LANCASTER   Possible case of spontaneous human combustion; 1 February 1943 (see Ch. 4)

LAWRENCEBURG   White Bigfoot seen at night in woods; footprints found later; 4 June 1984 (see Ch. 2)

LONG ISLAND SOUND   Witnesses at Rye saw large object with two white lights and one red light plunge into water; 22 June 1957 (see Ch. 10)

MIDDLETOWN   Crocodile caught in small creek; September 1927. Many other reports of crocodiles or alligators being caught, killed or seen, e.g. PORT JERVIS (2 July 1929), WOLCOTT (September 1929), PLEASANTVILLE (22 March 1931), BRONX RIVER (28 June 1932), CRESTWOOD LAKE, WESTCHESTER (1 July 1932), YONKERS (7 March 1935), EAST 123RD STREET, NEW YORK (alligator found in sewer, 9 February 1935 – see Ch. 14),

GRASS SPRAIN, WESTCHESTER (March 1935), EAST RIVER HARBOR, NEW YORK (1 June 1937), BROOKLYN MUSEUM SUBWAY STATION (6 June 1937), HUGUENOT LAKE, NEW ROCHELLE (11 August 1938), LAKE MINDOWASKIN, WESTFIELD (16 August 1942), RED HOOK, NEAR KINGSTON (4 August 1970), KENSICO RESERVOIR, VALHALLA (August 1982), BERNE (18 June 1983), CARROON LAKE, MASSAPEQUA, LONG ISLAND (July and August 1984)

NEWARK VALLEY   Dairy farmer Gary T. Wilcox was in fields when he saw shiny egg-shaped UFO 20 feet long on the ground, with two small men beside it. They carried trays of what looked like soil. One spoke and said they were from Mars and were interested in farming. He asked for fertilizer, and when Wilcox went to get some, the UFO took off. He left the fertilizer in the field and next day it had gone; 24 April 1964

NEW YORK   Table-tipping experiments followed by poltergeist outbreaks, with small objects like needles and pins flying around, some from a locked drawer; 11 December 1907–May 1909 (see Ch. 1). Ghostly woman in audience at Metropolitan Opera House spoke to her neighbour; c.1955 (see Ch. 11). Woman arriving early at an office on East 62nd Street on her first day at work saw the ghost of the late Angelo Donghia, interior designer, who she thought was the porter when he let her into the locked building; October 1987. Off New York, ship's crew saw flat UFO rise from the ocean; c. August 1954 (see Ch. 10)

NIAGARA FALLS   Fish found on ground after downpour; witness fed them to his cat; 24 May 1933

NORTH GREENBUSH   Papers bearing mathematical formulae floated slowly out of the sky; 24 July 1973 (see Ch. 13)

ROCKAWAY SHOALS, LONG ISLAND   Sea monster with head as large as a barrel seen close to yacht; 18 June 1913. Another seen off Montauk Point, 1929 (see Ch. 7)

ROUTE 22, ADIRONDACKS   Bigfoot dashed across road and was spotted by police officers in car; February 1982 (see Ch. 2)

SAGETOWN   Falls of foil/tinsel from sky; 27 August and 3 October 1956

SEAFORD, LONG ISLAND   Poltergeist outbreak; February and April 1958

SENECA LAKE   Phenomenon known as 'lake gun' heard for decades – like the explosion of a heavy piece of artillery, usually heard on hot, sultry days

SKANEATELES LAKE   Men fishing were bombarded by stones, which followed them to their homes; 28 October 1973 (see Ch. 16)

SYRACUSE   Ghosts seen in Loew's Theater; 1978. In the Syracuse area there have been occasional sightings of black panthers over many years; other locations where big cats have been seen include NEW ROCHELLE (1922), MALVERNE (June 1931), VAN ETTEN SWAMP (1977), GALWAY (November 1980), HAMMOND (black panther, March 1985), DEPOSIT (black panther, winter 1986–7)

TITICUS RESERVOIR, WESTCHESTER COUNTY   Couple fishing at night saw luminous sphere rise from the water only yards from their boat and splash back; there were other strange lights seen; 16–17 September 1955

VENICE CENTER   Craters appeared in field following loud explosions, all on 12 November in three consecutive years; third explosion heard 20 miles away and left crater 18 feet wide and 5 feet deep; 1966, 1967, 1968

North Carolina

ASHEBORO   UFO seen to settle in creek with bubbling sound; 19 July 1962

ASHEVILLE   Prisoners claimed jail was haunted; jailers admitted strange noises had been heard; April 1908 (see Ch. 5)

BILTMORE   Kangaroo seen, but not caught; 9 October 1981

BLADENBORO   Fire spook at house, with curtains, bedclothes, tablecloths, etc., spontaneously bursting into flame; January 1932 (see Ch. 4)

BLUE RIDGE MOUNTAINS, SOUTH OF ASHEVILLE   'Brown Mountain Lights' a famous mystery, with many experiments this century to try to identify them (see Ch. 8)

CAPE HATTERAS   East of Cape, steamer *Santa Clara* collided with sea monster and sea was stained red; 30 December 1947

CHARLOTTE   Foam-like object, one of five floating in sky, landed and was seen to be a slimy, thick liquid; 20 March 1957 (see Ch. 13)

CLAYTON   Strange lights, possibly of a poltergeist nature, flashed inside house; early June–16 July 1962

NEAR CONCORD   Glittering object descended into lake and was seen to disintegrate; September 1962 (see Ch. 10)

NEAR DREXEL   Deputy sheriff and volunteer deputy saw 6-foot grey Bigfoot cross road in front of their car; 14 January 1972. Other locations of pre-1981 Bigfoot sightings in the state include SOUTH MOUNTAIN (1974 and earlier years, and spring 1979), MOUNT HOLLY (30 July 1976), CAPE FEAR RIVER AREA, CHATHAM COUNTY (1976), CARPENTER'S KNOB, TOLUCA (December 1978), CASAR (December 1978 and January 1979)

DUNN   Boy saw little man in cornfield; 12 October 1976 (see Ch. 9)

FORT FISHER   Rumbling boom heard, shaking houses, sometimes as often as once or twice a week, along south-east coast

FRANKLIN   Taped messages from the dead obtained in Spiricom experiments; early 1980s (see Ch. 11)

GASTONIA French coin fell from the sky; October 1958 (see Ch. 13)

LITTLE TENNESSEE RIVER, VALLEY RIVER Water monster reports

NEAR MCADENVILLE Floating ghost light seen, associated with ghost story

MACO Ghost light reported along railway line, said to be ghost of railwayman with lantern (see Ch. 8)

MATTHEWS Man and daughter saw baboon walking along road on all fours; next day, boys saw 'monkey' drop out of tree; but police and several others found nothing; 8 and 9 August 1977

RAEFORD Giant cat was killing sheep; February 1953. Female big cat with kittens seen in PISGAH NATIONAL FOREST; 1975. In April 1984 a big cat with yellow fur and dark spots (cheetah?) was seen in WINSTON-SALEM

RED SPRINGS Man and two children saw disc-shaped UFO hovering close by with entity inside; December 1951

SIDNEY Non-human entity seen on several occasions, with red glowing eyes, grey face, pointed ears and hooked nose, with one hand missing and walking with a limp. It could leap 50–60 feet, and had a medallion on its chest used for communication and disappearing; 20–26 September 1973

STANLEY Fall of tiny toads from sky; summer 1961

NEAR SWAINSVILLE Possible Bigfoot seen by several witnesses; September 1981

THOMASVILLE Workers in furniture factory saw 6-foot ghost with blurred features; one man saw him 50 times; 1972–82 (see Ch. 5)

WALKER MOUNTAIN Huge glowing lights at least 200 feet in diameter seen; 1983 onwards

WARSAW Ghost train seen occasionally in early decades of the century

WILMINGTON Female ghost seen in library; 1982, 1983, 1985 (see Ch. 5)

North Dakota

ABSARAKA At night, boys peeked into abandoned Methodist church and saw a 'big light . . . in the sign of the cross'; adults came and saw it too, and could find no logical explanation; visitors were attracted from some distance; November 1987

NEAR CANNONBALL RIVER Men chased 8–9 foot Bigfoot in pickup. It ran 'as fast as a horse' and leapt across a creek; September 1977

DEVIL'S LAKE, LAKE SAKAKAWEA Lake monster reports

FARGO George T. Gorman, flying F-51 fighter plane, engaged in dogfight with 'UFO' which may have been a weather balloon and/or Jupiter; 1 October 1948 (see Ch. 3)

BETWEEN FARGO AND KINDRED Ghost light seen on road; 1968

KILLDEER MOUNTAINS People in sleigh saw large gorilla-like animal which first ran towards them, then ran off through snow leaving huge man-like tracks; c.1900

Ohio

ASHTABULA COUNTY Bigfoot-like creatures besieged lonely farmhouse; June 1981

AYERSVILLE Mysterious flows of water inside house – on floors, on top of piano, inside drawers – and plumber could find no leak; 5–10 July 1975 (see Ch. 1)

BRANCH HILL, NEAR LOVELAND Car headlights lit up three non-human figures by roadside; March 1955 (see Ch. 9)

CHARLES MILL LAKE, LAKE ERIE, OHIO RIVER, OLENTANGY RIVER, SLAVEN'S POND Water monster reports

CINCINNATI Rain of reddish oily liquid which damaged peach trees; 22 July 1955 (see Ch. 13)

CLEVELAND Miraculous music said to be heard from girl's grave in Calvary Cemetery; November 1936. Corrugated aluminium fell from sky; 25 July 1963

COLUMBUS Controversial poltergeist activity centring on fourteen-year-old Tina Resch; household items smashed; March 1984

COSHOCTON AREA Numerous Bigfoot sightings in 1987

CUYAHOGA RIVER Witnesses saw 18-foot python in fields between Akron and Cleveland; summer 1944 (see Ch. 14)

DEFIANCE 'Werewolf' seen: 7–9 feet tall, very hairy, with fangs. It ran 'from side to side' and carried a big stick over its shoulder, with which it hit a railway worker; July and August 1972

FINDLY 6-foot Nile monitor in pond was killed by shooting; February 1984 (see Ch. 14)

GREENSBURG Endless length of fishing line stretched up into the sky; September 1978 (see Ch. 13)

HARRISONVILLE Showers of stones fell on village over several days; October 1901 (see Ch. 16)

LITTLE MIAMI RIVER, NEAR LOVELAND Police officers saw giant frog or lizard; 3 March 1972 and two weeks later (see Ch. 14)

LOCKLAND Possible case of spontaneous human combustion; 3 August 1962 (see Ch. 4)

LORAIN COUNTY Big cat was killing dogs, cats and sheep; summer 1959. Other locations of big cat sightings include CROESBECK (lion, April 1971), BLUFFTON AREA (spring 1977), WESTERVILLE (June 1979), WELLSTON (early 1980s), NORTH OLMSTED, CLEVELAND (lion, July 1984), NORTH AVONDALE (November–December 1984)

NEAR LOUDONVILLE Ghost light seen over fields and woods over thirteen years

MANSFIELD Army helicopter crew narrowly missed colliding with UFO; 18 October 1973 (see Ch. 3)

NEAR MONROE Kangaroo hopped across road in front of car, but no trace could be found; late May 1968. One had also been seen outside GROVE CITY; January 1949

NEWCOMERSTOWN AREA Fifteen Bigfoot sightings within 5-mile radius of town during 1984–6

NEW PHILADELPHIA Ghostly voices heard in haunted house; 1970

NEAR PADANARAM Man saw tall, hairy creature, possibly Bigfoot, wade into water and swim to small island; 1954. Other locations of pre-1981 Bigfoot sightings include OHIO RIVER, CINCINNATI (February 1959), MANSFIELD (March 1959, 1963, August 1973), MILFORD (1964 and 4 April 1976), WAYNE NATIONAL FOREST (1966), CLEVELAND (22 April 1968), SALEM (spring 1968), POINT ISABEL (autumn 1968), LORAIN (9 November 1968), SOUTH OF HURON (October 1970), TOLEDO AND DEFIANCE (July and August 1972), BROOKSIDE PARK, CLEVELAND (August 1972), IRONTON (November 1972), DUBLIN (November 1972 and 1973), NEW LONDON (August 1973), OBERLIN (August 1973), MASSILLON (October 1973), WOODLAWN AREA (February 1976), ALLIANCE (March 1977), NELSON TOWNSHIP (8 March 1977), NEAR EATON (May 1977), BUTLER (July 1978), NEAR MINERVA (21 August 1978), UNION COUNTY (June 1980), RUSSELLS POINT (19 June 1980), LOGAN COUNTY (26 June 1980), NEAR LISBON (July 1980), SOUTH WAYNE NATIONAL FOREST (August and October 1980), NEAR LIMA (1980)

PLEASANTVILLE Possible case of spontaneous human combustion; 1956

ROME Reports of Bigfoot 7–9 feet tall which was terrorizing livestock; June–July 1981

WESTERVILLE White stone cylinder fell from sky; 1910 (see Ch. 13)

XENIA 3-foot crocodile caught in Huffman Pond; 6 July 1936

Oklahoma

ADA Ghost lights seen on Bushy Ranch; 1962

ALVA   Fire spook haunted invalid lady; March 1922 (see Ch. 4)

ARAPAHO   Ghostly voice heard in cemetery; 1972 onwards (see Ch. 11)

BEAVER COUNTY   Farmer often saw ghost lights; early years of century (see Ch. 8)

CALUMET   Woman saw 'cross between wolf and deer'; 1951 (see Ch. 14). Man saw 30-inch female chimpanzee in the woods several times; he left food for it and tried to catch it; February 1971

NEAR CHEYENNE   Men saw mystery animal, dark in colour and walking on four legs; 1982 (see Ch. 14)

NEAR CLAREMORE   Woman in car picked up young boy hitch-hiker who disappeared from the car; winter 1965 (see Ch. 5)

NEAR CONNERVILLE   Bigfoot sighting; August 1981

EAGLETOWN   9-foot crocodile killed in Rock Creek; July 1949

EL RENO   Black cat-like animal seen by farmer and son harvesting wheat; 1956. Other locations where big cats seen include DRUMRIGHT (black panther, 1976), TALIHINA (black panther, January 1977), MCCURTAIN COUNTY (black panther, June 1980)

LAKE EUFAULA   Lake monster reports; 1973

NEAR KENTON   Ghost lights seen 8 miles to east and 15 miles to south-west

LAWTON   Ape-like creature wearing trousers seen running through town and drinking from fish pond; February 1971

NOWATA AREA   Bigfoot encounters; autumn 1983

NEAR SAND SPRINGS   Ghost light seen 2 miles to west; 1954

SOUTH CANADIAN RIVER, NEAR NORMAN   4½-foot crocodile killed; November 1901

TULSA   Man saw two kangaroos and hit one (3½ feet tall) with his truck; he put it in the truck where two police officers and others saw it before he drove away; 31 August 1981. Family

in nearby OWASSO then said they often saw 3-foot kangaroos while making early morning newspaper deliveries

SOUTH OF VICI   Bigfoot sightings around rural property; the animal smelled like a sewer; early 1982

SOUTH-EAST OF WANN   Early sighting of Bigfoot near house gate; c.1915. Other locations of pre-1981 Bigfoot sightings in the state include NEAR GOODWATER (spring 1926), MOUNTAIN FORK RIVER (1926), NEAR WILBERTON (c.1956), NEAR NELAGONY (1967), BETWEEN OAKWOOD AND CANTON (November 1968), TALIHINA (1970), WATOVA SETTLEMENT NEAR NOWATA (1974–80), NEAR INDIANOLA (September 1975), NOXIE (September and October 1975), NEAR MOUTH OF YASHAU CREEK, LITTLE RIVER (1975), OKEMAH LAKE (spring 1976), STILWELL (August 1977)

Oregon

CRATER LAKE, CRESCENT LAKE, FORKED MOUNTAIN LAKE, HOLLOW BLOCK LAKE, UPPER KLAMATH LAKE, WALLOWA LAKE   Lake monster reports

GRANTS PASS   Motorcyclist saw Bigfoot on the road; 23 October 1983 (see Ch. 2)

MCMINNVILLE   Paul Trent photographed UFO; 11 May 1950 (see Ch. 3)

PORTLAND   Poltergeist outbreak; 28 October, 20 November 1909. China-like fragments fell from the sky; 21 July 1920 (see Ch. 13)

ROGUE RIVER, NEAR GOLD BEACH   Five people fishing saw 'silver dollar' UFO, and two of them, engineers, looked at it through binoculars. It had a fin, but no other details were noted; 24 May 1949

SIXES RIVER AREA   Miners saw 9-foot hairy 'animal-man' drinking at stream; 1900. This is probably the earliest Bigfoot sighting in Oregon this century, and was followed by dozens more sightings pre-1981, some other locations being YANKTON, TILLAMOOK HEAD, TOOD LAKE, MOUNT ASHLAND, WANOGA BUTTE, CONSER LAKE, ALPINE, LEBANON, ESTACADA, THE DALLES, CLACKAMAS RIVER, ROGUE RIVER, WILSONVILLE, COOS BAY, TIMOTHY LAKE, CASCADE MOUNTAINS, MCKENZIE RIVER VALLEY, COLLOWASH RIVER, ROWENA, DABNEY STATE PARK, RAINIER, MOUNT HOOD

TILLAMOOK AREA   Bad-smelling Bigfoot followed couple up hill; October 1981

TILLAMOOK HEAD   UFO seen to plunge into the sea several miles off shore; January 1965

NEAR WILLIAMETTE PASS   PhD in biochemistry climbing in mountains saw and photographed UFO – picture showed a triple image, which may indicate UFO appeared and disappeared several times during the 0.03 second exposure; 22 November 1966

Pennsylvania

ARNOLD   Children tried to catch little green entity; end February 1981 (see Ch. 9)

BOOTHWYN   Plaster statue of Christ bled at the hands, and continued to do so when hands were removed for examination; April 1975

BROAD TOP MOUNTAIN   40-foot snake seen by hikers; sightings began in 1919 (see Ch. 14)

CHESTNUT RIDGE, NEAR DERRY   Man camping in hills saw bad-smelling Bigfoot; 12 June 1982. Same witness found tracks in same area in May 1985. Many other reports from Chestnut Ridge (see Ch. 2)

NEAR CHRYSVILLE   Man saw landed UFO and pushed open door to see room with violet light and full of instruments, but no occupant; summer 1933

COUDERSPORT   Possible spontaneous human combustion of Dr J. Irving Bentley; 5 December 1966 (see Ch. 4)

DRIFTON AND FREELAND   During severe storm, many cases of ball lightning: ball lightning seen in houses, and dropping from sky and exploding on hitting ground. At Freeland telephone exchange, 'balls of fire' issued from plugs on switchboard; 22 June 1915

EAST PENNSBORO TOWNSHIP   Bigfoot seen standing outside house at night; also seen by motorist on road in same area; 29 September 1985 (see Ch. 2)

FLAT ROCK, NEAR RENOVA   Boy out target shooting saw black panther; 1958. Other locations where big cats sighted include OAKDALE (February 1978), NEAR TARENTUM, ALLEGHENY COUNTY (seen and video-taped by TV camera crew, 1 June 1982), NICHOLSON/CLARKS SUMMIT/NEWTON TOWNSHIP/JACKSON (tiger, July 1986), BETWEEN FERNDALE AND REVERE, and in LAKE NOCKAMIXON AREA (two policemen saw black panther in first location, August 1987)

GRAY STATION   Bigfoot threw wood at man on railway tracks; 13 December 1986. 8-foot Bigfoot walked in front of car; 1 February 1987

GREENSBURG   8-foot gorilla-like creature with glowing red eyes seen, and three-toed footprint found; July 1972. This is typical of most of the Bigfoot reports from Pennsylvania, the majority of which date from 1970 onwards. Some pre-1981 locations include NEW SEWICKLY TOWNSHIP, DERRY, HERMINIE, LUXOR, WHITNEY, BEAVER COUNTY, LATROBE, UNIONTOWN, MIDLAND, LANCASTER, JUMONVILLE SUMMIT, JEANETTE, CLAYSVILLE, GERMAN TOWNSHIP, SHALER, SPRING GROVE, YOUNGSTOWN, GARRISON, MCCLELLANDTOWN

HONEYBROOK   Monkey or ape first seen, 18 October; then shot on farm, 3 November 1987 (see Ch. 14)

LANGHORNE   Weird noises heard from small lake or woods around: shrieks, wails, moans, groans, heard nightly; searchers noticed the noises changed location as they proceeded; January 1934

NEAR LATROBE   Three sightings of Bigfoot over 8 feet tall, which stepped out of woods into clearing and could be seen by people eating on back porch; 3 July 1987

NEAR MILFORD   Woman working on farm at 6 a.m. saw 20-foot diameter UFO over barn, tilting towards her, with entity perched on rim, facing her. It soon streaked out of sight; May 1957

NEAR NEW ALEXANDRIA   Bigfoot seen at night by man on back road; 16 May 1987 (see Ch. 2)

NORTH ANNVILLE TOWNSHIP   Bigfoot-like creature seen in house yard; 6 September 1985

NORTH HUNTINGDON TOWNSHIP   Monkey seen by hunter; autumn 1987

PHILADELPHIA   Steamship *Mohican* was 'enshrouded in a strange vapour, which glowed like phosphorous' and played havoc with ship's compass. Decks were magnetized and ship glowed as if on fire. After half an hour the 'magnetic cloud' lifted and moved out to sea; 31 July 1904. Shower of stones fell in the evening on houses and people; July 1941. Patrolmen saw jelly-like mass fall into field; it gave off misty purplish glow, and soon evaporated; 26 September 1950 (see Ch. 13)

PITTSBURGH   Possible case of spontaneous human combustion: Albert Houck found his wife lying on a table, 'burned to a crisp'; 27 January 1907. Poltergeist activity with movement of objects and furniture, misty figures seen and laughter heard; *c.* July 1971–22 April 1972 (see Ch. 1)

WEST PHILADELPHIA   Possible case of spontaneous human combustion; 18 May 1957 (see Ch. 4)

WEST PITTSTON   Controversial case of poltergeist activity; August 1986

YORK   During thunderstorm, ball lightning came through open window into house and melted chain in washbasin; happened again several weeks later; summer 1921 (see Ch. 8)

Rhode Island

BAILEY'S BEACH   Man saw red sphere bobbing on the sea, which then rose into the air and moved quickly away out to sea; 29 April 1961

BLOCK ISLAND SOUND   Sighting of the Palatine Light during heavy gale, possibly a ghost ship; 27 December 1912

PROVIDENCE   Perch and other fish fell on to yards and streets during thunderstorm; 15 May 1900

South Carolina

BISHOPVILLE   'Lizardman', 7-foot, two-legged, scaly green creature, seen near swamp; July 1988

CHARLESTON   Ghostly light haunted barracks in military college; November 1980–February 1981

NEAR GREENVILLE   Possible case of spontaneous human combustion; victim was in car; 1 March 1953 (see Ch. 4)

LEXINGTON COUNTY   Big cat seen and pawprints found; August 1987

NEAR NEWBERRY   Boy fishing saw glowing cigar-shaped UFO 30 feet long settle on the surface of a stretch of water, before shooting away at speed; 15 July 1981

SPRINGFIELD   Family from Cleveland visited in-laws to escape poltergeist activity, but it followed them to Springfield, manifesting by pounding on walls and moving objects; July 1970

NEAR SUMMERVILLE   Ghost light seen on Sheep Island Road

TILLERS FERRY   Hundreds of little fish (catfish, perch, trout, etc.) fell during a heavy local shower, and were seen swimming in pools in the cotton fields; 27 June 1901

South Dakota

BIG SIOUX RIVER, NEAR BRUCE   Youngsters saw 3-foot brown Bigfoot-like creature on river bank; September 1979

CAMPBELL LAKE   Farmer saw giant four-legged dragon-like creature, and animals had been disappearing round the lake; huge tracks leading to lake seen in mud; 1934

GREEN GRASS   Policemen saw 6–7 foot hairy ape-like creature in creek bottom; 9 August 1977

NEAR JEFFERSON   Man watched Bigfoot dragging red furry object through alfalfa field; 6 September 1974

NEAR JOHNSON SIDING   Three men saw 10-foot shaggy white Bigfoot in car headlights. It picked up deer carcass and ran into undergrowth; November 1973

LITTLE EAGLE AREA   Many sightings of Bigfoot by local Indian residents, including police officers; August–December 1977. Boys out hunting saw three Bigfeet; October 1981 (see Ch. 2)

NEAR NEMO   Boys saw Bigfoot on hill; March 1974

RAUVILLE AREA   5-foot Bigfoot-type creature with dark red eyes seen sitting beside highway; other sightings in area; 22 October 1979

Tennessee

BETWEEN BRISTOL AND MOUNTAIN CITY   On 30-mile stretch of US421, 150 highway signs were stolen. New signs had just been put up following a similar theft seven months before; March 1983

DANTE   Twelve-year-old boy let dog out 6.30 a.m. and saw UFO in field, but thought he was dreaming. When he went out again twenty minutes later, he saw his and two other dogs by the UFO, with two men and woman, normally dressed, who were trying to grab his dog. It barked, so they grabbed another, which bit them. They seemed to walk straight through side of craft, which was long and round and took off silently. Reporter who visited the site saw 24 by 5-foot oblong of pressed grass. Witness did not know of Kearney (Nebraska) incident of previous day, which had not yet appeared in papers – details of craft and entities very similar; 6 November 1957

ELIZABETHON   About a ton of polyethylene film fell from sky; 25 November 1961

NEAR KNOXVILLE   Men fired at Bigfoot approaching house; September 1959. Other locations of pre-1981 Bigfoot sightings include RUTHERFORD COUNTY (August 1965), MONTEAGLE MOUNTAIN (spring 1968), GILES COUNTY (October 1975), NEAR FLINTVILLE (April 1976), NEAR WHITE HOUSE (September 1979), NASHVILLE (January 1980), BIG SANDY (October 1980)

MEMPHIS   Unnatural daytime darkness for fifteen minutes caused panic; 2 December 1904

ROBERTSON   6-foot kangaroo seen on Highway 49, making 10-foot-high bounces; June 1984

NEAR SUGAR TREE   Man walking home at night saw light 'rising out of nowhere' which made his hair stand on end; he banged his stick on the hollow tree stump where it was coming from, but nothing happened; 1922

Texas

ARLINGTON   Several residents claimed to see gorilla, but nothing found; October 1974. Two boys caught 3½-foot sand shark in creek; July 1976 (see Ch. 14)

BAILEY'S PRAIRIE   Ghost light associated with ghost of Bailey, a drinking man

BRAZOS RIVER, KLAMATH LAKE   Water monster reports

BROWNSVILLE   18-inch crocodile found in cotton bin; 21 September 1970. Office staff heard ghostly organ music and voices, and saw a black, hooded figure; 1982

CROSBY   Poltergeist activity in house allegedly built over graveyard; a neighbour saw ghosts in his bedroom; 1982–7

DALLAS   Possible case of spontaneous human combustion; victim was in car; October 1964 (see Ch. 4)

DALLAS–FORT WORTH   Fall of fish on Pentagon Parkway; 18 June 1958. Flaming blob fell on lawn, setting it on fire; 27 January 1964

ESPERANZA CREEK   Ghost light seen frequently, 1–3 feet above the ground

FARMERSVILLE   Children saw little green man, which the dogs then killed; May 1913 (see Ch. 9)

FORT WORTH   City street developed mysterious 20-foot-long bulge, 'like a giant earthworm' which swayed back and forth – it both appeared and disappeared suddenly. Excavations afterwards found soil layers intact to 8-foot depth and no trace of gas; July 1984. Lion seen by two men sitting in van near the zoo; two police officers also saw it, in spotlight – but no lions were missing from the zoo; February 1985. Man in back yard saw fish fall from the sky; 8 May 1985 (see Ch. 13)

FRISCO   Three purple blobs found in yard; probably fell from the sky; early September 1979 (see Ch. 13)

GAINESVILLE   Fishermen saw big hairy creature, which left six-toed footprints and had a long stride, possibly Bigfoot; 2 August 1984

HEARNE   Bigfoot seen around houses; October 1985

HOUSTON   Winged man seen in tree; 18 June 1953 (see Ch. 9)

NEAR HUFFMAN   Mrs Cash, Mrs Landrum and her grandson Colby were out at night when they saw a UFO giving out flames over the road. They stopped and watched. Later they were ill with a variety of symptoms; 29 December 1980 (see Ch. 6)

ISABEL   After religious revival meeting, people saw falling stars and figure of Jesus in the sky; 2 August 1927

JUNCTION   700-pound alligator found in shallow creek; mid-April 1977

LAMPASAS   Ghostly smell of frying liver and onions on Friday nights in old house; early 1980s (see Ch. 5)

LEVELLAND   Several reports of egg-shaped UFOs, which landed on the road in front of surprised motorists causing vehicle engine failure; 2/3 November 1957

NEAR LOS FRESNOS   Ambulance-driver saw 'bird' like a pterodactyl; 14 September 1983 (see Ch. 17)

MALONE   Two holes 20 feet apart found in field after farmer heard a roar from the sky; no trace of meteorites; 12 July 1983

MARFA   Ghost lights seen since at least last century in area of Mitchell Flat – earthquake lights or vehicle headlights or what? (see Ch. 8)

SAN ANTONIO   Teachers saw giant 'bird' like pterodactyl; 24 February 1976. Other similar sightings around this time in south-east Texas (see Ch. 17)

NORTH OF SAN ANTONIO   Man saw 8–9 foot Bigfoot with grey-white hair moving tree limbs near lake; autumn 1975. Other locations of pre-1981 Bigfoot sightings include LAMAR, GRAYSON and STEVENS COUNTIES (1969), SOUTH SULPHUR RIVER AREA (summer 1969 and September 1973), LAKE WORTH (July–November 1969), NEAR HALLSVILLE

(summer 1976), NEAR KELLY AIR
FORCE BASE (August 1976), NEAR
HAWLEY (July 1977), VIDOR (19 June
1978)

SARATOGA Ghost lights seen over
many years on Bragg Road, straight
road 8 miles long; linked with ghost
of headless railway brakeman (see
Ch. 8)

Utah

BEAR LAKE, GREAT SALT LAKE, MUD
LAKE, SEVIER LAKE, UTAH LAKE
Lake monster reports

NEAR CEDAR FORT Rancher saw
kangaroo which jumped away while
he was checking his sheep; June
1981

CUBERANT BASIN, NEAR NORTH OGDEN
Hikers saw tall, white-haired Bigfoot
and found partly eaten rabbit;
August 1977

NEAR ELIZABETH LAKE Three Bigfeet
were watched for ten minutes as
they played in meadow; 10 July
1977

LITTLE MALAD RIVER VALLEY
Cruciform hole 14 feet in diameter
found after earthquake, with clods
hurled 14 feet from hole; February
1979

NEAR MONTE CRISTO, EAST OF OGDEN
Elk-hunter saw white ape-like
creature at water hole and watched it
through rifle telescopic sight;
autumn 1979

MONTICELLO Deer-hunters saw
creature around 4 feet tall with
smoky-black short hair covering the
body, possibly a juvenile Bigfoot.
They were 40 feet away when it
went out of sight into sage brush;
October 1959

RIVERDALE Bigfoot ran across road;
25 February 1980

SALT LAKE CITY Fall of salty white
'goo' from sky; 25 March 1955 (see
Ch. 13)

NEAR SOUTH WEBER Sightings of
Bigfoot; 3 and 4 February 1980

TREMONTON Naval officer Delbert
Newhouse, experienced
photographer, filmed twelve objects
in the sky; 2 July 1952

Vermont

BURLINGTON Men talking in street saw
torpedo-shaped 'body' *c.*6 feet long
suspended in air about 50 feet above
buildings; tongues of fire issued
from it, and it was surrounded by
halo of dim light – ball lightning?;
*c.*1907

LAKE CHAMPLAIN, CONNECTICUT RIVER,
DEAD CREEK, LAKE MEMPHREMAGOG,
WINOOSKI RIVER Water monster
reports

NEAR RUTLAND Couple saw 8–10 foot
Bigfoot in meadow at night; police
also saw it run across road; July
1974

WEST PAULET Hunter saw panther;
November 1983

WEST RUTLAND Man smelled bad
odour and saw possible Bigfoot
under street light; it walked on two
legs. Seen by three others;
20 September 1985

WINDSOR Water from an unknown
source gathered on the furniture in a
house; when sponged off it quickly
returned; September 1955 (see
Ch. 1)

WOODSTOCK Spontaneous outbreaks of
fire in house which eventually
burned down; early April 1947

Virginia

ALEXANDRIA Witness was camping in
woods when she saw in her flashlight
a possible Bigfoot standing 15 feet
away. It ran into trees; July 1965

ARLINGTON Mystery animal, like a
medium-sized dog with no hair, no
tail, and big teeth, reportedly
roaming the area killing pets; June
1974

BLACKSTONE Beans and peas fell during a storm; August 1962 (see Ch. 13)

CHESAPEAKE BAY Many sightings of sea monster 'Chesapeake Chessie' or 'Potomac Patty'; favoured locations include HEATHSVILLE, RAPPAHANNOCK RIVER, POTOMAC RIVER (see Ch. 7)

COLONIAL BEACH Bigfoot seen by house on several occasions; June 1985–spring 1987 (see Ch. 2)

GALAX Garage bombarded with nails for four days; 10–13 July 1978 (see Ch. 16)

HAYMARKET Ball lightning entered kitchen and hit woman on chest; summer 1977. On 21 June 1978 the events were almost repeated (see Ch. 8)

HONEOYE CREEK, STAUNTON 2-foot crocodilian caught; 7 August 1939. 3- and 4-foot crocodilians seen at LAKE BRADFORD; August 1949. One caught in drainage channel at HAMPTON; 7 August 1982

NEWPORT NEWS Eight fiery red discs seen by captain and officer on board DC-4; 14 July 1952 (see Ch. 3)

NORTHWEST RIVER PARK, NEAR CHESAPEAKE 7-foot Bigfoot seen running through camping ground; 9 June 1981. Other sightings in the area

PEARISBURG Heavy furniture moved in poltergeist outbreak; late December 1976 (see Ch. 1)

NEAR PURGATORY MOUNTAIN Family saw cougar near their home several times; 1981. Other recent big cat sightings in BEDFORD and BOTETOURT COUNTIES

QUANTICO MARINE CORPS BASE Sightings of Bigfoot-type creature; January 1977

NEAR SUFFOLK Spook light first seen on Jackson Road; 5 March 1951

VIRGINIA BEACH Haunted fire station with doors slamming, bells sounding, sirens going off, mysterious clangs; 1972–82

WILLIAMSVILLE 'Coy-dog' killed; 2 October 1977 (see Ch. 14)

MOUNTAINS SOMEWHERE IN VIRGINIA Three people hunting at night were walking uphill, and scattered as 7–8 foot Bigfoot running on two legs passed them on its way down; 29 June 1972

Washington

ALDER DAM Possible Bigfoot tracks found in remote area; May 1981

APE CANYON, NEAR KELSO Prospectors in a cabin were bombarded with rocks by 'mountain devils'; they saw four Bigfeet and one was shot, this possibly causing the rock attack; July 1924. This famous case has caused much controversy, with some people claiming a hoax, but Fred Beck, who was there and shot at the creatures, still believed it really happened when he spoke to investigators 42 years later. More Bigfoot sightings have been made in Washington than in any other state. A few other pre-1981 sighting locations are MOUNT ST HELENS, WIND RIVER, ORCHARD, ORLEANS, YAKIMA, BOSSBURG, SATUS PASS, LAKE STEVENS, CRADLE LAKE, RICHLAND, MASON COUNTY, NOOKSACK RIVER, BELLINGHAM, MARIETTA, CHEHALIS RIVER, CLIPPER, EVANS, BEACON ROCK STATE PARK, SKAMANIA, KETTLE FALLS, DECEPTION PASS, NEAH BAY, NORTH BONNEVILLE, PORT ANGELES, KLICKITAT VALLEY, TOPPENISH RIDGE

BLUE MOUNTAINS Paul Freeman, Forest Service patrolman, saw Bigfoot, and found footprints which showed skin patterns; June 1982. He continued to find tracks regularly, e.g. April 1987 near INDIAN RIDGE (see Ch. 2)

BREMERTON Man hit by ball of fire which entered his room, setting objects alight and burning victim's arm; 6 November 1951 (see Ch. 8)

CHEHALIS Woman saw flying man with long silver wings; 6 January 1948 (see Ch. 9)

CHELAN LAKE, OMAK LAKE, QUINAULT

LAKE, ROCK LAKE, LAKE WASHINGTON
Lake monster reports

NEAR GRAND COULEE Large hole 2 feet
deep found, with plug of earth
standing on ground 75 feet away, as
if cut out by 'giant cookie cutter',
but no one could say what force tore
the 3-ton plug from the hole;
October 1984

GREEN LAKE, SEATTLE Two caimans,
the larger 2½ feet long, caught;
early June 1986

NEAR GREENWATER Couple camping
were chased off by Bigfoot which
spoke to them; 6 July 1985 (see
Ch. 2)

HOQUIAM Possible spontaneous
combustion of human corpse;
9 December 1973 (see Ch. 4)

STRAIT OF JUAN DE FUCA Two separate
witnesses, near Port Angeles, saw
large flaming object go down into
the sea; 9 March 1960 (see Ch. 10)

LONGVIEW Three flying men seen;
9 April 1948 (see Ch. 9). Black
panther seen by two men; July 1987

LUMMI ISLAND UFO splashed into sea,
and divers found object on sea bed,
which later disappeared;
31 December 1984 (see Ch. 10)

NEAR PASCO Ghost light seen

PUYALLUP Calf-sized blue-grey animal
seen, bounding fast across field,
possibly a kangaroo; 1967

MOUNT RAINIER Kenneth Arnold's
UFO sighting while he was piloting
his private plane is famous as the
event which triggered the name
'flying saucer'; 24 June 1947 (see
Ch. 3)

SPOKANE One house bombarded for a
week by golfball-sized rocks; August–
September 1977 (see Ch. 16)

TACOMA 5-pound steel ball fell from
sky; August 1951. Lion reportedly
seen in town, with shaggy black
mane, black tuft at end of long tail;
police caught a dog, part-collie
part-German shepherd, and said it
was the 'lion'; July 1976

LAKE WASHINGTON Two alligators seen
chasing ducks at south end of lake;
1967

West Virginia

BROWN'S MOUNTAIN Men walking as
night fell saw lights hovering just
above ground, and one man heard
voices jabbering; *c.* late 1920s (see
Ch. 8)

NEAR CHARLESTON Jet pilot saw
'rocket' 4 feet long with fins, which
flew past his plane at speed; 25 June
1987 (see Ch. 3)

CHIEF CORNSTALK HUNTING GROUNDS
Winged man-like figure seen
standing on Route 2 before taking
off straight up; 1960 or 1961 (see
Ch. 9)

DILLON'S MOUNTAIN Two hunters
claimed they were attacked by two
Bigfeet, a male and a female, and
scared them off by firing a gun in
the air; 25 October 1986 (see Ch. 2)

EAST LYNN LAKE Boy fishing caught
25-inch-long shark; 18 August 1977
(see Ch. 14)

FLATWOODS Boys and woman who
went to investigate landed UFO saw
huge figure with glowing eyes
floating towards them; 12 September
1952 (see Ch. 6)

KANAWHA RIVER, NEAR CHARLESTON
Men fishing from boat caught
octopus (in fresh water);
24 December 1933 (see Ch. 14)

PARSON AREA Sightings of 8-foot
Bigfoot with huge eyes 'like big balls
of fire'; summer 1960. Other
locations of pre-1981 Bigfoot
sightings in West Virginia include
NEAR DAVIS (summer 1960),
MONONGAHELA NATIONAL FOREST
(October 1960), NEAR HICKORY
FLATS (30 December 1960), MASON
COUNTY (November 1966), WESTON
(17 August 1976), OCEANA
(14 August 1978)

POINT PLEASANT Numerous sightings
of 'Mothman'; November and
December 1966 (see Ch. 9). Big cat
seen, and chickens disappeared;
September 1978. Other big cat
sighting locations include DOLLY
SODS (29 August 1980), HARDY
COUNTY (10 December 1978, 1986,

18 November 1987), RANDOLPH
COUNTY (15 August 1987)

WHARNCLIFFE Mysterious outbreaks of
fire in small town; summer 1983
(see Ch. 4)

Wisconsin

NEAR BARRON Boy carrying oil back to
stranded car saw twenty little men
walking along the road; summer
1919 (see Ch. 9)

BROWN'S LAKE, CHIPPEWA LAKE, DEVIL'S
LAKE, ELKHART LAKE, FOWLER LAKE,
LAKE GENEVA, MADISON FOUR LAKES,
MENDOTA LAKE, PEWAUKEE LAKE,
RED CEDAR LAKE, ROCK LAKE, LAKE
SUPERIOR, LAKE WAUBEAU, LAKE
WINNEBAGO, YELLOW RIVER Water
monster reports

EAGLE RIVER Chicken farmer Joe
Simonton saw entities in UFO
which landed in his garden; he filled
their water jug and they gave him a
cookie they had made; 18 April 1961
(see Ch. 6)

MANITOWOC 20-pound piece of steel
from sky crashed into street;
September 1962. Hunter caught
40-inch alligator on river bank near
Manitowoc; November 1978

MILWAUKEE 50-pound chunk of hot
metal fell from sky; 22 August 1974

MIRROW LAKE Ten-year-old girl
followed by man-like furry creature
in woods; c.1910. This may be
Wisconsin's earliest Bigfoot report;
other pre-1981 sighting locations
include STATE HIGHWAY 89, NEAR
ILLINOIS/WISCONSIN BORDER (July
1964), DELTOX MARSH, NEAR
FREMONT (October and November
1968), BENTON (August 1970), EAST
OF FORT ATKINSON (1972), COUNTY
ROAD W, NEAR FREDERIC (December
1974), NEAR CASHTON (September
1976), ST CROIX FALLS (8 October
1976)

OSHKOSH Footsteps heard and ghosts
seen in haunted Grand Opera
House; 1970s and 1980s

LAKE PEWAUKEE 30-inch crocodilian
caught; 9 July 1971

SOUTH OF STEVENS POINT Young
people spending holiday in cabin in
woods were terrorized by Bigfoot;
August 1981 (see Ch. 2)

WAUKESHA AREA Sightings of
kangaroo; first known sighting
5 April 1978, followed by many
others till 9 May. Then on 21 May a
kangaroo was seen in EAU CLAIRE
COUNTY, 185 miles away (see
Ch. 14)

Wyoming

LAKE DESMET, HUTTON LAKE, LAKE
KATHERINE, LAKE LA METRIE,
PATHFINDER LAKE, ALCOVA
RESERVOIR Water monster reports

NEAR JACKSON Woman saw Bigfoot
crossing field with giant strides;
summer 1972

NEAR LANDER Boys riding horses saw
Bigfoot running near them; summer
1972

MEDICINE BOW NATIONAL FOREST
Elk-hunter Carl Higdon saw 6-foot
entity in black who gave him pills to
satisfy his hunger before taking him
into UFO, where he was told he was
not what they needed, and taken
back; 24 October 1974

SNOW KING MOUNTAIN, JACKSON Two
men chased off mountain by 12-foot
Bigfoot with long dark hair and arms
hanging to the ground; 16 June 1980

TETON FOREST Students saw 'bear' and
shot it; found it was 7 feet tall, hairy
and human-like, a possible Bigfoot,
so they left the corpse; December
1967

USSR

ISLAND IN BALTIC SEA, OFF ESTONIA
Man working at factory noticed

landed UFO, glittering with colours, and close by stood two black cubes with a revolving 'pipe'. From one cube shot an orange beam which hit witness and made him fall over. UFO changed shape and disappeared. Witness felt sick afterwards; August 1980

BELORUSSKAYA (BYELORUSSIA) People on two airliners ten miles apart saw mysterious green cloud sending out shafts of light to the ground; January 1985

NEAR BUINAKSK, DAGHESTAN Lieutenant-Colonel Karapetyan saw tall, hair-covered naked 'man' captured in mountains as a possible spy. He would not eat, drink or speak, and was thought to be a wildman; late 1941 (see Ch. 12)

CAUCASUS MOUNTAINS Many reports of hairy man-beasts, possibly Neanderthal man (see Ch. 12). For example, Prof. V. K. Leontiev saw a Kaptar in JURMUT RIVER AREA – covered with long dark hair, walking upright, about 7 feet tall; July 1957. Mountaineers camping at 12,000 feet were visited by bright yellow blob, possibly ball lightning, which entered men's sleeping bags causing severe injuries and the death of one man; 17 August 1978 (see Ch. 8)

DARGANATA, TURKMENIYA Rain of frogs; June or July 1979

GORKI REGION Several thousand copecks-worth of silver coins fell from the sky during a storm; 17 June 1940 (see Ch. 13)

GRINKALNES/GIRKALNIS, LITHUANIA Four apparitions of the Blessed Virgin Mary were seen above the church; December 1943

IRKUTSK UFO shaped like rocket on four legs seen on ground, with two entities, and doctor took photograph; 1961

JUMINDA, ESTONIA Greenish-brown UFO 3 feet long watched until it suddenly disappeared; autumn 1938 or 1939

KARELIA Crater found on bank of frozen lake, 100 feet long, 50 feet wide, 10 feet deep – possibly something landed near lake, slid across ground and under the water, but no trace of craft (UFO?) was found; February 1961

KAZAN Chunk of ice fell from sky, narrowly missing witness who put it in refrigerator; analysis identified it as the remnants of a frozen gas meteorite; August 1984 (see Ch. 13)

KISLOVODSK, CAUCASUS Astronomers in astrophysical mountain station saw UFOs with vapour trails; 8 August, 4 September, 18 October 1967

LENINGRAD Man saw 'soap bubble' emerge from electric socket hole. It was bluish and milk-white, with vibration inside, and changing shape, and it moved to man's finger, under nail, shrank and disappeared; 1960

MOSCOW UFOs seen; December 1948, 27 November 1954, 14 February 1955. Saucer-shaped object on ground took off with spiral movement; 19 March 1958. Disc-shaped UFO fell with spiral motion; spring 1958. Three UFOs tracked on radar, but planes could not locate them; August 1959. 'Hot, bright, yellow ball' seen during storm over bell tower of cathedral in Kremlin; it entered through open door and flared up, vanishing with loud cracking noise, leaving strong smell of ozone; January 1978

NOVAYA ZEMLYA, BENNETT ISLAND Large icy clouds of mysterious origin form and dissipate within hours – from Soviet weapons tests, or naturally occurring? No signs of the former and scientists lack a natural explanation. One plume seen 12 March 1982 was 109 miles long and 6 miles high, moving against the wind

OGRE OBSERVATORY, LATVIA Three astronomers saw UFO which they knew was not a satellite; 26 July 1965

NEAR SOCHI Ball lightning passed

through plane in flight; January 1984 (see Ch. 8)

TAJIKISTAN   Reports of hairy hominoids in the Pamir mountains, e.g. General Topilski saw a dead one in 1925; prospector saw sleeping creature in 1934 (see Ch. 12)

TAMBOSK   Airliner struck by ball lightning when inside thundercloud; 12 August 1956 (see Ch. 8)

TIEN SHAN AND KIRGHIZ MOUNTAINS   Many reports of hairy man-beasts (see Ch. 12)

TIMANSKY RIDGE, KOMI   Recent reports of hairy hominoids; 1986 (see Ch. 12)

YEVPATORIYA, CRIMEA   Huge sea monster with horse-like head seen in Black Sea by fishermen who cut their nets and fled ashore; January 1934

Kazakhstan

Geophysical expedition camped in mountains saw orange lens-shaped UFO with diameter 50 per cent greater than moon's. It flew south, zigzagged to north-east, then disappeared behind mountains; 16 August 1960

Crew of jumbo jet saw UFO with lights – definitely not an aircraft said first officer; 22 April 1987 (see Ch. 3)

LAKE KOK-KOL, DZHAMBUL AREA   Lake monster reports, one witness being a scientist who saw snake-like body 50 feet long and head 6 feet long; 1975

PAVLODAR REGION   Woman saw flying man dressed in black; 1936 (see Ch. 9)

Siberia

KAMCHATKA PENINSULA   Search for mystery bear-like animal, the Irkuiem; 1987 (see Ch. 17)

LAKE KHYEYR   Biologist saw lake monster on shore eating grass. It had small head, long gleaming neck, huge bluish-black body with fin on its spine. Witness went to fetch colleagues, but when they returned with guns and cameras it had gone; 1964

KOMANDORSKIYE OSTROVA (COMMANDER ISLANDS), OFF KAMCHATKA   Sightings of 'extinct' Steller's sea-cow; early 1950s. Sightings near Cape Navarin in July 1962, and in Anapkinskaya Bay in summer 1976 (see Ch. 17)

LAKE LABINKIR, YAKUTIA   Lake monster reports

GULF OF OB   Huge black cloud caused daytime darkness lasting several hours over wide area of north-west Siberia; possibly 'a dense compact cloud of cosmic dust that entered the earth's atmosphere'; 18 September 1938

OB RIVER, NEAR VASYAKOVO   Man with dogs saw two 6-foot man-beasts come out of forest. Their eyes glowed dark red, and they were covered in black hair; 1960 or 1961 (see Ch. 12)

POLYARNYY   During thunderstorm, ball lightning went through room, through stone wall and into street, leaving burned edges to the hole it made in the wall; July 1972

SIBERIAN TAIGA   Hunter saw mammoths in forest; 1918 (see Ch. 17)

TUNGUSKA   30-megaton blast devastated hundreds of square miles of pine forest; ball of fire seen, and black clouds were followed by black rain. Next day, glowing clouds seen at high altitudes over Asia and Europe. No meteoritic debris found, so was the explosion caused by a comet striking the earth, or a space vehicle, or . . . ?; 30 June 1908

TYUMEN REGION   Maya Bykova saw 6-foot hairy hominoid in the forest; 16 August 1987 (see Ch. 12)

LAKE VOROTA   Geologist and companion saw 30-foot creature in lake; it was over 6 feet wide and had a dark grey body, with light patches on side of head, and a fin 20 inches high on its back; 1953

YAKUTIA Wildman known as Chuchunaa (fugitive or outcast) reported in area of Verkhoyansk (the coldest inhabited place on earth) (see Ch. 12). Triton, newt-like amphibian, said to have been found alive by gold miners 30 feet below surface of tundra; June 1987. A very similar report, where a lizard (*uglozub*) was found at 33 feet by geologists searching for gold, came out of KOLYMSKAYA in 1973

Ukraine

BRODY Poltergeist outbreak; 3 November–17 December 1922

GRUSHEVO/HRUSHIV Apparitions of Blessed Virgin Mary appeared in chapel to eleven-year-old girl and neighbours; 26 April 1987

ODESSA Air Force major saw UFO which also appeared on his radar, as he flew over city; also tracked on ground radar; April 1966

SEREDNE/SERIDNIA Twenty apparitions of the Blessed Virgin Mary, with messages; 20 December 1954– 21 November 1955

YENAKIYEVO Poltergeist activity broke out in presence of young boy – objects flew about, fires started, light bulbs exploded, and once a refrigerator turned upside-down; began November 1986

Airliner *en route* BETWEEN ZAPOROJE AND VOLGOGRAD began to glide earthwards when engines cut out after UFO seen overhead; it disappeared and engines restarted at 2500 feet above ground; 29 September 1967

CARACAS Nightwatchmen at prefect's office saw ghost of dancing cowboy who disappeared by a tree; November 1969

BETWEEN CARACAS AND PETARE Two lorry-drivers saw UFO hovering above road ahead; one of them had tussle with small entity with claws and glowing eyes. Two others gathered stones and other things while first attacked witness again. He fought back with a knife, but it did not harm the entity's hard skin. They took off while blinding him with a bright light; 28 November 1954 (see Ch. 6)

NEAR CHICO Four small hair-covered entities from landed UFO attacked two young men in a kidnap attempt; they were very strong and broke a rifle; 10 December 1954

ISLA ORCHILA North of the island, ship's crew saw UFO sink into sea; 13 December 1959 (see Ch. 10)

LOS LLANOS AREA Grey, hollow, kidney-shaped object fell from the sky; 22 July 1969

LAKE MARACAIBO Low-level nocturnal lights known as the Faro or Taro of Maracaibo, seen frequently. Glowing object (UFO?) seen to plunge into the lake; 23 March 1957

MARISELA, CARACAS Men saw UFO land and two entities emerge in light beams. They examined things, including plants, through instruments. Their belts sent out rays of light; 10 May 1966 (see Ch. 6)

SALINA Pastor saw UFO emerge from sea; 8 August 1967. Other similar sightings on 4 and 27 August along the coast, and again early in 1973 (see Ch. 10)

VENEZUELA

MOUNT ANTANA Explorers searched for 'dinosaur'; 1977 (see Ch. 17)

VIETNAM

ALONG BAY Sea monster sightings; 1903–4

NEAR DA NANG 'Bird-woman' with bat's wings seen by US marine; July or August 1969 (see Ch. 9)

DONG HOI Fishermen saw UFO fly over city, then fall into sea; 16 June 1909 (see Ch. 10)

PHAT-DIEM Poltergeist outbreak; 1924–5

'Wildman' (*Homo neanderthalensis pongoides*) shot in Vietnam in 1960s and then smuggled into USA where it was exhibited deep-frozen – a model may have been substituted at some stage (or it may always have been a model – a controversial point), but in 1968 Heuvelmans and Sanderson examined what they said was a genuine wildman

VIRGIN ISLANDS

ST THOMAS Passengers on liner saw sea monster with long neck and six or more humps, 60–80 feet long; 26 October 1934

WALES (see also *Modern Mysteries of Britain*)

Clwyd

EWLOE CASTLE Custodian saw ghost, and heard singing during thunderstorms (see Chs. 5 and 11)

PRESTATYN After baby christening, poltergeist activity broke out, with doors banging, footsteps heard, and a figure seen; October 1986

RHUDDLAN Man returning home from pub after midnight met dozens of ghostly monks who blocked his path. He dived through a hedge to escape.

Many years later, a Norman graveyard was found close by; July 1953

SHOTTON Ball lightning bounced through steelworks, hitting scrap shed and leaving dartboard shape on wall, 37 feet across with 'segments in place'; 1980

Dyfed

ABERARTH Orange ball seen to plunge into the sea, still glowing under water; 24 March 1955 (see Ch. 10)

TALLEY ABBEY Sound of ghostly chanting heard; probably 1970s (see Ch. 11)

Gwent

NEWPORT Mysterious death of Annie Thomas, a possible case of spontaneous human combustion; February 1980

TRELLECH Ten poltergeist incidents over two weeks at Crown Inn, ending with violent vibration of Christmas tree and top branch bending over; 10–24 December 1981

Gwynedd

CWMYGLO 'Thunderbolt' (ball lightning?) struck cottage and demolished chimney stack; 11 June 1987 (see Ch. 8)

RHOSLEFAIN, NEAR TYWYN Orange ball dropped into sea, then shot out again; 24 March 1955 (see Ch. 10)

TRAWSFYNYDD Ghostly carriage and horses seen; 30 December c.1979

Mid Glamorgan

KENFIG HILL Recordings made of voices and music trapped in walls of ancient inn; 1982 (see Ch. 11)

Powys

DYLIFE Humming noise heard and glowing figure seen in derelict mine; 1984 (see Ch. 5)

WEST GERMANY

ASCHAFFENBURG/DARMSTADT AREA Holes found in thick ice cover of several ponds; February 1986

NEAR BAD EMS Scout with group looking for wood found big toad sitting in cavity in tree stump when he cut into it, with no hole for it to get in or out; May 1975

BETWEEN BADEN-BADEN AND FRANKFURT On autobahn, witness saw small dark sedan car which vanished in an explosion with flames and smoke; 14 October 1987

BAVARIAN ALPS Reports of giant reptile known as Tatzelwurm (see Ch. 14)

BREMEN Poltergeist outbreak focusing on young apprentice; June 1965–c. July 1967

CHARLOTTENBURG, WEST BERLIN Poltergeist outbreak; 9 January–end April 1929

NEAR COLOGNE Crocodile found in washroom on Munich–Cologne express; February 1973

EICHSTÄTT Pure water flows October–February annually from sarcophagus of St Walburga, and is used for healing purposes (see Ch. 15)

GEROLSTEIN Poltergeist outbreak; 4 December 1901–20 February 1902

GROSSERLACH, NEAR SULZBACH Poltergeist outbreak; 30 April–mid-May 1916

HAMBURG Man saw cigar-shaped UFO with lighted windows in field near his house, with several dwarfs close by who went aboard when he approached; June 1914. Ball lightning entered house through closed window; 27 July 1952 (see Ch. 8). More than 30 people saw bear walking around; September 1974 (see Ch. 14). There were puma sightings in the Hamburg area, and a man at RANTRUM claimed he was attacked by one; hunters and policemen searched but found nothing; July–August 1982. Other locations where big cats have been seen include HANOVER AREA (July 1983), MERZIG-WADERN IN SAAR (August 1983), DELLIGSEN IN LOWER SAXONY (June 1985)

HEEDE Four young girls saw 100 apparitions of Blessed Virgin Mary; 1 November 1937–1940

HEROLDSBACH-THURN, BAVARIA Little girls, and later adults too, had many visions of Blessed Virgin Mary; 9 October 1949–1952

HOHENSCHAFTLERN, ISARTAL, BAVARIA During thunderstorm, ball lightning entered house through open window and rolled across floor, crept up stove and exploded leaving smell of ozone; 2 August 1921 (see Ch. 8)

KATTERBACH US Army Officers' Club haunted by ghostly Luftwaffe pilots; 1976

KEMPTON, NEAR DÜSSELDORF Icicle 6 feet long, 6 inches round, fell from sky, killing carpenter working on roof; 1951

LAUTER, BAVARIA Poltergeist outbreak; September–December 1946

LIMBURG Clergymen picked up 2000 marks in banknotes which fell from the sky; 1976 (see Ch. 13)

MUNICH Poltergeist outbreak; a few days in January 1927

NEUDORF, BADEN Poltergeist outbreak; 9 October–10 November 1952 (see Ch. 1)

NICKLHEIM, BAVARIA Poltergeist outbreak with objects passing through closed doors and windows; November 1968–February 1969 (see Chs. 1 and 16)

OPPAU Poltergeist outbreak; 9 October 1930–late February 1931

PEISSENBERG Poltergeist outbreak; October–November 1925

PURSRUCK Poltergeist outbreak;
November 1970–August 1971

REMAGEN Twenty children had vision
of Blessed Virgin Mary;
18 December 1950

NEAR RINKERODE, NEAR MUNSTER
Projectionist travelling home saw
landed cigar-shaped UFO and four
entities who seemed to be working
beneath craft; 9 October 1954

ROSENHEIM, BAVARIA Poltergeist
activity in lawyer's office, but only
in the presence of a young clerk –
lamps swinging, pictures rotating on
the walls, light bulbs exploding,
telephone disruption; November
1967–1968

SAARLOUIS Young puma seen by
several witnesses; March/April 1988

SCHERFEDE, WESTPHALIA Poltergeist
attack; September–December 1972

SPEICHER, RHEINLAND-PFALZ Ghostly
footsteps and evidence of anti-Nazi
ghost in house occupied by
American military family; 1965–6

VACHENDORF, BAVARIA Poltergeist
outbreak; 1948 (see Ch. 1)

WEST BERLIN Human finger fell from
sky and landed on car roof; March
1986 (see Ch. 13)

WILDBERG, NEAR STUTTGART
Poltergeist outbreak; ten days in late
1921

WILDENSTEIN CASTLE, NEAR HEILBRONN
'Goblins' seen; Baroness saw ghost
of child who died in 1890 at the
castle; 1 March 1953. Ghostly
woman in white seen in bathroom;
1945. Other ghosts seen and
phantom music heard

emitting coloured beams or flames
which flew over; 11 July 1970

NEAR CITLUK Visions of a 'golden-
haired Madonna' appeared to six
girls in fields; c.1980

KOMOVI FOREST UFOs seen in the
area, and said to have caused forest
fire which happened in rainy
weather – the flames from the
exhaust set the trees alight;
26 November 1967

LANEJEVO Crews of two planes saw
apparently metallic triangular object
in the sky above them;
20 September 1971

MEDJUGORJE Apparitions of Blessed
Virgin Mary appeared regularly to
teenage children; began 24 June
1981, still continuing in late 1980s

NICSJIC Bright conical UFO seen; 23
November 1967

PASMAN, DALMATIA Adults and
children saw apparition of Blessed
Virgin Mary, crowned with stars, in
a cloud; 11 June 1946

RIJEKA Radar and pilot sighting of
UFO; October 1971

SREMCICA Explosion heard, trees
burnt, and crater formed. In it was
oval object 8 inches in diameter,
ribbed and dark grey, possibly made
of magnesium; 18 February 1969

YUGOSLAVIA

BELGRADE Young astronomers
watched orange-red object for fifteen
minutes; 21 December 1968. Many
witnesses to oval, reddish UFO

ZIMBABWE

HARARE Fresh blood found beneath
coffin of man killed a week before;
10 September 1979

HWANGE GAME RESERVE Four men
going home through thick bush at
night saw bright light which came
down. It was a 'dish-shaped'
machine and two men came out of
the top and floated to the ground.
The witnesses ran away; 1983

LA ROCHELLE, NEAR MUTARE Ball of
fire (UFO?) visited estate, and men
in silver coveralls seen; bright light

from their heads caused witness to fall down; 15 August 1981

LAKE MCILWAINE   Pilot and student in Tiger Moth saw silver UFO, two saucers one above the other and about 40 feet long; it hovered, turned on its side and shot off at speed; 26 July 1954

WARREN HILLS, NEAR HARARE
Residents believed Warren Hills was haunted by spirits of people buried in graveyard underneath houses, and have reported poltergeist phenomena like showers of stones, broken windows, ice-cold houses on warm nights; 1983

Bibliography

Bord, Janet and Colin, *Alien Animals*, Granada Publishing, London, 1980; rev.
   edn Panther Books, London, 1985; Stackpole Books, Harrisburg, PA, 1981
—— *Bigfoot Casebook*, Granada Publishing, London, 1982; Stackpole Books,
   Harrisburg, PA, 1982
—— *The Evidence for Bigfoot and Other Man-Beasts*, The Aquarian Press,
   Wellingborough, 1984
—— *Modern Mysteries of Britain: 100 Years of Strange Events*, Grafton Books,
   London, 1987
Bowen, Charles (ed.), *The Humanoids: A Survey of World-Wide Reports of
   Landings of Unconventional Aerial Objects and their Alleged Occupants*, Neville
   Spearman, London, 1969; Henry Regnery Company, Chicago, 1969
Brandon, Jim, *Weird America*, E. P. Dutton, New York, 1978
Clark, Jerome, and Loren Coleman, *The Unidentified*, Warner Paperback Library,
   New York, 1975
Coleman, Loren, *Mysterious America*, Faber & Faber, Boston and London, 1983
—— *Curious Encounters*, Faber & Faber, Boston and London, 1985
Corliss, William R., *Handbook of Unusual Natural Phenomena*, The Sourcebook
   Project, PO Box 107, Glen Arm, MD 21057, USA, 1977
—— *Lightning, Auroras, Nocturnal Lights, and Related Luminous Phenomena: A
   Catalog of Geophysical Anomalies*, The Sourcebook Project, Glen Arm, MD,
   1982
—— *Tornados, Dark Days, Anomalous Precipitation, and Related Weather
   Phenomena: A Catalog of Geophysical Anomalies*, The Sourcebook Project,
   Glen Arm, MD, 1983
Costello, Peter, *In Search of Lake Monsters*, Garnstone Press, London, 1974;
   Panther Books, London, 1975
Cruz, Joan Carroll, *The Incorruptibles*, Tan Books and Publishers, Rockford, IL,
   1977
Dinsdale, Tim, *The Leviathans*, Routledge & Kegan Paul, London, 1966; Futura
   Publications, London, 1976
Eberhart, George M., *Monsters: A Guide to Information on Unaccounted for
   Creatures, Including Bigfoot, Many Water Monsters, and Other Irregular
   Animals*, Garland Publishing, New York and London, 1983
Evans, Hilary, *Gods, Spirits, Cosmic Guardians*, The Aquarian Press,
   Wellingborough, 1987
—— *Visions, Apparitions, Alien Visitors*, The Aquarian Press, Wellingborough,
   1984

—— with John Spencer (eds), *UFOs 1947–1987: The 40-year search for an explanation*, Fortean Tomes, London, 1987

Fairley, John, and Simon Welfare, *Arthur C. Clarke's World of Strange Powers*, William Collins, London, 1984

—— *Arthur C. Clarke's Chronicles of the Strange and Mysterious*, William Collins, London, 1987

Flammarion, Camille, *Haunted Houses*, T. Fisher Unwin, London, 1924

Fort, Charles, *The Complete Books of Charles Fort*, Dover Publications, New York, 1974

Gaddis, Vincent H., *Mysterious Fires and Lights*, David McKay Company, New York, 1967; Dell Publishing Co., New York, 1968

Gauld, Alan, and A. D. Cornell, *Poltergeists*, Routledge & Kegan Paul, London, 1979

Green, John, *Sasquatch: The Apes Among Us*, Hancock House Publishers, Saanichton, BC, and Seattle, WA, 1978

Halpin, Marjorie M., and Michael M. Ames (eds), *Manlike Monsters on Trial*, University of British Columbia Press, Vancouver and London, 1980

Hendry, Allan, *The UFO Handbook: A Guide to Investigating, Evaluating and Reporting UFO Sightings*, Sphere Books, London, 1980

Heuvelmans, Bernard, *In the Wake of the Sea-Serpents*, Rupert Hart-Davis, London, 1968

—— *On the Track of Unknown Animals*, Hill & Wang, Inc., New York, 1965; Paladin, London, 1970 (originally published in France as *Sur la Piste des Bêtes Ignorées*, Librairie Plon, Paris, 1955)

Holiday, F. W., *The Dragon and the Disc*, Sidgwick & Jackson, London, 1973

Hopkins, Budd, *Intruders: The Incredible Visitations at Copley Woods*, Random House, New York, 1987

—— *Missing Time: A Documented Story of UFO Abductions*, Richard Marek Publishers, New York, 1981

Hunter, Don, with René Dahinden, *Sasquatch*, McClelland & Stewart, Toronto, 1973

Keel, John A., *Strange Creatures from Time and Space*, Fawcett Publications, Greenwich, CT, 1970

Lorenzen, Coral and Jim, *Encounters with UFO Occupants*, Berkley Publishing Corporation, New York, 1976

McClure, Kevin, *The Evidence for Visions of the Virgin Mary*, The Aquarian Press, Wellingborough, 1983

McEwan, Graham J., *Mystery Animals of Britain and Ireland*, Robert Hale, London, 1986

MacKenzie, Andrew, *Hauntings and Apparitions*, William Heinemann, London, 1982

—— *The Seen and the Unseen*, Weidenfeld & Nicolson, London, 1987

Mackal, Dr Roy P., *A Living Dinosaur?: In Search of Mokele-Mbembe*, E. J. Brill, Leiden, The Netherlands, 1987

—— *Searching for Hidden Animals: An Inquiry into Zoological Mysteries*, Doubleday & Company, Garden City, NY, 1980

Marinacci, Mike, *Mysterious California*, Panpipes Press, Los Angeles, CA, 1988

Markotic, Vladimir (ed.), *The Sasquatch and Other Unknown Hominoids*, Western Publishers, Calgary, 1984

Meurger, Michel, and Claude Gagnon, *Lake Monster Traditions: A cross-cultural analysis*, Fortean Tomes, London, 1988

Michell, John, and Robert J. M. Rickard, *Living Wonders: Mysteries and Curiosities of the Animal World*, Thames & Hudson, London, 1982

—— *Phenomena: A Book of Wonders*, Thames & Hudson, London, 1977

Myers, Arthur, *The Ghostly Register*, Contemporary Books, Chicago, IL, 1986

Napier, John, *Bigfoot: The Yeti and Sasquatch in Myth and Reality*, Jonathan Cape, London, 1972

Persinger, Michael A., and Gyslaine F. Lafrenière, *Space-Time Transients and Unusual Events*, Nelson-Hall, Chicago, IL, 1977

Randles, Jenny, *Abduction*, Robert Hale, London, 1988

—— *The UFO Conspiracy: The First Forty Years*, Blandford Press, London, 1987; Javelin Books, London, 1988

—— and Peter Warrington, *Science and the UFOs*, Basil Blackwell, Oxford, 1985

Richards, John Thomas, *SORRAT: A History of the Neihardt Psychokinesis Experiments, 1961–1981*, The Scarecrow Press, Metuchen, NJ, and London, 1982

Rickard, Robert, and Richard Kelly, *Photographs of the Unknown*, New English Library, London, 1980

Rogo, D. Scott, *Miracles: A Parascientific Inquiry into Wondrous Phenomena*, The Dial Press, New York, 1982

—— *On the Track of the Poltergeist*, Prentice-Hall, Englewood Cliffs, NJ, 1986

—— *Phantoms*, David & Charles, Newton Abbot, 1976

—— and Raymond Bayless, *Phone Calls from the Dead*, Prentice-Hall, Englewood Cliffs, NJ, 1979

—— and Jerome Clark, *Earth's Secret Inhabitants*, Tempo Books, Grosset & Dunlap, New York, 1979

Roll, William G., *The Poltergeist*, Wyndham Publications, London, 1976

Sachs, Margaret, *The UFO Encyclopedia*, G. P. Putnam's Sons, New York, 1980

Sanderson, Ivan T., *Abominable Snowmen: Legend Come to Life*, Chilton Company, Philadelphia, 1961

—— *Investigating the Unexplained: A Compendium of Disquieting Mysteries of the Natural World*, Prentice-Hall, Englewood Cliffs, NJ, 1972

—— *Invisible Residents*, The World Publishing Company, Cleveland, OH, 1970; Nelson, Foster & Scott, Canada, 1970

Shackley, Myra, *Wildmen: Yeti, Sasquatch and the Neanderthal Enigma*, Thames & Hudson, London, 1983; published in USA by Thames & Hudson, New York, 1983, as *Still Living?*

Shuker, Dr Karl P. N., *Mystery Cats of the World: From Blue Tigers to Exmoor Beasts*, Robert Hale, London, 1989

Spencer, John, and Hilary Evans (eds), *Phenomenon: From flying saucers to UFOs – forty years of facts and research*, Futura Publications, London, 1988

Story, Ronald D. (ed), *The Encyclopedia of UFOs*, New English Library, London, 1980; Doubleday & Company, New York, 1980

—— *UFOs and the Limits of Science*, New English Library, London, 1981

Thurston, Herbert, S. J., *Ghosts and Poltergeists*, Burns Oates & Washbourne, London, 1953

—— *The Physical Phenomena of Mysticism*, Burns Oates & Washbourne, London, 1952

Vallee, Jacques, *Passport to Magonia: From Folklore to Flying Saucers*, Neville Spearman, London, 1970; Henry Regnery Company, Chicago, IL, 1969

Webster, Ken, *The Vertical Plane*, Grafton Books, London, 1989

Wylie, Kenneth, *Bigfoot: A Personal Inquiry into a Phenomenon*, The Viking Press, New York, 1980

Magazines specializing in strange phenomena worldwide

Fate   170 Future Way, Marion, Ohio 43305, USA

Forteana News   A section in the monthly reports of world-wide UFO newsclippings: UFO Newsclipping Service, Route 1, Box 220, Plumerville, Arkansas 72127, USA

Fortean Times   96 Mansfield Road, London NW3 2HX, UK

INFO Journal   International Fortean Organization, PO Box 367, Arlington, VA 22210-0367, USA

International UFO Reporter   J. Allen Hynek Center for UFO Studies, 2457 W. Peterson Ave., Chicago, IL 60659, USA

The ISC Newsletter and *Cryptozoology*   International Society of Cryptozoology, Box 43070, Tucson, AZ 85733, USA

MUFON UFO Journal   Mutual UFO Network, 103 Oldtowne Road, Seguin, TX 78155, USA

Pursuit   The Society for the Investigation of the Unexplained, PO Box 265, Little Silver, NJ 07739-0265, USA

Strange Magazine   PO Box 2246, Rockville, MD 20852, USA

Notes

See Bibliography for publication details of those books not fully described here.

1. *Things that go bump in the night . . .*

1. Flammarion, *Haunted Houses*, p. 196.
2. South Africa *Sunday Times*, January 1984, noted in *Fortean Times* 43, p. 16.
3. Hereward Carrington, *Psychic Oddities* (Rider, 1952), pp. 160–2.
4. Thurston, *Ghosts and Poltergeists*, pp. 172–5.
5. Cleveland, OH, *Plain Dealer*, 16 January 1977.
6. Angus Macnaghten, *Haunted Berkshire* (Countryside Books, 1986), pp. 92–3.
7. Gauld and Cornell, *Poltergeists*, pp. 107–8.
8. Roll, *The Poltergeist*, p. 88.
9. Roll, *The Poltergeist*, p. 93.
10. Gauld and Cornell, *Poltergeists*, p. 107.
11. Carrington, op. cit., p. 176.
12. *Ihmistiedon Rajamailla*, ed. Mrs Aikki Perttola-Flink (Helsinki, 1972), sent to *Fortean Times* by Tuuri Heporauta and used in issue no. 45, p. 49.
13. Gauld and Cornell, *Poltergeists*, p. 108.
14. Thurston, *Ghosts and Poltergeists*, p. 36.
15. Gauld and Cornell, *Poltergeists*, p. 114.
16. Thurston, *Ghosts and Poltergeists*, p. 36.
17. *Birmingham Times*, 20 September 1974, quoted in *Fortean Times* 7, p. 5.
18. Flammarion, *Haunted Houses*, p. 130.
19. Roll, *The Poltergeist*, p. 39.
20. Thurston, *Ghosts and Poltergeists*, p. 35.
21. Gauld and Cornell, *Poltergeists*, p. 106.
22. Macnaghten, op. cit., p. 91.
23. Thurston, *Ghosts and Poltergeists*, pp. 68–77.
24. Gauld and Cornell, *Poltergeists*, pp. 357, 358.
25. *Fortean Times*, 43, p. 16.
26. *Fate*, May 1977, p. 12.
27. Joan Krieger, 'This Poltergeist Uses the Phone', *Fate*, August 1980, pp. 87–91.
28. Gauld and Cornell, *Poltergeists*, p. 357.
29. Roll, *The Poltergeist*, pp. 135, 137.
30. Gauld and Cornell, *Poltergeists*, p. 115.
31. Flammarion, *Haunted Houses*, p. 161.
32. *Connecticut Herald*, 24 March 1974.
33. Thurston, *Ghosts and Poltergeists*, p. 15.
34. *The Sun*, 30 November 1972, noted in *Fortean Times* 17, p. 5.
35. *National Enquirer*, 2 September 1975, noted in *Fortean Times* 19, p. 6.
36. Both cases noted in Michell and Rickard, *Phenomena*, p. 23.

37. Montreal, *La Presse*, March or April 1985, quoted in *INFO Journal* 48.
38. *Sunday Express*, 16 February 1986, noted in *Fortean Times* 48, p. 6.
39. Lincoln, NB, *Journal*, 9 September 1987, quoted in *Journal of the Fortean Research Center*, vol. 2, no. 3, p. 9; *Detroit News*, 10 September 1987; *Indianapolis Star*, 11 September 1987.
40. R. S. Lambert, *Exploring the Supernatural* (Arthur Barker, 1954), p. 145.
41. Lambert, op. cit., p. 146.
42. Paul F. Eno, 'Besieged by a Demon', *Fate*, June 1985, p. 89.
43. Roll, *The Poltergeist*, pp. 47–9.
44. Roll, *The Poltergeist*, p. 84.
45. *The Post* (USA paper), 6 September 1981.
46. Flammarion, *Haunted Houses*, p. 302.
47. Thurston, *Ghosts and Poltergeists*, p. 71.
48. For more information on the achievements of SORRAT, see Richards, *SORRAT*.

2. Hairy man-beasts on the North American continent

1. Reporter Ed Pehhale, report published 2 December 1985.
2. Interview with Krantz in *The ISC Newsletter* (International Society of Cryptozoology), vol. 6, no. 2, summer 1987.
3. Report in *Bigfoot Co-op*, June 1981, p. 6, from Bob Chance and John Green.
4. Danville, IL, *Commercial-News*, 2 March 1981, reprinted in *Forteana News*, June 1981, p. 14.
5. Report from Dave Klakamp, included in Tim Curry's 'Bigfoot Index'.
6. Spokane, WA, *Chronicle*, 29 April 1981, reprinted in *Forteana News*, May 1981, p. 16.
7. Newark, NJ, *Star Ledger*, 29 June 1981, reprinted in *Forteana News*, July 1981, p. 19.
8. Baton Rouge, LA, *Advocate*, 28 May 1981, reprinted in *Forteana News*, July 1981, p. 18.
9. New Orleans, LA, *Times-Picayune/States-Item*, 31 October 1981, reprinted in *Forteana News*, November 1981, p. 20.
10. Racine, WI, *Shoreline Leader*, 27 August 1981, reprinted in *Forteana News*, September 1981, p. 19.
11. Vincennes, IN, *Sun-Commercial*, 4 October 1981, reprinted in *Forteana News*, November 1981, p. 20.
12. Fargo, ND, *Forum*, 12 October 1981, reprinted in *Forteana News*, December 1981, p. 16.
13. Report in *Pursuit*, vol. 14, no. 4, p. 187, compiled from press reports.
14. Port Huron, MI, *Times Herald*, 9 December 1981, reprinted in *Forteana News*, January 1982, p. 19.
15. Port Huron, MI, *Times Herald*, 15 December 1981, reprinted in *Forteana News*, February 1982, p. 18.
16. Bruce G. Hallenbeck, Bob Bartholomew and Paul Bartholomew, 'Bigfoot in the Adirondacks', *Adirondack Bits 'n Pieces*, vol. 1, no. 3, spring–summer 1984.
17. Details of Freeman case compiled from reports in *The Vancouver Sun*, 19, 22, 23 October 1982, and *The ISC Newsletter*, vol. 1, no. 2, summer 1982, and vol. 1, no. 3, autumn 1982.
18. PA, *The Latrobe Bulletin*, 15 May 1987.
19. *Fate*, March 1984, p. 46.
20. *Fate*, August 1983, p. 43.
21. Visalia, CA, *Times Delta*, 9 December 1982, reprinted in *Forteana News*, February 1983, p. 18.

22. Little Rock, AR, *Arkansas Democrat*, 25 October 1983, reprinted in *Forteana News*, November 1983, p. 16.
23. Newtown, CT, *Bee*, 22 June 1984, reprinted in *Forteana News*, June 1984, pp. 19–20.
24. Mark Opsasnick, 'Recent Bigfoot Activity in Colonial Beach, Virginia'.
25. *Fortean Times* 45, p. 34.
26. Investigation by Wayne King; reported in *Bigfoot Co-op*, December 1985, p. 4, and April 1986, p. 3.
27. Harrisburg, PA, *The Patriot*, 9 and 10 October 1985, noted in *Crux* no. 2, p. 14.
28. *Crux*, no. 2, p. 14.
29. CA, *San Francisco Examiner*, 10 August 1986.
30. Summerville, GA, *News*, 4 September 1986, reprinted in *Forteana News*, January 1987, p. 15.
31. Cacapon Bridge, WV, *The West Virginia Advocate*, November 1986.
32. Report by Stan Gordon in *PASU Data Exchange*, 4, p. 2.
33. Vancouver, BC, *The Province*, 18 and 19 March 1987; BC, *The Vancouver Sun*, 29 April 1987.
34. CA, *Reno Gazette-Journal*, 14 May 1987, noted in *Bigfoot Co-op*, April/June 1987, p. 4.
35. Concord, NH, *Monitor*, 13 November 1987.

3. *UFOs – mysterious or mundane?*

1. Hans Van Kampen, 'Case #17 Revised: What Did Kenneth Arnold Really See?', *UFO Brigantia* no. 28 (November/December 1987), pp. 28–31.
2. Story, *The Encyclopedia of UFOs*, p. 220; Sachs, *The UFO Encyclopedia*, p. 125.
3. Story, *The Encyclopedia of UFOs*, p. 71; Sachs, *The UFO Encyclopedia*, p. 203.
4. Sachs, *The UFO Encyclopedia*, p. 99.
5. Story, *The Encyclopedia of UFOs*, p. 243; Sachs, *The UFO Encyclopedia*, p. 218.
6. Willy Smith, PhD, 'Ufology in Uruguay and Brazil', *MUFON 1987 International UFO Symposium Proceedings*, pp. 88–91.
7. Story, *The Encyclopedia of UFOs*, pp. 93–5; Sachs, *The UFO Encyclopedia*, pp. 187–8.
8. Jerome Clark, 'The Strange Case of Carlos de los Santos', *UFO Report*, December 1980, p. 26.
9. Robert J. Kirkpatrick, 'Pilot's-Eye View . . . IFO Over California', *Fate*, June 1978, pp. 66–72.
10. Richard F. Haines, *Melbourne Episode: Case Study of a Missing Pilot* (L.D.A. Press, Los Altos, CA, 1987). This book contains full details of the event, plus fictionalized accounts of what might have happened. A summary of the facts appears in Story, *The Encyclopedia of UFOs*, p. 379.
11. Quentin Fogarty, *Let's Hope They're Friendly!* (Angus & Robertson, Australia, 1982); also the events are summarized in Story, *The Encyclopedia of UFOs*, pp. 392–5.
12. *Res Bureaux Bulletin*, No. 51 (September 1971), p. 1.
13. Full report with plane and flight control exchanges quoted in Bruce Maccabee, 'The Fantastic Flight of JAL 1628', *International UFO Reporter*, vol. 12, no. 2, March/April 1987, pp. 4–23.
14. London, *The Times*, 27 June 1987.
15. Cleveland, OH, *The Plain Dealer*, 27 June 1987.
16. Caroline Wise, 'Report from Poland', *Anomaly* 1 (1985), pp. 6–7.
17. Smith, op. cit., pp. 91–6.
18. Sachs, *The UFO Encyclopedia*, pp.

194–5; Story, *The Encyclopedia of UFOs*, pp. 223–6, contains a report by Bruce Maccabee, who conducted one of the analyses.

19. Story, *The Encyclopedia of UFOs*, pp. 41–4; Smith, op. cit., pp. 97–8.
20. Sachs, *The UFO Encyclopedia*, pp. 324–6; Story, *The Encyclopedia of UFOs*, pp. 366–9, including the text of an interview with Barauna, from which the quotation comes.
21. Richard F. Haines, 'Analysis of a UFO Photograph', a shortened version of this report being published in vol. 1 of *Journal of Scientific Exploration* (USA). Also personal correspondence with Dr Haines and Mrs McRoberts.
22. Joël Mesnard, 'The "Steel Airship" at Bois-de-Champ (April 1954)', *Flying Saucer Review*, vol. 32, no. 5, pp. 16–17.
23. More details of the analyses can be found in Sachs, *The UFO Encyclopedia*, pp. 329–30, and Story, *The Encyclopedia of UFOs*, pp. 374–5.

4. Spontaneous human combustion and other mysterious fires

1. New York, NY, *Herald*, 27–28 December 1916, noted in Gaddis, *Mysterious Fires and Lights* (Dell edn), pp. 191–2.
2. New York, NY, *Sun*, 24 January 1930, noted in *The Complete Books of Charles Fort*, p. 930.
3. Noted in 'Cases of Spontaneous Human Combustion', Appendix A in Sanderson, *Investigating the Unexplained*, pp. 273–6.
4. Ellsworth, ME, *American*, 14 January 1943, noted in Gaddis, *Mysterious Fires and Lights*, pp. 192–3.
5. Noted in *Doubt*, June 1943, p. 5.
6. AP report, 15 December 1949, noted in Gaddis, *Mysterious Fires and Lights*, p. 193.
7. *New Scientist*, 29 May 1986.
8. Vincent H. Gaddis devotes Chapter 14 of *Mysterious Fires and Lights* to the case of Mrs Reeser; the alternative view is put by Joe Nickell and John F. Fischer in 'Incredible Cremations: Investigating Spontaneous Combustion Deaths', *The Skeptical Inquirer*, vol. 9, no. 4, summer 1987, pp. 352–7.
9. Gaddis, *Mysterious Fires and Lights*, pp. 193–4.
10. Gaddis, *Mysterious Fires and Lights*, p. 193.
11. Gaddis, *Mysterious Fires and Lights*, p. 195.
12. Gaddis, *Mysterious Fires and Lights*, pp. 230–3.
13. Larry E. Arnold, ' "Zounds, Holmes! It's a Case of the Combustible Corpse!" ', *Pursuit*, vol. 10, no. 3, p. 75.
14. Gaddis, *Mysterious Fires and Lights*, p. 194.
15. Larry E. Arnold, 'The Flaming Fate of Dr John Irving Bentley', *Pursuit*, vol. 9, no. 4, pp. 75–9.
16. *Suburban Trib/Chicago Tribune*, 14 March 1980.
17. Gaddis, *Mysterious Fires and Lights*, p. 195.
18. Sanderson, *Investigating the Unexplained*, p. 276.
19. San Antonio, TX, *The Light*, 16 November 1980, quoted in *Pursuit*, vol. 13, no. 4, pp. 177–8.
20. *Doubt*, June 1943, p. 5.
21. The last four reports (Jones 1980–Angel 1974) come from Larry Arnold, 'Jack Angel, SHC Survivor', *Fortean Times* 39, pp. 12–15.
22. Thurston, *Ghosts and Poltergeists*, pp. 62, 65, 74.
23. R. S. Lambert, *Exploring the Supernatural* (Arthur Barker, London, n.d. c.1954), pp. 122–31.
24. Gaddis, *Mysterious Fires and Lights*, pp. 159–60.

25. Gaddis, *Mysterious Fires and Lights*, pp. 160–1.
26. Gaddis, *Mysterious Fires and Lights*, pp. 155–6.
27. Gaddis, *Mysterious Fires and Lights*, pp. 165–8.
28. *New York Post*, 10 February 1988.
29. *Fortean Times* 44, pp. 43–4; Columbus, OH, *Dispatch*, 24 July 1983.
30. *Fortean Times* 32, p. 40.
31. *Fortean Times* 44, p. 45.
32. *New York Times*, 25 August 1929, noted in *The Complete Books of Charles Fort*, pp. 924–5.
33. *The Complete Books of Charles Fort*, p. 924.
34. *New York Herald Tribune*, 11 April 1934, pp. 20–1.
35. 'The Human Flame-Thrower', *Fortean Times* 42, p. 21.
36. *Fortean Times* 42, p. 49.

5. Ghosts and hauntings

1. *New York Herald*, 15 May 1906.
2. South Yorkshire, *Record*, 28 August 1986.
3. Chester Butterworth, 'Outside Modern London', in Martin Ebon (ed.), *True Experiences with Ghosts* (New American Library, 1968), pp. 110–11.
4. Don Farrant, 'The Ghost of Heritage Hill', *Fate*, June 1980, pp. 46–50.
5. Frances Little, 'I Keep House for a Ghost', *Fate*, October 1978, pp. 46–50.
6. *Sydney Morning Herald*, 25 February 1970, reprinted in *INFO Journal*, vol. 2, no. 3, pp. 16–17.
7. Beaumont, TX, *Enterprise*, 22 August 1983.
8. Brandon, *Weird America*, pp. 56–7.
9. Charles Fairclough, *Chester Ghosts and Poltergeists* (privately published, n.d.), pp. 43–5.
10. MacKenzie, *The Seen and the Unseen*, p. 209.
11. The ladies wrote a book entitled *An Adventure*. Also worth consulting on this famous case is Chapter IX 'The Ghosts of Versailles' in MacKenzie, *Hauntings and Apparitions*, which also includes details of others' experiences and an analysis of the case.
12. Florence Carre, *Folklore of Lytchett Matravers, Dorset* (West Country Folklore No. 8, The Toucan Press, St Peter Port, Guernsey, 1975), p. 6.
13. MacKenzie, *The Seen and the Unseen*, pp. 241–6.
14. Peter Moss, *Ghosts over Britain* (Elm Tree Books, 1977), pp. 75–7.
15. J. R. W. Coxhead, *Devon Traditions and Fairy-Tales* (The Raleigh Press, Exmouth, 1959), pp. 91–2.
16. Fairley and Welfare, *Arthur C. Clarke's World of Strange Powers*, pp. 126–7.
17. London, *Sunday Express*, 23 December 1979.
18. *Sheffield Star*, 21 September 1987, reprinted in *Northern Earth Mysteries* 34, p. 26.
19. For a full account of the lore, especially in Britain, see Michael Goss, *The Evidence for Phantom Hitch-Hikers* (The Aquarian Press, Wellingborough, 1984).
20. Harry Lebelson, '"Phantom Hitchhikers Haunt World's Highways and Roads"', *Pursuit*, vol. 18, no. 2, pp. 74–7.
21. *ibid.*
22. Cynthia Hind, 'Girl-Ghost Hitches Ride . . .', *Fate*, July 1979, pp. 54–9.
23. *Ottawa Journal* and *Vancouver Province*, 11 April 1980, reported in *Res Bureaux Bulletin*, no. 60, p. 4.
24. Nancy Bradley, 'White Lady of the Haunted Forest', *Fate*, January 1983, pp. 53–6.
25. Craig C. Downer, 'The Horrible Ghost of Anchicaya', *Fate*, March 1982, pp. 48–52.
26. *New York Herald*, 18 April 1908.

27. Houston, TX, *Chronicle*,
    November 1982.
28. *The Charlotte Observer*, 9
    November 1986.
29. R. S. Lambert, *Exploring the
    Supernatural* (Arthur Barker,
    London, n.d., *c*.1954), pp. 142–3.
30. Fairley and Welfare, *Arthur C.
    Clarke's World of Strange Powers*,
    p. 149.
31. Aberdeen, Scotland, *Press &
    Journal*, 13 October 1987,
    reproduced in *Dear Mr Thoms . . .*
    no. 7.
32. Llowarch, 'A Mine of Experience',
    The Cambrian News (Wales),
    14 November 1986.
33. Grampian and Highland, Scotland,
    Press and Journal, 18 May 1987;
    Fortean Times 49, p. 25.
34. Bo Linus Orsjo, 'Ghost Hotel',
    Fate, December 1987, pp. 45–6.
35. New Haven, CT, *Evening Register*,
    16 November 1910.
36. *Res Bureaux Bulletin*, no. 43, p. 3.

6. *UFO landings and close encounters*

1. Aimé Michel, *The Truth About
   Flying Saucers* (Robert Hale,
   London, 1957), pp. 140–4.
2. Ted Phillips, *Physical Traces
   Associated with UFO Sightings*,
   Center for UFO Studies, Illinois,
   1975.
3. Phillips, op. cit., p. 79.
4. Erol A. Faruk, 'The Delphos
   landing: new evidence from the
   laboratory', part 1 in *International
   UFO Reporter*, vol. 12, no. 1,
   pp. 21–5, part 2 in vol. 12, no. 3,
   pp. 19–21. See also Ted Phillips,
   'Close Encounters of the Second
   Kind: Physical Traces – A Case in
   Point, Delphos, Kansas', in 1981
   MUFON UFO Symposium
   Proceedings (Texas, 1981),
   pp. 105–29.
5. J-J. Velasco, 'Scientific Approach
   and Results of Studies into
   Unidentified Aerospace Phenomena
   in France', MUFON 1987
   International UFO Symposium
   Proceedings (Texas, 1987), p. 56.
6. Correspondence, *The Journal of
   Transient Aerial Phenomena*
   (BUFORA, London), vol. 4,
   no. 4, p. 119.
7. Steuart Campbell, 'UFOs: the grip
   of fear', *The Unexplained* 150,
   pp. 2990–3, and 152, pp. 3026–8.
   Steuart Campbell, 'Livingston: A
   New Hypothesis', *The Journal of
   Transient Aerial Phenomena*
   (BUFORA, London), vol. 4,
   no. 3, pp. 80–7.
8. Bowen, *The Humanoids*,
   pp. 144–5.
9. Isabel Davis and Ted Bloecher,
   *Close Encounter at Kelly and
   Others of 1955*, Center for UFO
   Studies, Illinois, 1978. Case
   summarized in Coleman,
   Mysterious America, pp. 185–90.
10. Bowen, *The Humanoids*, pp. 90–1.
11. *Fortean Times* 33, p. 30.
12. A reappraisal of this fascinating
    case has been prepared by Chris
    Rutkowski; see his 'Burned by a
    UFO? The story of a bungled
    investigation', *International UFO
    Reporter*, vol. 12, no. 6,
    November/December 1987,
    pp. 21–4. See also the letter from
    Edward M. Barker in *International
    UFO Reporter*, vol. 13, no. 2,
    pp. 21–2.
13. The cases briefly reported in this
    chapter come from a vast quantity
    of UFO literature of the last four
    decades, much of it now
    unobtainable. For an up-to-date
    picture of all facets of the UFO
    phenomenon, two recent books
    should be read: both edited by
    John Spencer and Hilary Evans,
    the titles are *Phenomenon* and
    UFOs 1947–1987. Some years ago,
    Charles Bowen edited a book
    entitled *The Humanoids* which is a
    good source of entity reports.

7. Monsters in lakes, rivers and seas

1. Bernard Heuvelmans, 'Annotated Checklist of Apparently Unknown Animals with which Cryptozoology is Concerned', *Cryptozoology*, vol. 5 (1986), p. 10.
2. *The Tampa Tribune-Times*, 28 September 1986.
3. The search in Lough Nahooin is fully described in Holiday, *The Dragon and the Disc*, ch. 4.
4. Holiday, *The Dragon and the Disc*, pp. 37–8.
5. *Fate* (UK), July 1967, pp. 11–12.
6. *ISC Newsletter*, vol. 4, no. 4, p. 8.
7. New Haven *Register*, 7 November 1987.
8. *ISC Newsletter*, vol. 5, no. 3, pp. 7–8.
9. *New York Herald Tribune*, 8 January 1934.
10. Ulrich Magin, 'The "Sea Serpent" of Loch Ness – Resident or Visitor?', *Pursuit* 72, pp. 156–9.
11. Gary S. Mangiacopra, 'The Great Unknowns into the Twentieth Century', part one, *Of Sea and Shore*, spring 1980, p. 14.
12. Heuvelmans, *In the Wake of the Sea-Serpents*, pp. 370–1.
13. Heuvelmans, *In the Wake . . .* , pp. 395–6.
14. Heuvelmans, *In the Wake . . .* , p. 415.
15. Mangiacopra, op. cit., part two, *Of Sea and Shore*, summer 1980, p. 124.
16. Mangiacopra, op. cit., part three, *Of Sea and Shore*, fall 1980, p. 194.
17. *ibid.*, p. 196.
18. Mangiacopra, op. cit., part three continued, *Of Sea and Shore*, winter 1980–1, p. 259.
19. *New York Herald Tribune*, 6 October 1933.
20. *New York Herald Tribune*, 15 November 1933.
21. *New York Herald Tribune*, 7 December 1933.
22. Washington, DC, *Washington Post*, 24 August 1913.
23. Heuvelmans, *In the Wake . . .* , pp. 391–2.
24. Full story in Heuvelmans, *In the Wake . . .* , pp. 531–5.
25. Michael Bright, 'The Beaked Beast of Bungalow Beach', *BBC Wildlife*, August 1986, p. 382; Karl Shuker, 'The Gambian Sea-Serpent', *The Unknown*, September 1986, pp. 49–53, October 1986, pp. 31–6.
26. *Science and Mechanics*, November/December 1983.
27. Heuvelmans, 'Annotated Checklist . . .', p. 7.

8. Ball lightning and spook lights

1. Hal R. Aldrich, 'Ball Lightning and Explanations', *INFO Journal* 37, p. 2.
2. Theodore Charles Illert, 'The Parkside Lightning Ball', quoted in *Science Frontiers* 33, p. 4.
3. 'Ball Lightning at Salina, Kans.', *Monthly Weather Review* 47 (1919), p. 728, noted in Corliss, *Lightning, Auroras . . .* , p. 77.
4. North Wales *Daily Post*, 12 June 1987.
5. Gaddis, *Mysterious Fires and Lights*, p. 54.
6. Mark Stenhoff, 'Torro Ball Lightning Division Report: April 1987', *Journal of Meteorology* 12 (1987), p. 200, noted in *Science Frontiers* 54, p. 4.
7. P. W. Burbidge and D. J. Robertson, 'A Lightning-Associated Phenomenon and Related Geomagnetic Measurements', *Nature* 300 (1982), p. 623, noted in *Science Frontiers* 26, p. 2.
8. Frank Edwards, *Strange World* (Lyle Stuart, Inc., 1964).
9. James R. Powell and David Finkelstein, 'Ball Lightning',

American Scientist 58 (1970),
p. 262, noted in Corliss, *Lightning,
Auroras . . .* , p. 80.

10. Letter in *Pursuit* 67, p. 134.

11. Dallas, TX, *Times Herald*, 14
January 1984, reprinted in
Forteana News, January 1984,
p. 19. Further similar reports can
be found in William R. Corliss,
*The Unexplained: A Sourcebook of
Strange Phenomena* (Bantam
Books, 1976).

12. Edward U. Condon, *Scientific
Study of Unidentified Flying
Objects* (Bantam Books, New York,
1969), pp. 729–35, noted in
Corliss, *Lightning, Auroras . . .* ,
p. 58.

13. *Fortean Times* 31, p. 39.

14. MN, *Eagle Bend News*, 25 May
1961, noted in Gaddis, *Mysterious
Fires and Lights*, p. 202.

15. 'Ball Lightning', Royal
Astronomical Society of Canada
Journal 19 (1925), p. 213.

16. *Fate*, June 1953, noted in Gaddis,
Mysterious Fires and Lights,
pp. 202–3.

17. B. H. Bailey, 'Ball Lightning
Strikes Twice', *Weather* 39 (1984),
p. 76, quoted in *Science Frontiers*
41, p. 4.

18. p. 56.

19. *Round Robin*, October 1958,
quoted in Gaddis, *Mysterious Fires
and Lights*, pp. 54–5.

20. *Soviet Weekly*, 11 February 1984,
quoted in *Science Frontiers* 34,
p. 3.

21. Some of his writings on BOLs are:
'BOLs', *Probe Report*, July 1982;
excerpts from that in 'Mysterious
Spheres and Lights', *INFO Journal*
45, pp. 4–6, and 46, pp. 18–23;
'Seeing the Lights', *Fate*, October
1985, pp. 82–7, and November
1985, pp. 87–92.

22. *Journal of Meteorology*, vol. 10, no.
97, p. 89.

23. J. P. Painter, letter in *BUFORA
Journal* 2 (1963), quoted in *INFO
Journal* 9, p. 31.

24. Hilary Evans, 'Mysterious Spheres

and Lights', *INFO Journal* 46,
p. 21.

25. Little Rock, AR, *Arkansas
Democrat*, 8 July 1984, reprinted
in *Forteana News* 180, p. 20.

26. 'Strange Pipe and Ghost Lights in
West Virginia', *INFO Journal* 44,
p. 15.

27. Charles Gouiran, *et al.*, 'Report on
a Landing at Uzès', *Flying Saucer
Review*, vol. 24, no. 4, pp. 3–7.

28. Hilary Evans, 'Mysterious Spheres
and Lights', *INFO Journal* 46,
p. 22.

29. Account by a friend of Guy Lyon
Playfair, recorded in *Fortean Times*
31, p. 53.

30. Houston, TX, *Chronicle*, 31
October 1986.

31. *Wall Street Journal*, date
unknown.

32. *ibid.*; for a good general account
see Dennis Stacy, 'The Marfa
Lights', *MUFON UFO Journal*
235, pp. 3–7.

33. *Science Frontiers* 33, p. 3.

34. Brandon, *Weird America*, pp.
174–5.

35. Little Rock, AR, *Arkansas
Gazette*, 22 June 1980, reprinted in
Forteana News 132, p. 18.

36. Atlanta, GA, *Journal*, 29 October
1982, reprinted in *INFO Journal*
45, pp. 16–17.

37. Green Bay, WI, *Press-Gazette*,
1 October 1978, reprinted in
Forteana News, December 1978,
p. 17.

38. Gaddis, *Mysterious Fires and
Lights*, p. 77.

39. *Fate*, autumn 1948, reported in
Gaddis, *Mysterious Fires and
Lights*, pp. 90–1.

9. Winged people and other non-humans

1. Nigel Watson, *Phantom Aerial
Flaps and Waves*, Magonia

Occasional Paper No. 1 (1987), p. 12.

2. Alex Evans, 'Encounters with Little Men', *Fate*, November 1978, pp. 83–5.

3. *ibid.*, p. 85.

4. Perth, *West Mail*, 25 December 1982, reprinted in *UFO Newsclipping Service*, February 1983, no. 163, p. 12.

5. Vladimir V. Rubtsov, 'A "Flying 'Man' in Black" in Russia', *Flying Saucer Review*, vol. 24, no. 4, p. 13.

6. Dublin, *Irish Press*, 1938, reported in Clark and Coleman, *The Unidentified*, pp. 57–8.

7. Rogo and Clark, *Earth's Secret Inhabitants*, pp. 78–9.

8. *ibid.*, pp. 82–3.

9. 'Homens Alados em Pelotas', *SBEDV Bulletin* 112/115 (September 1976/April 1977).

10. Sinclair Taylor, 'The Bird Thing', *The World's Strangest Stories* (Fate magazine, Clark Publishing Company, 1983), pp. 27–8.

11. Reported in the *Houston Chronicle*, and in Keel, *Strange Creatures from Time and Space*, pp. 207–8.

12. *Flying Saucer Review*, vol. 19, no. 3, p. 29.

13. Isabel Davis and Ted Bloecher, *Close Encounter at Kelly and Others of 1955* (Center for UFO Studies, Illinois, 1978), pp. 149–60.

14. *Creature Chronicles* 6, pp. 6–7.

15. 'Winged Wonder Over Falls City?', *Journal* of the Fortean Research Center, vol. 1, no. 1, pp. 3–4.

16. Intcat 661, in *MUFOB* New Series 9 (winter 1977–8), p. 7.

17. Miguel Peyro Garcia, 'Strange Beings near Jerez de la Frontera (Province of Cadiz), Spain, in 1960', *APRO Bulletin*, vol. 29, no. 1 (July 1980), pp. 4–5.

18. Coral Lorenzen, 'UFO Occupants in the United States', in Bowen, *The Humanoids*, pp. 159–60.

19. Keel, *Strange Creatures from Time and Space*, p. 210.

20. The full story of the Mothman sightings can be found in John A. Keel, *The Mothman Prophecies* (Saturday Review Press, E. P. Dutton & Co., Inc., New York, 1975).

21. Don Worley, 'The Winged Lady in Black', *Flying Saucer Review* Case Histories 10, pp. 14–16.

22. Åke Franzen, 'The Little Man of Norrbotten', *Flying Saucer Review* Case Histories 4, pp. 13–14.

23. *Flying Saucer Review*, vol. 19, no. 6, p. 30.

24. Gordon Creighton, 'Tiny Entities Reported in Colombia', *Flying Saucer Review*, vol. 21, no. 5, p. 33.

25. Fred H. Bost, 'A Few Small Steps on the Earth: A Tiny Leap for Mankind?', *Pursuit*, vol. 10, no. 2, pp. 50–3.

26. Coleman, *Mysterious America*, pp. 41–56.

27. Robert A. Goerman, 'The Little Green Man Who Got Away', *Fate*, May 1982, pp. 61–5.

10. USOs – unidentified submarine objects

1. Munich, *Süddeutsche Zeitung*, 30 April 1988, noted in *BILK* 22.

2. Jacques Vallee, *Anatomy of a Phenomenon* (Henry Regnery Company, Chicago, 1965, and Neville Spearman, London, 1966), p. 141.

3. *INFO Journal* 13, p. 30.

4. Walter N. Webb, 'Radar/Sonar Contact', *MUFON UFO Journal* 199, pp. 7–9.

5. *Eastern Daily Press* report, noted in *Lantern* 16, p. 9.

6. (Neville Spearman, London, 1956), pp. 114–16.

7. London *Weekly Dispatch*, 10 July 1910, noted in *The Complete Books of Charles Fort*, p. 639.

8. *Gaceta Illustrada*, 31 July 1965,

noted in Vallee, *Passport to Magonia*, p. 308, case 651.

9. Madrid, *Pueblo*, 1 April 1981, noted in *UFO Newsclipping Service* 146, p. 12.

10. Vicente-Juan Ballester Olmos, 'Unusual Underwater Object', *Flying Saucer Review* Case Histories 6, pp. 5–7.

11. *Lumières dans la Nuit* Series 3 No. 5 (January 1971), reprinted in English in *Flying Saucer Review* Case Histories 14, p. 14.

12. *International UFO Reporter*, vol. 4, no. 3, p. 17.

13. *Zoologist*, 4 July 1938, noted in *INFO Journal*, vol. 1, no. 3, pp. 43–4, and Sanderson, *Invisible Residents*, p. 28.

14. Lieut.-Col. Lobet, 'Another Close Contact on Réunion', *Flying Saucer Review*, vol. 25, no. 3, p. 8.

15. Sanderson, *Invisible Residents*, p. 41.

16. All four Australian cases from H. J. Hinfelaar, 'Submarine Craft in Australasian Waters', *Flying Saucer Review*, vol. 12, no. 4, pp. 28–30.

17. *ibid.*, pp. 28–9.

18. *ibid.*, pp. 29–30.

19. John Prytz, 'I Spy With my Little Eye, Something Beginning with "S"', *Fortean Times* 42, p. 57.

20. *L'Astronomie* 22, p. 28, reported in Jacques Vallee, *Anatomy of a Phenomenon* (see note 2 above), p. 21.

21. *Naval Aviation News*, February 1951, noted in Sanderson, *Invisible Residents*, p. 36.

22. Samuel Norman, 'Recent UFOs Over Japan', *Fate*, June 1956, pp. 22–4, noted in Sanderson, *Invisible Residents*, p. 38.

23. Witness interviewed by oceanographer Dr Vladimir Azhazha, and the report is genuine despite having appeared in the *National Enquirer*. See *AFU Newsletter* 24, p. 10, and 27, p. 21.

24. *UFO Investigator*, vol. 4, no. 5, p. 4, noted in Sanderson, *Invisible Residents*, pp. 35–6.

25. *Seattle Times*, 9 March 1960, reported in Sanderson, *Invisible Residents*, p. 40.

26. 'Did Navy "Steal" UFO?', *APRO Bulletin*, vol. 33, no. 1, p. 1.

27. *Los Angeles Times*, 25 October 1962, reported in Jim and Coral Lorenzen, *UFOs Over the Americas* (New American Library, New York, 1968), pp. 51–2.

28. J. Antonio Huneeus, 'A Historical Survey of UFO Cases in Chile', MUFON UFO Symposium Proceedings 1987, pp. 191–2.

29. Joseph M. Brill, 'Are UFOs Operating from Underwater Bases off the Coast of Argentina?', *MUFON UFO Journal* 130, pp. 3–5.

30. Jim and Coral Lorenzen, *UFOs Over the Americas* (see note 27 above), pp. 52–3.

31. Sanderson, *Invisible Residents*, p. 49.

32. Gordon W. Creighton, 'Argentina 1962', *Flying Saucer Review*, vol. 10, no. 4, p. 13.

33. Brill, op. cit.

34. Robert A. Stiff, 'Tragic Sighting in Argentina', in Brad Steiger and Joan Whritenour, *The Allende Letters* (Universal 1968), noted in Sanderson, *Invisible Residents*, p. 58.

35. Charles Bowen, 'UFOs Over Water', *The Unexplained* 57, p. 1140.

36. *APRO Bulletin*, January 1964, p. 1, noted in Sanderson, *Invisible Residents*, pp. 74–6.

37. Oscar A. Galindez in *Flying Saucer Review*, vol. 14, no. 2, p. 22, quoted in Sanderson, *Invisible Residents*, pp. 23–5.

38. *APRO Bulletin*, vol. 29, no. 5, p. 7.

39. Jim and Coral Lorenzen, *UFOs Over the Americas* (see note 27 above), pp. 50–1.

40. *ibid.*, pp. 54–5.

41. Gordon Creighton, 'Underwater UFO Base off Venezuela?', *Flying Saucer Review*, vol. 21, no. 1, pp. 11–12.
42. Walter N. Webb, 'Radar/Sonar Contact', *MUFON UFO Journal* 199, pp. 9–10.
43. Santa Ana, CA, *The Register*, 14 November 1973, reported in *INFO Journal* 13, p. 31.
44. *Fate*, March 1955, p. 18, noted in Sanderson, *Invisible Residents*, p. 37.
45. Port Chester, NY, *Item*, 22 June 1957, noted in Sanderson, *Invisible Residents*, p. 39.
46. *New York Times*, 5 November 1906, quoted in Livingston Gearhart, 'Bombed by Meteors', *Fate*, March 1965, p. 80.
47. Yarmouth, NS, *Light Herald*, 12 October 1967, quoted in Sanderson, *Invisible Residents*, pp. 44–5.
48. Clas Svahn and Anders Liljegren, 'The Kölmjärv Ghost Rocket Crash Revisited', *AFU Newsletter* 27, pp. 1–5.
49. *Fortean Times* 24, p. 41.
50. *INFO Journal* 25, p. 5.
51. *Fortean Times* 45, p. 47.
52. Both *Fortean Times* 24, p. 41.
53. *INFO Journal* 30, p. 4.
54. Brandon, *Weird America*, p. 170.
55. *International UFO Reporter* in *Frontiers of Science*, vol. 3, no. 5, pp. 13–14.
56. *Skylook* (predecessor to *MUFON UFO Journal*) 82 (September 1974), p. 8.

11. *Ghostly voices*

1. (Gerald Duckworth & Co. Ltd, London, 1953), p. 78.
2. p. 112.
3. Danton Walker, *Spooks De Luxe* (Franklin Watts, USA, 1956), reprinted in *Fate*, August 1979, p. 51.
4. Jarl Fahler, 'The Return of Finland's President', in Martin Ebon (ed.), *True Experiences with Ghosts* (New American Library, 1968), pp. 74–7.
5. *Daily Express*, 3 March 1971, noted in *Fortean Times* 10, p. 5.
6. Charles Fairclough, *Chester Ghosts and Poltergeists* (n.d. – 1970s or 1980s), p. 4.
7. W. H. Allen, London, 1978.
8. Long report by Neil Bartlem in *Chester Observer*, 24 December 1985, and personal contact with Ken Webster and colleagues.
9. MacKenzie, *The Seen and the Unseen*, pp. 167–9.
10. Angus Macnaghten, *Haunted Berkshire* (Countryside Books, Newbury, 1986), p. 59.
11. MacKenzie, *The Seen and the Unseen*, pp. 85–6.
12. *Fortean Times* 10, p. 3.
13. Margaret A. Blair, 'A Ghost Sings in Ireland', *Fate*, June 1979, pp. 41–6.
14. Charles Fairclough, *Chester Ghosts and Poltergeists*, pp. 43–5.
15. Llowarch, 'Weird Wonders of Wales', *Cambrian News*, 30 January 1987.
16. Gerald J. Sword, 'Who Goes There? (Ghostly Manifestations at Point Lookout)', *Chronicles of St Mary's*, Monthly Bulletin of the St Mary's County Historical Society, vol. 30, no. 7 (July 1982), pp. 465–71.
17. *New York Herald Tribune*, 12 July 1924.
18. *Daily Telegraph*, 24 February 1981, noted in *Fortean Times* 35, p. 36.
19. *Rand Daily Mail*, 30 July 1982, noted in *Fortean Times* 43, p. 42.
20. Martin A. De Harte, ' "Robina Has Not Been Saved!" ', *Fate*, February 1982, pp. 44–6.
21. R. S. Lambert, *Exploring the Supernatural* (Arthur Barker, London, 1954), pp. 106–21.
22. *National Enquirer*, 4 September 1984, noted in *Fortean Times* 43, p. 16.

23. Peter A. Jordan, 'The Hackettstown Haunting', *Fate*, October 1980, pp. 49–55.

24. Joan Krieger, 'This Poltergeist Uses the Phone', *Fate*, August 1980, pp. 87–91.

25. Ian Stevenson, 'Are Poltergeists Living or Dead?', *Fate*, February 1988, pp. 73–4.

26. MacKenzie, *The Seen and the Unseen*, p. 26.

27. Cruz, *The Incorruptibles*, pp. 100–1; personal communication from the Suore Minime dell' Addolorata.

28. Personal correspondence.

29. MacKenzie, *Hauntings and Apparitions*, pp. 156–61.

30. The experiments featured in an American TV series 'That's Incredible', and have also been filmed by Japanese and Canadian television, and by the English BBC TV 'Newsnight' programme. We have heard a tape of some of the sounds and corresponded with John Marke.

31. Lexington Park, MD, *The Enterprise*, 31 October 1986.

32. Lexington Park, MD, *The Enterprise*, 22 October 1986.

33. Southern Maryland Psychic Investigations report by Lori Mellott.

34. *South Yorkshire Times*, 29 August 1986.

35. Lesley Sussman, 'Did Voice from Grave Name Killer?', *Fate*, July 1978, pp. 61–7.

36. General historical background in D. Scott Rogo, *Phantoms*, pp. 78–9, and Fairley and Welfare, *Arthur C. Clarke's World of Strange Powers*, pp. 272–4. Techniques used by one researcher, G. Gilbert Bonner, appear in his article 'Radio Link with the Dead', in *Fate*, September 1979, pp. 46–53. Books have also been written, including several by Jürgenson and Raudive, most notably Raudive's *Breakthrough* (Colin Smythe, Gerrards Cross, 1971; Taplinger, New York, 1971). See also Peter Bander, *Voices from the Tapes* (Drake Publishers, New York, 1973) and D. J. Ellis, *The Mediumship of the Tape Recorder* (privately published, 1978).

37. This theory is set out in Terrence Peterson, 'Spiricom or Spiricon?', *Fate*, January 1987, pp. 92–7, and there are answering letters in the April 1987 issue. A book on Spiricom is John G. Fuller's *The Ghost of 29 Megacycles* (Souvenir Press, London, 1985).

38. *New Frontiers Newsletter*, fall–winter 1986, noted in *INFO Journal* 54, p. 31.

39. *Indianapolis Star*, 21, 22, 23 October 1987.

12. *Hairy man-beasts around the world*

1. Sanderson, *Abominable Snowmen*, pp. 164–5.

2. New York Botanical Garden *Newsletter*, fall 1987, noted in *INFO Journal* 53, p. 28.

3. Sanderson, *Abominable Snowmen*, pp. 174–7.

4. Lt.-Col. P. H. Fawcett, *Exploration Fawcett* (Hutchinson & Co., London, 1953), pp. 200–2.

5. Pablo Latapi Ortega, 'Ucumar, the Argentinian Yeti', in *Contactos Extraterrestres*, 16 April 1980.

6. *London Evening Standard*, 15 March 1976, noted in Eberhart, *Monsters*, p. 197.

7. Sanderson, *Abominable Snowmen*, p. 194.

8. Chicago *Tribune*, 11 October 1978; Winnipeg, Manitoba, *Free Press*, 16 October 1978; and many other press reports; also *Fortean Times* 27, p. 48.

9. Librairie Plon, Paris, 1980.

10. For more details see Heuvelmans, *On the Track of Unknown Animals*, ch. 16, and Sanderson, *Abominable Snowmen*, ch. 9.

11. Welfare and Fairley, *Arthur C. Clarke's Mysterious World*, pp. 18–19.

12. *Fortean Times* 17, p. 21; Welfare and Fairley, *Arthur C. Clarke's Mysterious World*, p. 15.

13. Tim Kirby, 'The Littlest Yeti', *BBC Wildlife*, vol. 5, no. 5 (May 1987), p. 251.

14. *BBC Wildlife*, September 1987, p. 443.

15. Heuvelmans, *On the Track . . .* , pp. 117–21.

16. Heuvelmans, *On the Track . . .* , pp. 101–2.

17. Heuvelmans, *On the Track . . .* , pp. 104–6.

18. More information on sightings, footprints and possible identifications will be found in Heuvelmans, *On the Track of Unknown Animals*, ch. 6, and Sanderson, *Abominable Snowmen*, ch. 12.

19. 'What is it? . . . Myth or Reality?', *Technical Journal for Youth*, 6.

20. Shackley, *Wildmen*, p. 129. More information on the Siberian wildman can be found in Chapter 8 of *Wildmen*.

21. Report by Dmitri Bayanov and Nikolai Avdeyev in *Bigfoot Co-op*, April/June 1987, pp. 6–9.

22. Report by Maya Bykova in *Bigfoot Co-op*, April 1988, pp. 5–8. Also Dmitri Bayanov's updating and comment in *Bigfoot Co-op*, June 1988, pp. 6–10.

23. See, for example, her report in Markotic, *The Sasquatch and other Unknown Hominoids*.

24. Shackley, *Wildmen*, p. 115; Henry Gris and William Dick, *The New Soviet Psychic Discoveries* (Prentice-Hall, Inc., USA, 1978; Souvenir Press, London, 1979), p. 193.

25. Gris and Dick, *The New Soviet Psychic Discoveries* (see note 24 above), p. 187.

26. *ibid.*, ch. 16, which gives full details of the author's interview with Karapetyan.

27. Dmitri Bayanov, 'A Field Investigation into the Relict Hominoid Situation in Tajikistan, USSR', *Cryptozoology*, vol. 3 (1984), pp. 74–9.

28. Shackley, *Wildmen*, pp. 118–19.

29. Sanderson, *Abominable Snowmen*, pp. 310–11.

30. Dmitri Bayanov in Markotic, *The Sasquatch . . .* , p. 73.

31. On the Almas in Mongolia, see Shackley, *Wildmen*, ch. 5, and Michael Heaney, 'The Mongolian Almas: A Historical Reevaluation of the Sighting by Baradiin', *Cryptozoology*, vol. 2 (1983), pp. 40–52.

32. Zhou Guoxing, 'The Big Wildman and the Little Wildman', *BBC Wildlife*, September 1987, pp. 443–4.

33. Zhou Guoxing, 'The Status of Wildman Research in China', *Cryptozoology*, vol. 1 (1982), pp. 13–23. For a more detailed account of the 1940 encounter, see Shackley, *Wildmen*, p. 82.

34. Shackley, *Wildmen*, p. 84.

35. Yuan Zhenxin and Huang Wanpo, *Wildman: China's Yeti*, *Fortean Times* Occasional Paper No. 1, pp. 11–12.

36. In addition to the references cited, useful accounts of the Chinese wildman can also be found in Shackley, *Wildmen*, ch. 4; Frank E. Poirier, Hu Hongxing, Chung-Min Chen, 'The Evidence for Wildman in Hubei Province, People's Republic of China', *Cryptozoology*, vol. 2 (1983), pp. 25–39; John Green, 'The Search in China for Unknown Hominoids', in Markotic, *The Sasquatch and other Unknown Hominoids*, pp. 87–99.

37. According to Bernard Heuvelmans in his chapter on the Orang pendek (ch. 5) in *On the Track of Unknown Animals*.

38. *ibid.*, pp. 85–7. This encounter is also reported in Sanderson, *Abominable Snowmen*, pp. 222–4,

Chapter 10 of his book being devoted to 'The East'.

39. Bernard Heuvelmans, 'Annotated Checklist of Apparently Unknown Animals with which Cryptozoology is Concerned', *Cryptozoology*, vol. 5 (1986), p. 23.

40. *Sydney Morning Herald*, 23 October 1912, quoted in Dmitri Bayanov, 'The Case for the Australian Hominoids', in Markotic, *The Sasquatch and other Unknown Hominoids*, pp. 101–26.

41. Greg Hunter, 'The Great Yowie Hunt', *Australian Penthouse*, vol. 4, no. 9 (August 1983), pp. 34–41.

42. Australian newspaper report, name unknown, 7 April 1978.

43. Lismore, NSW, *Northern Star*, 23 May 1981.

44. A. G. Thorne, P. G. Macumber, 'Discoveries of Late Pleistocene Man at Kow Swamp, Australia', *Nature*, vol. 238 (no. 5363, 11 August 1972), pp. 316–19.

45. *New York Times*, 2 June 1987.

13. *Unexpected objects falling from the sky*

1. *Doubt* 14, p. 212.

2. Houston, TX, *Chronicle*, 25 July 1982.

3. Tass report dated 13 August 1984, quoted in full in Fairley and Welfare, *Arthur C. Clarke's Chronicles of the Strange and Mysterious*, p. 72.

4. Ronald J. Willis, 'Ice Falls', *INFO Journal*, vol. 1, no. 3, pp. 12–23.

5. Christopher F. Chyba, 'The Cometary Contribution to the Oceans of Primitive Earth', *Nature* 330 (1987), p. 632, noted in *Science Frontiers* 56, pp. 2–3. Jeff Hecht, 'Snowballs from space "filled Earth's oceans"', *New Scientist*, no. 1612, 12 May 1988, p. 38.

6. Palm Beach, FL, *Post*,

12 September 1978, noted in *Res Bureaux Bulletin* 40, p. 7.

7. Vancouver, BC, *Province*, 3 February 1986, noted in *INFO Journal* 50, p. 22.

8. Mike Rowe, 'The Whirlwind Theory of Fish Falls', *Fortean Times* 38, pp. 42–3; Derek Elsom, 'Catch a falling frog', *New Scientist* 108 (no. 1615, 2 June 1988), pp. 38–40.

9. Brandon, *Weird America*, p. 96.

10. Chicago, IL, *Tribune*, 3 July 1901.

11. Forth Worth, TX, *Star-Telegram*, 9 May 1985.

12. 'The Chilatchee, Alabama Fish Fall', *INFO Journal* 46, p. 24.

13. *Daily Telegraph*, 25 August 1986, reported in *Fortean Times* 48, p. 16.

14. Los Angeles, CA, *Times*, 22 May 1911.

15. Brandon, *Weird America*, p. 28.

16. San Francisco, CA, *Chronicle*, 27 October 1956, reported in *INFO Journal* 7, p. 45.

17. *Fortean Times* 44, p. 27.

18. From Gilbert Whitley's list of 'Rains of Fishes in Australia', reprinted in *INFO Journal* 10, pp. 22–5.

19. *New York Post*, 20 August 1941, noted in Sanderson, *Investigating the Unexplained*, p. 294.

20. Nigel Rimes in *Flying Saucer Review*, vol. 14, no. 6, back cover.

21. *Shropshire Star*, 10 March 1986.

22. Brandon, *Weird America*, p. 98.

23. *Daily Telegraph*, 10 January 1952, noted in Sanderson, *Investigating the Unexplained*, p. 296.

24. Michael A. Persinger and Gyslaine F. Lafrenière, *Space-Time Transients and Unusual Events* (Nelson-Hall Inc., Chicago, 1977), p. 30.

25. *Detroit Free Press*, 11 March 1958, noted in Sanderson, *Investigating the Unexplained*, p. 296.

26. Persinger and Lafrenière, op. cit., p. 30.

27. *New York Times*, 11 July 1971, noted in *INFO Journal* 8, p. 26.

28. Robert C. Warth, 'Corn Falls from Sky', *Pursuit* 76, p. 173.
29. *Greeley Tribune* report, noted in *Fate*, March 1988, p. 24.
30. St Louis, *Post-Dispatch*, 10 November 1965, noted in Michell and Rickard, *Phenomena*, p. 19.
31. *Fortean Times* 25, p. 11.
32. *Sunday Express*, 15 April 1957, noted in Michell and Rickard, *Phenomena*, p. 19.
33. Brandon, *Weird America*, p. 170.
34. *Fate* (UK), September 1976, p. 31.
35. *Bath Chronicle*, 7 January 1976, noted in Michell and Rickard, *Phenomena*, p. 19.
36. Los Angeles, CA, *Times*, 7 January 1909.
37. *Popular Mechanics*, 14-801, noted in *The Complete Books of Charles Fort*, p. 639.
38. Persinger and Lafrenière, op. cit., p. 31.
39. ' "Pseudo"-Meteorites', *INFO Journal* 11, pp. 9–10.
40. ibid., p. 9.
41. Rickard and Kelly, *Photographs of the Unknown*, pp. 32–3.
42. *Fate*, April 1955, p. 13, noted in Sanderson, *Investigating the Unexplained*, p. 280.
43. *Sacramento Union*, 29 July 1955, noted in Sanderson, *Investigating the Unexplained*, p. 279.
44. Brandon, *Weird America*, p. 125.
45. ibid., p. 63.
46. ibid., pp. 154–5.
47. *Indianapolis News*, 18 May 1984, quoted in *Pursuit* 67, p. 133.
48. AP report carried in various papers, and noted in *Fortean Times* 42, p. 14.
49. *The Cambridge Encyclopedia of Astronomy* (Jonathan Cape, London, 1977), pp. 244–8.
50. *American Journal of Science* 4-34-437, noted in *The Complete Books of Charles Fort*, p. 504.
51. *Nature* 105-759, noted in Sanderson, *Investigating the Unexplained*, p. 285.
52. *Australian Flying Saucer Review* no. 3 (December 1970), noted in *INFO Journal* 9, p. 22.
53. *Baltimore Sun*, 27 June 1956, noted in Sanderson, *Investigating the Unexplained*, p. 286.
54. *Birmingham Evening Mail*, 13 May 1969, noted in *Fortean Times* 25, p. 11.
55. Belgium, *Le Soir*, 15 July 1975, noted in *Fortean Times* 25, p. 11.
56. *Toronto Star*, 21 and 22 August 1978, noted in *Res Bureaux Bulletin* 38, p. 2.
57. Quincy, MA, *Patriot Ledger*, 5 November 1983, reprinted in *Forteana News* 174, p. 19.
58. Persinger and Lafrenière, op. cit., p. 30.
59. AP report, noted in Sanderson, *Investigating the Unexplained*, p. 289.
60. Brandon, *Weird America*, pp. 178–9.
61. Numerous press reports, noted in *Fortean Times* 27, p. 5, and *Pursuit* 45, p. 42.
62. Gaddis, *Mysterious Fires and Lights*, p. 42.
63. *Miami Herald*, 28–29 February 1958, quoted in Gaddis, *Mysterious Fires and Lights*, pp. 42–3.
64. Gaddis, *Mysterious Fires and Lights*, p. 43.
65. For more on these beliefs, see 'Pwdre Ser or the "Rot of the Stars" ', Chapter 14 of William R. Corliss, *The Unexplained: A Sourcebook of Strange Phenomena* (Bantam Books, New York, 1976).
66. Houston, TX, *Post/Sun*, 9 September 1979, noted in Corliss, *Tornadoes, Dark Days . . .* , p. 59.
67. *INFO Journal* report, noted in Brandon, *Weird America*, p. 32.
68. Brandon, *Weird America*, pp. 105–6.
69. *Pursuit*, vol. 4, no. 1, p. 6.
70. *Pursuit*, vol. 5, no. 3, pp. 53–4.
71. *Atlanta Journal & Constitution*, 11 June 1972, quoted in *Pursuit*, vol. 5, no. 3, p. 54.
72. *St Louis Post-Dispatch*,

24 September 1978, quoted in
Pursuit 45, p. 40.

14. *Out-of-place big cats and other mystery animals*

1. *Cincinnati Enquirer*, 21 November
   1985, reproduced in *Creature
   Chronicles* 8, p. 3.
2. Loren E. Coleman, 'Mystery
   Animals in Illinois', *Fate*, July
   1971, pp. 13–18.
3. Coleman, *Mysterious America*,
   ch. 12, pp. 106–16.
4. *ISC Newsletter*, vol. 5, no. 3,
   p. 10.
5. Victor Lott, 'A Fisher in Florida',
   INFO Journal 44, p. 9.
6. *The Conservationist* July/August
   1982, reprinted in *INFO Journal*
   41, p. 17.
7. Loren Coleman has researched into
   black cats in the States; see his
   article 'Black "Mountain Lions" in
   California?', *Pursuit* 46, pp. 61–2,
   and Chapter 11 of his *Mysterious
   America*.
8. Ulrich Magin, 'Continental
   European Big Cats', *Pursuit* 71,
   pp. 114–15.
9. *Berrima District Post*, 7 June 1978.
10. A survey of the reports from the
    Southern Highlands is given in
    Paul Cropper, 'The Panthers of
    Southern Australia', *Fortean Times*
    32, pp. 19–21.
11. Coffs Harbour, NSW, *Advocate*,
    9 March 1982.
12. Michael Goss, 'The Queensland
    Tiger', *Fate*, March 1987,
    pp. 38–47.
13. Michell and Rickard, *Living
    Wonders*, pp. 64–6.
14. *Melbourne Herald*, 3 February
    1983.
15. *Sunday*, 18 February 1979.
16. *Melbourne Argus*, 3 November
    1933.
17. *Fortean Times* 25, p. 36.
18. *Melbourne Sun*, 2 January 1980.
19. For more information see
    'Thylacine Reports Persist After 50
    Years', *ISC Newsletter*, vol. 4,
    no. 4, pp. 1–5, and Michael Goss,
    'Tracking Tasmania's Mystery
    Beast', *Fate*, July 1983, pp. 34–43.
20. *New Scientist*, 24 April 1986;
    details of the criticisms are given in
    Bob Rickard, 'The return of the
    tiger?', *Fortean Times* 49, pp. 5–7.
21. *Perth Sunday Times*, probably
    February 1972.
22. *Perth West Australian*, 24 August
    1982.
23. Coleman, *Mysterious America*, pp.
    117–18; see the rest of his Chapter
    13 for more information on
    'Mystery Kangaroos'.
24. *ibid.*, pp. 131–4.
25. *Boston Globe & Boston
    Herald-America*, 30 May 1979,
    noted in *Res Bureaux Bulletin* 48,
    p. 4.
26. *ISC Newsletter*, vol. 1, no. 1,
    pp. 10–11.
27. *New York Times*, 10 February
    1935, reported in *INFO Journal* 37
    in Loren Coleman's 'Alligators-
    in-the-Sewers: A Journalistic
    Origin', pp. 4–7.
28. Both in *Fortean Times* 42, p. 26.
29. Brandon, *Weird America*, p. 105.
30. Coleman, *Mysterious America*,
    pp. 57–60.
31. Columbus, OH, *Dispatch*,
    26 February 1984, reported in
    Fortean Times 42, p. 43.
32. Richmond, VA, *Times-Dispatch*,
    26 December 1933, reported in
    INFO Journal 49, p. 3.
33. *Res Bureaux Bulletin* 24, p. 6.
34. *Res Bureaux Bulletin* 6, p. 5.
35. *Res Bureaux Bulletin* 24, p. 6.
36. *Arizona Republic*, 1 July 1978,
    noted in *Res Bureaux Bulletin* 36,
    p. 3.
37. *Res Bureaux Bulletin* 44, p. 2.
38. Michael A. Persinger and Gyslaine
    F. Lafrenière, *Space-Time
    Transients and Unusual Events*
    (Nelson-Hall Inc., Chicago, 1977),
    p. 139.
39. *Süddeutsche Zeitung*, 23

September 1974, noted in Ulrich Magin, 'Continental European Big Cats', *Pursuit* 71, p. 114.

40. Coleman, *Curious Encounters*, p. 67.

41. See Chapter 15, 'The North American Ape', in his *Mysterious America*, pp. 155–70.

42. Earlier reports in Coleman, *Mysterious America*, pp. 155–70; last from Greensburg, PA, *Tribune-Review*, 22 November 1987.

43. Philadelphia, PA, *Enquirer*, 4 November 1987.

44. Jerome Clark, 'A Message from Magonia', *Fortean Times* 8, p. 5.

45. *Fate*, July 1977, p. 18.

46. *Fate*, October 1979, p. 47.

47. Okmulgee, OK, *Exposure*, 17 September 1983, reprinted in *Forteana News* 178, p. 15.

48. Annie P. Gray, *Mammalian Hybrids* (Commonwealth Agricultural Bureau, Slough, 1971); G. B. Kolenosky, 'Hybridisation between Wolf and Coyote', *J. Mammal.* 52 (1971), pp. 446–9.

49. *Covington Virginian*, 4 October 1977, noted in *Res Bureaux Bulletin* 27, p. 6.

50. *Pursuit*, vol. 5, no. 1, p. 13.

51. *New York Herald Tribune*, 3 July 1924.

52. Woodbury, NJ, *Daily Times*, 15 December 1925.

53. *Delaware Leader*, 19 September 1979, reproduced in *Pursuit* 50, p. 93.

54. East Hartford, CT, *Gazette*, 4 September 1986, and Hartford, CT, *Courant*, 11 September 1986, reprinted in *Forteana News*, December 1986 and January 1987.

55. *Falls City Journal*, 31 October 1968.

56. *INFO Journal*, vol. 2, no. 2, p. 20; Marinacci, *Mysterious California*, p. 59.

57. C. Louis Wiedemann, 'Difficulties of Tracking Down the Lizardman', *Vestigia Newsletter* 3, p. 3.

58. Coleman, *Curious Encounters*, p. 73.

59. *Creature Chronicles* 4 and 9; Coleman, *Curious Encounters*, pp. 75–6.

60. Rex Gilroy, 'Australia's Lizard Monsters', *Fortean Times* 37, pp. 32–3.

61. Ulrich Magin, 'European Dragons: The Tatzelwurm', *Pursuit* 73, pp. 16–22.

62. Turin, *La Stampa*, 28 and 29 June 1975, reported in *Pursuit* 35, p. 62.

63. Magin, 'European Dragons', op. cit., p. 18.

64. *ibid.*, p. 17.

65. *ibid.*, p. 19.

66. *ibid.*, p. 19.

67. Coleman, *Mysterious America*, p. 76.

68. *ibid.*, p. 34.

69. *ibid.*, pp. 74–5.

70. Great Falls, MT, *Tribune*, 28 October 1978, reproduced in *Forteana News*, December 1978, p. 18.

15. *Religious phenomena, including visions of the Virgin Mary*

1. *The Universe*, 12 February 1988.

2. PA, *The Philadelphia Enquirer*, 4 August 1985, reproduced in *Pursuit* 71, p. 133.

3. Rogo, *Miracles*, pp. 221–32.

4. Zsolt Aradi, *The Book of Miracles* (Monarch Books, Inc., Derby, CT, 1961), p. 242.

5. *Miraculous Lady of the Roses*, p. 6.

6. McClure, *Evidence for Visions . . .* , pp. 44–5.

7. *ibid.*, p. 35.

8. *ibid.*, pp. 98–104.

9. *Miraculous Lady of the Roses*, p. 7.

10. For more information on holy wells in Britain, see Janet and Colin Bord, *Sacred Waters* (Grafton Books, 1985, and paperback edition 1986).

11. *The Scapular*, March/April 1949, and *Philippine Trends*, December 1948.
12. *Miraculous Lady of the Roses*, pp. 6–7.
13. Quoted in Rogo, *Miracles*, p. 231.
14. *ibid.*, p. 227.
15. *ibid.*, p. 227.
16. Gordon Creighton, 'An Unprepossessing Creature seen in Canada', *Flying Saucer Review*, vol. 15, no. 3, pp. 20–1.
17. John Brent Musgrave, *UFO Occupants and Critters* (Global Communications, New York, 1979), p. 47.
18. Gene Duplantier, 'Report from Canada', *Saucer News*, vol. 16, no. 4, p. 34.
19. Persinger and Lafrenière, *Space-Time Transients . . .*, pp. 207–12.
20. Rogo, *Miracles*, pp. 250–7.
21. John S. Derr and Michael A. Persinger, 'Temporal Association between the Zeitoun Luminous Phenomena and Regional Seismic Activity', *The Explorer* 4 (October 1987), p. 15, summarized in *Science Frontiers* 55, p. 4.
22. *Fortean Times* 49, p. 33.
23. *Res Bureaux Bulletin* 37, p. 2.
24. Milwaukee, WI, *Journal*, 20 April 1974, noted in *Fortean Times* 7, p. 11.
25. Reuters report.
26. *London Evening News*, 15 August 1973, noted in *The News* (later *Fortean Times*) 1, p. 10.
27. St Louis, MO, *Post-Dispatch*, 1 September 1987.
28. Rickard and Kelly, *Photographs of the Unknown*, pp. 94–5.
29. Statement written by Abbé Gueniot in 1908, quoted in Rogo, *Miracles*, p. 145.
30. D. Scott Rogo devotes Chapter 6, pp. 140–58, of his book *Miracles* to this phenomenon; also see his article 'The Virgin of the Hailstones' in *Fate*, July 1987, pp. 59–65.
31. *San Francisco Chronicle*, 15 January 1974, noted in *Fortean Times* 7, p. 5.
32. Rogo, *Miracles*, pp. 173–8.
33. *Daily Telegraph*, 4 July 1987.
34. 'The Scientist Who Makes Icons Weep', *Newsweek*, 26 October 1987.
35. *Grit*, 26 July 1970, noted in Michell and Rickard, *Phenomena*, p. 21.
36. *The Guardian*, 8 September 1980, noted in *Fortean Times* 33, p. 5.
37. Rogo, *Miracles*, pp. 159–60.
38. *ibid.*, pp. 161–2.
39. *The Guardian*, 14 February 1983, noted in *Fortean Times* 42, p. 6.
40. Robert S. Carswell, 'The Hoax of the Bleeding Statue', *The Skeptical Inquirer*, vol. 10, no. 4, pp. 295–6.
41. *The Plain Dealer*, 28 October 1987.
42. Plattsburgh, NY, *Press Republican*, 28 December 1983, noted in *Fortean Times* 42, p. 6.
43. *Orthodox News*, vol. 4 no. 7, March 1987.
44. Michell and Rickard, *Phenomena*, p. 20.
45. Revd Albert J. Hebert, S.M., *Mary, Why Do You Cry?* (1985), p. 32.
46. G. Tomaselli, *Prodigious Tears*.
47. D. Scott Rogo, 'Natuzza Evolo Works Miracles', *Fate*, May 1982, pp. 40–6.
48. IL, *Worcester Telegram*, 10 May 1970, noted in Michell and Rickard, *Phenomena*, p. 20.
49. Francis Johnson, 'Charbal Maklhouf: Saint of the Mass' (Catholic Truth Society, London); Cruz, *The Incorruptibles*, pp. 294–9.
50. For much more information, see Chapter 8, 'The Miracle of St Januarius', in Rogo, *Miracles*.
51. Ian R. Grant, *The Testimony of Blood* (Burns Oates & Washbourne, 1929).
52. Mary F. Ingoldsby, 'The Eucharistic Miracle of Lanciano', *Voice of Padre Pio*, vol. 15, no. 2 (1985), pp. 6–7.

53. Revd Edmond Crapez, C.M.,
*Blessed Catherine Labouré,
Daughter of Charity of St Vincent
de Paul* (St Joseph's Provincial
House, Emmitsburg, MD, 1933),
pp. 235–41. See also Cruz, *The
Incorruptibles*, pp. 281–5.

54. *London Standard*, 27 February
1985, noted in *Fortean Times* 46,
p. 15.

55. Glenn H. Mullin, *Death and
Dying in the Tibetan Tradition*
(Arkana, 1987), p. 231, note 43.

56. Peter Ratazzi, 'Healing Waters
from the Tomb', *Fortean Times*
28, pp. 38–41.

57. Maria Anna Birgitta zu Münster
OSB and Prof. Dr Andreas Bauch,
*Saint Walburga, Her Life and
Heritage* (The Abbey of St
Walburg, Eichstätt, 1979, rev.
1985).

58. *Sunday Express Magazine*, 18
December 1983.

16. *Stones thrown by invisible
assailants*

1. Recent edition, edited and with a
commentary by Stewart Sanderson,
published 1976 by D. S. Brewer
Ltd, Suffolk, and Rowman &
Littlefield, New Jersey.

2. The case is described in detail in
Thurston, *Ghosts and Poltergeists*,
pp. 125–35.

3. Reprinted in Dwight Whalen,
'Stoned on Annie Taylor', *Fortean
Times* 45, p. 62.

4. *Journal SPR*, vol. 12, pp. 260–6,
quoted in Nandor Fodor, *An
Encyclopaedia of Psychic Science*
(The Citadel Press, Secaucus, NJ,
1966), pp. 293–4.

5. Port of Spain, Trinidad, *Mirror*
and *Gazette*, noted in *The
Complete Books of Charles Fort*,
p. 936.

6. *Derry Journal* and *Coleraine
Constitution*, noted in *ibid.*, p. 575.

7. *Annales des Sciences Psychiques*
(1913), p. 152, quoted in
Flammarion, *Haunted Houses*,
pp. 278–80.

8. *Gazette de Lausanne*, 1 May 1914,
quoted in Flammarion, *Haunted
Houses*, pp. 301–3.

9. Ian Stevenson, 'Are Poltergeists
Living or Dead?', *Fate*, February
1988, pp. 71, 73.

10. Letter from the pastor, M. Laval,
quoted in Flammarion, *Haunted
Houses*, pp. 76–81.

11. *The Complete Books of Charles
Fort*, pp. 533–4 – Ms de Ford's
letter was written to Fort; see also
Thelma Hall Quast, 'Rocks Rain on
Chico, California', in *Fate* (UK),
February 1976, pp. 25–8.

12. *Rand Daily Mail*, 29 May 1922,
noted in *The Complete Books of
Charles Fort*, pp. 564–5.

13. Fodor, op. cit., p. 294.

14. Thurston, *Ghosts and Poltergeists*,
pp. 6–7.

15. Gauld and Cornell, *Poltergeists*,
p. 109.

16. Ivan T. Sanderson, *More "Things"*
(Pyramid Books, New York, 1969),
pp. 149–50.

17. Quotation from *The West Indian*,
23 September 1934, and later
events were reported in later issues;
see full report in Thurston, *Ghosts
and Poltergeists*, pp. 136–42.

18. R. S. Lambert, *Exploring the
Supernatural* (Arthur Barker,
1954), pp. 140–2.

19. Gaddis, *Mysterious Fires and
Lights*, pp. 200–1.

20. Mrs Spears' letter to NICAP dated
25 July 1950, quoted in Hal R.
Aldrich, 'Fireball and Rockfalls',
INFO Journal 38, pp. 4–5.

21. Roll, *The Poltergeist*, pp. 35–6.

22. *Daily Express*, 22 March 1957,
noted in Michell and Rickard,
Phenomena, p. 17.

23. *Wellington Evening Post*, 25, 26, 27
March 1963, reported in *INFO
Journal*, vol. 2, no. 2, pp. 43–4.

24. More details of the case will be
found in Guy Lyon Playfair, *The*

Indefinite Boundary (Souvenir Press, London, 1976, Panther paperback 1977), pp. 250–4 of latter edition; the quotation also comes from Playfair's book.

25. *Fate* (UK), March 1970, p. 9.
26. *New York Times*, 8 January 1968, quoted in *INFO Journal*, vol. 1, no. 3, p. 59.
27. Chicago, IL, *Sun-Times*, 11 October 1968, quoted in *Pursuit*, vol. 2, no. 2, pp. 26–7.
28. Roll, *The Poltergeist*, p. 93.
29. *INFO Journal* 14, reported in Michell and Rickard, *Phenomena*, pp. 16–17.
30. Playfair, op. cit., pp. 265–8.
31. *Victoria Colonist*, 4 September 1977, and *Vancouver Province*, 6 September 1977, noted in *Res Bureaux Bulletin* 24, pp. 2–3.
32. Shrewsburg, NJ, *The Sunday Register*, 9 July 1978, and investigated by Robert Warth of SITU, noted in *Pursuit* 44, p. 170.
33. NC, *Winston-Salem Journal and Sentinel*, 14 and 15 July 1978, noted in *Pursuit* 44, p. 170.
34. South Africa *Sunday Times*, 20 July 1980, noted in *Fortean Times* 35, pp. 42–3.
35. *Fortean Times* 35, p. 43.
36. Fairley and Welfare, *Arthur C. Clarke's World of Strange Powers*, p. 40.
37. David Barritt, 'Tales from Africa', *Fortean Times* 44, pp. 36–7.
38. D. Scott Rogo, 'Rock-Throwing Poltergeist', *Fate*, November 1984, pp. 61–6, and December 1984, pp. 88–93.
39. Chicago, IL, *Tribune*, 12 May 1986, reprinted in *Pursuit* 74, p. 89.
40. London, *Sunday Express*, 17 May 1987, reported in *Flying Saucer Review*, vol. 32, no. 5, p. 25.

17. Is extinction the end?

1. J. Tessier-Yandell, 'Rediscovery of the Pygmy Hog', *Animals* 13, no. 20, pp. 956–8 (1971); *BBC Wildlife*, August 1986, p. 396.
2. *ISC Newsletter*, vol. 5, no. 2, pp. 3–5.
3. *New York Times*, 14 October 1986.
4. For further details of British boar sightings, see our *Modern Mysteries of Britain*.
5. Stephen Pile, 'How they scotched the great auk story', *Sunday Times*, 11 May 1986.
6. For other examples see *Fortean Times* 38, pp. 26–7.
7. *Washington Post*, 28 September 1987.
8. Jared Diamond, 'In Quest of the Wild and Weird', *Discover*, March 1985, p. 38; J. Seebeck and M. K. Morcombe, 'Rediscovery of two "extinct" marsupials', *Animals* 10 (no. 6), pp. 271–4 (1967).
9. TX, *Houston Chronicle*, 2 and 21 July 1986.
10. James H. Powell, Jr, 'On the trail of the Mokele-Mbembe', *Explorers Journal*, vol. 59, no. 2 (June 1981), pp. 84–91.
11. Marcellin Agnagna was interviewed by J. Richard Greenwell for the *ISC Newsletter*, vol. 3, no. 2, pp. 7–9.
12. Chapter 17.
13. Chapter 18.
14. Chapter 19.
15. Chapters 20 and 21.
16. Mackal, *A Living Dinosaur?*, p. xviii.
17. For more details of these sightings, see our book *Alien Animals*, pp. 134–5.
18. *ISC Newsletter*, vol. 2, no. 4, p. 8.
19. Brandon, *Weird America*, p. 220.
20. Chapter 3.
21. Ronald Rosenblatt, 'Africa's Flying Dragon', *INFO Journal* 48, pp. 14–15; Michell and Rickard, *Living Wonders*, p. 50.
22. Ivan T. Sanderson, *More "Things"* (Pyramid Books, New York, 1969), ch. 3 'Three Toes – Model B'. Hoax details in St Petersburg, FL, *Floridian*, 11 June 1988.

23. *Sunday Express*, 9 June 1985.
24. Michel Raynal, 'Does the Steller's Sea Cow Still Survive?', *INFO Journal* 51, pp. 15–19.
25. S. K. Klumov, 'Do large unknown animals still exist on the earth?' (in Russian), *Priroda magazine*, August 1962, no. 8, pp. 65–75, quoted in Raynal, op. cit., p. 17.
26. A. A. Berzin, E. A. Tikhomirov, V. I. Troinine, 'Has Steller's Sea Cow Disappeared?' (in Russian), *Priroda magazine* 8 (Moscow, 1963), pp. 73–5, quoted in Raynal, op. cit., p. 18, and in *Pursuit*, vol. 2, no. 1, p. 13.
27. Full witness report quoted in Fairley and Welfare, *Arthur C. Clarke's Chronicles of the Strange and Mysterious*, pp. 104–5.
28. A chapter (17) describing the discovery of the sea-cow can be found in Richard Carrington, *Mermaids and Mastodons* (Chatto & Windus, London, 1957).
29. Dominic Belfield, 'Latest Odds on the Modern Mammoth', *BBC Wildlife*, March 1988, p. 148.
30. 'Is the mammoth extinct?', *Soviet Life*, December 1978, p. 66.
31. Heuvelmans, *On the Track . . .*, pp. 221–38.
32. UPI report, 29 September 1987. Discussion of its possible identification as *Arctodus simus* by Loren Coleman in *Strange Magazine* no. 2, p. 24.
33. Michell and Rickard, *Living Wonders*, pp. 66–7; Heuvelmans, *On the Track . . .*, pp. 138–40.
34. *Fortean Times* 48, p. 11.
35. Librairie Plon, Paris, 1978.
36. *Liverpool Daily Post*, 3 January 1976, noted in *Fortean Times* 15, pp. 11–12.
37. Letter from J. Harrison to Michell and Rickard, noted in their *Living Wonders*, p. 50.
38. *Toronto Star*, 12 November 1977, noted in *Res Bureaux Bulletin* 27, p. 5.
39. *Pursuit* 10, pp. 60–1; 12, pp. 105–9; 13, p. 95.
40. Percy H. Fawcett, *Lost Trails, Lost Cities* (Funk & Wagnalls, New York, 1953), p. 187.
41. Heuvelmans, *On the Track . . .*, ch. 10.

Picture Credits

Larry E. Arnold/Fortean Picture
Library, p. 69
Dmitri Bayanov, p. 202
Trevor Beer/Fortean Picture
Library, p. 233
Ray W. Boeche, p. 245
Janet & Colin Bord/Wales Scene,
pp. 83, 184
Michael Buhler/Fortean Picture
Library, pp. 51, 104
Loren Coleman/Fortean Picture
Library, pp. 153, 158, 159, 238
James Crocker/Fortean Picture
Library, p. 142
René Dahinden/Fortean Picture
Library, pp. 27, 28, 30, 31, 43,
112, 204, 205, 207, 208
Mary Evans Picture Library, p. 19
Mary Evans Picture Library/Guy
Lyon Playfair, pp. 12, 17, 72, 74
Fortean Picture Library, pp. 56, 57,
58, 65, 66, 80, 100, 101, 120, 129,
134, 156, 224, 226, 234, 235, 254,
255, 258, 262, 264, 265, 270, 302
Fort Worth Star–Telegram, p. 219
Glasgow Herald & Evening Times,
p. 98
Cynthia Hind/Fortean Picture
Library, p. 87
Kalle Kultala/Collection of the
Photographic Museum of Finland,
p. 180
Robert Le Serrec/Fortean Picture
Library, p. 121
Hannah McRoberts/Fortean Picture
Library, p. 60

André Martinez/Fortean Picture
Library, p. 140
Maryland Tourism, p. 185
Drawing by David Miller from *A
Living Dinosaur?: In Search of
Mokele-Mbembe* by Dr Roy P.
Mackal, © 1987 by E. J. Brill,
Leiden, The Netherlands, p. 294
Mutual UFO Network (MUFON),
p. 177
Ivor Newby/Fortean Picture
Library, p. 113
Guy Lyon Playfair/Fortean Picture
Library, p. 285
Dr J. T. Richards/Fortean Picture
Library, pp. 25, 88
Ron Schaffner/Fortean Picture
Library, p. 247
Dr Karl Shuker/Fortean Picture
Library, p. 300
South Wales Echo, p. 192
Dennis Stacy/Fortean Picture
Library, p. 111
Clas Svahn/Fortean Picture Library,
p. 174
Western Mail & Echo, Cardiff,
p. 215
West Highland News Agency, p. 92
Nicholas Witchell/Fortean Picture
Library, pp. 118, 119
Marie T. Womack from *A Living
Dinosaur?: In Search of
Mokele-Mbembe* by Dr Roy P.
Mackal, © 1987 by E. J. Brill,
Leiden, The Netherlands,
p. 295

Index of Places